# International Rare Book Prices

# SCIENCE & MEDICINE

## Volume 1

# International Rare Book Prices

# SCIENCE & MEDICINE

## Volume 1

**Edited by Michael Cole**

R.R. Bowker (UK) Ltd

© **Picaflow Ltd.,**
7 Pulleyn Drive,
York YO2 2DY, United Kingdom

ISBN 0-859-35113-0


First published in 1987 by
**R.R. Bowker (UK) Ltd.**
an imprint of
Butterworth & Co (Publishers) Ltd.,
88 Kingsway, London WC1, United Kingdom


Printed and bound in Great Britain by
Biddles Ltd, Guildford and King's Lynn

# Contents

# Introduction and Notes

*Science & Medicine* is the fourth title in the annual series *International Rare Book Prices.* The other titles are *The Arts & Architecture, Early Printed Books, Modern First Editions, Voyages, Travel & Exploration.*

*IRBP* has been established so as to provide annual records of the international pricing levels of out-of-print, rare or antiquarian books within a number of specialty subject areas and to furnish details of likely sources for such books. Information of this nature, a basic necessity for anyone engaged in any branch of librarianship, collecting or commerce involving finding, purchasing or selling out-of-print or early books, has, hitherto, not been readily obtainable in discrete, single-subject, form.

## Sources of information:

The books recorded in the various subject volumes in the 1987 *IRBP* series have been selected from catalogues issued during 1986 by some 190 bookselling firms in Britain and the United States. These firms range in nature from the highly specialized, handling books solely within closely defined subject areas, through to large concerns with expertise across a broad spectrum of type of book.

## Extent of coverage:

In planning editorial policy, I have been aware from the outset of the need, expressed by many librarians and booksellers, to include records of books falling within the lower to middle range of the pricing scale rather than restricting selection to the unusually fine and expensive. Over-much publicity is often given to this latter category, usually to the exclusion of the real world inhabited by librarians, collectors and booksellers to whom budgetary considerations are all-important. It should be recognised, that, within the world of books as a whole, many more individual items change hands at less than a three-figure sum, whether sterling or dollars, than reach that level. It is intended that *IRBP* should provide a realistic overview of the norm, rather the exception, within the booktrade.

The recorded titles, totalling 30,000 or so in the complete series, combine to present an accurate reflection of the diversity of books offered for sale each year within each discipline. These titles are not, therefore, dry bibliographical listings of books which are unlikely to come onto the open market and whose theoretical existence is therefore of mere academic interest. The books listed in *IRBP* are demonstrably obtainable.

## Authorship and cross-references:

Authors are listed alphabetically by surname.

Whenever possible, the works of each author are noted under a single form of name irrespective of the various combinations of initials, forenames and surname by which the author is known.

Works published anonymously, or where the name of the author is not recorded on the title-page, are suitably cross-referenced by providing the main entry under the name of the author (when mentioned by the bookseller) with a corresponding entry under the first main word of the title. Thus, Christopher Pitt's anonymously published *The plague at Marseilles* will be found under *Pitt, Christopher*, with a secondary reference under *Plague*. In cases of unknown, or unmentioned, authorship, entry is made under the first main word. *A letter from a gentleman at Rome* will thus be found under *Letter*.

Books with dual authorship are provided with ancillary cross-referencing under the name of the second author in cases when this is considered to be of assistance.

## Full-titles:

Editorial policy has been to eschew, whenever possible, short-title records in favour of full-, or at least more complete and explanatory, titles. Short-title listings do little to convey the flavour, or even the content, of many books - particularly those published prior to the nineteenth century.

## Descriptions:

Books are listed alphabetically under each author's name, using the first word of the title ignoring, for alphabetical purposes, the definite and indefinite articles *the, a* and *an*. Within this alphabetical grouping of titles, variant editions are not necessarily arranged in chronological order, i.e., a 2nd, 3rd or 4th edition might well be listed prior to an earlier edition.

Subject to restrictions of space and to the provisos set out below, the substance of each catalogue entry giving details of the particular copy offered for sale has been recorded in full.

The listings have been made so as to conform to a uniform order of presentation, viz: Title; place of publication; publisher or printer; date; edition; size; collation or elements of content worthy of note; description of contents including faults, if any; binding; description of binding; bookseller; price.

Abbreviations of description customary within the booktrade have generally been used, although the individual context has been allowed to dictate the extent of such use. A list of these abbreviations will be found on page *x*.

## Collations:

Collations, when provided by the bookseller, are repeated in toto although it should be borne in mind that booksellers employ differing practices in this respect; some by providing complete collations and others by indicating merely the number of pages in the main body of the work concerned. The same edition of the same title catalogued by two booksellers could therefore have two apparently different collations and care should be taken not to regard any collation recorded in *IRBP* as being a definitive or absolute record of total content. Such details as *are* recorded, however, will often prove invaluable for comparison and identification purposes.

**Prices:**

Although it will be understood by all readers that the price, or "value", of any work is not absolute and immutable, the prices asked for the titles recorded in *IRBP* represent a fair assessment by the booksellers concerned, based upon their own - usually considerable - expertise and experience, of the appropriate marketplace level. Having said this, it should also be recognised that each bookseller operates in a different milieu. That two booksellers should choose to offer what is apparently an identical title for sale at differing prices is cause, perhaps, for observation; it is not necessarily indicative of the relative standing of the booksellers concerned.

It is also as well to bear in mind that the titles have been taken out of their cataloguing context. In many circumstances, individual titles can well bear a legitimate and reasonable pricing premium. The costs of providing the additional benefits and services that specialist booksellers in any field offer to their customers must necessarily be reflected in the prices that they charge.

The condition of any individual copy naturally pays an important role in determining its price. Whilst (as mentioned earlier), major faults in any listed item have been recorded, it would be impracticable, both for the bookseller and for *IRBP* to attempt to describe every nuance of condition that might apply.

**Acknowledgments:**

I am indebted to the booksellers who have provided their catalogues during 1986 for the purposes of *IRBP*. A list of these booksellers forms an appendix at the rear of this volume.

This appendix provides a handy reference of international contacts with proven experience of handling books within the individual specialist fields encompassed by the series. The booksellers listed therein are able, between them, to offer advice on any aspect of the rare and antiquarian booktrade.

A secondary aspect of *IRBP* is that the individual titles in the series provide annual substantial subject-related listings of items recently offered for sale. Many of the listed books will still, at the time of publication, be available and readers with a possible interest in acquiring any of the items way well find it worth their while communicating with the booksellers concerned to obtain further and complete details.

**Caveat**

Whilst the greatest care has been taken in transcribing entries from catalogues, it should be understood that, in a compilation of this nature, it is inevitable that an occasional error will have passed unnoticed. Obvious mistakes, usually typographical in nature, observed in catalogues have been corrected. I have not questioned the accuracy in bibliographical matters of the cataloguers concerned.

Michael Cole
*Series Editor IRBP*

# Abbreviations

| | | | |
|---|---|---|---|
| advt(s) | advertisement(s) | inscrbd | inscribed |
| addtn(s) | addition(s) | inscrptn | inscription |
| a.e.g. | all edges gilt | iss | issue |
| altrtns | alterations | jnt(s) | joint(s) |
| Amer | American | lge | large |
| bibliog(s) | bibliography(ies) | lea | leather |
| b/w | black & white | lib | library |
| bndg | binding | ltd | limited |
| bd(s) | board(s) | litho(s) | lithograph(s) |
| b'plate | bookplate | ms(s) | manuscript(s) |
| ctlg(s) | catalogue(s) | mrbld | marbled |
| chromolitho(s) | chromo-lithograph(s) | mod | modern |
| ca | circa | mor | morocco |
| cold | coloured | mtd | mounted |
| coll | collected | n.d. | no date |
| contemp | contemporary | n.p. | no place |
| crnr(s) | corner(s) | num | numerous |
| crrctd | corrected | obl | oblong |
| cvr(s) | cover(s) | occas | occasional(ly) |
| dec | decorated | orig | original |
| detchd | detached | p (pp) | page(s) |
| diag(s) | diagram(s) | pict | pictorial |
| dw(s) | dust wrapper(s) | port(s) | portrait(s) |
| edn(s) | edition(s) | pres | presentation |
| elab | elaborate | qtr | quarter |
| engv(s) | engraving(s) | rebnd | rebind/rebound |
| engvd | engraved | rec | recent |
| enlgd | enlarged | repr(d) | repair(ed) |
| ex lib | ex library | roy | royal |
| f (ff) | leaf(ves) | sep | separate |
| fig(s) | figure(s) | sgnd | signed |
| fldg | folding | sgntr | signature |
| ft | foot | sl | slight/slightly |
| frontis | frontispiece | sm | small |
| hand-cold | hand-coloured | t.e.g. | top edge gilt |
| hd | head | unif | uniform |
| ill(s) | illustration(s) | vell | vellum |
| illust | illustrated | vol(s) | volume(s) |
| imp | impression | w'cut(s) | woodcut(s) |
| imprvd | improved | wrap(s) | wrapper(s) |

# Science & Medicine
# 1986 Catalogue Prices

**Abbott, Maude**
- History of medicine in the province of Quebec. Toronto: 1931. 1st edn.
*(Scientia)* **$45**

**Abel, A.L.**
- Oesophagael obstruction; its pathology, diagnosis and treatment. Oxford: 1929. xi,234 pp. 2 cold plates, 132 ills in text.
*(Whitehart)* **£15**

**Abel, John Jacob**
- Chemistry in relation to biology and medicine with especial reference to insulin. Balt: 1939. Tall 8vo. 79 pp. Cloth. *(Argosy)* **$35**

**Abell, Sydney George, et al.**
- A bibliography of the art of turning and lathe and machine tool history. Society of Ornamental Turners, 1956. 2nd edn, revsd & enlgd. Folio. vii,89 pp. Mimeographed text. Cloth-backed printed bds, as issued.
*(Weiner)* **£75**

**Abercrombie, John**
- Inquiries concerning the intellectual powers and the investigation of truth. London: 1833. 4th edn. xv,441 pp. Full calf gilt, sl rubbed.
*(Jenner)* **£60**
- Pathological and practical researches on the diseases of the stomach, the intestinal canal ... other viscera of the abdomen. Phila: Carey, Lea & Blanchard, 1838. 3rd Amer from 2nd London edn, enlgd. 320 pp. Little foxing. Contemp calf, sl worn & stained.
*(Diamond)* **$45**

**Abercromby, Hon. R.**
- Seas and skies in many latitudes: or wanderings in search of weather. 1888. xvi,447 pp. 8 photographs, 3 maps, 33 ills. Orig pict cloth, inner hinge cracked, spine torn. *(Whitehart)* **£15**

**Abernethy, John**
- Memoirs of John Abernethy, F.R.S., with a view of his lectures, writings and character ... New York: Harper & Brothers, 1853. 8vo. viii,434 pp. 10 pp pub ctlg. *(Poitras)* **$75**
- The new family physician, and guide to health and long life; with a variety of valuable tables on medical statistics. 1838. 1st edn. Port. Lower jnt torn. *(Robertshaw)* **£10**
- Physiological letters, exhibiting a general view of Mr. Hunter's Physiology, and his researches in comparative anatomy. Hartford: 1825. 1st Amer edn. 144 pp. Disbound.
*(Fye)* **$40**
- Surgical observations on diseases resembling syphilis; and on diseases of the urethra. London: 1814. 3rd edn. 234 pp. Uncut. Disbound. *(Jenner)* **£30**
- Surgical observations on the constitutional origin and treatment of local diseases; and on aneurisms ... Phila: 1811. 1st Amer edn. 325 pp. Lea. *(Fye)* **$200**
- Surgical observations on the constitutional origin and treatment of local diseases ... Phila: 1811. 1st Amer edn. 8vo. Half-title, ix,[2],325 pp. Contemp tree calf, rubbed, front jnt cracked. *(Elgen)* **$150**

**Abney, Capt. W. de W.**
- Colour measurement and mixture. London: SPCK, 1891. x,11-207, [i],2,[vi] pp. Frontis, 45 ills. *(Pollak)* **£16**

**Abraham, J. Johnston**
- The surgeon's log: impressions of the Far East. New York: 1912. 44 ills. *(Argosy)* **$35**

**Abraham, J.J.**
- Lettsom. His life, times, friends and descendents. London: 1933. Ills. Bevelled bds. *(Winterdown)* **£35**

**Abrahamson, Ira A.**
- Color atlas of anterior segment eye diseases. New York: 1964. 8vo. Many color plates. Fabricoid, loose leaf notebook. *(Argosy)* **$35**

**Academy ...**
- The academy of arts and sciences, or new preceptor. Edinburgh: 1810. 2 vols. xii,959; 871 pp. 84 plates (6 fldg), 6 fldg maps. No title to vol II (published?). Half-calf gilt, worn.        *(Weiner)* **£50**

**Account ...**
- An account of persons remarkable for their health ... See Graham, T.J.
- Account of the experiments tried by the Board of Agriculture in the composition of various sorts of bread ... 1795. 4to. 34 pp. 2 fldg plates. Few leaves sl spotted. New buckram.        *(Weiner)* **£85**

**Accum, Frederick**
- Elements of crystallography, after the method of Hauy. London: Longman ..., 1813. 1st edn. 8vo. lxiii,396 pp. 4 engvd plates, text figs. Some foxing on plates. Orig bds, rebacked.        *(Antiq Sc)* **$350**

**Accum, Friedrich Christian**
- A treatise on adulterations of food, and culinary poisons ... and methods of detecting them ... London: Printed by J. Mallett ..., 1820. 12mo. [1]f,xvi,372 pp. Color vignette on title, 2 text ills. Old cloth, rebacked. Water-stains & browning on a few leaves.        *(Zeitlin)* **$275**

**Achenhurst, Thos. R.**
- A practical treatise on weaving and designing of textile fabrics. Bradford: n.d. [ca 1879?]. 246 ills. Half-calf, mrbld edges, bds sl soiled, rubbed.        *(Quinto Charing Cross)* **£35**

**Ackerknecht, Erwin**
- Medicine at the Paris Hospital: 1794-1848. Balt: 1967. 1st edn. 242 pp. Dw.  *(Fye)* **$25**

**Ackerman, W.**
- See Hilbert D. & Ackerman, W.

**Ackworth, A.T.**
- The manufacture of roofing tiles. N.d. [possibly 1910, or 1924]. 146 pp. Ills, plate.        *(Weiner)* **£25**

**Adair, Frank (ed.)**
- Cancer in four parts ... comprising international contributions to the study of cancer in honor of James Ewing. Phila: 1931. 1st edn. 484 pp. Ex lib.        *(Fye)* **$75**

**Adami, J. G.**
- Medical contributions to the study of evolution. London: 1918. 372 pp. Ills. Ex lib.        *(Argosy)* **$40**

**Adami, J. George & Martin, C.F.**
- Report on observations made upon the cattle

at the experimental station at Outremont, P.Q. Recognized to be tuberculous by the tuberculin test. Ottawa: 1899. 32 pp. Printed wraps, worn.        *(Argosy)* **$25**

**Adami, J. George & McCrae, John**
- A text-book of pathology. Phila: [1912]. 1st edn. 8vo. x,[17]-759 pp. 11 cold plates. Spine edge & crnrs frayed. Ex lib.        *(Elgen)* **$50**

**Adams, Daniel (ed.)**
- The medical and agricultural register for the years 1806 and 1807. Containing practical information on husbandry ... the preservation of health. Boston: Manning & Loring, 1808-07. Vol I, 24 numbers, all published. Contemp calf-backed mrbld bds.        *(Robertshaw)* **£68**

**Adams, Francis**
- The genuine works of Hippocrates, translated from the Greek with a preliminary discourse ... New York: William Wood & Company, 1886. 2 vols. 388; 348 pp. 8 full-page plates.        *(Poitras)* **$150**
- The genuine works of Hippocrates, translated from the Greek with a preliminary discourse ... New York: William Wood, 1929. Lge 8vo. v,390; 366 pp. 3 plates. Orig cloth, upper bd with sm deep scratch.        *(Jenner)* **£45**

**Adams, George**
- Geometrical and graphical essays, containing, a general description of the mathematical instruments used in geometry ... London: for W. & S. Jones, 1803. 3rd edn, crrctd & enlgd. Engvd frontis. 14pp ctlg of instruments. Contemp polished calf, gilt spine.        *(McDowell)* **£240**

**Adams, J. Howe**
- History of the life of D. Hayes Agnew. Phila: 1892. 1st edn. Ills. Half lea.  *(Argosy)* **$75**

**Adams, J.C.**
- Lectures on the lunar theory. Cambridge: 1900. [2],88 pp. Orig cloth, faded & marked.        *(Whitehart)* **£25**

**Adams, P.H.**
- Pathology of the eye. London: 1912. 1st edn. 12mo. Ills. Fabricoid. Oxford Medical Publication.        *(Argosy)* **$35**

**Adams, Raymond D., et al.**
- Diseases of muscle: a study in pathology. New York: [1953]. 8vo. 556 pp. Color frontis, 347 ills. Some ink underlining. Buckram. Dw.        *(Argosy)* **$35**

**Adams, Wellington**
- Electricity: its application in medicine and surgery. Detroit: 1891. 12mo. 113 pp. Text.

Orig pict wraps. *(Argosy)* **$35**

**Adams. George**
- A treatise, describing the construction and explaining the use of new celestial and terrestrial globes. London: 1810. xxiv,242 pp. Frontis, 13 plates. Old damp-stain at top edge of last few leaves. Orig speckled calf, spine gilt, some wear to spine ends. *(Pollak)* **£80**

**Addison, Thomas**
- On the constitutional and local effects of the supra-renal capsules. London: Samuel Highley, 1855. 1st edn. Lge 4to. 11 hand-cold litho plates, with light spotting. Some margins lightly soiled. Orig cloth, crnrs & hinges reprd. Wellcome Library stamps.
*(Quaritch)* **$10,500**

**Addison, Joseph**
- The evidences of the Christian religion ... with a preface containing the sentiments of Mr. Boyle, Mr. Lock, and Sir Isaac Newton. London: Tonson, 1730. 1st edn. Sm. 8vo. One marginal wormhole. Contemp calf, jnts worn. *(Marlborough)* **£40**

**Adler, Alfred**
- Study of organ inferiority and its psychical compensation: a contribution to clinical medicine. New York: 1917. 1st edn in English, x,86,[2] pp. *(Gach)* **$75**

**Adler, Francis Head**
- Clinical physiology of the eye. New York: 1933. 1st edn. 8vo. 406 pp. Ills. Cloth.
*(Argosy)* **$35**

**Adler, Lewis**
- See Willard, de Forest & Adler, Lewis

**Adorno, J.N.**
- Introduction to the harmony of the universe; or, principles of physico-harmonic geometry. 1851. viii,[1],160 pp. 18 fldg plates. Orig cloth rebacked, orig spine laid on.
*(Whitehart)* **£25**

**Adrian, Edgar D.**
- The mechanism of nervous action; electrical studies of the neurone. Phila: 1932. 1st edn.
*(Scientia)* **$85**

**Agassiz, Louis**
- An essay on classification. London: 1859. 381 pp. *(Scientia)* **$125**
- An essay on classification. London: Longman, &c., 1859. 1st edn thus. 8vo. Pub pebbled cloth. *(McDowell)* **£45**

**Agnew, D. Hayes**
- Classification of the animal kingdom. A lecture introductory to the course of anatomy,

in the Philadelphia School of Anatomy. Phila: 1860. 16 pp. Wraps. *(Argosy)* **$30**
- The principles and practice of surgery. Phila: 1878-83. 1st edn. 3 vols. Lea. *(Fye)* **$150**
- The principles and practice of surgery ... Phila: 1878-83. 1st edn. 3 vols. Profusely illustrated. Orig sheep, rubbed. *(Elgen)* **$200**

**Aikin, Lucy**
- Memoir of John Aikin. With a selection of his miscellaneous pieces, biographical, moral and critical. Phila: 1824. 1st Amer edn. 8vo. 487 pp. Orig bds. Ex lib. *(Argosy)* **$50**

**Aikin, William**
- An introductory lecture, delivered before the medical class of the University [of Maryland], November, 1837. Balt: 1837. 8vo. 20 pp. Mod wraps. *(Argosy)* **$25**

**Air-ship ...**
- The air-ship City of New York ... See Lowe, T.S.C.

**Airy, George Biddell**
- Gravitation. An elementary explanation of the principal perturbations of the solar system. London: Macmillan, 1884. 2nd edn. xvi,173, [iii], 32 [ctlg] pp. Orig cloth, old rebacking, worn. *(Pollak)* **£15**
- Gravitation; an elementary explanation of the principal perturbations in the solar system. 1834. xxiii,215 pp. Few notes in contemp hand in some margins. Later cloth.
*(Whitehart)* **£18**
- Mathematical tracts on the lunar and planetary theories, the figure of the earth ... Cambridge: Deighton, 1831. 2nd edn. v,410 pp. 5 plates. Prize calf, spine & jnts taped.
*(Pollak)* **£30**
- On the algebraical and numerical theory of errors of observations and the combination of observations. Cambridge, 1861. 1st edn. Orig cloth, dull & sl defective. *(Whitehart)* **£18**
- On the undulatory theory of optics, designed for the use of students in the University. London & Cambridge: Macmillan, 1866. New edn. viii,159,29 [ctlg] pp. 2 fldg plates. New cloth. *(Pollak)* **£30**

**Aiton, William**
- A treatise on the origin, qualities, and cultivation of moss-earth, with directions for converting it into manure ... Air: Wilson & Paul, 1811. [viii],xxxix, 357,[1] pp. 8vo. Sl worming with loss of text, general browning. New grey bds, paper label. *(Blackwell's)* **£75**

**Akert, Konrad**
- See Emmers, Raimond & Akert, Konrad

**Albee, Fred H.**
- Bone-graft surgery. Phila: 1915. 1st edn. 332

ills, 3 in color.          *(Argosy)* **$125**
- Orthopedic and reconstruction surgery: industrial and civilian. Phila: 1919. Tall 8vo. 1138 pp. 804 ills. Ex lib.          *(Argosy)* **$75**

**Alcott, William A.**
- Vegetable diet as sanctioned by medical men, and by experience in all ages. Boston: 1838. 1st edn. xi,276 pp. Lightly foxed. Contemp patterned cloth, rubbed.          *(Weiner)* **£150**

**Alden, Ebenezer**
- The early history of the medical profession in the county of Norfolk, Mass. An address ... Boston: 1853. 8vo. 48 pp. Orig printed wraps, rebacked.          *(Argosy)* **$40**

**Alexander, A.F.O'D.**
- The planet Saturn, a history of observation, theory and discovery. 1962. 474 pp. 11 double-sided plates, figs in text.
          *(Whitehart)* **£18**

**Alexander, Franz**
- Psychoanalysis of the total personality: application of Freud's theory of the ego to the neuroses. Translated ... New York: 1935. Tall 8vo. Printed bds.          *(Argosy)* **$27.50**
- The scope of psychoanalysis 1921 - 1961. Selected papers. New York: 1961. 1st edn.
          *(Robertshaw)* **£10**

**Alexander, Franz & Eisenstein, Samuel (eds.)**
- Psychoanalytic pioneers. New York & London: 1966. 1st edn. Dw. *(Robertshaw)* **£15**

**Alexander, Franz & Selesnick, S.**
- The history of psychiatry: an evolution of psychiatric thought and practice from prehistoric times to the present. New York: [1966]. 1st edn. 8vo. Cloth. Dw. *(Argosy)* **$27**

**Alexis of Piemount [Ruscelli, Girolamo]**
- The secrets of ... Alexis of Piemount contayning excellent remedies ... second part ... thyrde and last part ... London: ..., 1568-63-[66]. 4to. [6],117,[11]; [2],79,[7]; 75,[9]ff (some mispagination). Sep w'cut titles. Few stained leaves. Calf, gilt.
          *(Rootenberg)* **$1,250**

**Alford, Charles J.**
- Mining law in the British Empire. London: Griffin, 1906. xii,300. Advts.   *(Pollak)* **£15**

**Alison, William Pulteney**
- Outlines of physiology and pathology; with a supplement to the physiology, embracing an account of the most recent additions ... Edinburgh & London: 1836. 2nd edn. xvi,650,73 pp. Half-calf, mrbld bds, sl rubbed & bumped.          *(Jenner)* **£40**

**Allan, Major W.D.**
- List of the sheep marks for the County of Argyll. Oban: 1926. 184 pp. Red cloth.
          *(Phenotype)* **£18**

**Allbutt, T. Clifford**
- Notes on the composition of scientific papers. London: 1923. Cloth, front cvr creased.
          *(Argosy)* **$30**
- On professional education with special reference to medicine. London: 1906. 12mo. 80 pp. Cloth.          *(Argosy)* **$35**
- A system of surgery, by many writers. 1896. 8 vols. Some foxing on prelims. New maroon cloth, spines very sl sunned.   *(Jenner)* **£125**

**Allchin, W.H.**
- The nature and causes of duodenal indigestion. London: 1892. 12mo. 72 pp. Printed wraps. Bradshaw Lecture for 1891.
          *(Argosy)* **$35**

**Allen, A.H. Burlton**
- Pleasure and instinct: a study in the psychology of human action. New York: Harcourt, 1930. 1st Amer edn. Worn dw.
          *(Gach)* **$27.50**

**Allen, Alfred A.**
- Chemistry of urine. A practical guide to the analytical examination of diabetic, albuminous and gouty urine. London: Churchill, 1895. xi,212 pp. 19 text figs. A trifle slack.          *(Pollak)* **£12**

**Allen, Carroll**
- Local and regional anesthesia. Phila: 1914. 1st edn. 625 pp.          *(Fye)* **$50**

**Allen, Grant**
- The colour-sense: its origin and development. An essay in comparative psychology. Boston: Houghton: Osgood, 1879. 1st U.S. edn. [ii],xii, 282,[2] pp. Dec green cloth.
          *(Gach)* **$65**

**Allen, J. Adams**
- Observations on the medical platform. Detroit: 1853. 29 pp. 8vo. Sewn. Ex lib.
          *(Argosy)* **$30**
- Steps to the medical platform. Ann Arbor, 1854. 8vo. 32 pp. Printed wraps. Ex lib.
          *(Argosy)* **$30**

**Allen, Rev. John**
- Euclid's elements of geometry ... elements of plain and spherical trigonometry. A system of conick sections ... and elements of astronomy, with notes. Balt: 1822. 1st edn. 494,[6] pp. Num text figs. Contemp tree calf.
          *(M&S)* **$27.50**

**Allen, Nathan**
- Essay on the opium trade, including a sketch of its history, extent, effects, etc., as carried out in India and China. Boston: Jewett, 1850. 1st edn. 68 pp. Wraps, backstrip worn. Sgnd "With respects of the Author". *(Xerxes)* **$100**
- The prevention of disease, insanity, crime and pauperism. Boston: 1878. 25 pp. Orig printed wraps. Ex lib. *(Argosy)* **$25**
- State medicine in its relation to insanity. Boston: 1875. 1st edn. 31 pp. Printed wraps. *(Argosy)* **$25**

**Allen, Peter**
- Lectures on oral catarrh; or the commonest forms of deafness and their cure. New York: 1872. 1st Amer edn. 277 pp. Shaken, top of backstrip torn, name boldly written on title. *(Fye)* **$30**

**Allen, Ted & Gordon, Sidney**
- The scalpel, the sword. The story of Dr. Norman Bethune. Boston: [1952]. 8vo. Cloth. Dw. *(Argosy)* **$25**

**Allingham, William**
- Fistula, haemorrhoids, painful ulcer ... and other diseases of the rectum. Phila: 1873. 2nd edn. 265 pp. *(Fye)* **$65**
- Fistula, haemorrhoids, painful ulcer ... and other diseases of the rectum. Phila: 1882. 4th edn (1st to include an index). 252 pp. *(Fye)* **$50**

**Allis, Oscar**
- Dislocations of the hip. 1896. 1st edn. 171 pp. Ills. Orig pebbled cloth, bottom of spine sl worn. Author's sgnd & inscrbd copy. *(Oasis)* **$75**
- An inquiry into the difficulties encountered in the reduction of dislocations of the hip. Phila: 1896. 1st edn. 171 pp. Inscribed by the author. *(Fye)* **$150**
- An inquiry into the difficulties encountered in the reduction of dislocations of the hip. Phila: 1896. 1st edn. Tall 8vo. Ex lib. *(Argosy)* **$45**

**Allison, R.S.**
- The senile brain: a clinical study. London: [1962]. 1st edn. Preface underlined. *(Argosy)* **$30**

**Allport, Gordon W. & Vernon, Philip, E.**
- Studies in expressive movement ... with a chapter on matching sketches of personality with script ... New York: Macmillan, 1933. 1st edn. 12mo. xiv,269,[5] pp. Blue cloth. Inscription by Allport. *(Gach)* **$75**

**Allport, Noel L.**
- The chemistry and pharmacy of vegetable drugs. Newnes, 1943. viii,264 pp. Num text

ills. Cvrs faded. *(Pollak)* **£15**

**Allshorn, George Edward**
- A handy book for homeopathic domestic practice, or, hints how to use a few of the principle medicines ... London: 1868. 3rd edn. 208 pp. Orig purple cloth, spine sunned & loose. *(Jenner)* **£16**

**Allsop, F.C.**
- Practical electric-light fitting. 1892. xv,275 pp. Frontis, 3 fldg plates, ills. Shaken. *(Weiner)* **£20**

**Alsop, G.F.**
- History of the Women's Medical College, Philadelphia, Pa., 1850-1950. Phila: Lippincott, 1950. 4to. xi,256 pp. 6 ills. *(Poitras)* **$40**

**Alt, Adolf**
- Lectures on the human eye in its normal and pathological conditions. London: 1884. 8vo. xvi,208 pp. 95 text ills. Spine edges & crnrs frayed. *(Elgen)* **$45**

**Althaus, Julius**
- Influenza: its pathology, symptoms, complications and sequels. Its origin ... treatment. 1892. 2nd edn. xii,408 pp. Cvrs dust stained & marked. *(Whitehart)* **£18**
- The spas of Europe. 1862. xix,494,[32 advts] pp. Foxing at rear. Orig green cloth, loose in casing, spine & crnrs bumped. *(Jenner)* **£35**
- A treatise on medical electricity, theoretical and practical, and its use in the treatment of paralysis, neuralgia, and other diseases. London: Trubner & Co., 1859. 1st edn. 8vo. xvi,352 pp. Mostly unopened. Orig cloth, spine worn. *(Rootenberg)* **$250**
- A treatise on medical electricity, theoretical and practical, and its use in the treatment of paralysis, neuralgia, and other diseases. Phila: 1870. 2nd edn, revsd & partly rewritten. *(Scientia)* **$65**

**Alvarez, Walter C.**
- The mechanics of the digestive tract. New York: 1922. 1st edn. Small 8vo. 22 ills. Cloth. *(Argosy)* **$85**
- The mechanics of the digestive tract. An introduction to gastroenterology. New York: 1928. 2nd edn, revsd. xix,447 pp. 100 ills. Orig cloth. Sgnd presentation copy from author. *(Whitehart)* **£25**
- Nervous indigestion. New York: 1930. 1st edn. 8vo. Cloth. *(Argosy)* **$35**
- Nervousness, indigestion, and pain. New York: n.d. [ca 1943]. 500 pp. *(Argosy)* **$35**
- The neuroses: diagnosis and management of functional disorders and minor psychoses. Phila: [1951]. 667 pp. *(Argosy)* **$35**

**Alvis, Bennet**
- See Weiner, Meyer & Alvis, Bennet

**Amar, Jules**
- The physiology of industrial organisation and the re-employment of the disabled. Translated ... London: Library Press, 1918. xxv,[iii],371 pp. 135 ills. Jnts a little weak.
*(Pollak)* **£25**

**Amesbury, Joseph**
- Practical remarks on the causes, nature and treatment of deformities of the spine, chest, and limbs ... London: Longman, &c., 1840. Sole edn. Sq 4to. 36 litho plates (2 fldg). Lib stamps on title & plates. Pub cloth, rebacked.
*(McDowell)* **£180**

**Amory, Robert**
- A treatise on electrolysis and its applications to therapeutical and surgical treatment in disease. New York: [1886]. 1st edn. 8vo. vii,307 pp. Ills. Inner hinge starting.
*(Elgen)* **$50**
- A treatise on electrolysis and its application to therapeutical and surgical treatment in disease. New York: 1886. 1st edn. 307 pp.
*(Fye)* **$50**

**Anatomical Dialogues ...**
- Anatomical dialogues; or, a breviary of anatomy: wherein all the parts of the human body are concisely and accurately described ... by a gentleman of the Faculty. 1796. 4th edn. viii,387, [10]. 10 plates. Mod lea.
*(Whitehart)* **£65**

**Anatomy ...**
- The anatomy of melancholy ... See Burton, Robert
- The anatomy of the human body ... See Keill, James

**Ancrade, E.N. da C.**
- The structure of the atom. London: Bell, 1923. 1st edn. xiv,314 pp. 49 text figs. Orig cloth much faded. *(Pollak)* **£20**

**Anderson, Andrew**
- Inaugural dissertation on the Eupatorium Perfoliatum of Linnaeus. New York: 1813. 75 pp. Printed wraps, uncut. *(Argosy)* **$75**

**Anderson, Fannie**
- Doctors under three flags. Detroit: Wayne U.P., [1951]. 1st edn. 8vo. 8 plates. Cloth. Ex lib. *(Argosy)* **$35**

**Anderson, J.W.**
- The prospector's handbook. A guide for the prospector or traveller in search of metal-bearing or other valuable minerals. 1888. 3rd edn, revsd with additions. Sm 8vo. Several

text figs, pub advts at rear. Gilt illust cloth.
*(Edwards)* **£35**

**Anderson, Miles H.**
- Functional bracing of the upper extremities. Springfield: [1958]. 1st edn. 4to. Hundreds of ills. Cloth. Dw. *(Argosy)* **$37.50**

**Anderson, Miles, et al.**
- Prosthetic principles - above knee amputations. Springfield: [1960]. 4to. Profusely illust. Cloth. Dw. *(Argosy)* **$35**

**Anderson, T. M'Call**
- Contributions to clinical medicine. Edited by J. Hinshelwood. Edinburgh: 1898. xi,416 pp. Orig cloth. "With the Author's compliments" on half-title. *(Whitehart)* **£28**

**Andrade, E.N. da C.**
- The structure of the atom. London: G. Bell, 1927. 3rd edn, revsd & enlgd. xviii,[ii], 750,[ii]. 8 plates, fldg chart, 114 text figs.
*(Pollak)* **£20**

**Andral, Gabriel**
- A treatise on pathological anatomy. Translated by Richard Townsend and William West. New York: 1832. 1st Amer edn. 2 vols. 8vo. viii,424; 507 pp. Foxing, in some leaves heavy. Orig sprinkled sheep, worn. *(Hemlock)* **$100**

**Andrews, C.W.**
- A descriptive catalogue of the marine reptiles of the Oxford clay ... in the British Museum. 1910-13. 2 vols. 4to. 25 plates. Ex lib.
*(Wheldon & Wesley)* **£65**

**Andrews, J.**
- Astronomical and nautical tables, with precepts, for finding the longitude and latitude of places, by lunar distances, double altitudes ... 1805. 1st edn. xxiii,263 pp. Orig bds, stained & worn. Contemp signature on title. *(Whitehart)* **£35**

**Andrews, W.S.**
- Magic squares and cubes. Chicago: Open Court Publishing, 1908. vi,199,[iii] pp. Spine faded. *(Pollak)* **£25**

**Andrews. Edmund & Lacey, Thomas**
- The mortality of surgical operations in the Upper Lake States, compared with that of other regions. Chicago: 1877. 123 pp. Printed wraps, lacks end wrap. *(Argosy)* **$27.50**

**Andry, Nicholas**
- An account of the breeding of worms in human bodies. Their nature, and several sorts ... from the French original with figures. London: 1701. Title mtd & disfigured with

some loss of text. Plates, one or two torn with loss, final lf reprd. New half-calf.
*(Goodrich)* **$95**

**Angevine, Jay B., et al.**
- The human cerebellum: an atlas of gross topography in serial sections. Boston: [1961]. 1st edn. Obl folio. 100 plates. Two-tone brown cloth. *(Argosy)* **$45**

**Annals ...**
- Annals of medical history. New York: 1929-42. 2nd & 3rd series complete, 14 vols. Orig cloth-backed bds (one vol in orig wraps).
*(Fye)* **$600**
- Annals of the astronomical observatory of Harvard College vol VIII. Results of observations ... Cambridge: 1876. Roy 4to. viii,65 pp. 10 plates & 6 plates of photographs. Part II ... 8pp. Part III ... 7pp, 35 plates. Lightly browned, damp-staining. Disbound. *(Zeitlin)* **$150**
- The annals of the Royal Statistical Society, 1834 - 1934. London: for the Society, 1934. xii,308 pp. 8 plates. *(Pollak)* **£25**

**Annandale, Thomas**
- Observations on the operation for congenital cleft palate, with cases. Edinburgh: 1869. 8vo. 8 pp. Wraps. Ex lib. *(Argosy)* **$27.50**

**Anson, Barry**
- See Bast, Theodore & Anson, Barry

**Anson, Barry & Donaldson, James**
- The surgical anatomy of the temporal bone and ear. Phila: 1967. 1st edn. 4to. 211 pp. Ills. *(Fye)* **$20**

**Appert, Charles**
- The art of preserving all kinds of animal and vegetable substances for several years ... translated from the French. London: for Black, Parry & Kingsbury, 1812. 12mo. xxv,[1],100, [4 advts] pp. Contemp speckled calf, rubbed. *(Burmester)* **£75**
- The art of preserving all kinds of animal and vegetable substances for several years. London: for Black, Parry & Kingsbury, 1812. 8vo. Fldg engvd frontis. Title foxed. Contemp calf, rebacked. *(McDowell)* **£110**

**Appleyard, Rollo**
- The history of the Institution of Electrical Engineers (1871 - 1931). For the Institution, 1939. 342 pp. Cold frontis, 37 plates. White linen gilt, lea label. *(Pollak)* **£16**

**Aran, F.A.**
- Practical manual of the diseases of the heart and great vessels. Translated ... Phila: 1843. 1st edn in English, 8vo. 164 pp. Foxing. Cloth-backed stiff printed wraps. *(Elgen)* **$50**

**Arber, Agnes**
- Herbals, their origin and evolution. A chapter in the history of botany. Cambridge: University Press, 1912. 1st edn. 4to. Extensively illust. Some pencil annotations. Pub dec cloth, sl grubby. *(McDowell)* **£65**
- Herbals, their origin and evolution. A chapter in the history of botany 1470 - 1670. Cambridge: 1912. xviii,253 pp. Frontis, 21 plates, 113 figs in text. Orig pict cloth, t.e.g. *(Whitehart)* **£55**

**Arbuthnot, John**
- An essay concerning the effects of air on human bodies. London: for J. Tonson, 1733. 1st edn. 8vo. Errata slip pasted down on A8 verso. Contemp panelled calf, rebacked with later gilt spine, orig spine label preserved. *(Quaritch)* **$450**
- An essay concerning the nature of aliments, and the choice of them, according to the different constitutions of human bodies ... To which are added, practical rules of diet ... 1735. 3rd edn. [xxiv],436 pp. Calf, rebacked, crnrs rubbed. *(Jenner)* **£90**
- An essay concerning the nature of aliments, and the choice of them, according to the different constitutions of human bodies. London: for J. & R. Tonson, 1756. 4th edn. 8vo. xxxii,365,[1] pp, [1 pub advts]f. Contemp sprinkled calf. *(Zeitlin)* **$195**

**[Arbuthnot, John]**
- An essay on the usefulness of mathematical learning, in a letter from a gentleman ... printed at the Theatre in Oxford for Anth. Peisely ... 1701. 1st edn. 8vo. Half-title, title, 57 pp. Contemp calf, rebacked.
*(Pickering)* **$650**

**Arcana ...**
- Arcana Fairfaxiana manuscripta. [Manuscript volume of 16th/17th c apothecaries' lore and housewifery, reproduced in facsimile, with an introduction]. Newcastle: 1890. Sm 4to. Orig mor, rubbed, upper jnt partially split. Bodleian Library duplicate. *(Robertshaw)* **£18**

**Archbold, J.F.**
- The Statutes relating to lunacy comprising the law with respect to pauper lunatics, hospitals and licensed houses, inquisitions in lunacy and criminal lunatics. 1890. 3rd edn. [39], [clxi], 660 pp. Orig cloth, spine worn. *(Whitehart)* **£18**

**Archibald, R.G.**
- See Balfour, Andrew & Archibald, R.G.

**Archives ...**
- Archives of gynaecology, obstetrics and pediatrics. 1889-92. 2 vols. 733; 563 pp. Half lea. *(Fye)* **$20**

**Argyll, Duke of**
- Autobiography and memoirs. New York: 1906. 1st Amer edn. 2 vols. 602; 635 pp.
  *(Scientia)* **$45**
- The reign of law. London: 1867. 5th edn. 435 pp. Spine worn.    *(Scientia)* **$27.50**

**Aristotle**
- Aristotle's last legacy, unfolding the mysteries of nature in the generation of man ... London: R. Ware, 1749. 12mo. [6],112,[2 advts] pp. Frontis. Mod full calf.    *(Dailey)* **$225**
- Medical knowledge: The works of the famous philosopher, containing his complete master piece, and family physician ... J. Smith, High Holborn, n.d. [ca 1880?] 12mo. 352 pp. Cold ills. Orig brown cloth, spine cracked inside, gatherings rather slack.    *(Jenner)* **£12**
- The works of Aristotle, the famous philosopher, in four parts ... a new edition. New England, for the Proprietor, 1813. 16mo. 264 pp. Text browned. Contemp calf, quite rubbed, spine ends sl chipped.
  *(M&S)* **$100**

**Armatage, George**
- The cattle doctor. 1899. 7th edn. Revsd & enlgd. xx,928 pp. Ills, some cold. Qtr roan, purple cloth, gilt dec.    *(Phenotype)* **£25**
- Memoranda for emergencies; or, the veterinarian's pocket remembrancer: being concise directions for the treatment of urgent or rare cases ... 1870. Pocket size. xi,168 pp. New cloth.    *(Whitehart)* **£25**

**Armstrong, Harry G.**
- Principles and practice of aviation medicine. Balt: 1939. 496 pp. Ills.    *(Argosy)* **$40**

**Armstrong, John**
- Facts, observations ... puerperal fever, scarlet fever, pulmonary consumption, and measles ... Phila: 1826. 2nd Amer edn. vi,[2],120; iv,[4],216; 11 pp, half-title, 80 pp. Contemp lea, front jnt tender.    *(Elgen)* **$75**
- Facts, observations, and practical illustrations, relative to puerperal fever, scarlet fever, pulmonary consumption, and measles. A general view of the pathology ... Hartford: 1823. 1st Amer edn. 120,216,80 pp. Contemp mottled calf.    *(M&S)* **$40**
- Facts, observations, and practical illustrations, relative to puerperal fever, scarlet fever, pulmonary consumption, and measles. A general view ... Hartford: Cooke, 1823. 1st Amer edn. vi[1],120, iv,[3], 216,80 pp. Foxed, staining. Orig bds, spine reprd.
  *(Diamond)* **$75**
- Facts, observations, and practical illustrations, relative to puerperal fever, scarlet fever, pulmonary consumption, and measles ... Hartford: 1823. 1st Amer edn. vi,[2],120; iv,[4],216; 11 pp, half-title, 80 pp.

Contemp lea, front hinge cracked. *(Elgen)* **$90**
- Lectures on the morbid anatomy, nature, and treatment, of acute and chronic diseases ... edited by Joseph Rix ... Phila: Haswell, 1837. 8vo. 687 pp. Contemp tree calf. Ex lib.
  *(Zeitlin)* **$75**
- Practical illustrations of the scarlet fever, measles, and pulmonary consumption; with observations on the efficacy of sulphureous waters in chronic complaints. 1818. 2nd edn. xii,468 pp. Roughtrimmed, calf-backed cloth with new endpapers.    *(Jenner)* **£65**
- Practical illustrations of typhus fever, of the common continued fever and of inflammatory diseases, &c., with notes, critical and explanatory ... Phila: James Webster, 1822. 2nd Amer edn. 8vo. xvi,17-434 pp. Browning & foxing. Lea, rubbed.    *(Elgen)* **$75**
- Practical illustrations of typhus fever, of the common continued fever, and of inflammatory diseases &c., &c. With notes critical and explanatory, ... Phila: J. Webster, 1822. 2nd Amer edn. 8vo. xvi,17-434 pp. Contemp sheep, worn, hinges weak.
  *(Hemlock)* **$75**
- Practical illustrations of typhus fever, of the common continued fever and of inflammatory diseases, &c., with notes, critical and explanatory by Nathaniel Potter, M.D. ... Phila: James Webster, 1822. 8vo. 434 pp. Contemp full tree calf, rubbed. *(Zeitlin)* **$125**
- Practical illustrations of typhus fever, of the common continued fever and of inflammatory diseases ... New York: Duyckinck 1824. 432 pp. Browned. Calf, bds re-attached.
  *(Xerxes)* **$70**

**Arnott, Neil**
- On warming and ventilating; with directions for making and using the thermometer-stove, or self-regulating fire and other new apparatus. London: Longman, 1838. 1st edn. viii,138 pp, a few w'cuts in text. Orig cloth-cvrd bds, rebacked.    *(Antiq Sc)* **$150**

**Arrhenius, Svante**
- Theories of chemistry: being lectures delivered ... edited by T. Slater Price. London: 1907. 1st edn. 212 pp. Spine stained.    *(Scientia)* **$55**
- Theories of solutions. New Haven: 1923. 4th printing. 247 pp. Spine frayed. Silliman Lectures.    *(Scientia)* **$27.50**
- Worlds in the making. London & New York: 1908. xiv,230 pp. Ills.    *(Weiner)* **£40**

**Arruga, H.**
- Ocular surgery. New York: 1956. 1st English translation. 948 pp.    *(Fye)* **$50**

**Art ...**
- The art of cookery ... See Glasse, Hannah
- The art of preserving the feet, or practical

instructions for the prevention and cure of corns, bunnions ... by an experience chiropodist. 1818. 1st edn. Uncut in orig bds, some wear. *(Robertshaw)* **£36**

**Arthur Foundation, James**
- Time and its mysteries ... Washington Square, New York & London: NYU Press, Milford, OUP, 1936-49. 1st edns. 3 vols. 8vo. viii,1202; viii,137; x,126 pp. 6 ills vol I. Cloth. *(Zeitlin)* **$30**

**Arthur, David**
- A manual of practical X-ray work. 1908. xii,244 pp. Ills. Title almost detchd. Orig brown cloth. *(Jenner)* **£20**

**Ash, Edwin**
- The problem of nervous breakdown. London: 1919. 1st edn. *(Gach)* **$20**

**Ash, J.E.**
- See Decoursey, Elbert & Ash, J.E.

**Ashburn, Percy**
- A history of the medical department of the United States Army. Boston: 1929. 1st edn. Spine lettering dull. *(Scientia)* **$35**

**Ashburner, R.W.**
- The shorthorn herds of England 1885, 86, 87. Warwick: 1888. 460,xxxii [breeders' advts]. Cloth gilt. Spine faded. *(Phenotype)* **£35**

**Ashe, Thomas**
- Memoirs of mammoth, and various other extraordinary and stupendous bones, of incognital, or non-descript animals, found in the vicinity of Ohio ... and Red Rivers. Liverpool: G.F. Harris, 1806. 1st edn. 8vo. Uncut. 12,60 pp. Orig bds, mod paper backstrip. *(Dailey)* **$200**

**Ashley, C.G. & Hayward, C.B.**
- Wireless telegraphy and wireless telephony. Chicago: 1914. 141 pp. Ills, diags. *(Weiner)* **£20**

**Ashton, T.J.**
- On the diseases, injuries and malformations of the rectum and anus; with remarks on habitual constipation. Phila: 1865. 2nd Amer edn. 287 pp. *(Fye)* **$50**

**Ashwell, Samuel, M.D.**
- A practical treatise on the diseases peculiar to women, illustrated by cases ... Boston: T.R. Marvin, 1843. 1st Amer edn. 8vo. 312 pp. Some foxing. Orig cloth, soiled. *(M&S)* **$37.50**

**Aston, Francis William**
- Isotopes. London: Arnold, 1923. 1st edn.

viii,152,8 [ctlg] pp. 4 plates, 21 text figs. *(Pollak)* **£125**
- Isotopes. London: Arnold, 1924. 2nd edn. xi,182,8 [ctlg] pp. 23 text figs. *(Pollak)* **£50**
- Isotopes. London: Edward Arnold & Co., 1922. 1st edn. 8vo. viii,152 pp. 4 plates, text diags. Orig blue cloth. *(Pickering)* **$200**
- Isotopes. 1922. 1st edn. viii,152 pp. Plates, diags. *(Weiner)* **£75**
- Mass spectra and isotopes. New York: 1933. 1st Amer edn. 248 pp. 8 plates. Bottom of front cvr frayed. *(Oasis)* **$25**
- Mass spectra and isotypes. London: Arnold, 1942. 2nd edn xii,276 pp. 12 plates, 48 text figs. Sgnd by author on front paste-down. [plus] 3 sides 8vo Trinity College notepaper in (?) Aston's ms giving details of lecture course on isotopes. *(Pollak)* **£75**
- Mass-spectra and isotopes. 1933. xii,248 pp. 8 plates, diags. *(Weiner)* **£30**

**Astrologer ...**
- The astrologer of the nineteenth century ... See Smith, R.C., et al.

**Astruc, Jean**
- A general and compleat treatise on all the diseases incident to children from the birth to the age of fifteen ... London: John Nourse, 1746. 1st edn. 8vo. x,229 pp, plus pub advts. Contemp calf, rebacked. *(Rootenberg)* **$850**
- A general and compleat treatise on all the diseases incident to children from the birth to the age of fifteen ... London: for John Nourse, 1746. 1st, and only, edn. 8vo. Some light marginal browning. Contemp sheep, rebacked. *(Quaritch)* **$625**

**Atcheson, Nathaniel**
- A letter addressed to Rowland Burdon, Esq., M.P. on the present state of the carrying part of the coal trade, with tables of several of the duties on coals ... Thomas Davison, 1802. 8vo. iv,34 pp. 2 fldg tables. Sl worn & stained. Uncut. Orig wraps. *(Deighton Bell)* **£120**

**Atkinson, E. Miles**
- Abscess of the brain: its pathology, diagnosis and treatment. London: 1934. 1st edn. 289 pp. *(Fye)* **$50**

**Atkinson, J.**
- Telephony. A detailed exposition of the telephone exchange system of the British Post Office. N.d. [1948-50]. 2 vols. xii,511; xii,872 pp. Spine of vol II torn, edges worn. *(Whitehart)* **£18**

**Atlay, J.B.**
- Sir Henry Wentworth Acland, Bart ... a memoir. London. 1903. 1st edn. 8vo. viii,507 pp. Frontis, 5 plates. *(Elgen)* **$35**

**Atlee, Washington L.**
- The chemical relations of the human body with surrounding agents. Phila: 1845. 8vo. 16 pp. Mod wraps.                    *(Argosy)* **$40**

**Aubertin, J.J.**
- By order of the sun to Chile to see his total eclipse April 16, 1893. London: Kegan Paul, 1894. [xii],152, 80 [pub ctlg]. Frontis, 4 plates, 1 of which torn. Blue dec cloth, silver & gilt. Author's pres copy.   *(Pollak)* **£12.50**

**Auginbaugh, William E.**
- I swear by Apollo; a life of medical adventure. New York: n.d. [ca 1938]. 1st edn. Dw.
                                        *(Argosy)* **$25**

**Austin, William**
- A treatise on the origin and component parts of the stone in the urinary bladder. London: W. Bulmer for G. Nicol, 1791. Sole edn. 8vo. [4],123,[1] pp. Some browning. Mrbld bds, rubbed.                          *(Dailey)* **$250**

**'Avion' (pseud.)**
- Aeroplanes and aero engines. An introduction to the study of flight in simple language for the man in the street. 1918. 1 plate, 43 ills. Spine faded, cloth dust-stained.
                                    *(Whitehart)* **£18**

**Axenfeld, Theodor**
- The bacteriology of the eye. Translated ... London: Bailliere, Tindall & Cox, 1908. xv,[1],402,[iv] pp. 3 cold plates. 87 text ills.
                                        *(Pollak)* **£25**

**Aylett, Stanley**
- Surgery of the caecum and colon. Edinburgh: 1954. 1st edn. 295 pp.            *(Fye)* **$15**

**Ayres, J.G.**
- See Gray, Horace & Ayres, J.G.

**Ayres, S.C.**
- Tumors of the optic nerve. Cincinnati: 1890. 12mo. 2 plates, sev text ills. Printed wraps.
                                        *(Argosy)* **$35**

**Babbage, Charles**
- The ninth Bridgewater treatise. A fragment. London: J. Murray, 1837. 1st edn. 240,[1] pp. With the half-title. Mod cloth, uncut.
                                    *(Antiq Sc)* **$175**
- The ninth Bridgewater treatise. A fragment. London: John Murray, 1837. 2nd edn. viii,xii, 23-270,[4] pp. 8 pp advts. Uncut. Orig ribbed brown cloth, rebacked, orig spine laid down. Pres copy from Babbage's son.
                                    *(Pickering)* **$300**
- The ninth Bridgewater treatise. A fragment. London: J. Murray, 1837. 1st edn. [iv],xxii,23-240,[i ctlg],[i blank]. 3 plates,

various text figs. Orig cloth, paper label, sl wear on spine, one gathering a little weak.
                                        *(Pollak)* **£120**
- The ninth Bridgewater treatise. A fragment. London: J. Murray, 1837. 1st edn. Lacking the half-title. Contemp half-mor, pebbled cloth bds. Armorial device in gilt on front bd.
                                    *(McDowell)* **£60**
- The ninth Bridgewater treatise. A fragment. London: John Murray, 1838. 2nd edn. Contemp tree calf, rebacked. *(McDowell)* **£140**
- On the economy of machinery and manufactures ... London: Charles Knight, 1833. 3rd edn enlgd. 8vo. Engvd title, text w'cut, Orig purple cloth, spine sl faded.
                                    *(Quaritch)* **$750**
- On the economy of machinery and manufactures ... London: Charles Knight ..., 1833. 3rd edn in 8s. xxiv,392,[2 advts] pp. Engvd title, sl foxed. Orig cloth, a little worn, spine faded & sl damaged.
                                    *(Pickering)* **$400**
- On the economy of machinery and manufactures ... London: Charles Knight ..., 1846. 3rd printing of 4th edn enlgd. 8vo. xxiv,408 pp. Engvd title. Orig cloth, rebacked preserving the orig spine. Royal Institution Library stamps.          *(Pickering)* **$500**
- Table of logarithms of the natural numbers, from 1 to 108,000. Stereotyped edition. London: Spon, 1872. xx,201,[ii] pp. Faint mark at lwr edge of prelims. New cloth.
                                        *(Pollak)* **£30**
- Table of logarithms of the natural numbers, from 1 to 108,000. Stereotyped edition. London: E. & F.N. Spon, 1889. Roy 8vo.
                                    *(McDowell)* **£24**

**Babcock, Harriet**
- Time and the mind: Personal tempo - the key to normal and pathological mental conditions. Cambridge: Sci-Art Publishers, [1941]. 1st edn. 304 pp. Spine faded. Sgnd copy.
                                        *(Gach)* **$25**

**Bache, Franklin**
- Introductory lecture to the course of chemistry, delivered in Jefferson Medical College. Phila: 1852. 8vo. 16 pp. Sewed.
                                        *(Argosy)* **$30**

**Bacon, Francis**
- The philosophical works .. with occasional notes. London: J.J. & P. Knapton, &c., 1733. 1st coll edn. 3 vols. 4to. Rebacked, orig labels preserved.                      *(McDowell)* **£275**
- The works. 1819. 10 vols. Port. A few stains in vols I & II. Near-contemp dark blue half-calf.                        *(Robertshaw)* **£150**

**Bacon, R.N.**
- The report on the agriculture of the County of Norfolk ... 1844, 416 pp. 2 ports, 5 fldg

maps, 12 full page plates, 4 fldg plans, many ills. Orig cloth, faded, rebacked.
*(Phenotype)* £75

**B[adcock] W[illiam]**
- A touch-stone for gold and silver wares, or, a manual for Goldsmiths ... with the particular weights, allay, and value of each coyn. London: for John Bellinger, 1677. 1st edn. Engvd frontis, engvd plate. Penult leaf reprd. Contemp calf, rebacked.    *(McDowell)* £550

**Baden-Powell, Major B.**
- Practical aero-dynamics and the theory of the aeroplane. London: n.d. [ca 1907]. [viii],57 pp. Frontis. Plate, text figs. Orig limp cloth, sl damage to fore-edge of half-title.
*(Pollak)* £20

**Badgley, Carl E.**
- Collected works: selected scientific publications, papers, speeches and letters. Edited by Joe M. Abell. Ann Arbor: [1962]. 4to. Many ills. Cloth.    *(Argosy)* $35

**Bailey Radium Labs Inc.**
- Modern treatment of arthritis and kindred conditions with radium water. N.J.: 1927. 8vo. 31 pp. Orig printed wraps. *(Argosy)* $30
- Radium in rejuvenescence. N.J.: 1929. 8vo. 30 pp. Ills. Orig printed wraps. *(Argosy)* $25

**Bailey, J. & Culley, G.**
- General view of the agriculture of Northumberland ... Cumberland ... Westmorland ... [3 parts in 1, Westmorland by A. Pringle]. 1797. 1st 8vo edn. viii,319 pp. Frontis, fldg map, 10 plates. Contemp half-calf. Jnts split.    *(Phenotype)* £90

**Bailey, Pearce**
- Accident and injury, their relations to diseases of the nervous system. New York: 1899. 1st edn. 430 pp.    *(Fye)* $100
- Diseases of the nervous system resulting from accident and injury. New York: 1906. 627 pp. Num photographs. Half lea.    *(Fye)* $65
- Diseases of the nervous system resulting from accident and injury. New York: 1906. 1st edn.    *(Scientia)* $35
- Diseases of the nervous system resulting from accident and injury. 1909. xii,627 pp. 94 figs & plates. Orig cloth.    *(Whitehart)* £40

**Bailey, Percival**
- Intracranial tumors. Springfield: 1933. 1st edn. 475 pp. Scattered pencil underlining. Ex lib. Wells Eagleton's copy with his b'plate.
*(Fye)* $250
- Intracranial tumors. Springfield: 1948. 2nd edn. 478 pp. 16 plates. Dw.    *(Oasis)* $60
- Intracranial tumors. Springfield: 1948. 2nd edn. 478 pp. Plates.    *(Fye)* $50

- Intracranial tumors. Springfield: 1948. 2nd edn. xxiv,478 pp. Frontis, 16 plates, bibliog. Recased in orig cloth.    *(Whitehart)* £40

**Bailey, Percival & Von Bonin**
- The isocortex of man. Urbana: University of Illinois Press, 1951. Lge 8vo. Num ills. Printed wraps.    *(Argosy)* $37.50

**Baillie, G.H.**
- Watches, their history, decoration and mechanism. London: Methuen, [1929]. 1st edn. Connoisseur's Library Edition. 8vo. xxiii, 383 pp. Cold frontis, 75 plates (6 in colour). Orig blind-stamped crimson cloth, gilt spine, t.e.g. Dw. Sgnd pres copy.
*(Zeitlin)* $400
- Watchmakers and clockmakers of the world. London: Methuen, [1929]. 1st edn. Connoisseur's Library Edition. 8vo. xiv, 415 pp. Orig crimson cloth, gilt spineine, rebacked with orig spine laid down, t.e.g.
*(Zeitlin)* $225
- Watchmakers and clockmakers of the world. London: N.A.G. Press, [1951]. 3rd edn, enlarged. 8vo. xxxv, 388 pp. Maps at rear. Orig cloth, Spine faded and chipped.
*(Zeitlin)* $40

**Baillie, Matthew**
- The morbid anatomy of some of the most important parts of the human body. Walpole, N.H.: G.W. Nichols, 1808. 2nd Amer edn. 271 pp. Contemp calf cvrs, worn & rehinged.
*(Diamond)* $75

**Bain, Alexander**
- Education as a science. London: Kegan Paul, 1879. xxviii,453,32 [pub advts] pp. 1st edn. 12mo. Dec red cloth. International Scientific Series.    *(Gach)* $50
- Mind and body. The theories of their relation. New York: D. Appleton & Co., 1873. 196 pp. Spine chipped.  *(Poitras)* $20
- The senses and the intellect. London: Parker, 1855. 8vo. xxxi,[1],614 pp, [1 advts]f. Orig cloth, rebacked.    *(Zeitlin)* $150

**Bainbridge, William**
- The cancer problem. New York: 1915. 1st edn. 534 pp. Autographed by the author.
*(Fye)* $60

**Baines, Arthur E.**
- Studies in electrophysiology (animal and vegetable). New York: 1918. 31 cold plates, many other text ills. 8vo. Cloth. Ex lib.
*(Argosy)* $30

**Baines, Edward**
- History of the cotton manufacture in Great Britain. With a notice of its early history in the east, and in all quarters of the globe ...

N.d. 18 plates, 11 w'cuts. Orig cloth, rebacked.          *(Edwards)* **£60**

**Baird Television Ltd.**
- Instructions for connecting and operating the Baird 'Televisor' home reception "set. N.d. [ca 1930]. 4to. [8] pp. 6 diags. Stapled as issued. Baird Television Ltd., 133 Long Acre.
*(Weiner)* **£150**

**Baker, George**
- An essay, concerning the cause of the endemial colic of Devonshire. London: J. Hughs, 1767. 1st edn. Slim 8vo. Contemp half-calf, rebacked.          *(McDowell)* **£160**

**Baker, Henry**
- Of microscopes, and the discoveries made thereby. London: J. Dodsley, 1785. 1st coll edn. 2 vols. 8vo. xxii,[1],324; xx,442,[10, index] pp. Fold-out frontis, 30 engvd plates, many fldg. Full calf, gilt spineine.
*(Dailey)* **$450**

**Baker, J.L.**
- An essay on the farming of Northamptonshire. 1852. 64 pp. Fldg cold map. Card cvrs, new cloth spine.
*(Phenotype)* **£28**

**Baker, John Wynne**
- Considerations upon the exportation of corn: written at the request of the Dublin Society. Dublin: S. Powell, printer to the Society, 1771. 1st edn. 8vo. 48 pp. Disbound.
*(Burmester)* **£75**

**Baker, T. Thorne**
- The spectroscope and its uses in general analytical chemistry. London: 1923. 2nd edn. 98 figs.          *(Winterdown)* **£10**
- The telegraphic transmission of photographs. 1910. xi,146 pp. Ills, diags.      *(Weiner)* **£50**

**Baker, Thomas**
- The geometrical key: or, the gate of equations unlock'd; a new discovery of the construction of all equations ... London: ... for R. Clavel, 1684. 1st edn. Sm 4to. Fldg leaf synopsis, 10 fldg engvd plates. Lightly browned & foxed. Contemp calf, rebacked.      *(Zeitlin)* **$1,350**

**Bakewell, Frederick C.**
- Philosophical conversations: in which are familiarly explained the cause of numerous daily occuring natural phenomena. London: Harvey & Darton, [1842]. 2nd edn. xiv,310,[ii] pp. Title vignette, text figs. Occas foxing. Gilt dec cloth.      *(Pollak)* **£25**

**Balbi, C.M.R.**
- Loud speakers, their construction, performance and maintenance, a practical

handbook for wireless manufacturers. 1926. 96 pp. Ills, diags.          *(Weiner)* **£25**

**Baldwin, H.R.**
- Precision in diagnosis, an essay read before the Medical Society of New Jersey. Newark: 1875. 8vo. 16 pp. Orig printed wraps. Ex lib.
*(Argosy)* **$25**

**Baldwin, James Mark**
- The individual and society, or psychology and sociology. London: Redman, 1911. 1st British edn. 210 pp. Pub rose cloth, spine faded.          *(Gach)* **$35**

**Bale, M. Powis**
- Woodworking machinery. Its rise, progress and construction, with hints on the management of saw mills. 1894. 2nd edn with additions. Fldg frontis & plates. Cloth, gilt, bds soiled.      *(Quinto Charing Cross)* **£36**

**Balfour, Andrew**
- First report of the Wellcome Research Laboratories at the Gordon Memorial College, Khartoum. Khartoum: 1904. Lge 8vo. 83 pp. Frontis. Plates, some cold. Cvrs sl soiled.          *(Jenner)* **£20**
- Third report of the Wellcome Research Laboratories at the Gordon Memorial College, Khartoum. Khartoum: 1908. Lge 8vo. 477 pp. Frontis. Plates, some cold. Cvrs sl soiled.          *(Jenner)* **£15**

**Balfour, Andrew & Archibald, R.G.**
- Review of some of the recent advances in tropical medicine, hygiene and tropical veterinary science ... in the Anglo-Egyptian Sudan. 1908. Lge 8vo. 251 pp. Frontis. Cvrs worn.          *(Jenner)* **£10**

**Balfour, F.M.**
- A treatise on comparative embryology. 1885. 2nd edn. 2 vols. xi,583,xxii; xi,792,xxiv pp. Vol II sl worn.          *(Whitehart)* **£50**

**Balfour, Francis**
- A collection of treatises on the effects of sol-lunar influence in fevers; with an improved method of curing them. Cupar: ... R. Tullis, 1815. 3rd edn. 8vo. [2]ff,12,xxxii,[4], 383 pp. 2 fldg tables. Sprinkled calf, black lea label.
*(Zeitlin)* **$375**

**Balfour, J.H.**
- Introduction to the study of palaeontological botany. Edinburgh: 1872. xvi,118 pp. 4 plates, ills.          *(Weiner)* **£25**
- Introduction to the study of palaeontological botany. Edinburgh: 1872. 8vo. 4 plates, 102 text figs. Lacks front free endpaper. Cloth.
*(Wheldon & Wesley)* **£18**

**Ball, J.**
- Forcible and rapid dilation of the cervic uteri for the cure of dysmenorrhea, with a new method of treatment for the permanent relief of flexion. New York: 1873. 8vo. 16 pp. 2 text w'cuts. Sewed. *(Argosy)* **$25**

**Ball, John**
- A new compendous dispensatory: or a select body of the most useful, accurate and elegant medicines ... for the several disorders incident to the human body ... 1769. 1st edn. 12mo. Contemp sheep, jnts torn, front inner hinge reprd. *(Robertshaw)* **£28**

**Ball, Walter W. Rouse**
- A short account of the history of mathematics. London: Macmillan, 1888. xxiii,464 pp. Orig cloth, darkened & a little worn at spine ends. *(Pollak)* **£30**

**Ballance, Charles & Edmunds, Walter**
- A treatise on the ligation of the great arteries in continuity with observations on the nature, progress and treatment of aneurism. London: 1891. 1st edn. 566 pp. Lib stamp on half-title. Rebound in cloth, lea label. *(Fye)* **$300**

**Ballhatchet, A.V.**
- Wireless apparatus making ... design, construction and operation. [1922]. viii,187 pp. Ills, diags. *(Weiner)* **£20**

**Bampfield, R.W.**
- An essay on curvature and diseases of the spine, including all the forms of spinal distortion ... Phila: 1845. 1st Amer edn. 223 pp. Sheep, rebacked. *(Goodrich)* **$125**

**Bancroft, Frederic & Pilcher, Cobb (eds.)**
- Surgical treatment of the nervous system. Phila: 1946. 1st edn. 534 pp. *(Fye)* **$50**

**Banfield, T.C.**
- The statistical companion for 1854. London: Longman, 1854. Sm 8vo. Orig cloth. *(Marlborough)* **£45**

**Bangs, L.B. & Hardaway, W.A. (eds.)**
- An American text-book of genito-urinary disease, syphilis and diseases of the skin. Phila: 1898. 1st edn. 4to. 1229,32 [pub ctlg] pp. 20 cold plates, 300 engvs. Rebacked. *(Elgen)* **$75**

**Bankoff, George**
- Plastic surgery. 1943. 372 pp. 560 ills. Orig blue cloth. *(Jenner)* **£17**
- The story of surgery. London: [1947]. 8vo. 16 plates. Cloth. *(Argosy)* **$35**

**Banting, Frederick G.**
- See MacLeod, John J.R. & Banting,

Frederick G.

**Barba, Albaro Alonso**
- A collection of scarce and valuable treatises upon metals, mines, and minerals. London: J. Hodges, 1740. 2nd coll edn. 8vo. [14],319,[1] pp. Engvd frontis. Contemp calf. Preserved in a cloth slipcase. *(Antiq Sc)* **$475**

**Barber, Elmer**
- Osteopathy complete. Kansas City: Barber, 1900. 3rd edn. 566 pp. Ills. Index. Cvr worn, front hinge cracked. *(Xerxes)* **$45**

**Barbour, A.H. Freeland**
- Spinal deformity in relation to obstetrics. New York: n.d. [ca 1885]. Thin folio. 39 plates, 15 in tint. Orig cloth, rebacked. *(Argosy)* **$125**

**Bard, Philip**
- Patterns of organisation in the central nervous system. Balt: 1952. 580 pp. 268 ills, 12 tables. *(Argosy)* **$60**

**Bardeen, Charles**
- Anatomy in America. Madison: 1905. 1st edn. 205 pp. Uncut. Wraps. *(Fye)* **$75**

**Bardsley, James Lomax**
- Hospital facts and observations, illustrative of the efficacy of the new remedies ... London: Burgess & Hill, 1830. Sole edn. 8vo. ix,[1],223 pp. Frontis. Mod qtr mor. *(Dailey)* **$150**

**Bardsley, Samuel Argent**
- Medical reports of cases and experiments, with observations, chiefly derived from hospital practice: ... canine madness ... London: R. Bickerstaff, 1807. 1st edn. 8vo. Contemp half-calf. *(Quaritch)* **$225**

**Barker, A.F.**
- The prospective development of Peru as a sheep breeding and wool growing country. Leeds. 1927. xii,174 pp. Ills, charts & graphs. Cloth samples on card. Orig cloth, somewhat faded, stained. *(Phenotype)* **£42**

**Barker, John**
- An essay on the agreement betwixt ancient and modern physicians: or a comparison between the practice of Hippocrates, Galen, Sydenham and Boerhaave ... 1748. xii,290 pp. Marginal stains to 26 leaves. Blind-tooled panelled calf, sl rubbed. *(Jenner)* **£100**

**Barker, Lewellys F.**
- Treatment of the commoner diseases met with by the general practitioner. Phila: Lippincott, 1934. 319 pp. Dw. *(Poitras)* **$17.50**

**Barker, Lewellys F. & Sprunt, Thomas P.**
- The degenerative diseases: their causes and prevention. New York & London: Harper & Brothers, 1925. 4to. 254 pp. Cvrs faded.
*(Poitras)* **$30**

**Barlow, Nora (ed.)**
- Charles Darwin's diary of the voyage of H.M.S. Beagle. Cambridge: 1934. 2nd printing. 451 pp.          *(Scientia)* **$50**

**Barlow, Peter**
- A new mathematical and philosophical dictionary; comprising an explanation of the terms and principles of pure and mixed mathematics ... 1814. Thick roy 8vo. 13 plates, diags. Uncut. Mod paper-covrd bds, amateurishly lettered.          *(Weiner)* **£65**

**Barlow, William**
- Magneticall advertisements: or divers pertinent observations ... concerning the nature and properties of the load-stone ... London: for Timothy Barlow, 1616. Sole edn. 4to. [xvi],86,[2] pp. Errata leaf. W'cut diags in text. Contemp sheep.          *(Pickering)* **$9,000**

**Barnaby, S.W.**
- Marine propellers. 1887. 2nd edn. xiii,78 pp. 4 plates (3 fldg), ills.          *(Weiner)* **£15**

**Barnard, Fordyce**
- Experts as witnesses. A lecture delivered before the New York Medico-Legal Society. New York: 1874. 8vo. 28 pp. Orig printed wraps.          *(Argosy)* **$30**

**Barnard, George P.**
- The selenium cell, its properties and applications. 1930. 8vo. xxix,331 pp. Frontis, Num ills & diags, bibliogs.          *(Weiner)* **£38**

**Barnard, Henry**
- Papers on Froebel's Kindergarten, with suggestions on principles and methods of child culture in different countries. Hartford: 1881. [ii],799,[3] pp. Frontis. Printed brown cloth.          *(Gach)* **$30**

**Barnard, J.E. & Welch, F.V.**
- Practical photo-micrography. 1936. 3rd edn. xii,352 pp. 23 plates. Cloth sl dust-stained.
*(Whitehart)* **£15**

**Barnard, J.G.**
- The phenomena of the gyroscope, analytically examined. With two supplements, on the effects of initial gyratory velocities, and of retarding forces on the motion of the gyroscope. New York: Van Nostrand, 1858. 1st coll edn. 8vo. 42 pp. Orig printed wraps.          *(Antiq Sc)* **$90**

**Barnes, Francis M.**
- An introduction to the study of mental disorders. St. Louis: C.V. Mosby Company, 1923. 2nd edn. 295 pp.          *(Gach)* **$25**

**Barnes, Irene H.**
- Between life and death: The story of C.E.Z.M.S. medical missions in India, China and Ceylon. London: 1901. Ills. (Church of England Zenana Missionary Society).
*(Argosy)* **$45**

**Barnes, R.**
- A clinical history of the medical and surgical diseases of women. 1878. xix,918 pp. 181 figs. Orig cloth, spine faded. *(Whitehart)* **£40**

**Barnes, Robert**
- Lectures on obstetric operations. London: 1871. 2nd edn. 508 pp.          *(Fye)* **$50**

**Barnett, Adam**
- Doctor Harry; the story of Dr. Herman Lorber. New York: [1958]. Cloth. Dw.
*(Argosy)* **$25**

**Barnett, S.A. (ed.)**
- A century of Darwin. London: Heinemann, 1959. 2nd edn. Frontis. 8vo. Dw.
*(McDowell)* **£18**

**Barnhill, John Finch**
- Surgical anatomy of the head and neck. Balt: 1937. 1st edn. 4to. xiii,921 pp. Frontis, 431 ills, sev in colour.          *(Elgen)* **$65**

**Baron, John**
- The life of Edward Jenner ... with illustrations of his doctrines and selections from his correspondence. 1838. 2 vols. 624; 471 pp. 2 frontis. Some foxing. New half lea.
*(Jenner)* **£200**

**Barrett, A.W.**
- Dental surgery for medical practitioners and students of medicine. 1905. 4th edn. xii,159,[i], 16 [advts] pp. 85 text ills. 2 leaves with discoloured edges.          *(Pollak)* **£10**

**Barrough, Philip [or Barrow]**
- The methode of physicke containing the causes, signes, and cures of inward diseases in mans body from the head to the foote ... London: ... Vautrolier, 1583. 1st edn. Folio in sixes. [8]ff,303 pp. Orig limp vell. Title & 1 leaf supplied in facsimile.          *(Zeitlin)* **$2,875**

**Barrow, Isaac**
- Euclid's elements; the whole fifteen books, compendiously demonstrated ... London: For W. & J. Mount, 1751. [viii],384 pp. Frontis, 9 plates. Occas foxing. Contemp calf, rubbed.
*(Pollak)* **£75**

- Geometrical lectures ... translated ... corrected and amended by ... Isaac Newton. By Edmund Stone, F.R.S. London: for Stephen Austen, 1735. 1st English trans. 8vo. [1]f,vi, 309,[1] pp (some misnumbering),[1]f. Engvd frontis, 11 fldg plates. Old calf rebacked. *(Zeitlin)* **$375**

**Barrow, Philip [or Barrough]**
- See Barrough, Philip

**Barrus, Clara**
- Nursing the insane. New York: Macmillan, 1908. 1st edn. xii,409 pp. *(Gach)* **$25**

**Barsky, Arthur**
- Plastic surgery. Phila: 1938. 1st edn. 355 pp. *(Fye)* **$100**

**Bartholow, Roberts**
- Medical electricity: a practical treatise on the applications of electricity to medicine and surgery. Phila: 1882. 2nd edn. 291 pp. *(Fye)* **$40**
- Treatise on the practice of medicine. New York: 1887. 6th edn revsd & enlgd. Large thick 8vo. xxvi,990,8 [pub ctlg] pp. 54 ills. Full sheep, rubbed. *(Elgen)* **$30**

**Bartlett, Elisha**
- The history, diagnosis, and treatment of the fevers of the United States. Phila: Blanchard & Lea, 1852. 3rd edn, revsd. 595 pp. Embossed bds, faded, sl chip in spine. *(Poitras)* **$250**
- Sketches of the character and writings of eminent living surgeons and physicians of Paris, Translated from the French ... Boston: 1831. 1st edn. 2 litho ports by Pendleton. Foxed. Old bds, worn & soiled. *(M&S)* **$30**

**Bartlett, John**
- A discourse on the subject of animation delivered before the Humane Society. Boston: 1792. Sq 12mo. 40 pp. Sewed. *(Argosy)* **$85**

**Bartlett, John Russell**
- The progress of ethnology, an account of recent archaeological, philological and geographical researches in various parts of the globe, tending to elucidate the physical history of man. New York: 1847. 1st edn. 8vo. 151 pp. Orig printed wraps, loose. *(M&S)* **$75**

**Barton-Chapple, H.J.**
- Popular television. 1935. xiii,112 pp. Ills, diags. 18pp illust advts for television components. *(Weiner)* **£20**
- See Moseley, Sydney A. & Barton-Chapple, H.J.

**Baruch, Simon**
- Principles and practice of hydrotherapy. New York: Wood, 1899. 435 pp. Ills. A few pencil notes on endpapers & index. Final leaf detchd. *(Xerxes)* **$55**

**Barzilai, Gemma**
- Atlas of ovarian tumors, New York: 1949. 1st edn. 4to. 261 pp. 58 photomicrograph plates, some cold. *(Fye)* **$40**

**Bashford, H.H.**
- Harley Street calendar. London: 1930. 8vo. Cloth. *(Argosy)* **$35**

**Bass, Charles C.**
- See Dock, George & Bass, Charles C.

**Bast, Theodore & Anson, Barry**
- The temporal bone and the ear. Springfield: 1949. 1st edn. 478 pp. *(Fye)* **$45**

**Bastian, H. Charlton**
- The brain as an organ of mind. London: Kegan Paul, Trench & Co., 1885. Thick sm 8vo. [viii],[xvi], 708 pp. 44 pp ctlg. Dec red cloth. *(Gach)* **$50**
- The nature and origin of living matter. London: Fisher Unwin, 1905. 1st edn. 8vo. Ills. Pub cloth, rubbed. *(McDowell)* **£28**

**Bateman, John Frederic & Revy, Julian John**
- Channel Railway. Description of a proposed cast-iron tube for carrying a railway across the Channel between the coast of England and France. Vacher & Sons, August 1869. 59, [v blank] pp. Lge fldg plate. Orig printed wraps. *(Pollak)* **£200**

**Bateman, Thomas**
- A practical synopsis of cutaneous diseases according to the arrangement of Dr. Willan. London: 1813. 2nd edn. xxiv,342 pp. Cold frontis. Orig green pebbled cloth, crnrs bumped, spine sl stained, upper bd damp-stained. *(Jenner)* **£100**
- A practical synopsis of cutaneous diseases according to the arrangement of Dr. Willan ... London: 1824. 6th edn. 8vo. Cold frontis. xxiv,343 pp. Contemp mottled calf, crnrs bruised. *(Hemlock)* **$100**

**Bateman, William**
- Magnacopia; or a library of useful and profitable information for the chemist and druggist, surgeon-dentist, oilman, and licensed victualler. 1835. 1st edn. 12mo. Orig bds, some wear. *(Robertshaw)* **£9**

**Bates, Cadwallader John**
- Thomas Bates and the Kirklevington Shorthorn. A contribution to the history of

pure Durham cattle. Newcastle: 1897. xxii,513 pp. 2 maps, 7 pedigrees, 6 plates.
*(Phenotype)* **£70**

**Bates, Henry W.**
- The naturalist on the River Amazon. London: 1863. 1st edn. 2 vols. 351; 423 pp. Fldg map. Rebnd in cloth. Cvrs rubbed.
*(Scientia)* **$300**
- The naturalist on the River Amazon. With a memoir of the author by Edward Clodd. New York: 1892. Abrgd reprint of 1st edn. lxxxix,395 pp. Spine worn. Ex lib.
*(Scientia)* **$60**

**Bates, William**
- See Judovich, Bernard & Bates, William

**Bateson, Beatrice**
- William Bateson, F.R.S., naturalist. His essays and addresses together with a short account of his life. Cambridge: 1928. 4 plates.
*(Winterdown)* **£25**

**Bateson, William**
- The law of heredity. A study of the cause of variation and the origin of living organisms. Balt: n.d.. 2nd edn, revsd. *(Scientia)* **$65**
- The law of heredity. A study of the cause of variation and the origin of living organisms. Balt: 1883. 1st edn. 336 pp. *(Scientia)* **$85**
- Materials for the study of variation, treated with especial regard to discontinuity in the origin of species. London: 1894. 1st edn. 598 pp. Inner rear hinge cracked. *(Scientia)* **$200**
- Materials for the study of variation ... London: 1894. 8vo. xvi, 598 pp. 209 text figs. Few pencil annotations. Orig cloth, sl worn, inner jnts cracked. Ex lib.
*(Wheldon & Wesley)* **£70**
- Materials for the study of variation, treated with especial regard to discontinuity in the origin of species. London: 1894. 8vo. xvi, 598 pp. 209 text figs. Sgntr on half-title. Orig cloth. *(Wheldon & Wesley)* **£85**
- Mendel's principles of heredity. Cambridge: University Press, 1909. 1st edn. xiv,[2],396 pp. Half-title, 3 photog ports, 6 cold plates, text figs & errata. Orig cloth rebacked with orig spine laid down. *(Rootenberg)* **$250**
- Mendel's principles of heredity. Cambridge: University Press, 1909. 1st edn. Roy 8vo. 3 ports, 6 cold plates, 38 figs. Pub dark green cloth. *(McDowell)* **£80**
- Mendel's principles of heredity. Cambridge: University Press, 1909. 1st edn, 2nd printing. 3 ports, 6 cold plates, many figs in text. Pub cloth, crnrs bumped, front bd sl snagged.
*(McDowell)* **£60**
- Mendel's principles of heredity. Cambridge: 1909. 1st edn, 2nd printing. xiv,396 pp. Frontis, 6 cold plates, text ills. *(Elgen)* **$150**
- Mendel's principles of heredity. Cambridge;

1913. 3rd imp, with addtns. Roy 8vo. xiv,396 pp. 3 ports, 6 cold plates, 38 text figs. Half-title sl browned. Orig cloth, trifle used.
*(Wheldon & Wesley)* **£30**
- Mendel's principles of heredity: a defence. Cambridge. 1st edn. *(Scientia)* **$300**

**Baudelocque, J.L.**
- An abridgement of Mr. Heath's translation of Baudelocque's midwifery. With notes by William P. Dewees. Phila: 1811. 588 pp. 7 engvd plates. Full lea. *(Fye)* **$275**

**Baudoin, Charles**
- The birth of the psyche. Translated by Fred Rothwell. London: George Routledge, 1923. 1st edn in English. 12mo. Cloth-backed rose bds. *(Gach)* **$20**
- Suggestion and autosuggestion; A psychological and pedagogical study ... 1922. 6th imp. 288 pp. Sl spotting. Orig blue cloth.
*(Jenner)* **£9**

**Bauer, Louis**
- Lectures on orthopaedic surgery. Phila: Lindsay & Blakiston, 1864. 1st edn. 8vo. [2],108 pp. Frontis, text ills. Light browning, ownership stamp on title. Orig cloth, rebacked. Sgnd by the author on front fly leaf.
*(Rootenberg)* **$250**

**Bauer, Louis H.**
- Aviation medicine. Balt: 1926. 1st edn. xv,241 pp. Ills, plates. *(Elgen)* **$55**

**Bauerman, H.A.**
- A treatise on the metallurgy of iron ... history of iron manufacture ... 1882. 5th edn. xii,515 pp. Orig cloth. *(Whitehart)* **£18**

**Baume, Antoine**
- A manual of chemistry or a brief account of the operations of chemistry and their products, translated from the French ... Warrington: 1786. 2nd edn, crrctd, with addtns. 12mo. vi,399 pp, pub ctlg. Old calf, very worn, bds loose. *(Weiner)* **£40**

**Baumeister, R.**
- The cleaning and sewerage of cities. Adapted from the German ... New York: Engineering News Pub. Co., 1895. vii,293 pp. Ills. Minor cvr rubbing & staining. *(Diamond)* **$35**

**Baur, Erwin, et al.**
- Human heredity. Translated ... London: 1931. 1st edn in English. 734 pp.
*(Scientia)* **$37.50**

**Bausch & Lomb**
- Ophthalmic lenses. Their history, theory and application. Rochester: Bausch & Lomb Optical Co., 1935. 88 pp. *(Poitras)* **$30**

**[Baxter, Andrew]**
- Matho; or, the Cosmotheoria puerilis ... in which ... philosophy and astronomy are accomodated to the capacity of young persons ... London: A. Millar, 1740. 1st edn. 2 vols. 8vo. [12],432; [6],395,[1] pp. Contemp calf, spine lightly worn.          *(Rootenberg)* **$350**

**Baylis, Benjamin**
- On puddling, by a practical puddler. For the Author, 1866. Sm 8vo. 56 pp. Fldg frontis. Orig dec blind-stamped cloth.  *(Weiner)* **£38**

**Bayliss, Jones & Bayliss**
- Illustrated catalogues of solid and tubular wrought iron hurdles, patent continuous flat & round bar fencing, for horses, cattle, sheep ... Wolverhampton: Victoria Works, 1891. Dec title, ills throughout. Orig printed wraps.
*(McDowell)* **£45**

**Bayliss, W.M.**
- Intravenous injection in wound shock; being the Oliver-Sharpey Lectures ... May 1918. London: 1918. 1st edn. Half-title, xi,172 pp. 59 ills.          *(Elgen)* **$85**

**Bayliss, Sir William M.**
- The vaso-motor system. 1923. [vi],163 pp. Num ills. Occas pencilling. New red cloth, new endpapers.          *(Jenner)* **£20**

**Baynard, Edward**
- Health. A poem shewing how to procure, preserve and restore it. To which is annex'd the Doctor's Decade. Manchester: R. Whitworth, 1740. 8th edn. 12mo. 31 pp. Mod paper bds, lea spine.   *(Xerxes)* **$45**
- See Floyer, Sir John

**Baynes, H.G.**
- Analytical psychology and the English mind, and other papers ... with a foreword by C.G. Jung. London: 1950. ix,242 pp. Orig green cloth.          *(Jenner)* **£12**
- Mythology of the soul. A research into the unconscious from schizophrenic dreams and drawings. 1949. Reprinted. xii,939 pp. Frontis, 49 plates. Orig cloth. *(Whitehart)* **£25**
- Mythology of the soul. A research into the unconscious from schizophrenic dreams and drawings. London: Routledge & Kegan Paul, [1955]. 2nd imp.          *(Gach)* **$75**

**Beach, W.**
- The new guide to health; embracing a ... treatise on the healing art, on reformed or botanic principles ... without mercury, the lancet or the knife. 1852. 1st edn. Frontis. Some browning. Orig cloth, worn inner hinges broken.   *(Robertshaw)* **£10**

**Beadle, E.R.**
- Sacredness of the medical profession. Phila: 1865. 31 pp. Wraps.          *(Argosy)* **$20**

**Beale, L.J.**
- The laws of health, in relation to mind and body: a series of letters from an old practitioner to a patient. 1851. xv,306 pp. Orig blind-stamped cloth, rebacked.
*(Whitehart)* **£35**

**Beale, L.S.**
- How to work with the microscope. London: Harrison, 1868. 4th edn. xix,383 pp. Photographic frontis, 69 plates. Cvrs shabby, jnts weak. A working copy.   *(Pollak)* **£10**
- How to work with the microscope. London: 1868. 4th edn. 8vo. xix,383 pp. Over 400 ills. Cloth, trifle used, inner jnts weak.
*(Wheldon & Wesley)* **£35**

**Beale, Lionel John**
- Observations on distortions of the spine; with a few remarks on deformities of the legs. London: John Wilson, 1831. 1st edn. 8vo. Litho frontis, litho plate. Without the half-title (?). Mod half-calf. Inscribed "from the Author" at hd of title.   *(Quaritch)* **$325**

**Beale, Lionel S.**
- On slight ailments, and on treating disease. 1890. 3rd edn. viii,374 pp. Cvrs sl soiled.
*(Jenner)* **£10**
- On slight ailments: their nature and treatment. Phila: 1880. 8vo. Cloth.
*(Argosy)* **$35**
- Our morality and the moral question, chiefly from the medical side. London & Phila: 1887. 12mo. Cloth.          *(Argosy)* **$35**

**Beaman, A. Gaylord**
- A doctor's odyssey. A sentimental record of Le Roy Crummer: physician, author, bibliophile, artist in living. Balt: John Hopkins, 1935. 8vo. ix,340 pp. Frontis, ills.
*(Poitras)* **$45**
- A doctor's odyssey. A sentimental record of Le Roy Crummer: physician, author, bibliophile, artist in living. Balt: 1935. 8vo. Cloth.          *(Argosy)* **$35**

**Beard, G.M. & Rockwell, A.**
- The medical use of electricity with special reference to general electricization as a tonic in neuralgia ... New York: 1867. 65 pp. Some leaves a bit brittle. Orig cloth. Ex lib.
*(Goodrich)* **$45**
- Practical treatise on the medical and surgical uses of electricity. New York: 1884. 4th edn. 4to. 758 pp. 200 ills.   *(Argosy)* **$100**

**Beard, George M.**
- American nervousness. Its causes and

consequences: a supplement to Nervous Exhaustion. New York: G.P. Putnam's Sons, 1881. 1st edn. 12mo. [iv],xxii, 352,[2] pp. Pebbled green cloth.          *(Gach)* **$125**
- Certain queries in electro-physiology & electro-therapeutics. N.p.: 1872. 8vo. 13 pp. Mod wraps. Ex lib.          *(Argosy)* **$35**
- A new method of treating malignant tumors by electrolyzing the base. New York: 1874. 8vo. 16 pp. Orig printed wraps. Ex lib.          *(Argosy)* **$35**
- A practical treatise on nervous exhaustion. New York: William Wood, 1880. 1st edn. 8vo. xx,198 pp. Orig cloth.          *(Dailey)* **$145**
- A practical treatise on nervous exhaustion (neurasthenia). New York: William Wood, 1880. 2nd, revsd, edn. xxviii,198 pp. Bevelled brown cloth, hinges broken. Somewhat musty.          *(Gach)* **$85**
- The study of trance, muscle-reading and allied nervous phenomena in Europe and America. ... New York: 1882. 16mo. 40 pp. Text ills. Orig printed wraps.          *(Argosy)* **$40**

**Beatson, Major-General Alexander**
- A new system of cultivation without lime or dung or summer fallows, as practiced at Knowle-Farm, in the county of Sussex. Printed by B.W. Bulmer & W. Nicol, 1820. 8vo. Half-title. xvi,162 pp. 4 engvd plates, some browning. Uncut. New bds, paper label.          *(Deighton Bell)* **£80**

**Beatson, George Thomas**
- Congenital deformity of both thumbs. N.p.: n.d. [ca 1897]. 8vo. 6 pp. 3 photographic plates. Wraps.          *(Argosy)* **$20**

**Beaumont, R.**
- Woollen and worsted. The theory and technology of the manufacture of woollen, worsted and union yarns and fabrics. 1916. 2 vols. xxxvi,640 pp. 42 plates, 469 ills in text. Light staining on prelims, sm lib stamps on some pages.          *(Whitehart)* **£40**

**Beaumont, William**
- Experiments and observations on the gastric juice, and the physiology of digestion. Plattsburgh: F.P. Allen, 1833. 1st edn. 226 x 135 mm. 280 pp. Foxing. Stamps on title. Foxing. Orig linen-backed bds, paper label, hinges cracked.          *(Hemlock)* **$1,400**
- Experiments and observations on the gastric juice, and the physiology of digestion. Boston: Lilly, Waite & Co., 1834. 8vo. 280 pp. Occas spotty foxing. Contemp cloth-backed bds, paper label, spine faded, jnts sl loosened.          *(M&S)* **$1,000**

**Bechterev, V.M.**
- General principles of human reflexology. Translated ... New York: [1932]. 467 pp. Ills.

*(Argosy)* **$40**
- General principles of human reflexology: an introduction to the objective study of personality. Translated ... New York: [1933]. 1st US edn. 467,[3] pp. Frontis. Black cloth, shelfworn, front hinge cracked.          *(Gach)* **$50**

**Beck, Carl**
- The crippled hand and arm. Phila: 1925. 1st edn. 243 pp. Cold frontis. 302 ills. Orig cloth.          *(Oasis)* **$80**

**Beck, Conrad**
- The microscope, theory and practice. London: 1938. 217 pp. Cloth sl worn.          *(Winterdown)* **£10**
- The microscope. A simple handbook. 1921. 1st edn. 131 figs.          *(Winterdown)* **£10**
- The microscope. A simple handbook. 1921. 1st edn. 144 pp. 131 ills. Cloth sl stained.          *(Whitehart)* **£15**

**Beck, Richard**
- A treatise on the construction, proper use, and capabilities of Smith, Beck, and Beck's achromatic microscopes. London: John Van Voorst, 1865. Sole edn. 8vo. viii,144 pp. 28 engvd plates (some cold), with descriptive letterpress. Blind-stamped cloth.          *(Dailey)* **$450**

**Beckmann, John**
- A history of inventions and discoveries. Translated from the German ... London: R. Lea, 1814. 2nd edn, enlgd. 4 vols. 8vo. Contemp half-calf, mrbld bds.          *(McDowell)* **£250**
- A history of inventions, discoveries and origins. London: R. Bohn, 1846. 4th edn. 2 vols. 8vo. Port frontis in each vol. Pub blind-stamped cloth.          *(McDowell)* **£40**
- A history of inventions, discoveries and origins. Translated from the German ... London: Bohn, 1846, [and] George Bell, 1880. 4th edn, revsd & enlgd. 2 vols. xxiii,518 pp; xii,548 pp. 2 frontis. Orig blind-stamped cloth.          *(Pollak)* **£40**

**Bedford, Gunning**
- Clinical lectures on the diseases of women and children. New York: 1856. 4th edn. 602 pp.          *(Fye)* **$50**
- Lectures of obstetrics and the diseases of women and children. New York: 1846. 26 pp. Orig printed wraps.          *(Argosy)* **$25**

**Bedini, Silvio**
- Early American scientific instruments and their makers. Wash. DC: 1964. 1st edn. 184 pp.          *(Scientia)* **$60**

**Beebe, W.**
- Galapagos, world's end. New York &

London: 1924. 1st edn. xxi,443 pp. Roy 8vo.
9 cold plates, 83 other ills. Cloth, trifle used.
*(Wheldon & Wesley)* £50

**Beer, Arthur & Beer, Peter (eds.)**
- Kepler, four hundred years. Proceedings of
conferences held in honour of Johannes
Kepler. Oxford: 1975. 1st edn. 1034 pp.
Vistas in Astronomy vol 18. *(Scientia)* $95

**Beer, T.**
- Atmospheric waves. 1974. xvi,300 pp. 73 ills.
*(Whitehart)* £15

**Begbie, J. Warburton**
- Address in medicine: ancient and modern
practice of medicine. Edinburgh: 1875. 58
pp. *(Argosy)* $25

**Behan, Richard J.**
- Pain: its origin, conduction, perception and
diagnostic significance. New York: 1914. 1st
edn. 920 pp. *(Fye)* $50
- Pain: its origin, conduction, perception and
diagnostic significance. New York: 1914. 1st
edn. 920 pp. 191 text ills, many charts.
*(Argosy)* $40
- Pain: its origin, conduction, perception and
diagnostic significance. New York & London:
1920. Thick 8vo. 2nd edn. xxviii,920 pp. 191
ills & charts. Spine sl faded. *(Jenner)* £18

**Behrens, Charles F.**
- Atomic medicine. New York: [1949]. Ills. Ex
lib. *(Argosy)* $35

**Belcher, Geo. E.**
- Observations on membranous croup with
cases. New York: 1857. 30 pp. Orig printed
wraps. Author's pres copy. *(Argosy)* $30

**Bell, A.N.**
- Climatology and mineral waters of the United
States. New York: Wood, n.d. [ca 1885]. 4
w'engvs, 11 maps. *(Argosy)* $35
- Medical progress. Brooklyn: 1870. 33 pp.
Printed wraps. Oration, 47th anniversary
Kings County Medical Society. *(Argosy)* $25

**Bell, Alex. M.**
- Visible speech: the science of universal
alphabetics ... for the writing of all languages
in one alphabet ... inaugural edition. London
& New York: 1867. 1st edn. 4to. 126 pp. 16
plates. Orig cloth, 1 signature loose.
*(M&S)* $175

**Bell, Alexander Graham**
- Memoir upon the formation of a deaf variety
of the human race. [?New Haven, Ct.:
National Academy of Sciences, 1883]. 1st
edn. 4to. 86 pp. Fldg table. Orig cloth spotted
& stained. *(M&S)* $100

- Upon the production of sound by radiant
energy. Washington, DC: Gibson Brothers,
1881. 1st edn. 8vo. 45 pp. Ills. Orig printed
wraps, stamped "With the author's
compliments.". *(Rootenberg)* $225

**Bell, Benjamin**
- A system of surgery. Phila: 1791. 1st Amer
edn. 570,xxx pp. Inner hinges taped, front
outer hinge cracked, half of lea backstrip
missing. *(Fye)* $150
- A treatise on gonorrhoea virulenta and lues
venerea. Phila: for Robert Campbell, 1795.
First Amer edn. 2 vols. 8vo. Browned, with sl
worming. Contemp mottled calf.
*(Zeitlin)* $250
- A treatise on the theory and management of
ulcers: with a dissertation on white swellings
of joints. To which is prefixed, an essay ...
chirurgical treatment of inflammation ...
Edinburgh: 1789. New edn. xvi,484,[1] pp. 1
plate. Contemp lea, rubbed, worn.
*(Whitehart)* £85
- A treatise on the theory and management of
ulcers. Boston: Thomas & Andrews, 1791. 1st
Amer edn. 8vo. 295pp. Engvd plate. Linen-
backed blue bds, paper label, antique style.
*(Antiq Sc)* $145
- A treatise on the theory and management of
ulcers: with a dissertation on white swellings
of the joints. To which is prefixed an essay ...
on inflammation ... Boston: 1797. 264 pp.
Lea. *(Fye)* $300

**Bell, Charles**
- The anatomy and philosophy of expression as
connected with the fine arts. London: John
Murray, 1844. 3rd edn, enlgd. Roy 8vo. 4
engvd plates, ills in text. Advt slip at end. Pub
blind-stamped cloth, hd of spine reprd.
*(McDowell)* £110
- The anatomy and philosophy of expression as
connected with the fine arts. London: 1877.
7th edn. 254 pp. Num engvd plates. Prize lea.
*(Fye)* $100
- Engravings of the arteries ... Phila: 1833. 3rd
Amer edn. 64 pp text. 11 cold engvd plates (1
torn at fold). Minimal foxing. Half-calf, spine
badly broken. $100
- Engravings of the arteries; illustrating the
anatomy of the human body, and serving as an
introduction to the surgery of the arteries.
Phila: 1816. 2nd Amer edn. 78 pp text. 12
plates (11 cold, 1 fldg with short tear). Some
foxing, Contemp lea, sl rubbed. *(Elgen)* $185
- An exposition of the natural system of the
nerves of the human body ... Phila: 1825. 1st
Amer edn. 165 pp. 3 plates (2 fldg, with sm
tear), text w'cuts. Contemp lea, sl rubbed, jnt
tender. *(Elgen)* $235
- The hand - its mechanism and vital
endowments as evincing design. London:
1833. 2nd edn. 314 pp. Orig cloth, paper

label, inner hinge cracked.         *(Fye)* **$400**
- The hand - its mechanism and vital endowments as evincing design. London: 1834. 3rd edn. 348 pp. Orig cloth, paper label.         *(Fye)* **$350**
- The hand, its mechanism and vital endowments as evincing design. 1833. 2nd edn. xvi,314 pp. Orig bds, rebacked.
          *(Whitehart)* **£80**
- The hand, its mechanism and vital endowments, as evincing design. Phila: Carey, Lea & Blanchard, 1835. New edn. 12mo. 213,[5] pp. Orig cloth, somewhat soiled.         *(Gach)* **$75**
- A system of dissections, explaining the anatomy of the human body ... Balt: 1814. 1st Amer edn. 2 vols. 12mo. 265; 264 pp. One leaf of introductory material missing. Lea. Bds detchd, one spine defective. *(Fye)* **$150**

**Bell, Charles & Bell, John**
- The anatomy and physiology of the human body. New York: 1827. 5th Amer edn. 2 vols. 584; 475 pp. Engvd plates. Lea. Wear to extremities of binding, front hinge cracked on Vol I, labels missing.         *(Fye)* **$200**

**Bell, E.T.**
- The development of mathematics. New York: McGraw-Hill, 1945. 2nd edn. 8vo.
          *(McDowell)* **£25**

**Bell, G.J.**
- A practical treatise on segmental and elliptical oblique or skew arches setting forth the principles and methods to be followed in dealing with them. Carlisle: 1896. Sm 4to. [3],125 pp. 8 fldg plates, figs in text. Orig cloth stained & marked.     *(Whitehart)* **£18**

**Bell, Isaac Lothian**
- Chemical phenomena of iron smelting. An experimental and practical examination ... 1872. 3 fldg charts (1 cold). Text annotations, foxed.         *(Edwards)* **£15**
- Chemical phenomena of iron smelting. An experimental and practical examination ... the capacity of the blast furnace ... London: Geo. Routledge, 1872. 1st edn. xxiv,432 pp, errata leaf. 2 fldg diags, fldg table. Spine sl faded, ink name on title.     *(Diamond)* **$75**

**Bell, J. & Redwood, T.**
- Historical sketch of the progress of pharmacy in Great Britain. 1880. i,415 pp. Orig cloth, sl dust stained.     *(Whitehart)* **£35**
- Historical sketch of the progress of pharmacy in Great Britain. London: 1880.
          *(Winterdown)* **£30**
- Historical sketch of the progress of pharmacy in Great Britain. London: 1880. Sm 8vo. 415 pp. Cloth.         *(Argosy)* **$85**

**Bell, John**
- The anatomy of the human body. London: 1802-04. 4 vols. 3rd, 2nd & 1st edns. Lge 8vo. Num copperplates (lacking one plate). Contemp mottled calf, worn. *(Argosy)* **$150**
- The principles of surgery. New York: 1812. 2nd Amer edn. 562 pp. Lea binding scuffed, worn, front hinge broken.     *(Fye)* **$150**
- See Bell, Charles & Bell, John

**Bell, [John]**
- The general and particular principles of animal electricity and magnetism, &c... [London]: for the Author, 1792. 1st edn. 8vo. 80 pp. Sm tear in title reprd. Mrbld wraps.
          *(Rootenberg)* **$350**

**Bell, John & Condie, D. Francis**
- All the material facts in the history of epidemic cholera: a report of the College of Physicians of Philadelphia, to the Board of Health. Phila: 1832. 2nd enlgd edn. 8vo. Orig printed bds, rebacked.     *(Argosy)* **$75**

**Bell, Louis**
- The telescope. New York & London: McGraw-Hill, 1922. 1st edn, 7th imp. 8vo. Frontis, many ills. Pub blue textured cloth.
          *(McDowell)* **£26**
- The telescope. New York: 1922. viii,287. 190 ills.         *(Whitehart)* **£25**

**Bell, Luther V.**
- An attempt to investigate some obscure and undecided doctrines in relation to smallpox, varioloid and vaccination. Boston: Marsh, Capen & Lyon, 1836. 72 pp. Lacks backstrip. Ex lib.         *(Xerxes)* **$70**

**Bell, T.**
- The history of improved shorthorns, or Durham Cattle and of the Kirklevington Herd ... Newcastle: 1871. ix,373 pp. Frontis, 7 engvs. Red cloth, very faded.
          *(Phenotype)* **£28**

**Bell, Thomas**
- The anatomy, physiology, and diseases of the teeth. London: S. Highley, 1829. 1st edn. 8vo. xiii,[2],329 pp. 11 plates, 1f pub advts. Uncut in mod half-calf.   *(Rootenberg)* **$850**
- The anatomy, physiology, and diseases of the teeth. Phila: Carey & Lea, 1831. 2nd Amer edn. 8vo. xiii,[1],351,[1] pp. 11 engvd plates. Stamp on title, sporadic browning. Half-mor.
          *(Rootenberg)* **$250**

**Bell, Walter George**
- The Great Plague in London in 1665. London & New York: 1924. 4to. ix,374 pp. Frontis, 30 ills.     *(Poitras)* **$60**

**Bell, Whitfield J., Jr.**
- Early American science. Needs and opportunities for study. Williamsburg, VA: 1955. 1st edn. 85 pp. *(Scientia)* **$25**

**Bellasis, E.S.**
- River and canal engineering. The characteristics of open flowing streams ... 1913. x,215 pp. 72 ills. Orig cloth badly stained. *(Whitehart)* **£12**

**Bender, Lauretta**
- Psychopathology of children with organic brain disorders. Springfield: [1956]. Thin 8vo. Ills. Buckram. Dw. *(Argosy)* **$40**

**Benedict, F.G.**
- See Dodge, Raymond & Benedict, F.G.

**Benedict, Francis G.**
- Mental effort in relation to gaseous exchange, heart rate, and mechanics of respiration. Washington: 1933. 1st edn. Ills. Cloth-backed bds. *(Argosy)* **$35**

**Beneventi, Francis A.**
- Retropubic prostatectomy, for benign enlargement of the prostate gland. Springfield: [1954]. 4to. Ills. Buckram. *(Argosy)* **$27.50**

**Bennett, A.E. & Purdy, Avis B.**
- Psychiatric nursing technic. Phila: 1940. 8vo. Ills. Cloth. *(Argosy)* **$20**

**Bennett, A.R.**
- The telephone systems of the Continent of Europe. 1895. xiv,436 pp. Frontis, ills, tables. *(Weiner)* **£50**

**Bennett, John Hughes**
- Researches into the action of mercury, podophyllin, and taraxacum on the biliary secretion ... Chicago: 1874. 1st Amer edn. 80 pp. Marginal staining, not affecting text. Limp pebble cloth, rubbed & edges frayed. *(Elgen)* **$175**

**Bennett, R. & Elton, J.**
- History of corn milling. Handstones, slave and cattle mills. 1898. xix, 246 pp. Many ills. Green cloth gilt. *(Phenotype)* **£35**

**Bennion, Elisabeth**
- Antique medical instruments. London: 1979. 1st edn. 355 pp. Dw. *(Fye)* **$75**

**Benson, Reuel A.**
- A nursery manual: the care and feeding of children in health and disease. Phila: Boericke & Tafel, 1908. 12mo. 184 pp. Orig green cloth, spine & bds with some water-stains. *(Jenner)* **£12**

**Benson, William**
- Principles of the science of colour concisely stated to aid and promote their useful application in the decorative arts. 1868. Lge 4to. ix,48 pp. 5 plates (hand-cold?), other ills. Orig blind-stamped cloth, sl stained. *(Whitehart)* **£35**

**Bent, Silas**
- An address delivered ... upon the thermal paths to the Pole, the currents of the ocean and ... the climates of the world. Saint Louis: Studley, 1872. 8vo. 40 pp. 2 fldg litho maps in blue & red. Orig green pebbled cloth, gilt, crnrs sl worn. *(Zeitlin)* **$75**

**Berdoe, Edward**
- The origin and growth of the healing art. A popular history of medicine ... London: 1893. 1st edn. Half-title, frontis, xii,509 pp. 3 plates. Partly unopened. *(Elgen)* **$90**

**Berens, C. & Zuckerman, J.**
- Diagnostic examination of the eye. Phila: 1946. 1st edn. 711 pp. *(Fye)* **$30**

**Berg, Ernst Julius**
- Heaviside's operational calculus as applied to engineering and physics. New York: McGraw-Hill, 1929. 3rd imp. xiii,214 pp. 65 text figs. *(Pollak)* **£25**

**Bergen, W.C.**
- Practice of navigation and nautical astronomy. [1872]. xii,593 pp. Fldg plate, other ills. Half-mor, spine rubbed & marked. Inscribed by author. *(Whitehart)* **£25**

**Bergman, Torbern Olof**
- A dissertation on elective attractions ... translated ... London: for J. Murray, 1785. 1st edn in English. 8vo. xiv,[2],382, pp,[1]f. "Emendanda". 7 fldg tables (3 lge, 1 with sm tear). Outer margin frayed on first few leaves. Orig bds, shagreen backed. *(Zeitlin)* **$375**

**Bergmann, Ernst von, et al.**
- A system of practical surgery ... translated and edited ... New York: [1904]. 1st edn in English. 5 vols. Profusely illustrated, many cold plates. Orig full sheep. *(Elgen)* **$175**
- A system of practical surgery. New York: 1904. 1st edn in English. 5 vols. *(Fye)* **$200**

**Bergson, Henri**
- An introduction to metaphysics. London: 1913. 1st English edn. 79 pp. Pencil & crayon underscoring. Orig blue cloth. *(Jenner)* **£16**

**Berkeley, Edmund C.**
- Giant brains, or machines that think. New York: J. Wiley, [1949]. 8vo. xvi,270 pp. Orig cloth. *(Antiq Sc)* **$75**

**Berkeley, George**
- A treatise concerning the principles of human knowledge. Part 1 [all published]. Dublin, 1710. 1st edn. 8vo. [8],214 pp. Early leaves sl browned. Contemp panelled calf, rebacked.
*(M&S)* **$2,500**

**Berkeley, George, Lord Bishop of Cloyne**
- Siris: a chain of philosophical reflexions and inquiries concerning the virtues of tar water. London: 1744. New edn, with additions & emendations. 8vo. Mod wraps. *(Argosy)* **$100**

**Bermingham, Edward J.**
- Chronic nasal catarrh, and what the general practitioners can do for it. New York: 1893. 12mo. 45 pp. 18 ills. Printed wraps.
*(Argosy)* **$20**

**Bernays, Thelka**
- Augustus Charles Bernays: a memoir. Port St. Louis: 1912. 1st edn.        *(Argosy)* **$35**

**Bernhardt, F.A.**
- Questions relating to fires in general, the draught of smoke, and the saving of fuel. London: 1835. 8vo. 15 pp. Sm piece torn from crnr of title without loss. Mod bds.
*(Deighton Bell)* **£55**

**Bernheim, Bertram**
- Blood transfusion, hemorrhage and the anaemias. Phila: 1917. 1st edn. 259 pp.
*(Fye)* **$75**

**Bernheim, Bertrams M.**
- A surgeon's domain. Kingswood: [1949]. 12mo.        *(Argosy)* **$20**

**Bernutz, M. Gustave & Goupil, M. Ernest**
- Clinical memoirs on the diseases of women. New Sydenham Society, 1866. xiv,276; xii,270,83 pp. Ills. Little foxing in vol II. Orig cloth, spine sl worn at hd. *(Jenner)* **£35**

**Berry, R.J.A.**
- Brain and mind; or, the nervous system of man. New York: 1928. 1st edn. xii,608 pp. Ills.        *(Elgen)* **$45**
- Brain and mind; or, the nervous system of man. New York: 1928. 1st edn. 608 pp.
*(Argosy)* **$40**

**Berry, Richard J.A.**
- A cerebral atlas, illustrating the differences between the brains of mentally defective and normal individuals ... London: Oxford University Press, 1938. Atlas folio. xxvi,425 pp. 430 photographs. Orig blue cloth, bds rather buckled.        *(Jenner)* **£45**

**Bert, Paul**
- Barometric pressure: researches in experimental physiology. Translated ... Columbus: 1943. 1st edn in English. xxxii,1055 pp. Ills. Ex lib.        *(Elgen)* **$150**
- Barometric pressure: researches in experimental physiology. Translated ... Columbus: 1943. 4to. 1087 pp. Buckram. Ex lib.        *(Argosy)* **$125**

**Besant, Annie**
- The law of population, its consequences and its bearing upon human conduct and morals. 34th thou. New American edition from the 35th thou., English edn. Valley Falls, Kansas: Fair Play Publishing Co., 1889. 12mo. 47 pp. Orig printed wraps.        *(M&S)* **$60**

**Besse, H.**
- Diploteratology; or a history of some of the most wonderful human beings that have ever lived in double form ... strange freaks of nature and the causes of same. Delaware: 1874. 12mo. Text ills. Embossed cloth. Ex lib.        *(Argosy)* **$75**

**Best, William Newton**
- The science of burning liquid fuel. A practical book for practical men. N.p.: 1913. 1st edn. 8vo. [9],159 pp. Profusely illus. Orig cloth, spine faded.        *(M&S)* **$50**

**Bethan-Edwards, M.**
- Travels in France by Arthur Young during the years 1787, 1788, 1789. With an introduction ... 1889. lix,366,24 [pub advts] pp. Frontis. Dark green cloth, rear inner jnt split.        *(Phenotype)* **£18**

**Betton**
- Directions for taking and using the true and genuine British oil ... Betton's oil. London: n.d. [ca 1750]. 8pp. One folio sheet paginated & folded, but not cut or bound. Some edges frayed, affecting the text, browned & soiled, worn along fold lines.        *(Xerxes)* **$125**

**Beverley, E.**
- The Darwinian theory of the transmutation of species examined by a graduate of the University of Cambridge. 1868. 2nd edn. 386 pp. Orig cloth.        *(Whitehart)* **£35**

**Bianchi, Leonardo**
- A text-book of psychiatry for physicians and students. New York: William Wood, 1906. 1st edn in English. xvi,904 pp. 106 text ills. Pub cloth.        *(Gach)* **$75**

**Bichat, Xavier**
- Pathological anatomy. The last course of Xavier Bichat ... account of life and labours of Bichat ... Translated ... Phila: 1827. 1st edn in English. 232 pp. Browning, foxing. Contemp calf.        *(Elgen)* **$175**

- Physiological researches on life and death. Translated from the French by F. Gold. London: Longmans ..., [1815]. [viii],283,[i blank] pp. *(Pollak)* **£90**
- A treatise on the membranes in general, and on different membranes in particular. Boston: 1813. 1st edn in English. 260 pp. Full lea, hinges cracked, some chipping of spine. *(Fye)* **$400**
- A treatise on the membranes in general, and on different membranes in particular ... Translated ... Boston: 1813. 1st edn in English. xix,[1], [21]-259 pp, errata leaf. Marginal worming in 30 pages. Some foxing. Contemp tree calf, sl chipped. *(Elgen)* **$400**

**Bick, Edgar**
- History and source book of orthopedic surgery. New York: 1933. 1st edn. 254 pp. *(Goodrich)* **$65**

**Bickerton, Thomas H.**
- A medical history of Liverpool from the earliest days to the year 1920. 1936. 4to. xx,313 pp. 2 cloth-backed fldg maps (one sl curled), 6 other maps. Plates & ills. Pages uncut, tiny cut on top cvr. *(Jenner)* **£25**

**Bicknell, Franklin & Prescott, Frederick**
- The vitamins in medicine. 1942. Lge 8vo. [vi],662 pp. Frontis, ills. Hinges cracked, cvrs sl soiled. *(Jenner)* **£15**

**Bidwell, S.**
- Curiosities of light and sight. 1899. xii,226 pp. 50 ills. Light foxing. Orig cloth, unopened. *(Whitehart)* **£35**

**Biedl, Artur**
- The internal secretory organs. Their physiology and pathology. New York: William Wood & Co., 1913. 1st Amer edn. viii,[2],606 pp. Bevelled cloth cvrs, sl worn. Ex lib. *(Diamond)* **$75**

**Bigelow, Henry J.**
- Rapid lithotrity with evacuation. Boston: 1878. 1st edn. 41 pp. *(Fye)* **$40**
- Science and success. A valedictory address ... Boston: 1859. 2nd edn. 24 pp. Wraps. *(Fye)* **$35**

**Bigelow, Jacob**
- Brief expositions of rational medicine: Prefixed by the Paradise of Doctors, a fable. Boston: 1860. 12mo. 75 pp. Cloth. Ex lib. *(Argosy)* **$35**
- Florula Bostoniensis: a collection of plants of Boston and its vicinity. Boston: 1814. 1st edn. Old bds, reprd, uncut. *(Argosy)* **$175**
- A treatise on the materia medica, intended as a sequel to the pharmacopoiea of the United States Boston: Charles Ewer, 1822. 1st edn.

8vo. 424 pp. Some minor stains & soiling. Contemp calf, lea label, a little rubbed. *(M&S)* **$175**

**Biggs, Rosemary & Macfarlane, R.G.**
- Human blood, coagulation & its disorders. Oxford: [1953]. Ills. *(Argosy)* **$20**

**Billard, C.M.**
- A treatise on the diseases of infants, founded on recent clinical observations ... in pathological anatomy ... translated ... New York: 1839. 1st edn in English. viii,620 pp. Sl foxing. *(Elgen)* **$300**

**Billings, Archibald**
- First principles of medicine. Phila: Lea & Blanchard, 1851. 2nd Amer edn. 4to. xi,246 pp. 32 pp pub ctlg. Embossed cvrs, sl chipping at top. *(Poitras)* **$40**

**Billings, Frank**
- Focal infection. The Lane Medical Lectures. Delivered on September 20-24, 1915, Stanford University Medical School, San Francisco. New York: 1916. 1st edn. 8vo. Ills. *(Argosy)* **$85**

**Billings, J.S., et al.**
- The composition of expired air and its effects upon animal life. Washington: Smithsonian Institution, 1895. 1st edn. Sm folio. [4],80,[1] pp. Index. Title a little soiled. Lacks wraps, stitching nearly broken. *(M&S)* **$50**

**Billroth, Th.**
- Clinical surgery: extracts from the reports of surgical practice between the years 1860 - 1876. New Sydenham Society, 1881. xx,518 pp. 9 litho plates, 29 ills. *(Jenner)* **£35**
- General surgical pathology and therapeutics. New York: 1874. 2nd Amer edn. 697 pp. Ex lib. *(Fye)* **$100**
- General surgical pathology and therapeutics. New York: 1871. 1st edn in English. 676 pp. Half lea. Front free endpapers lacking, title discold & nearly detchd. *(Fye)* **$75**
- Historical studies on the nature and treatment of gunshot wounds from the fifteenth century to the present time (1859). Translated by C.P. Rhoads. New Haven: 1933. 1st edn in English. *(Scientia)* **$50**
- Lectures on surgical pathology and therapeutics. London: 1877-78. 1st edn in English. 2 vols. 438; 543 pp. Sev leaves damp-soiled, leaf of text missing. Cvrs worn, backstrip missing, shaken. *(Fye)* **$50**

**[Bindon, David]**
- Some thoughts on the woollen manufactures of England: in a letter from a clothier to a member of Parliament. London: for J. Roberts, 1731. 1st edn. 8vo. Half-title, 19 pp.

Tables. Mod mrbld wraps.
*(Deighton Bell)* £68

**Binet, Alfred & Simon, Th.**
- Mentally defective children ... with an appendix containing the Binet-Simon tests of intelligence. New York & London: [1914]. 2nd imp. xii,[179.[1] pp. 12mo. Red cloth, dusty & somewhat spotted.   *(Gach)* $37.50

**Binz, C.**
- Lectures on pharmacology for practitioners and students. London: New Sydenham Society, 1895-97. 1st English edn. 2 vols. 8vo. Pub blind-stamped cloth.   *(McDowell)* £75
- Lectures on pharmacology. London: New Sydenham Society, 1895-97. 1st edn in English. 2 vols. 389; 451 pp. Text ills. Orig cloth.   *(Oasis)* $60

**Bird, Golding**
- Elements of natural philosophy; being an experimental introduction to the study of the physical sciences. London: Churchill, 1839. xl,407,8 [ctlg] pp. Some margins marked. New cloth. A good working copy.
*(Pollak)* £10

**Birtwhistle, George**
- The principles of thermodynamics. Cambridge University Press, 1925. 1st edn. 8vo. Pub black cloth, some rubbing.
*(McDowell)* £26

**Bischof, Gustav**
- Elements of chemical and physical geology. Translated ... Cavendish Society, 1854. 3 vols. 8vo. Orig cloth, gilt, faded, stitching becoming loose in all vols, t.e.g.
*(Blackwell's)* £110

**Bishop, E. Stanmore**
- Uterine Fibromyomata. Their pathology, diagnosis and treatment. New York: 1904. 1st Amer edn. 323 pp.   *(Fye)* $25

**Black, Joseph**
- Experiments upon magnesia alba ... To which is annexed, An essay on the cold produced by evaporating fluids ... by William Cullen. Edinburgh: W. Creech, 1777. 1st edn in book form of both parts. 12mo. Some staining. Black calf, lea label, antique style.
*(Antiq Sc)* $1,350
- Lectures on the elements of chemistry ... Edinburgh: ... William Creech, 1803. 1st edn. 2 vols. 4to. lxxvi (misnumbered lxvi), [4],556; [2],762 pp. Port, 3 engvd plates. Without the 20 pp index. Water-staining 1st few leaves, occas foxing. Contemp tree calf.
*(Pickering)* $3,000

**Blackburn, Isaac Wright**
- Illustrations of the gross morbid anatomy of the brain in the insane. A selection of 75 plates showing the pathological conditions ... Washington: 1908. Roy 8vo. Orig cloth. Ex lib.   *(Argosy)* $75

**Blackburne, William**
- Facts and observations concerning the prevention and cure of scarlet fever, with some remarks on the origin of acute contagions in general. 1803. 166 pp. Unbound, in paper cvrs.   *(Jenner)* £50

**Blacker, C.P.**
- Eugenics: Galton and after. 1952. 349 pp. Port frontis, few ills. Bibliog of Dalton's papers. Sl worn. Dw.   *(Jenner)* £10
- Eugenics: Galton and after. Cambridge: 1952. 1st Amer edn. 349 pp. Dw.
*(Scientia)* $35
- Human values in psychological medicine. London: 1933.   *(Argosy)* $25
- Human values in psychological medicine. London: Oxford University Press, 1933. vii,179 pp. Orig maroon cloth. Author's inscrbd copy.   *(Jenner)* £10

**Blackfan, Kenneth D. & Diamond, Louis K.**
- Atlas of the blood in children. New York: 1944. 2nd imp. xiv,320 pp. 70 cold plates. Orig brown cloth. Dw.   *(Jenner)* £16

**Blackmore, Sir Richard**
- Creation. A philosophical poem. Demonstrating the existence and providence of a God. In seven books. London: J. Tonson, 1715. 3rd edn. 12mo. lxvi,[iv],237, [iii advts] pp. Some foxing throughout. Speckled calf, newly rebacked.   *(Pollak)* £40
- A treatise of consumptions and other distempers belonging to the breast and lungs. 1735. 3rd edn, crrcted. xxiv, dedicatory poem, 211 pp. Full calf gilt, sl rubbed.
*(Jenner)* £110

**Blackrie, Alexander**
- A disquisition on medicines that dissolve the stone. In which Dr. Chittick's secret is considered and discovered. London: D. Wilson: 1766. 12mo. [iv],123,[i blank] pp. Contemp calf, a little rubbing, lge ring mark on front bd.   *(Pollak)* £70

**Blackwell, Elizabeth**
- Pioneer work in opening the medical profession to women. Autobiographical sketches. London: 1895. 1st edn.
*(Scientia)* $150

**Blackwood, A.L.**
- The food tract, its ailments, and diseases of

the peritoneum. Phila: Boericke & Tafel, 1909. viii,359 pp. Orig red cloth, spine chipped at tail, hinges cracked. *(Jenner)* **£10**

**Blackwood, William, et al.**
- Atlas of neuropathology. Edinburgh: 1949. Thin 8vo. Profusely illust. Cloth.
*(Argosy)* **$50**

**Blaine, R.G.**
- Aetheric or wireless telegraphy. [1906]. 228,iv pp. Ills, diags. *(Weiner)* **£40**

**Blair, Vilray P.**
- Surgery and diseases of the mouth and jaws; a practical treatise on the surgery and diseases of the mouth and allied structures. St. Louis: 1912. 1st edn. *(Scientia)* **$125**
- Surgery and diseases of the mouth and jaws. St. Louis: 1914. 2nd edn. 638 pp. *(Fye)* **$200**

**Blake, Joseph**
- Fractures; being a monograph on gunshot fractures of the extremities. New York: 1919. 1st edn. 150 pp. *(Fye)* **$25**

**Blake, Robert**
- An essay on the structure and formation of the teeth in man and various animals. Dublin: William Porter, 1801. 1st English edn. 8vo. [10],xii,240,[4] pp. 9 engvs (7 fldg), errata & advt leaves. Orig half-calf, spine elab gilt.
*(Rootenberg)* **$850**

**Blakeman, Rufus**
- A philosophical essay on credulity and superstition; and also on animal fascination and charming. New York: Appleton, 1849. 1st edn. 12mo in 6's. [vi],206,[8] pp. Cloth-backed bds. *(Gach)* **$50**

**Blakey, Robert**
- History of the philosophy of the mind: embracing the opinions of all writers of mental science ... 1848. 4 vols. xlix,478; viii,520; viii,560; viii,676 pp. Lib cloth, stamps on titles, labels on spines, new endpapers, crnrs bumped. *(Jenner)* **£50**

**Blakiston, Peyton**
- Practical observations on certain diseases of the chest and on the principles of auscultation. Phila: 1848. 1st Amer edn. 384,32 [pub ctlg] pp. Mild occas damp-staining. Orig cloth, worn. Front hinge split.
*(Oasis)* **$60**

**Blancard, S.**
- The physical dictionary. Wherein the terms of anatomy ... causes of diseases ... instruments and their uses are accurately described ... virtues of medicinal plants ... London: 1726. 7th edn. [1], 370,[1] pp. Fldg

plate. Contemp panelled calf, very worn.
*(Whitehart)* **£120**

**Bland, Miles**
- Algebraical problems, producing simple and quadratic equations ... Cambridge: 1820. [vi],375 pp. Old damp stain on last few leaves. Orig bds, new cloth spine. *(Pollak)* **£20**
- The elements of hydrostatics: with their applications to the solutions of problems. Cambridge: Deighton, 1827. viii,359 pp. Half-calf, spine taped. Working copy.
*(Pollak)* **£20**

**Bland-Sutton, John**
- Evolution and disease. London: 1890. 1st edn. 8vo. 136 ills. Orig cloth. *(Argosy)* **$30**
- Gall-stones and diseases of the bile-ducts. New York: 1908. 12mo. 46 ills. Flexible calf, chipped. *(Argosy)* **$40**
- Tumours innocent and malignant. Chicago: 1903. 3rd edn. 556 pp. Engvs. Orig cloth, a little worn. *(Oasis)* **$35**
- Tumours innocent and malignant. London: 1917. 6th edn. ix,790 pp. 383 ills. Orig green cloth, sl tear in spine. Inscribed by author.
*(Jenner)* **£12**

**Blandford, George Fielding**
- Insanity and its treatment. Lectures on the treatment, medical and legal, of insane patients. Edinburgh: Oliver & Boyd, 1884. 3rd edn. 12mo. viii,507 pp. Pub red cloth, extremities worn, shelfworn. *(Gach)* **$50**

**Blane, Gilbert**
- Elements of medical logick, illustrated by practical proofs and examples. London: Thomas & George Underwood, 1819. 1st edn. 8vo. vii,[1], 219, [1 blank, 6 index], 8 pp advts. Orig bds. *(Dailey)* **$150**
- A lecture on muscular motion read at the Royal Society the 13th and 20th November, 1788. London: Joseph Cooper, [1788]. 1st edn. Folio. Title, 57 pp. Contemp soft wraps. Later pres copy to Sir Hans Krebs (1953 Nobel Prize in medicine). *(Hemlock)* **$250**
- Observations on the diseases of seamen. London: Joseph Cooper, 1789. 2nd edn, with crrctns & addtns. 8vo. 8,560,16 pp. Fldg table. Occas light foxing, lib stamp & contemp sgntr on title. Orig bds, spine partly perished, upper cover nearly detchd.
*(M&S)* **$200**

**Blanton, Wyndham B.**
- Medicine in Virginia in the Seventeenth Century.. New York: 1972. 4to. xvii,337 pp. Ills. *(Poitras)* **$20**

**Blatchford, Thomas W.**
- Hydrophobia: its origin and development, as influenced by climate, season, etc. Phila:

1856. 104 pp. Damp-stains. Stitched. Ex lib.
*(Argosy)* **$25**

**Blatz, William E. & Bott, Helen**
- Parents and the pre-school child. London &
Toronto: Dent, 1928. xii,306,[2] pp. 1st edn.
Worn dw.                       *(Gach)* **$17.50**

**Blech, G.M. & Lynch, Charles**
- Medical tactics and logistics. Springfield &
Balt: [1934].                  *(Argosy)* **$25**

**[Blenkinsop, Adam]**
- A hot-water cure, sought out in Germany in
the summer of 1844. The journal of a patient.
London: 1845. 12mo. Ills. Uncut. Orig
embossed cloth.                *(Argosy)* **$50**

**Bleuler, Eugen**
- Dementia praecox, or the group of
schizophrenias. Translated ... New York:
IUP, [1952]. 1st printing in English. [xii],548
pp. Several gatherings protruding. Crimson
cloth.                         *(Gach)* **$25**

**Blith, Walter**
- The English improver improved or the
survey of husbandry surveyed, all clearly
demonstrated from principles of reason ...
London: for J. Wright, 1652. 3rd imp. Sm
4to. [iii],262,[20] pp. 2 pp title, 4 w'engvd
plates, 1 defective. Contemp sheep, worn.
*(Deighton Bell)* **£225**
- The English improver, or a new survey of
husbandry ... London: J. Wright, 1649. 1st
edn. Sm 4to. W'cut head-pieces & initial
letters. Contemp calf, mrbld bds, newly
rebacked, red lea label.    *(Blackwell's)* **£400**

**Blogg, M.W.**
- Bibliography of the writings of Sir William
Osler ... revised and enlarged with an index.
Balt: 1921. 96 pp.            *(Goodrich)* **$85**

**Blumenbach, Johann F.**
- Elements of physiology. To which is
subjoined, by the translator, an appendix,
exhibiting a brief and compendious view ...
animal electricity. Phila: T. Dobson, 1795.
1st edn in English. 2 vols in 1. 8vo.
xvi,229,[1]; 247 pp. Contemp tree calf.
*(Antiq Sc)* **$275**

**Blundell, James**
- The principles and practice of obstetricy. In
five parts ... to which is added notes and
illustrations by Thomas Castle. Washington:
1834. 1st Amer edn. 520 pp. Text w'cuts. Sl
foxing, browning. Contemp calf, rubbed.
*(Elgen)* **$95**

**Blyth, Alexander Wynter**
- Poisons; their effects and detection. New

York: Wood, 1885. 2 vols. 668 pp. Table.
Cvrs worn, bumped.             *(Xerxes)* **$50**

**Boase, H.S.**
- A treatise on primary geology. 1834. 8vo.
xi,390 pp. Contemp calf, edges rubbed,
rebacked.             *(Wheldon & Wesley)* **£50**

**Boba, Antonio**
- Hypothermia for the neurosurgical patient.
Springfield: 1960. 1st edn. 124 pp. Dw.
*(Fye)* **$15**

**Bobst, Elmer Holmes**
- Bobst: the autobiography of a pharmaceutical
pioneer. New York: [1973]. 8vo. Ills. Cloth.
Pres copy.                     *(Argosy)* **$25**

**Bockshammer, Gustavus Ferdinand**
- Bockshammer on the freedom of the will.
Translated from the German, with additions
... Andover: Gould & Newman, 1835. 1st edn
in English. 12mo. [ii],199,[3] pp. Cloth-
backed bds. Ex lib.            *(Gach)* **$30**

**Bodansky, Meyer**
- Biochemistry of disease. New York: [1944].
684 pp. Ills.                  *(Argosy)* **$35**

**Bodian, D.**
- See Howe, H.A. & Bodian, D.

**Boelter, W.R.**
- The rat problem. London: John Bale ... 1909.
vii,[i], 165,[i],[vi advts] pp. Dec cloth, new
endpapers.                     *(Pollak)* **£20**
- The rat problem. Published under the
auspices of the Society for the Destruction of
Vermin. London: 1909. vii,165,[7 advts] pp.
Orig buff cloth, fairly grubby.  *(Jenner)* **£20**

**Boerhaave, Hermann**
- Academical lectures on the theory of physic.
Being a genuine translation of his Institutes
and explanatory comments ... London: W.
Innys, 1751-43-46. 6 vols. 2nd edn vol 1; 1st
edn vols 2-6. 8vo. Contemp calf, red & green
mor labels.                    *(Dailey)* **$635**

**Boericke, William & Dewey, Willis A.**
- The twelve tissue remedies of Schussler ...
homeopathically      and      bio-chemically
considered. Phila: 1925. 6th edn. 450 pp.
Cvrs sl worn.                  *(Jenner)* **£10**

**Boghurst, William**
- Loimographia. An account of the Great
Plague of London in the year 1665. London:
Shaw & Sons, 1894. 1st edn. 8vo. Pub cloth.
*(McDowell)* **£35**

**Bogomolets, A.A.**
- The prolongation of life. New York: [1946].

8vo. 96 pp. Port. Cloth.        *(Argosy)* **$20**

**Bogue, Benjamin N.**
- Stammering; its cause and cure. Indianapolis: 1926. 12mo. Port. Cloth.        *(Argosy)* **$25**

**Bohler, Lorenz**
- Medullary nailing of Kuntscher. Translated ... Balt: 1948. 1st edn in English. Tall 8vo. Ills. Cloth.        *(Argosy)* **$35**
- The treatment of fractures. Vienna: 1930. 2nd edn. 185 pp. Outer hinges torn. *(Fye)* **$30**

**Bohr, Niels**
- Atomic theory and the description of nature. Four essays with an introductory survey. Cambridge: 1934. 1st edn. 119 pp.
        *(Scientia)* **$65**
- On the quantum theory of line spectra, Parts I,II,III, 1918-22. Copenhagen: 1928. Reissue. 118 pp. Orig wraps.        *(Scientia)* **$75**

**Boileau, Capt. J.T.**
- A new and complete set of travers tables: shewing the difference of latitude ... together with tables ... useful to the surveyor and civil engineer. 1839. Sm lib stamp on title. Orig bds, lea spine, crnrs worn.        *(Whitehart)* **£15**

**Bolton, Joseph Shaw**
- The brain in health and disease. London: 1914. 1st edn. Lge 8vo. 479 pp. 99 ills. Cloth. Ex lib.        *(Argosy)* **$50**
- The brain in health and disease. London: Edward Arnold, 1914. 1st edn. xiv,479 pp. 99 text ills. Very worn reading copy. *(Gach)* **$30**

**Bolton, Lyndon**
- Time measurement, an introduction to means and ways of reckoning physical and civil time. London: G. Bell & Sons, 1924. 1st edn. 8vo. vii,166 pp. 8 plates, 28 figs, index. Red cloth, blind-stamped front cvr.        *(Zeitlin)* **$30**

**Bonaparte, Marie**
- Female sexuality. New York: [1953]. 8vo. Cloth. Dw.        *(Argosy)* **$30**

**Bond, Allen Kerr**
- When the Hopkins came to Baltimore. Balt: 1927. 84 pp. Half-cloth.        *(Argosy)* **$25**

**Bond, Henry**
- The longitude found: or, a treatise shewing an easie and speedy way ... to find the longitude ... London: ... Robert Green [etc] ..., 1676. 1st edn. Sm 4to. [viii],65,[2 advts],[1], pp. 8 engvd plates. Title & 2 leaves sl frayed. Antique style sheep.        *(Pickering)* **$3,000**

**Bonet, Theophile**
- A guide to the practical physician: shewing ... the truest and safest way of curing all diseases

... whether by medicine, surgery or diet ... 1684. 1st edn in English. Folio. [xii],868 pp. Sl browning throughout. Title reprd. Mod half-mor, mrbld bds.        *(Jenner)* **£225**

**Bonime, Ellis**
- Tuberculin and vaccine in tubercular affections. Troy, NY: 1917. 1st edn. xv,267 pp. Ills, plates (some cold). Cloth spotted.        *(Elgen)* **$35**

**Bonner, Thomas**
- The Kansas doctor: a century of pioneering. Lawrence: 1959. 1st edn. 334 pp. Dw.
        *(Fye)* **$20**

**Bonney, T.G.**
- Annals of the Philosophical Club of the Royal Society written from its minute books. London: Macmillan, 1919. x,286 pp.
        *(Pollak)* **£15**
- Volcanoes, their structure and significance. 1899. xiii,391 pp. 13 plates. Cloth, spine faded.        *(Wheldon & Wesley)* **£18**

**Bonnycastle, John**
- An introduction to astronomy ... illustrated with copper-plates. The second edition, corrected and improved. London: for J. Johnson, 1788. 8vo. 6,[2],437,[3] pp. Frontis, 19 fldg plates. Contemp calf, upper hinge cracked.        *(M&S)* **$125**
- An introduction to astronomy. In a series of letters, from a preceptor to his pupil. London: for J. Johnson, 1807. 5th edn, crrctd & impvd. 8vo. vi,[ii],385 pp. 19 plates. Paper discoloured in gutter. Orig tree calf, inner jnts weak.        *(Pollak)* **£35**

**Book, William Frederick**
- The psychology of skill. With special reference to its application in typewriting. New York: Gregg Publishing Company, [1925]. 1st edn. [x],257,[5] pp. *(Gach)* **$28.50**

**Boole, George**
- A treatise on the calculus of finite differences. Cambridge: Macmillan, 1860. 1st edn. 8vo. [iv],248 pp. Orig cloth, rebacked.
        *(Antiq Sc)* **$250**

**Boorse, H. & Motz, L.**
- The world of the atom. New York: 1965. 1st edn. 2 vols. 1873 pp. Text ills. Slipcase.
        *(Oasis)* **$40**

**Booth, E.R.**
- History of osteopathy and twentieth century medical practice. Cincinnati: [1905]. 1st edn. Frontis, xx,835 pp. Num ills, ports.
        *(Elgen)* **$40**

**Booth, James**
- The theory of elliptic integrals, and the properties of surfaces of the second order ... London: Bell, 1851. xi,159,[i advts] pp. Orig cloth-backed bds. Working copy. *(Pollak)* **£20**

**Boothby, Walter**
- Nitrous oxide - oxygen anesthesia, with a description of a new apparatus. 1911. 1st edn. 15 pp. Wraps. *(Fye)* **$75**

**Borchers, W.**
- Electric furnaces. The production of heat from electrical energy and the construction of electric furnaces. 1908. ix,224 pp. 282 ills. *(Whitehart)* **£15**

**Borden, Simeon**
- A system of useful formulae, adapted to the practical operations of locating and constructing railroads: A paper read before the Boston Society of Civil Engineers. December 1840. Boston: 1851. 8vo. 12,118 pp. 28 figs in text. Orig cloth, sl worn & dusty. *(Deighton Bell)* **£75**

**Borges, Albert F.**
- Elective incisions and scar revision. Boston: [1973]. 1st edn. 4to. Profusely illust. Cloth. *(Argosy)* **$50**

**Boring, Edwin G.**
- Sensation and perception in the history of experimental psychology. New York: n.d. [ca 1942]. 644 pp. Port, ills. *(Argosy)* **$40**

**Borland, J. Nelson & Cheever, David**
- First medical and surgical report of the Boston City Hospital. Boston: 1870. 1st edn. 688 pp. 2 mounted orig photographs. *(Fye)* **$325**

**Borlase, William**
- The natural history of Cornwall. The air, climate ... mining ... trade, tenure and arts. Oxford: W. Jackson, 1758. Folio. xix,326,[ii errata & drctns to binder]. Fldg map, 28 engvd plates. Sl foxing throughout. Contemp calf, sometime rebacked, crnrs worn. *(Blackwell's)* **£185**

**Borough, William**
- See Norman, Robert & Borough, William

**Bossut, John**
- A general history of mathematics. London: 1803. 1st edn in English. 540 pp. Chronological table. Half-mor, mrbld bds, a little worn. *(Oasis)* **$100**

**Bosworth, T.O.**
- Geology of the Tertiary and Quaternary periods in the North-West of Peru. London:

Macmillan, 1922. [ii],xxii,434, [i advts] pp. 26 plates, 11 fldg maps, 150 ills. Cvrs badly faded, hd of spine with sm tear. *(Pollak)* **£20**

**Both, Carl**
- Consumption and its treatment in all its forms. Practical application of the cellular principle. Boston: 1873. 1st edn. Tall 8vo. Ills. Ex lib. *(Argosy)* **$50**

**Bott, Helen**
- See Blatz, William E. & Bott, Helen

**Bottone, S.R.**
- Wireless telegraphy and Hertzian waves. [1912] 4th edn. xii,136 pp. Ills, diags. *(Weiner)* **£20**

**Bouchard, Charles**
- Lectures on auto-intoxication in diseases, or self-poisoning of the individual. Translated ... Phila: 1894. 1st edn in English. 8vo. Cloth. *(Argosy)* **$25**

**Boule, Marcellin**
- Fossil men: elements of human palaeontology. Translated ... Edinburgh: 1923. 1st edn in English. 504 pp. *(Scientia)* **$40**

**Bourne, Geoffrey**
- An introduction to medical history & case taking. Edinburgh: 1931. 1st edn. Sm 8vo. Cloth. *(Argosy)* **$35**

**Bourne, John**
- A treatise on the steam engine in its application to mines, mills, steam navigation and railways. 1849. 3rd edn. 4to. vii,258 pp. 33 plates (many fldg), fldg table, num w'cuts. Orig pict green cloth, worn, recased. *(Weiner)* **£80**
- A treatise on the steam engine in its application to mines, mills, steam navigation and railways. London: Longman, Brown, &c., 1851. New edn. 4to. Lge fldg engvd frontis (torn at fold), 32 engvd plates. Lib stamps on title & plates. Rebound in cloth. *(McDowell)* **£55**

**Bourne, John C.**
- Drawings of the London and Birmingham railway. With an historical and descriptive account by John Britton. 1839. Folio. Litho title, 2 maps on 1 page, 29 litho plates containing 36 views. Dec cloth gilt, rebacked in gilt edged mor. *(Edwards)* **£2,100**

**Bovinine Co.**
- A practical treatise on how to preserve perfect nutrition in health and disease by natural means. [New York: ca 1900]. 12mo. 110 pp. Orig pict wraps. *(Argosy)* **$30**

**Bowden, B.V. (ed.)**
- Faster than thought. A symposium on digital computing machines. London: 1953. 1st edn. 416 pp. Worn dw. *(Scientia)* **$65**
- Faster than thought. A symposium on digital computing machines. London: Pitman, 1953. 1st edn. 8vo. Frontis, ills. Pub cloth, faded. *(McDowell)* **£18**

**Bowdich, Thomas Edward**
- Excursions in Madeira and Porto Santo during the autumn of 1823, while on his third voyage to Africa ... London: George B. Whittaker, 1825. 1st edn. 4to. xii,278 pp. 28 litho plates (4 cold, 3 fldg). Light browning on prelims. Contemp calf, spine gilt. *(Rootenberg)* **$950**

**Bowditch, N.I.**
- A history of the Massachusetts General Hospital. Boston: 1872. 2nd edn. *(Scientia)* **$100**

**Bowditch, Nathaniel**
- The new American practical navigator; being an epitome of navigation ... Newburyport: Edmund Blunt, 1802. 1st edn. 8vo. 589,[4] pp. 3 pp advts. Fldg chart, 7 plates. Chart strengthened at folds, foxing & offsetting to text & plates. Rec cloth, lea label. *(M&S)* **$1,400**

**Bowen, Wilbur Pardon**
- Applied anatomy and kinesiology, the mechanism of muscular movement. Phila: Lea & Febiger, 1919. 2nd, revsd, edn. 334 pp. Photo ills. Sl shaken. *(Xerxes)* **$35**

**Bowles, R.L.**
- A method for treating the apparently drowned. Together with remarks in discussion on the phenomena attending death from drowning. London: 1904. 14 pp. Plates. *(Goodrich)* **$60**

**Bowman, F.H.**
- The structure of the wool fibre, in its relation to the use of wool for technical purposes. Manchester: 1885. 2nd edn. xviii,366,10 [pub advts] pp. Ills. A little foxed. Dark green cloth, gilt spine. *(Phenotype)* **£38**

**Boyd, C.R.**
- Resources of South-West Virginia, showing the mineral deposits of iron, coal, zinc, copper and lead ... New York: Wiley, 1881. 1st edn. xiv,321 pp. W'cut plates, tables. Some pages stained. Orig bevelled cloth, rebacked, with sl wear & staining. *(Diamond)* **$45**

**Boyland, G. Halstead**
- Buffalo lithia water from the Buffalo Hills of Virginia, its uses and effects. N.p.: 1886. 11 pp. Orig printed wraps. *(Argosy)* **$30**

**Boyle, Robert**
- Certain physiological essays and other tracts ... the second edition ... London: for Henry Herringman, 1669, 2nd enlgd edn. 4to. Collation as in Fulton, with the final blank. 18th c signature on title, some browning. Contemp calf, rebacked, orig spine. *(Pickering)* **$650**
- Certain physiological essays, written at distant times, and on several occasions. London: Henry Herringman, 1661. 1st edn. 4to. Contemp calf, rebacked. *(Quaritch)* **$3,000**
- An essay about the origins & virtues of gems. London: Moses Pitt, 1672. 1st edn. 12mo. [14],185 pp. 19th c mrbld bds with recent lea back. Title sl dust-soiled, traces of damp-staining. *(Antiq Sc)* **$1,100**
- Essays of the strange subtilty, determinate nature, great efficacy of effluviums. To which are annext ... London: by W.G. for M. Pitt, 1673. 1st edn, 2nd iss. Complex collation. First 4ff ink-stained, occas damp-stains, dusty. Disbound, stitching broken. *(Pollak)* **£200**
- Experiments, notes, &c. about the mechanical origine or production of divers particular qualities ... London: E. Flesher, for R. Davis ...,1676. 8vo. Collation as called for. Cancel title-page. Mod polished calf. Minor defect in 1 leaf, neatly reprd. *(Zeitlin)* **$3,200**
- Medicinal experiments: or, a collection of choice and safe remedies for the most part simple, and easily prepared ... in three parts ... London: W. & J. Innys, 1718. 6th edn, crrctd. 12mo. 12ff,168 pp, 11ff,61 pp. Blind-stamped panelled calf, rebacked. *(Hemlock)* **$225**
- Medicinal experiments; or, a collection of choice remedies ... The third and last volume. London: J. Taylor, 1694. 1st edn. 12mo. [18],76 pp. Crushed niger mor. *(Antiq Sc)* **$450**
- Medicinal experiments; or, a collection of choice and safe remedies ... London: for W. Innys, 1712. 5th edn, corrected. 12mo. 3 vols in 1. Contemp calf, rebacked, worn at edges. *(Zeitlin)* **$275**
- New experiments and observations touching cold, or an experimental history of cold, begun ... and an examen of Mr. Hob's doctrine about cold ... London: John Crook, 1665. 1st edn. 8vo. 2 engvd plates, one fldg. Contemp calf. *(Quaritch)* **$2,150**
- Occasional reflections upon several subjects ... London: for Henry Herringman, 1665. 1st edn. 8vo. [40],80, 161-264, [230],[10]. Red & blacks title. Contemp unlettered calf, hd & ft of spine reprd. *(Pickering)* **$1,500**
- Short memoirs for the natural and

experimental history of mineral waters ...
London: for Samuel Smith, 1684-85. 1st edn.
8vo. [xviii],112, [13],[1] pp. Tear in F1 reprd.
Contemp calf, cvrs rubbed, jnts cracking, hd
of spine chipped.          *(Pickering)* **$1,000**
- Some considerations touching the usefulnesse
of experimental naturall philosophy. Oxford:
Hen. Hall for Ric. Davis, 1663. 1st edn. 4to.
1 f, 2 half-titles, title, 6 ff, 127,[12] pp; title,
sub-title, 417,[16] pp. 1f [errata]. Later calf,
blind-stamped.             *(Hemlock)* **$1,350**
- Some considerations touching the usefulnesse
of experimental naturall philosophy. Oxford:
H. Hall for R. Davis, 1663. 1st edn. 4to. [8]ff,
127,[1] pp, [4]ff; 417 (i.e. 409) pp,[1] pp, [9]ff.
Lacks fol A1-2. Old calf, rebacked, crnrs
reprd. Sl worm trail vol 2.   *(Zeitlin)* **$2,250**
- Some considerations touching the usefulnesse
of experimental naturall philosophy. Oxford:
H. Hall for R. Davis, 1664-71. 1st complete
edition (2nd edn, issue 'B' of 1st vol, 1st edn
of 2nd vol). 4to. Complex collation. Contemp
calf, rebacked, crnrs renewed. *(Antiq Sc)* **$850**
- Some considerations touching the usefulnesse
of experimental naturall philosophy. Oxford:
H. Hall for R. Davis, 1664. 2nd edn, issue 'A'.
Numbering erratic. Title mounted & soiled
with sm hole. Some marginal foxing. Mod
sprinkled calf, gilt.          *(Zeitlin)* **$650**
- Some        considerations       upon       the
reconcileableness of reason and religion. By
T.E. a lay-man ... London: ..., 1675. 1st edn.
8vo.   [iv],xviii,[i    blank],[i    errata],126,[2
blank],[5],[2 blank],[1 errata],39 pp. Title
browned. Contemp mottled calf, jnts reprd.
                             *(Pickering)* **$625**
- Tracts ... about cosmicall qualities of things
... Oxford: for Ric. Davis, 1671. 1st edn, 1st
iss. 6 parts in 1. 16mo. [6],42; [2],27,[1]; 28;
[2],[4] 43,[1]; 21,[1]; [2],16 pp. Half-titles for
each part & 2nd gen title for the last 3.
Contemp calf, rebckd.       *(M&S)* **$1,600**
- Tracts consisting of observations about the
saltness of the sea. An account of a statical
hygroscope and its uses ... London: E.
Flesher, 1674. 1st edn. Sm 8vo. Unobtrusive
water-stain in foremargin throughout. Very
early sheep.                  *(Dailey)* **$850**
- The works of the Honourable Robert Boyle ...
to which is prefixed the life of the Author
...London: for A. Millar, 1744. 1st coll edn.
Folio. 5 vols. Frontis port, 5 ports, 23 engvd
plates. Red & black titles. Contemp calf,
worn, hinges split, bd detchd. *(Zeitlin)* **$1,250**
- The works of the Honourable Robert Boyle ...
to which is prefixed the life of the Author.
London: A. Millar, 1744. 1st coll edn. Folio.
5 vols. Engvd port, vignettes on titles, 24
engvd plates on 15 fldg sheets. Occas light
foxing. Contemp˙calf.      *(Quaritch)* **$2,250**
- The works of the Honourable Robert Boyle ...
To which is prefixed the life of the Author.
London: J. & F. Rivington, et al., 1772. 2nd

edn. Lge 4to. 6 vols. ccxxxviii,799; 800; 803;
821; 750; 796 pp, index. Frontis, 24 engvd
plates. Contemp calf, rebacked.
                           *(Rootenberg)* **$1,250**
- The works of the Honourable Robert Boyle ...
to which is prefixed the life of the Author
...London: for J. & F. Rivington, &c, 1772.
2nd edn. 6 vols. 4to. Contemp calf, jnts of Vol
I reprd. From the lib of Edward Gibbon with
his b'plate.                *(Pickering)* **$3,000**

## Boys, C.V.
- Soap-bubbles and the forces which mould
them. 1890. 1st edn. viii,9-178 pp. Frontis,
68 figs in text, lge fldg plate. Orig pale green
pict cloth. Romance of Science Series.
                            *(Whitehart)* **£15**

## Bracegirdle, B.
- A history of microtechnique, The evolution
of the microtome and the development of
tissue preparation. London: 1978. 28 plates, 4
cold. 150 figs.          *(Winterdown)* **£35**

## Bracken, H.
- Farriery improved, or, a compleat treatise
upon the art of farriery ... 1756, 8th edn. 2
vols. x,396; xvi,321 pp. Orig full calf,
rebacked, new labels. Sl marginal staining vol
II.                          *(Phenotype)* **£42**

## Bradbury, Fred
- Carpet manufacture. Belfast: for the Author,
1904. 301,19 [advts] pp. Plates (2 cold), num
ills & diags.                 *(Weiner)* **£30**

## Bradford, Edward & Lovett, Robert
- Orthopedic surgery. New York: 1911. 1st
edn. 410 pp. More than 300 photographic
ills. Pub pres copy.            *(Fye)* **$125**

## Bradley, F.H.
- Appearance and reality: a metaphysical essay.
London: Swan Sonnenschein & Co., 1893. 1st
edn. 8vo. 24,558 pp. Unopened in orig cloth.
                              *(M&S)* **$225**
- The principles of logic. Oxford: 1922. 2nd
edn, revsd. 2 vols. xxviii,739 pp. Cloth sl
dust-stained, edges sl worn. Ex Signet Library
with b'plates.             *(Whitehart)* **£35**

## Bradley, Lonsdale
- An enquiry into the deposition of lead ore, in
the mineral veins of Swaledale, Yorkshire.
1862. Lge 8vo. vii,40 pp. Cold geological
map, 10 cold plates, cold reference plate. Orig
gilt-lettered cloth.          *(Weiner)* **£40**

## Bradley, Richard
- The plague at Marseilles consider'd. With
remarks upon the plague in general, shewing
its cause and nature of infection ... London:
for W. Mears, 1721. 1st edn. 8vo. [viii],60 pp.

Half-calf. *(Burmester)* £75

**Brady, Francis**
- Dover coal boring; observations on the correlation of the Franco-Belgian, Dover & Somerset coal fields, with reports ... N.d. (ca 1892). 36 pp. Lge (90 cm) fldg map, very lge (300 cm) fldg section of boring. Cloth-backed printed bds, worn. *(Weiner)* £35

**Bragg, Sir William**
- An introduction to crystal analysis. London: Bell, 1928. 1st edn. vii,168 pp. 8 plates, 105 text figs. *(Pollak)* £45
- Old trades and new knowledge. London: G. Bell, 1926. 1st edn. 8vo. Cold frontis. Dw. Royal Institution Christmas Lectures 1925. *(McDowell)* £18
- The world of sound. Six lectures delivered before a juvenile auditory at the Royal Institution, Christmas 1919. 1920. 1st edn. viii,196 pp. Num ills. Orig pict cloth, spine dull. *(Whitehart)* £15

**Bragg, Sir William Henry, et al.**
- X-rays and crystal structure. London: Bell, 1916. 2nd edn. vii,228,[iv] pp. 4 plates, 75 text figs. *(Pollak)* £45
- X-rays and crystal structure. London: 1925. 5th edn. xi,324 pp. Tables, etc., throughout text. Orig red cloth, upper hinge cracked. *(Jenner)* £10
- X-rays and crystal structure. London: G. Bell, 1925. 5th edn. xi,324 pp. 8 plates, 105 text figs. Sev sm cvr stains. *(Diamond)* $50

**Bragg, William L.**
- Atomic Structure of Minerals. Ithaca, N.Y.: Cornell Univ Press, 1937. 1st edn. 8vo. xiii,[1],292 pp. Frontis, 9 plates, text figs. Orig cloth. *(Antiq Sc)* $60
- Atomic Structure of Minerals. Ithaca, N.Y.: Cornell Univ Press, 1950. 2nd printing of 1937 edn. xiii,[1],292 pp. Frontis, 144 figs. *(Pollak)* £20

**Brain, W. Russell**
- Mind, perception and science. Oxford: [1951]. 12mo. 90 pp. Cloth. *(Argosy)* $25

**Bramwell, Byrom**
- Diseases of the spinal cord. Edinburgh: 1884. 2nd edn. 359 pp. *(Fye)* $75
- Diseases of the spinal cord. Edinburgh: 1895. 3rd edn, revsd & extnded. 659 pp. *(Fye)* $75
- Practical medicine and medical diagnosis. Edinburgh: 1887. [1],149 pp. 41 ills. Contemp mor, badly marked. *(Whitehart)* £35

**Bramwell, J.M.**
- Hypnotism, its history, practice and theory. 1906. 2nd edn. xvi,478,4 pp. Orig cloth, t.e.g. *(Whitehart)* £18

**Brande, W.T. & Cox, Rev. G.W.**
- A dictionary of science, literature and art. 1875. New edn, revsd. 3 vols. xiii,945; 952; 1068 pp. Mod cloth. *(Whitehart)* £50

**Brande, William Thomas**
- A dictionary of materia medica and practical pharmacy; including a translation of the formulae of the London Pharmacopoeia. 1839. 1st edn. Orig cloth, spine sl faded. *(Robertshaw)* £20
- A manual of chemistry. 1819. xlvii,652 pp. 3 fldg plates (inc frontis), w'cuts. New buckram. *(Weiner)* £85
- A manual of chemistry. 1848. 6th edn, greatly enlgd. 2 vols in 1. W'engvd ills. Contemp half-calf. *(Robertshaw)* £20
- A manual of pharmacy. 1833. 3rd edn, crrctd & enlgd. Orig cloth-backed bds, jnts split at hd & ft. *(Robertshaw)* £12
- A manual of pharmacy. London: 1825. 1st edn. xi,556 pp. 3/4 lea, mrbld bds. *(Elgen)* $95

**Brannt, W.T.**
- The metallic alloys. A practical guide for the manufacture of all kinds of alloys, amalgams, and solders, used by metal-workers ... Phila: 1896. New edn, revsd & enlgd. xxviii,527 pp. 34 engvs. Orig cloth. *(Whitehart)* £15

**Brasch, Frederick (ed.)**
- Sir Isaac Newton, 1727-1927. A bi-centenary evaluation of his work. Balt: 1928. 1st edn. 351 pp. Unopened. *(Scientia)* $30

**Brasset, Edmund A.**
- A doctor's pilgrimage. An autobiography. Phila: [1951]. Dw. *(Argosy)* $20

**Braun, Heinrich**
- Local anesthesia. Its scientific basis and practical use. Phila: 1914. 1st edn in English. 399 pp. Ills. Orig cloth. *(Oasis)* $100

**Braun, Wernher von**
- History of rocketry and space travel. New York: 1966. 1st, & ltd, edn. 4to. 244 pp. Ills in color & b/w. Boxed in simulated lea. *(Oasis)* $50

**Brecher, Gerhard**
- See Galetti, Pierre & Brecher, Gerhard

**Bree, Charles Robert**
- An exposition of fallacies in the hypothesis of Mr. Darwin. London: Longmans, 1872. xviii,418 pp. 32 pp inserted advts dated March, 1872. 2 frontis (one fldg, one sl torn), 34 w'engvs. Orig green cloth gilt, lower jnt & hinge almost gone. Worn ex lib. *(Blackwell's)* £45

**Bree, Robert**
- A practical inquiry into disordered respiration; distinguishing the species of convulsive asthma, their causes and indications of cure. London: for Richard Phillips, 1807. 4th edn. xxiv,373,[i advt],[ii blank]. Half-calf, spine edges worn.
*(Pollak)* £40
- A practical inquiry into disordered respiration; distinguishing the species of convulsive asthma, their causes and indications of cure. Phila: 1811. 1st Amer edn. [5],x-xxiii, [25]-260 pp. Browning. Contemp calf, jnt tender, hd of spine chipped. *(Elgen)* **$175**

**Bremner, M.D.K.**
- The story of dentistry from the dawn of civilisation to the present. Brooklyn, New York & London: 1946. 2nd edn. 8vo. Pub cloth, sl discoloured. *(McDowell)* £40

**Brewer ...**
- The brewer. A familiar treatise ... See Loftus, William R.

**Brewster, David**
- Letters on natural magic addressed to Sir Walter Scott, bart. 1838. 4th edn. viii,351 pp. Figs in text. Orig printed bds dull & dust-stained, spine dull, edges worn.
*(Whitehart)* £25
- The life of Sir Isaac Newton. London: 1831. 1st edn. 366 pp. Lea, scuffed. *(Scientia)* **$55**
- Memoirs of the life, writings and discoveries of Sir Isaac Newton. Edinburgh: 1855. 1st edn. 2 vols. 478; 564 pp. Spines chipped.
*(Scientia)* **$95**
- Memoirs of the life, writings, and discoveries of Sir Isaac Newton. Edinburgh: Edmonston & Douglas, 1860. 2nd edn. 2 vols. 8vo. xxi,[iii],430; xi,[i],434 pp. Frontis in each vol, w'engvd ills. Contemp half-calf.
*(Burmester)* £75
- A treatise on new philosophical instruments for various purposes in the arts and sciences. Edinburgh & London: 1813. 1st edn. 8vo. 20,427 pp. 12 plates. Lacks half-title. Contemp 3/4 calf, mrbld bds. *(M&S)* **$600**

**Brickel, A.C.J.**
- Surgical treatment of hand and forearm infections. St. Louis: 1939. 1st edn. 300 pp. Ills. *(Oasis)* **$30**
- Surgical treatment of hand and forearm infections. St. Louis: 1939. 1st edn. 300 pp. Num photographic & X-ray ills. Ex lib.
*(Fye)* **$50**

**Brickner, R.M.**
- Intellectual functions of the frontal lobes. New York: 1936. 1st edn. Ills. Dw.
*(Argosy)* **$50**

**Bridgman, Percy**
- Dimensional analysis. New Haven: 1922. 1st edn. 112 pp. Spine shelfworn. *(Scientia)* **$85**

**Brierley, Marjorie**
- Trends in psycho-analysis. London: Hogarth Press, 1951. 8vo. Cloth. *(Argosy)* **$35**

**Brierre de Boismont, A.J.F.**
- Hallucinations: or, the rational history of apparitions, visions, dreams, ecstasy, magnetism and somnambulism. Phila: Lindsay & Blakiston, 1853. 1st Amer edn. Library stamp on title & spine. Victorian cloth, jnts frayed. *(Gach)* **$150**

**Briggs, Henry, et al.**
- Mathematical tables, contrived after a most comprehensive method. London: for R. & W. Mount, 1717. 4to. [x],64,[300], 39,[i advt] pp. Occas foxing. Contemp calf, some wear, spine ends reprd. The 2nd iss of the 1st edn of 1705, with cancel title. *(Pollak)* £135

**Briggs, L. Vernon**
- The manner of man that kills: Spencer - Czolgosz - Richeson. Boston: Richard G. Badger, [1921]. 444 pp. Green cloth, front hinge broken. *(Gach)* **$35**

**Briggs, Richard**
- The English art of cookery, according to the present practice; being a complete guide to all housekeepers, on a plan entirely new. London: for G.G. & J. Robinson, 1794. 3rd edn. 8vo. 12 copper-plates. Title dusty. Contemp half-calf, red label, bds rubbed.
*(McDowell)* £300

**Brill, A.A.**
- Fundamental conceptions of psychoanalysis. London: 1922. 1st English edn. vii,344 pp. Marginal spotting. Orig maroon cloth.
*(Jenner)* £18
- Lectures on psychoanalytic psychiatry. New York: 1946. 1st edn. Sm 8vo. Cloth. Dw.
*(Argosy)* **$35**
- Psychoanalysis: its theories and practical application. Phila: 1912. 1st edn.
*(Argosy)* **$35**

**Brim, Charles, J.**
- Medicine in the Bible. The Pentateuch, Torah. New York: 1936. 1st edn. Sgnd by author. *(Scientia)* **$85**

**Bristowe, John S.**
- Diseases of the intestines and peritoneum. New York: 1879. 1st Amer edn. 243 pp.
*(Fye)* **$25**

**British ...**
- The British dispensatory, containing a

faithful translation of the new London pharmacopoeia ... useful remarks relating to the preparation of the medicines. London: Edward Cave, 1747. 12mo. xii,136,83, [i blank] pp. Some foxing. New cloth, lea label.
*(Pollak)* £40
- British Pharmacopoeia 1867. 1867. xxiv,434 pp. Orig cloth, dust stained. Spine sl defective, inner back hinge cracked.
*(Whitehart)* £25
- British Pharmacopoeia 1867. 1867. xxiv,434 pp. Orig blind-stamped pebbled cloth, small tears at jnt. Ex lib.
*(Elgen)* $75
- British Pharmacopoeia 1867. 1877. 3rd reprint, with additions made in 1874. xxviii,457 pp. Orig cloth, dust stained.
*(Whitehart)* £15

**Britten, F.J.**
- Old clocks and watches and their makers. Being an historical and descriptive account of the different styles of clocks and watches of the past, In England and abroad ... London, New York: B.T. Batsford ... 1899. 1st edn. 8vo. viii,500,10. Orig cloth. *(Zeitlin)* $275
- Old clocks and watches and their makers ... London, New York: B.T. Batsford ... [1919]. 4th edn. 8vo. x,597 pp. 433 figs, diagrams, monograms, index. Rebnd in brown buckram. *(Zeitlin)* $100
- Old clocks and watches and their makers ... London, New York: Spon, 1932. 6th [and best] edn. 8vo. viii,891,[1] pp. 913 text figs. Orig red cloth, binding worn, shaken, loose.
*(Zeitlin)* $200

**Broad, C.D.**
- The mind and its place in nature. London: 1937. 3rd imp. 674,[20 advts] pp. Orig black cloth. *(Jenner)* £10.50

**Broadbent, W.H.**
- The pulse. Phila: Lea Bros. [1890]. 1st Amer edn. 12mo. vi,[2],312 pp. Ills. Orig cloth, hinges cracked, spine a little worn.
*(Antiq Sc)* $60

**Broca, A.**
- Ligations and amputations. Bristol: 1917. 1st edn in English. 285 pp. Over 500 ills.
*(Fye)* $40

**Broca, P.**
- Phenomena of hybridity in the Genus Homo. 1864. xiv,148 pp. Orig blind-stamped cloth, rebacked, t.e.g. Lib stamp on title.
*(Whitehart)* £45

**Brock, R.C.**
- The anatomy of the bronchial tree. Oxford University Press, 1947. 2nd imp. [vi],96 pp. Num plates & ills. Cvrs sl worn. *(Jenner)* £18

**Brock, Samuel (ed.)**
- Injuries of the skull, brain and spinal cord. Balt: 1940. 1st edn. 632 pp. *(Oasis)* $45
- Injuries of the skull, brain and spinal cord: neuro-psychiatric, surgical and medico-legal aspects. Balt: 1940. 1st edn. *(Argosy)* $85

**Brockbank, Edward Mansfield**
- A centenary history of the Manchester Medical Society with biographical notices ... Manchester: 1934. 101 pp. Frontis, few plates. Cvrs sl soiled. *(Jenner)* £9

**Brockbank, William**
- Portrait of a hospital, 1752 - 1948 ... bicentenary of the Royal Infirmary, Manchester. 1952. x,218 pp. Cold frontis, ills. Orig blue cloth, a little worn.
*(Jenner)* £15

**Brodie, Sir Benjamin C.**
- Clinical lectures on surgery, delivered at St. George's Hospital. Phila: 1846. 1st Amer edn. Cloth. Ex lib. *(Argosy)* $40

**Broedel, Max**
- Three unpublished drawings on the anatomy of the human ear. Phila: 1946. 1st edn. 4to.
*(Fye)* $20

**Broglie, Louis de**
- An introduction to the study of wave mechanics. Translated by H.T. Flint. London: 1930. 1st edn in English. 249 pp.
*(Scientia)* $95
- Matter and light. The new physics. London: Allen & Unwin, 1939. 1st English edn. 300,[iv] pp. *(Pollak)* £25

**Brookbank, Edward M.**
- Centenary history of the Manchester Medical Society, with biographical notices. Manchester: 1934. 1st edn. 101 pp. Ports.
*(Argosy)* $30

**Brooks, William K.**
- The foundations of zoology. New York: 1899. 1st edn. 339 pp. Spine torn. *(Scientia)* $45
- The foundations of zoology. New York: 1915.
*(Scientia)* $30

**Broomwell, I. Norman & Fischelis, Philipp**
- Anatomy and histology of the mouth and teeth. Phila: Blakiston, 1917. 5th edn revsd. 467 pp. Ms notes not affecting text. Sl staining in gutter. *(Poitras)* $30

**Brophy, Truman**
- Oral surgery: a treatise on the diseases, injuries, and malformations of the mouth and associated parts. Phila: 1915. 1st edn. 1090 pp. Num cold plates. *(Fye)* $200

**Brose, Henry L.**
- The theory of relativity. An introductory sketch based on Einstein's original writings. Oxford: Blackwell, 1919. 1st edn. 32 pp. 3 text figs. Orig wraps.        *(Pollak)* **£25**

**Brougham, Henry, Lord**
- Lives of men of letters and science who flourished in the time of George III. London: 1845. 1st edn. 516 pp, Errata. Rebnd in blue cloth.        *(Scientia)* **$50**

**Broughton, W.B.**
- The biology of brains. Proceedings of a symposium ... 1972. 290 pp. Ills. Ex lib.
        *(Poitras)* **$30**

**Broussais, F.J.V.**
- A treatise on physiology applied to pathology ... translated ... Phila: 1826. 1st edn in English. viii,[9]-555 pp. Browning, light foxing. Contemp calf, edges rubbed.
        *(Elgen)* **$150**

**Brown, Benjamin H.**
- Vibratory technique. Chicago: Vibratory Publishing, 1910. Sm 8vo. 103 pp. (Colitis, eczema, obesity, rheumatism, &c.).
        *(Xerxes)* **$50**

**Brown, George**
- The surgery of oral and facial diseases and malformations: their diagnosis and treatment including plastic surgical reconstruction. Phila: 1938. 4th edn. 778 pp.        *(Fye)* **$75**

**Brown, Harcourt**
- Scientific organisation in seventeenth century France. (1620 - 1680). Balt: 1934. 1st edn. 306 pp. Crnrs bumped.        *(Scientia)* **$30**

**Brown, Rev. J. Wood**
- An enquiry into the life and legend of Michael Scot. Edinburgh: 1897. xvi,281 pp. Frontis. Cvrs sl rubbed, t.e.g.        *(Jenner)* **£30**

**Brown, J.B. & McDowell, F.**
- Plastic surgery of the nose. Springfield: 1951. 1st edn. 427 pp.        *(Fye)* **$75**
- Plastic surgery of the nose. Springfield: 1965. 2nd edn. 432 pp. Dw.        *(Fye)* **$40**
- Plastic surgery of the nose. St. Louis: 1951. 1st edn. 427 pp. Ills.        *(Oasis)* **$30**
- Skin grafting of burns. Phila: 1944. 1st edn, 2nd printing. 204 pp.        *(Fye)* **$75**
- Skin grafting of burns. Primary care. Treatment. Repair. Phila: Lippincott, 1943. xi,[4],204 pp.        *(Poitras)* **$60**
- Skin grafting. Phila: 1958. 3rd edn. 411 pp.        *(Fye)* **$60**

**Brown, John**
- The elements of medicine of John Brown,

M.D. ... Portsmouth, N.H.: William & Daniel Treadwell, 1803. New edn, revsd & crrctd. 8vo. 2 vols in 1. lxxxv,463 pp, [5]ff (lacks last blank). Lge fldg table. Contemp mottled calf, jnt reprd.        *(Zeitlin)* **$125**
- Locke and Sydenham. Edinburgh: 1866. Thick 12mo. Cloth.        *(Argosy)* **$35**

**Brown, O. Phelps**
- The complete herbalist; or, the people their own physicians. 1874. 8vo. 504 pp. Port, text figs, Cloth, a trifle worn & contents refixed.
        *(Wheldon & Wesley)* **£15**
- The complete herbalist; or, the people their own physicians by the use of nature's remedies ... Jersey City: published by the author, 1880. 504 pp. Ills.        *(Poitras)* **$40**

**Brown, P.**
- New illustrations of zoology, containing plates of new, curious, and nondescript birds, ... reptiles and insects. London: 1776. 4to. [viii],136 pp. 50 hand-cold plates. Contemp calf, rebacked, crnrs rubbed. Thomas Pennant's copy, with ms note & b'plate.
        *(Wheldon & Wesley)* **£1,750**

**Brown, Percy**
- American martyrs to science through the roentgen rays. Springfield: Charles C. Thomas, 1936. Back cvr creased. (Ex lib.
        *(Poitras)* **$50**

**Brown, Samuel**
- Lectures on the atomic theory and essays scientific and literary. Edinburgh: 1858. 1st edn. 2 vols. 12mo. Disbound.        *(M&S)* **$40**

**Brown, Thomas**
- Lectures on the philosophy of the human mind ... Edinburgh: W. & C. Tait, 1824. 2nd edn. 8vo. 4 vols. Contemp half-calf, rubbed with sl wear.        *(Zeitlin)* **$125**

**Brown, William & Thomson, Godfrey H.**
- The essentials of mental measurement. Cambridge: University Press, 1925. 3rd edn. x,224 pp. Orig cloth.        *(Gach)* **$25**

**Browne & Sharpe Mfg Co.**
- A treatise on the use and construction of milling machines made by ... Providence, R.I.: 1891. 162 pp. Many ills. Occas light foxing. Orig bevelled pict cloth, gilt.
        *(Weiner)* **£25**

**Browne, Edward, M.D.**
- An account of several travels through a great part of Germany: in four journeys ... London: B. Tooke, 1677. 1st edn. 8vo. 3 fldg plates. Old red mor, gilt tooled. (Browne: physician to Charles II).        *(Argosy)* **$350**

**Browne, Edward. G.**
- Arabian medicine. Cambridge: 1921. viii,138 pp. New cloth, t.e.g. Fitzpatrick Lectures, November 1919/1920.    *(Whitehart)* **£25**

**Browne, Richard [Brown]**
- Medicina musica: or, a mechanical essay on the effects of singing ... on human bodies ... to which is annex'd, a new essay on the nature and cure of the spleen ... London: ... Knapton, 1729. New edn. Sm 8vo. xvi,[1], 125,[1] pp. Mod sprinkled calf. *(Zeitlin)* **$550**

**Browne, Thomas**
- A full and true coppy of ... Religio Medici. 2nd authorised edn, Crooke, 1645. Sm 8vo. Title sl worn, lacks blanks & crnrs of engv. Later vell, red lea label.    *(Oasis)* **$500**
- Hydriotaphia, urne-buriall; or, a discourse of the sepulchrall urnes ... Together with the Garden of Cyrus ... London: for Hen Brome ... 1658. 1st edn. Sm 8vo. Title leaf, [12],202,[4] pp. Engvd frontis, 2 engvd plates. Lacks longitudinal label. Mod calf.    *(Elgen)* **$325**
- Pseudodoxia epidemica ... the fourth edition ... whereunto are now added ... newly written. London: for Edward Dod, 1658. 4to. [8]ff,468 (i.e. 440)pp,[8]ff; [4]ff,73,[3]pp. 2 engvd plates. Lacks longitudinal label. Title mtd. Contemp calf, rebacked.    *(Zeitlin)* **$200**
- Pseudodoxia epidemica: or, enquiries into very many received tenets ... London: For Edw. Dod ... 1650. 2nd edn, crrctd & enlgd. Folio. [xvi],329,[xi] pp. Lower edge staining of rear leaves, 1 leaf with sm tear. Contemp calf, later rebacking. Crnrs reprd.    *(Pollak)* **£180**
- Pseudodoxia epidemica: or, enquiries into very many received tenets and commonly presumed truths ... London: 1672. 6th ('and last') edn. [xx],440, [11],144 pp. Minor spotting & prelims sl stained. Full calf, recased, mor label. Upper hinge cracked.    *(Jenner)* **£100**

**[Browne, Thomas]**
- Religio medici, the fifth edition ... With annotations never before published. Also, observations ... now newly added. London: ... for Andrew Cook, 1659. Sm 8vo. [9]ff, inc engvd frontis, [1]f, 75,[3] pp. Contemp sprinkled calf, rebacked. A few stains.    *(Zeitlin)* **$450**

**Browning, Wm.**
- Medical heredity: distinguished children of physicians (U.S. to 1910). Balt: 1925.    *(Argosy)* **$35**

**Bruce, Alexander**
- A topographical atlas of the spinal cord. London: Williams & Norgate, 1901. 1st edn.

4to. 32 photogravure plates. Pub qtr brown mor, brown ribbed cloth, gilt lettered.    *(McDowell)* **£60**

**Bruce, R.**
- Fifty years among Shorthorns, with over 30 pen pictures of notable sires. 1907. 214 pp. Ills. Green cloth.    *(Phenotype)* **£30**

**Brucke, Ernst**
- The human figure; its beauties and defects. Authorised translation, revised by the author. London: 1891. 8vo. Gilt pict cloth. Ex lib.    *(Argosy)* **$35**

**Bruhl, Gustav**
- Atlas and epitome of otology. Phila: 1902. 1st English translation. 292 pp. 244 cold figs.    *(Fye)* **$75**

**Bruhns, Karl (ed.)**
- Life of Alexander von Humboldt ... Translated by J. & C. Lassell. London: 1873. 1st edn in English. 2 vols. 412; 447 pp. Ex lib.    *(Scientia)* **$65**

**Brunschwig, Alexander**
- Radical surgery in advanced abdominal cancer. Chicago: 1947. xii,324 pp. Ills. Cvrs sl faded.    *(Jenner)* **£10**
- The surgery of pancreatic tumors. St. Louis: 1942. 1st edn. 421 pp.    *(Fye)* **$20**

**Brunswik, Egon**
- Perception and the representative design of psychological experiments. Berkeley CA: University of California Press, 1956. 2nd edn, revsd & enlgd. [ii],xii,154 pp. Tall 8vo.    *(Gach)* **$50**

**Brunton, Sir T. Lauder**
- Lectures on the action of medicines ... New York: 1897. 1st Amer edn. xv,673 pp. Ills. Spine edges chipped off, top bd nearly detchd.    *(Elgen)* **$65**
- Lectures on the action of medicines ... London: Macmillan, 1901. xv,688 pp. Reprint of 1897 1st iss with crrctns. Little wear to spine ends.    *(Pollak)* **£15**

**Brush, E.F.**
- The association of human and bovine tubercolosis. New York & Albany: Wynkoop, Hallenbeck, Crawford, 1898. 144 pp.    *(Xerxes)* **$45**

**Bryan, Benjamin**
- The British vivisectors' directory; a Black Book for the United Kingdom. London: 1890. 1st edn.    *(Scientia)* **$75**

**Bryan, G.**
- Stability in aviation. An introduction to

dynamical stability as applied to the motions of aeroplanes. 1911. x,[1],192 pp. 9 ills, 38 figs in text. Orig cloth, water-stained on edges.                                    *(Whitehart)* **£18**

**Bryant, Thomas**
- On diseases of the breast. London: 1887. 1st edn. 358 pp. 8 cold lithos.        *(Fye)* **$50**

**Bryce, James**
- An account of the yellow fever, with a successful method of cure ... Edinburgh: ... W. Creech, 1796. 1st edn. Sm 4to. [2]ff, 97pp. Orig mrbld bds, upper cvr det. Small portion of outer margin of first few leaves gnawed slightly.                 *(Zeitlin)* **$350**

**[Buch'hoz, Pierre Joseph]**
- The toilet of flora; or, a collection of the most simple and approved methods of preparing baths, essences, pomatums ... receipts of cosmetics ... for the use of the ladies. 1779. New edn, imprvd. 12mo. Half-title, frontis. Mod mor.                  *(Robertshaw)* **£155**

**Buchan, A.**
- A handy book of meteorology. Edinburgh: 1867. 204 pp. 5 plates, 53 ills. Orig cloth, spine sl defective.            *(Whitehart)* **£15**

**Buchan, William**
- Domestic medicine: or, a treatise on the prevention and cure of diseases ... Ninth edition, to which is now added ... 1786. Lacking f.e.p. Contemp calf, worn, upper cvr loose, jnt cracked.        *(Robertshaw)* **£10**
- Domestic medicine: or, a treatise on the prevention and cure of diseases ... to which is now added such useful discoveries ... as have transpired since the demise of the author. 1828. 511 pp. Sev ills. Rebound in mor.
                                          *(Jenner)* **£40**

**Buchanan, Charles**
- Antisepsis and antiseptics. Newark: 1895. 1st edn. 352 pp.                        *(Fye)* **$45**

**Buchanan, Thomas**
- An engraved representation of the anatomy of the human ear ... The whole designed as a guide to acoustic surgery. Hull: Thomas Topping, 1823. 1st edn. Folio. 38,[10] pp. 2 plates. Uncut in orig bds, lightly soiled. Inscrbd to Thomas Gillespie.
                                    *(Rootenberg)* **$550**

**Bucher, Elmer E.**
- Practical wireless telegraphy. New York: 1917. vii,322 pp. Ills, diags. Lacks front free endpaper. Soiled & shaken.    *(Weiner)* **£25**
- Vacuum tubes in wireless communication. New York: 1919. viii,202 pp. Ills, diags.
                                       *(Weiner)* **£25**

- The wireless experimenter's manual incorporating how to conduct a radio club ... New York: 1920. 350 pp. Ills, diags, advts. Front cvr discoloured.            *(Weiner)* **£25**

**Buck, Albert**
- Diagnosis and treatment of ear diseases. New York: 1880. 1st edn. 411 pp.    *(Fye)* **$25**

**Buck, Albert (ed.)**
- A reference handbook of the medical sciences being a complete and convenient work of reference ... New York: 1885. 1st edn. 8 vols. Lea.                             *(Fye)* **$200**

**Buck, Albert Henry**
- The growth of medicine from the earliest times to about 1800. New Haven & London: 1917. xviii,582 pp. Ills.      *(Poitras)* **$50**

**Buck, G.W.**
- A practical and theoretical essay on oblique bridges ... revised. 1880. New edn. v,76 pp. 13 lge fldg plates. New cloth. *(Whitehart)* **£25**

**Bucke, Richard Maurice**
- Cosmic consciousness: a study in the evolution of the human mind. New York: 1935. 4to. Orig cloth.          *(Argosy)* **$25**

**Buckingham, Clyde E.**
- For humanity's sake. Story of the early development of the League of Red Cross Societies. Washington: [1964].    *(Argosy)* **$20**

**Buckingham, John**
- Matter and radiation with particular reference to the detection and uses of the infra-red rays. London: 1930.   *(Argosy)* **$35**

**Buckland, William**
- Geology and mineralogy considered with reference to natural theology. London: Pickering, 1836. 1st edn. 2 vols. xvi,599; viii,128 pp. 87 plates, many double-page or fldg, hand-cold fldg section. Plates foxed. Uncut. Orig cloth, v rubbed, rebacked.
                                       *(Pollak)* **£75**
- Reliquiae diluvianae; or observations on the organic remains contained in caves, fissures and diluvial gravel, and on other geological phenomena, attesting the action of a universal deluge. London: 1824. 2nd edn. 303 pp. 27 plates. Half lea, mrbld bds.    *(Scientia)* **$150**

**Buckley, Arabella, B.**
- A short history of natural science and of the progress of discovery ... Stanford, 1879. 2nd edn, with crrctns, addtns. xxix,505 pp. Cold plate, Orig cloth, jnts weak.      *(Pollak)* **£20**
- A short history of natural science and of the progress of discovery ... Stanford, 1888. 4th edn. xxix,509 pp. Cold plate, 74 text figs.

Orig dec cloth, rear jnt a little weak.
*(Pollak)* **£15**

**Buckley, C.F.**
- Cerebral hyperaemia, a consideration of some views of Dr. William A. Hammond. New York: Putnam, 1882. 1st edn. 129 pp. Author's pres copy, sgnd.      *(Xerxes)* **$65**

**Buckley, J.M.**
- Faith-healing, Christian Science and kindred phenomena. New York: The Century Co., 1892. 1st edn. 308 pp. Pub dec cloth, lea label, worn.      *(Gach)* **$25**

**Buckley, J.P.**
- Modern dental materia medica, pharmacology and therapeutics ... London: Rebman Ltd., 1911. 3rd edn. Pub green cloth, sl rubbed.      *(McDowell)* **£30**

**Buckman, James**
- Science and practice in farm cultivation. London: R. Hardwicke, 1865. 8vo. viii,358 pp. 7 engvd plates (foxed), 44 engvs in the text. Orig green mor-grained cloth, gilt, blocked in blind.      *(Blackwell's)* **£65**

**Bucy, Paul (ed.)**
- The precentral motor cortex. Urbana: 1949. 2nd edn. 615 pp.      *(Fye)* **$30**

**Buehler, Karl**
- The mental development of the child. New York: 1930. 1st edn in English. 8vo. Cloth.      *(Argosy)* **$35**

**Buerger, Leo**
- The circulatory disturbances of the extremities, including gangrene, vasomotor and trophic disorders. Phila: 1924. 1st edn. Lge 8vo. 628 pp. 192 ills, 5 in color. Cloth.      *(Argosy)* **$50**

**Buerger, M.J.**
- X-ray crystallography. An introduction to the investigation of crystals by their diffraction of monochromatic X-radiation. New York: 1942. xxi,531 Many text ills. Orig blue cloth.      *(Jenner)* **£20**

**Buffon, Comte de**
- Buffon's natural history. Containing a theory of the earth, a general history of man ... From the French ... London: J.S. Barr, 1792. 1st edn of Barr translation. 10 vols. 8vo. 83 copperplates. Few light stains in vol 6. Contemp calf, red & green labels.      *(Rootenberg)* **$450**
- A natural history, general and particular ... translated by William Smellie ... London: Thomas Kelly, [1781]. New edn, crrctd & enlgd. 2 vols. viii,682; viii,462 pp. 2 ports, 51

(ex 52) hand-cold plates. Occas light foxing. Contemp half-calf, rebacked.
*(Blackwell's)* **£150**

**Bulkley, L. Duncan**
- Cancer of the breast with a study of 250 cases. Phila: 1924. 1st edn. 336 pp.      *(Fye)* **$50**
- Clinical notes on psoriasis, with especial reference to its prognosis and treatment. New York: 1895. 8vo. 14 pp. Wraps. *(Argosy)* **$20**
- Notes on some of the newer remedies used in diseases of the skin. N.p.: n.d. [ca 1895]. 12mo. 13 pp. Wraps.      *(Argosy)* **$20**
- On the management of infantile eczema. N.p.: n.d. [ca 1880]. 8vo. 12 pp. Wraps.
*(Argosy)* **$20**
- On the relations of diseases of the skin to internal disorders. New York: 1906. 8vo. Cloth.      *(Argosy)* **$20**
- On the use of the solid rubber bandage in the treatment of eczema and ulcers of the leg. New York: 1878. 12mo. 21 pp. Sewed.
*(Argosy)* **$25**
- Sleep in its relations to diseases of the skin. [New York: ca 1895]. 8vo. 16 pp. Wraps.
*(Argosy)* **$20**
- Syphilis in the innocent. Clinically and historically considered, with a plan for legal control. New York: [1894]. 1st edn. Sm stain on front cvr.      *(Argosy)* **$45**

**Bulloch, William**
- The history of bacteriology. London: Oxford University Press, 1960. 2nd printing.
*(Scientia)* **$50**
- The history of bacteriology. London: Oxford University Press, 1938. 1st edn. 8vo. Pub dark green cloth, spine bruised.
*(McDowell)* **£30**

**Bumstead, Freeman**
- Pathology and treatment of venereal diseases. Phila: Blanchard & Lea, 1861. 1st edn. Roy 8vo. 686 pp. W'cut ills. Some staining. Spine ends worn.      *(Xerxes)* **$75**

**Bunnell, Sterling**
- Surgery of the hand. Phila: 1944. 1st edn. 734 pp.      *(Fye)* **$100**
- Surgery of the hand. Phila: 1956. 3rd edn. 1079 pp.      *(Fye)* **$100**

**Bunsen, Robert W.**
- Gasometry ... translated by Henry E. Roscoe. London: Walton & Maberly, 1857. 1st edn in English. 8vo. xii,298 pp,[1]f, 8 pp pub list. 60 text ills, 11 tables. Some light foxing. Orig red cloth, gilt, somewhat stained.   *(Zeitlin)* **$425**
- Gasometry comprising the leading physical and chemical properties of gases. London: Walton & Maberly, 1857. 1st edn in English. 8vo. xii,298,[1 errata] pp. 60 w'cuts in text. Orig cloth, sm nick in spine. *(Antiq Sc)* **$275**

**Burbury, S.H.**
- See Watson, H.W. & Burbury, S.H.

**Burch, George E. & DePasquale, N.P.**
- A history of electrocardiography. Chicago: 1964. 1st edn.        *(Scientia)* **$75**

**Burdell, Harvey & John**
- Observations on the structure, physiology, anatomy and diseases of the teeth. In two parts. New York: 1838. 1st edn. 96 pp. Text w'cuts, half-title to Part 2. Foxing. Orig cloth, spine ends frayed.        *(Elgen)* **$225**

**Burdon-Sanderson, J.S.**
- The School of Medical Science in Oxford. Oxford: 1892. 8vo. 36 pp. Printed wraps.
        *(Argosy)* **$25**

**Burgess, Perry**
- Who walk alone. New York: [1946]. Profusely illust. (Leper colony at Culion).
        *(Argosy)* **$25**

**Burgess, Thomas H.**
- The physiology or mechanism of blushing; illustrative of the influence of mental emotion on the capillary circulation. London: Churchill, 1839. Sole edn. 8vo. viii,202 pp. Contemp half-calf.        *(Dailey)* **$125**

**Burgh, N.P.**
- Link-motion and expansion-gear practically considered. 1872. Lge 8vo. 90 plates (many fldg), 229 w'cuts. Orig half-mor, worn.
        *(Weiner)* **£85**

**Burke, Richard M.**
- An historical chronology of tubercolosis. Springfield: [1955]. 2nd edn. 12mo. 125 pp. Cloth.        *(Argosy)* **$25**

**Burkhard, Oscar**
- Readings in medical German. New York: n.d. [ca 1930]. 8vo. Cloth.        *(Argosy)* **$25**

**Burland, C.A.**
- The arts of the alchemists. New York: 1968. 1st Amer edn. 224 pp. Dw.        *(Scientia)* **$30**

**Burlingame, Dorothy**
- Twins: a study of three pairs of identical twins. New York: n.d. [1952]. Tall 8vo. 92 pp. 30 charts. Cloth.        *(Argosy)* **$25**

**Burlingame, Josiah**
- The poor man's physician. The sick man's friend, or nature's botanic garden ... Norwich, N.Y.: Wm. G. Dyer, 1826. 1st edn. 12mo. 239 pp. Spotting & browning, one leaf torn & reprd. Contemp calf.        *(Hemlock)* **$150**

**Burmeister, H.**
- The organisation of tribolites, translated ... Ray Society, 1846. Folio. 6 plates, water-stained. Bds, sl worn.
        *(Wheldon & Wesley)* **£20**

**Burness, Alexander G. & Mavor, F.J.**
- The specific action of drugs on the healthy system; an index to their therapeutic value, as deduced from experiments on man and animals. London: Bailliere, Tindall & Cox, 1874. x,184,28 [ctlg] pp. Spine faded, spine ends & crnrs worn.        *(Pollak)* **£15**

**Burnet, Sir F.M.**
- The clonal selection theory of acquired immunity. Cambridge: 1959. ix,209 pp. 12 figs in text.        *(Whitehart)* **£18**

**Burnet, Frank M. & Fenner, Frank.**
- The production of antibodies. Melbourne: 1949. 2nd edn. Spine faded.        *(Scientia)* **$55**

**Burnett, Charles (ed.)**
- System of diseases of the ear, nose and throat. Phila: 1893. 1st edn. 2 vols. 789; 858 pp. Full lea.        *(Fye)* **$75**

**Burnett, Charles H., et al.**
- A text-book of diseases of the ear, nose and throat. Phila: 1901. 1st edn. xiii,716 pp. 14 plates (3 cold), num text ills. Inner hinges cracked.        *(Elgen)* **$65**

**Burnett, J. Compton**
- Delicate, backward, puny and stunted children - their developmental defects ... London: 1895. Lge 16mo. iv,164 pp. Prelims heavily browned. Orig maroon cloth, hinges cracked.        *(Jenner)* **£10**

**Burnham, Curtis**
- See Kelly, Howard & Burnham, Curtis

**Burns, Allen**
- Observations on some of the most frequent and important diseases of the heart ... distribution of some of the large arteries of the human body. Edinburgh ... for Thomas Bryce, 1809. 1st edn. 8vo. iv,[2],322 pp. Lib stamp on title. Contemp half-calf.
        *(Rootenberg)* **$1,600**
- Observations on the surgical anatomy of the head and neck ... with a life of the author; and additional cases and observations ... Balt & Phila: 1823. 1st Amer edn. 8vo. xxix,31-512,[1] pp. 10 engvd plates, stamps on verso. Foxing. Contemp sheep, worn.
        *(Hemlock)* **$175**

**Burns, John**
- The anatomy of the gravid uterus. With practical inferences relative to pregnancy and

labour ... Salem (Mass.): 1808. 1st Amer edn. 8vo. xxi,1 [blank],248 pp. 2 plates. Uncut in orig bds, linen back with paper label.
*(Hemlock)* **$150**
- Dissertations on inflammation. Albany, N.Y.: E.F. Backus, 1812. 1st Amer edn. 2 vols in one. 213; 214 pp. Contemp calf, sl worn & stained. *(Diamond)* **$75**
- Observations on abortion ... Springfield (Mass.): Isaiah Thomas, jun., 1809. 2nd Amer edn. 16mo. 138 pp. Contemp full calf.
*(M&S)* **$42.50**
- The principles of midwifery, including the diseases of women and children. London: 1817. 4th edn.xvi, 648 pp. Old calf, rebacked.
*(Goodrich)* **$85**
- Principles of midwifery, including the diseases of women and children. London: Longman, Hurst, 1814. 3rd edn, greatly enlgd. Some age staining in text. New cloth, mrbld bds. *(Diamond)* **$75**

**Burns, Robert Scott (ed.)**
- Working drawings and designs in mechanical engineering and machine making. Edinburgh & London: n.d. [ca 1863]. Lge folio. 200 pp. 49 v lge double-page plates (2 numbered 38), num engvs & w'cut diags in the text. Half-calf, worn, ends of jnts cracked. *(Weiner)* **£220**

**Burnside, William S. & Panton, Arthur W.**
- The theory of equations. Dublin: Hodges, Figgis, 1899 - 1901. 4th edn. 2 vols. xiv,286; xi,292 pp. Orig cloth. *(Pollak)* **£25**

**Burr, C.B. (ed.)**
- Medical history of Michigan. Minneapolis: 1930. 1st edn. 2 vols. *(Scientia)* **$100**

**Burr, George O.**
- See Evans, Herbert McLean & Burr, George O.

**Burrage, Walter**
- A history of the Massachusetts Medical Society, with brief biographies of the founders and chief officers 1781 - 1922. Privately printed (The Plimpton Press, Norwood, Mass.). Tall thick 8vo. xii,505 pp. Stamp on title. Orig blue cloth. *(Hemlock)* **$60**

**Burrall, F.A.**
- Asiatic cholera. New York: Wood, 1866. 1st edn. 155 pp. Minor water stains throughout. *(Xerxes)* **$75**

**Burrow, Trigant**
- The social basis of consciousness: a study in organic psychology based upon a synthetic and societal concept of the neuroses. New York: Harcourt, 1927. 1st U.S. edn. xviii,256 pp. Dw. Ex lib. *(Gach)* **$25**

**Burrows, Harold**
- Biological actions of sex hormones. Cambridge: 1945. 1st edn. 4to. 514 pp. Buckram. *(Argosy)* **$40**
- Mistakes and accidents of surgery. London: 1923. 1st edn. viii,470 pp. Sl shelf wear. *(Elgen)* **$30**

**Burrows, Harold & Horning, Eric**
- Oestrogens and neoplasia. Springfield: 1952. 1st edn. 189 pp. Extensive bibliog. *(Fye)* **$30**

**Burstall, Francis H.**
- See Morgan, Sir Gilbert & Burstall, Francis H.

**Burton, E.F. & Kohl, W.H.**
- The electron microscope. An introduction to its fundamental principles and applications. London: 1946. 2nd edn. Num plates. Bibliog. *(Winterdown)* **£12**

**[Burton, Robert]**
- The anatomy of melancholy. What it is, with all the kinds, causes, symptomes, prognostickes, & severall cures of it ... Oxford: for Henry Cripps, 1638. Folio. [5]ff, 78,[2] pp. Engvd title. Contemp calf, worn, jnts cracked. 1 leaf loose. *(Zeitlin)* **$750**
- The anatomy of melancholy: What it is, with all the kinds, causes, symptomes, prognostickes, & severall cures of it. By Democritus Junior. London: for H. Cripps, 1660. 7th edn. Folio. Engvd title. vi,723,[10] pp. Early calf, spine worn, mod lea label. *(Gach)* **$550**
- The anatomy of melancholy: What it is, with all the kinds, causes, symptoms ... London: E. Blake, 1836. 16th edn. viii,744 pp. Frontis. Contemp calf-backed mrbld bds, shelfworn. *(Gach)* **$50**

**[Burtt, G.F.]**
- The locomotives of the London, Brighton & South Coast Railway, 1839-1903. 1903. vii,245 pp. Plates, ills. Orig wraps, worn, soiled & shaken. *(Weiner)* **£30**

**Bury, Edward**
- Death improv'd and immoderate sorrow for deceased friends and relations reprov'd. 1693. Sm 8vo. [viii],272 pp. Title stained & soiled, lower outer crnr defective, one leaf torn, few sl shaved headlines, rather soiled & stained. Half-calf, worn. *(Jenner)* **£80**

**Bury, Judson**
- Diseases of the nervous system. Manchester: 1912. xx,7728 pp. Cold frontis, 8 plates, 216 ills. Cvrs rubbed. *(Jenner)* **£25**

**Butler, Charles**
- An easy introduction to the mathematics; in

which the theory and practice are laid down and familiarly explained. Oxford: Bartlett & Newman, 1814. 2 vols in 1. xlvi,470; v,[iii],508 pp. Some foxing. Half-calf, sl wear to spine head.          *(Pollak)* **£35**

**Butler, Richard**
- An essay concerning blood-letting shewing the various effects and peculiar advantage of bleeding in different parts ... London: for W. Mears, 1734. 1st edn. 8vo in 4s. [4]ff, 148pp. Large paper copy. Dedication binding full red mor, front hinge cracking.     *(Zeitlin)* **$850**

**Butler, Samuel**
- Evolution old and new; or the theories of Buffon, Erasmus Darwin and Lamarck, as compared with that of Mr. Charles Darwin. London: 1879. 1st edn. 384 pp. Spine shelfworn.          *(Scientia)* **$75**
- Evolution old and new; or the theories of Buffon ... as compared with that of Mr. Charles Darwin. London: 1911. New edn, with author's revisions. 430 pp.
          *(Scientia)* **$27.50**
- Luck, or cunning as the main means of organic modification? London: 1922. 2nd edn, 2nd printing. 282 pp. *(Scientia)* **$27.50**

**Butlin, Henry Trentham**
- Diseases of the tongue. London: Cassell, 1885. 8vo. viii,451,[8 advts] pp. 8 chromo-litho plates, num text engvs. Orig cloth, jnts split.          *(Dailey)* **$85**

**Butterworth, Benj. (comp.)**
- The growth of industrial art ... Washington: G.P.O., 1888. 1st edn. Lge folio. [4],200 pp. Over 2,000 ills. Orig cloth. Sm shelf label on spine.          *(M&S)* **$225**

**BW**
- See Badcock, William

**[Byam, Lydia]**
- A collection of exotics, from the island of Antigua. By a Lady. [London: 1797]. 1st, & sole, edn. Folio. 3ff, 6 (of 12) hand-cold engvd plates numbered in contemp ms 1-6. Title sl soiled, two short tears in plate 6 reprd. Mod half-vell, mrbld bds.     *(Dailey)* **$1,500**

**Byerley, William Elwood**
- An elementary treatise on Fourier's series ... Boston: Ginn, 1893. ix,287,[vii] pp. Cloth dulled.          *(Pollak)* **£20**

**Byford, William**
- A treatise on chronic inflammation and displacements of the unimpregnated uterus. Phila: 1871. Ills. Ex lib.     *(Argosy)* **$45**
- A treatise on the chronic inflammation and displacements of the unimpregnated uterus.

Phila: 1871. 2nd edn. 248 pp.     *(Fye)* **$50**
- A treatise on the theory and practice of obstetrics. New York: 1873. 2nd edn. 469 pp.
          *(Fye)* **$20**

**Cabanes, Dr.**
- Curious bypaths of history, being medico-historical studies and observations. Paris: 1898. 1st English edn. Ltd (500). Frontis. Some foxing. Orig cloth, rubbed.
          *(Robertshaw)* **£15**

**Cabell, James L.**
- A brief historical notice of the origin and progress of international hygiene. Boston: 1882. 18 pp. Orig blue printed wraps.
          *(Argosy)* **$25**

**Cabinet-maker ...**
- The cabinet-maker's guide: or, rules and instructions in the art of varnishing, dying, staining, japanning ... London: printed ... Greenfield, Mass: Reprinted by Ansel Phelps, 1825. 1st Amer edn. 16 mo. 108 pp. Orig printed bds, hinges cracked.
          *(M&S)* **$450**

**Cabot, A.T.**
- Papers upon abdominal surgery. Boston: 1891. 1st edn. 59 pp. Wraps.     *(Fye)* **$75**

**Cabot, Richard**
- Differential diagnosis presented through an analysis of 383 cases. Phila: 1911. 1st edn. 753 pp.          *(Fye)* **$50**

**Cabot, Richard C. (ed.)**
- Diseases of metabolism and of the blood; animal parasitology; toxicology. New York: 1909. 649 pp. Cold plate, ills. *(Argosy)* **$75**

**Cadogan, William**
- A dissertation on gout, and all chronic diseases, jointly considered ... London: for J. Dodsley, 1771. Sm 4to. viii,88 pp. Some old marginal inking, last 2 leaves reprd, final leaf trimmed & dusty on verso. Half-calf, mrbld bds.          *(Pollak)* **£75**
- A dissertation on the gout. 1771. 1st edn. 88 pp. Half-title & final page reinforced at margins. Mod qtr calf.     *(Oasis)* **$350**
- A dissertation on the gout, and all chronic diseases, jointly considered, as proceeding from the same causes. Phila: [1772]. Text quite stained. Half-calf, jnts worn. *(Allen)* **$50**

**Caird, F.M.**
- See Cathcart, Charles W. & Caird, F.M.

**Caird, Francis**
- Hints on the antiseptic management of wounds. Edinburgh: 1880. 27 pp. 1st edn. Wraps.          *(Fye)* **$75**

**Cairns, Hugh**
- A study of intracranial surgery. London: H.M.S.O., 1929. 83,viii pp. 30 plates. Orig wraps, recased.                    *(Pollak)* **£35**

**Cajori, Florian**
- A history of the conceptions of limits and fluxions in Great Britain from Newton to Woodhouse. Chicago: Open Court Publishing, 1919. viii,299 pp. Frontis, plate. Orig cloth.                          *(Pollak)* **£30**

**Caldwell, W.H.**
- The Guernsey [cattle]. Peterborough, New Hampshire: 1941. 393 pp. Ills. Cloth. Author's sgnd copy.           *(Phenotype)* **£48**

**Calhoun, A.W.**
- Report of seventy cataract operations. Atlanta: 1876. 8vo. 28 pp. Printed wraps.
                                   *(Argosy)* **$40**

**Calkins, Gary N.**
- Protozoology. New York: Lea & Febiger, 1909. 349 pp. 125 engvs, 4 cold plates.
                                    *(Poitras)* **$25**

**Calkins, Leroy**
- See Scammon, Richard & Calkins, Leroy

**Callahan, Alston**
- Surgery of the eye: injuries. Springfield: 1950. 1st edn. 4to. 217 pp.      *(Fye)* **$60**

**Callcott, Maria**
- A Scripture herbal. 1842. xxii,544 pp. Many ills. Inscription on title. Rebound in calf-backed mrbld bds.              *(Jenner)* **£80**

**Callis, Robert**
- The reading of the famous and learned Robert Callis, Esq. upon the statute of 23 H.8. cap. 5. of sewers. As it was delivered by him at Grays Inn, in August 1622 ... 1685. 2nd edn. Damp-staining affecting title & prelims. Calf, upper bd badly mkd & warped.
                                  *(Edwards)* **£65**

**Callon, J.**
- Lectures on mining, delivered at the School of Mines, Paris. Translated ... 1876-81-86. 3 text vols, 3 atlas volumes of plates. xix,459; xiv,540; viii,231 pp. 119 double-page plates. Some spines faded, some sl defective.
                                *(Whitehart)* **£150**

**Calne, Donald B.**
- Therapeutics in neurology. Oxford: [1975]. 8vo. Cloth. Author's pres copy. *(Argosy)* **$45**

**Calverton, V.F. & Schmalhausen (eds.)**
- The new generation. Introduction by Bertrand Russell. New York: Macaulay Co.,

1930. 1st edn. 717 pp. Ex lib.      *(Gach)* **$25**

**Camac, C.N.B.**
- Epoch-making contributions to medicine, surgery and the allied sciences. Phila: 1909. 1st edn. 35 pp. Some underlining. Backstrip worn, inner hinges cracked.        *(Fye)* **$40**

**Cameron, Charles**
- The cholera microbe and how to meet it. London: 1884. 8vo. 26 pp. Orig printed wraps.                           *(Argosy)* **$30**

**Cameron, Charles A.**
- Chemistry of agriculture, the food of plants: including the composition, properties and adulteration of manures. Dublin: 1857. 144 pp. Lacks rear free endpaper. *(Weiner)* **£18**

**Cameron, G.R.**
- Pathology of the cell. 1952. 1st edn. xv,840 pp. 64 plates, 41 figs, extensive bibliog.
                               *(Whitehart)* **£35**

**Cameron, J.**
- Shorthorns in Central and Southern Scotland. 1921. xv,335 pp. Many ills. Brown cloth.
                                *(Phenotype)* **£38**

**Cammidge, P.J.**
- Glycosuria and allied conditions. London: 1913. vi,467 pp. Some ills. Orig red cloth.
                                   *(Jenner)* **£12**
- See Robson A.W. Mayo & Cammidge, P.J.

**Campbell, Alfred W.**
- Histological studies on the localisation of cerebral functions. Cambridge: 1905. 1st edn. 4to. Half-title, xix,360 pp. 29 full-page plates. Tape repairs, some crude, affecting text. New cloth. Ex lib.                    *(Elgen)* **$275**

**Campbell, Dorothy Adams, et al.**
- Eyes in industry. A comprehensive book on eyesight, written for industrial workers. 1951. viii,234 p. Ills throughout. Some cold plates. Orig blue cloth.              *(Jenner)* **£12**

**Campbell, Henry F.**
- Registration and sanitation; their value. A preliminary report read before the Board of Health of the State of Georgia. Augusta: 1881. 23 pp. Printed wraps. Author's pres copy.                       *(Argosy)* **$25**

**Campbell, Henry Fraser**
- Blood-letting in puerperal eclampsia. Pathology and therapeutics: the old and the new. New York: 1876. 48 pp. Orig blue printed wraps.              *(Argosy)* **$27.50**
- Resume of a report on position, pneumatic pressure and mechanical appliance in uterine displacements. Augusta: 1876. 18 pp. 4 figs.

Printed wraps. Author's pres copy.
*(Argosy)* **$27.50**
- The soft rubber spring-stem pessary in the treatment of uterine flexions. Atlanta: 1879. 10 pp. Printed wraps. *(Argosy)* **$20**
- The widespread influence of the cerebro-spinal centers over the ganglionic plexuses. Richmond, Va: 1880. 11 pp. Printed wraps. Author's pres copy. *(Argosy)* **$25**
- The yellow fever quarantine of the future, based upon the portability of atmospheric germs, and the non-contagiousness of the disease. Cambridge: 1880. 16 pp. Orig printed wraps. *(Argosy)* **$25**

**Campbell, J. Menzies**
- A dental bibliography British and American 1682 - 1880. London: David Low, 1949. 1st edn. Slim 8vo. Orig blue slip-case.
*(McDowell)* **£55**

**Campbell, Lewis & Garnett, William**
- The life of James Clerk Maxwell, with a selection from his correspondence ... and a sketch of his contributions to science. London: 1882. 1st edn. 662 pp. Rebnd in buckram. *(Scientia)* **$40**

**Canetti, Elias**
- Crowds and power. Translated from the German ... New York: The Viking Press, 1962. 1st U.S. edn. 495,1 pp. *(Gach)* **$25**

**Canning, Edward**
- Orthodontia, or treatment of malposition of the teeth. Denver: 1912. 8vo. 64 pp. Orig printed wraps. *(Argosy)* **$30**

**Cannon, Walter**
- Traumatic shock. New York: 1923. 1st edn. 201 pp. *(Fye)* **$75**

**Cantlie, Sir N.A.**
- A history of the Army Medical Department. 1974. 2 vols. 519; 448 pp. 28 plates, maps.
*(Whitehart)* **£35**

**Canton, Edwin**
- Surgical and pathological observations. London: 1855. 1st edn. Tall 8vo. 106 pp. Plates & text engvs. Lacks backstrip.
*(Argosy)* **$35**

**Cantor, Georg**
- Contributions to the founding of the theory of transfinite numbers, translated ... Chicago & London: 1915. ix,211 pp. Cloth soiled. (Open Court Classics of Science & Philosophy No. 1) *(Weiner)* **£40**
- Contributions to the founding of the theory of transfinite numbers, translated ... Chicago: Open Court Publishing, 1915. ix,211 pp. Cloth sl worn & dull. *(Pollak)* **£25**

**Cantor, Meyer**
- Intestinal intubation. Springfield: 1949. 533 pp. Dw. *(Fye)* **$75**

**Capellmann, Carl**
- Pastoral medicine. Translated ... Cincinnati: 1879. *(Argosy)* **$30**

**Carey, Mathew**
- A short account of the malignant fever, lately prevalent in Philadelphia. Phila: for the Author, 1793. 1st edn. 8vo. 103,[9] pp. A little foxing, leaf 97/98 lacking part of margin. Linen-backed blue bds with paper label, antique style. *(Antiq Sc)* **$425**
- A short account of the malignant fever, lately prevalent in Philadelphia. Phila: for the Author, 1794. 4th edn improved. 8vo. 164 pp. Mottled calf, jnt reprd. *(Argosy)* **$175**

**Carling, E.R. & Ross, J.P. (eds.)**
- British surgical practice, 1947 - 1961. 8 vols, index vol, 11 annual supp vols. Lge 8vo.
*(Jenner)* **£40**

**Carlisle, Anthony**
- An essay on the disorders of old age and on the means for prolonging human life. London: Longman ... & Brown, 1817. 1st edn. 8vo. Red & black title. Half calf, gilt spine. *(Quaritch)* **$100**

**Carlson, Elof A.**
- The gene: A critical history. Phila: 1966. 1st edn. 301 pp. *(Scientia)* **$40**

**Carman, E.A., et al.**
- Special report on the history and present condition of the sheep industry of the United States. U.S.D.A. Washington: 1892. 1000 pp. 95 engvs. *(Phenotype)* **£85**

**Carmichael, T.H.**
- Treatment of arthritis. Phila: n.d. [ca 1927]. 12mo. 24 pp. Stitched. *(Argosy)* **$20**

**Carnochan, J.M.**
- Address on the study of science, delivered in the New York Medical College ... New York: 1857. 43 pp. Orig printed wraps. *(Argosy)* **$35**

**Carpenter, Alfred**
- On London fogs. Croydon: 1890. 46 pp. Orig printed wraps. Ex lib. *(Argosy)* **$25**

**Carpenter, G. Hale & Ford, E.B.**
- Mimicry. London: 1933. 1st edn. 134 pp.
*(Scientia)* **$45**

**Carpenter, J.**
- See Nasmyth, J. & Carpenter, J.**Carpenter, Nathaniel**
- Geographie delineated forth in two bookes ...

the second edition corrected ... Oxford: ...,
1635. 2nd edn. Sm 4to. [xvi],272, [2
blank],[14],386,[2 blank]. 4 fldg tables. Title
sl frayed. Leaf torn & reprd without loss.
Contemp calf, rebacked. *(Pickering)* **$1,200**

**Carpenter, P.H.**
- See Etheridge, R. & Carpenter, P.H.

**Carpenter, William B.**
- The microscope and its revelations. London:
1852. 3rd edn. 10 plates, 395 figs.
*(Winterdown)* **£35**
- The microscope and its revelations. 1875. 5th
edn. xxxii,848 pp. 25 plates, 494 ills. Some
foxing. Rebacked, orig spine laid down.
*(Jenner)* **£28**
- The microscope and its revelations. 1881. 6th
edn. xxxii,882 pp. Frontis, 25 plates, 502 figs
in text. Half-title torn, reprd. New cloth.
*(Whitehart)* **£38**
- Nature and man. Essays scientific and
philosophical. New York: 1889. 1st Amer
edn. 483 pp. Ex lib. *(Scientia)* **$35**
- On the use and abuse of alcoholic liquors, in
health and disease. Phila: Henry C. Lea.
1866. [ii],178,[2],12 pp. 4 pp pub ctlg. Orig
green cloth, worn. *(Gach)* **$37.50**
- The physiology of alcoholics: an address.
New York: National Temperance Society,
1883. 23 pp. Printed wraps. Ex lib.
*(Argosy)* **$25**
- Principles of comparative physiology. 1854.
4th edn. xxviii,770 pp. 300 figs in text. Orig
blind-stamped cloth, sl faded & worn.
*(Whitehart)* **£15**
- Principles of human physiology. Phila: 1847.
3rd Amer edn. 752,32 [pub advts] pp. Num
text ills. Orig sheep, scuffed. *(Oasis)* **$50**
- Principles of mental physiology, with their
applications to the training and discipline of
the mind, and the study of its morbid
conditions. New York: Appleton, 1889.
lxvi,737,[3] pp. Shelfworn. *(Gach)* **$25**

**Carpue, J.C.**
- An introduction to electricity and galvanism;
with cases, shewing their effects in the cure of
diseases: to which is added, a Description ...
London: sold by A. Phillips ..., 1803. 1st edn.
8vo. 3 fldg engvd plates. Contemp lea-backed
mrbld bds, rubbed. *(Antiq Sc)* **$575**

**Carque, Otto**
- Foundation of all reform; a guide to health,
wealth and freedom. Chicago: Kosmos, 1904.
66 pp. Ills. Wraps. *(Xerxes)* **$35**

**Carr, G.S.**
- A synopsis of elementary results in pure
mathematics. London: Hodgson, 1886.
xxxvi,[ii], 935 pp. 193 plates. Good working
copy. *(Pollak)* **£20**

**Carr, W.**
- The history of the rise and progress of the
Killerby, Studley and Warlaby Herds of
Shorthorns. 1867. Cr 8vo. vii, 158 pp.
Frontis. Green cloth, recased. *(Phenotype)* **£38**

**Carrel, Alexis & Dahelly, G.**
- The treatment of infected wounds. New
York: 1917. 1st edn in English. 238 pp.
*(Fye)* **$100**

**Carroll, Alfred L.**
- The question of quarantine: the nature and
prevention of communicable zymotic
diseases. New York: 1872. 21 pp. Orig
printed wraps. Ex lib. *(Argosy)* **$25**

**Carson, Joseph**
- Synopsis of the ... lectures on materia medica
and pharmacy delivered in the University of
Pennsylvania. Phila: Blanchard & Lea, 1851.
1st edn. 204 pp. Rubbed & worn. Interleaved
throughout, with Dr. Lewis L. Wolken's ms
notes & comments. *(Xerxes)* **$225**

**[Carter, Elizabeth (trans.)]**
- Sir Isaac Newton's philosophy explained for
the use of the ladies. In six dialogues on light
and colours. From the Italian ... London: for
E. Cave, 1739. 1st edn in English. 2 vols.
12mo. [iv],xvi,iv, 232; 247 pp. Half-title. 19th
c half-calf, minor wear. *(Burmester)* **£325**
- Sir Isaac Newton's philosophy explained for
the use of the ladies. In six dialogues ... From
the Italian ... London: for E. Cave, 1739. 1st
edn in English. 2 vols. 12mo. [iv],[iv], 232;
247 pp. Browning, occas dusty, sm tears. 19th
c half-calf, mrbld bds. *(Pollak)* **£100**

**Carter, Henry Rose**
- Yellow fever. An epidemiological and
historical study of its place of origin. Balt:
Williams & Wilkins, 1931. 4to. xii,308 pp.
Dw. *(Poitras)* **$30**

**Carter, J. Bailey**
- The fundamentals of electrocardiographic
interpretation. Springfield: 1937. 1st edn.
8vo. Ills. Cloth. *(Argosy)* **$30**

**Case, Calvin S.**
- A practical treatise on the technics and
principles of dental orthopedia, including
drawings and working details of appliances ...
Chicago: C.S. Case Company, 1908. xv,406
pp. Num ills. Qtr lea, sl scuffed. *(Poitras)* **$45**

**Casper, J.L.**
- A handbook of the practice of forensic
medicine based on personal experience. New
Sydenham Society, 1861-65. 4 vols. 8vo.
xvi,317; vi,331; ix,417; xv,364 pp. Orig
blind-stamped cloth, vols 3 & 4 rebacked.

Dust stained & sl worn.     *(Whitehart)* **£65**

**Castell, Evans**
- Physico-chemical tables for the use of analysts, physicists, chemical manufacturers and scientific chemists. Griffin, 1902. 2 vols. xxii,548; xiv,549-1235 pp. Spine ends worn, jnts slack.                    *(Pollak)* **£25**

**Castigliani, Arturo**
- A history of medicine. New York: 1941. 1st edn in English.              *(Scientia)* **$85**
- A history of medicine. New York: 1947. 2nd edn in English, revsd & enlgd. Spine lettering dull, shelfworn.            *(Scientia)* **$75**

**Castle, W.E.**
- Genetics and eugenics. A text-book for students of biology and a reference book for animal and plant breeders. Cambridge, Mass.: 1920.                 *(Argosy)* **$50**

**Castle, William, et al.**
- Heredity and eugenics: a course of lectures summarizing recent advances in knowledge in variation, heredity and evolution ... Chicago: 1912. 1st edn. 315 pp.         *(Scientia)* **$40**

**[Catalogues]**
- For catalogues of equipment, instruments, &c., See Trade catalogue ...

**Cathcart, Charles W. & Caird, F.M.**
- Johnston's students' atlas of bones and ligaments. Edinburgh: W. & A.K. Johnston, [1885]. 1st edn. Sm folio. 30 double-page litho ills.                 *(McDowell)* **£30**

**Cathell, D.W.**
- Book on the physician himself from graduation to old age. Phila: 1924.
                              *(Argosy)* **$35**

**Cattell, John**
- A treatise on the culture and treatment of American plants, by John Cattell, Nurseryman & Seedsman, Westerham, Kent. [London: John Nichols, ca 1845]. 8vo. 4 pp. Disbound.                *(Burmester)* **£25**

**Cattell, Richard & Warren, Kenneth**
- Surgery of the pancreas. Phila: 1954. 1st edn. 374 pp. Ex lib.              *(Fye)* **$15**

**Caudill, William & Lin, Tsung-Yi**
- Mental health research in Asia and the Pacific. Honolulu: East-West Center Press, [1969]. xvi,487 pp. Library pocket in rear. Worn dw.                  *(Gach)* **$25**

**Caustic, Christopher (pseud.)**
- See Fessenden, Thomas Green

**Cavallo, Tiberius**
- A complete treatise of electricity in theory and practice with original experiments. London: Edward & Charles Dilly, 1777. 1st edn. 8vo. xvi,viii, 412,[4] pp. 3 fldg plates, errata, advt leaf. Sm split in fold of one plate. Half-calf.              *(Rootenberg)* **$585**
- An essay on the theory and practice of medical electricity. London: Printed for the author, 1780. 1st edn. 8vo. xvi,112 pp. 1 fldg engvd plate. Old half-calf. *(Offenbacher)* **$300**
- A treatise on the nature and properties of air and other permanently elastic fluids ... London: for the author, 1781. 1st edn. 4to. xii,835,[1] pp, [4]ff. 3 fldg engvd plates, 1 fldg table. Light foxing, plates lightly offset. Old bds, chipped, rebacked.     *(Zeitlin)* **$450**

**Cavendish, Henry**
- The electrical researches ... written between 1771 and 1781, edited ... Cambridge: University Press, 1879. 1st edn. 8vo. lxvi,454 pp. Advt leaf. Prize binding in tree calf, ornate gilt spine, by Sayer & Wilson. Cambridge award to J.J. Thomson.
                          *(Rootenberg)* **$500**
- Observations on Mr. Hutchin's experiments for determining the degree of cold at which quicksilver freezes. London: J. Nicols, 1784. 1st edn. 4to. 26 pp. Orig printed sheet (conjugate with last leaf); uncut & unopened as issued.           *(Rootenberg)* **$300**
- The scientific papers ... Cambridge: University Press, 1921. 1st edn. 2 vols. Lge 8vo. xxviii,452; xii,496 pp. 2 frontis, 6 plates & ills in the text. Orig maroon cloth. Royal Society of Edinburgh stamps on titles.
                            *(Pickering)* **$1,000**
- The scientific papers of the Honourable Henry Cavendish ... Cambridge: University Press, 1921. 1st comprehensive edn. 2 vols. 4to. xxvii,452; xii,496 pp. 2 frontis, 6 fldg plates in vol II, text diags throughout. Orig cloth, lib stamps.      *(Rootenberg)* **$600**

**Cayley, Arthur**
- An elementary treatise on elliptic functions. George Bell, 1895. 2nd edn. xii,[ii],386 pp. Orig cloth.                  *(Pollak)* **£25**

**Celsus, A. Cornelius**
- Of medicine. In eight books. Translated, with notes critical, and explanatory, by James Creive, M.D. London: Wilson, 1756. 1st edn in English. 8vo. Errata leaf. Contemp calf, rebacked.            *(McDowell)* **£130**

**Certain ...**
- Certain necessary directions, as well for the cure of the plague as for preventing the infection; with many easie medicines of small charge ... London: John Bill & Christopher Barker, 1665. 4to. [4],35 pp. Black letter.

Lightly browned. Qtr calf. *(Rootenberg)* **$525**

**Cescinsky, Herbert & Webster, Malcolm R.**
- English domestic clocks, Illustrated from drawings and photographs by the authors. London: Routledge & Sons, 1914. 2nd edn. Folio. 353 pp. Cold frontis, 407 figs, index. Orig 3/4 black mor, green cloth, t.e.g.
*(Zeitlin)* **$210**

**Chadwick, Edwin**
- On preventive administration, as compared with curative administration as practised in Germany. [London]: 1889. 12mo. 19 pp. Orig printed wraps. *(Argosy)* **$20**
- The present condition of sanitary science. London: 1889. 12mo. 10 pp. Orig printed wraps. Ex lib. *(Argosy)* **$20**
- Sanitary progress ... on the prevention of epidemics. London: 1882. 12 mo. 23 pp. Orig printed wraps. Ex lib. Pres copy. *(Argosy)* **$30**

**[Chadwick, Edwin]**
- Report to Her Majesty's Principal Secretary of State for the Home Department ... on an inquiry into the sanitary conditions of the labouring population of Great Britain. London: William Clowes, 1842. 8vo. Fldg maps, plans, plates. Pub cloth.
*(McDowell)* **£750**

**Chadwick, J.**
- Radioactivity and radioactive substances. An introduction to the study of ... With a foreword by Sir Ernest Rutherford. London: Pitman, 1921. 1st edn. xii,111,[viii ctlg] pp. 30 text figs. *(Pollak)* **£100**
- Radioactivity and radioactive substances ... With a foreword by Sir Ernest Rutherford. London: Pitman, 1934. 3rd edn. xii,116,32 [ctlg] pp. 32 text figs. *(Pollak)* **£25**

**Chadwick, Mary**
- Nursing psychological patients. London: 1931. 8vo. Cloth. *(Argosy)* **$27.50**

**Chamberlain, Paul M.**
- It's about time. New York: Richard R. Smith, 1941. 1st edn. Roy 8vo. 490 pp. Frontis, num diags & photographs. Orig buckram gilt.
*(Zeitlin)* **$300**

**Chamberlaine, William**
- Tirocinium medicum; or a dissertation on the duties of youth apprenticed to the medical profession. 1812. 1st edn. Fldg plate. Some browning & spotting. Later cloth.
*(Robertshaw)* **£25**

**Chambers, George**
- A handbook of descriptive and practical astronomy. London: Murray, 1861. 1st edn.

xlvi,514,[ii advts] pp. Frontis, 52 plates. Orig cloth, rebacked. Good working copy.
*(Pollak)* **£12**

**Chambers, R.**
- Ancient sea margins, as memorials of changes in the relative level of sea and land. 1848. 8vo. vi,337 pp. Frontis, cold map, text figs. Orig cloth, sl used. *(Wheldon & Wesley)* **£50**

**[Chambers, Robert]**
- Vestiges of the natural history of creation. London: John Churchill, 1850. 8th edn. vi,319 pp. Contemp half-mor, half-title discarded by binder. *(Pollak)* **£25**

**Chambers, Thomas K.**
- Digestion and its derangements. The principles of rational medicine applied to disorders of the alimentary canal. New York: 1856. 1st Amer edn. x,441,6[pub ctlg] pp. Blind-stamped cloth, spotted & discolored.
*(Elgen)* **$55**
- The renewal of the clinical lectures illustrative of a restorative system of medicine, given at St. Mary's Hospital. London: 1863. 2nd edn. 420 pp. Orig photograph of Chambers pasted inside front cvr. *(Argosy)* **$50**

**Champlin, James Tilt**
- Text-book in intellectual philosophy ... containing an outline of the science with an abstract of its history. Boston: Crosby, Nichols, Lee, 1860. 1st edn. 240,[2] pp. Pebbled cloth, jnts frayed. *(Gach)* **$35**

**Chandler, Asa C.**
- Hookworm disease: distribution, biology, epidemiology, pathology, diagnosis, treatment and control. New York: 1929. 1st edn. 494 pp. Ills. *(Argosy)* **$40**

**Channing, W.F.**
- Notes on the medical application of electricity. Boston: Davis, 1849. 199 pp. 8 text engvs. Orig cloth, rebacked.
*(Goodrich)* **$75**

**Channing, Walter**
- A physician's vacation; or, a summer in Europe. Boston: 1856. 1st edn. 568 pp. Orig embossed cloth, lacks backstrip. *(Argosy)* **$85**
- A treatise on etherization in childbirth. Boston: 1848. 1st edn. Cloth worn.
*(Scientia)* **$325**

**Channing, William F.**
- The American fire-alarm telegraph: a lecture ... before the Smithsonian Institution ... Boston: Redding & Co., 1855. 1st sep edn. 8vo. 19 pp. Orig printed wraps. *(M&S)* **$65**

**Chapin, John Bassett**
- A compendium of insanity. Phila: W.B. Saunders, 1898. 1st edn. 12mo. Pub red cloth.                    *(Gach)* **$35**

**Chaplin, Arnold**
- On medicine in the century before Harvey. London: 1922. 8vo. 28 pp. Stiff printed wraps.                    *(Argosy)* **$25**

**Chapman, Henry**
- Thermae Redidive; or, the City of Bath Described ... See Guidott, Thomas

**Chapman, Henry C.**
- Manual of medical jurisprudence and toxicology. Phila: Saunders, 1893. Sm 8vo. 237 pp. Ills.                    *(Xerxes)* **$45**

**Chapman, Nathaniel**
- Lectures on the more important diseases of the thoracic and abdominal viscera. Phila: Lea & Blanchard, 1844. 4to. vii,383 pp. Water staining. Full lea, sl scuffed.
                    *(Poitras)* **$75**
- Lectures on the more important eruptive fevers, haemorrhages and dropsies, and on gout and rheumatism. Phila: Lea & Blanchard, 1844. 4to. 448,30 [pub ctlg] pp. Some foxing.                    *(Poitras)* **$75**

**Chapman, W. Louis**
- Auto-intoxication as a cause and complication of disease. Providence: 1903. Tall 8vo. 92 pp. Cloth-backed bds, front cvr torn. *(Argosy)* **$25**

**Chapman, William**
- Observations on the advisable measures to be adopted in forming a communication for the transit of merchandise and the produce of land, to and from Carlisle, in a letter ... Newcastle: Edward Walker, 1824. 1st edn. 8vo. 10 pp. Mod calf-backed mrbld bds.
                    *(Deighton Bell)* **£140**

**Chapuis, Alfred & Jaquet, Eugene**
- The history of the self-winding watch 1770-1931. Neuchatel & New York: 1956. 4to. 246 pp. Cold frontis, 154 figs. Orig green cloth gilt.                    *(Zeitlin)* **$52.50**

**Charaka Club ...**
- See Proceedings of the Charaka Club ...

**Charcot, J.M.**
- Clinical lectures on senile and chronic diseases. Translated ... London: New Sydenham Society, 1881. 1st British edn. xvi,307 pp. 6 plates. Blind embossed cloth.
                    *(Gach)* **$135**
- Clinical lectures on senile and chronic diseases. Translated ... New Sydenham Society, 1881. 1st edn in English. xvi,307 pp.

6 plates. Orig cloth.            *(Whitehart)* **£75**
- Clinical lectures on senile and chronic diseases. Translated ... London: New Sydenham Society, 1881. 1st English edn. 8vo. Pub cloth, small snag to rear bd.
                    *(McDowell)* **£40**
- Lectures on localisation of cerebral and spinal diseases delivered at the Faculty of Medicine of Paris. Translated ... New Sydenham Society, 1883. 1st edn in English. xxxii,341 pp. 89 figs in text. Orig cloth, spine sl worn.
                    *(Whitehart)* **£65**
- Lectures on localization in diseases of the brain ... translated ... New York: 1878. 1st edn in English. viii,133 pp. 45 text w'cuts. Orig cloth, spine ends & crnrs frayed.
                    *(Elgen)* **$200**

**Charlesworth, J.K.**
- The geology of Ireland, an introduction. Edinburgh: Oliver & Boyd, 1953. 1st edn. Frontis, extensively illust. Pub green cloth.
                    *(McDowell)* **£28**

**Charpentier, A.**
- A practical treatise on obstetrics. Translated ... New York: Wood, 1887. 4 vols. 509; 381; 348; 404 pp. Cold & b/w ills. Some wear.
                    *(Xerxes)* **$85**

**Chase, A.W.**
- Dr. Chase's recipes; or information for everybody. An invaluable collection of about 800 practical recipes. Ann Arbor: 1870. 384 pp.                    *(Poitras)* **$40**

**Chase, Heber**
- The final report of the committee of the Philadelphia Medical Society on the construction of instruments ... radical cure of hernia. Phila: 1837. 243 pp. Cloth-backed bds, front outer hinge weak, label missing.
                    *(Fye)* **$200**

**Chase, Robert H.**
- The ungeared mind. Phila: 1918. Ills.
                    *(Argosy)* **$27**

**Chatelin, C. & de Martel, T.**
- Wounds of the skull and brain, their clinical forms and medical and surgical treatment. London: 1918. 1st English translation. 313 pp. Dw.                    *(Fye)* **$50**

**Chatley, Herbert**
- The problem of flight: a text-book of aerial engineering. London: Charles Griffin, 1907. x,119 pp. Frontis, 61 ills. Half-mor, t.e.g., top edge of cvrs bleached by damp.
                    *(Pollak)* **£20**

**Cheadle, W.B.**
- On the principles and exact conditions to be

observed in the artificial feeding of infants ...
London: Hospital for Sick Children, Great
Ormond Street, 1889. 209 pp. Recased.
*(Goodrich)* **$75**

**Cheatle, G.L. & Cutler. Max**
- Tumors of the breast. Their pathology,
symptoms, diagnosis and treatment. Phila:
1931. 1st Amer edn. 596 pp. 468 ills.
*(Fye)* **$100**

**Cheesman, J.E.**
- Bailliere's synthetic anatomy. London:
Bailliere, Tindall & Cox, n.d. [ca 1920]. 100
pp. Hundreds of cold transparent overlays.
Cloth cvrd bds, 14 sections bound together
with string. *(Xerxes)* **$100**

**Cheever, David**
- See Borland, J. Nelson & Cheever, David
- Surgical cases in 1869. Boston: 1869. Tall
8vo. 33 pp. Printed wraps. *(Argosy)* **$27.50**
- Surgical cases. Boston: 1869. 33 pp. Wraps.
Inscribed by the author. *(Fye)* **$40**

**Chemist ...**
- Chemists' windows. An illustrated treatise on
the art of displaying pharmaceutical and
allied goods in chemists' shop windows. With
chapters on ticket writing ... business-
promoting accessories. 1915. vi,[1],208 pp.
194 ills in text. Orig cloth. *(Whitehart)* **£18**
- Chemists' windows. An illustrated treatise on
the art of displaying pharmaceutical and
allied goods in chemists' shop windows. 1915.
1st edn. 194 ills in text. *(Robertshaw)* **£12**

**Chemistry ...**
- Chemistry, theoretical, practical and
analytical as applied to arts and manufactures
by writers of eminence. N.d [ca 1880]. 8 vols.
1008 pp. Num full-page plates, some fldg.
Orig pict cloth gilt. One spine torn, reprd.
*(Whitehart)* **£40**

**Cheselden, William**
- The anatomy of the human body, with forty
copperplates. Boston: Manning & Loring,
1795. 1st Amer edn. 8vo. 5.[1],350 pp. 40
plates. Text & plates foxed, 1 plate torn.
Contemp sheep, lea label, rubbed.
*(M&S)* **$150**
- The anatomy of the human body. Boston:
1806. 2nd Amer edn. 352 pp. 40 full-page
engvd plates. Full lea. *(Fye)* **$400**
- Osteographia; or, the anatomy of the bones.
London: 1733. 1st edn. Lge folio. [28]ff, 56
engvd plates, text on verso. Additional plate
on verso of LVI, 9 further full-page plates,
engvd frontis & title. Sporadic foxing. Half-
calf, edges worn. Lge paper.
*(Rootenberg)* **$1,250**

**Chester, John, Bishop of**
- Of the principles and duties of natural
religion. 1675. xx,410,55 pp. Frontis. Lower
crnr of one page torn without loss. Mod 3/4
calf, antique style, gilt spine, lea label.
*(Whitehart)* **£120**

**Chesterton, G.K.**
- Eugenics and other evils. London: 1922. 1st
edn. 188 pp. Foxed. *(Scientia)* **$35**

**Chevers, Norman**
- A manual of medical jurisprudence for Bengal
and the North-Western Provinces. Calcutta:
F. Carberry, 1856. 1st edn. 8vo. viii,608 pp.
Half-calf, mrbld bds. Lib stamps.
*(Zeitlin)* **$200**

**Chew, Samuel**
- Lectures on medical education, or on the
proper method of studying medicine. Phila:
1864. 12mo. Orig cloth. Ex lib. *(Argosy)* **$45**

**Cheyne, George**
- An essay of health and long life. London: for
George Strahan, 1724. 1st edn. 8vo. Ink blot
on title & 2 other preliminary leaves. Sm
wormhole to lower margin of some early
leaves. Contemp panelled calf.
*(Quaritch)* **$325**
- An essay of health and long life. London:
1725. 4th edn. 232 pp. Title wrinkled &
stained, old repair of tear. Recent qtr lea.
*(Fye)* **$150**
- An essay of health and long life. London:
1725. 2nd edn. xx,232 pp. Extensive contemp
underscoring & annotation in pencil & ink.
Textured cloth amateurishly applied over orig
calf bds, crnrs bumped, hinges cracked.
*(Jenner)* **£150**
- An essay of health and long life. London:
George Strahan, 1725. 7th edn. [48],232 pp.
Old calf, rebacked in mor. *(Dailey)* **$75**

**Cheyne, W. Watson (ed.)**
- Recent essays by various authors on bacteria
in relation to disease. New Sydenham Society,
1886. xvi,650 pp. 9 plates. Orig blind-
stamped cloth. *(Whitehart)* **£18**
- Recent essays by various authors on bacteria
in relation to disease. London: New
Sydenham Society, 1886. 1st edn. 8 litho
plates, most with hand-cold details. Pub
blind-stamped cloth. *(McDowell)* **£55**

**Child, C.M.**
- Patterns and problems of development.
Chicago: 1941. 1st edn. 811 pp. *(Scientia)* **$45**

**Child, Maurice**
- Small power wireless installations. [1913].
123 pp. Ills, diags, advts. Orig pict bds, very
worn & shaken. *(Weiner)* **£20**

**Chisolm, A. Stuart**
- Recreations of a physician. New York: 1914. 1st coll edn. Tall 8vo. Cloth.        *(Argosy)* **$30**

**Chisolm, Julian J.**
- Neurotomy; a substitute for enucleation. A new operation in ophthalmic surgery. Richmond: 1879. 8vo. 16 pp. Printed wraps.        *(Argosy)* **$35**

**Chittenden, R.H.**
- Papoid. Epitome of a report on papoid digestion. New York: 1892. 46 pp. Printed wraps.        *(Argosy)* **$25**
- Physiological economy in nutrition. 1905. xi,478 pp. 16 plates. Orig cloth, inner hinge sl cracked.        *(Whitehart)* **£18**

**Chittenden, Russell**
- History of the Sheffield Scientific School of Yale University 1846 to 1922. New Haven: 1928. Ltd (100). 2 vols. Half lea.        *(Scientia)* **$85**

**Chorobski, Jerzy (ed.)**
- Neurological problems: a jubilee volume in honour of Eufemius Josef Herman. Warsaw: 1967. x,444 pp. Port frontis, ills throughout. Orig grey cloth. Dw.        *(Jenner)* **£14**

**Choulant, Ludwig**
- History and bibliography of anatomic illustration, in its relation to anatomic science and the graphic arts. Translated ... University of Chicago Press, [1920]. Title & inner back hinge mended. Ex lib.        *(Argosy)* **$100**

**Christian, Henry A.**
- The diagnosis and treatment of diseases of the heart. New York: [1928]. Tall 8vo. Cloth. Ex lib.        *(Argosy)* **$35**

**Christian, Henry A. (ed.)**
- Psychiatry for practitioners. By various authors. New York: Oxford University Press, 1936. 1st edn. x,646 pp. Spine faded.        *(Gach)* **$30**

**Christie, Alex Turnbull**
- Observations on the nature and treatment of cholera: and on the pathology of mucous membranes. Edinburgh: 1828. 127 pp. Faint offsetting, ink stain on title verso & preface page. Rebound half-calf, mrbld bds, crnrs rubbed.        *(Jenner)* **£25**

**Christison, R.**
- Dispensatory, or commentary on the Pharmacopoeias of Great Britain. 1848. 2nd edn. xlii,1003 pp. Orig blind-stamped cloth, sl dust stained & worn.        *(Whitehart)* **£40**

**Christison, Robert**
- A treatise on poisons in relation to medical jurisprudence ... Edinburgh: 1845. 4th edn. viii,986 pp. Plate. Mod cloth.        *(Weiner)* **£40**

**Church, A.H.**
- On the relation of phyllotaxis to mechanical laws. 1901-04. 1st edn. 3 vols. Plates & ills. Orig wraps, faded & sl torn. Inscribed by the author.        *(Whitehart)* **£45**

**Church, Archibald & Peterson, Frederick**
- Nervous and mental diseases. Phila: 1908. 6th edn. 945 pp. Ills. Orig cloth. Ex lib.        *(Oasis)* **$35**
- Nervous and mental diseases. Phila: F.A. Davis, 1911. 932 pp. Cloth, tips rubbed.        *(Gach)* **$25**

**Churchill, F.**
- Essays on the puerperal fever and other diseases peculiar to women. Sydenham Society, 1849. vii,552 pp. Orig blind-stamped cloth, rebacked, new spine.        *(Whitehart)* **£40**

**Churchill, Fleetwood**
- On the diseases of women, including diseases of pregnancy and childbed. Phila: 1852. 683 pp.        *(Fye)* **$40**
- On the theory and practice of midwifery. Phila: 1843. 1st Amer edn. 519 pp. Full lea.        *(Fye)* **$75**
- On the theory and practice of midwifery. Phila: 1851. 3rd Amer edn. 510 pp. Full lea.        *(Fye)* **$75**

**Churchill, James Morss**
- Cases illustrative of the immediate effects of acupuncturation, in rheumatism, lumbago, sciatica ... London: 1828. Sm 8vo. [iv],101,[2] pp. Sm stain near beginning. Orig paper wraps, almost detchd.        *(Jenner)* **£75**

**CIBA**
- The story of the chemical industry in Basle. Olten: CIBA, 1959. 1st edn. 4to. 233 pp. Boxed.        *(Scientia)* **$65**

**Clagett, Marshall**
- The science of mechanics in the Middle Ages. Madison: 1959. 1st edn. 711 pp. Dw.        *(Scientia)* **$55**

**Clagett, Marshall (ed.)**
- Critical problems in the history of science. Madison: 1959. 1st edn. 555 pp. Dw worn.        *(Scientia)* **$25**

**Clapp, George Wood**
- Prosthetic articulation. New York: Dentists' Supply Co., 1914. 3rd edn. 8vo. Photographic & other plates. *(McDowell)* **£25**
- Prosthetic articulation. New York: 1914. 1st

edn. 8vo. Cloth.                  *(Argosy)* **$25**

**Clark, A.J.**
- Comparative physiology of the heart.
Cambridge: 1927. 1st edn. Graphs & charts.
*(Argosy)* **$25**

**Clark, Alfred J.**
- The mode of action of drugs on cells.
London: 1933. 1st edn.    *(Scientia)* **$100**

**Clark, Alonzo**
- The Parish will case: a medical consideration
of the physical conditions of Henry Parish, as
bearing upon the question of his mental
capacity. Albany: 1860. 4to. 135 pp. Printed
wraps detchd. Ex lib.          *(Argosy)* **$75**

**Clark, Austin H.**
- The new evolution. Zoogenesis. Balt:
Williams & Wilkins, 1930. Ltd (250) sign
copies. Sm 4to. xiv,293,3 pp. Ills. Orig 3/4
calf, mrbld bds. T.e.g. Sl cvr wear.
*(Diamond)* **$50**

**Clark, Charles H.**
- Water analysis for sanitary purposes.
Chemical and biological. Boston: 1892. 1st
edn. 12mo. 88 pp. Cloth.    *(Argosy)* **$20**

**Clark, Daniel Kinnear**
- The steam engine. [1890-91]. 2 vols. Lge 8vo.
iv,788; iv,806 pp. 21 fldg plates, diags. Ex lib.
*(Weiner)* **£45**

**Clark, F. Le Gros**
- Outlines of surgery: being an epitome of the
lectures on the principles and practice of
surgery delivered at St. Thomas's Hospital.
1863. xxii,258 pp. Orig blind-stamped cloth,
a little dust stained.      *(Whitehart)* **£38**

**Clark, James**
- The sanative influence of climate: with an
account of the best places or resort for
invalids in England, the South of Europe, &c.
London: John Murray, 1841. 8vo.
xxvii,[1],377,[3], [4 advts] pp. Contemp
blind-stamped cloth. Lib stamps.
*(Dailey)* **$100**
- A treatise on pulmonary consumption
comprehending an inquiry into the causes,
nature, prevention and treatment of
tuberculosis and scrofulous diseases in
general. 1835. xxiii,339 pp. Sl soiled, few
stamps. Half-calf, very worn & rubbed.
Binding copy.              *(Jenner)* **£45**

**Clark, Sir James**
- The sanative influence of climate. 1846. 4th
edn. xix,412 pp. Orig blind-stamped cloth.
*(Whitehart)* **£35**

**Clark, James B.**
- Some personal reflections of Dr. Janeway.
New York: 1917. 1st edn. 36 pp. *(Argosy)* **$15**

**Clark, L. Pierce**
- The nature and treatment of amentia:
psychoanalysis and mental arrest in relation
to the science of intelligence. Balt: 1933. 1st
edn. 8vo. Frontis. Pencil underlining. Cloth.
*(Argosy)* **$40**

**Clark, W.E., et al.**
- The hypothalmus. Morphological,
functional, clinical and surgical aspects. 1838.
Lge 8vo. xii,211 pp. Hinges weak, cvrs worn.
Ex lib.                    *(Jenner)* **£18**

**Clarke, Sir Arthur**
- An essay on warm, cold and vapour bathing,
with practical observations on sea bathing ...
Dublin: 1816. 3rd edn. 8vo. 118 pp. Title sl
soiled. Uncut in orig bds, rebacked.
*(Deighton Bell)* **£28**
- The mother's medical assistant containing
instructions for ... treatment of the diseases of
infants and children. London: 1820. 148 pp.
Uncut.                     *(Goodrich)* **$85**

**Clarke, Charles Manfield**
- Observations on those diseases of females
which are attended by discharges. London:
1831. 2 vols. Copperplates by Heath. Bds
worn.                      *(Argosy)* **$60**

**Clarke, Edward Goodman**
- The modern practice of physic. London:
1805. 1st edn. xvi,454 pp. Foxing. Contemp
mottled calf, some scuffing, inner hinges
cracked.                   *(Elgen)* **$95**

**Clarke, Edward H.**
- The building of a brain. Boston: 1874. 1st
edn. 12mo. Cloth.          *(Argosy)* **$75**
- The relation of drugs to treatment. Boston:
1856. 1st edn. 28 pp. Printed wraps.
*(Argosy)* **$25**
- Visions: a study of false sight (pseudopia).
With an introduction ... by Oliver Wendell
Holmes. Boston: 1878. 1st edn. Sm 8vo.
xxii,315 pp. Frontis.        *(Elgen)* **$75**

**Clarke, W. Fairlie**
- A manual of the practice of surgery. New
York: 1879. 1st Amer edn. 316 pp. 168
w'cuts.                     *(Fye)* **$20**

**Clarkson, Arthur**
- Textbook of histology, descriptive and
practical, for the use of students. Bristol:
1896. Thick 8vo. Cold ills. Green cloth,
upper hinge cracked, first gathering coming
loose.                     *(Jenner)* **£12**

**Clarkson, Patrick & Pelly, Anthony**
- The general and plastic surgery of the hand ... Phila: [1962]. 1st edn. xiv,428pp. Num ills, plates.                                    *(Elgen)* **$125**

**Clausius, R.**
- The mechanical theory of heat, with its applications to the steam-engine and to the physical properties of bodies. London: Van Voorst, 1867. 1st English edn. xvi,376, [ii advts] pp. 16 text figs.          *(Pollak)* **£150**

**Claxton, Timothy**
- Memoir of a mechanic. Being a sketch of the life of ... written by himself. Together with miscellaneous papers. Boston: George W. Light, 1839. 12mo. [2],179, 8[pub advts] pp. Frontis port, ills. Orig blind-stamped cloth.
                                             *(M&S)* **$60**

**Cleaveland, Parker**
- An elementary treatise on mineralogy and geology. Boston: Cummings & Hilliard, 1816. 1st edn. 8vo. xii,688 pp. 5 fldg engvd plates, hand-cold geological map. Contemp tree calf, rubbed. In cloth box, with label.
                                           *(Antiq Sc)* **$500**

**Cleaves, Margaret A.**
- Light energy: its physics, physiological action, and therapeutic applications. New York: 1904. 827 pp. Ills.        *(Argosy)* **$40**
- The record of four years in an exclusively electro-therapeutic clinic. New York: [1899]. 37 pp. Printed wraps.        *(Argosy)* **$25**

**Cleghorn, George**
- Observations on the epidemical disease in Majorca, 1744-49. London: 1769. 8vo. Contemp calf, hinges reprd. Ex lib.
                                           *(Argosy)* **$150**

**Cleghorn, Thomas**
- The hydro-aeronaut, or navigator's life-buoy: being an easy and effectual method of preventing the loss of lives by drowning ... London: for J.M. Richardson, 1810. 1st edn. 8vo. With the half-title, vignette title, aquatint frontis. Orig bds, rebacked.
                                     *(Deighton Bell)* **£225**

**Cleveland, Reginald M.**
- America fledges wings: the history of the Daniel Guggenheim Fund for the Promotion of Aeronautics. New York: 1942. Deluxe edn, ltd (750). Spine faded.          *(Scientia)* **$35**

**Clifford, William K.**
- Lectures and essays. Edited by Leslie Stephen & Frederick Pollock. London: 1879. 2 vols. 340; 321 pp. Half lea, mrbld bds.
                                          *(Scientia)* **$75**

**Clinch, George**
- English hops, a history of cultivation and preparation for the market from the earliest times. London: McCorquodale, 1919. 1st edn. Slim 8vo. Frontis, ills. Pub green cloth.
                                        *(McDowell)* **£28**

**Cline, J.M.**
- Climatic causation of disease, with chart showing the pathological distribution of climate in the United States. Galveston: 1895. 8vo. 23 pp. Cold chart. Printed wraps.
                                          *(Argosy)* **$20**

**Close, Major C.F.**
- Text book of topographical and geographical surveying. London: H.M.S.O., 1905. Roy 8vo. vi,288 pp. 33 plates, 71 figs. Spine faded.
                                          *(Pollak)* **£25**

**Clossy, Samuel**
- Observations on some of the diseases of the parts of the human body. Chiefly taken from the dissections of morbid bodies. London: G. Kearsly, 1763. 1st edn. xi,[5],195 pp (mispaginated 192). Text ills. Lightly browned. Polished calf.      *(Rootenberg)* **$450**

**Clouston, Thomas Smith**
- Clinical lectures on mental diseases. London: 1904. 6th edn. 738 pp. Crnrs bent.
                                            *(Gach)* **$25**
- How pleasant surroundings and conditions affect the health and happiness. Edinburgh: n.d. [ca 1897]. 12mo. 22 pp. Wraps.
                                          *(Argosy)* **$25**
- The hygiene of mind. New York: Dutton, 1907. 2nd edn. xxiii,284 pp. Cloth.
                                           *(Gach)* **$22.50**
- Unsoundness of mind. London: Methuen, [1911]. 1st edn. xxxi,360 pp.   *(Gach)* **$30**

**Clow, A. & N.L.**
- The chemical revolution. A contribution to social technology. 1952. xii,680 pp. 110 plates, 16 diags. Sm lib mark on spine.
                                        *(Whitehart)* **£25**

**Clydesdale Horse ...**
- History of the Clydesdale Horse. Glasgow: William Love, 1884. xii,212 pp. Cr 8vo. Half red mor.                          *(Phenotype)* **£75**

**Clymer, Meredith**
- Epidemic cerebro-spinal meningitis. Phila: 1872. 1st edn. 59 pp. Lge fldg cold map. Ex lib.                              *(Argosy)* **$45**

**Coates, Benjamin H.**
- An oration on certainty in medicine. Phila: 1830. 29 pp. Wraps.       *(Argosy)* **$27.50**

**Coates, J.B. & Havens, W.P. (eds.)**
- Internal medicine in Word War II. Washington, D.C.: Office of the Surgeon General, 1961-63. 2 vols. Many ills.
*(Argosy)* **$45**

**Coates, J.B., et al. (eds.)**
- Orthopaedic surgery in the Mediterranean theatre of operations. Washington, DC.: 1957. Tall 8vo. 95 ills. Fabricoid.
*(Argosy)* **$35**

**Cobbe, William Rosser**
- Doctor Judas. A portrayal of the opium habit. Chicago: S.C. Griggs, 1895. 1st edn. 8vo. 320 pp. Orig cloth, recased. *(Dailey)* **$85**

**Cochrane, W.A.**
- Orthopaedic surgery. New York: 1926. 1st Amer edn. 528 pp. *(Fye)* **$25**

**[Cock, Simon]**
- Observations on the report of the Select Committee of the House of Lords, relative to the timber trade. By a British merchant. London: J.M. Richardson, 1821. 1st edn. 8vo. vii,[i blank],118 pp. With the half-title. Disbound. *(Deighton Bell)* **£58**

**Cocker, Edward**
- Cocker's arithmetick, being a plain and familiar method suitable ... for the full understanding ... London: for T. Passinger & T. Lacy, 1678. 1st edn. 12mo. [5]ff,334 pp, [1]f. Frontis port. Ownership inscrptn, ex lib. Sprinkled calf by F. Bedford. *(Zeitlin)* **$2,400**

**Cocking, W.T.**
- Television receiving equipment. [1940]. viii,298 pp. Ills, diags (2 fldg). *(Weiner)* **£15**

**Codman, E.A.**
- Bone sarcoma, an interpretation of the nomenclature used by the Committee on the Registry of Bone Sarcoma of the American College of Surgeons. New York: 1925. 93 pp.
*(Goodrich)* **$65**
- The shoulder. Boston: 1934. 1st edn, 2nd printing. 513,29 pp. *(Fye)* **$200**
- A study in hospital efficiency as demonstrated by the case report of the first five years of a private hospital. [Boston: ca 1917]. 8vo. 179 pp. Orig printed wraps. *(Argosy)* **$35**

**Cogan, Thomas**
- The haven of health. Chiefly gathered for the comfort of students, and consequently of all those that have a care of their health ... London: by Anne Griffin, 1636. Sm 4to. [8]ff, 321pp, [11]ff. Title-page in photostat facsimile. Staining. Orig calf. *(Elgen)* **$400**

**Coghill, G.E.**
- Anatomy and the problem of behaviour. Cambridge: University Press, 1929. xii,113,[3] pp. 1st edn. Green cloth.
*(Gach)* **$35**

**Cohen, Barnett**
- Chronicles of the Society of American Bacteriologists: 1899 - 1950. Balt: 1950. 29 pp text, 50 photographs. Qtr cloth.
*(Argosy)* **$35**

**Cohen, I. Bernard**
- Scientific instruments of the 17th and 18th centuries and their makers. From the French. London: 1972. 62 plates, figs. Cloth.
*(Winterdown)* **£30**
- Some early tools of American science. An account of the early scientific instruments ... in Harvard University. Cambridge, Mass: 1950. 32 plates. *(Winterdown)* **£30**
- Some early tools of American science. An account of the early scientific instruments ... in Harvard University. Cambridge, Mass: 1950. 1st edn. 201 pp. Dw. *(Scientia)* **$30**

**Cohn, Alfred E.**
- Medicine, science and art. Studies in interrelations. Chicago: University of Chicago Press, 1931. 212 pp. Ex lib.
*(Poitras)* **$27.50**
- Medicine, science and art. Studies in interrelations. Chicago: [ca 1931]. 1st edn. Tall 8vo. Half buckram. *(Argosy)* **$35**

**Cohn, Alfred E. & Lingg, Claire**
- The burden of diseases in the United States. New York: 1950. 2 vols (1 text, 1 lge fldg charts). 4to. *(Argosy)* **$35**

**Cohn, Ferdinand**
- Bacteria: the smallest of living organisms. Translated ... Balt: 1939. 44 pp. Ills. Printed bds. Ex lib. *(Argosy)* **$25**

**Coit, Henry L.**
- Relations between Medical Milk Commissions and the Municipal Boards of Health. Cincinnati: 1916. 11 pp. Printed wraps. *(Argosy)* **$25**

**Coke, John Redman**
- The American dispensatory, containing the operations of the pharmacy ... Phila: Thomas Dobson & Son, 1818. 4th edn, much improved. 4to. clv,735 pp. 6 plates. Paper sl stained, some pencilling. Lea & spine worn & chipped. *(Poitras)* **$125**

**Colbatch, Sir John**
- Novum lumen chirurgicum: or, a new light of chirurgery. Wherein is discovered, a much more safe and speedy way of curing wounds

... London: D. Brown, 1695. 1st edn. Sm 8vo.
Contemp calf, jnts reprd.     *(Quaritch)* **$775**

**Colburn, Zerah**
- An inquiry into the nature of heat, and into its
mode of action in the phenomena of
combustion, vaporisation, &c. London: 1863.
1st edn (?). 8vo. 99 pp. Orig printed bds,
becoming disbound.        *(M&S)* **$27.50**
- An inquiry into the nature of heat, and into its
mode of action in the phenomena of
combustion, vaporisation, &c. 1863. Orig
bds, worn. Upper bd detchd. *(Edwards)* **£20**

**Colby, Benjamin**
- Guide to health, an exposition of the
Thomsonian system of practice. Milford,
N.H.: 1846. W'cut plates throughout. Calf
scuffed.        *(Argosy)* **$50**

**Colby, R.A.**
- Color atlas of oral pathology. Phila: 1956. 188
pp.        *(Fye)* **$40**

**Cole, F.J.**
- Early theories of sexual generation. Oxford:
1930. 1st edn. 230 pp. Ex lib. Spine frayed &
rubbed.        *(Scientia)* **$50**
- A history of comparative anatomy, from
Aristotle to the 18th century. London: 1944.
viii,524 pp. 200 figs. Orig green cloth, crnrs
bumped. Torn dw.        *(Jenner)* **£35**

**Cole, Frank**
- Milestones in anesthesia. Readings in the
development of surgical anesthesia,
1665-1940. Lincoln: 1965. 1st edn. Dw.
        *(Scientia)* **$37.50**

**[Cole, Henry G.]**
- Confessions of an American opium eater.
From bondage to freedom. Boston: James H.
Earle, 1895. 1st edn. 8vo. [2],v,245 pp. Port
frontis, 7 plates. Orig cloth. cvrs lightly
soiled.        *(Dailey)* **$75**

**Cole, Lewis Gregory**
- Lung dust lesions (pneumoconiosis) versus
tubercolosis. New York: 1848. 474 pp. Ills.
        *(Poitras)* **$25**
- Serial radiography of the stomach and
duodenum ... London: 1911. Tall 8vo. 4 fldg
plates. Orig printed wraps.   *(Argosy)* **$30**

**Cole, M.J.**
- See Cross, M.I. & Cole, M.J.

**Cole, Mary**
- The lady's complete guide; or cookery in all
its branches .. the complete brewer ... likewise
the family physician. London: Kearsley,
1791. 3rd edn, very much improved. 8vo.
Half-title. Last leaf of index in facsimile. Mod

qtr calf, buckram bds.     *(McDowell)* **£180**

**Cole, Michael & Maltzman, Irving (eds.)**
- A handbook of contemporary Soviet
psychology. New York: [1969]. 1st edn.
Thick 8vo. 887 pp. Cloth. Dw. *(Argosy)* **$35**

**Cole, Warren**
- See Everson, Tilden & Cole, Warren

**Coleman, G.**
- Lunar and nautical tables arranged and
adapted for determining the latitude at sea;
also the variation of the compass ... 1865. 3rd
edn. xvi,104, xxxviii,317,[22] pp. Orig cloth,
new endpapers.        *(Whitehart)* **£18**

**Coleman, J.**
- Cattle of Great Britain: being a series of
articles on the various breeds of cattle ...
1875. Roy 4to. iv,162,8 [advts]. 18 plates.
Green dec cloth.        *(Phenotype)* **£120**

**Coles, Alfred C.**
- The blood: how to examine and diagnose its
diseases. 1898. xii,260 pp. 6 cold plates.
Backstrip sl frayed.        *(Jenner)* **£15**
- Critical microscopy. How to get the best out
of the microscope. London: 1921.
        *(Winterdown)* **£10**

**Coley, Bradley**
- Neoplasms of bone and related conditions.
New York: 1949. 1st edn. 765 pp. *(Fye)* **$30**

**Coley, Bradley & Higinbotham, Norman**
- Tumors of bone: a roentgeno-graphic atlas.
New York: 1953. 1st edn. 216 pp. *(Fye)* **$30**
- Tumors of bone; a roentgeno-graphic atlas.
New York: [1953]. 4to. 172 ills. *(Argosy)* **$45**

**Coley, James Millman**
- A practical treatise on the diseases of
children. Phila: 1846. 1st Amer edn. 414 pp.
Marginal browning, some foxing. Orig paper-
cvrd bds, rebacked in cloth.     *(Elgen)* **$85**

**Collection ...**
- A collection of exotics ... See Byam, Lydia

**Colles, Abraham**
- Lectures of the theory and practice of surgery
... Edited ... Phila: 1845. 1st Amer edn.
viii,420 pp. Foxing, staining in margin.
Cloth-backed printed stiff wraps. *(Elgen)* **$95**
- Lectures on the theory and practice of
surgery. Phila: 1845. 420 pp. Full lea.
        *(Fye)* **$150**
- Selections from the works of Abraham Colles
... edited, with annotations by Robert
McDowell. London: 1891. 1st edn. 431 pp.
        *(Fye)* **$125**

- Treatise on surgical anatomy. Phila: 1831. 2nd Amer edn. 186 pp. Lea, bds detchd, backstrip worn. *(Fye)* **$50**

**Collett, L.W.**
- The structure of the Alps. 1927. 8vo. xii,290 pp. 12 plates, 63 text figs. A little foxing. Cloth, trifle used. *(Wheldon & Wesley)* **£15**

**Collignon, Charles**
- Moral and medical dialogues. Cambridge: 1769. 116 pp. Lacking free endpapers & both bds, o/w complete & clean. *(Jenner)* **£24**

**Collin, V.**
- Manual for the use of the stethoscope. A short treatise on the different methods of investigating the diseases of the chest. Translated ... Boston: 1829. 12mo. 1st edn in English. 4 engvd plates. Uncut & partly unopened. Orig cloth-backed bds. *(Argosy)* **$350**

**Collins, J.H.**
- Principles of metal mining. [1875]. 152 pp. Ills. *(Weiner)* **£20**

**Collins, Joseph**
- The doctor looks at life and death. New York: [1931]. 1st edn. *(Argosy)* **$25**
- The doctor looks at love and life. New York: n.d. [ca 1926]. 1st edn. Cloth. Dw. *(Argosy)* **$20**

**Collins, Mary**
- Colour-blindness: with a comparison of testing different methods of colour-blindness. New York: Harcourt, Brace & Company, 1925. 1st Amer edn. xxxii,237,[3] pp. Cold plate. Green cloth. *(Gach)* **$35**

**Collins, Samuel**
- A systeme of anatomy, treating of the body of man, beasts, birds, fish, insects ... [London]: ... Thomas Newcomb, 1685. 1st edn. Folio. 2 vols. Engvd title, frontis port, imprim leaf all present. 74 copperplates. Old mottled calf, some splitting, wearing. *(Zeitlin)* **$3,500**

**Colson, C.**
- Notes on docks and dock construction. 1894. x,426 pp. 365 ills. Orig cloth. *(Whitehart)* **£18**

**Colville, W.J.**
- Spiritual science of health and healing. Boston: n.d. [ca 1887]. 218 pp. *(Xerxes)* **$45**

**Colwell, Hector A.**
- An essay on the history of electrotherapy and diagnosis. London: 1922. 180 pp. Cloth rubbed. Author's pres copy. *(Goodrich)* **$125**
- An essay on the history of electrotherapy and diagnosis. London: Heinemann, 1922. xv,180

pp. Frontis, 115 ills. Spine worn, faded. *(Pollak)* **£20**

**Combe, Andrew**
- The physiology of digestion, considered with relation to the principles of dietetics. New York: 1843. 16 mo. Cloth. Ex lib. *(Argosy)* **$40**
- The physiology of digestion, considered with relation to the principles of dietetics. Edinburgh: 1881. 10th edn. W'engvd ills. Orig blind-stamped cloth, gilt. *(Robertshaw)* **£10**
- Principles of physiology applied to the preservation of health and to the movement of physical and mental education. New York: Fowler & Wells, 1847. 320 pp. 5 w'cuts. Foxed. *(Xerxes)* **$45**

**[Combe, George]**
- Essays on phrenology. Edinburgh: Bell & Bradfute; & London: Longman, Hurst ..., 1819. 1st edn. xxiv,392 pp. Plate at end, foxed. Old half-calf. Lib stamps on verso of title. *(Dailey)* **$125**

**Combe, George, et al.**
- Moral and intellectual science. New York: Fowler & Wells, 1848. 8vo. iv,112 pp. Frontis. Some foxing. Disbound. *(Dailey)* **$30**

**Comings, B.N.**
- Nervousness: heredity, school pressure and worry. Hartford: 1885. 12mo. 19pp. Orig printed wraps. Ex lib. *(Argosy)* **$27.50**

**Comparative ...**
- A comparative view of the state and faculties of man ... See Gregory, John

**Complete ...**
- The complete farmer; or, general dictionary of husbandry in all its branches: containing the various methods of cultivating ... 1769. 2nd edn. 4to. Unpaginated. 27 fldg plates. Contemp reversed calf, jnts cracked. *(Phenotype)* **£140**
- The complete farmer; or, general dictionary of agriculture and husbandry: comprehending the most improved methods of cultivation ... 1807. 5th edn, wholly re-written & enlgd. 2 vols, 4to. Unpaginated. 109 full-page plates. New paper bds. Uncut. *(Phenotype)* **£150**

**Compton, Arthur E.**
- X-rays and electrons: an outline of recent X-ray theory. New York: 1926. 1st edn. 403 pp. 2 pages sl defaced. *(Scientia)* **$95**

**Comrie, John Dixon**
- History of Scottish medicine. London: 1932. 2nd edn. 2 vols. 852 pp. Ills. *(Poitras)* **$45**
- History of Scottish medicine. London: 1932.

2nd edn. 2 vols. 8vo. 852 pp. Cold frontis,
num ills. Orig cloth, t.e.g.
*(Bow Windows)* **£55**
- History of Scottish medicine. Wellcome
Historical Medical Museum, 1927. 1st edn.
Num ills.          *(Robertshaw)* **£12.50**

**Comroe, Bernard**
- Arthritis and allied conditions. Phila: 1940.
1st edn. 752 pp.          *(Fye)* **$75**

**Comstock, John L.**
- A history of the precious metals ... with
directions for testing their purity ... Together
with ... speculations concerning the mineral
wealth of California. Hartford: Belknap &
Hamersley, 1849. 1st edn. 8vo. 222 pp. Orig
cloth, frayed.          *(Antiq Sc)* **$110**

**Comstock, Joseph**
- Tongue of time, and star of the states. New
York: 1838. 1st edn. 487 pp. Lacks front
blank endpapers, a few pencil notes in
margins. Disbound.          *(Xerxes)* **$160**

**Condie, D. Francis**
- Annual oration delivered before the
Philadelphia Medical Society ... Session
1844-45. Phila: 1845. 24 pp. Foxing. Sewed.
*(Argosy)* **$27.50**
- A practical treatise on diseases of children.
Phila: 1847. 2nd edn. 657,32 [pub ctlg] pp.
Orig lea, sl rubbed.          *(Oasis)* **$50**
- See Bell, John & Condie, D. Francis

**Confessions ...**
- Confessions of an American opium eater ...
See Cole, Henry G.

**Conklin, W.J.**
- The influence of school-life upon the
eyesight, with special reference to the public
schools of Dayton, Ohio. 1880. Author's pres
copy.          *(Argosy)* **$25**
- A page of medical history: Moliere and the
Doctors. Toledo: 1891. 8vo. 32 pp. Orig
printed wraps.          *(Argosy)* **$25**

**Connor, Frank Powell**
- Surgery in the tropics. Phila: 1929. 1st Amer
edn. 293 pp. Ex lib.          *(Fye)* **$40**

**Connor, Leartus**
- Hot water in the management of eye diseases.
Some suggestions.. Detroit: 1887. 16 pp. Orig
blue printed wraps. Ex lib.          *(Argosy)* **$35**

**Conolly, John**
- An introductory lecture delivered in the
University of London ... London: 1829.
12mo. 36 pp. Stitched. Ex lib. *(Argosy)* **$25**

**Conversations ...**
- Conversations on natural philosophy ... See
Marcet, Mrs. Jane

**Converse, J.M.**
- See Kasanjian, V.H. & Converse, J.M.

**Cook, A.B.**
- Joined twins: obstetrical and surgical
management. Lousville: 1869. 1st edn. 8vo.
26 pp. Orig printed wraps. A.l.s. laid in.
*(Argosy)* **$75**

**[Cook, Henry]**
- Patent artificial slate manufactury, Woodford
Bridge, Essex, for covering roofs, fronts of
houses, and ricks ... [London: ca 1794]. 8vo.
[2],28 pp. Inserted leaf after C2 on new
method of laying the slates. Occas ms
corrections in contemp hand. Disbound.
*(Burmester)* **£150**

**Cook, Marc**
- The wilderness cure. New York: 1881. 1st
edn. 12mo. Cloth. Ex lib.          *(Argosy)* **$40**

**Cook, Moses**
- The manner of raising, ordering, and
improving forest trees ... and measure timber
and other solid bodies. London: Daniel
Browne, 1717. 2nd edn, v much crrctd. 8vo.
xix,[i],276 pp. Contemp panelled calf, cvrs
little stained & worn, jnts cracking.
*(Blackwell's)* **£85**

**Cooke, C.J. Bowen**
- British locomotives, their history,
construction and modern development. 1894.
2nd edn. xvi,381 pp. Fldg plates (few cold),
num ills. A bit worn & loose.  *(Weiner)* **£25**

**Cooke, William**
- A commentary on medical and moral life, or
mind and the emotions ... Phila: 1853. 1st
U.S. edn. 327 pp. Some sl pencilling. Upper
front jnt & top of spine chipped. *(Gach)* **$30**

**Cooke, Sir William Fothergill**
- The electric telegraph: was it invented by
Professor Wheatstone? London: W.H. Smith
& Sons, 1854. 1st edn. 8vo. 48 pp. Orig
wraps. Inscribed by the author.
*(Rootenberg)* **$135**

**Cooke, Wm.**
- Remarks on a recent effort to subvert the
charter of the Royal College of Surgeons.
London: 1826. 1st edn. 89 pp. Wraps.
*(Argosy)* **$25**

**Cooley, Arnold James**
- A cyclopaedia of practical receipts, and
collateral information in the arts,

manufactures and trades, including medicine ... 1845. 2nd edn. Orig cloth, rebacked with orig spine, new endpapers. Some wear.
*(Robertshaw)* £15
- Instructions and cautions respecting the selection and use of perfumes, cosmetics ... 1868. Orig cloth, worn. *(Robertshaw)* £12.50

**Cooper, Astley**
- The anatomy and surgical treatment of abdominal hernia. Phila: 1844. 427 pp. 26 litho plates. Lea bndg v worn, lower right crnr damp-stained not affecting text or plates.
*(Oasis)* $80
- The anatomy of the thymus gland. London: 1832. 1st edn. 4to. [6],47, 5 leaves of explanation of plates. 5 lge litho plates, 3 with heightened color. Some leaves loose, spotting. Orig bds, backstrip loose. *(Hemlock)* $825

**Cooper, Bransby**
- Lectures on the principles and practice of surgery. London: 1851. 1st edn. 964 pp.
*(Fye)* $90

**Cooper, Irving S.**
- Parkinsonism: its medical and surgical therapy. Springfield: [1961]. 4to. Many ills. Light blue cloth. *(Argosy)* $30

**Cooper, Jack R., et al.**
- The biochemical basis of neuropharmacology. New York: Oxford University Press, 1974. 12mo. Ills. Cloth.
*(Argosy)* $20

**Cooper, Phillip (ed.)**
- The craft of surgery. Boston: [1964]. 1st edn. 2 vols. 4to. Buckram. *(Argosy)* $60

**Cooper, Samuel**
- A dictionary of practical surgery ... with notes and additions by John Syng Dorsey. Phila: 1816. 2 vols. 531; 522 pp. Lea. *(Fye)* $325
- The first lines of the practice of surgery, designed as an introduction ... a concise book of reference ... London: 1819-20. 4th edn. xxviii,663; xliii,496 pp. 17 plates. Titles soiled & torn, free endpapers missing. Disbound. A binding copy, w.a.f.
*(Jenner)* £55
- The first lines of the practice of surgery ... with notes by Alexander H. Stevens. New York: 1822. 2nd Amer edn. 2 vols. 680; 511 pp. Engvd plates. Lea. *(Fye)* $150

**Cooper, Thomas Sidney**
- Groups of cattle drawn from nature. Ackerman & Co, 1839. Imp folio. 25 tinted lithos. Very light foxing on a few plate surrounds. Orig qtr green mor.
*(Phenotype)* £650

**Cooper, W. & Nephews**
- The world's sheep farming for 50 years, 1843 - 1893. In commemoration of the Jubilee Cooper's Sheep Dipping Powder. Berkhamsted: 1893. 104 pp. Many ills. Dec card cvrs. Pres copy. *(Phenotype)* £30

**Cooper, William**
- Practical remarks on near sight, aged sight, and impaired vision; with observations upon the use of glasses and on artificial light. London: 1847. 1st edn. 216 pp. *(Fye)* $100

**Cope, Edward D.**
- The origin of the fittest. Essays on evolution. New York: 1887. 1st edn. 467 pp. Spine sl shelfworn. *(Scientia)* $65
- The primary factors of organic evolution. Chicago: 1904. 8vo. xvi,547 pp. 120 text figs. Cloth. *(Wheldon & Wesley)* £20

**Cope, Zachary**
- The history of St. Mary's Hospital Medical School, or, a century of medical education. Toronto: 1954. 1st edn. 8vo. Ills. Cloth.
*(Argosy)* $45
- A history of the acute abdomen. London: 1965. 1st edn. Dw. *(Scientia)* $45

**Copeland, S.**
- Agriculture ancient and modern. A historical account of its principles and practice. 1866. 4to. 2 vols. x,784; 800 pp. Engvd title, 43 plates, text ills. Orig half-calf. *(Phenotype)* £75

**Copeland, Thomas**
- Observations on some of the principal diseases of the rectum and anus ... Phila: 1811. 1st Amer edn. 120 pp. Disbound.
*(Fye)* $100
- Observations on some of the principal diseases of the rectum and anus ... Phila: 1811. 1st Amer edn. 12mo. 120 pp. Orig bds, calf spine. *(Hemlock)* $125

**Copeman, W.S.C.**
- A short history of gout and the rheumatic diseases. Berkeley: 1964. 1st edn. Dw.
*(Scientia)* $30
- The Worshipful Society of Apothecaries of London: a history 1617 - 1967. Oxford: [1967]. Sq 8vo. 19 plates, 20 line ills. Cloth. Dw. *(Argosy)* $27.50

**Copland, M.**
- See Geschickter, C. & Copland, M.

**Corfe, George**
- The apothecary, ancient and modern, of the City of London. London: 1885. 1st edn. 38 pp. Printed wraps. *(Argosy)* $22.50
- The physiognomy of diseases. London: James Nisbet, 1849. 1st edn. 4to. viii,151 pp. Hand-

cold frontis. Sm lib stamp in blind on frontis & title. New bds.          *(Rootenberg)* **$150**

**Coriat, Isador Henry**
- Abnormal psychology. New York: Moffat, Yard & Company, 1916. 428 pp. Frontis. Red cloth.                                 *(Gach)* **$25**

**Corlett, William T.**
- Diseases of the skin due to defective alimentation. Cleveland: 1888. 10 pp. Unopened. Orig printed wraps. Ex lib.
                                      *(Argosy)* **$20**
- The medicine-man of the American Indian and his cultural background. Springfield: 1935. 1st edn.          *(Scientia)* **$75**

**Corn Laws ...**
- Corn Laws. The battle for native industry. The debate upon the Corn Laws ... in Session, 1846. Reprinted ... from Hansard. Office of the Society for the Protection of Agriculture & British Industry, 1846. Roy. 8vo. 2 vols. xii,790; xii 728 pp. Mod buckram.                     *(Phenotype)* **£45**

**Cornaro, Luigi**
- See Lessius, Leonardus & Cornaro, Luigi

**Cornell, William M.**
- An introductory lecture ... to the ... Female Medical College of Pennsylvania. Phila: 1852. 12mo. 16 pp. Mod wraps.
                                   *(Argosy)* **$27.50**

**Corner, George**
- The hormones in human reproduction. Princeton: 1942. 1st edn. 265 pp. *(Fye)* **$50**

**Cornil, A. Victor & Ranvier, Louis**
- A manual of pathological histology. Translated, with notes & additions by E.O. Shakespeare & J. Simes. Phila: 1880. 1st edn in English. Top of spine frayed, crnrs of cvrs worn.                            *(Scientia)* **$75**

**Corning, J. Leonard**
- Carotid compression and brain rest. New York: [1882]. 39 pp. Printed wraps. Ex lib.
                                      *(Argosy)* **$25**

**Corry, John**
- The detector of quackery; or, analyser of medical, philosophical, political, dramatic, and literary imposture ... London: B. Crosby ..., 1802. 2nd edn. 8vo. [4],164,[4 index] pp. Old qtr calf, jnts split.      *(Dailey)* **$125**

**Corson. John W.**
- Paper on the management of shoulders in examination of the chest. Including a new physical sign ... New York: 1859. 32 pp. Ills. Printed wraps.                    *(Argosy)* **$20**

**Cosslett, V.E.**
- Introduction to electron optics. The production, propagation and focussing of electron beams. Oxford: 1946. 8 plates, 155 figs. Ex lib.               *(Winterdown)* **£20**

**Cotterell, E.**
- On some common injuries to limbs, their treatment and after-treatment including bone-setting ... 1885. x,108 pp. 7 figs. Orig cloth, sl stained.                     *(Whitehart)* **£18**

**Cotting, Benjamin E.**
- Professional reminiscences. Boston 1888. 1st edn. 112 pp. Orig printed wraps, crudely rebacked. Ex lib.               *(Argosy)* **$35**

**Cotton, Henry A.**
- The defective delinquent and insane: the relation of focal infections to their causation, treatment, and prevention. Princeton: 1921. 1st edn. xvi,201 pp.          *(Gach)* **$25**

**Coues, Elliot & Shute, D.K.**
- Neuromyology: classification of the muscles of the human body with reference to their innervation, and new nomenclature of the muscles. New York: 1887. 48 pp. Printed wraps.                          *(Argosy)* **$25**

**Coulson, Walter J.**
- Treatise on syphilis. London: Churchill, 1869. 373 pp. Some signatures loose. Front hinge cracked, paper label on spine covering the word "syphilis".           *(Xerxes)* **$60**

**Coulter, John S.**
- Physical therapy. New York: 1932. 1st edn. Clio Medica Series.            *(Scientia)* **$25**

**Counsell, George**
- The London new art of midwifry: or, the midwife's sure guide ... London: John Anderson, 1758. 1st edn. 8vo. xxviii, 195,[3] pp. 2 full-page ills. Early sgntrs & ms notes. Contemp calf, rebacked.   *(Rootenberg)* **$625**

**Coupland, Sidney**
- Harveian Oration, 1915. London: 1915. 67 pp.                               *(Argosy)* **$20**

**Coursey, Philip R.**
- Telephony without wires. 1919. ix,414 pp. Ills, diags, bibliog. Cloth sl discoloured.
                                     *(Weiner)* **£30**

**Courville, Cyril**
- Cerebral palsy. A brief introduction to its history, aetiology, and pathology, with some notes ... Los Angeles: 1954. ix,80 pp. Orig red cloth, crnrs a little bumped. *(Jenner)* **£15**
- Commotio cerebri. Cerebral concussion and the postconcussion syndrome in their medical

and legal aspects. Los Angeles: San Lucas Press, 1953. 161 pp. Ills.  *(Poitras)* **$40**
- Intracranial tumors. Providence: 1931. 158 pp. 1st edn. Ink underlining throughout. Wraps.  *(Fye)* **$50**
- Untoward effects of nitrous oxide anesthesia with particular reference to residual neurologic and psychiatric manifestations. Mountainview: 1939. 1st edn. 174 pp.
*(Fye)* **$45**

**Cowper, William**
- The anatomy of human bodies ... curiously engraved in 114 copper plates. Leyden: J.A. Langerak, 1737. 2nd edn. Atlas folio. Extra engvd title, 114 full-page & fldg plates. Contemp mottled calf, considerable wear at spine.  *(Argosy)* **$2,500**

**Cox, Rev. G.W.**
- See Brande, W.T. & Cox, Rev. G.W.

**Cox, Homersham**
- A rudimentary treatise on the integral calculus. London: John Weale, 1852. xii,120,12 [ctlg]. Orig cloth, paper label.
*(Pollak)* **£15**

**Cox, Joseph Mason**
- Practical observations on insanity: in which some suggestions are offered towards ... treating diseases of the mind ... Phila: 1811. 1st Amer edn. Sm 8vo. xi,[1], [13]-238 pp. Orig calf, sl rubbed.  *(Elgen)* **$275**

**Coxe, John Redman**
- Practical observations on vaccination: or inoculation for the cow-pock. Phila: James Humphreys, 1802. 1st edn. 8vo. 152 pp, inc 2 fldg tables. Cold frontis. Advts leaf. Title lightly foxed. Uncut. Orig bds, paper spine chipped.  *(M&S)* **$500**

**Crabb, George**
- Universal technological dictionary or, familiar explanations of the terms used in all arts and sciences, containing definitions drawn from the original writers. 1823. Lge 4to. 2 vols. 36 full-page plates. Contemp bds, sl stained, rebacked. Paper labels.
*(Whitehart)* **£180**

**Crabtree, Harold**
- An elementary treatment of the theory of spinning tops and gyroscopic motion. London: Longmans ..., 1909. 1st edn. 8vo. 3 plates, text ills. Orig cloth.  *(Antiq Sc)* **$45**

**Craft ...**
- The craft and frauds of physick expos'd ... See Pitt, Robert

**Craig, G.Y. (ed.)**
- The geology of Scotland. 1965. Roy 8vo. xv,556 pp. Fldg cold geolog map, many maps, tables, photos, text figs. Cloth.
*(Wheldon & Wesley)* **£30**

**Cramer, John Andrew**
- Elements of the art of essaying metals. London: 1741. 8vo. 470 pp. 6 fldg copper plates, 1 with sm tear. Contemp calf, worn, front cvr detchd.  *(Argosy)* **$100**

**Cramer, W.**
- Fever, heat regulation, climate and the thyroid-adrenal apparatus. London: 1928. 1st edn. 8vo. 40 plates. Cloth.  *(Argosy)* **$30**

**Crawford, Adair**
- An experimental enquiry into the effects of tonics. Edited by Alexander Crawford. London: G. Hayden, 1816. Sole edn. 8vo. [2], ii,iii, [1], viii,124 pp. Engvd plate. Orig bds with paper label.  *(Dailey)* **$175**

**Crawford, John B.**
- An essay on the indigenous malarial diseases of Wyoming Valley. Read by appointment before the Luzerne County Medical Society. Wilkes-Barre, Pa: 1881. Orig printed wraps. Author's pres copy.  *(Argosy)* **$25**

**Crawley, Chetwode**
- From telegraphy to television. 1931. xii,212 pp. Num plates.  *(Weiner)* **£18**

**Creighton, C.**
- The natural history of cow-pox and vaccinal syphilis. 1887. viii,160 pp. Orig cloth, stained.  *(Whitehart)* **£25**

**Cremona, Luigi**
- Elements of projective geometry. Translated by Charles Leudesdorf. Oxford University Press, 1885. Many text figs. Prize calf, gilt, sl rubbed.  *(Edwards)* **£15**

**Cresson, Joshua**
- Meditations written during the prevalence of the yellow fever in Philadelphia, 1793. London: Phillips, 1803. 23 pp. Full lea, raised bands.  *(Xerxes)* **$150**

**Cresswell, D.**
- A supplement to the elements of Euclid. With an appendix ... Dambridge: Deighton, 1825. xv,582 pp. 8 pp ctlg. Some foxing. Orig cloth-backed bds.  *(Pollak)* **£25**

**Crighton-Browne, James**
- Stray leaves from a physician's portfolio. London: n.d. [ca 1900]. Lge 8vo. Cloth. Ex lib.  *(Argosy)* **$35**

**Crile, George**
- Experimental research into the surgery of the respiratory system. Phila: 1900. 2nd edn. 114 pp. Inscrbd & autographed by Crile.
*(Fye)* **$100**
- Hemorrhage and transfusion: an experimental and clinical research. New York: 1909. 1st edn. 560 pp. *(Fye)* **$150**
- Man - an adaptive mechanism. New York: 1916. 1st edn. 387 pp. Ills. Inner hinges cracking. *(Oasis)* **$40**
- Man - an adaptive mechanism. New York: 1916. 1st edn. 8vo. Orig cloth. *(Argosy)* **$40**
- Problems in surgery. Phila: 1928. 1st edn. Tall 8vo. Ills. Cloth. *(Argosy)* **$30**

**[Crile, George]**
- The thyroid gland: Clinics of George W. Crile and associates. Phila: 1922. 1st edn. 288 pp. Ills. *(Oasis)* **$45**

**Crile, George & Lower, W.E.**
- Anoci-association. Phila: 1914. 1st edn. 259 pp. *(Fye)* **$50**
- Anoci-association. Phila: 1914. 1st edn. 8vo. Ills. Cloth. *(Argosy)* **$50**
- Surgical shock and the shockless operation through anoci-association. Phila: 1920. 2nd edn, revised, of 'Anoci-Association'. 8vo. Cloth. *(Argosy)* **$35**

**Crile, George, & associates.**
- Diagnosis and treatment of diseases of the thyroid gland. Phila: 1932. 1st edn. 508 pp. Ills. *(Oasis)* **$35**
- Diagnosis and treatment of diseases of the thyroid gland. Phila & London: W.B. Saunders Co., 1932. 4to. 508 pp. Ills. *(Poitras)* **$30**

**Crocker, Henry Radcliffe**
- Atlas of the diseases of the skin in a series of illustrations from original drawings ... Edinburgh & London: Young J. Pentland, [1893]-1896. 1st edn. 16 fascicles, lge folio. 97 chromo-litho plates. Margins lightly spotted. Unbound as issued, in mahogany box.
*(Quaritch)* **$850**

**Crohn, Burrill B.**
- Regional ileitis. London: Staples Press, 1949. 1st edn. 8vo. Dw. *(McDowell)* **£35**

**Croll, J.**
- Climate and time in their geological relations. A theory of secular changes of the earth's climate. 1875. xvii,577 pp. Frontis, 7 cold plates, 1 fldg. Orig cloth, spine reprd.
*(Whitehart)* **£35**

**Crombie, A.C. (ed.)**
- Scientific change. Historical studies in the intellectual, social and technical conditions

for scientific discovery ... New York: 1963. 1st edn. 896 pp. Dw. Upper crnrs of pages badly bumped. *(Scientia)* **$25**

**Crookes, William**
- On radiant matter. A lecture delivered ... at Sheffield, Friday, August 22, 1879 [London: printed by E.J. Davey]. 1st edn. 8vo. 30 pp. 21 w'engvs in the text. Title torn. Orig printed blue-grey wrapper, spine splitting & frayed, laid into mor-backed case.
*(Pickering)* **$650**

**Crookshank, F.G.**
- Migraine and other common neuroses: a psychological study. London: Kegan Paul, Trench, Trubner, 1926. [ii],101,[1] pp. Advt leaf. 1st edn. Bds, cloth spine, paper label. Psyche Miniatures Medical Series No. 1.
*(Gach)* **$20**

**Cross, John**
- Sketches of the Medical Schools of Paris. London: Callow, 1815. xv,207 pp. Half-title, 2 engvd plates. Ex lib. *(Goodrich)* **$250**

**Cross, Louise Montgomery**
- The preparation of medical literature. Phila: [1959]. Tall 8vo. 80 ills. Dw. Pres copy, sgnd by author. *(Argosy)* **$35**

**Cross, M.I. & Cole, M.J.**
- Modern microscopy. A handbook for beginners, in two parts ... 1893. xii,104,[42 advts] pp. Orig red cloth, bds stained.
*(Jenner)* **£10**
- Modern microscopy. A handbook for beginners and students. Combining ... 1903. 3rd edn, entirely revsd & enlgd. xvi,292 pp. Frontis, num ills in text. New cloth.
*(Whitehart)* **£18**

**Crotte, A.**
- Disease of the thyroid, parathyroids and thymus. Phila: 1938. 3rd edn. 1229 pp. Half lea. *(Fye)* **$50**

**Crowther, James Arnold**
- Ions, electrons, and ionizing radiations. London: Arnold, 1920. 2nd edn. xi,276 pp. 2 plates. 95 text figs. *(Pollak)* **£20**

**Cullen, Thomas**
- Adenomyoma of the uterus. Phila: 1908. 1st edn. 270 pp. Autographed by Cullen with a lengthy inscrptn. *(Fye)* **$300**
- Cancer of the uterus: its pathology, symptomatology, diagnosis, and treatment ... diseases of the endometrium. New York: 1900. 1st edn. 693 pp. Sev hundred w'cuts by Broedel, chromo-lithos. Inscrbd & autographed by Cullen. *(Fye)* **$350**
- Cancer of the uterus: its pathology, symptomatology, diagnosis, and treatment ...

New York: 1909. 1st edn, 2nd printing. 693 pp. W'cuts & chromo-lithos. Rebnd in leatherette. *(Fye)* **$100**
- Cancer of the uterus: its pathology, symptomatology, diagnosis, and treatment ... diseases of the endometrium. Phila & London: Saunders, 1909. 693 pp. 11 litho plates, over 300 cold & b/w plates by Max Brodel & Herman Becker. *(Poitras)* **$65**
- The distribution of adenomyomas containing uterine mucosa. Chicago: 1920. 1st edn. 69 pp. *(Fye)* **$15**
- See Kelly, Howard & Cullen, Thomas

**Cullen, Thomas Stephen**
- Early medicine in Maryland. [Balt: 1927]. 1st edn. 4to. 15pp. Bds. Ex lib. *(Argosy)* **$17.50**

**Cullen, William**
- First lines of the practice of physic ... Dublin: Luke Whire, 1784. 4th edn, crrctd & enlgd. Vol I, Book I, 238 pp, Vol II, Book II, 284 pp. Some staining. Full lea, hinges sl worn. *(Poitras)* **$125**
- Lectures on the materia medica. London: T. Lowndes, 1772. 1st edn. 4to. [2],v,[2],512 pp. With ctlg, index, & pub advts. Early sgntr on title, b'plate removed from front pastedown. Contemp calf, rebacked. *(Rootenberg)* **$550**
- See Black, Joseph (Experiments upon ...)
- A treatise of the materia medica. Edinburgh: for Charles Elliot ..., 1789. 1st edn. 4to. 2 vols. Lge uncut copy in orig bds. Wellcome library duplicate with release stamp on verso of titles. *(Quaritch)* **$525**
- A treatise of the materia medica. Edinburgh: for Charles Elliot ..., 1789. 1st edn. 4to. 2 vols. xxiii,432; 610,[2 pub advts] pp. With half-titles. Orig calf bds, rebacked. *(Elgen)* **$450**

**Culley, G.**
- Observations on livestock: containing hints for choosing and improving the best breeds. 1807. 4th edn. 274,6[index] pp. 2 plates. Full tree calf, rebacked. *(Phenotype)* **£80**
- See Bailey, J. & Culley, G.

**Culley, R.S.**
- A handbook of practical telegraphy. 1878. 7th edn. xi,468 pp. 18 plates, some fldg, 147 figs in text. Orig cloth, spine faded, cloth sl marked, inner hinges cracked. *(Whitehart)* **£25**

**Culp, Dr.**
- Dr. Culp's catechism on smallpox and vaccination. [Tampa, Fla.]: 1899. 12mo. 31 pp. Printed wraps. Ex lib. *(Argosy)* **$20**

**Culpeper, Nicholas**
- Complete herbal and English physician ... Manchester: J. Gleave, 1826. 4to. vi,240,44

pp. 2 ports, 36 plates containing 255 cold figs. Much soiling & foxing. Half calf, recently rebacked, dull green lea label. *(Blackwell's)* **£105**
- The complete herbal. 1850. New edn. 4to. vi,398,[4] pp. Port, 20 hand-cold plates. Marginal staining of port & plates. New bds. *(Wheldon & Wesley)* **£75**
- Complete herbal, to which is now added, upwards of one hundred additional herbs, with a display of their medicinal and occult qualities. 1815. 4to. Frontis, 40 cold plates. Buckram. *(Allen)* **$100**
- Culpeper's complete herbal ... to which is now first annexed his English Physician enlarged ... London: 1815. vi,398,[4] pp. Port, 40 hand-cold plates. Crnr of port stained. Mod cloth. *(Wheldon & Wesley)* **£120**
- Culpeper's English physician; and complete herbal. To which are now first added upwards of one hundred additional herbs ... forming a complete family dispensary ... London: Lewis ... 1805. Port frontis, 2 titles, 42 engvd plates. Contemp half-calf. *(McDowell)* **£165**
- The English physician enlarged with 369 medicines made of English herbs that were not in any impression until this. London: Ballard et al., 1752. 12mo. 394 pp. Occas soiling. Later patterned wraps. *(Argosy)* **$125**
- Pharmacopoeia Londinensis: or, the London dispensatory further adorned by the studies and collections of the Fellows ... London: P. Cole, 1656. 8vo. 12ff,1-341 pp,2ff,343-377 [i.e. 295] pp. 16ff. Some leaves frayed. Contemp calf, dull, hinges worn. *(Hemlock)* **$250**
- Pharmacopoeia Londinensis: or, the London dispensatory further adorned by the studies and collections of the Fellows ... London: 1659. 28,107,[1 blank], 191-342, [4], 343-377, [32]. 3 worm holes, without loss. Full calf, spine scuffed, hinge part cracked. *(Jenner)* **£110**

**Cumings, John N.**
- Heavy metals and the brain. Springfield: Charles, C. Thomas, 1959. 4to. 161 pp. Ex lib. *(Poitras)* **$20**

**Cumming, Alexander**
- The elements of clock and watch-work. Adapted to practice. In two essays. London: ... for the Author, 1766. 1st edn, 4to. [4]ff, 192pp, 16 engvd plates, [8]ff. Lightly browned, damp-stains & w'stains thr'out. Contemp calf, hinges cracked. *(Zeitlin)* **$600**

**Cummings, N.F.**
- Study of country convalescent treatment of 100 neuropsychiatric patients, Washington, D.C.: 1923. 20 pp. Wraps. Ex lib. *(Argosy)* **$25**

**Cumston, Charles Greene**
- An introduction to the history of medicine ...
New York: Knopf, 1926. 390 pp. Ills. Cvrs
scuffed.                                    *(Poitras)* **$50**

**Cuneo, H.M. & Rand, C.W.**
- Brain tumors of childhood. Springfield: 1952.
1st edn. 224 pp. Dw.                       *(Fye)* **$25**

**Cunningham, D.J.**
- Edinburgh stereoscopic atlas of anatomy.
Meadville, Pa.: Keystone View Co., n.d. [ca
1910]. New revsd edn. 10 vols. 322 3" x 6"
stereo photos mounted on 7" x 9" cards with
accompanying text on each card. Slipcases
worn, rubbed, one backstrip detchd.
                                           *(Xerxes)* **$550**

**Cunningham, F.D.**
- Defective vision, and the principles on which
it may be corrected by optical means.
Virginia: 1872. 12mo. 188 pp. Wraps.
Author's pres copy.                        *(Argosy)* **$25**

**Curie, Eve**
- Madame Curie: a biography. Translated by
Vincent Sheehan. Garden City: [1940]. Ills.
                                           *(Argosy)* **$20**

**Curie, Marie Sklodowska**
- Radioactive substances. New York: [1961].
Sm 8vo. Ills. Cloth. Dw      *(Argosy)* **$20**

**Curling, T.B.**
- A practical treatise on the diseases of the testis
and of the spermatic cord and scrotum. Phila:
1856. 2nd Amer edn. 419 pp.      *(Fye)* **$75**

**Curr, John**
- The coal viewer, and engine builder's
practical companion ... Sheffield: ... Taylor,
1797. 1st edn. 4to. 96 pp. 5 fldg engvd plates
(1 soiled & sl torn in the fold). Uncut in orig
bds, rebacked.                 *(Pickering)* **$2,650**

**Currie, J.R. & Long, W.H.**
- An agricultural survey in South Devon.
Totnes: 1929. 204 pp. Card cvrs.
                                           *(Phenotype)* **£25**

**Currie, James**
- Medical reports, on the effects of water, cold
and warm, as a remedy in fever and other
diseases ... from the 4th London edn, crrctd
& enlgd. Phila: James Humphreys, 1808. 2
vols in 1. 8vo. xvi,17-430 pp. Minimal
spotting. Calf, worn, hinges split.
                                           *(Hemlock)* **$150**

**Curtis**
- Curtis's botanical magazine, a set from the
beginning in 1787 to 1904. Vols 1 to 130.
7994 hand-cold plates, bound in 109 vols.

8vo. Mod cloth, in the style of the publisher's
binding. Occas foxing & soiling.
                              *(Wheldon & Wesley)* **£20,000**

**Curtis, Asa**
- Synopsis of a course of lectures on medical
science, at the Botanico-Medical College of
Ohio. Cincinnati: for the Author, 1846. 8vo.
464 pp. Orig calf, crudely rebacked.
                                           *(Argosy)* **$45**
- Synopsis of a course of lectures ... on medical
science, delivered to students of the Botanico-
Medical College of Ohio. Cincinnati: E.
Shepard, 1846. 4to. xvi,464 pp. Half calf,
patterned bds.                 *(Hemlock)* **$100**

**Curtis, Charles E.**
- Estate management. A practical handbook for
landlords, agents, and pupils. London: Cox,
1889. 3rd edn. xix,[i],420 pp. 28 pp pub ctlg.
Jnts a little weak.            *(Pollak)* **£12**

**Curtis, Lawrence**
- See Ivy, Robert & Curtis Lawrence

**[Curtis, William]**
- Instructions for collecting and preserving
insects; particularly moths and butterflies ...
nets and apparatus ... London: for the Author
..., 1771. 1st edn. 8vo. iv,44 pp. Engvd
frontis. Some staining on endpapers. Old
mrbld bds, black calf spine. *(Burmester)* **£275**

**Curwen, E. Cecil (ed.)**
- The journal of Gideon Mantell, surgeon and
geologist covering the years 1818 - 1852.
London  Oxford  University  Press,  1940.
xii,315,[i] pp. Frontis, 3 plates, map. Dw.
                                           *(Pollak)* **£30**
- The journal of Gideon Mantell, surgeon and
geologist, covering the years 1818 - 1852.
Edited ... by E.C. Curwen. London: 1940. 1st
edn. 315 pp.                   *(Scientia)* **$45**

**Curwen, J.C.**
- Hints  on  agricultural  subjects,  and  ...
improving the condition of the labouring
classes. London: Johnson & Crosby, 1809.
2nd edn. 8vo. xxiv,286,2 [drctns to binder]
pp. Aquatint, 4 engvd plates, 4 fldg tables.
Half-titles. Orig bds, rebacked, rubbed.
                                           *(Blackwell's)* **£125**
- Observations  on  the  state  of  Ireland,
principally directed to its agriculture and
rural population, in a series of letters ... 1818.
821 pp. Rebnd half-calf, cloth sides.
                                           *(Phenotype)* **£65**

**Curwen, M.D.**
- See Molloy, Edward & Curwen, M.D.

**Cushing, Clinton**
- Preventive medicine and surgery in lying-in
chamber. Sacramento: 1881. 8vo. 16 pp.

Printed wraps. *(Argosy)* **$30**

**Cushing, Harvey**
- A bibliography of Andreas Vesalius. 1943. 1st edn. Ltd (800). 230 pp. Ills. Mild damp-staining bottom margin throughout. Orig 3/4 mor, sl rubbed. *(Oasis)* **$160**
- Consecratio medici and other papers. Boston: 1928. 2nd printing. 276 pp. Chipped dw. *(Oasis)* **$35**
- Consecratio medici and other papers. Boston: 1929. 1st edn, reprinted. 276 pp. Autographed by author. *(Fye)* **$250**
- From a surgeon's journal. Boston: 1936. 1st edn. 534 pp. Autographed by author. *(Fye)* **$250**
- From a surgeon's journal. Boston: 1936. 1st edn. 534 pp. *(Fye)* **$50**
- The life of Sir William Osler ... Oxford: Clarendon Press, 1925. 1st edn. 2 vols. 8vo. 41 plates. Orig blue cloth, gilt lettering. *(Zeitlin)* **$350**
- The life of Sir William Osler ... Oxford: Clarendon Press, 1925. 2nd imp. 2 vols. 8vo. xiii,685; 728 pp. Ills. *(Poitras)* **$100**
- The life of Sir William Osler ... Oxford: Clarendon Press, 1925. 3rd edn. 2 vols. 685; 728 pp. Photo ills. *(Xerxes)* **$85**
- The life of Sir William Osler. Oxford: 1925. 1st edn, 1st printing. 2 vols. 685; 728 pp. Pres copy inscrbd in Cushing's hand & sgnd "The Author". *(Fye)* **$650**
- The life of Sir William Osler. Oxford: 1926. 4th imp. 2 vols. 685; 728 pp. Num plates. *(Zeitlin)* **$75**
- The medical career and other papers. Boston: 1940. 1st edn, reprinted. 302 pp. *(Fye)* **$50**
- The meningiomas arising from the olfactory groove and their removal by aid of electrosurgery. Glasgow: 1927. 1st edn. 53 pp. Wraps. *(Fye)* **$150**
- Papers relating to the pituitary body, hypothalamus and parasympathetic nervous system. Springfield: 1932. 1st edn. 234 pp. Dw. *(Fye)* **$300**
- The pituitary body and its disorders. Phila: 1912. 1st edn. 341 pp. *(Fye)* **$325**
- Selected papers on neurosurgery. Edited by Donald Matson. New Haven: 1969. 1st edn. 66p pp. Ills. *(Oasis)* **$60**
- Selected papers on neurosurgery. New Haven: 1969. 1st edn. 669 pp. Ills. Dw. *(Oasis)* **$50**
- Studies in intracranial physiology and surgery. London: Oxford University Press, 1926. 4to. xii,146 pp. 15 ills. *(Poitras)* **$125**
- Studies in intracranial physiology and surgery. The third circulation. The hypophysics ... London: 1926. 1st edn. 146 pp. Buckram, with orig wraps bound in. Ex lib. *(Fye)* **$250**
- Tumors of the nervus acusticus. Phila: 1917. 1st edn. 269 pp. *(Fye)* **$300**

**Cutbush, James**
- A system of pyrotechny, comprehending the theory and practice, with the application of chemistry; designed for exhibition and for war. In four parts ... Phila: 1825. 8vo. Engvd plate. Half-sheep, front hinge mended. *(Argosy)* **$150**

**Cuthbertson, John**
- Description of an improved air-pump, and an account of some experiments made with it ... For the author ..., n.d. [ca 1787]. 8vo. [2],41,[1] pp. 2 fldg engvd plates. Sm hole in title without loss, plates reprd along folds. Mod qtr calf. *(Deighton Bell)* **£350**

**Cutler, C.W.**
- The hand: its disabilities and diseases. Phila: 1942. x,572 pp. 274 ills. *(Whitehart)* **£35**
- The hand: its disabilities and diseases. Phila: 1942. 1st edn. 572 pp. *(Fye)* **$100**

**Cutler, Elliott & Zollinger, Robert**
- Atlas of surgical operations. New York: 1940. 1st edn, 3rd printing. Folio. 181 pp. *(Fye)* **$35**

**Cutler, Max**
- See Cheatle, G.L. & Cutler, Max
- Tumors of the breast. Phila: 1962. 1st edn. 488 pp. *(Fye)* **$40**

**Cuvier, Georges**
- A discourse on the revolution of the surface of the globe, and the changes thereby produced in the animal kingdom. Phila: 1831. 252 pp. Bds with linen spine. *(Scientia)* **$55**
- A discourse on the revolutions of the surface of the globe and the changes thereby produced in the animal kingdom. London: Whittaker, Treacher & Arnot, 1829. 1st edn in English. 8vo. [2],261 pp. 4 wood engvs, many text ills. Contemp half-calf. *(Rootenberg)* **$200**
- Essay on the theory of the earth ... with mineralogical notes ... and an account of Cuvier's geological discoveries by Professor Jameson. Edinburgh: W. Blackwood, 1813. 1st edn in English. 8vo. xiii,262,[1] pp. 2 engvd plates. Plates spotted. Orig bds. *(Antiq Sc)* **$300**
- Essay on the theory of the earth, translated from the French ... Edinburgh: 1813. 1st edn in English. 8vo. xiii,265,[1] pp. 2 plates. Plates & title rather foxed, inscrptn on front free endpaper. Mod calf-backed bds, uncut. *(Wheldon & Wesley)* **£65**

**Cyclopaedia ...**
- Cyclopaedia of automobile engineering. Chicago: 1913. 4 vols. Over 400 pp per vol. Num plates & ills. Hd of 2 spines defective, one backstrip partly detchd. *(Weiner)* **£75**
- Cyclopaedia of obstetrics and gynaecology.

New York: 1887. 12 vols. Many w'engvs.
*(Elgen)* **$495**
- The cyclopaedia of practical receipts in all the useful and domestic arts ... by a practical chemist. 1841. 1st edn. A few crrctns & addtns in ink. *(Robertshaw)* **£15**

**Da Costa, Bernardo F. Bruto**
- Sleeping sickness in the Island of Principe. Sanitation, statistics, hospital services ... Translated ... 1913. viii,90 pp. Tables. Pub file copy label on wraps, sl faded. *(Jenner)* **£9**
- Sleeping sickness in the Island of Principe. London: 1913. 8vo. Frontis, fldg charts. Orig wraps. *(Argosy)* **$20**

**Dabney, Charles W.**
- The cotton plant. Its history, botany, chemistry, culture, enemies, and uses. Washington: 1896. Fldg cold chart, cold map, 2 plates, 32 figs. Half-calf. *(Edwards)* **£25**

**Dadd ...**
- Dadd's pocket library for car owners, 1927. Ten small booklets, each 16 pp, on carburation, lubrication, insurance, &c., each in cold card wraps, the set contained in a card slipcase, rubbed. *(Weiner)* **£50**

**Dahelly, G.**
- Carrel, Alexis & Dahelly, G.

**Dalby, W.B.**
- Lectures on diseases and injuries of the ear. 1885. 3rd edn. xii,260 pp. 28 figs in text. Spine sl worn. *(Whitehart)* **£18**

**Daldy, T.M.**
- See Wilks, S. & Daldy, T.M.

**Dalgedo, D.G.**
- The climate of Portugal, and notes on its health resorts. Lisbon: 1914. 8vo. 479 pp. 6 maps. New buckram, orig wraps bound in. Ex lib. *(Argosy)* **$40**

**Dalton, Edward B.**
- Inaugural thesis on the disorder known as bronzed skin; or disease of the supra-renal capsules. New York: 1860. 8vo. 20 pp. Printed wraps in lib binder. *(Argosy)* **$35**

**Dalton, John**
- Meteorological observations and essays. London: W. Richardson, J. Phillips & W. Pennington, 1793. 1st edn, 1st iss. 8vo. Num diags in text. Uncut in orig bds, backstrip renewed. *(Quaritch)* **$850**
- Meteorological observations and essays ... London: ... Pennington, 1793. 1st edn, 1st iss. 8vo in 4s. xvi,208 pp. Several w'cut diags in the text. Uncut. Orig lavender bds, a little worn, in a mor-backed case. Inscribed by

Dalton to William Fothergill.
*(Pickering)* **$2,500**
- A new system of chemical philosophy. London: 1842, 1810, 1827. 8vo. 3 pts. Vol 1 pt 1, 2nd ed, vi,[2],220 pp; Vol 1 pt 2, 1st ed, [4]ff,221-560 pp. 8 plates; Vol 2 pt 1 (all published), 1st edn, xii,257 pp,[1]f. Orig cloth, rebacked. Author's inscrbd pres copy.
*(Zeitlin)* **$5,000**

**Dalton, John C.**
- History of the College of Physicians and Surgeons in the City of New York ... New York: 1888. 1st edn. 8vo. 208 pp. 20 ills. Cloth sl w'stained. *(Argosy)* **$50**
- Introductory address to the medical class of 1860-61 of the College of Physicians and Surgeons. New York: 1860. 24 pp. Wraps. *(Argosy)* **$20**
- The origin and propagation of disease. New York: 1874. 30 pp. Orig printed wraps. Ex lib. *(Argosy)* **$25**
- A treatise on physiology and hygiene; for schools, families, and colleges. New York: 1883. 8vo. Engvd frontis, num text ills. Contemp cloth, rebacked. *(Argosy)* **$50**

**Daly, R.A.**
- Igneous rocks and the depths of the earth. New York: 1933. 2nd edn. 8vo. xxii,342 pp. Frontis, 187 ills. Cloth.
*(Wheldon & Wesley)* **£15**
- Our mobile earth. New York: 1926. 8vo. xxii,342 pp. Frontis, 187 ills. A little minor foxing. Cloth. *(Wheldon & Wesley)* **£18**

**Dana, Alexander Hamilton**
- Inductive inquiries in physiology, ethics and ethnology, relating to subjects of recent research of speculation. New York: A.S. Barnes, 1873. 1st edn. 12mo. [ii],308,[2] pp. Black cloth. *(Gach)* **$30**

**Dana, Charles L.**
- The peaks of medical history: an outline of the evolution of medicine for the use of medical students and practitioners. New York: 1926. 1st edn. 8vo. 40 full-page plates, 16 text ills. Cloth. *(Argosy)* **$75**

**Dana, Charles Loomis**
- Text-book of nervous diseases and psychiatry: for the use of students and practitioners of medicine. New York: William Wood, 1908. 7th edn. 782 pp. Red cloth, rubbed, hinges broken. *(Gach)* **$35**

**Dana, J. Freeman & Dana, Samuel L.**
- Outlines of the mineralogy and geology of Boston and its vicinity. Boston: Cummings & Hilliard, 1818. 1st edn. Tall 8vo. 108 pp. Fldg hand-cold engvd map. Blue bds with linen back, antique style. *(Antiq Sc)* **$285**

**Dana, James D.**
- Characteristics of volcanoes, with contributions of facts and principles from the Hawaiian Islands ... New York: Dodd, Mead & Co., 1890. 1st edn. Lge 8vo. xvi,399 pp. 16 plates (many fldg), num text ills. Uncut in orig cloth.         *(Rootenberg)* **$175**
- Manual of mineralogy, including observations on mines, rocks, reduction of ores ... London: Trubner, 1862. New edn, revsd & enlgd. xii,13-456 pp. Text figs. Occas foxing. Orig cloth.         *(Pollak)* **£35**

**Dana, James Dwight**
- A system of mineralogy: including an extending treatise on crystallography. New Haven: Durrie & Peck and Herrick & Noyes, 1837. 1st edn. 8vo. xiv,144, 144*-152*, 145-452,119,[1] pp. 4 fldg engvd plates. Contemp sheep, neatly rebacked.
         *(Antiq Sc)* **$450**

**Dana, Samuel L.**
- A muck manual for farmers. Lowel, Mass: D. Bixby, 1842. 1st edn. 244 pp. Spine tips defective, spine soiled & a little cvr staining.         *(Diamond)* **$75**

**Dandy, Walter**
- Benign tumors in the third ventricle of the brain: diagnosis and treatment. Springfield: 1933. 1st edn. 172 pp. Ills.    *(Oasis)* **$150**
- Benign tumors in the third ventricle of the brain: diagnosis and treatment. Springfield: 1933. 1st edn. 171 pp. Ex lib.    *(Fye)* **$150**
- Intracranial arterial aneurysms. Ithaca: 1947. 1st edn, 3rd printing. 147 pp. Num fldg charts.         *(Fye)* **$100**

**Danforth, I.N.**
- Nathan Smith Davis. Chicago: 1907. 1st edn. 4to. Ills. Cloth. Ex lib.    *(Argosy)* **$35**

**Daniell, J. Frederic**
- Meteorological essays and observations. London: 1823. 1st edn. 19,643 pp. 5 fldg plates. Contemp 3/4 calf, worn. *(M&S)* **$115**
- Meteorological essays and observations. London: Underwood, 1827. 2nd edn, revsd & enlgd. viii,643 pp. 6 plates, num text figs & tables, some fldg. 4 leaves with sm tear, occas foxing. Contemp half-calf, rubbed.
         *(Pollak)* **£50**

**Daniell, William C.**
- Observations upon the autumnal fevers of Savannah. Savannah: W.T. Williams, 1826. 1st edn. 8vo. Heavily foxed. Mottled calf.         *(Argosy)* **$400**
- Observations upon the autumnal fevers of Savannah. Savannah: 1826. 1st edn. 8vo. 152 pp. Errata slip pasted to last leaf of text. Foxed. Contemp calf, rebacked with cloth.

**Dana, James D.**         *(M&S)* **$325**

**Darbishire, A.D.**
- Breeding and the Mendelian discovery. 1911. 8vo. xii,282 pp. 4 cold plates.
         *(Wheldon & Wesley)* **£20**

**Darby, H.C.**
- The draining of the fens. Cambridge University Press, 1956. 2nd edn. 8vo. Frontis, many ills. Dw.    *(McDowell)* **£18**

**Darkness ...**
- Darkness at noon; or, the Great Solar Eclipse, of the 16th of June, 1806 ... by an inhabitant of Boston. Boston: Carlisle & Newell, May, 1806. 1st edn. 12mo. Plate, 34 pp. Untrimmed. Mod cloth.    *(M&S)* **$200**

**Darlington, C.D.**
- Evolution of genetic systems. Cambridge: 1939. 1st edn. 149 pp.    *(Scientia)* **$30**
- Recent advances in cytology. Phila: 1932. 1st Amer edn. 559 pp.    *(Scientia)* **$40**

**Darrach, W.**
- Drawings of the anatomy of the groin: with anatomical remarks. Phila: 1844. 2nd edn. 8vo. 127 pp. 4 litho plates. Orig cloth, spine worn.         *(M&S)* **$42.50**
- Drawings of the anatomy of the groin: with anatomical remarks. Phila: 1844. 2nd edn. 8vo. 4 litho plates. Orig cloth. Ex lib.
         *(Argosy)* **$50**

**Darwin, C.G.**
- The new conceptions of matter. London: Bell, 1931. 1st edn. viii,192 pp. 6 plates, 46 text figs.         *(Pollak)* **£20**

**Darwin, Charles**
- Darwinism stated by Darwin himself. Characteristic passages ... New York: Appleton, 1884. 1st edn. xv,351,16 [advts] pp. Orig brown dec cloth, minor rubbing.
         *(Diamond)* **$25**
- The descent of man, and selection in relation to sex. London: Murray, 1871. 1st edn, 2nd iss. 2 vols. 8vo. Pub green cloth, spines a little rubbed, hds of spines pulled.
         *(McDowell)* **£180**
- The descent of man, and selection in relation to sex. London: 1881. 2nd edn, 14th thous. 693 pp.    *(Scientia)* **$40**
- The descent of man, and selection in relation to sex. London: 1882. 2nd edn, 15th thous. 693 pp. Ills. Orig green cloth.    *(Oasis)* **$50**
- The descent of man, and selection in relation to sex. 1882. xvi,693 pp. 78 ills. Orig cloth, sl damaged,         *(Whitehart)* **£15**
- The descent of man, and selection in relation to sex. London: Murray, 1888. 2nd edn, revsd & augmntd, 22nd thous. 1st iss of the

Library Edition. Half-titles present. 8vo. Orig cloth, gilt.        *(Blackwell's)* **£85**
- The descent of man, and selection in relation to sex. London: 1889. 2nd edn, 25th thous. Orig cloth.        *(Wheldon & Wesley)* **£30**
- The descent of man, and selection in relation to sex. London: 1894. 2nd edn, 31st thous. Orig cloth, trifle used.
        *(Wheldon & Wesley)* **£20**
- The descent of man, and selection in relation to sex. 1906. xix,1031 pp.        *(Weiner)* **£10**
- The different forms of flowers on plants of the same species. New York: Appleton, 1877. viii,352,10 [advts] pp. 15 ills. Orig brown cloth, minor rubbing.        *(Diamond)* **$35**
- The different forms of flowers on plants of the same species. New York: 1877. 1st Amer edn. 352 pp.        *(Scientia)* **$75**
- The different forms of flowers on plants of the same species. London: Murray, 1877. 1st edn. 8vo. viii,352 pp. Lacks the advts. Prize calf gilt, sometime rebacked & backstrip laid down, arms in gilt on sides. *(Blackwell's)* **£75**
- The different forms of flowers on plants of the same species. New York: 1896. 352 pp. Text ills. Half-mor. Extremities very sl worn.
        *(Oasis)* **$40**
- The effects of cross and self fertilisation in the vegetable kingdom. London: Murray, 1876. 1st edn, 1st iss. 8vo. viii,482 pp. 109 tables, 1 diag, errata. Orig green cloth.
        *(Rootenberg)* **$475**
- The effects of cross and self fertilisation in the vegetable kingdom. New York: 1892. 482 pp.
        *(Scientia)* **$40**
- The expression of the emotions in man and animals. London: Murray, 1872. 1st edn, 2nd iss. 7 heliotype plates, 3 fldg. Full mor prize bndg, King's College, London, Arms in gilt.
        *(McDowell)* **£100**
- The expression of the emotions in man and animals. New York: Appleton, 1873. 1st Amer edn. [ii],[viii], 374,[16] pp. 7 heliotypes, 21 text ills. Embossed brown cloth, upper front jnt frayed.        *(Gach)* **$175**
- The expression of the emotions in man and animals. New York: 1873. 1st Amer edn. 374 pp. Rear cvr somewhat stained. *(Scientia)* **$85**
- The expression of the emotions in man and animals ... New York: Appleton, 1873. [vii],374,12 [advts] pp. 7 heliotype plates, text ills. Sl repair to one plate. Orig brown cloth, rebacked. Some shelf wear & rubbing.
        *(Diamond)* **$125**
- The expression of the emotions in man and animals. London: 1873. 10th thous. vi,374 pp. 7 plates. Light foxing & soiling. Orig cloth, sl used.        *(Wheldon & Wesley)* **£55**
- The expression of the emotions in man and animals. London: 1873. 10th thous. vi,374 pp. 7 plates. 19th c half-calf, trifle rubbed. Advts discarded by binder.
        *(Wheldon & Wesley)* **£40**

- The expression of the emotions in man and animals. 1890. 2nd edn edited by Francis Darwin. viii,394 pp. 7 plates (1 loose). Inscribed on flyleaf "J.D. Duff from F. Darwin Feb 1890".        *(Weiner)* **£150**
- The expression of the emotions in man and animals. London: 1890. 2nd edn, edited by F. Darwin. 394 pp.        *(Scientia)* **$100**
- The expression of the emotions in man and animals. London: 1892. 11th thous. viii,394 pp. 7 plates. Orig cloth, sl marked.
        *(Wheldon & Wesley)* **£20**
- The expression of the emotions in man and animals. New York: 1896. "Authorized Edition". 374 pp. Photographic ills.
        *(Oasis)* **$30**
- The expression of the emotions in man and animals. New York: 1898. 372 pp. *(Fye)* **$40**
- The formation of vegetable mould, through the actions of worms, with observations on their habits. London: Murray, 1881. 1st edn. Area cut from front blank (to remove name?) Pub green cloth.        *(McDowell)* **£130**
- The formation of vegetable mould ... London: 1881. 3rd thous. viii,326 pp. 15 text figs. Prize calf, gilt. *(Wheldon & Wesley)* **£30**
- The formation of vegetable mould, through the actions of worms, with observations on their habits. London: 1881. 4th thous. 326 pp.        *(Scientia)* **$50**
- The formation of vegetable mould, through the actions of worms, with observations on their habits. London: Murray, 1881. 5th thous, crrctd. Pub green cloth.
        *(McDowell)* **£50**
- The formation of vegetable mould, through the action of worms. London: Murray, 1883. 8th thous, crrctd. Sm 8vo. vii.328,[i advts] pp. Orig green cloth, rec recased.
        *(Blackwell's)* **£45**
- The formation of vegetable mould through the action of earth worms. New York: 1896. 326 pp. Text ills. Half-mor.        *(Oasis)* **$35**
- The formation of vegetable mould through the action of worms with observations on their habits. 1904. viii,198 pp. 15 ills.
        *(Whitehart)* **£10**
- Formation of vegetable mould ... London: 1904. viii,298 pp. 10 plates. Orig cloth.
        *(Wheldon & Wesley)* **£15**
- Insectivorous plants. London: Murray, 1875. 1st edn, 1st iss. 8vo. x,462 pp. 30 text w'cuts. Orig green cloth. Charles Jenner's b'plate.
        *(Rootenberg)* **$350**
- Insectivorous plants. New York: 1875. 1st Amer edn. 462 pp.        *(Scientia)* **$75**
- Insectivorous plants. London: 1875. 2nd thous. x,462 pp. 30 figs. Inscrptn on half-title. Orig cloth, jnts a trifle weak.
        *(Wheldon & Wesley)* **£60**
- Insectivorous plants. London: Murray, 1876. 4th thous. Sm 8vo. x,462. Errata slip. Orig green cloth, recently recased.

*(Blackwell's)* **£55**
- Insectivorous plants. New York: 1896. "Authorized Edition". 462 pp. Half-mor. Top of spine sl worn. *(Oasis)* **$35**
- Insectivorous plants, revised by Francis Darwin. 1908. xiv,377 pp. Diags. *(Weiner)* **£10**
- Journal of researches into the natural history and geology of the countries visited ... 1845. 2nd edn, crrctd with addtns. vii,519 pp. Half-mor, sl rubbed, sm tears in jnts. Half-title & advts discarded by binder. *(Wheldon & Wesley)* **£80**
- Journal of researches into the natural history and geology of the countries visited during the voyages of H.M.S. Beagle round the world ...New York: Harper & Bros, 1846. 1st Amer edn. 2 vols. 12mo. vii,[1],351; 324,8,4 pp. Text w'cuts. Cloth, little worn. *(Antiq Sc)* **$275**
- Journal of researches into the geology and natural history ... New York: 1890. New edn. 551 pp. *(Scientia)* **$75**
- Journal of researches into the natural history and geology ... New York: D, Appleton, 1890. New edn. xvi,551 pp. 8 pp advts. Orig light green gilt dec cloth, sl soiled. *(Blackwell's)* **£85**
- Journal of researches into the natural history and geology of the countries visited during the voyages of H.M.S. Beagle round the world ...London: Newlson, 1893. Sq 8vo. Plates, some fldg. Contemp full calf, spine rubbed, gilt faded, front hinge weak. *(McDowell)* **£24**
- Journal of researches into the natural history and geology of the countries visited ... 1893. 615 pp. Frontis, 21 plates, text figs. Orig blue cloth, sl used. *(Wheldon & Wesley)* **£25**
- The movements and habits of climbing plants. London: 1875. 2nd edn, revsd. 1st edn in book form. *(Scientia)* **£185**
- The movements and habits of climbing plants. London: Murray, 1876. 2nd thous. Sm 8vo. viii,208,32 [ctlg] pp. Orig green cloth gilt, recently recased. *(Blackwell's)* **£50**
- The movements and habits of climbing plants, London: 1888. 3rd thous. x,208 pp. 13 text figs. Orig cloth. *(Wheldon & Wesley)* **£40**
- The movements and habits of climbing plants. New York: 1891. 208 pp. Not in Freeman. *(Scientia)* **$27.50**
- A naturalist's voyage. Journal of researches ... London: 1889. x,519 pp. Port. Orig cloth, trifle used. *(Wheldon & Wesley)* **£20**
- On the origin of species. London: J. Murray, 1859. 1st edn. 8vo. ix,502 pp. Pub advts, fldg chart. Orig cloth, recased. very slight foxing & wear. Preserved in a half-mor box. *(Antiq Sc)* **$7,500**
- On the origin of species by means of natural selection ... New York: Appleton, 1860. 1st

Amer edn. 12mo. 432 pp. Fldg table. Occas browning. Orig cloth, spine strengthened. *(Rootenberg)* **$550**
- On the origin of species by means of natural selection. London: Murray, 1860. 2nd edn, 5th thous. x,502 pp. Murray's ctlg dated Jan 1860 at end. Fldg diag. Orig green cloth, trifle used, refixed. Bndg variant b. *(Wheldon & Wesley)* **£160**
- On the origin of species by means of natural selection ... London: Murray, 1866. 4th edn, with crrctns & addtns. 8th thous. 8vo. Pub green cloth, sm snags to hd & ft of spine. *(McDowell)* **£65**
- The origin of species by means of natural selection. London: Murray, 1872. 6th edn, with crrctns & addtns. 12th thous. 8vo. A little browning to prelims. Pub cloth. *(McDowell)* **£30**
- The origin of species by means of natural selection. 1880. xxi,458 pp. Rear jnt shaken. *(Weiner)* **£12**
- The origin of species. 1890. 6th edn, 39th thous. 8vo. xxi,458 pp. Fldg diag. Orig cloth. *(Wheldon & Wesley)* **£28**
- The origin of species. London: 1899. 56th thous. 8vo. xxi,432 pp. Fldg diag. Orig green cloth. *(Wheldon & Wesley)* **£18**
- The origin of species. 1900. 8vo. xxxi,703 pp. Port, fldg table. Orig cloth. *(Wheldon & Wesley)* **£15**
- On the various contrivances by which British and foreign orchids are fertilized by insects. London: J. Murray, 1862. 1st edn (1st iss). 8vo. vi,365 pp. 1 fldg plate, text w'cuts. 32 pp advts at rear dated December 1861. Orig cloth, spine a bit chipped. *(Antiq Sc)* **$375**
- On the various contrivances by which British and foreign orchids are fertilised ... London: 1862. 1st edn. Freeman 800 variant b, without the advt at end. vi,365 pp. Fldg plate, 33 text figs. Orig plum cloth, reprd. *(Wheldon & Wesley)* **£220**
- The power of movement in plants, assisted by Francis Darwin. London: 1880. 2nd edn, 2nd thous. x,592 pp. 196 text figs. A little foxing at beginning. Orig cloth, 2 tiny tears in spine. *(Wheldon & Wesley)* **£55**
- See Krause, Ernst (Erasmus Darwin ...)
- See Muller, Hermann (The fertilisation of flowers...)
- See Romanes, George J. (Mental evolution in animals ... )
- See Weissmann, August (Studies in the theory of descent ...)
- The structure and distribution of coral reefs ... New York: 1898. 3rd edn. *(Scientia)* **$27.50**
- The variation of animals and plants under domestication. London: Murray, 1868. 1st edn, 1st iss. 2 vols. 8vo. viii,411,[32]; viii,486,[2] pp. With pub advts. Text ills throughout. Orig green cloth, rebacked,

retaining orig spines.      *(Rootenberg)* **$400**
- The variation of animals and plants under domestication. London: Murray, 1868. 1st edn, 2nd iss, with Freeman's points. (Freeman 878). Orig green cloth gilt, vol 2 bumped, sl w'stained, lib label removed from upper cover.      *(Blackwell's)* **£200**
- The variation of animals and plants under domestication. New York: O. Judd, n.d. [1868]. 1st Amer edn. 2 vols. 8vo. iv,iii-iv, v-x, 11-494, [6 pub advts]; 568, [8 pub advts]. Orig cloth.      *(Antiq Sc)* **$125**
- The variation of animals and plants under domestication. London: Murray, 1885. 2nd edn, 5th thous. 2 vols. 8vo. Discreet blind-stamps on title. Pub green cloth.
      *(McDowell)* **£58**
- The variation of animals and plants under domestication. 1885. 2nd edn, 5th thous. 8vo. 2 vols.      *(Wheldon & Wesley)* **£55**
- The variation of animals and plants under domestication. New York: 1896. "Authorized Edition". 2 vols. 473; 494 pp. Text ills. Half-mor, top of spines sl rubbed.      *(Oasis)* **$50**
- The variation of animals and plants under domestication. 1899. 8th imp of 2nd edn, revsd. 2 vols. Text figs. Orig cloth, sl marked.      *(Wheldon & Wesley)* **£30**
- The variation of animals and plants under domestication. London: 1899. 2nd edn, 8th imp. 2 vols. 473; 495 pp.    *(Scientia)* **$37.50**
- The various contrivances by which orchids are fertilised by insects. New York: 1877. 1st Amer edn. 300 pp.      *(Scientia)* **$75**
- The various contrivances by which orchids are fertilised by insects. Second edition, revised. New York: Appleton, 1877. 1st Amer edn. xvi,300,8 [advts] pp. 38 ills. Orig brown cloth, little shelf wear. Old lib b'plate & blind-stamp.      *(Diamond)* **$45**
- The various contrivances by which orchids are fertilised ... London: Murray, 1882. 2nd edn, revsd. xvi,300 pp. 32 pp ctlg inserted. Orig green cloth gilt.      *(Blackwell's)* **£65**
- The various contrivances by which orchids are fertilised by insects. London: 1888. 2nd edn, 4th thous. xvi,300 pp. Ills. Orig cloth, tear in lower jnt.      *(Wheldon & Wesley)* **£30**
- The various contrivances by which orchids are fertilised by insects. London: 1904. Popular edn. xvi,300,[iv list of books] pp. 38 text w'cuts.      *(Pollak)* **£25**

**Darwin, Erasmus**
- Phytologia; or, the philosophy of agriculture and gardening, with the theory of draining morasses, and with an improved construction of the drill plough. J. Johnson, 1800. viii, 612, [xii] pp. 12 engvd plates, some fldg, all foxed & stained. Contemp calf.
      *(Blackwell's)* **£210**
- Zoonomia or the laws of organic life. London: 1801. 3rd edn. 4 vols. 516; 565; 512; 493 pp.

4 engvd, 6 cold plates. Sl worming end of vol II not affecting text. Old calf, rebacked, worn.
      *(Oasis)* **$250**

**Darwin, Francis & Seward, A.C. (eds.)**
- More letters of Charles Darwin; a record of his work in a series of hitherto unpublished letters. New York: 1903. 1st Amer edn. 2 vols. 494; 508 pp.      *(Scientia)* **$75**

**Darwin, Francis (ed.)**
- Charles Darwin, his life told in an autobiographical chapter, edited by ... London: 1908. 8vo. viii,348 pp. Port, facsimile. Orig cloth.
      *(Wheldon & Wesley)* **£20**
- The life and letters of Charles Darwin ... London: 1888. 7th thous, revsd. 3 vols. 385; 393; 418 pp. Spines faded.      *(Scientia)* **$75**
- The life and letters of Charles Darwin ... New York: D. Appleton, 1896. 8vo. 2 vols. 2 ports, 3 plates. Orig 3/4 lea, mrbld bds. *(Zeitlin)* **$65**
- The life and letters of Charles Darwin ... New York: 1896. 2 vols. Half lea, mrbld bds.
      *(Scientia)* **$35**

**Daubeny, Charles**
- Sketch of the geology of North America, being the substance of a memoir read before the Ashmolean Society. Oxford: 1839. 1st edn. Slim 8vo. Lge fldg frontis map. Orig wraps, sl torn.      *(McDowell)* **£35**

**Daukes, S.H.**
- The medical museum. Modern developments, organisation and technical methods. London: Wellcome Foundation, [1929]. 4to. Ills.      *(Argosy)* **$35**

**Daumas, Maurice**
- Scientific instruments of the 17th and 18th centuries. Translated & edited by Mary Holbrook. New York: 1972. 1st edn in English. 361 pp. Dw.      *(Scientia)* **$60**

**Dausset, J., et al. (eds.)**
- Advances in transplantation. Proceedings of the First International Congress of the Transplantation Society. Balt: Williams & Wilkins Co., 1968. 779 pp. Ills. *(Poitras)* **$75**

**Davenport, Charles B.**
- The feebly inhibited. Washington: 1915. 1st edn. 4to. 158 pp. Tables & genetic charts. Cloth.      *(Argosy)* **$40**
- Heredity in relation to eugenics. New York: 1911. 1st edn. 298 pp.      *(Scientia)* **$35**

**Davey, M.J.B.**
- Interpretative history of flight. A survey of the history and development of aeronautics with particular reference to contemporary influence and conditions. HMSO, 1937.

208pp. Frontis, 30 plates. Bds, marked & sl stained, linen spine.  *(Whitehart)* **£15**

**Davey, N.**
- The gas turbine. 1914. xiv,248 pp. 100 ills. Orig cloth, stained.  *(Whitehart)* **£18**

**Davidoff, Leo M.**
- See Epstein, Bernard S. & Davidoff, Leo M.

**Davidson, Wm. & Hudson, Alfred**
- Essays on the sources and mode of action of fever. Phila: 1843. 8vo. Foxed. Half-sheep.  *(Argosy)* **$50**

**Davies, John**
- A pamphlet on patents, containing all the necessary information for persons desirous of obtaining letters patent for inventions ... Weale, Simpkin & Co., 1850. 8vo. iv,16 pp. Glassine wraps, disbound. *(Deighton Bell)* **£30**
- Selections in pathology & surgery; or, an exposition of the nature and treatment of local diseases. Phila: A. Waldie, 1839. 4to. 119 pp. Sl foxing. Qtr lea, mrbld bds, front bd detchd.  *(Poitras)* **$65**
- Selections in pathology & surgery; or, an exposition of the nature and treatment of local diseases. Phila: 1839. 58 pp. Wraps. Ex lib.  *(Argosy)* **$35**

**Davies, Porter**
- Doctors of the old school: being curiosities of medicine and ancient practice. Akron, Ohio: 1905. 1st edn. 4to. 4 plates. Half-mor, rubbed.  *(Argosy)* **$35**

**Davies, Stanley P.**
- Social control of the feeble-minded: a study of social programs and attitudes in relation to the problems of mental deficiency. New York: 1923. 8vo. 222 pp. Orig printed wraps, chipped & reprd.  *(Argosy)* **$20**

**Davies, Thomas S.**
- Solutions of the principal questions of Dr. Hutton's course of mathematics. London: Longman, Orme, 1840. xii,551,32 [ctlg] pp. New paper bds, orig cloth spine, uncut.  *(Pollak)* **£25**

**Davis [Daniel]**
- Davis's manual of magnetism. Including also electro-magnetism ... with a description of the electrotype process ... Boston: Daniel Davis, 1842. 1st edn. 12mo. [8],218 pp. Frontis, ills, index. Orig cloth, some wear to extremities. Ex lib.  *(M&S)* **$75**

**Davis, David**
- See Young, Hugh & Davis, David

**Davis, Edward**
- Complications of pregnancy. New York: 1923. 1st edn. 277 pp.  *(Fye)* **$20**

**Davis, George E.**
- A handbook of chemical engineering. 1901-02. 2 vols. Lge thick 8vo. Approx 780 pp. Ills, diags. New buckram. Ex lib.  *(Weiner)* **£25**

**Davis, Harold T.**
- The theory of linear operators from the standpoint of differential equations of infinite order. Bloomington: Principia Press, 1936. xiv,628 pp.  *(Pollak)* **£25**

**Davis, James W. & Lees, F. Arnold**
- West Yorkshire: an account of its geology, physical geography, climatology and botany. London: Reeve, 1878. xl,414 pp. 5 fldg cold plates, 16 other plates, 2 fldg maps in pockets on pastedowns. Orig green cloth, gilt, backstrip dulled.  *(Blackwell's)* **£25**

**Davis, John S.**
- Plastic surgery: its principles and practice. Phila: 1919. 1st edn. 770 pp. 864 ills. Orig cloth.  *(Oasis)* **$250**
- Plastic surgery: its principles and practice. Phila: 1919. 1st edn. 770 pp.  *(Fye)* **$500**

**Davis, Nathan Smith**
- History of medicine with the code of medical ethics. Chicago: [1903]. 1st edn. Port. Tall 8vo. Uncut & unopened. Cloth. *(Argosy)* **$85**

**Davis, Robert H.**
- Breathing in irrespirable atmospheres ... including a short history of gas and incendiary warfare ... London: n.d. [ca 1945]. Lge 8vo. 386 pp. Profusely illust. Buckram.  *(Argosy)* **$60**

**Davison, C.**
- A study of recent earthquakes. 1905. xii,355 pp. 80 ills. One section loose. Sl foxing. Contemporary Science Series.  *(Whitehart)* **£15**

**Davison, Charles & Smith, Franklin**
- Autoplastic bone surgery. Phila: 1916. 1st edn. 369 pp.  *(Fye)* **$100**

**Davson, Hugh**
- The physiology of the eye. London: 1949. 1st edn. 8vo. 451 pp. 301 ills. Cloth. Dw. Author's pres copy, sgnd.  *(Argosy)* **$35**

**Davson, Hugh (ed.)**
- The eye. New York & London: 1962. 1st edn. 4 vols. 8vo. Cloth. Dw.  *(Argosy)* **$125**

**Davy, Humphry**
- Elements of agricultural chemistry, in a course of lectures for the Board of Agriculture. 1813. 1st edn. 4to. viii,323, lxiii,[4 index] pp. 10 plates. Plates sl foxed & offset. Contemp calf, rebacked.
  *(Whitehart)* £150
- Elements of agricultural chemistry. London: 1813. 1st edn. 4to. 323,lxiii,[4] pp. 10 engvd plates (1 fldg). Lge paper copy, untrimmed, in orig bds, cloth spine worn at extremities.
  *(Oasis)* $200
- Elements of agricultural chemistry, in a course of lectures for the Board of Agriculture. London: 1813. 1st edn. 4to. [v]-viii, 323,lxiii, [4] pp. 10 engvd plates. Sl foxing. Mod half-calf, new endpapers. Armorial b'plate. *(Deighton Bell)* £140
- Elements of agricultural chemistry London: Longmans, 1821. 3rd edn. x,415 pp. 9 plates. 3 leaves washed, margins dusty & marked. New half-calf, mrbld bds, uncut.
  *(Pollak)* £40
- Elements of chemical philosophy. 1812. Part 1, Vol 1 (all published). xiv,511 pp. 12 plates, errata leaf. Uncut. Orig paper-cvrd bds, worn, rebacked. *(Antiq Sc)* £380
- On the safety lamp for coal miners; with some researches on flame. London, R. Hunter, 1818. 1st edn. 8vo. viii,148 pp. Half-title, fldg engvd frontis. Linen-backed blue bds, antique style. *(Antiq Sc)* $875

**[Davy, Sir Humphry]**
- A syllabus of a course of lectures on chemistry, delivered at the Royal Institution of Great Britain. London: ... Royal Institution, 1802. 1st edn. 8vo. [vi],91 pp. Minor age-stains. Mod grey bds, red mor label. *(Deighton Bell)* £185

**Dawbarn, R.H.M.**
- An aid to materia medica. New York: Putnam, 1894. 3rd ed, revsd & enlgd by Wolsey Hopkins. Sm 8vo. 133 pp. Interleaved with ms notes of Emil A. Muller of the College of Physicians and Surgeons.
  *(Xerxes)* $45
- Treatment of certain malignant growths by excision of external carotids. Phila: 1903. Cold frontis. *(Argosy)* $40

**Dawkins, W.B.**
- Early man in Britain and his place in the Tertiary Period. 1880. xxiii,537 pp. 168 text ills. Contemp sgntrs on title. *(Whitehart)* £25

**Dawson, C.C.**
- Saratoga: Its mineral waters. New York: 1874. Revsd edn. 16mo. 64 pp. Views & maps. Ex lib. Inscrbd by author. *(Argosy)* $40

**Dawson, P.**
- Electric railways and tramways, their construction and operation. A practical handbook ... 1897. 4to. xxvi,[1],677 pp. 503 figs in text, 183 tables. New cloth. Lib stamps. *(Whitehart)* £40

**Dax, E. Cunningham**
- Experimental studies in psychiatric art. London: [1953]. 1st edn. 100 pp. 51 ills, some cold. Dw. *(Argosy)* $40

**Day, Albert**
- Methomania: treatise on alcoholic poisoning. Boston: 1867. 1st edn. 70 pp. *(Argosy)* $40

**de Allande, I. & Orias, O.**
- Cytology of the human vagina. New York: 1950. 1st English translation. 286 pp.
  *(Fye)* $30

**de Beer, Gavin**
- Embryos and ancestors. Oxford: 1940. 1st edn. 108 pp. *(Scientia)* $35

**de Beer, Gavin (ed.)**
- Evolution: essays on aspects of evolutionary biology presented to E.S. Goodrich on his seventieth birthday. Oxford: 1938. 1st edn. 351 pp. *(Scientia)* $45

**de Fleury, Maurice**
- Medicine and the mind. Translated ... 1900. xi,373 pp. 14 figs & diags. Orig cloth, sl worn. One section loose. *(Whitehart)* £35
- Medicine and the mind. Translated ... London: 1900. 8vo. Ills. Cloth spotted.
  *(Argosy)* $40

**De Ford, W.H.**
- Lectures on general anaesthesia in dentistry ... Pittsburgh: 1912. Port, text ills.
  *(Argosy)* $45

**De Forest, Lee**
- Television today and tomorrow. 1945. 176 pp. Diags. Ex lib. *(Weiner)* £25

**de Martel, T.**
- See Chatelin, C. & de Martel, T.

**De Moivre, Abraham**
- Annuities upon lives: or, the valuation of annuities upon any numbers of lives ... London: ..., 1725. 1st edn. 8vo. 4,viii, 108,[2 tables]. Errata slip pasted down. W'staining in margins. Contemp calf, rebacked, crnrs rubbed. *(Pickering)* $650
- The doctrine of chances: or, a method of calculating the probabilities of events in play. London: for the author ..., 1738. 2nd, enlgd, edn. [iv],xiv, [ii blank],258,[i errata]. Some foxing. Lge copy in contemp calf, rebacked &

recrnrd.                    *(Pickering)* **$800**
- The doctrine of chances: or, a method of
calculating the probabilities of events in play.
London: Frank Cass, 1967. Facsimile reprint
of 2nd, 1738, edn. Cloth gilt.    *(Pollak)* **£20**

**de Morgan, Augustus**
- A budget of paradoxes. London: Longmans,
Green, 1872. vii,511 pp. Half-mor, rubbed.
Ex Inner Temple lib. very good working
copy.                         *(Pollak)* **£75**
- A budget of paradoxes. Chicago: 1915. 2nd
edn, edited by David E. Smith. 2 vols. 402;
387 pp.                     *(Scientia)* **$55**
- The differential and integral calculus. 1842.
Thick 8vo. xx,785,64 pp. Lib stamp on title,
last leaf & front pastedown. Orig dec blind-
stamped cloth, a little worn, front hinge loose.
                              *(Weiner)* **£40**
- The differential and integral calculus,
containing differentiation, integration ...
London: Robert Baldwin, 1842. 1st edn.
xx,785, [iii],64. A little foxing at front. Orig
cloth, rebacked with old spine relaid.
                              *(Pollak)* **£50**
- The differential and integral calculus,
containing differentiation, integration ... with
applications to algebra ... and mechanics ...
London: Robert Baldwin, 1842. 1st edn.
Thick 8vo. xx,785,64 pp. Orig cloth.
                           *(Rootenberg)* **$185**
- Elementary illustrations of the differential
and integral calculus. Chicago: Open Court
Publishing, 1899. New edn. viii,144 pp.
                              *(Pollak)* **£25**
- An essay on probabilities and on their
application to life contingencies and
insurance offices. London: Longman, Orme,
et al., 1838. 1st edn. 8vo. xviii,306 pp, 40 pp
appendix. Engvd title, text diags. Occas
browning. Lacks pub ctlg. Orig cloth.
                           *(Rootenberg)* **$200**
- An essay on probabilities and on their
application to life contingencies and
insurance offices. London: Longman, Orme,
1838. xviii, 306,xl pp. New full calf gilt.
                              *(Pollak)* **£55**
- An essay on probabilities and on their
application to life contingencies and
insurance offices. London: n.d. 306,xl pp.
Spine chipped.             *(Scientia)* **$55**
- On the study and difficulties of mathematics.
Chicago: Open Court Publishing, 1910. 3rd
reprint edn. Faded.          *(Pollak)* **£25**

**De Quincey, Thomas**
- Confessions of an English opium-eater.
London: Taylor & Hessey, 1822. 1st edn.
vi,206,[2 advts] pp. Old half-mor, mrbld
edges. A trivial stain on first few leaves. With
the half-title & advts.      *(Dailey)* **$500**

**Deaderick, W.H. & Thompson, L.**
- Endemic diseases of the Southern States.
Phila: 1916. 1st edn. 546 pp. 1st edn. 4to.
Cloth. Ex lib.               *(Argosy)* **$40**

**Dean, C.G.T.**
- The Royal Hospital, Chelsea. London: 1950.
1st edn. Cloth. Dw.          *(Argosy)* **$25**

**Dearborn, George van Ness**
- Moto-sensory development: observations on
the first three years of a child. Balt: Warwick
& York Inc., 1910. 1st edn. viii,215,[1] pp.
12mo. Green cloth. Lacking frontis
photograph.                    *(Gach)* **$35**

**Deaver, John**
- Enlargement of the prostate: its history,
anatomy ... technique of operations, and after-
treatment. Phila: 1905. 1st edn. 266 pp. 108
full-page plates.             *(Fye)* **$100**

**Deaver, John B., et al.**
- The breast: its anomalies, its diseases, and
their treatment. Phila: 1917. 1st edn. 724 pp.
Ex lib.                       *(Fye)* **$100**
- The breast: its anomalies, its diseases, and
their treatment. Phila: P. Blakiston's Son,
1917. 217 ills, 8 cold plates.    *(Fye)* **$45**

**Deaver, John D.**
- A treatise on appendicitis. Phila: 1896. 1st
edn. 168,32 [ctlg] pp. 32 plates, mostly cold.
Orig cloth.                   *(Oasis)* **$80**

**Deavitch, Eugene**
- In search of complications. An
autobiography. New York: 1940. Tall 8vo.
Cloth.                       *(Argosy)* **$35**

**DeBakey, Michael**
- See Elkin, Daniel C. & DeBakey, Michael
- See Kilduffe, Robert & DeBakey, Michael

**Debierre, C.**
- Malformations of the genital organs of
women. Phila: 1905. 1st English translation.
182 pp. 85 w'cuts.            *(Fye)* **$75**

**Debye, Peter**
- Polar molecules. New York: 1929. 1st edn.
172 pp. Spine frayed.      *(Scientia)* **$75**

**Decoursey, Elbert & Ash, J.E.**
- Atlas of ophthalmic pathology. Omaha: 1942.
3rd edn. 4to. Ills. Cloth.    *(Argosy)* **$50**

**Dedekind, Richard**
- Essays on the theory of numbers. Translated
... Chicago: Open Court Publishing, 1909.
[viii], 115,[v] pp.          *(Pollak)* **£20**

**Dee, Arthur**
- Fasciculus chemicus: or chymical collections, expressing the ingress ... of the secret hermetick science ... London: ... for Richard Mynne, 1650. 1st edn in English. 8vo. [50],268 pp. Engvd title & horoscope. Sep title for 2nd part. Contemp half-calf.
*(Dailey)* **$3,500**

**Deecke, Theodore**
- The condition of the brain in insanity. N.p.: [1881]. 32 pp. Diag. Orig printed wraps.
*(Argosy)* **$27.50**

**Deeny, James (ed.)**
- Tubercolosis in Ireland. Report of the National Tubercolosis Survey. [Dublin]: 1954. Tall 8vo. Ills.          *(Argosy)* **$35**

**Defoe, Daniel**
- An abridgement of the history of the Great Plague in London ... London: for C. & J. Rivington, 1824. New edn. 12mo. [vi],192 pp. Contemp tree calf, some rubbing. Mor prize label inset to front cvr.   *(Pollak)* **£16**
- An essay upon publick credit. London: by the Booksellers, 1710. 3rd edn. 8vo. New wraps.
*(Marlborough)* **£350**

**Degensheim, G.A.**
- See Hurwitz, Alfred & Degensheim, G.A.

**Dejerine,, J.J. & Gauckler, E.**
- The psychoneuroses and their treatment by psychotherapy. Translated ... Phila: n.d. [ca 1913]. 1st edn in English. Tall 8vo. Cloth.
*(Argosy)* **$40**

**Delafield, John, et al.**
- Journal of the proceedings of a convention of literary and scientific gentlemen, held in the common council chamber of the City of New York. New York: Leavitt & Carvill, 1933. 2nd edn. Tall 8vo. Reproduction of 1831 edn.
*(McDowell)* **£40**

**Delaval, Edward Hussey**
- An experimental inquiry into the cause of the changes of colours in opake and coloured bodies ... [second part: A letter ... 1756]. London: for J. Nourse, 1777. 1st edn. 4to. [ii],lxxv,138 pp. Without the errata leaf. Contemp calf, worn, jnts weak.
*(Pickering)* **$400**

**Delavan, David B.**
- Early days of the Prebyterian Hospital, New York City. N.p.: Privately printed, 1926.
*(Argosy)* **$60**

**DeLucchi, M.R., et al.**
- A stereotaxic atlas of the chimpanzee brain ... Berkeley and Los Angeles: University of

California Press, 1965. 1st edn. Sq 4to. [78]ff. Cold frontis, photographs & outline plates throughout. Orig cloth.       *(Zeitlin)* **$100**

**Demikhov, V.P.**
- Experimental transplantation of vital organs. New York: 1962. 1st English translation. 285 pp. Ex lib.                     *(Fye)* **$50**

**Democritus Junior**
- See Burton, Robert

**Dempster, J.H.**
- Pathfinders of physiology. Detroit Medical Journal Co.: 1914. 66 pp. Ports. *(Argosy)* **$25**

**Dench, Edward**
- Diseases of the ear. New York: 1894. 1st edn. 645 pp. ills.                      *(Fye)* **$20**

**Dendy, Walter Cooper**
- The philosophy of mystery. New York: Harper & Brothers, 1845. [iv],442 pp. Orig cloth, chipped at extremities.   *(Gach)* **$50**

**Denison, Charles**
- Rocky Mountains health resorts. An analytic study of high altitudes in relation to the arrest of chronic pulmonary diseases. Boston: 1881. 2nd edn. 8vo. Ills. Orig cloth. Ex lib.
*(Argosy)* **$45**

**Denman, Thomas**
- Aphorisms on the application and use of the forceps and vectis; on preternatural labours ... and with convulsions. Phila: 1803. 1st Amer edn. 108 pp.                 *(Fye)* **$400**
- Collection of engravings, tending to illustrate the generation and parturition of animals, and of the human species. London: J. Johnson, 1787. Folio. 15 (only) engvd plates, explanatory text in English & French. Half-calf.                        *(Argosy)* **$400**
- An introduction to the practice of midwifery. With notes ... New York: 1821. 683 pp. 16 engvd plates. Full lea.          *(Fye)* **$175**

**Dennis, Frederic S.**
- Selected surgical papers (1876 - 1914). New York: Private printed, 1934. 1st edn. 2 vols. Thick 4to. Port, num ills, bibliog. Cloth-backed bds.                    *(Argosy)* **$60**

**Dennis, Wayne**
- The Hopi child. New York & London: 1940. 1st edn. xii,204 pp. 8 half-tones. Red cloth, some shelfwear. Sgnd by author on half-title.
*(Gach)* **$50**

**Denny-Brown, D.**
- Diseases of the basal ganglia and subthalamic nuclei. New York: Oxford University Press, [1946]. Sm 8vo. 71 pp. Cloth. *(Argosy)* **$35**

**Denslow, L.N.**
- A surgical treatment of locomotor ataxia. London: Bailliere, Tindall & Cox, 1912. 8vo. ix,118 pp. *(Poitras)* **$30**

**Denton, William**
- Is Darwin right? Or, the origin of man. Wellesley, Mass: 1881. 1st edn. 12mo. 193 pp. Orig cloth, somewhat worn, spine faded, shaken. *(M&S)* **$22.50**

**DePalma, Anthony**
- Surgery of the shoulder. Phila: 1950. 1st edn. 438 pp. *(Fye)* **$25**

**DePasquale, N.P.**
- See Burch, George E. & DePasquale, N.P.

**Dercum, Francis X.**
- A clinical manual of mental diseases. Phila: W.B. Saunders, 1913. 1st edn. 425 pp. *(Gach)* **$37.50**
- An essay on the physiology of mind: an interpretation based on ... physical and chemical considerations. Phila: W.B. Saunders, 1922. 1st edn. [ii],150 pp. Orig cloth. *(Gach)* **$30**
- An essay on the physiology of mind. An interpretation ... Phila: 1922. 2nd edn. 12mo. Cloth. *(Argosy)* **$25**

**Derenzy, George Webb**
- Enchiridion: or a hand for the one-handed. London: 1823. 8vo. 20 pp. 20 w'cut ills. Mod mrbld bds, mor label. Offprint of The Pamphleteer, with its own pagination. *(Deighton Bell)* **£55**

**Derham, William**
- The artificial clock-maker. A treatise of watch, and clock-work ... London: for James Knapton, 1696. 1st edn. 8vo in 4s. [12],132 pp. W'cut plate, 2 other w'cut ills in text. Some w'staining, dust-soiled throughout. Contemp calf, spine chipped, rubbed. *(Pickering)* **$2,500**

**Desault, P.J.A.**
- A treatise on fractures, luxations and other affections of the bones. Translated ...Phila: 1817. 398 pp. 3 copperplates. New wraps. Ex lib. *(Argosy)* **$60**

**Deschweinitz, G.E.**
- Diseases of the eye. Phila: 1897. 2nd edn. 679 pp. *(Fye)* **$20**

**Descriptive ...**
- A descriptive catalogue of the minerals ... of Scarborough ... See Kendall, Francis

**Despard, L.L.**
- Textbook of massage and remedial

gymnastics. London: Henry Frowde, 1914. 2nd edn. Sm 4to. 413 pp. Cold & b/w ills. Upper front hinge tearing, inner hinges cracking. *(Xerxes)* **$45**

**Detwiler, Samuel R.**
- Neuroembryology: an experimental study. New York: 1936. 1st edn. Text ills, graphs. Pencil underlining. *(Argosy)* **$30**

**Deutsch, Albert**
- The mentally ill in America: a history of their care and treatment from colonial times. Garden City: 1937. 1st edn. 530 pp. Ills. *(Argosy)* **$35**

**Deutsch, Helene**
- Psycho-analysis of the neuroses. Translated ... London: Hogarth Press, 1932. 1st edn. *(Argosy)* **$40**

**Dewees, William P.**
- A compendious system of midwifery ... Phila: Carey, Lea & Carey, 1828. 3rd edn. 4to. 644 pp. 18 plates (2 reprd at inner edge). Foxing. Full lea. *(Poitras)* **$75**
- A compendious system of midwifery ... Phila: 1828. 3rd edn. 644 pp. 18 engvd plates. Full lea. *(Fye)* **$100**
- A compendious system of midwifery ... Phila: 1835. 7th edn. 660 pp. 18 engvd plates. Full lea. *(Fye)* **$100**
- An essay on the means of lessening pain and facilitating certain cases of difficult parturition. Phila: 1819. 2nd edn. 156 pp. Some w'stains. Orig bds, paper backstrip cracked and worn. *(Fye)* **$250**
- A practice of physic ... Phila: 1833. 2nd edn. Thick 8vo. 819 pp. Foxing. Ex lib. *(Argosy)* **$45**
- A practice of physic, comprising most of the diseases not treated of in "Diseases of Females" and "Diseases of Children". Phila: 1830. 1st edn. 2 vols. 8vo. Contemp calf. *(Argosy)* **$175**
- A treatise on the diseases of females. Phila: 1828. 2nd edn. 542 pp. 12 engvd plates. Full lea. *(Fye)* **$200**
- Treatise on the diseases of females. Phila: Carey & Lea: 1831. 3rd edn, revsd & crrctd. 8vo. Orig sheep, worn. Ex lib. *(Argosy)* **$100**
- Treatise on the physical and medical treatment of children. 1829. 3rd edn with crrctns. Sheep. *(Allen)* **$25**

**Dewey, Evelyn**
- Behaviour development in infants. A survey of the literature on prenatal and postnatal activity 1920 - 1934. New York: 1935. viii,321 pp. *(Jenner)* **£20**

**Dewey, Willis A.**
- Essentials of homeopathic therapies ... Phila:

**Boericke & Tafel**, 1898. 2nd edn. 283 pp.
Orig red cloth, spine & jnts a little rubbed.
*(Jenner)* £16
- See Boericke, William & Dewey, Willis A.

**Dewhurst, Kenneth**
- Dr. Thomas Sydenham (1624 - 1689), his life
and original writings. London: Wellcome,
1966. 1st edn. 8vo. Frontis & ills. Dw.
*(McDowell)* £24

**Diamond, Louis K.**
- See Blackfan, Kenneth D. & Diamond, Louis
K.

**Dibblee, George Binney**
- Instinct and intuition - a study in mental
duality. London: 1939. 394 pp. Ills, some
cold. Sl foxing. Orig black cloth. *(Jenner)* £10

**Dibdin, W.J.**
- Practical photometry: a guide to the study of
the measurement of light. 1889. 1st edn.
xv,227 pp. 2 fldg plates, 32 ills. Owner's
name stamped on title. Orig cloth, sl dust-
stained, two crnrs worn.     *(Whitehart)* £18

**Dick, Robert**
- Derangements, primary and reflex, of the
organs of digestion. Phila: 1842. 1st Amer
edn. 8vo. Half-calf. Ex lib.   *(Argosy)* $45
- Derangements, primary and reflex, of the
organs of digestion; with an addition ... [and]
a new method of treating cases of functional
neuralgia. London: 1843. xliii,384 pp. Orig
brown cloth. Bds worn & stained, spine torn,
hinge cracked.      *(Jenner)* £15

**Dick, Thomas**
- The Christian philosopher; or, the
connection of science and philosophy with
religion. Glasgow: Collins, [1846]. New edn,
revsd & greatly enlgd. 2 vols in 1. xii,17-314;
viii,9-333,[iii] pp. Frontis, 55 ills. Spine ends
& crnrs a little worn.      *(Pollak)* £25

**Dickinson, H.W. & Jenkins, R.**
- James Watt and the steam engine. The
memorial volume prepared for the Committee
of the Watt Centenary Commemoration at
Birmingham, 1919. Oxford: 1927. 1st edn.
Lge 4to. xvi,415 pp. Frontis, 104 full-page
plates, 2 maps, 39 ills. Orig cloth, marked.
*(Whitehart)* £125

**Dickinson, W.H.**
- A treatise of albuminaria. New York: 1881.
300 pp. Cold lithos.      *(Fye)* $40

**Dickinson, William H.**
- Medicine old and new. London: 1899. 47 pp.
*(Argosy)* $20
- Occasional papers on medical subjects, 1855

- 1896. London: 1896.     *(Argosy)* $35

**Dickson, Leonard E.**
- Linear groups, with an exposition of the
Galois field theory. Leipzig: B.G. Teubner,
1901. 1st edn. x,312 pp. Sl cvr rubbing.
*(Diamond)* $75

**Dickson, R.W.**
- The farmer's companion. 1813. 2 vols. 946
pp. 103 plates (40 fldg, 2 cold). Sl worming in
vol I, not affecting text). Full speckled calf.
*(Phenotype)* £160
- Improved system of management of livestock
and cattle: or, a practical guide to the
perfecting and improvement of the several
breeds and varieties ... [1824]. 4to. iv,504;
510 pp. Port, engvd title. 32 plates. Rebnd
half-mor. Portion of p 364 lacking.
*(Phenotype)* £165

**Dickson, S.**
- The fallacies of the faculty, with the chromo-
thermal system of medicine. 1862. New edn.
lii,188 pp. Orig cloth. Author's pres copy.
*(Whitehart)* £35

**Dickson, Samuel**
- The unity of disease analytically and
synthetically proved: with facts and cases
subversive of the received practice of physic
... [1839]. xxii,200 pp. Orig cloth-backed bds,
paper label. May lack leaf after title (?
dedication).      *(Weiner)* £30

**Dickson, Samuel H.**
- Essays on life, sleep, paint, etc. Phila: 1852.
1st edn. Orig cloth.      *(Argosy)* $40

**Dickson, Samuel Henry**
- Studies in pathology and therapeutics. New
York: William Wood & Co., 1867. 8vo. 201
pp.      *(Poitras)* $30

**Diday, Charles J.P.E.**
- A treatise on syphilis in newborn children and
infants at the breast. Translated ... London:
New Sydenham Society, 1859. 1st English
edn. 8vo. xii,272 pp. Some upper crnrs
folded, sgntr on flyleaf. Orig cloth, hinges
strained, spine stained. *(Bow Windows)* £25
- A treatise on syphilis in newborn children.
London: New Sydenham Society, 1859. 1st
edn in English. 272 pp. Orig cloth, rebacked.
*(Oasis)* $60
- A treatise on syphilis in newborn children and
infants at the breast. Translated ... New York:
Wood & Co., 1883. xii,310 pp. Color frontis.
Dec cloth, sl cvr soiling.      *(Diamond)* $25

**Didusch, William**
- A collection of urogenital drawings. New
York: 1952. 1st edn. 4to 222 pp. Inscrbd &

autographed by author.          *(Fye)* **$175**

**Diethelm, Oskar**
- Treatment in psychiatry. New York: 1936.
1st edn. 8vo. 476 pp. Cloth.    *(Argosy)* **$30**

**Dieulafait, Louis**
- Diamonds and precious stones, a popular
account of gems. 1874. xii,291 pp. Ills, diags.
Cloth worn, spine defective.     *(Weiner)* **£15**

**Digby, Kenelm**
- Immunity in health. London: 1919. 1st edn
*(Argosy)* **$30**

**Digby, Sir Kenelm**
- Chymical secrets, and rare experiments in
physick & philosophy, with figures ...
containing many rare and unheard of
medicines ... Printed Will. Cooper, 1683-82.
1st edn. A-S8; [16],272 pp. 4 etched plates.
Separate title to part II. Half-calf, antique.
*(Dailey)* **$1,750**

**[Digby, Kenelm]**
- Two treatises: In the one of which, the nature
of bodies, in the other, the nature of mans
soule, is looked into ... London: John
Williams, 1645. 1st English edn. 8vo.
[11]ff,429; [4]ff,143,[26] pp. 2 sep titles.
Lacks engvd port. Contemp calf, rebacked.
*(Rootenberg)* **$850**

**Diller, Theodore**
- Pioneer medicine in Western Pennsylvania.
New York: Hoeber, 1927. 8vo. xiv,230 pp. 26
full-page ills.              *(Poitras)* **$40**
- Pioneer medicine in Western Pennsylvania.
New York: 1927. 1st edn. Many ills.
*(Argosy)* **$60**

**Dimbleby, J.B.**
- All past time ... containing a classification of
all eclipses and transits from creation ... 1897.
Port frontis, charts & diags throughout. Sl
foxing. Cloth gilt. *(Quinto Charing Cross)* **£10**

**Dingley, Amasa**
- An oration on the improvement of medicine.
New York: printed by John Buel, [1794]. 1st
edn. 8vo. 39 pp, with the half-title. Loss in
margin of one leaf not affecting text. Linen-
backed blue bds with paper label, antique
style.                    *(Antiq Sc)* **$185**

**Dinsdale, Alfred**
- First principles of television. 1932. 1st edn.
xv,241 pp. Many plates, ills. Ex lib with
stamps on plate margins.      *(Weiner)* **£45**
- Television (seeing by wire or wireless). 1926.
62 pp. Plates. Orig printed bds. Lacking the
orig dw.                     *(Weiner)* **£90**
- Television. With a foreword by Dr. J.A.

Fleming. London: Television Press, 1928.
2nd edn. xx,180,[ii advts]. Sm lib stamp on
title.                       *(Pollak)* **£35**

**Dirac, Paul**
- The principles of quantum mechanics.
Oxford: 1930. 1st edn. 257 pp. *(Scientia)* **$100**
- The principles of quantum mechanics.
Oxford: 1935. 2nd edn. 300 pp. *(Scientia)* **$50**
- The principles of quantum mechanics.
Oxford: 1947. 3rd edn. 311 pp. *(Scientia)* **$30**

**Dircks, Henry**
- The life, times, and scientific labours of the
second Marquis of Worcester. To which is
added, a reprint of his Century of Inventions,
1663 ... London: Quaritch, 1865. One of 30
copies on lge paper. 4to. xxiv,[2],624 pp. 2
plates, ills. Mod buckram.     *(Zeitlin)* **$150**
- The life, times, and scientific labours of the
second Marquis of Worcester. To which is
added, a reprint of his Century of Inventions,
1663 ... London: Quaritch, 1865. Thick 8vo.
1st edn. Frontis. engvs. Pub cloth,
untrimmed.                 *(McDowell)* **£110**

**Directions ...**
- Directions for preparing manure ... See
Maconochie, Allan, Lord Meadowbank

**[Directory ...]**
- American electrical directory for 1886. Being
a complete book of reference of the electric
lighting interests of North America. Ft.
Wayne: 1886. 2nd edn. 495 pp. Gilt dec red
mor, worn. A.e.g.             *(Elgen)* **$95**
- The dentists register. London: Dental Board
of the United Kingdom, 1939. lxxxi,376,[iv]
pp. Additional 16 pp listing of corporate
bodies & directors at end. Lacks 1st leaf of
prelims, some red underlining, spine torn at
head, crnrs worn.            *(Pollak)* **£25**
- Medical directory, 1936. London: Churchill,
1936. 92nd annual issue. lxviii,2379 pp.
Faded.                       *(Pollak)* **£15**
- Medical directory, 1946. London: Churchill,
1946. 102nd annual issue. xcii,2559 pp.
*(Pollak)* **£15**

**Diseases ...**
- Diseases and remedies. A concise survey of
the most modern methods of medicine.
Written especially for the drug trade by
physicians and pharmacists. 1898. Orig blind-
stamped cloth, rebacked.    *(Whitehart)* **£18**

**Ditton, Humphry**
- An institution of fluxions: containing the first
principles ... Revised, corrected and
improved, by John Clarke. London: for James
& John Knapton, 1726. 2nd edn. [xvi],240
pp. Contemp calf, rebacked with remains of
old spine relaid.            *(Pollak)* **£125**

**Dixey, G.A.**
- Epidemic influenza. A study in comparative statistics. Oxford, 1892. xiv,29,[34] pp. 11 fldg charts, 22 tables. Orig cloth.
*(Whitehart)* £18

**Dixon, Edward H.**
- Scenes in the practice of a New York surgeon. New York: [1855]. 12mo. 8 plates by Darley. Cloth, spine ends worn. *(Argosy)* $40
- Scenes in the practice of a New York surgeon. New York: 1855. 1st edn. 407 pp. W'cuts by Darley. Front free endpaper missing. Inner hinges cracked. *(Fye)* $40
- Some abnormal conditions of the sexual and pelvic organs, which impair virility. New York: n.d. [ca 1890]. Tall 8vo. 40 pp. Uncut & partially unopened. Printed wraps. Ex lib. *(Argosy)* $30
- A treatise on diseases of the sexual organs: Adapted to popular and professional reading, and the exposition of quackery ... New York: Wm. Taylor, 1845. 1st edn. 12mo. [1],12,260 pp: 4 full page ills. Orig cloth, spine faded. Scattered foxing. *(M&S)* $35

**Dixon, Joshua**
- The literary life of William Brownrigg ... an account of the coal mines near Whitehaven: and observations on ... epidemic fevers. London: Longman & Rees, 1801. 1st edn. 8vo. 13.[1].239 pp, errata leaf. Num figs in text. Contemp bds, rebacked. *(Dailey)* $385

**Dobell, Horace**
- On loss of weight, blood-spitting and lung disease. 1878. viii,274 pp. Cold frontis, lge table. Sm tear inside front cvr. One gathering loose, sl warped & torn. *(Jenner)* £25

**Dobzhansky, Theodosius**
- Genetics and the origin of species. New York: 1937. 1st edn. 364 pp. *(Scientia)* $60
- Heredity and the nature of man. New York: 1964. 1st edn. 179 pp. Dw. *(Scientia)* $20

**Dock, George & Bass, Charles C.**
- Hookworm disease: etiology, pathology, diagnosis, prognosis and prophylaxis. St. Louis: C.V. Mosby, 1910. 4to. 250 pp. Cold plate, 49 engvs. *(Poitras)* $75

**[Dodd, George]**
- Dodd's curiosities of industry. London: H. Lea, n.d. [1870?]. 1st edn. 8vo. Pub blind-stamped cloth, gilt. *(McDowell)* £48

**Dodd, H. & Cockett, F.B.**
- The pathology and surgery of the veins of the lower limb. 1976. 4to. [5],323 pp. Many ills. *(Whitehart)* £18

**Dodge, Raymond & Benedict, F.G.**
- Psychological effects of alcohol. Washington: 1915. Tall 8vo. 32 ills. Cloth. *(Argosy)* $50

**Dodoens, Rembert**
- A new herbal, or historie of plants ... now translated ... in English by Henry Lyte ... London: Edward Griffin, 1619. 4th English edn. Sm folio. [12]ff, 564pp. Title-page mounted. Some browning. Mod calf. *(Zeitlin)* $2,250

**Dods, John B.**
- The philosophy of electrical psychology. New York: Fowler & Wells, 1850. 1st edn. 168 pp. Initial 5 pp w'stained, foxing at end. *(Xerxes)* $60
- The philosophy of electrical psychology, in a course of twelve lectures. New York: 1851. 8vo. Frontis port. Orig blind-stamped cloth. Ex lib. *(Argosy)* $50

**Dolan, Thomas M.**
- Vaccination: its place and power. London: 1883. 1st edn. 8vo. 45 pp. Printed wraps. *(Argosy)* $25

**Dole, George T.**
- A discourse occasioned by the death, and embracing a sketch of the life of, Dr. Joseph Torrey. Salem: 1851. 8vo. Orig printed wraps, rebacked. *(Argosy)* $30

**Dollard, John, et al.**
- Frustration and aggression. New Haven & London: 1939. 1st printing. xii,209,[3] pp. Puncture to gutter of 1st 5 leaves. Owner's signature on flyleaf. Red cloth, shelfworn. *(Gach)* $25

**Domeier, Wm.**
- Observations on the climate, manners & amusements of Malta, for invalids repairing to that island for the recovery of health. London: 1810. 116 pp. Wraps. *(Argosy)* $50

**Donaldson, Henry Herbert**
- The growth of the brain: A study of the nervous system in relation to education. [20],374 pp. 77 ills, 64 tables. Orig cloth, sl faded & dust stained. Front inner hinge cracked. *(Whitehart)* £25
- The growth of the brain: a study of the nervous system ... London: 1895. 1st edn. Sm 8vo. Num text ills. Cloth. *(Argosy)* $100
- The growth of the brain; A study of the nervous system in relation to education. London: 1895. 1st edn. *(Scientia)* $55
- The growth of the brain; A study of the nervous system in relation to education. London & New York: 1914. 12mo. 374,[2] pp. Advts. Red cloth. *(Gach)* $25
- The growth of the brain. New York: 1914.

Text ills. *(Argosy)* **$50**

**Donaldson, James**
- See Anson, Barry & Donaldson, James
- View of the agriculture of the county of Elgin or Moray, lying between the Spey and the Findhorn ... for the consideration of the Board of Agriculture. London: C. Clarke, 1794. 1st 4to edn. 43 pp. Half-title. Sewed as issued, outer leaves a little soiled.
*(Blackwell's)* **£50**

**Donaldson, Peter**
- A review of the present systems of medicine and chirurgy of Europe and America ... New York: 1821. 1st edn. x,440 pp. Browning & foxing. Contemp calf, rubbed. *(Elgen)* **$160**

**Donders, F.C.**
- An essay on the nature and ... anomalies of refraction. Phila: 1899. Revised edn. 81 pp. Half mor, sl worn. *(Oasis)* **$30**
- An essay on the nature and the consequences of anomalies of refraction. Phila: 1899. 81 pp. Half lea. *(Fye)* **$40**
- On the anomalies of accomodation and refraction of the eye. With a preliminary essay on physiological dioptics. 1864. xvii,635 pp. Diags. 3 leaves not caught in binding.
*(Weiner)* **£50**
- On the anomalies of accomodation and refraction of the eye. With a preliminary essay on physiological dioptics. New Sydenham Society, 1864. xvii,635 pp. Orig cloth, spine sl worn. *(Whitehart)* **£70**

**Donkin, A.S.**
- On the relation between diabetes and food and its application to the treatment of the disease. 1875. viii,186 pp. Orig cloth dull, front inner hinge cracked. *(Whitehart)* **£20**

**Donkin, W.F.**
- An essay on the theory of the combination of observations. Oxford: Ashmolean Society, 1844. 71 pp. Errata slip. Orig printed wraps.
*(Weiner)* **£8**

**Donne, Alphonse**
- Change of air and scene; a physician's hints. London: 1873. Ex lib. *(Argosy)* **$40**

**Donovan, Edward**
- Instructions for collecting and preserving various subjects of natural history ... together with a treatise on the management of insects ... London: for the Author ... 1794. 1st edn. 8vo. [iv],86 pp. 2 engvd plates. Contemp mrbld bds, rebacked. *(Burmester)* **£285**
- The natural history of British shells. London: 1799-1803. 5 vols in. 8vo. 180 hand-cold plates. A few pencil annotations, 1 plate badly foxed. Half blue mor. *(Wheldon & Wesley)* **£850**

- The natural history of British shells. London: 1799-1800. 5 vols in 2. 8vo. 180 hand-cold plates. 3 plates rather foxed. Titles to vols 3-5 discarded by the binder. Contemp full calf.
*(Wheldon & Wesley)* **£800**

**Doremus, R. Ogden**
- Report of elaborate experiments made with burnt ammonia alum in baking powders. [New York]: 1881. 15 pp. Orig printed wraps.
*(Argosy)* **$25**

**Dorham, William Henry**
- Results of a series of experiments on the comparative strength of Marriott & Atkinson's boiler-plate cast steel, lowmoor iron and puddled steel ... 1862. 8vo. v,58 pp. Many tables. Orig blind-stamped cloth cvrs, spine faded. *(Deighton Bell)* **£32**

**[Dossie, Robert]**
- The elaboratory laid open, or, the secrets of modern chemistry and pharmacy revealed: containing many particulars ... to be known to all practitioners in medicine. London: for J. Nourse, 1758. 1st edn. [xvi],375,9 [index] pp. Contemp calf, jnts reprd.
*(Deighton Bell)* **£250**

**Doty, Alvah H.**
- A manual in the principles of prompt aid to the injured. Designed for military and civil use. New York: Appleton, 1889 224 pp. Ills.
*(Poitras)* **$35**

**Douglas, Charles & Anne**
- The Shetland Pony. With an appendix on the making of the Shetland Pony ... Edinburgh: 1913. 1st edn. xi,176 pp. Many plates. Orig red cloth. *(Phenotype)* **£42**

**Douglas, D.M.**
- Wound healing and management. A monograph for surgeons. 1963. vii,175 pp. Ills, some cold. *(Jenner)* **£10**

**Douglas, General Sir Howard**
- An essay on the construction of military bridges and the passage of rivers in military operations. 1853. 3rd edn. xx,431 pp. Engvd frontis, num figs on 14 fldg plates. Lib stamps. Contemp half-mor, worn.
*(Weiner)* **£85**

**Douglas, James**
- Myographiae comparatae specimen: or, a comparative description of all the muscles in a man and in a quadruped. London: ... for G. Strachan, 1707. 1st edn, 2nd issue corrected. 12mo. [1],xxxvi, 216,16 pp. Wormtrail, without loss. Contemp calf, gilt spine.
*(Rootenberg)* **$285**

**Douglas, Richard**
- Surgical diseases of the abdomen. Phila: 1903. 1st edn. xii,17-883 pp. 20 full-page plates. T.e.g. Inner hinges cracked, tear at lower spine edge.            *(Elgen)* **$140**

**Dowding, G.V. (ed.)**
- Book of practical television. 1935. 320 pp. 231 ills, 62 plates.      *(Whitehart)* **£18**

**Dowler, Bennet**
- Tableau of the yellow fever of 1853, with topographical, chronological, & historical sketches of the epidemics of New Orleans ... New Orleans: 1854. 8vo. 66 pp. Sewed. Author's pres on title.       *(Argosy)* **$60**

**Downie, Major William**
- Hunting for gold. Reminiscences of personal experiences and research in the early days of the Pacific Coast from Alaska to Panama. The California Publishing Co., 1893. Frontis, num ills & ports. Orig cloth, sl worn.
         *(Edwards)* **£200**

**Dowsett, H.M.**
- Wireless telegraphy and telephony. 1920. xxxi,331 pp. Ills, diags.      *(Weiner)* **£18**
- Wireless telephony and broadcasting. 1924. 2 vols. xi,210; ix,233 pp. Plates (several cold), ports, very many ills, diags.   *(Weiner)* **£75**

**Doyen, E.**
- Surgical technique. Phila: [1900]. 38 pp. Orig printed wraps.       *(Argosy)* **$25**

**Drachmann, A.G.**
- Ktesibios, Philon and Heron. A study in ancient pneumatics. Copenhagen: 1948. 1st edn. 197 pp. Orig wraps. Last few leaves defective.       *(Scientia)* **$50**
- The mechanical technology of Greek and Roman antiquity. A study of literary sources. Copenhagen: 1963. 1st edn. 220 pp.
         *(Scientia)* **$30**

**Drake, Daniel**
- Discourses delivered by appointment before the Cincinnati Medical Library Association, Jan 9th & 10th, 1852. Cincinnati: 1852. 12mo. 93 pp. Limp cloth, chipped. Ex lib.         *(Argosy)* **$125**
- A systematic treatise ... on the principal diseases of the Interior Valley of North America, as they appear in the Caucasian, African, Indian, and Esqimaux varieties of its population. Cincinnati: 1850. 1st edn. Thick 8vo. 19 plates & maps. Mod half-calf.
         *(Argosy)* **$850**

**Drake, Nathan**
- Essays biographical, critical and historical, illustrative of the rambler, adventurer & idler

... and of the various periodical papers ... to 1809. Buckingham & London: 1809-10. 1st edn. 2 vols. Thick 16mo. 3/4 calf. Gilt top.
         *(Argosy)* **$125**
- Literary hours; or sketches critical, narrative, and poetical. Sudbury: 1800. 2nd edn, crrctd & enlgd. 2 vols. Contemp mottled calf, backs worn, inner hinges mended, armorial blindstamp.       *(Argosy)* **$85**

**Draper, John C.**
- Text-book on anatomy, physiology and hygiene, for the use of schools and families. New York: 1870. 8vo. 170 text ills. Cloth. Ex lib           *(Argosy)* **$45**

**Draper, John William**
- Human physiology, statical and dynamical; or, the conditions and course of the life of man. New York: 1856. Tall 8vo. 649 pp. Nearly 300 text w'cuts. Orig cloth, worn, jnts mended. Ex lib.       *(Argosy)* **$75**

**Drayson, A.W.**
- Cause of the supposed proper motion of the fixed stars and an explanation of the apparent acceleration of the moon's mean motion ... 1874. xxiv,311 pp. Diags. Ex lib.
         *(Weiner)* **£15**
- Untrodden ground in astronomy and geology. Giving further details of the second rotation of the earth ... London: 1890. 1st edn. 8vo. xii,305 pp. 82 figs. Orig cloth.
         *(Bow Windows)* **£20**

**Dredge, James (ed.)**
- Electric illumination by Conrad Cooke ... and H. Vivarez, with abstracts of specifications ... [1882]-1885. 2 vols. 4to. xx,693,cxc; xv,455, cccxciv,xiii pp. Fldg plates, num ills & diags. Vol II shaken in bndg & little worn at spine ends.       *(Weiner)* **£240**

**Dressler, Wilhelm & Roesler, H.**
- An atlas of electrocardiography, Springfield: 1949. 1st edn. Obl 8vo. 503 pp. Cloth.
         *(Argosy)* **$35**

**Drewitt, F.D.**
- The romance of the Apothecaries' Garden at Chelsea. London: 1924. 2nd edn. Ills.
         *(Argosy)* **$27.50**

**Drewry, G. Overend**
- Consumption and wasting diseases successfully treated by 'Hydrated Oil". London: [1877]. 24mo. 48 pp. Printed wraps. Ex lib.       *(Argosy)* **$25**

**Dreyer, J.L.E.**
- Tycho Brahe: a picture of scientific life and work in the sixteenth century. Edinburgh: 1890. 1st edn. 405 pp.   *(Scientia)* **$60**

**Drinker, Cecil K.**
- Carbon monoxide asphyxia. New York: [1938]. 1st edn. Tall 8vo. Ills. Cloth.
*(Argosy)* **$35**

**Drinkwater, H.**
- Fifty years of medical progress 1873 - 1922. 1924. ix,183 pp. Cloth dull. *(Whitehart)* **£15**
- Fifty years of medical progress 1873 - 1922. London: 1924. 1st edn. Ills.  *(Argosy)* **$35**

**Drude, Paul**
- The theory of optics, translated from the German ... 1902. x,546 pp. Diags.
*(Weiner)* **£35**

**Druitt, Robert**
- The principles and practice of modern surgery. Phila: 1850. 2nd Amer edn. 576 pp. Final 20 leaves sl defective. Full lea. *(Fye)* **$30**
- Report on the cheap wines from France, Germany, Italy ... and Australia. London: Henry Renshaw, 1873. 2nd edn. 8vo. xii,180,[8 advts] pp. Frontis, vignettes in text. Orig green cloth.  *(Dailey)* **$175**

**Drysdale, A.L.**
- Greater profits from land, the secret of successful farming ... Edinburgh: 1914. 4to. viii,187 pp. Red cloth.  *(Phenotype)* **£18**

**Du Moncel (Th.)**
- Electric lighting, translated from the French by Robert Routledge. 1882. xv,318 pp. Orig dec cloth, a little worn. Lib stamps.
*(Weiner)* **£35**

**Dubois, Paul**
- The psychic treatment of nervous disorders. (the psychoneuroses and their moral treatment). Translated ... New York & London: 1905. 8vo. Orig cloth. *(Argosy)* **$35**

**Dubois, Rene J. (ed.)**
- Bacterial and mycotic infections of man. Phila: [1948]. 4to. 785 pp. 101 ills, inc 3 cold plates. Cloth.  *(Argosy)* **$45**

**Dubreuil, Jean**
- The practice of perspective. Or, an easy method of representing natural objects according to the rules of art. Applied ... buildings, appendages, parts, furniture, &c. ... 1749. 3rd edn. 4to. 150 copper plates, many fldg. Full calf, sm split in spine.
*(Edwards)* **£150**

**Ducamp, Theodore**
- Treatise on retention of urine, caused by strictures in the urethra. Translated from French ... New York: Samuel Wood & Sons, 1827. 219 pp. Brown stain on top margin throughout. Uncut. Lacks cvr & backstrip.

*(Xerxes)* **$85**

**Duchene, Captain**
- The mechanics of the aeroplane. A study of the principles of flight, translated from French. London: Longmans, Green, 1912. 1st edn. x,231 pp, errata slip. 91 text figs.
*(Diamond)* **$45**
- The mechanics of the aeroplane. A study of the principles of flight, translated from French. London: Longmans, Green, 1912. 1st English edn. x,231 pp, 91 figs. Orig cloth.
*(Pollak)* **£20**

**Duckworth, Sir Dyce**
- The influence of character and right judgement in medicine: the Harveian Oration ... London: 1898. 53 pp. Holograph pres from the author.  *(Argosy)* **$35**

**Duckworth, Dyce (ed.)**
- Selections from the works of the late J. Warburton Begbie. New Sydenham Society, 1882. xxiv,422 pp. Frontis. Spine sl chipped & soiled. Dw.  *(Jenner)* **£25**

**Dudley, Emilius C.**
- The medicine man: being the memoirs of 50 years of medical progress. New York: n.d. [ca 1927]. 1st edn. Thick 8vo. Ills. *(Argosy)* **$30**

**Dugdale, Robert L.**
- The Jukes: a study in crime, pauperism, disease and heredity. New York: 1888. 4th edn. 121 pp.  *(Scientia)* **$37.50**
- The Jukes: a study in crime, pauperism, disease and heredity. New York: Putnam's Sons, 1910. 4th edn. v,[i],120,[i index].[iii] pp. 4 fldg tables, Spine ends a bit worn.
*(Pollak)* **£15**

**Dugdale, William**
- The history of imbanking and draining of divers fens and marshes ... and of the improvements thereby. London: Bowyer & Nichols, 1772. 2nd edn. Folio. xii,469 pp. 10 double-page maps, 1 fldg map. Blind-stamped calf, hinges renewed. *(Frew Mackenzie)* **£295**

**Duhem, Pierre**
- Thermodynamics and chemistry. Translated by G.K. Burgess. New York: 1903. 1st edn in English. 445 pp.  *(Scientia)* **$40**

**Duhring, Louis A.**
- Case of dermatitis herpetiformis (multiformis), aggravated by pregnancy and irregular menstruation. [Phila: 1884]. 16mo. 7 pp. Wraps.  *(Argosy)* **$25**
- Case of lepra maculosa et tuberosa. N.p.: n.d. [ca 1890]. 12mo. 6 pp. Wraps. *(Argosy)* **$20**
- Case of typical dermatitis herpetiformis. N.p.: [1880]. 8vo. 3 pp. Wraps. *(Argosy)* **$15**

**Duke, Marc**
- Acupuncture. New York: [1972]. 1st edn. 8vo. Ills. Cloth.                *(Argosy)* **$20**

**Duke-Elder, Stewart**
- The practice of refraction. London: 1935. 2nd edn. 8vo. 180 ills. Cloth. Ex lib.
*(Argosy)* **$25**

**Duke-Elder, Sir W.S.**
- Recent advances in ophthalmology. Phila: 1927. 1st edn. 6 cold plates, 133 ills.
*(Argosy)* **$35**

**Dunbar, Helen Flanders**
- Emotions and bodily changes: a survey of literature on psychosomatic inter-relationships 1910-33. New York: Columbia University Press, 1935. 1st edn. [ii],xviii,595 pp. Worn dw.                *(Gach)* **$50**

**Duncan, Alexander**
- Memorials of the Faculty of Physicians and Surgeons of Glasgow, 1599 - 1850, with sketch of the rise and progress of Glasgow Medical School and of the profession in the West of Scotland. Glasgow: 1896. 1st edn. Sq 4to. 4 plates.           *(Argosy)* **$85**

**Duncan, Andrew**
- Elements of therapeutics: or, first principles of the practice of physic. Edinburgh: 1773. 2nd edn. 2 vols in 1. xvi,192; 225 pp. Calf rebacked, endpapers worn.        *(Jenner)* **£32**
- Medical cases. Edinburgh: 1784. 3rd edn. viii,436. Port frontis laid down but now detchd. Heavy foxing on frontis & early pages. Mod brown cloth, red lea label.
*(Jenner)* **£50**

**Duncan, David (ed.)**
- Life and letters of Herbert Spencer. London: 1908. 1st edn. 621 pp. Partly unopened, some pages roughly cut.            *(Scientia)* **$45**
- Life and letters of Herbert Spencer. New York: 1908. 1st Amer edn. 2 vols. 414; 444 pp.                      *(Scientia)* **$45**

**Duncan, H.O.**
- The world on wheels. Paris: n.d. [ca 1926]. 2 vols. 4to. xxxii,1200 pp. Port, num ills. Margins of first 50 leaves very sl cockled. Mod qtr calf.            *(Weiner)* **£175**

**Duncan, J. Matthews**
- Cases of extra-uterine gestation & uterne haematocele. Edinburgh: 1868. 8vo. 14 pp. Wraps. Inscribed by author on title.
*(Argosy)* **$30**
- On the life of William Hunter: the Harveian Address, 13th April, 1876. Edinburgh: 1876. 8vo. 21 pp. Frontis port. Wraps. *(Argosy)* **$25**
- On the mortality of childbed and maternity

hospitals. Edinburgh: 1870. 1st edn. Half-title, xii,172 pp. Orig cloth, back reprd.
*(Elgen)* **$125**

**Duncan, John**
- Introductory address, delivered at the opening of the Edinburgh Medical School on 30th October 1877. Edinburgh: 1877. 8vo. 13 pp. Wraps.                   *(Argosy)* **$30**

**Duncan, Louis C.**
- Medical men in the American Revolution 1775-1783. Carlisle Barracks, PA: 1931. 1st edn. Army Medical Bull. No. 25. Orig wraps, cloth tape on spine.          *(Scientia)* **$75**

**Duncan, Peter Martin & Millard, William**
- A manual for the classification, training and education of the feeble-minded, imbecile, and idiotic. London: Longmans, Green, 1866. 1st edn. [xvi],191,[1] pp. Advts dated July 1865. Mauve cloth, somewhat musty, sl discolored.
*(Gach)* **$150**

**Duncan, T.C.**
- Paedophygea: the feeding and management of infants and children, and the homeopathic treatment of their common diseases. Chicago: 1888. 5th edn, revsd. 426 pp. Hinges cracked.
*(Xerxes)* **$50**

**Dunell, H.**
- British wire-drawing and wire-working machinery. 1925. 4to. xv,188 pp. 181 figs & plates, fldg map. Orig cloth, sl marked. The Engineer Series.         *(Whitehart)* **£25**

**Dunglison, Robley**
- Human physiology. Phila: Blanchard & Lea, 1856. 8th edn. 4to. 2 vols. xxiii,729,32 [pub ctlg]; xv,755 pp. Ills throughout. Full lea, sl scuffed.                      *(Poitras)* **$125**
- New remedies: the method of preparing and administering them, their effects on the healthy and diseased economy, &c. Phila: Lea & Blanchard, 1841. 3rd edn, with num modifications & addtns. 4to. xii,541,6 [pub ctlg] pp. 5 ills. Foxing. Lea.   *(Poitras)* **$50**
- On the influence of atmosphere and locality, change of air and climate; seasons; food ... elements of hygiene. Phila: Blanchard & Lea, 1835. 1st ed. 514 pp. Lea, some scuffing.
*(Poitras)* **$150**
- Syllabus of the lectures of medical jurisprudence and on the treatment of poisoning and suspended animation. University of Virginia, 1827. 142 pp. Qtr lea, mrbld bds. Ex lib.          *(Poitras)* **$100**

**Dunham, Carroll**
- Lectures on materia medica. New York: Hart, 1878. 1st edn. 2 vols. 419; 409 pp. Frontis port. Cvrs worn, backstrip of one vol coming

off. *(Xerxes)* **$75**

**Dunham, George C.**
- Military preventive medicine. Carlisle Barracks: 1938. 4to. 329 ills. 1198 pp.
*(Argosy)* **$35**

**Dunlap, Knight**
- A system of psychology. New York: Scribner's, 1912. 1st edn. xvi,368 pp.
*(Gach)* **$25**

**Dunn, Matthias**
- An historical, geological and descriptive view of the coal trade of the North of England ... Newcastle-upon-Tyne: 1844. ix,248 pp. Hand-cold fldg diag. Binder's cloth, front cvr with unsightly fading & cockling.
*(Weiner)* **£75**

**Dupytren, Guillame**
- Lectures on clinical surgery ... translated from the French ... Washington: Duff Green, 1835. 4to. vi,548 pp. Foxing. Qtr lea, mrbld bds.
*(Poitras)* **$250**

**Durant, Ghislani**
- Hygiene of the voice: its physiology and anatomy. New York: G. Schirmer, 1870. 1st edn.
*(Argosy)* **$50**
- Sea-bathing: its use and abuse. New York: 1878. 16mo. 60 pp. Printed wraps.
*(Argosy)* **$25**

**Durant, Thomas M.**
- The days of our years: short history of medicine and the American College of Physicians, 1915-65. N.p.: [1965]. 32 pp. Printed wraps.
*(Argosy)* **$25**

**Duveen, Denis & Klickstein, Herbert**
- A bibliography of the works of Antoine Laurent Lavoisier, 1743 - 1794. London: William Dawson, 1954 & 1965. 1st edn. 2 vols. 4to. With the supplement. Orig blue cloth.
*(McDowell)* **£140**

**Duvernoy, Henri M.**
- Human brainstem vessels. Berlin: 1978. Sq 4to. profusely illust. Cloth.
*(Argosy)* **$85**

**Duvries, Henri**
- Surgery of the foot. St. Louis: 1965. 2nd edn. 4to. 586 pp. Num ills. Cloth.
*(Argosy)* **$35**

**Dyer, Isadore**
- Art of medicine and other addresses, papers, &c. New Orleans: 1913. 1st edn. Frontis.
*(Argosy)* **$35**

**Dyer, K.F.**
- The biology of racial integration. Bristol: 1974. ix,46 pp. Some ills. Orig yellow cloth.

Dw. *(Jenner)* **£10**

**Dyson, Frank & Woolley, R.**
- Eclipses of the sun and moon. Oxford: 1937. 1st edn. 160 pp.
*(Scientia)* **$37.50**

**Earle, Sir James**
- A short account of the life of Mr. Percival Pott. [London: 1790]. 1st edn. 8vo. 45 pp. Port. Old wraps. Ex lib.
*(Argosy)* **$45**

**Earle, Pliny**
- History, description and statistics of the Bloomingdale Asylum for the Insane. New York: 1848. 1st edn. 136 pp. Wraps.
*(Argosy)* **$20**
- History, description and statistics of the Bloomingdale Asylum for the Insane. New York: Egbert, Hovey & King, 1848. 1st edn. 8vo. [2],136 pp. Frontis. Orig printed wraps.
*(M&S)* **$100**

**Eastcott, H.H.G.**
- Arterial surgery. Phila: 1973. 2nd edn.
*(Poitras)* **$50**

**Eaton, Amos**
- A manual of botany for the Northern and Middle States of America. Albany: Webster & Skinners, 1824. 4th edn, revsd & crrctd. 8vo. xi,12-539 pp. Infrequent small spotting. Contemp mottled calf.
*(Hemlock)* **$100**

**Eaton, Amos & Wright, John**
- North American botany, comprising the native and common cultivated plants north of Mexico. Troy: 1840. 625 pp. Full contemp sheep.
*(Argosy)* **$125**

**Ebbard, Richard J.**
- How to acquire and strengthen will-power ... a rational course of training of volition and development of energy after the methods of the Nancy School. 1902. 3rd edn rvsd. x,275 pp. Uncut, cvrs sl rubbed. *(Jenner)* **£12**

**Eberle, John**
- Notes of lectures on the theory and practice of medicine, delivered in the Jefferson Medical College, at Philadelphia. Cincinnati: 1834. 2nd edn, crrctd. 8vo. Sheep, worn.
*(Argosy)* **$60**
- A treatise of the materia medica and therapeutics. Balt: 1824-25. 2nd edn, with crrctns. 2 vols. xi,327; 401 pp. Browning & foxing. Lea, rubbed & scuffed. *(Elgen)* **$130**
- Treatise of the materia medica and therapeutics. Phila: 1836. 4th edn, enlgd & crrctd. 2 vols. Contemp calf, sl rubbed, lea labels.
*(Argosy)* **$60**
- A treatise on the diseases and physical education of children. Phila: 1848. 3rd edn. 8vo. 555 pp. Sheep. *(Hemlock)* **$50**

- A treatise on the practice of medicine. Phila:
1835. 3rd edn. 2 vols. Full calf. *(Argosy)* **$50**

**Ebstein, Wilhelm**
- The regimen to be adopted in cases of gout.
Translated by John Scott. London: Churchill,
1885. [viii],68,16 [advts] pp.   *(Pollak)* **£20**

**Eccles, W.H.**
- Wireless telegraphy and telephony, a
handbook. 1918. 2nd edn. xxiv,514 pp. Ills,
diags, advts.   *(Weiner)* **£20**

**Eck, Justus**
- The application of arc lamps to practical
purposes, a manual for arc lamp users. 1910.
101 pp. Ills, diags. 15 pp illus advts.
*(Weiner)* **£25**

**Ecker, Arthur**
- The normal cerebral angiogram. Springfield:
1951. 1st edn. Ills. 2 stereo photos inserted at
rear.   *(Oasis)* **$25**
- The normal cerebral angiogram. Springfield:
[1951]. 1st edn. Sm 8vo. Profusely illust. Red
cloth.   *(Argosy)* **$25**

**Eclectic ...**
- The eclectic and general dispensatory:
comprehending a system of pharmacy,
materia medica, the formulae of the London,
Edinburgh, and Dublin pharmacopoeias.
Phila: Tower & Hogan, 1827. 4to. 627 pp. 7
plates. Some staining.   *(Poitras)* **$75**

**Economo, Constantin von**
- Encephalitis lethargica. Its sequelae and
treatment. Translated ... London: Oxford
University Press, 1931. xiv,[ii],200 pp. 21
ills.   *(Pollak)* **£25**

**Eddington, Arthur S.**
- Fundamental theory. Oxford: 1953. 292 pp.
3rd printing. Dw   *(Scientia)* **$75**
- The internal constitution of the stars.
Cambridge: University Press, 1926. 1st edn.
8vo. viii,407 pp. Orig blue cloth, cvrs lightly
worn. Pub pres copy James Edward Clark.
*(Rootenberg)* **$250**
- New pathways in science. The Messenger
Lectures for 1934. Cambridge: University
Press, 1935. x,333 pp. 4 plates. *(Pollak)* **£20**
- The philosophy of physical science. The
Tarner lectures 1938. Cambridge: University
Press, 1939. 1st edn. ix,230 pp. A few
marginal pencil notes.   *(Pollak)* **£20**
- Space, time and gravitation. An outline of the
general theory of relativity. Cambridge: 1920.
1st edn. vi,218 pp. 1 plate. Orig cloth.
*(Whitehart)* **£25**
- Space, time and gravitation. An outline of the
general theory of relativity. Cambridge:
University Press, 1935. Reprint of 1920 1st

edn. vi,218 pp. Frontis, 20 text figs.
*(Pollak)* **£15**
- Stars and atoms. Oxford: 1927. 127 pp.
Plates.   *(Weiner)* **£25**
- Stellar movements and the structure of the
universe. 1914. xii,266 pp. 4 plates, diags.
*(Weiner)* **£85**
- Stellar movements and the structure of the
universe. London: 1914. 1st edn. 266 pp.
*(Scientia)* **$125**
- The theory of relativity and its influence on
scientific thought. The Romanes Lectures for
1922. Oxford: Clarendon Press, 1922. 1st
edn. 32 pp. Orig wraps.   *(Pollak)* **£25**

**Edebohls, George M.**
- Surgical treatment of Bright's disease. New
York: 1904. 1st coll edn.   *(Argosy)* **$100**

**Eder, Josef F.**
- History of photography. Translated by E.
Epstean. New York: 1945. 1st edn in English.
860 pp.   *(Scientia)* **$75**

**Edes, Robert T.**
- Text-book of therapeutics and materia
medica. Phila: Lea & Blanchard, 1887. 1st
edn. 552 pp. Hinges cracked, cvrs soiled.
*(Xerxes)* **$45**

**Edinburgh ...**
- The Edinburgh new dispensatory, containing
I: the elements of pharmaceutical chemistry;
II:The materia medica; III: ... the London
and Edinburgh pharmacopoeia. Edinburgh:
William Creech, 1797. 5th edn. 4to. xxxi,622
pp. Lea, hinges weak, new endpapers.
*(Poitras)* **$125**

**Edleston, I.**
- Correspondence of Sir Isaac Newton and
Professor Cotes ... 1850. 1st edn. xcviii,316
pp. Frontis. Orig cloth, rebacked.
*(Whitehart)* **£40**

**Edmunds, Walter**
- See Ballance, Charles & Edmunds, Walter

**Edwardes, Ernest L.**
- The grandfather clock. An archaeological and
descriptive essay on the long-case clock with
its weight-driven precursors and
contemporaries. Altrincham: John Sherratt &
Son, [1952]. 2nd edn. Cr 8vo. 253 pp. 54
plates. Orig cloth. Dw.   *(Zeitlin)* **$60**

**Edwards, E.**
- The American steam engineer, theoretical
and practical with examples of the latest and
most approved American practice in the
design and construction of steam engines of
every description ... Phila: 1888. xlix,50-419
pp. 77 ills & plates. Orig cloth.

*(Whitehart)* £38

**Edwards, J.J. & Edwards, M.J.**
- Medical museum technology. London: 1959.
8vo. 23 plates. Cloth. Dw.  *(Argosy)* $30

**Edwards, Joseph F.**
- How a person threatened or afflicted with
Bright's disease ought to live. Phila: 1881. 1st
edn. 16mo. 87 pp. Cloth.  *(Argosy)* $35

**Eggerth, Arnold H.**
- History of Hoagland Laboratory. Brooklyn:
1960. 12mo. Sev ills.  *(Argosy)* $25

**Eggleston, Wilfrid**
- Scientists at war. London: 1950. 291 pp.
Rubbed & sl shelfworn. Ex lib.
*(Epistemologist)* $37.50

**Ehrenfest, Hugo**
- Birth injuries of the child. New York: 1922.
1st edn. 221 pp.  *(Fye)* $45

**Ehrenwald, Jan (ed.)**
- The history of psychotherapy: from healing
magic to encounter. New York: [1976]. 1st
edn.  *(Argosy)* $30

**Eichhoff, P. Joseph**
- On new medicinal soaps. [Leipzig: ca 1890].
8vo. 16 pp. Wraps.  *(Argosy)* $20

**Eichhorn, Gustave**
- Wireless telegraphy. 1906. x,116 pp. Ills,
diags. Hd of spine worn.  *(Weiner)* £40

**Eigenmann, Carl**
- Cave vertebrates of America: a study in
degenerative evolution. Washington, D.C.:
1909. 4to. Num plates, several in color.
*(Argosy)* $45

**Eimer, G.H. Theodor**
- Organic evolution as the result of the
inheritance of acquired characteristics
according to the laws of organic growth.
Translated ... London: 1890. 1st edn in
English. 435 pp.  *(Scientia)* $50

**Einhorn, Max**
- Diagnosis and treatment of stenosis of the
pylorus. New York: 1895. 24mo. 32 pp. Ills.
Orig printed wraps.  *(Argosy)* $25
- Diseases of the intestines: a text book for
practitioners and students of medicine. New
York: 1900. 1st edn. 66 ills.  *(Argosy)* $40
- Diseases of the stomach. New York: 1896. 1st
edn.  *(Scientia)* $40
- Practical problems of diet and nutrition. New
York: 1905. 1st edn. 8vo. 64 pp. Cloth.
*(Argosy)* $25

**Einstein, Albert**
- Investigations on the theory of the Brownian
movement. Edited with notes by R. Furth.
Translated by A.D. Cowper. New York: n.d.
124 pp.  *(Scientia)* $45
- Relativity. The special and general theory. A
popular exposition, translated ... London:
Methuen, 1921. 4th edn. xiii,[iii], 138,[ii], 8
[ctlg] pp. Frontis, 5 text figs.  *(Pollak)* £26
- See Planck, Max (Where is science going?)
- Sidelights on relativity. Ether and relativity
[1920]; Geometry and experience [1921].
Translated by G.B. Jeffrey and W. Perrett.
London: 1922. 1st edn in English. 56 pp.
Spine faded.  *(Scientia)* $45
- Sidelights on relativity. Translated ...
London: Methuen, 1922. 1st edn. [iv],56,[iv]
pp. Foxed.  *(Pollak)* £35
- The theory of relativity. Its formal content
and present problems. The Rhodes Lectures
for 1931. N.p., n.d. 8 pp. An abridgement of
the three lectures of the series. Stapled as
issued. Faint vertical fold.  *(Pollak)* £30

**Einstein, Albert & Infeld, Leopold**
- The evolution of physics. The growth of ideas
from the early concepts to relativity and
quanta. Cambridge: University Press, 1938.
1st edn. x,319 pp. 3 plates, num text figs. Dw.
*(Pollak)* £30

**Eisenstein, Samuel**
- See Alexander, Franz & Eisenstein, Samuel

**Eissler, K.R.**
- Leonardo da Vinci: psychoanalytic notes on
the enigma. New York: [1961]. 1st edn. Tall
8vo. Ills. Cloth.  *(Argosy)* $35

**Ela, Walter**
- Fractures of the elbow-joint. Cambridge:
1873. 1st edn. 57 pp. Wraps.  *(Fye)* $25

**Elaboratory ...**
- The elaboratory laid open ... See Dossie,
William

**Elderton,. NP.**
- Frequency curves and correlation. 1927. 2nd
edn. vii,239 pp. Fldg table, fldg diags. Errata
slip. Spine torn.  *(Weiner)* £20

**Eldridge-Green, F.W.**
- The Hunterian lectures on colour-vision and
colour-blindness. New York: 1912. 1st Amer
edn. 76 pp.  *(Fye)* $30

**Elger, T.G.**
- The moon. A full description and map of its
principal physical features. 1895. 1st edn.
viii,173 pp. 4 double-page plates. Orig pict
cloth, v sl marked.  *(Whitehart)* £35

**Eliot, Walter Graeme**
- Portraits of the noted physicians of New York, 1750-1900. New York: 1900. 1st edn. Ltd (250). 200 pp. 199 ports. Orig linen, sl rubbed, inner hinges cracked. *(Elgen)* **$125**

**Elkin, Daniel C. & DeBakey, Michael E. (eds.)**
- Vascular surgery. Washington, D.C.: 1955. Tall 8vo. 56 ills, 52 tables. Fabricoid. *(Argosy)* **$40**

**Eller, Joseph Jordan**
- Tumors of the skin, benign and malignant. Phila: [1939]. Tall 8vo. 607 pp. 403 plates. Buckram. *(Argosy)* **$40**

**Elliot, T.J.**
- The land question: its examination and solution from an agricultural point of view ... 1884. Roy 8vo. 132 pp. Brown cloth. *(Phenotype)* **£18**

**Elliotson, John**
- On the recent improvements in the art of distinguishing the various diseases of the heart ... London: Longman ... & Green, 1830. 1st edn. Folio. 8 engvd plates. Foxed, title dust-soiled. Later half-calf. *(Quaritch)* **$1,150**

**Elliott, John**
- The medical pocket-book ... virtues and doses of medicinal compositions ... third American edition. Boston: 1795. 18mo. 154 pp. Old calf, front cvr very worn. *(M&S)* **$30**

**Elliott, Robert Henry**
- The Indian operation of couching for cataract ... 1917. 1st Amer edn. xii,94 pp. Half-title, 7 plates. Ex lib. *(Elgen)* **$85**

**Ellis, Asa**
- The country dyer's assistant. Brookfield, Mass.: for the author, [1798]. 1st edn. 16mo. 139,[4] pp. Some stains & foxing, tear in one leaf crudely sewn, without loss. Orig sheep, worn, hinges weak. *(M&S)* **$350**

**Ellis, Benjamin**
- The medical formulary: being a collection of prescriptions, derived from the writings and practice of many of the most eminent physicians in America and Europe. Phila: 1826. 1st edn. 148,4 pp. Contemp calf. *(M&S)* **$50**
- The medical formulary: being a collection of prescriptions ... Phila: 1826. 1st edn. Contemp calf, lea label. *(Argosy)* **$75**
- The medical formulary: being a collection of prescriptions ... Phila: 1846. 4th edn, with num addtns. Cloth, sl rubbed, paper label. *(Argosy)* **$40**

**Ellis, G.**
- Modern practical joinery: a comprehensive treatise on the practice of joiner's work by hand and machine ... 1928. 7th edn. xi,502, lxiii pp. Over 1400 ills, inc 20 double-page & 41 photog plates. *(Whitehart)* **£35**

**Ellis, George E.**
- Memoir of Sir Benjamin Thompson, Count Rumford, with notices of his daughter. Phila: 1871. 1st edn. 680 pp. *(Scientia)* **$60**

**Ellis, George Viner & Ford, G.H.**
- Illustrations of dissections, in a series of orig coloured plates the size of life, representing the dissection of the human body. London: 1867. 1st edn. Atlas folio. 58 chromo-litho plates. Mod black half-mor. *(Argosy)* **$1,500**
- Illustrations of dissections ... New York: Wood, 1882. 2nd edn. 2 vols. Tall 8vo. 58 cold lithos. Cloth, top of backstrip chipped. Ex lib. *(Argosy)* **$45**

**Ellis, H.**
- See Feldman, Stanley & Ellis, H.

**Ellis, Havelock**
- Man and woman: a study of human secondary sexual characteristics. Boston & New York: 1929. 488 pp. 23 ills. *(Argosy)* **$75**
- Studies in the psychology of sex. Phila: 1904-28. 7 vols. Cloth. *(Argosy)* **$85**

**Ellis, John**
- The avoidable causes of disease, insanity and deformity. New York: Mason Brothers, 1860. 1st trade edn. 12mo. *(Gach)* **$35**

**Ellis, William**
- The practical farmer; or, the Hertfordshire husbandman: containing many new improvements in husbandry, etc. London: for Weaver, Bickerton ..., 1732. Sm 8vo. 171,5 [advts] pp. Light browning of early leaves. Orig calf, lacking spine label. *(Ivelet)* **£110**

**Ellis, William D. (ed.)**
- A source book of gestalt psychology. London: Routledge & Kegan Paul, [1974]. xvi,403,[1] pp. *(Gach)* **$27.50**

**Elmer, A.W.**
- Iodine metabolism and thyroid function. 1938. xviii,605 pp. 23 figs, 86 tables. Orig cloth, spine faded. *(Whitehart)* **£18**

**Elsberg, Louis**
- Introductory address delivered before the Medical Class of Dartmouth Collage, August 1, 1883. Hanover, N.H.: 1883. 23 pp. Orig blue printed wraps. Author's complimentary copy. *(Argosy)* **$25**
- Laryngoscopal medication; or, the local

diseases of the throat, larynx, and neighboring organs, under sight. New York: 1864. 38 pp. 7 ills. Orig blue printed wraps. *(Argosy)* **$30**

**Elsberg. Charles**
- Diagnosis and treatment of surgical diseases of the spinal cord and its membranes. Phila: 1916. 1st edn. 330 pp.          *(Fye)* **$175**
- Tumors of the spinal cord and the symptoms of irritation and compression of the spinal cord and nerve roots. New York: 1925. 1st edn. 421 pp. Water damage to margins with many leaves stuck together.          *(Fye)* **$50**

**Elsholtz, Johann Sigismund**
- The curious distillatory: or, the art of distilling coloured liquids, spirits, oyls ... with divers other collateral experiments. London: ... Boulter, 1677. 1st edn in English. 8vo. [14],111,[3] pp. Frontis, engvd plate. Contemp calf, stitching loose.
          *(Rootenberg)* **$1,500**

**Elton, Charles**
- Animal ecology. New York: 1927. 1st Amer edn. 209 pp.          *(Scientia)* **$40**

**Elwyn, Herman**
- Diseases of the retina. Phila: 1947. 1st edn. 587 pp.          *(Fye)* **$100**

**Ely, Leonard**
- Inflammation in bones and joints. Phila: 1923. 1st edn. 433 pp.          *(Fye)* **$30**

**Emanuel, H.**
- Diamonds and precious stones: their history, value and distinguishing characteristics. 1867. xxii,266 pp. Plates, extra litho title, diags, 28 pp bibliog. Orig pict cloth, worn & soiled.          *(Weiner)* **£25**

**Emerson, Charles**
- Pneumorthrax; a historical, clinical and experimental study. Balt: 1903. 150 pp. Disbound. Inscrbd & autographed by author.          *(Fye)* **$60**

**Emerson, R.L.**
- Legal medicine and toxicology. New York: 1909. 1st edn. xiii,593 pp. 8 cold plates.          *(Elgen)* **$50**

**Emerson, William**
- The doctrine of fluxions: not only explaining the elements thereof, but also ... London: Robinson & Roberts, 1768. 3rd edn. Contemp calf, worn.          *(Pollak)* **£100**
- The elements of geometry, in which the principle propositions of Euclid, Archimedes and others are demonstrated ...To which is added ... London: for F. Wingrave, 1794. New edn. viii,216 pp. 14 fldg plates, some

dusty in folds. Orig calf, rebacked.
          *(Pollak)* **£55**

**Emme, Eugene M. (ed.)**
- The history of rocket technology. Essays on research, development and utility. Detroit: 1964. 1st edn. 320 pp. Dw. *(Scientia)* **$22.50**

**Emmers, Raimond & Akert, Konrad**
- A sterotaxic atlas of the brain of the squirrel monkey. Madison: University of Wisconsin Press, 1963. Tall folio. 102 pp. Num plates.          *(Argosy)* **$40**

**Emmet, Thomas**
- The principles and practice of gynaecology. Phila: 1879. 1st edn. 855 pp.          *(Fye)* **$175**

**Emmet, Thomas Addis**
- Birthday dinner given by his professional friends at Delmonico's, 29 May. With autobiographical narrative. New York: 1905. 1st edn. 4to. Many ports. Cloth. Ex lib. Author's sgnd pres copy.          *(Argosy)* **$75**
- Prolasus uteri, its chief causes and treatment. New York: 1871. 1st edn. 34 pp. Plain wraps. Pres copy.          *(Argosy)* **$45**
- Reduction of inverted uteri by a new method. New York: 1866. 1st edn. 15 pp. Wraps.          *(Argosy)* **$35**
- A study of the etiology of perineal laceration, with a new method for its repair. N.p.: 1883. 1st sep edn. 8vo. 12 pp. Printed wraps. Reprint from Vol VIII of Gynecological Transactions, 1883.          *(Argosy)* **$75**

**Eng, Helena**
- The psychology of child and youth drawing from the ninth to the twenty-fourth year. London: 1957. 4to. viii,205 pp. 118 ills, many cold. Cloth. Ex lib.          *(Jenner)* **£12**

**Engelbach, William**
- Endocrine medicine. Springfield: 1932. 4 vols, inc index vol. 4to. 933 ills. *(Argosy)* **$40**
- Endocrine medicine. With a foreword by Lewellys F. Barker. Springfield: 1932. 1st edn. 4 vols, inc index vol. Profusely illust. Dws with sl tears.          *(Elgen)* **$125**

**England, J.W. (ed.)**
- Philadelphia College of Pharmacy: First Century, 1821 - 1921. [Phila]: 1922. 1st edn. 4to. 728 pp. Num ills.          *(Argosy)* **$30**

**English, Frank P. & Keats, W.A.**
- Reconstructive and plastic surgery of the eyelids. Springfield: [1975]. 95 pp. Profusely illust. Cloth. Dw.          *(Argosy)* **$35**

**Epidemic ...**
- Epidemic cholera, its mission and mystery,

haunts and havocs, pathology and treatment.
New York: Carleton, 1866. 1st edn. 120 pp.
*(Xerxes)* **$70**

**Epiphanus**
- Epiphanus' treatise on weights and measures,
the Syriac version. Edited by James E. Dean.
Chicago: 1935. 1st edn. 145 pp. Orig wraps.
*(Scientia)* **$22.50**

**Eppinger, Hans & Hess, Leo**
- Vagotonia: a clinical study in vegetative
neurology. Translated ... New York: 1917.
Wraps. *(Argosy)* **$45**

**Epps, John**
- Consumption (phthisis): its nature and
treatment. London: Sanderson, 1859. 1st edn.
292 pp. Cvrs faded. *(Poitras)* **$45**

**Epstein, Bernard S. & Davidoff, Leo M.**
- An atlas of skull roentgenograms. Phila:
1953. 4to. 415 pp. 603 ills on 315 engvs.
Cloth. *(Argosy)* **$50**

**Epstein, D.W.**
- See Maloff, I.G. & Epstein, D.W.

**Ercker, Lazarus**
- Treatise on ores and assaying [1580].
Translated by A.G. Sisco & Cyril S. Smith.
Chicago: 1951. xxxiii,360 pp. Dw torn.
*(Scientia)* **$45**

**Erdman, Frederick**
- The control of the circulation by
physiological methods. Germantown:
Privately printed, 1921. Ills. *(Argosy)* **$35**

**Erich, John**
- See New, Gordon & Erich, John

**Erichsen, John**
- On concussion of the spine, nervous shock
and other obscure injuries of the nervous
system, in their clinical and medico-legal
aspects. New York: 1882. 2nd edn. 300 pp.
*(Fye)* **$45**

**Erichsen, John (trans. & ed.)**
- Observations on aneurism selected from the
works of the principal writers on that disease.
London: Sydenham Society, 1844. 1st edn.
8vo. xii,524 pp. Orig dec cloth. *(Antiq Sc)* **$75**

**Erichsen, John Eric**
- The science and art of surgery. Being a
treatise on surgical injuries, diseases and
operations. 1857. 2nd edn. xxiii,1040 pp. 410
ills. Orig blind-stamped cloth, rebacked.
*(Whitehart)* **£40**
- The science and art of surgery. Phila: 1860.
2nd Amer edn. 996 pp. Full lea. *(Fye)* **$75**

- The science and art of surgery. Phila: Lea,
1869. Thick sm 4to. 1228 pp. 630 w'engvs.
Full lea. *(Xerxes)* **$48**
- The science and art of surgery. Phila: 1873. 2
vols. Full lea. *(Fye)* **$75**

**Ernest, Maurice**
- The longer life. London: n.d. [ca 1938]. 8vo.
Ills. Cloth. *(Argosy)* **$30**

**Erskine-Murray, James**
- A handbook of wireless telegraphy ... 1913.
4th edn. Thick 8vo. xvi,442 pp. Ills, diags (1
fldg). Cloth sl stained. *(Weiner)* **£20**

**Erving, Henry Wood**
- The discoverer of anaesthesia: Dr. Horace
Wells of Hartford. New Haven: Yale
University Press, 1933. 8vo. 13 pp. Printed
wraps. *(Argosy)* **$25**

**Eschauzier, J.S. & Jennings, H.C.**
- Life-preserving bed, or mattrass, for sea-
faring people. By His Majesty's Royal Letter
Patent. Shacklewell: T. Rutt, 1813. 8vo. 20
pp. 2 hand-cold plates (on 1 double-fldg leaf).
Orig printed wraps, edges somewhat chipped.
*(Rootenberg)* **$350**

**Essay ...**
- An essay on capacity and genius ... See
Mitchell, William Andrew
- An essay on the usefulness of mathematical
learning ... See Arbuthnot, John

**Essays ...**
- Essays on phrenology ... See Combe, George
- Essays, mathematical and physical ... See
Mansfield, Jared

**Essman, Walter B.**
- Neurochemistry of cerebral electroshock.
New York: [1973]. 8vo. Cloth. Dw.
*(Argosy)* **$35**

**Etheridge, R. & Carpenter, P.H.**
- Catalogue of the Blastoidea in the Geological
Department of the British Museum. 1886.
4to. xvi,322 pp. 20 plates. Cloth. Ex lib.
*(Wheldon & Wesley)* **£20**

**Etheridge, Robert**
- Fossils of the British Islands stratigraphically
and zoologically arranged. Volume 1 [all
published] ... Oxford: 1888. Lge 4to. viii,468
pp. Tables. Sl wear at hd of spine.
*(Weiner)* **£60**

**Eugenics ...**
- Eugenics in race and state: Scientific papers
of the 2nd International Conference of
Eugenics. Balt: 1923. 1st edn. 2 vols. 439;
472 pp. Ex lib. *(Scientia)* **$65**

**Euler, Leonard**
- A complete theory of the construction and properties of vessels, with practical conclusions ... 1790. 8 pp, 6ff, 281 pp. 11 fldg plates, Frontis port (inserted?). Old calf, worn, rebacked, remains of old spine laid on.
*(Weiner)* **£175**

**Evans, Arthur**
- See Stewart, J. Purves & Evans, Arthur

**Evans, Edward Payson**
- Evolutionary ethics and animal psychology. London: Heinemann, 1898. 1st British edn. 12mo. viii,386 pp. Straight grained blue cloth. *(Gach)* **$40**

**Evans, Frankis & Gray Cecil**
- General anaesthesia. London: 1959. 2 vols. Tall 8vo. Ills. Dw. *(Argosy)* **$45**

**Evans, George A.**
- A hand-book of historical and geographical phthisology, with special reference to distribution of consumption in the United States. New York: 1888. 1st edn. 8vo. Cloth. Ex lib. *(Argosy)* **$35**

**Evans, Herbert McLean & Burr, George O.**
- The antisterility vitamine fat soluble E. Berkeley: 1927. 1st edn. 4to. 176 pp. 12 full-page plates. First few pp sl torn, without loss. Some extra ills pasted-in. Orig half-mor, spine sl worn & hinges weak. Pres copy from Evans.
*(Oasis)* **$80**

**Evans, Sir John**
- The ancient stone implements, weapons and ornaments of Great Britain. London: Longmans, Green, 1897. 2nd edn, revsd. xviii,747 pp. 2 fldg plates, 477 text figs. Orig cloth gilt, tiny hole in spine edge. *(Pollak)* **£25**

**Evans, Joseph**
- Acute head injury. Springfield: 1950. 1st edn. 116 pp. *(Fye)* **$50**
- Acute head injury. Springfield: [1950]. 8vo. 116 pp. Ills. *(Argosy)* **$35**

**Eve, Paul F.**
- A collection of remarkable cases in surgery. Phila: 1857. 1st edn. xi,[33]-858 pp. Text ills. Some browning. Orig full sheep, sl scuffed.
*(Elgen)* **$195**

**Evelyn, John**
- A philosophical discourse of earth, relating to the culture and improvement of it for vegetation ... London: John Martyn, 1676. 1st edn. Sm 8vo. Imprim leaf laid down, lacks final blank. Title reprd, marginal ink notes. Some discoloration. Contemp sheep.

*(Blackwell's)* **£400**
- Silva: or ... forest-trees ... terra ... pomona ... kalendarium hortense ... London: John Martyn, 1679. 3rd edn, much enlgd & imprvd. Folio. [lxix],412, 38,[i] pp. 5 engvs. Sub-titles. Errata fragile. Sm hole in 2S2. Marginal staining. Mod half-calf.
*(Blackwell's)* **£140**
- Silva: or, a discourse of forest-trees, with notes by A. Hunter, a new edition, to which is added the Terra. York: 1786. 2nd of Hunter's edns. 2 vols. 4to. 3 fldg tables, 42 engvd plates. Later half-calf.
*(Wheldon & Wesley)* **£150**
- Silva: or, a discourse of forest-trees, and the propagation of timber in His Majesty's dominions. York: 1786. New edn. 2 vols. Lge 4to. [41],311; 343,[74] pp. Port frontis, num plates (3 fldg). Half-calf, gilt spine, hinges cracked. *(Whitehart)* **£125**

**Everett, George H.**
- Health fragments or, steps toward a true life embracing health, digestion, disease, and the science of the reproductive organs. New York: by the author, 1877. 6th edn. 125 ills.
*(Poitras)* **$25**

**Everson, Tilden & Cole, Warren**
- Spontaneous regression of cancer. Phila: 1966. 1st edn. 560 pp. *(Fye)* **$15**

**Ewald, C.A.**
- Diseases of the digestive organs. London: New Sydenham Society, 1891-92. 1st edn in English. 2 vols. 680 pp. Orig cloth, spine of vol II sl mis-shapen. *(Oasis)* **$70**

**Ewbank, Thomas**
- A descriptive and historical account of hydraulic and other machines for raising water. New York: D. Appleton, 1842. 1st edn. 8vo. xvi,582,14 [pub advts]. Numerous w'cuts in text. Orig cloth, gilt illust spine. Cloth a little frayed. *(Antiq Sc)* **$100**

**Ewing, James**
- Lectures on tumor pathology. Cornell University Medical School, n.d. [ca 1934]. Port. Wraps. *(Argosy)* **$75**
- Neoplastic diseases. Phila: 1941. 4th edn. 1160 pp. *(Fye)* **$60**

**Examination ...**
- Examination of William Vaughan, Esq., in a committee of the hon. House of Commons, April 22 1796, on the commerce of the Port of London, and the accomodation for shipping &c. 1796. 8vo. 23 pp. New mrbld bds. *(Deighton Bell)* **£55**

**Exposures ...**
- Exposures of quackery: being a series of

articles upon, and analyses of, various patent medicines. By the Editor of "Health News". n.d. [ca 1893]. 2 vols in 1. Half-mor, worn, cvrs detchd.                    *(Robertshaw)* **£15**

**Faber, Knud Helge**
- Nosography on modern internal medicine. New York: 1923. 8vo. 21 ports. Cloth. Reprinted, with addtns, from Annals of Medical History.            *(Argosy)* **$35**

**Faber, Seymour, et al.**
- Cytologic diagnosis of lung cancer. Springfield: 1950. 1st edn. 4to. 59 pp. 10 cold plates.                      *(Fye)* **$60**

**Facts ...**
- Facts and arguments on the transmission of intellectual and moral qualities from parent to offspring. New York: Wiley & Putnam, 1843. 1st edn. 8vo. vii,[2],10-191, [1] pp. Some foxing. Pub cloth, blind-stamped.
                              *(Dailey)* **$100**
- Facts and arguments on the transmission of intellectual and moral qualities from parent to offspring. New York: Wiley & Putnam, 1843. 1st edn. 8vo. 191 pp. Sl foxing. B'plate removed.                  *(Diamond)* **$45**
- Facts and arguments respecting the great utility of an extensive plan ... See Macartney, Sir J.

**Fagge, Charles H.**
- The principles and practice of medicine. Phila: 1886. 1st Amer edn. Full lea.
                            *(Scientia)* **$100**

**Fahnestock, Wm. Baker**
- Artificial somnambulism. Hitherto called mesmerism ... Phila: Barclay & Co., [1869]. 1st edn. Sm 8vo. [41]-326 pp. Orig cloth, worn.                    *(M&S)* **$47.50**

**Faingold, Joseph E.**
- The chiropodial formulary and prescription writing. Containing nearly 600 ailments ... Chicago: Universal Publishers, 1935. 195 pp.
                            *(Poitras)* **$35**

**Fairbairn, William**
- An account of the construction of the Britannia and Conway tubular bridges, with a complete history of their progress ... 1849. xii,291 pp. 20 fldg plates (inc frontis: plates numbered 1-20, but plate 9 not published), diags. Orig qtr mor, worn.   *(Weiner)* **£185**
- Iron: its history, properties, and processes of manufacture. Edinburgh: 1861. xi,235 pp. Fldg plates, ills. Orig blind-stamped cloth, little worn, rebacked, orig spine laid on.
                              *(Weiner)* **£50**
- Remarks on canal navigation, illustrative of the advantages of the use of steam, as a

moving power on canals ... London: Longman ..., 1831. 8vo. 93 pp. 5 fldg lithos, foxed, mostly marginal. Orig bds, upper cvr detchd.                    *(Zeitlin)* **$450**
- Useful information for engineers; being a series of lectures delivered to the working engineers of Yorkshire and Lancashire ... 1856. 2nd edn. xvi,376 pp. 5 plates, many figs. New cloth.          *(Whitehart)* **£25**

**Fairbank, Thomas**
- An atlas of general affections of the skeleton. Edinburgh: 1951. 4to. 411 pp. 510 ills. Cloth.
                              *(Argosy)* **$50**

**Faitthorn, John**
- Facts an observations on liver complaints and bilious disorders. Phila: 1822. 2nd edn. Sheep, jnt repaired.         *(Argosy)* **$40**

**Fajans, Kasimir**
- Radio-elements and isotopes: chemical forces and optical properties of substances. New York: 1931. 1st edn. 125 pp.   *(Oasis)* **$60**

**Falck, N.D.**
- A treatise on the venereal disease, in three parts. London: 1772. 474 pp. 4 plates (1 fldg). All plates rather dirty, 2 detchd & fldg plate creased. Foxing throughout.   *(Jenner)* **£130**

**Falconer, William**
- Observations on Dr. Cadogan's dissertation on the gout and all chronic diseases. Bath: R. Cruttwell, 1772, 2nd edn, with crrctns & addtns. 115 pp. Title browned, crnr of last leaf cut without loss. Mod mor-backed cloth, unlettered.              *(Robertshaw)* **£45**

**Falkner, H.G.**
- Actinotherapy for general practitioners. New York: 1927. 8vo. 36 ills. Cloth. *(Argosy)* **$35**

**Falta, Wilhelm**
- The ductless glandular diseases. Translated ... Phila: [1916]. 1st English translation. 673 pp. 101 text ills.         *(Argosy)* **$85**

**Familiar ...**
- A familiar treatise on scrofula, scurvy, consumption, dropsy and rheumatism ... powerful and salutary virtues of the vegetable syrup of de Velnos ... n.d. [ca 1830]. 1st edn. Orig cloth.          *(Robertshaw)* **£20**

**Family Physician ...**
- The family physician. A manual of domestic medicine by physicians and surgeons of the principal London hospitals ... N.d. [ca 1879]. Subscription edn. 4 vols. Woodburytype ports. Orig cloth, a.e.g.   *(Whitehart)* **£30**

**Faraday, Michael**
- The chemical history of a candle. Edited by William Crookes. London: 1894. New edn. 226,32 [pub ctlg] pp. Text ills. Orig red cloth, blind-stamped & gilt. *(Oasis)* **$60**
- Chemical manipulation; being instructions to students in chemistry on the methods of performing experiments of demonstration or of research with accuracy and success. London: 1827. 1st edn. vii,ix, 11-256 pp. Lib stamp removed from title. Mod cloth. *(Whitehart)* **£120**
- A course of six lectures on the chemical history of a candle: To which is added a lecture on platinum. Delivered before a juvenile auditory ... edited by William Crookes. New York: 1861. 1st Amer edn. 16mo. 223 pp, ills. Orig cloth, spine little worn. *(M&S)* **$60**
- A course of six lectures on the chemical history of a candle ... London: Griffin, Bohn, 1861, viii,208,8 [pub ctlg] pp. 37 w'cuts. Cloth a little shabby. *(Pollak)* **£35**
- Experimental researches in chemistry and physics. London: Taylor & Francis, 1859. 1st edn in book form. 8vo. viii,496 pp. 3 plates. A few later annotations. Orig cloth. *(Rootenberg)* **$400**
- Experimental researches in electricity. Reprinted from the Philosophical Transactions of 1831-38. London: 1839-44-55. Quaritch "Facsimile edition". 3 vols. 8vo. viii,574,8; viii,302,5; viii,588,4 pp. 17 engvd plates. Half-titles in Vols II & III. Cloth. *(Rootenberg)* **$550**
- Experimental researches in electricity. Reprinted from the Philosophical Transactions of 1831-38. London: 1839-44-55. 1st edn in book form. 3 vols. 8vo. viii,574,8; viii,302,5; viii,588,4 pp. 17 engvd plates. Half-titles in Vols II & III. Orig cloth. *(Rootenberg)* **$1,500**
- Experimental researches in electricity. 1839. 1st edn. viii,574 pp. 8 fldg plates, plate 1 foxed. Orig cloth, dull & dust-stained. *(Whitehart)* **£150**
- Manipulation: being instructions to students in chemistry on the methods of performing experiments of demonstration ... Edited by J.K. Mitchell. New York: 1831. 1st Amer edn. 689 pp. Recent half lea, mrbld bds. Internal damp-staining. *(Scientia)* **$100**

**[Faraday, Michael]**
- Faraday's diary, being the various philosophical notes of experimental investigations made ... during the years 1820 - 1862. London: G. Bell, 1932-36. 8 vols. All with dws. *(Pollak)* **£300**
- Faraday's diary, being the various philosophical notes of experimental investigations made ... during the years 1820 - 1862. London: G. Bell, 1932-36. 8 vols (inc

index vol). Roy 8vo. Plates, ills. Pub cloth, sl rubbed. *(McDowell)* **£130**

**Farber, Eduard (ed.)**
- Great chemists. New York: 1961. 1st edn. *(Scientia)* **$60**

**Faries, John Culbert**
- Limbs for the limbless. A handbook on artificial limbs for layman and surgeon. New York: 1934. 104 pp. Few ills. Ex lib. *(Poitras)* **$25**

**Farlow, John W.**
- The history of the Boston Medical Library. Norwood, Mass.: privately printed at the Plimpton Press, 1918. 1st edn. Tall 8vo. 31 plates. Half cloth. *(Argosy)* **$50**

**Farmer's ...**
- The farmer's compleat guide, through all the articles of his profession; the laying out, proportioning, and cropping his ground ... London: G. Kearsley, 1760. 8vo. vi,418 pp. Contemp sprinkled calf, jnts starting to crack, cvrs sl rubbed & stained. *(Blackwell's)* **£150**

**Farquharson, Eric L.**
- Illustrations of surgical treatment. Instruments and appliances. Edinburgh: 1939. Roy 8vo. xi,338 pp. Num ills. *(Jenner)* **£18**
- Illustrations of surgical treatment. Instruments and appliances. Edinburgh: 1939. 57 plates, 259 figs. *(Jenner)* **£16.50**

**Farr, Robert E.**
- Practical local anaethesia and its surgical technic. Phila: 1929. 611 pp. 16 plates, 268 ills. *(Argosy)* **$45**

**Farr, William**
- Vital statistics: a memorial volume. London: 1885. xxiv,563,[i] pp. Port frontis laid down. Orig cloth, rebacked, new endpapers. *(Pollak)* **£90**

**[Fatio de Duillier]**
- Fruit walls improved, by inclining them to the horizon ... whereby they receive sunshine, and heat ... London: 1699. 1st edn. 4to. Engvd frontis (detchd), title, iii-xxviii, [ii],128 pp. 2 fldg engvs. Contemp mor. W'staining affecting bds & some text. *(Pickering)* **$350**

**Faught, F.A.**
- Blood pressure from the clinical standpoint. Phila: 1913. Ills. *(Argosy)* **$27.50**

**Faulconer, Albert & Keys, Thomas E.**
- Foundations of anesthesiology. Springfield: 1965. 1st edn. 2 vols. Dws. *(Scientia)* **$125**

**Faulkner, Frank**
- The art of brewing, practical and theoretical. London: F.W. Lyon, 1876. 2nd edn. 8vo. viii,199 pp. 5 photo-litho plates. Orig green cloth, blocked in gilt & black.
(*Blackwell's*) £30

**Fauntleroy, A.M.**
- Report on the medico-military aspects of the European War; from observations taken behind the Allied armies in France. Washington: 1915. vii,146pp. 218 figs in text & plates. Orig cloth, spine faded.
(*Whitehart*) £35

**Fauth, P.**
- The moon in modern astronomy. A summary of twenty years selenographic work, and a study of recent problems. [1907]. 160 pp. Frontis, 66 ills. Orig cloth. (*Whitehart*) £18

**Fay, Dudley Ward**
- A psychoanalytic study of psychoses with endocrinoses. New York: 1922. Tall 8vo. Lib buckram, orig wraps bound in. (*Argosy*) $30

**Fayrer, Sir Joseph**
- Recollections of my life. Edinburgh: 1900. xii,508 pp. Frontis, 25 plates. Orig cloth, stained. Spine worn.          (*Whitehart*) £18

**Fearing, Franklin**
- Reflex action; a study in the history of physiological psychology. Balt: 1930. 1st edn.
(*Scientia*) $65

**Fearne, Anne**
- My days of strength: an American woman doctor's forty years in China. New York: 1939. 8v0. Ills. Buckram, Ex lib. (*Argosy*) $30

**Federspiel, Matthew**
- Harelip and cleft palate: cheiloschisis, uranoschesis and staphyloschesis. St. Louis: 1927. 1st edn. 200 pp. More than 100 drawings & photographs.          (*Fye*) $200

**Feinagle, Gregor von**
- The new art of memory, founded upon the principles taught by M. Gregor von Feinagle ... London: 1812. 1st edn. 12mo. xii,408 pp. 3 plates (of 5), plate 4 torn. Qtr polished calf, mrbld bds, hinges split.          (*Zeitlin*) $125
- The new art of memory, founded upon the principles taught by ... Feinagle ... London: R. Edwards, 1813. 3rd edn. 12mo. xviii[2], 467,[1 advt] pp. Frontis, 5 fldg plates. Contemp 3/4 calf, mrbld bds, rebacked. Some cvr wear.          (*Diamond*) $75

**Feinblatt, Henry**
- Transfusion of blood. New York: 1926. 1st edn. 137 pp.          (*Fye*) $30

- Transfusion of blood. New York: Macmillan, 1926. 137 pp. 24 engvs.     (*Poitras*) $22.50

**Feldman, Maurice**
- Clinical roentgenology of the digestive tract. Balt: 1938. 1st edn. 1014 pp. 8vo. Cloth.
(*Argosy*) $40

**Feldman, Stanley & Ellis, H.**
- Principles of resuscitation. Phila: F.A. Davis, 1967. 128 pp. Ills. Ex lib.     (*Poitras*) $20

**Felix, A.H.**
- Television, its methods and uses. New York: 1931. x,272 pp. Num ills & diags. Lib stamp.
(*Weiner*) £30

**Felkin, R.W.**
- On the geographical distribution of some tropical diseases. Edinburgh: 1889. 8vo. 16 fldg maps. Cloth.          (*Argosy*) $50

**Felkin, William**
- A history of the machine-wrought hosiery and lace manufactures. 1867. xxvii,559 pp. 20 plates, many fldg. Several cold lace designs, usually blue. Subscribers' list. Orig cloth, worn at crnrs, rebacked.     (*Weiner*) £110

**Female ...**
- The female instructor or, young woman's companion: being a guide to all the accomplishments which adorn the female character ... Liverpool: n.d. [ca 1820?]. Frontis, vignette title, 7 plates. Browning, spotting. Polished calf, bds worn, hinges cracked.     (*Quinto Charing Cross*) £35

**Fenichel, Otto**
- Collected papers, first and second series. London: [1954-55]. 2 vols. Lge 8vo. Dw.
(*Argosy*) $40
- Psychoanalytic theory of neurosis. London: [1946]. 703 pp.          (*Argosy*) $35

**Fenn, Wallace O.**
- History of the International Congresses of Physiological Sciences, 1889 - 1968. [Balt: 1968]. Thin 8vo. Cloth.     (*Argosy*) $35

**Fenner, Frank.**
- See Burnet, Frank M. & Fenner, Frank

**Fere, Charles**
- The evolution and dissolution of the sexual instinct. Paris: Charles Carrington, 1904. 1st edn in English. Half crimson levant, uncut.
(*Argosy*) $85

**Ferenczi, Sandor**
- Further contributions to the theory and technique of psychoanalysis. Hogarth Press, 1926. 1st English edn. 473,[1] pp. Some

spotting on prelims. Orig green cloth, upper bd sl w'stained. *(Jenner)* **£35**

**Fergus, A.F.**
- The origin and development of the Glasgow School of Medicine ... Glasgow: 1911. 8 ports. *(Whitehart)* **£15**

**Ferguson, Alexander**
- The technic of modern operations for hernia. Chicago: 1907. 1st edn. 366 pp. *(Fye)* **$50**

**Ferguson, Eugene S.**
- Bibliography of the history of technology. Cambridge: 1968. 1st edn. 347 pp. Dw. *(Scientia)* **$37.50**

**Ferguson, James**
- Astronomy explained upon Sir Isaac Newton's principles ... to which are added, a plain method of finding the distances of all the planets ... The eighth edition. London: for Rivington [et al], 1790. 8vo. [8],503 pp. Fldg front, 17 fldg plates. Contemp sheep. *(M&S)* **$125**
- An introduction to astronomy for young gentlemen & ladies ... Phila: 1805. 1st Amer edn. 178 pp, 7 fldg plates (1 torn). Contemp calf, lacking spine. *(M&S)* **$25**
- Lectures on select subjects in mechanics, pneumatics, hydrostatics and optics ... London: for A. Millar, 1764. (with) A supplement ... London: 1767. 2nd & 1st edns. 4to. viii,252,[4]; 40. 36 fldg plates (some frayed at margins). Contemp calf, rebacked. *(Pickering)* **$350**
- Select mechanical exercise: Shewing how to construct different clocks, orreries, and sundials ... London: W. Strahan & T. Cadell, 1773. 1st edn. 8vo. [1],3,xliii, 272 pp. 9 fldg engvd plates, text ills, errata, directions to the binder. Half-calf. *(Rootenberg)* **$550**

**Ferguson, John**
- Bibliotheca chemica. A bibliography of books on alchemy, chemistry and pharmaceutics. London: Derek Verschoyle, 1954. 1st edn. 2 vols. Roy 8vo. Dw. *(McDowell)* **£120**

**Ferrel, W.**
- A popular treatise on the winds: comprising the general motions of the atmosphere, monsoons, cyclones, tornadoes, waterspouts, hail-storms, &c., &c. 1893. 1st edn. vii,505 pp. Frontis, 36 figs, 7 tables. Orig cloth, sl marked & worn, inner hinges cracked. *(Whitehart)* **£35**

**Ferriar, John**
- An essay towards a theory of apparitions. London: for Cadell & Davies, 1813. 1st edn. [ii],139,[3] pp. Mod qtr lea. *(Gach)* **$85**

**Ferris, Floyd T.**
- Treatment on epidemic cholera, as observed in the Duane-Street Cholera Hospital, New York ... 1834. New York: 1835. 1st edn. Tall 8vo. 70 pp. 4 cold litho plates. Cloth. Ex lib. *(Argosy)* **$50**

**Ferster, C.B. & Skinner, B.F.**
- Schedules of reinforcement. New York: Appleton-Century-Crofts, [1957]. 1st edn. *(Gach)* **$50**

**[Fessenden, Thomas Green]**
- Terrible tractoration. A poetical petition against galvanizing trumpery ... addressed to the Royal College of Physicians by Christopher Caustic. New York: for Stansbury, 1804. 12mo. 1st Amer edn. iv,xxxvi,192,[4] pp. 4 engvs (foxed). Mod drab wraps. *(Gach)* **$175**

**Feuchtersleben, Baron E. von**
- The principles of medical psychology, being the outlines of a course of lectures ... Translated ... Sydenham Society, 1847. xx,[12], 392 pp. Orig blind-stamped cloth, rebacked. Crnrs worn. *(Whitehart)* **£40**

**Feuerbach, Anselm von**
- Caspar Hauer; an account of an individual kept in a dungeon, separated from all communication with the world ... to about the age of seventeen ... 1834. 2nd edn. 12mo. xiv,173 pp. Frontis, port (w'stained). Half-calf, worn. *(Weiner)* **£50**

**Ficarra, Bernard J.**
- Essays on historical medicine. New York: 1948. Ills. *(Argosy)* **$35**

**Field, Henry**
- Memoirs historical and illustrative of the Botanick Garden at Chelsea; belonging to the Society of Apothecaries of London. 1820. 1st edn. Contemp cloth. *(Robertshaw)* **£38**

**Field, Henry & Semple, R.H.**
- Memoirs of the Botanick Garden at Chelsea belonging to the Society of Apothecaries. revised, corrected and continued to the present time. 1878. Port, plate, 3 plans. Sm tear at hd of spine. *(Robertshaw)* **£36**

**Field, John (ed.)**
- Neurophysiology. Washington, D.C.: 1959.4o. 3 vols. Ills. Cloth. *(Argosy)* **$150**

**Fieser, Louis**
- The scientific method: a personal account of unusual projects in war and peace. New York: 1964. 1st edn. 242 pp. *(Scientia)* **$50**

**Figuier, L.**
- The world before the deluge, translated from the 4th French edition, with numerous illustrations. 1865. 8vo. Cloth, trifle worn.
*(Wheldon & Wesley)* £15

**Filby, Frederick**
- A history of food adulteration and analysis. London: 1934. 1st edn. Dw. *(Scientia)* $50

**Findlay, Leonard**
- Syphilis in childhood. London: 1919. 1st edn. Sm 8vo. Ills, some cold. Cloth. Author's pres copy, sgnd. *(Argosy)* $35

**Findlay, William**
- Robert Burns and the medical profession. London: 1898. 1st edn. Sq 8vo. 13 full-page ports. Uncut. Cloth. Ex lib. *(Argosy)* $50

**Findley, Palmer**
- Story of childbirth. Garden City: 1933. 1st edn. Ills. Cloth. *(Argosy)* $35

**Fink, D.G.**
- See Miller, S.C. & Fink, D.G.

**Fischelis, Philipp**
- See Broomwell, I. Norman & Fischelis, Philipp

**Fischer, Martin H.**
- Death and dentistry. Springfield: 1940. Tall 8vo. 62 ills. Cloth, uncut. *(Argosy)* $40

**Fishbein, M.A.**
- A history of the American Medical Association 1847 to 1947 ... Phila: 1947. xvi,1226 pp. Frontis, plates. *(Whitehart)* £40

**Fishbein, Morris**
- An autobiography. Garden City: 1969. Tall 8vo. 505 pp. Ills. Cloth. dw. *(Argosy)* $35
- Frontiers of medicine. Balt: 1933.
*(Argosy)* $30
- Joseph B. de Lee: Crusading obstetrician. New York: 1949. 1st edn. Port. *(Argosy)* $30
- Medical follies. New York: 1925.
*(Argosy)* $25
- Medical writing: the technic and the art. Chicago: AMA, 1938. Ills. *(Argosy)* $35
- See Simmons, George H. & Fishbein, Morris

**Fishbein, Morris (ed.)**
- Doctors at war. 1945. 1st edn. 82 photos, charts. Spine crudely reprd. Ex lib.
*(Argosy)* $25

**Fisher, George P.**
- Life of Benjamin Silliman, late Professor of chemistry, mineralogy, and geology in Yale College ... New York: 1866. 1st edn. 2 vols. 407; 408 pp. *(Scientia)* $75

**Fisher, R.A.**
- The genetical theory of natural selection. Oxford: At the Clarendon Press, 1930. 1st edn. 8vo. [8],xiv,272 pp. 2 cold plates, text ills. Orig cloth. *(Rootenberg)* $275

**Fisher, Richard B.**
- Joseph Lister, 1827 - 1912. 1977. 351 pp. 16 plates. Orig cloth. Dw. *(Jenner)* £15

**Fisher, Seymour**
- Body experience in fantasy and behavior. New York: Appleton-Century-Crofts, [1970]. xii,690,[2] pp. *(Gach)* $17.50

**Fisher, W.A.**
- Cataract: senile, traumatic and congenital. Chicago: 1917. 1st edn. 119 pp. *(Fye)* $15

**Fishman, Alfred & Richard, D.W. (eds.)**
- Circulation of the blood: Men and ideas. New York: 1964. 1st edn. Ex lib. Stamp marks on all fedges. Dw. *(Scientia)* $65
- Circulation of the blood: Men and ideas. New York: 1964. 247 figs. Bibliogs.
*(Winterdown)* £35

**Fisk, Dorothy**
- Dr. Jenner of Berkeley. 1959. vii,288 pp. 9 ills. Port frontis. Orig red cloth. Dw.
*(Jenner)* £12

**Fister, Gordon B.**
- Half-century: the 50 year story of the Allentown Hospital, 1899 - 1949. Allentown, Pa: 1949. Ills. Ex lib. *(Argosy)* $35

**Fitch, Samuel S.**
- Family physician: teaching how to prevent and cure disease, and prolong life and health to 100 years. New York: 1875. 12mo. 120 pp. Orig printed wraps. *(Argosy)* $45
- Popular treatise upon the diseases of the heart, apoplexy, dyspepsia, and other chronic diseases, with proofs of their curability ... New York: 1859. 1st edn. 112 pp. Ills. Orig embossed cloth, cvr & first few pages damp-stained. *(Argosy)* $75
- Six discourses on the functions of the lungs ... pulmonary consumption, asthma, and diseases of the heart ... New York: 1853. 1st edn. 368 pp. Orig cloth. *(M&S)* $25
- Six lectures on the use of the lungs: and causes, prevention, and cure of pulmonary consumption, asthma, and diseases of the heart ... New York: 1847. 1st edn. 27 ills. Orig cloth. *(Argosy)* $40

**Fitzroy, Rear Admiral**
- The weather book. A manual of practical meteorology. 1863. 2nd edn. 16 plates, mainly fldg. 40 pp pub advts. Orig cloth, worn, rebacked. *(Edwards)* £30

**Fitzwilliams, Duncan**
- On the breast. St. Louis: 1925. 1st Amer edn. 440 pp. *(Fye)* **$40**
- The tongue and its diseases. London: 1927. 1st edn. 505 pp. *(Fye)* **$75**
- The tongue and its diseases. London: Oxford University Press, 1927. xvi,505 pp. 6 cold plates, 166 text figs. [together with] Offprint by same author; The modern treatment of carcinoma of the tongue. 1930. 16 pp. *(Pollak)* **£30**

**[Flachat, E. & Petiet, J.]**
- The railway-engine driver's guide: being an explanation of the action and mechanisms of the several parts of locomotives and observations on their management. Paris: 1840. 4ff, 142 pp. 72 plates. Some pencilling on plates, & some light foxing. Later cloth. *(Weiner)* **£75**

**Flagg, P.J.**
- The art of anaesthesia. Phila: Lippincott, 1922. 3rd edn. 371 pp. Ills. *(Xerxes)* **$45**
- The art of anaesthesia. Phila: n.d. [ca 1919]. 161 ills. Ex lib. *(Argosy)* **$40**

**Flatt, Adrian**
- The care of the rheumatoid hand. St. Louis: 1963. 1st edn. 222 pp. *(Fye)* **$40**

**Flaxman, John**
- Anatomical studies of the bones and muscles, for the use of artists, engraved by Henry Landseer; with two additional plates ... London: M.A. Nattali, 1833. 1st edn. Folio. 13 pp. Engvd frontis port, 21 engvd plates. Contemp red cloth, sl faded. *(Rootenberg)* **$450**

**Fleet, John**
- A discourse relative to the subject of animation delivered before the humane society ... Boston: 1797. Sq 12mo. 25 pp. Sewed. *(Argosy)* **$85**

**Fleischer, Dr. Emil**
- A system of volumetric analysis. Translated ... London: Macmillan, 1877. 1st edn in English. 12mo. xix, errata page, 274,48 [pub ctlg] pp. 14 text ills. Cvrs sl worn & stained. *(Diamond)* **$75**

**Fleming, A.P.M. & Brocklehurst, H.J.**
- A history of engineering. London: 1925. 1st edn. 312 pp. Dw. *(Scientia)* **$17.50**

**Fleming, Alexander**
- On the antibacterial action of cultures of a penicillium, with special reference to their use in the isolation of B. Influenziae ... [London: 1944]. Square 8vo. 12 pp. Ills, tables. Offprint without cvrs, wire-sewn as issued. Qtr red mor slipcase. *(Zeitlin)* **$1,000**
- Penicillin, Its practical application. London: Butterworth, 1946. 8vo. 1st edn. x,[2],380 pp. Text ills. Orig green cloth, gilt. *(Zeitlin)* **$85**
- Penicillin: Its practical applications. London: Butterworth, 1946. 1st edn. Sl dusty blue cloth. *(McDowell)* **£35**
- Penicillin: Its practical applications. Phila: 1946. Ills. Ex lib. *(Argosy)* **$75**
- Penicillin: Its practical applications. 1946. 1st edn. x,[2],380 pp. Orig cloth. *(Whitehart)* **£25**
- Penicillin: Its practical applications. London: Butterworth, 1946. 1st edn. x,[2],380 pp. 59 ills. Orig cloth, new front endpapers. *(Pollak)* **£25**

**Fleming, George**
- Rabies and hydrophobia: their history, nature, causes, symptoms, and prevention. London: 1872. 1st edn. Half-title, xiii,405,32 [pub ctlg, dated June 1884] pp. 2 chromo plates, text ills. Sl foxing, some shelf wear. *(Elgen)* **$85**
- The wanton mutilation of animals. London: George Bell, 1898. 4to. 24 pp. 7 plates. Orig printed wraps, spine browned, some worming. *(Dailey)* **$37.50**

**Fleming, J.A.**
- An elementary manual of radiotelegraphy and radiotelephony for students and operators. 1916. 3rd edn. xiv,360 pp. Num figs in text. Orig cloth, spine sl faded. *(Whitehart)* **£15**
- Magnets and electric currents. An elementary treatise for the use of electrical artisans and science teachers. 1898. xv,408 pp. 134 figs in text. *(Whitehart)* **£15**
- The principles of electric wave telegraphy and telephony. Longmans, Green, 1910. 2nd edn, revsd & extnded. xviii,906 pp. Frontis, 8 fldg plates, profuse text ills. Recased. *(Pollak)* **£25**
- The wonders of wireless telegraphy. 1913. xi,279 pp. Ills, diags. *(Weiner)* **£18**

**Fletcher, Robert**
- Medical lore, in the older English dramatists and poets (exclusive of Shakespeare). Balt: Johns Hopkins, 1895. 8vo. 35 pp. printed wraps. *(Argosy)* **$20**

**Flexner, James Thomas**
- Doctors on horseback: pioneers of American medicine. New York: 1937. 1st edn. Ports. *(Argosy)* **$40**

**Flexner, Simon & Flexner, James**
- William Henry Welch and the heroic age of medicine. New York: 1941. 1st edn. Ills. *(Argosy)* **$35**

**Flint, Austin**
- Clinical medicine: A systematic treatise on

the diagnosis and treatment of diseases ... Phila: 1879. 1st edn. Tall 8vo. 795 pp. Full sheep, lea label.              *(Argosy)* **$100**
- Handbook of physiology: for students and practitioners of medicine. New York: 1905. 1st edn. Tall 8vo. 877 pp. 247 ills. Cloth.
 *(Argosy)* **$35**
- Manual of auscultation and percussion, embracing the physical diagnosis of diseases of the lungs and heart, and of thoracic aneurism. Phila: Lea, 1890. 5th edn. 268 pp. Ills.                                *(Xerxes)* **$50**
- A practical treatise on the physical exploration of the chest and the diagnosis of diseases affecting the respiratory organs. Phila: 1866. 2nd edn, 595,32 [pub ctlg]. Extremities worn.             *(Oasis)* **$45**
- Treatise on the principles and practice of medicine. Phila: 1881. Thick 8vo. 1070 pp. Mod buckram. Ex lib.      *(Argosy)* **$50**

**Florey, M.E.**
- The clinical application of antibiotics - penicillin. London: Oxford University Press, 1952. 730 pp. Ills.         *(Poitras)* **$60**

**Florey, Sir Howard**
- Lectures on general pathology delivered at the Sir William Dunn School of Pathology, University of Oxford. London: Lloyd-Luke, 1954. 1st edn. 4to. Ills. Dw. *(McDowell)* **£28**

**Floyer, Sir John**
- The history of cold bathing: both ancient and modern. In two parts. London: William Innys, 1715. xx,426 pp. Lea, spine reprd, sl chipped.                     *(Poitras)* **$75**
- Psykrolosia: or the history of cold bathing ... [and, the second part written by Edward Baynard] Treating of the genuine use of hot and cold baths ... 1706. 2nd edn. (1st edn thus). [xxxiv],192; 240 pp. Index. Browning. Contemp calf, rubbed & worn. *(Jenner)* **£110**

**Fluckiger, Friedrich A. & Hanbury, Daniel**
- Pharmacographia. A history of the principal drugs of vegetable origin, met with in Great Britain and British India. London: 1874. 1st edn. 8vo. 704 pp. Mod green lib cloth. Some ms notations in ink & sev addtnl printed & ms sheets of related material.   *(Argosy)* **$100**
- Pharmacographia. A history of the principal drugs of vegetable origin, met with in Great Britain and British India. 1879. 2nd edn. Orig mor-backed cloth.        *(Robertshaw)* **£40**

**Fluegel, J.C.**
- Psycho-analytic study of the family. London: 1921. 1st edn.               *(Argosy)* **$30**
- The psychology of clothes. London: Hogarth Press, 1950. Ills.            *(Argosy)* **$35**

**Fluegge, Carl G.F.W.**
- Micro-organisms, with special reference to the etiology of the infective diseases. Translated ... London: New Sydenham Society, 1890. 826 pp. 144 ills. Cloth worn.
 *(Argosy)* **$50**
- Micro-organisms with special reference to the etiology of the infective diseases ... Translated ... London: New Sydenham Society, 1890. 1st English edn. Thick 8vo. Ills. Pub cloth.
 *(McDowell)* **£35**

**Foltz, Jonathan M.**
- The endemic influence of evil government, illustrated in a view of the climate, topography, & diseases, of the Island of Majorca. New York: 1843. 65 pp. Frontis. Wraps.                      *(Argosy)* **$35**

**Fomon, Samuel**
- Cosmetic surgery: principles and practice. Phila: 1960. 1st edn. 651 pp.    *(Fye)* **$75**
- The surgery of injury and plastic repair. Balt: Williams & Wilkins, 1939. 1409 pp. Ills.
 *(Poitras)* **$50**

**Fonda, Sebastian F.**
- Analysis of Sharon Waters, Schoharie County, with directions for invalids. New York: 1857. 96 pp. Orig embossed cloth. Ex lib.                      *(Argosy)* **$35**

**Fontaine, W.M.**
- The Potomac or younger mesozoic flora. Washington: 1889. 4to. 2 vols. 180 plates. U.S. Geological Survey.
 *(Wheldon & Wesley)* **£45**

**Foote, Edward**
- A text-book of minor surgery. New York: 1908. 1st edn. 752 pp. Half lea.   *(Fye)* **$40**

**Foote, Edward B.**
- Medical common sense ... causes, prevention and cure of chronic diseases and unhappiness in marriage. New York: for the Author, 1863. 390 pp.                      *(Xerxes)* **$35**

**Foote, J.S.**
- A contribution to the comparative histology of the femur. Washington: 1916. 4to. 35 plates. Buckram. Ex lib.      *(Argosy)* **$40**

**Forbes, Charles S.**
- Iceland; its volcanoes, geysers and glaciers. London: John Murray, 1860. 1st edn. 8vo. Fldg map, engvd frontis, other ills. A little spotting. Pub textured cloth, spine faded.
 *(McDowell)* **£90**

**Forbes, George**
- A course of lectures on electricity delivered before the Society of Arts. London:

Longmans, Green, 1891. vi,163, [iv ctlg] pp.
17 text figs.                    *(Pollak)* £15

**Forbes, John**
- The theory of the differential and integral
calculus. Glasgow: Collins, 1837. x,[ii],240
pp. Orig cloth, spine ends worn, a little dusty.
                                 *(Pollak)* £30

**Forbes, Sir John**
- Of nature and art in the cure of diseases.
London: 1857. 1st edn. Cloth, rubbed.
                                 *(Argosy)* $45

**Forbes, Litton**
- Diseases of the nose and naso pharynx. 1891.
2nd edn. 208 pp. Ills. Orig brown cloth, a
little shaken. Incorrect half-title ('On deafness
and its curative treatment').      *(Jenner)* £10

**Ford, E.B.**
- Mendelism & evolution. New York: 1931. 1st
Amer edn. 116 pp. A.F. Shull's copy.
                                 *(Scientia)* $35
- See Carpenter, G. Hale & Ford, E.B.

**Ford, Frank**
- Diseases of the nervous system in infancy,
childhood and adolescence. Springfield:
1937. 1st edn. Lge 8vo. 953 pp. Profusely
illust.                           *(Argosy)* $40

**Ford, Frank, et al.**
- Birth injuries of the central nervous system.
Balt: 1927. 1st edn. Thin 8vo. Ills.
                                 *(Argosy)* $30

**Ford, G.H.**
- See Ellis, George Viner & Ford, G.H.

**Ford, Simon**
- A discourse concerning God's judgments ...
(published to accompany the annexed
narrative concerning the man whose hands
and legs lately rotted off ... by another
author). London: 1678. 2 tracts, sep titles &
pagination but continuous signatures. 12mo.
Contemp calf.                    *(Argosy)* $350

**Ford, William W.**
- Text-book of bacteriology. Phila: 1927. 1st
edn. 8vo. 1069 pp. Ills. Cloth. *(Argosy)* $45

**Fordyce, George**
- Elements of the practice of physic, in two
parts. London: 1741. 8vo. Old calf, spine
split. Ex lib.                    *(Argosy)* $100
- Five dissertations on fever. Boston: 1815. 1st
Amer edn. 8vo. [2],ii. [3]-442,[1] pp. Half-title
for each paper. Contemp calf, sl rubbed.
                                 *(Elgen)* $225
- Five dissertations on fever. Boston: Bradford
& Read, 1815. 1st coll edn. 8vo. 442,[2] pp.

Orig bds, uncut. Backstrip near gone.
                                 *(Antiq Sc)* $175
- Five dissertations on fever. Boston: 1815. 1st
Amer edn.                         *(Argosy)* $85
- Five dissertations on fever. Boston: 1823.
8vo. 444 pp. Orig tree calf, worn. Ex lib.
                                 *(Argosy)* $45
- Five dissertations on fever. Boston: T.
Bedlington & C. Ewer, 1823. 2nd Amer edn.
iv,[3]-442,2 pp. Some age staining. Contemp
tree calf, cvrs worn, spine tip defective.
                                 *(Diamond)* $75

**Fordyce, William**
- A new inquiry into the causes, symptoms, and
cure, of putrid and inflammatory fevers; with
an appendix ... London: for Cadell et al.,
1777. 4th edn. xvi,228,16 [ctlg of books for
1791]. Contemp calf, spine ends sl worn.
From the lib of Jonathan Couch. *(Pollak)* £60

**Forel, August**
- The sexual question. A scientific,
psychological, hygienic and sociological
study. New York: 1924. 8vo. Ills. Cloth.
                                 *(Argosy)* $25
- The social world of the ants compared with
that of man. Translated ... New York: 1930.
1st Amer edn. 2 vols. 551,445 pp. Reprd
spine Vol I.                      *(Scientia)* $65

**Forkner, Claude E.**
- Leukemia and allied disorders. New York:
1938. 1st edn. Ills, bibliog. Pres copy.
                                 *(Argosy)* $40

**Forrest, H.E.**
- The Atlantean continent, its bearing on the
great ice age and the distribution of species.
1935. 2nd edn.     *(Wheldon & Wesley)* £15

**Forsyth, A.R.**
- Lectures introductory to the theory of
functions of a complex variable. Delivered to
the University of Calcutta during January and
February 1913. Cambridge: University Press,
1914. xvi,281,[iii] pp. Orig cloth. *(Pollak)* £25
- The theory of functions of a complex
variable. Cambridge: University Press, 1906.
2nd edn. xxiv,782 pp. Plate, text figs. Orig
cloth, v sl wear to spine ends.   *(Pollak)* £30
- Theory of functions of a complex variable.
Cambridge: University Press, 1893. 1st edn.
xxii,682 pp. Plate, text figs. Occas foxing.
Orig cloth, recased.              *(Pollak)* £30

**Fort, George F.**
- History of medical economy during the
Middle Ages ... New York & London: 1883.
Lge 8vo. xii,488 pp. Uncut in orig cloth.
                                 *(Hemlock)* $100

**Fossier, A.E.**
- History of the Orleans Parish Medical Society 1878-1928. Privately printed: 1930. 1st edn. A little worn.                    *(Scientia)* **$35**
- History of the Orleans Parish Medical Society 1878-1928. Privately printed: 1930. Thin tall 8vo. Cloth.                     *(Argosy)* **$75**

**Foster, J.**
- Treatise on the evaporation of saccharine chemical and other liquids by the multiple system in vacuum and open air ... Sunderland: [1895]. 2nd edn. Thick 8vo. 759 pp. 49 lge fldg plates, 181 figs in text. New cloth.                    *(Whitehart)* **£25**

**Foster, Sir Michael**
- Lectures on the history of physiology during the 16th, 17th and 18th centuries. Cambridge, Mass: 1901. 1st edn. 8vo. 3/4 calf.                       *(Argosy)* **$125**
- Lectures on the history of physiology during the 16th, 17th and 18th centuries. Cambridge: 1924. Reprinted. 306 pp. Frontis.                   *(Whitehart)* **£18**
- A text book of physiology. London: 1877. xvi,559pp. Few ills. Few pencil marks. Cvrs sl worn, spine sl frayed.          *(Jenner)* **£25**
- A text book of physiology. London: 1879. 3rd edn. xii,722, [2 advts] pp. Edges uncut & rather grubby. Orig green cloth, upper hinge cracked inside.              *(Jenner)* **£18**

**Foster, William D.**
- A short history of clinical pathology. Edinburgh: 1961. 1st edn. Dw. *(Scientia)* **$35**

**Fothergill, John**
- An account of the sore-throat attended with ulcers. 1751. 3rd edn. 72 pp. Sl browned. Mod half-calf, mrbld bds.       *(Oasis)* **$150**

**Fothergill, William Edward**
- Manual of midwifery for the use of students and practitioners. New York: Macmillan, 1896. 484 pp. Cold plate, 69 text ills. Cvrs fading, some staining.          *(Poitras)* **$20**

**Fourier, Joseph**
- The analytical theory of heat. Translated ... Cambridge: University Press, 1878. 1st English edn. [iv],466,[ii] pp. 20 text figs.
                              *(Pollak)* **£150**

**Fournier d'Albe, E.E.**
- The moon element, an introduction to the wonders of selenium. 1924. 1st edn. 166 pp. Frontis, plates. ills, tables.    *(Weiner)* **£30**

**Fowler, F.C.**
- Life: how to enjoy and how to prolong it. Moodus, Conn.: 1896. Sm 8vo. Ills. Cloth, warped.                       *(Argosy)* **$45**

**Fowler, George**
- A treatise on appendicitis. Phila: 1894. 1st edn. 190 pp.                      *(Fye)* **$100**

**Fowler, Orson Squire & Lorenzo, N.**
- New illustrated self-instructor in phrenology and physiology ... with the chart and character ... New York: Fowler & Wells, [1859]. 1st edn. Sm 8vo. viii,[9]-176, [4 advts] pp. Text ills throughout. Orig blind-stamped cloth.                      *(Zeitlin)* **$75**

**Fox, Cornelius B.**
- The disposal of the slop water of villages. London: 1875. 12mo. 32 pp. Ills. Bds.
                           *(Argosy)* **$27.50**

**Fox, George Henry**
- Photographic atlas of diseases of the skin. Physician's edition. Phila: 1902. Sm folio. iv,228 pp text. 80 full-page cold plates, other ills. 3/4 lea, rubbed, crnrs worn, jnts started.                      *(Elgen)* **$75**
- Photographic atlas of diseases of the skin. Phila: [1905]. 4 vols. 4to. 96 cold plates with tissue guards. Buckram.    *(Argosy)* **$100**

**Fox, Joseph**
- The natural history of the human teeth ...; The history and treatment of the diseases of the teeth ... London: Thomas Cox, 1803-06. 1st edn. 2 vols in 1. 4to. vii,100; [2],170 pp. 22 engvd plates. Contemp calf, rebacked. Lge paper copy.            *(Rootenberg)* **$3,000**
- A new medical dictionary; containing a concise explanation of all the terms used in medicine, surgery, pharmacy ... and chemistry. London: J. Callow, 1808. Revsd edn. 8vo. Pub bds, rebacked. *(McDowell)* **£30**

**Fox, Joseph & Harris, Chapin A.**
- The diseases of the human teeth: natural history and structure with the mode of applying artificial teeth, etc. etc.... Phila: Lindsay & Blakiston, 1855. 4to. xix,440 pp. Frontis, 30 engvd plates. Sporadic browning. Mod qtr mor.          *(Rootenberg)* **$250**

**Fox, R. Dacre**
- Bone-setting so-called and the treatment of sprains. Manchester: Heywood, 1883. 15 pp. New wraps.                   *(Pollak)* **£10**

**Fox, Sidney A.**
- Ophthalmic plastic surgery. New York: 1952. Tall 8vo. 133 ills. Cloth. Ex lib. *(Argosy)* **$35**

**Fox, William Tilbury**
- Acne and its treatment. N.p.: [1873]. 8vo. 12 pp. Wraps.                   *(Argosy)* **$25**

**Frank, Robert M. & Wrotnowska, D. (eds.)**
- Correspondence of Pasteur and Thuillier

concerning anthrax and swine fever vaccinations. Alabama: 1968. 16 plates.
*(Winterdown)* £15

**Frankel, J. & Hutter, R.**
- A practical treatise on the manufacture of starch, glucose, starch-sugar, and dextrine. Phila: 1881. xvi,17-344 pp. 58 figs in text. New cloth. *(Whitehart)* £18

**Frankenstein, Carl**
- Psychopathy: a comparative analysis of clinical pictures. New York: Grune & Stratton, 1959. 1st edn. viii,198 pp. Ex lib.
*(Gach)* $22.50

**Frankland, Edward**
- Experimental researches in pure, applied and physical chemistry. London: Van Voorst, 1877. 1st edn. 8vo. xliv, 1047 pp. Fldg tables, charts, plates & text w'cuts. Orig cloth gilt.
*(Antiq Sc)* $275
- Experimental researches in pure, applied and physical chemistry. 1877. xliv, 1047 pp. 23 ills including 2 fldg cold plates. Scattered foxing. Orig blind-stamped cloth, partially unopened. *(Whitehart)* £60

**Franz, J. Ch.**
- The eye: a treatise on the art of preserving this organ in a healthy condition, and of improving the sight ... London: J. Churchill, 1839. 1st edn. 8vo. xix,296 pp, 4 pp pub advts. Frontis. Endleaves discolored. Orig cloth. *(Rootenberg)* $165

**Franz, Shepherd Ivory**
- Handbook of mental examination methods. New York: 1912. Tall 8vo. Orig printed wraps, chipped. *(Argosy)* $30

**Fraser, Patrick**
- Treatise upon penetrating wounds of the chest. London: 1859. 1st edn. 8vo. 140 pp. Red cloth. *(Argosy)* $50

**Frazier, Charles**
- Surgery of the spine and spinal cord. New York: 1918. 1st edn. 971 pp. Inner hinges cracked, shaken. *(Fye)* $125

**Frederick, Christine**
- Household engineering; scientific management in the home. Chicago: 1919. 527 pp. Num ills. *(Weiner)* £40

**Freeman, Albert**
- The planning of fever hospitals and disinfecting and cleansing stations. London: 1920. 8vo. Many ills, fldg plans, maps, graphs, &c. Cloth. *(Argosy)* $35

**Freeman, Leonard**
- Skin grafting. St. Louis: 1912. 1st edn. 139 pp. *(Fye)* $175

**Freeman, Walter**
- Neuropathology: the anatomical foundation of nervous diseases. Phila: 1913. 1st edn.
*(Scientia)* $50

**Freeman, Walter & Watts, J.W.**
- Psychosurgery in the treatment of mental disorders and intractable pain. Springfield: 1950. *(Scientia)* $37.50
- Psychosurgery: intelligence, emotion and social behaviour following prefontal lobotomy for mental disorders. Springfield: 1942. 1st edn. *(Scientia)* $75

**Freind, John**
- Emmenologia. Translated from Latin by Thomas Dale. 1729. [xvi],216 pp., index. Illustration. Sl soiled. Contemp calf gilt.
*(Jenner)* £120
- Nine commentaries upon fevers: and two epistles concerning the small-pox, addressed to Dr. Mead ... translated into English (from the Latin) by Thomas Dale. London: for T. Cox, 1730. 1st edn in English. 8vo. Contemp polished sheep, upper cvr detchd.
*(M&S)* $125

**Freke, Henry**
- The dependence of life on decomposition. Dublin: 1871. 12mo. 55 pp. Sewed, mod wraps. *(Argosy)* $35

**Freke, John**
- An essay on the art of healing, in which pus laudabile or matter ... and the causes of various diseases are endeavoured to be accounted for ... London: 1748. xiv,15-272 pp. Full calf, cvrs worn. red mor label.
*(Jenner)* £125

**French, Gilbert J.**
- The life and times of Samuel Crompton, inventor of the spinning machine called the Mule ... Manchester: Thomas Dinham, 1860. 2nd edn. 8vo. Port frontis, 2 fldg plates, 4 other plates. Contemp full calf.
*(McDowell)* £45

**French, J.W.**
- Modern power generators, steam, electrical and internal combustion and their application to present-day requirements. 1908. 1st edn. 2 vols. xix,210; xiv,203 pp. Many diags & ills. Series of composite sectional models. Orig green pict cloth. *(Whitehart)* £85

**French, Sidney J.**
- Torch and crucible: the life and death of Antoine Lavoisier. Princeton University

Press: [1941].                  *(Argosy)* **$35**

**French, Thomas M. & Alexander, Franz**
- Psychogenic factors in bronchial asthma.
[Washington, D.C.]: 1941. 2 vols. 8vo. Orig
printed wraps.               *(Argosy)* **$50**

**Frerichs, F. Theodor**
- A clinical treatise on diseases of the liver.
1860-61. 2 vols. xxvii,402; xx,584 pp. 2
frontis, 68 figs. New cloth. *(Whitehart)* **£40**

**Fresenius, C. Remigius**
- Elementary instruction in chemical analysis
... 1843. First English edn. xii,284 pp. Few
w'cuts. Lib label on front pastedown.
                              *(Weiner)* **£40**

**Freud, Anna**
- The psycho-analytical treatment of children.
Translated ... London: Imago, [1946]. 8vo. 98
pp. Cloth. Dw.               *(Argosy)* **$30**

**Freud, Sigmund**
- An autobiographical study. Translated ...
London: Hogarth Press, 1935. 8vo. Port.
Cloth. International    Psycho-Analytical
Library.                      *(Argosy)* **$35**
- Beyond the pleasure principle. Translated ...
London: 1922. 1st edn in English. Tall 8vo.
90 pp. International Psycho-Analytical
Library.                      *(Argosy)* **$50**
- Civilisation and its discontents. 1930. 1st edn
in English. 144pp. Orig cloth.
                              *(Whitehart)* **£25**
- The collected papers. London: 1949-50. 5
vols. 5th & 6th impressions (vol V, 1st edn).
Orig green cloth, edges uncut. Dws rather
tatty.                        *(Jenner)* **£45**
- Collected papers: Volumes 1-4. Translated ...
New York & London: 1924-34. 4 vols. Sm
4to. International Psycho-Analytical Library.
                              *(Argosy)* **$100**
- Collected papers: Volumes 1-5. Translated ...
London: Hogarth Press, 1953-56. 5 vols.
International Psycho-Analytical Library.
                              *(Argosy)* **$125**
- The Ego and the Id. 1927. 1st edn in English.
88 pp. Orig cloth.           *(Whitehart)* **£28**
- The ego and the id. Translated ... London:
Hogarth Press, 1935. 88 pp.  *(Argosy)* **$30**
- The future of an illusion. Translated by W.D.
Robson-Scott. [New York]: 1928. 1st Amer
edn. 8vo. 98 pp. Cloth. International Psycho-
Analytical Library.          *(Argosy)* **$50**
- A general introduction to psychoanalysis.
Authorised translation ... New York: [1920].
1st edn in English. 8vo. Orig cloth, backstrip
spotted.                      *(Argosy)* **$50**
- Group psychology and the analysis of the
Ego. Authorised translation ... London &
Vienna: International Psycho-Analytical
Library, 1922. 1st edn. [7],134,[1 advt] pp.

Orig green cloth, cvr sl soiled & rubbed.
                             *(Diamond)* **$75**
- Group psychology and the analysis of the
Ego. 1922. 1st edn in English. 134 pp. Orig
cloth.                        *(Whitehart)* **£28**
- Group psychology and the analysis of the ego.
Translated ... New York: n.d. [ca 1925]. 8vo.
Cloth. International    Psycho-Analytical
Library.                      *(Argosy)* **$25**
- Group psychology and the analysis of the ego.
Translated ... London: 1940. 2nd edn. 8vo.
Cloth. International    Psycho-Analytical
Library.                      *(Argosy)* **$30**
- Infantile cerebral paralysis (1897). Translated
by L.A. Russin. Coral Gables, FL: 1968. 1st
edn in English.              *(Scientia)* **$65**
- Introductory lectures on psycho analysis. A
course of twenty-eight lectures ... London:
Allen & Unwin, 1923. 1st reprint. 395,[v
advts] pp. Frontis. Some foxing. Orig cloth,
faded.                        *(Pollak)* **£20**
- New introductory lectures on psycho-
analysis. Translated by W.J.H. Sprott. New
York: [1933]. 8vo. Cloth.     *(Argosy)* **$35**
- On war, sex, and neurosis. Edited by Sander
Katz & P. Goodman. New York: [1947]. 1st
Amer edn. 8vo. Cloth. Dw.     *(Argosy)* **$35**
- Psychology of everyday life. Translated by
A.A. Brill. New York: 1919. 1st Amer edn.
Cloth.                        *(Argosy)* **$35**
- Selected papers on hysteria and other
psychoneuroses. Translated ... New York:
1920. Tall 8vo. 225 pp. Printed wraps,
chipped. Nervous and Mental Disease
Monograph Series. 3rd, enlgd, edn.
                              *(Argosy)* **$40**
- Three contributions to the theory of sex.
Translated by A.A. Brill. Washington: 1920.
Tall 8vo. 100 pp, with 17 pp index. Printed
wraps. Nervous and Mental Disease
Monograph Series.            *(Argosy)* **$50**
- Totem and taboo. Resemblances between the
psychic lives of savages and neurotics.
Translated ... New York: 1919. Cloth.
                              *(Argosy)* **$75**
- A young girl's diary. Translated ... New
York: 1923. Half-cloth.      *(Argosy)* **$25**

**Freundlich, Herbert**
- New conceptions in colloidal chemistry.
London: Methuen, 1926. 47 ills. A little
slack.                        *(Pollak)* **£15**

**Friedenwald, Harry**
- Jewish luminaries in medical history and a
catalogue of works bearing on the subject of
the Jews and medicine ... Balt: 1946. 1st edn.
Dw.                           *(Scientia)* **$40**
- The Jews and medicine. Balt: 1944. 1st edn.
2 vols.                       *(Scientia)* **$85**

**Friedenwald, James S.**
- Pathology of the eye. New York: 1929. 1st

edn. 252 ills, chiefly micro-photographs by H. Campbell. *(Argosy)* **$60**

**Friedman, Ruben**
- A history of dermatology in Philadelphia, including a biography of Louis A. Duhring. Fort Pierce Beach, Fla,: 1955. Tall 8vo. 556 pp. Ills. Cloth. Ex lib. *(Argosy)* **$45**

**Frisinger, H.H.**
- The history of meteorology to 1800. New York: 1977. x,148 pp. Ills & figs in text. *(Whitehart)* **£18**

**Fritsch, H.**
- The diseases of women. New York: 1883. 1st English translation. 355 pp. 159 w'cuts. *(Fye)* **$15**

**Froebel, Friedrich Wilhelm August**
- The education of man. Translated ... New York: A. Lovell & Company, 1885. 1st edn in English. 12mo. vi,273,[1] pp. Pebbled olive cloth, shelfworn. *(Gach)* **$50**

**Frolov, Y.P.**
- Pavlov and his school: the theory of conditioned reflexes. Translated ... New York: 1937. 8vo. 27 ills. Dw. *(Argosy)* **$35**
- Pavlov and his school: the theory of conditioned reflexes. London: 1938. 291 pp. Torn dw. *(Epistemologist)* **$30**

**Frost, W. Adams**
- The fundus oculi with an ophthalmoscopic atlas illustrating its physiological & pathological conditions. Edinburgh: 1896. 1st edn. 4to. 228 pp. *(Fye)* **$250**
- The fundus oculi with an ophthalmoscopic atlas illustrating its physiological & pathological conditions. Edinburgh, Glasgow & London: 1901. 4to. xviii,[ii],228 pp. 47 cold plates, 46 text figs. Sl wear & a little slack. *(Pollak)* **£27**

**Fruit ...**
- Fruit walls improved, by inclining them to the horizon ... See Fatio de Duillier

**Fuchs, Adalbert**
- Atlas of the histopathology of the eye. Leipzig: 1924. 1st edn. 337 pp. Shaken, tear at top of spine. *(Fye)* **$40**
- Text-book of ophthalmology. Phila: 1913. 4th edn. 989 pp. Inner hinges cracked, shaken. Inscribed & autographed by Fuchs. *(Fye)* **$50**

**Fuchs, H. Ernst**
- Text-book of ophthalmology. Translated ... New York: 1924. 997 pp. 455 ills. Binding spotted. *(Argosy)* **$75**

**Fullarton, Col. William**
- A letter addressed to the Right. Hon. Lord Carrington, President of the Board of Agriculture [on turning grassland into tillage]. London: J. Debrett, 1801. 8vo. [iii],100 pp. Name on verso of half-title. Recent qtr cloth, bds, black lea label. *(Blackwell's)* **£55**

**Fuller, Francis**
- Medicina gymnastica: or, every man his own physician. A treatise concerning the power of exercise ... 1740. 7th edn imprvd. Contemp calf, short split at hd of lower jnt. *(Robertshaw)* **£75**

**Fuller, Samuel**
- Practical astronomy in the description and use of both globes, orrery and telescopes ... Dublin: 1732. Title, 4ff,237 pp. 10 fldg plates, 2 printed in red. Overall, grubby, stained & used but complete, excepting plate IV lacking one-third of engvd area. *(Weiner)* **£120**

**Fuller, Thomas**
- Pharmacopoiea domestica. 1723. 1st edn. 12mo, Contemp calf, rebacked. Old stamp of Queen's College, Oxford, on title. *(Robertshaw)* **£55**
- Pharmacopoiea extemporanea: or, a body of medicines, containing a thousand select prescripts, answering most intentions of cure. 1730. 4th edn. Port. Contemp calf, rebacked. Blind stamp on title. *(Robertshaw)* **£55**

**Fullmer, June**
- Sir Humphrey Davy's published works. Cambridge, Mass: Harvard University Press, 1969. 1st edn. 8vo. Dw. *(McDowell)* **£25**

**Fullum, S.W.**
- The marvels of science and their testimony to Holy Writ. London: Hurst & Blackett, 1854. 7th edn, revsd. vi,349 pp. Frontis, 9 plates. Some marginal marks. Orig cloth, recased, crnrs worn. *(Pollak)* **£15**

**Fulton, John F.**
- Aviation medicine in its preventive aspects. An historical survey. London: 1948. 1st edn. *(Scientia)* **$40**
- The great medical bibliographers: A study in humanism. Phila: 1951. 1st edn. *(Scientia)* **$80**
- Harvey Cushing. A biography. Springfield: 1946. 1st edn. Ills, Dw, a little torn. Pres copy to Edward Glover. *(Robertshaw)* **£24**
- Muscular contraction and the reflex control of movement. Balt: 1926. 1st edn. Dw badly torn. *(Scientia)* **$125**
- Muscular contraction and the reflex control of movement. Balt: Bailliere, Tindall & Cox,

1926. xv,644 pp. Num ills. Cvrs patchily marked. *(Pollak)* **£75**
- Physiology of the nervous system. New York: 1949. 3rd, revsd, edn. 8vo. 614 pp. Ills, bibliog. Cloth. *(Argosy)* **$85**
- Selected readings in the history of physiology. Springfield: 1930. xx,317 pp. Frontis, 60 figs in text. Orig cloth, spine sl marked & worn. *(Whitehart)* **£25**

**Fulton, John F. & Keller, A.**
- The sign of Babinski; A study of the evolution of cortical dominance in primates. Springfield: 1932. 1st edn. Sgnd by Fulton. *(Scientia)* **$75**

**Fulton, John F., et al. (eds.)**
- The frontal lobes. Balt: 1948. 901 pp. 237 ills, 39 tables. *(Argosy)* **$85**
- The hypothalmus and central levels of autonomic function. Balt: 1940. 319 ills, 35 tables. *(Argosy)* **$85**

**Fulton, Robert**
- A treatise on the improvement of canal navigation; exhibiting the numerous advantages to be derived from small canals ... London: 1796. 1st edn. 4to. 16,144 pp. 17 engvd plates, some foxing. Contemp calf, rebacked, orig lea label with title in French. *(M&S)* **$850**

**Fyfe, Andrew**
- A system of the anatomy of the human body; illustrated by upwards of two hundred tables ... Edinburgh: J. Pillans, 1805. 2nd edn, with alterations & improvements. 3 vols. 4to. 213 engvs. Occasional spotting. Contemp half-calf, rebacked. *(McDowell)* **£420**

**Gabor, D.**
- The electron microscope. Its development, present performance and future possibilities. New York: 1948. viii,164 pp. 54 ills. *(Whitehart)* **£15**

**Galen**
- Galen's method of physick: or, his great master peece; being the very marrow and quintessence of all his writings ... whereunto is annexed ... Translatour, Peter English: Edinburgh: 1656. 12mo. 2ff,344 pp. Occas mild browning. Contemp calf, cvr detchd. *(Hemlock)* **$525**
- On anatomical procedures. Translated, with introduction & notes, by Charles Singer. London: 1956. 1st edn. Dw. *(Scientia)* **$60**
- On anatomical procedures; the later books. Translated by W.L.H. Duckworth. Cambridge: 1962. 1st edn. Dw. *(Scientia)* **$55**

**Galetti, Pierre & Brecher, Gerhard**
- Heart-lung bypass, principles and technique

of extracorporeal circulation. 1962. 1st edn. 391 pp. Ex lib *(Fye)* **$30**

**Gall, Franz Joseph**
- On the functions of the brain and of each of its parts: with observations of the possibility of determining the instincts, propensities and talents ... Translated. Boston: 1835. Sole edn. 6 vols. All vols foxed & shelfworn, some damp-stained, vol 1 recased. *(Gach)* **$375**

**Gallup, Joseph A.**
- Outlines of the institutes of medicine: founded on the philosophy of the human economy, in health and disease. Boston: 1839. 2 vols. Tall 8vo. 416; 460 pp. Litho port. Uncut & unopened in orig green cloth. *(Hemlock)* **$175**

**Galton, Capt. Douglas**
- Report to the Lords of the Committee of Privy Council for Trade and Foreign Plantations, on the railways of the United States. 1857. Folio. 40 pp. 7 plates, lge cold fldg map, fldg table. Old cloth-backed bds, worn, rebacked. *(Weiner)* **£125**

**Galton, Francis**
- English men of science, their nature and nurture. 1874. 1st edn. xiii,270 pp. Orig cloth, spine worn. *(Whitehart)* **£85**
- Hereditary genius: an inquiry into its laws and consequences. London: Macmillan, 1869. 1st edn. 8vo. vi,[2],390,[2], 56 [pub ctlg] pp. 2 fldg tables. Orig gilt cloth, rebacked. *(Antiq Sc)* **$275**
- Hereditary genius: an inquiry into its laws and consequences. 1869. 1st edn. vi,[1],390. Fldg chart. Mod half-mor. *(Whitehart)* **£220**
- Hereditary genius: an inquiry into its laws and consequences. London: Macmillan, 1869. 1st edn. 8vo. Inscrbd on the half-title. *(Frew Mackenzie)* **£125**
- Hereditary genius: an inquiry into its laws and consequences. London: Macmillan, 1869. 1st edn. 8vo. 2 fldg tables. Mod half red crushed mor. *(McDowell)* **£140**
- Hereditary genius: an inquiry into its laws and consequences. London: Macmillan, 1869. 1st edn. 8vo. vi,[2], 390,[2], 39 [pub ctlg] pp. 2 fldg tables. Orig cloth, rebacked. *(Rootenberg)* **$325**
- Hereditary genius: an inquiry into its laws and consequences. 1892, reprinted 1914. 2nd edn. xxix,379 pp. Orig cloth. *(Whitehart)* **£35**
- Inquiries into human faculty and its development. 1883. 1st edn. xii,[1],387 pp. Frontis, 4 plates. Orig cloth, spine sl faded. *(Whitehart)* **£200**
- Inquiries into human faculty. New York: 1883. 1st Amer edn. 387 pp. *(Scientia)* **$175**

**Galvani, Luigi**
- Commentary on the effects of electricity on muscular motion, translated ... Norwalk: 1953. 4to. Ltd (1,000). 176 pp. Fldg plates. Ills, bibliog. Crnr bumped.  *(Weiner)* £50

**Gamgee, A.**
- A text-book of the physiological chemistry of the human body including an account of the chemical changes occuring in disease. 1880. 2 vols. xix,487; xix,528 pp. 88 figs, 2 cold plates. Orig blind-stamped cloth, sl faded & stained.  *(Whitehart)* £35

**Gamow, George**
- Constitution of atomic nuclei and radioactivity. Oxford: Clarendon Press, 1931. 1st edn. 114 pp. Text ills.  *(Oasis)* $100

**Ganot, A.**
- Natural philosophy for general readers and young people. Translated and edited ... Longmans, 1896. 8th edn. xii,731 pp. 24 pp ctlg. Cold frontis, 6 plates (1 cold), 24 text ills. Little foxing. Orig cloth.  *(Pollak)* £25

**Gant, Frederick James**
- The science and practice of surgery. 1886. 2 vols. Lge 8vo. xxviii,1089; xxv,1183 pp. Ills. Ex lib stamps on titles, b'plates on pastedowns.  *(Jenner)* £35

**Gant, S.E.**
- Diagnosis and treatment of diseases of the rectum, anus and contiguous textures. Phila: 1900. 1st edn. 399 pp. Binding rubbed.  *(Fye)* $25

**Gantt, W. Horsley**
- A medical review of Soviet Russia. London: ... British Medical Association, 1928. 4to. 112 pp.  *(Poitras)* $25
- Russian medicine. New York: 1937. 1st edn. Clio Medica Series.  *(Scientia)* $30

**Gardiner, John**
- Observations on the animal oeconomy, and on the causes and cure of diseases. Edinburgh: 1784. xxx,[1],458 pp. Contemp bds.  *(Whitehart)* £60

**Garner, Richard Lynch**
- The speech of monkeys. New York: Charles L. Webster, 1892. [ii],xiv,217,[9] pp. Frontis. Pict grey cloth, shelfworn.  *(Gach)* $40

**Garnett, F.W.**
- Westmorland agriculture, 1800 - 1900. Kendal: 1912. 4to. xvi,320 pp. 64 ills, 6 maps & tables. Orig qtr vell, a little darkened.  *(Phenotype)* £95

**Garnett, Thomas**
- A lecture on the preservation of health. Liverpool: printed by J. M'Creery, 1797. 1st edn. 8vo. 72 pp. With the half-title. Sl foxing, age-staining of a few leaves. Newly rebound in mrbld bds, red mor label.  *(Deighton Bell)* £155

**Garnett, William**
- See Campbell, Lewis & Garnett, William

**Garrigues, Henry**
- Gynecology, medical and surgical. Phila: 1905. 1st edn. 461 pp. 343 ills.  *(Fye)* $20

**Garrison, F.H.**
- An introduction to the history of medicine ... Phila: 1929. 4th edn, revised & enlarged. [16],996 pp. Various plates. *(Whitehart)* £40
- An introduction to the history of medicine ... Phila: 1929. 4th edn, reprinted. 996 pp.  *(Fye)* $35

**Garrod, A.B.**
- The essentials of materia medica and therapeutics. 1864. 2nd edn. xxxi,391 pp. New cloth.  *(Whitehart)* £18

**Garrod, A.E.**
- See Ord, W.M. & Garrod, A.E.

**Garrod, Archibald E.**
- The inborn factors in disease. An essay. Oxford: Clarendon Press, 1931. 160 pp. Dw.  *(Pollak)* £40

**[Garth, Samuel]**
- The dispensary: a poem in six cantos. Second edition, corrected by the author, 1699. Title a little soiled. Contemp calf, rebacked.  *(Robertshaw)* £75

**Gaskell, W.H.**
- The involuntary nervous system. 1920. New edn. ix,178 pp. 9 figs (8 cold). Orig cloth, sl faded.  *(Whitehart)* £18
- The origin of vertebrates. 1908. 1st edn. ix,537 pp. 168 figs in text, bibliog, index of authors. Orig cloth.  *(Whitehart)* £25

**Gassendri, Pierre**
- The mirrour of true nobility & gentility, being the life of the renowned Nicolaus Claudius Fabricius ... London: ... for Humphrey Moseley, 1657. Sm 8vo. [10]ff,216 pp; 296 pp,[8]ff,[10]ff. Engvd port. Upper margins trimmed. Contemp calf, worn, spine damaged.  *(Zeitlin)* $490

**Gatland, K.**
- Development of the guided missile. 1954. 2nd edn. 292 pp. 103 figs in text, 11 full-page ills.  *(Whitehart)* £18

**Gatty, Mrs. Alfred**
- Parables from nature. Bell & Daldy, 1868. Frontis, 14 w'engvd plates. Full polished calf gilt, a.e.g.                    *(Pollak)* £20

**Gaubius, Hieronymous David**
- A complete extemporaneous dispensatory, or, the method of prescribing, compounding and exhibiting extemporaneous medicines ... many accurate specimens of each. London: 1741. 1st English edn. xvi,432,[36] pp. Full calf, bds badly scuffed, lea peeling.
                                    *(Jenner)* £60

**Gauckler, E.**
- See Dejerine, J.J. & Gauckler, E.

**Gauger, Nicholas**
- Fires improved: being a new method of building chimneys, so as to prevent their smoking ... London: for J. Senex & E. Curll, 1715. 1st edn in English. 8vo. [vi],161,[19],[2 advts] pp. Contemp unlettered calf, jnts cracked but sound.        *(Pickering)* $550

**Geerligs, H.C. Prinsen**
- Cane sugar and its manufacture. Altrincham: 1909. Lge 8vo. xii,350,xvi pp. Tables. Bottom outer crnr of cvr & first few leaves damp-affected.            *(Weiner)* £25

**Geikie, A.**
- Text-book of geology. 1903. 4th edn, revsd. 2 vols. 8vo. 1472 pp. Plate, 508 text figs. Cloth.
                        *(Wheldon & Wesley)* £20

**Geikie, J.**
- The antiquity of man in Europe, being the Munro Lectures, 1913. 1914. 8vo. xx,328 pp. 4 maps, 21 plates, 9 text figs. Cloth.
                        *(Wheldon & Wesley)* £25
- Earth sculpture or the origin of land forms. 1909. 8vo. 2nd revsd edn. xvi,320 pp. 10 plates, 88 text figs. Orig cloth.
                        *(Wheldon & Wesley)* £20

**Geikie, James**
- Prehistoric Europe, a geological sketch. Edward Stanford, 1881. 8vo. xviii,592 pp. 2 plates, 3 maps, 12 text figs. Orig blue cloth, blocked in gilt & black. B'plates.
                        *(Blackwell's)* £55

**General Board of Health**
- Minutes of information collected with reference to works for the removal of soil water or drainage of dwelling houses ... sewage and cleansing of ... towns. 1852. 207 pp. Fldg map, diags (1 as fldg plate). Orig blue wraps, dusty & worn, sewing defective.
                                    *(Weiner)* £40

**Genet, Edmond Charles**
- Memorial on the upward forces of fluids, and their applicability to several arts, sciences and public improvements. Albany [N.Y.]: Packard & Van Benthuysen, 1825. 1st edn. 8vo. 112 pp. Full-page ill, 5 plates, fldg table. Orig printed bds, lightly soiled.
                                    *(M&S)* $2,000

**Gerarde, J.**
- The herball, or generall historie of plantes ... much enlarged and amended by Thomas Johnson ... London: 1633. Engvd title. Sl worming at beginning affecting few letters, 1 text-margin reprd, minor stains. Lacks 1st & last blanks. 18th c calf, rebacked.
                        *(Wheldon & Wesley)* £1,400
- The herball, or generall historie of plantes ... much enlarged and amended by Thomas Johnson ... London: 1636. Folio. Engvd title, nearly 3,000 w'cuts. Some marginal w'staining. Lacks 1st & last blanks. Contemp calf, rebacked.    *(Wheldon & Wesley)* £1,100

**Gerster, Aped**
- The rules of aseptic and antiseptic surgery. New York: 1891. 3rd edn. 365 pp. Photographically illust. Half lea.    *(Fye)* $75

**Geschickter, C. & Copland, M.**
- Tumors of bone. New York: 1936. 2nd edn. 832 pp.                        *(Fye)* $30

**Gesell, Arnold, et al.**
- Vision: its development in infant and child. New York: 1949. 1st edn. 329 pp. *(Fye)* $20

**Gesner, Conrad**
- The newe levell of health, wherein is contayned the most excellent secretes of phisicke and philosophie ... corrected ... by George Baker. London: Henrie, Denham, 1576. 1st English translation. 8vo. [12],258ff. Mod calf. 2 sm wormholes, minor loss.
                                    *(Zeitlin)* $4,500
- The practise of the new and old phisicke, wherein is contained the most excellent secrets of phisicke and philosophie ... London: Peter Short, 1599. 2nd edn in English. 4to. [12]ff,[1 blank], 265ff. Frontis, w'cut ills. Contemp vell. Minor defects.
                                    *(Zeitlin)* $2,500

**Getchell, F.H. (ed.)**
- An illustrated encyclopaedia of the science and practice of obstetrics. With 84 large plates and numerous woodcuts. Phila: Gebbie, 1885. Folio. 276 pp. Orig 3/4 lea, bndg v stained.                *(M&S)* $75

**Gibbs, J. Willard**
- The scientific papers. London: 1906. 1st edn. 2 vols. xxviii,434; viii,284 pp. Photogravure

trport. Uncut in lea-backed fitted cloth solander case.          *(Elgen)* **$350**

**Gibbs, Joseph**
- Cotton cultivation. In its various details, the barrage of great rivers, and instructions for irrigating, embanking, draining ... adapted to the ... soils of India. 1862. Sm 8vo. 5 fldg plates. Orig cloth, worn.          *(Edwards)* **£20**

**Gibson, R.W.**
- Francis Bacon. A bibliography of his works and of Baconiana to the year 1750. Oxford: The Scrivenor Press, 1950. 1st edn. 4to. Ills.          *(McDowell)* **£90**

**Gibson, William**
- The institutes and practice of surgery: being an outline of a course of lectures. Phila: 1824-1825. 1st edn. 2 vols. xvi,469; viii,542 pp. Half-title, 18 plates (4 cold). Some foxing. Contemp calf, sl rubbed & scuffed.
          *(Elgen)* **$225**
- The institutes and practice of surgery. Phila: 1850. 8th edn. 2 vols. 503; 478 pp. Num engvd plates, some hand-cold. Full lea.
          *(Fye)* **$100**

**Gihon, A.L.**
- Practical suggestions in naval hygiene. Washington: 1871. [8],151 pp. Orig linen bds.          *(Whitehart)* **£20**

**Gilbert, Grove Karl, et al.**
- The San Francisco earthquake and the fire of April 18, 1906, and their effects on structures and structural materials. Reports ... Washington, DC: Govt Printing Office, 1907. 1st edn. xii,170 pp. 57 plates (3 fldg). New cloth & bds, orig wraps bound in.
          *(Diamond)* **$75**

**Gilbert, William of Colchester**
- On the magnet, magnetic bodies also ... London: Chiswick Press, 1960. Facsimile of 1600 edn, ltd (250). Folio. Num figs in text. Orig limp vell, with ties.          *(Pollak)* **£250**

**Gilbreth, Frank B.**
- Motion study. A method for increasing the efficiency of the workman. New York: 1911. 1st edn. 8vo. 23,116 pp. Ills. 32 pp cctlg. Rust mark on title. Orig cloth.          *(M&S)* **$75**

**Gillespie, W.M.**
- A manual of the principles and practice of road-making: Comprising the location, construction, and improvement of roads ... and railroads. New York: 1847. 1st edn. 336 pp. Orig cloth.          *(M&S)* **$60**

**Gillies, Harold D.**
- Plastic surgery of the face. London: 1920. 1st

edn. 4to.          *(Scientia)* **$400**

**Gillilan, L.A.**
- Clinical aspects of the autonomic nervous system. Boston: 1954. 1st edn. 316 pp. Ills. Dw.          *(Oasis)* **$30**

**Gillis, Leon**
- Amputations. London: Heineman, 1954. 423 pp. Ills. Ex lib.          *(Poitras)* **$50**

**Gillmore, Quincy Adams**
- Practical treatise on limes, hydraulic cements, and mortars ... New York: Van Nostrand, 1863. 1st edn. 333 pp. 57 text figs, 41 tables. Marginal damp-staining, Spine tips defective, some shelf wear.          *(Diamond)* **$45**

**Gilman, Daniel C.**
- The life of James Dwight Dana. New York: 1899. 1st edn. 409 pp. Top & bottom of spine worn.          *(Scientia)* **$22.50**

**Girdlestone, G.R.**
- Tubercolosis of bone and joint. Oxford University Press, 1940. 265 pp. Ills. B'plate. Cvrs sl faded.          *(Jenner)* **£12**

**Gladstone, R.J. & Wakeley, C.P.G.**
- The pineal organ. The comparative anatomy of median and lateral eyes, with special reference to the origin of the pineal body ... 1940. Lge 8vo. xvi,528 pp. Ills. Ex lib.
          *(Jenner)* **£25**

**Glaister, J. & Logan, D.D.**
- Gas poisoning in mining and other industries. Edinburgh: 1914. xi,471 pp. Plans, cold plates, other ills. Orig cloth. *(Whitehart)* **£15**

**Glanvill, Joseph**
- Scepsis scientifica: or, confest ignorance, the way to science ... London: by E. Cotes, for Henry Eversden, 1665. Sm 4to. [16]ff, 184 pp; [8]ff,92 pp; [2]ff. Imprimatur & errata leaves. Leaf with longitudinal title. Marginal stains. Contemp calf, sl wear. *(Zeitlin)* **$1,250**

**[Glasse, Hannah]**
- The art of cookery, made plain and easy. London: A. Millar [&c.], 1765. Ninth edn. Some staining to edge of title & prelims. Some spotting. Contemp calf, rebacked.
          *(McDowell)* **£70**

**Glasser, Otto**
- Medical physics. Chicago: 1944. 1st edn. Ills. Spine sl faded.          *(Oasis)* **$50**
- The science of radiology. Springfield: 1933. 1st edn. xiii,450 pp. Ills. Cvr sl soiled.
          *(Elgen)* **$85**
- Wilhelm Conrad Roentgen and the early history of the Roentgen rays. Springfield:

1934. 1st Amer edn. 494 pp. *(Scientia)* **$85**

**Glauber, Johann Rudolph**
- The works of the highly experienced and famous chymist, John Rudolf Glauber: Containing ... choice secrets in medicine ... Translated ... London: Thomas Milbourn ... 1689. 1st edn in English. Folio. [12],440; [4],220,92,[11]. 11 engvd plates. Mod lea. *(Antiq Sc)* **$1,500**

**Glenn, William, et al.**
- Thoracic and cardiovascular surgery with related pathology. New York: 1975. 3rd edn. 1345 pp. Profusely illus. Ex lib. *(Poitras)* **$75**

**Gliddon, Geo. R.**
- See Nott, Josiah Clark & Gliddon, Geo. R.

**Glimpses ...**
- Glimpses of the San Francisco disaster ... great Californian cataclysm and fire ... which spread consternation along the golden sands of the land of promise ... Chicago: 1906. Obl 8vo. Frontis, 111 plates, fldg panoramic view, torn & detchd. *(Weiner)* **£20**

**Glyn-Jones, W.S.**
- The law relating to poisons and pharmacy with notes and cases. 1909. 1st edn. Hd of spine snagged. Pres copy. *(Robertshaw)* **£12**

**Goddard, Henry**
- The Kallikak family: a study in the heredity of feeble-mindedness. New York: 1913. 2nd printing. 121 pp. *(Scientia)* **$40**

**Goddard, Henry Herbert**
- Psychology of the normal and the subnormal. New York: Dood, Mead & Company, 1924. [ii],xxiv,349 pp. 56 half-tone plates. Printed orange cloth. *(Gach)* **$25**

**Goddard, Paul B.**
- The anatomy, physiology and pathology of the human teeth; with the most approved methods of treatment ... New York: S. & Wm. Wood, 1854. 2nd edn. Sm folio. 227 pp. 30 litho plates. Text foxed & tide-mark throughout. Orig cloth, rebacked, faded & soiled. *(M&S)* **$450**

**Goddard, Robert H.**
- The papers of Robert H. Goddard. Edited by Esther C. Goddard & G.E. Pendray. New York: 1970. 1st edn. 3 vols. Boxed. Sgnd by Esther Goddard. *(Scientia)* **$175**
- Rocket development. Liquid-fuel rocket research 1929-41. Edited by Esther C. Goddard & G.E. Pendray. Englewood Cliffs, NJ: 1961. 222 pp. Dw. *(Scientia)* **$30**

**Godfray, H.**
- An elementary treatise on the lunar theory with a brief sketch of the history of the problem up to the time of Newton. 1859. 2nd edn revsd. xi,119 pp. Diags in text. Orig cloth. *(Whitehart)* **£15**

**Godlee, Sir Rickman John**
- Lord Lister [Joseph Lister]. 1917. xix,676 pp. Frontis, 33 plates. Uncut, edges spotted. Orig blue cloth. *(Jenner)* **£18**

**Goldberg, A. & Rimington, C.**
- Diseases of porphyrin metabolism. Springfield: Charles C. Thomas, 1962. 231 pp. Ills. *(Poitras)* **$25**

**Goldschmidt, Richard**
- In and out of the ivory tower. Seattle: 1960. 1st edn. 352 pp. Dw. Ex lib. *(Scientia)* **$45**
- Lymantria. Berlin: 1933. 1st edn. 186 pp. *(Scientia)* **$60**
- The material basis of evolution. New Haven: 1940. 1st edn. 436 pp. *(Scientia)* **$55**
- Physiological genetics. New York: 1938. 2nd printing. 375 pp. *(Scientia)* **$45**
- Theoretical genetics. Berkeley: 1958. 2nd printing. 563 pp. *(Scientia)* **$35**

**Goldstein, Kurt**
- The organism; An holistic approach to biology derived from pathological data in man. New York: 1939. Spine faded. *(Scientia)* **$55**
- The organism; An holistic approach to biology derived from pathological data in man. New York: American Book Company, [1939]. 1st edn. Sm 8vo. xviii,533,[1] pp. Russet cloth. *(Gach)* **$35**

**Goldzieher, Max**
- The endocrine glands. New York: 1939. 1st edn. *(Scientia)* **$60**

**Gooch, Robert**
- A practical compendium of midwifery; being the course of lectures on midwifery and on diseases of women and infants delivered at St. bartholemew's Hospital. Phila: 1832. 1st Amer edn. 8vo. [2],xii, [7],319 pp. 4 pp pub ctlg. Contemp sheep, hinges split. *(Hemlock)* **$125**

**Good, M.E.**
- Hear with your eyes by reading word-forms on the face. Appleton, 1930. 1st edn. 12mo. 40 pp. Ills. Dw. *(Xerxes)* **$35**

**Goodchild, G.F. & Tweney, C.F.**
- A technological and scientific dictionary. Newnes, [1906]. viii,875 pp. Num figs. Half-mor, spine & crnrs a little worn. *(Pollak)* **£15**

**Goodhart, James Frederic**
- On common neuroses, or the neurotic elements in disease and its rational treatment. London: H.K. Lewis, 1892. viii,128 pp. Printed wraps. Inscrbd by the author.
*(Gach)* **$35**

**Goodison, Nicholas Proctor**
- English barometers 1680 - 1860. A history of domestic barometers and their makers. London: Cassell, [1969]. 1st edn. 4to. xiii,353 pp. 158 ills, 8 drawings. Orig cloth. Dw.
*(Zeitlin)* **$100**

**Goodman, Nathan**
- Notable contributors to the knowledge of syphilis. New York: 1943. 1st edn.
*(Scientia)* **$45**

**Goodnow, Minnie**
- Nursing history in brief. Phila: W.B. Saunders, 1943. 2nd edn, rvsd. 338 pp, 103 ills.
*(Poitras)* **$25**

**Goodrich, E.S.**
- Studies on the structure and development of vertebrates. London: 1930. 1st edn. 837 pp.
*(Scientia)* **$50**

**Gordon, E.H.**
- A practical treatise on electric lighting. 1884. xvi,228 pp. 23 plates. Ills. Lacks front free endpaper.
*(Weiner)* **£40**

**Gordon, G.F.C.**
- Clockmaking past and present, with which is incorporated ... 'Clocks, Watches and Bells" by the late Lord Grimethorpe ... 1925. viii,232 pp. 35 plates, 29 figs in text. 1 plate loose. Orig cloth.
*(Whitehart)* **£35**

**Gordon, James Edward Henry**
- A physical treatise on electricity and magnetism ... London: Sampson, Low ..., 1880. 1st edn. 2 vols. 8vo. xx,323; xx,296 pp. 52 plates. Orig cloth, gilt lettered, spines a little rubbed, sl shaken.
*(Pickering)* **$200**
- A physical treatise on electricity and magnetism ... London: Sampson, Low, 1880. 1st edn. 2 vols. xvii,323; xvi,295 pp. 52 plates, 255 text figs. 32 pp ctlg at end.
*(Pollak)* **£50**

**Gordon, John**
- Engravings of the skeleton of the human body. Edinburgh: 1818. 1st edn. [2],135,[1] pp.22 plates. Some foxing. Ex lib, rebnd in buckram.
*(Elgen)* **$95**

**Gordon, Sidney**
- See Allen, Ted & Gordon, Sidney

**Gordon, Thomas**
- Philosophical essays, in two volumes. London: for the Author, 1808-09. 1st edn. 2 vols. 4to. [2],xiii,[1],297; [2],297 pp. 2 fldg engvd plates. Contemp tree calf, backs richly gilt. One cvr loose & other jnts cracked.
*(Antiq Sc)* **$600**

**Gore, George**
- Theory and practice of electro-deposition; including every known mode of depositing metals, preparing metals for immersion ... London: C. Griffin, [ca 1856]. viii,104 pp. 36 text figs. Dec blind-stamped cvrs. "Orr's Circle of the Sciences".
*(Diamond)* **$75**

**Gorgas, Ferdinand J.S.**
- Dental medicine. A manual of dental materia medica and therapeutics. Manchester, John H. King & Son, 1906. 7th edn, revsd & enlgd. 624 pp. Occas dusty margin. Half-calf, crnrs worn.
*(Pollak)* **£16**

**Gorton, David Allyn**
- An essay on the principles of mental hygiene. Phila: Lippincott, 1873. 1st edn. Pub brown cloth.
*(Gach)* **$35**

**Gosney, E.S. & Popenoe, Paul**
- Sterilization for human betterment: a summary of results of 6000 operations in California, 1909-1929. New York: 1930. 202 pp. Dw.
*(Scientia)* **$25**

**Goss & Company**
- The aegis of life, a non-medical commentary of the indiscretions arising from human frailty ... practical observations of sexual debility. 1824. 17th edn. Uncut in orig bds, jnts cracked, spine defective.
*(Robertshaw)* **£20**

**Gosselin, L.**
- Clinical lectures on surgery. Phila: 1878. 1st English translation. 350 pp. Full lea.
*(Fye)* **$60**

**Gottstein, J.**
- Diseases of the larynx. Edinburgh: 1883. 1st English translation. 274 pp.
*(Fye)* **$40**

**Goudsmit, Samuel**
- See Pauling, Linus & Goudsmit, Samuel

**Goulard, Thomas**
- A treatise on the ... various preparations of lead ... for different chirurgical disorders. London: 1770. 2nd edn. 222 pp. (Bound with "Arnoud, G. Remarks on the extract of lead". 25pp). Armorial b'plate. Contemp calf, worn & chipped, hinge cracked.
*(Oasis)* **$100**
- A treatise on the effects ... of lead. A new edition. 1773. 232 pp. Title sl soiled. Rebnd

qtr calf, mrbld bds.          *(Oasis)* **$100**
- A treatise on the effects and various preparations of lead ... for different chirurgical disorders. 1772. 3rd edn. Some dampstains on last few leaves. Contemp sheep, hd of spine worn. *(Robertshaw)* **£35**
- A treatise on the effects and various preparations of lead ... for different chirurgical disorders. 1777. New edn. 12mo. viii,7,231 pp. Full calf gilt, sl worn.
*(Jenner)* **£90**

**Gould, R.T.**
- The marine chronometer. Its history and development. London: J.D. Potter, 1923. 1st edn. [2]ff, xvi,287,[1] pp. Frontis, 38 plates. Orig cloth, hd & ft of spine chipped, crnrs bumped.          *(Zeitlin)* **$300**

**Goupil, M. Ernest**
- See Bernutz, M. Gustave & Goupil, M. Ernest

**Gowers, William R.**
- Epilepsy and other chronic convulsive diseases; Their causes, symptoms and treatment. New York: 1885. 1st Amer edn. Tear at top of spine.          *(Scientia)* **$85**

**Gowers, Sir William Richard**
- Lectures on the diagnosis of diseases of the brain, delivered at University College Hospital. London: F. & A. Churchill, 1887. 2nd edn. 8vo. vii,[1],254 pp. [1]f,14 [advts] pp,[1]f. 18 text figs. Orig black cloth, gilt.          *(Zeitlin)* **$225**

**Grace, J.H. & Young, A.**
- The algebra of invariants. Cambridge: University Press, 1903. 1st edn. 8vo.
*(McDowell)* **£30**

**Graetz, Leo**
- Recent developments in atomic theory. Translated by Guy Barr. 1923. 39 ills, 1 fldg table.          *(Edwards)* **£12**

**Graham, Harvey**
- Eternal Eve. The history of gynaecology and obstetrics. New York: 1951. 1st edn. 699 pp. Ills. Frayed dw.          *(Oasis)* **$40**
- The story of surgery. New York: 1939. 1st edn. 425 pp.          *(Fye)* **$25**

**Graham, James**
- The general state of medical and chirurgical practice, shewing them to be inadequate, ineffectual, absurd and ridiculous. London: 1779. "6th edn". 12mo. 248 pp. Recent leatherette.          *(Hemlock)* **$250**

**Graham, Sylvester**
- Lectures on the science of human life. New

York: Fowler & Wells, 1851. 1st edn. 651 pp. Many ills. Lightly foxed throughout.
*(Xerxes)* **$55**

**Graham, T.J.**
- Sure methods of improving health and invigorating life; by regulating the diet and regimen ... illustrated by cases. 1838. 4th edn. Lea.          *(Whitehart)* **£38**

**[Graham, T.J.]**
- An account of persons remarkable for their health and longevity; exhibiting their habits, practices and opinions ... 1829. 2nd edn. xii,313 pp. Mod cloth.          *(Whitehart)* **£40**

**Graham, Thomas**
- Chemical and physical researches. Collected and printed for presentation only. Preface and analytical contents by Dr. Angus Smith. Edinburgh: 1876. Lge thick 8vo. lvi,660 pp. Collotype port, 3 fldg plates. Orig dec cloth, a little worn & shaken.          *(Weiner)* **£100**
- Chemical and physical researches. Collected and printed for presentation only. Preface and analytical contents by Dr. Angus Smith. Edinburgh: 1876. Only coll edn. Thick roy 8vo. lvi,660 pp. Collotype port, 3 double-page plates. Orig dec cloth.
*(Offenbacher)* **$350**
- A treatise on indigestion ... with notes and an appendix by an American physician. Phila: 1831. 1st Amer edn. 206 pp. Orig cloth-backed bds, text damp-stained. *(M&S)* **$40**
- A treatise on indigestion, with observations on some painful complaints ... London: Simpkin & Marshall, 1838. 4th edn. xii,198 pp. Some browning. Old half-cloth, bds soiled & rubbed.          *(Dailey)* **$100**

**Graham, Thomas (ed.)**
- Chemical reports and memoirs, on atomic volume: isomorphism ... and volcanic activity. For the Cavendish Society, 1848. vii,370,15 pp. 2 fldg plates. Ex lib. Report of the first meeting of the Cavendish Society bound in.          *(Weiner)* **£35**

**Graham, Thomas John**
- A chemical catechism: in which the elements of chemistry, with the recent discoveries in the science, are clearly and fully explained. London: Simpkin & Marshall, 1829. 2nd ed. xi,616 pp. Plate. A little foxing. Lacks half-title. Full mor, rebacked.          *(Pollak)* **£50**
- Modern domestic medicine; or, a popular treatise, illustrating the character, symptoms ... of all diseases ... 1827. 3rd edn, much enlgd. xii,619 pp. Diced calf, spine gilt, sl rubbed, hinges cracked.          *(Whitehart)* **£40**
- Modern domestic medicine; or, a popular treatise, illustrating the character, symptoms ... of all diseases ... 1829. 4th edn. Sl foxing,

espec on prelims & appendix. Half-calf, mrbld bds.      *(Jenner)* **£33**

**Grainger, R.D.**
- Elements of general anatomy, containing an outline of the organization of the human body. 1829. 1st edn. xxvi,526 pp. New bds.     *(Whitehart)* **£40**

**Grant, Robert**
- History of physical astronomy, from the earliest ages to the middle of the nineteenth century ... London: Henry G. Bohn, [n.d.]. 8vo. xx,637,[1] pp, [1 ctlg]f. Some pencil marks. Orig green stamped cloth, gilt lettered spine, worn.     *(Zeitlin)* **$75**
- Outlines of comparative anatomy, presenting a sketch of the present state of knowledge, and of the progress of discovery in that science. London: 1841. 656 pp. 137 figs. Prelims spotted. Paste bds, cloth-backed, crnrs rubbed & bumped.     *(Jenner)* **£60**

**Grantham, John**
- Facts and observations in medicine and surgery ... 1844. viii,216 pp. Ills. Sl foxing. Roughtrimmed, spine split, cvrs worn.     *(Jenner)* **£20**

**Granville, Augustus Bozzi**
- Graphic illustrations of abortion and the diseases of menstruation ... London: for John Churchill, 1834. 1st edn, 2nd iss. 4to. 14 hand-cold plates, 12 lithod & 2 engvd, 1 double-page & fldg. Contemp half-calf, hd & tail of spine reprd.     *(Quaritch)* **$750**

**Granville, Joseph Mortimer**
- Common mind-problems. Salem & New York: 1879. 102 pp. Pub ctlg. Orig printed cloth, spine tips rubbed.     *(Gach)* **$35**

**Gratry, A.**
- Logic. Translated by Helen and Milton Singer. La Salle, Ill: Open Court Publishing, 1944. xii,628 pp. Dw.     *(Pollak)* **£25**

**Grauvogl, V.**
- Textbook of homeopathy. Translated ... Chicago: C.S. Halsey, 1870. 1st edn. 2 parts in 1 vol. Roy 8vo. 341; 438 pp. Fldg chart. List of subscribers. Mtd orig photo frontis. V worn.     *(Xerxes)* **$85**

**Graves, R.J.**
- Clinical lectures on the practice of medicine. To which is prefixed a criticism by Professor Trousseau of Paris. Dublin, 1864. xxvi,873 pp. Orig cloth, rebacked.     *(Whitehart)* **£45**

**Gray, Andrew**
- The theory and practice of absolute measurements in electricity and magnetism.

London: Macmillan, 1888-93. 2 vols in 3. xiv,518; xxiii,4,346; xx,347-868 pp. 197 text figs. 2 vols faded.     *(Pollak)* **£50**
- A treatise on gyrostatics and rotational motion. London: Macmillan, 1918. xx,530 pp. 121 text figs.     *(Pollak)* **£20**

**Gray, Andrew & Mathews, G.B.**
- A treatise on Bessel functions and their applications to physics. London: Macmillan, 1895. x,291 pp. Cloth faded.     *(Pollak)* **£20**

**Gray, Asa**
- The botanical text-book ... comprising Part I ... Part II ... New York & Boston: 1842. 1st edn. 12mo. 413,3 [pub advts] pp. 78 wood engvs. Lightly browned. Orig cloth.     *(Rootenberg)* **$185**

**Gray, Cecil**
- See Evans, Frankis & Gray, Cecil

**Gray, George J.**
- A bibliography of the works of Sir Isaac Newton ... Cambridge: 1907. 2nd edn, revsd & enlgd. Obl 8vo. 80pp. Frontis. Cloth-backed paper-cvrd bds, edges rubbed.     *(Elgen)* **$125**

**Gray, George W.**
- Frontiers of flight: The story of NACA research. New York: 1948. 1st edn. 362 pp. (NACA: National Advisory Committee for Aeronautics).     *(Scientia)* **$40**

**Gray, H.**
- Anatomy, descriptive and surgical. 1866. 4th edn. xxxiv,788 pp. 394 ills in text. Orig cloth worn, rebacked.     *(Whitehart)* **£40**

**Gray, Henry**
- Anatomy, descriptive and applied. Phila: 1913. 1502 pp.     *(Fye)* **$50**
- Anatomy, descriptive and surgical. Phila: 1862. 2nd Amer edn. 816 pp. Mod half lea.     *(Fye)* **$300**
- Anatomy, descriptive and surgical. Phila: 1870. New Amer edn. 876 pp. Full lea.     *(Fye)* **$75**
- Anatomy, descriptive and surgical. Phila: 1878. New Amer edn. 983 pp. Full lea.     *(Fye)* **$75**

**Gray, Horace & Ayres, J.G.**
- Growth in private school children with averages and variabilities ... from the ages of one to nineteen years. Chicago: [1931]. 1st edn. xvi,282,[2] pp. Dw.     *(Gach)* **$25**

**Gray, Jane L. (ed.)**
- The letters of Asa Gray. Boston: 1893. 1st edn. 2 vols. 838 pp.     *(Scientia)* **$85**
- The letters of Asa Gray. Boston: 1894. 2 vols.

838 pp.                    *(Scientia)* **$65**

**Gray, Landon Carter**
- A treatise on nervous and mental diseases.
Phila: 1893. 687,32 [pub ctlg] pp. 168 ills. 2
pp damaged without loss. Cloth stained & sl
worn.                       *(Oasis)* **$30**
- A treatise on nervous and mental diseases.
Phila: Lea Brothers, 1895. 2nd edn, revsd &
enlgd. Thick heavy 8vo. Hinges broken. Ex
lib.                        *(Gach)* **$30**

**Gray, Samuel Frederick**
- A supplement to the pharmacopoeia: being a
treatise on pharmacology in general;
including not only the drugs and compounds
... London: 1821. 2nd (?) edn. xxxii,480,[48]
pp. Some foxing throughout. Half-calf, cloth
bds, crnrs & edges rubbed.     *(Jenner)* **£38**
- A supplement to the pharmacopoeia: being a
treatise on pharmacology in general;
including not only the drugs and compounds
... London: 1828. 4th edn. lvi,528,[1] pp.
Newly rebnd in roan.        *(Whitehart)* **£45**

**Greef, R.**
- Atlas of external diseases of the eye. New
York: [1914]. vi,175 pp. 84 cold ills on 54
plates. Orig cloth, dull.     *(Whitehart)* **£35**
- Guide to the microscopic examination of the
eye. Translated from the second German
edition ... London: Rebman, 1901. xiv,171,[i]
pp. 5 text figs. Faint traces of signature on
title.                       *(Pollak)* **£16**

**Green, C.E. & Young, D. (eds.)**
- Encyclopaedia of agriculture. 1907. 4to. 4
vols. Qtr mor. One spine torn & reprd.
                           *(Phenotype)* **£35**

**Green, Horace**
- Observations on the pathology of the croup:
with remarks on its treatment by tropical
medications. New York: 1852. 2nd edn. Sm
8vo. vii,115 pp. Frontis. Foxing & some
pencilling. Front hinge loose, cvrs rubbed &
bumped.                      *(Jenner)* **£30**
- A treatise of diseases of the air passage:
comprising an inquiry into the history,
pathology, causes, and treatment ... New
York: 1852. 3rd edn, revsd & enlgd. xvii,314
pp. 7 plates (6 hand-cold), Sl shelf wear.
                           *(Elgen)* **$100**

**Green, T. Henry**
- An introduction to pathology and morbid
anatomy. 1871. Sm 8vo. xvi,303 pp. Ills. Cvrs
& spine sl worn & frayed.     *(Jenner)* **£9**

**Greenhill, Sir G.**
- Notes on dynamics. London: H.M.S.O.,
1908. 2nd edn. Folio. 221,11 [advts] pp. 15
fldg plates. Orig bds, front cvr with sm tear.

Sgntr of Rollo Appleyard on front cvr.
                           *(Pollak)* **£35**

**Greenhow, Edward H.**
- On diptheria. 1860. xii,274 pp. Lib stamp on
title.                      *(Whitehart)* **£15**
- On diptheria. London: J.W. Parker & Son,
1860. 1st edn. 8vo. xii,274 pp. Orig cloth.
Author's engvd b'plate.      *(Antiq Sc)* **$150**
- On diptheria. New York: 1861. 1st Amer edn.
160 pp.                      *(Fye)* **$45**

**Greenish, Henry G.**
- A text book of materia medica ... designed for
students of pharmacy and medicine. London:
Churchill, 1909. 2nd edn. xii,640. 269 pp.
Orig cloth, rear cvr sl marked.  *(Pollak)* **£20**

**Greenwood, Major**
- Epidemics and crowd-diseases. An
introduction to the study of epidemiology.
London: 1935. 1st edn.      *(Scientia)* **$60**
- Epidemics and crowd-diseases. An
introduction to the study of epidemiology.
London: Williams & Norgate, 1935. 409,[ii].
Fldg graph.                  *(Pollak)* **£25**
- The medical dictator and other biographical
studies. London: 1936. 1st edn. Dw.
                           *(Scientia)* **$35**
- Medical statistics from Graunt to Farr.
Cambridge: 1948. 1st edn. Dw. *(Scientia)* **$60**
- Some British pioneers of social medicine.
London: 1948. 1st edn.      *(Scientia)* **$37.50**

**Greenwood, Nicholas**
- Astronomia Anglicana: containing an
absolute and entire piece of astronomy ...
London: for William Hebsman, 1689. 1st
edn. Folio. viii,260. Num w'cuts diags &
printed tables. Sl soiled in places. Contemp
panelled calf, a little worn, red mor label.
                           *(Pickering)* **$1,200**

**Gregory, Alva**
- Spondylotherapy simplified. Oklahoma City:
Gregory, 1914. 180 pp. Cvr worn.
                           *(Xerxes)* **$40**

**Gregory, D.F.**
- Examples of the processes of the differential
and integral calculus. Cambridge: Deighton,
1846. 2nd edn, edited by William Walton.
x,529 pp. 4 plates. Half-calf, bds faded,
worn.                        *(Pollak)* **£25**

**Gregory, David**
- A treatise of practical geometry, in three
parts. (Translated from the Latin, with
additions). Edinburgh: for Elphinston
Balfour, 1796. 11th edn. 143 pp. 5 plates.
New half-calf.               *(Pollak)* **£30**

**Gregory, George**
- The economy of nature explained and illustrated on the principles of modern philosophy ... London: J. Johnson, 1796. 1st edn. 3 vols. 8vo. 46 engvd plates. Crnrs of pages in vol II a little crushed. Contemp full calf, spines somewhat worn, hinge split.
*(Zeitlin)* **$350**

**Gregory, John**
- Observations on the duties and offices of a physician and on the method of prosecuting enquiries in philosophy ... London: for W. Strahan & T. Candell, 1770. viii,182 pp. Some foxing. New bds, new endpapers.
*(Poitras)* **$175**

**[Gregory, John]**
- A comparative view of the state and faculties of man with those of the animal world. London: for J. Dodsley, 1765. 1st edn. 16mo in 8s. [iv],203,[5] pp. Some pencil-lining, first few leaves browned & edge-tattered. Mod calf-backed mrbld bds.
*(Gach)* **$100**

**Gregory, Olinthus**
- Mathematics for practical men: being a common-place book ... for the use of civil engineers, architects and surveyors. London: John Weale, 1848. 3rd edn, revsd & enlgd. xix,392,[ii], 118 pp. Fldg table, 12 plates, some being dusty in folds. Half-mor.
*(Pollak)* **£35**

**Gregory, Samuel**
- Letters to ladies, in favour of female physicians for their own sex. Boston: the [American Medical Education] Society, 1854. 2nd edn. 48 pp. Sm faint stain in upper margin. Orig printed wraps.
*(M&S)* **$125**

**Gresswell, D.A.**
- A contribution to the natural history of scarlatine, derived from observations on the London epidemic of 1887-88. Oxford: 1890. viii,205 pp. Many tables, Cvrs sl worn, lib label on spine.
*(Jenner)* **£20**

**Grew, Nehemiah**
- The anatomy of plants with an idea of the philosophical history of plants ... read before the Royal Society. [London]: W. Rawlins, 1682. 1st edn. Folio. 83 engvd plates, 5 fldg. Lower crnr of one leaf torn away, without loss. Contemp calf, spine reprd.
*(Quaritch)* **$800**

**Grey, John**
- A view of the past and present state of agriculture in Northumberland. 1841. 42 pp. Card cvr.
*(Bow Windows)* **£32**

**Grey, Dr. R.**
- Memoria technica or method of artificial memory, applied to and exemplified in chronology, geography, history and astronomy ... 1851. Half calf, mrbld bds, inner hinge cracked.
*(Quinto Charing Cross)* **£25**

**Griesinger, Wilhelm**
- Mental pathology and therapeutics. London: New Sydenham Society, 1867. 1st edn in English. xiv,503 pp. Pub embossed brown cloth, some wear to jnts.
*(Gach)* **$175**

**Griffin, J.**
- A plain and popular system of practical navigation and nautical astronomy ... including a journal of a voyage from London to Madeira ... 1852. 1st edn. x,234, [329],[52] pp. Frontis, many ills & tables. Orig 3/4 roan, sl rubbed & worn.
*(Whitehart)* **£25**

**Griffin, R.B. & Little, A.D.**
- The chemistry of paper making. Together with the principles of general chemistry. New York: 1894. 1st edn. 8vo. 6,517,[7], [2],[2] pp. 4 plates (1 fldg), ills. Orig cloth.
*(M&S)* **$150**

**Griffith, J.P. Crozer**
- The diseases of infants and children. Phila: 1920. 1st edn, 2nd printing. 2 vols. Lge 8vo. 885; viii,657 pp. 20 cold plates, over 400 ills.
*(Elgen)* **$35**

**Griffith, J.W. & Henfrey, Arthur**
- The micrographic dictionary; a guide to the examination and investigation of microscopic objects. London: Van Voorst, 1875. 3rd edn. 2 vols in 1. 48 engvd plates, some hand-cold, hundreds of w'cuts. Contemp mor, mrbld edges. *(McDowell)* **£60**
- The micrographic dictionary; a guide to the examination and investigation of the structure and nature of microscopic objects. London: 1875. 3rd edn. 2 vols in 1. 8vo. [xlii],845 pp. 48 engvd plates (15 cold). W'cuts in text. Recent half-calf.
*(Bow Windows)* **£70**

**Griffiths, E.H.**
- The thermal measurement of energy. Lectures delivered at the Philosophical Hall, Leeds. Cambridge: University Press, 1901. viii,135 pp. 19 text figs.
*(Pollak)* **£20**

**Griffiths, Thomas**
- Chemistry of the four ancient elements, fire air earth and water: an essay ... London: John W. Parker, 1851. 2nd edn. 12mo. xii,240 pp. 87 text figs on 16 plates. Contemp prize calf gilt, a little wear.
*(Diamond)* **$50**

**Grigg, E.R.N.**
- The trail of the invisible light. From X-

Strahlen to radio(bio)logy. Springfield: 1965. Lge 4to. xliii,974 pp. Many ills.
*(Whitehart)* £45

**Grimes, G.**
- The lily of the West: on human nature, education, the mind, insanity ... Nashville: n.p., 1846. 96 pp. Mod drab wraps, orig yellow printed wraps preserved. *(Gach)* $185

**Grimes, James Stanley**
- Etherology; or, the philosophy of mesmerism and phrenology: including a new philosophy of sleep and of consciousness ... New York, Phila ... & Boston: 1845. 8vo. xvi,350 pp. Frontis. Some staining. Embossed bds.
*(Poitras)* $70

**Grinker, Lt. Col. Roy R. & Spiegel, Capt. J.**
- War neuroses in North Africa, the Tunisian Campaign (January - May, 1943). Army Air Forces, September, 1943. 300 pp. 'Restricted: Not to be republished." Ex lib. Every page marked 'Restricted" *(Xerxes)* $85

**Grollman, Arthur**
- The cardiac output of man in health and disease. Springfield: 1932. 1st edn.
*(Scientia)* $65

**Gross, Robert**
- See Ladd, William & Gross, Robert
- The surgery of infancy and childhood. Phila: 1953. 1st edn. 1000 pp. Occas red underlining. *(Fye)* $75

**Gross, Samuel David**
- The anatomy, physiology, and diseases of the bones and joints. Phila: 1830. 1st edn. Tall 8vo. v, half-title, 390 pp. 2 pp pub ctlg. Contemp signature on title, foxing. Contemp calf, hinges rubbed. *(Hemlock)* $200
- Elements of pathological anatomy. Phila: Blanchard & Lea, 1857. 3rd edn, modified & thoroughly revised. 4to. xxv,771,32 [pub ctlg] pp. 342 engvs on wood. Full lea.
*(Poitras)* $150
- Memorial oration in honour of Ephraim McDowell (the father of ovariotomy). Louisville: John P. Morton, 1879. 22 pp. 2 ills. Inscription to Dr. Rodman by Dr. Colman Rogers. *(Poitras)* $85
- A system of surgery: pathological, diagnostic, therapeutic and operative. Phila: 1866. 4th edn. 2 vols. 1049; 1087 pp. Free endpaper missing in one vol. Full lea, scuffed & rubbed.
*(Fye)* $100

**Gruber, Howard E., et al. (eds.)**
- Contemporary approaches to creative thinking: a symposium held at the University of Chicago. New York: Atherton, [1962]. 223

pp. Dw. *(Gach)* $27.50

**Grunwald, Ludwig**
- Atlas and epitome of diseases of the mouth ... and nose. Phila: 1903. 2nd edn. 219 pp. Ills.
*(Fye)* $75
- A treatise on nasal supportation; or, supportative diseases of the nose and its accessory sinuses. 1900. Translated from the 2nd German edn. xii,229 p. 2 plates, 1 table. 8 ills. Cvrs sl worn. ex lib. *(Jenner)* £10

**Guerini, Vincenzo**
- A history of dentistry. Phila: Lea & Febiger, 1909. 1st edn. Lge 8vo. 355 pp. Red & black title, 20 plates, 104 text figs. Orig cloth.
*(Antiq Sc)* $100

**Guerra, Francisco**
- American medical bibliography 1639 - 1783. 1962. Thick sm 4to. 885 pp. *(Jenner)* £75

**Guidott, Thomas**
- A collection of treatises relating to the City and Waters of Bath ... to which is now added Thermae Redivive; or, the City of Bath Described, &c., by Henry Chapman. London: 1725. [xxx],430 pp. 4 plates (1 fldg). Blind-dec calf. 5 treatises. *(Jenner)* £120

**Guillemin, Amedee**
- The applications of the physical forces. Translated from the French by Mrs. Norman Lockyer ... 1877. Roy 8vo. 4 cold plates, 467 ills. prize calf gilt, rubbed & worn.
*(Edwards)* £35
- The forces of nature. A popular introduction to the study of physical phenomena. Translated from the French by Mrs. Norman Lockyer ... 1872. Roy 8vo. 11 cold plates, 455 w'cuts. Rebnd qtr mor. *(Edwards)* £35
- The heavens. An illustrated handbook of popular astronomy. Edited by J. Norman Lockyer. 1867. Roy 8vo. 39 plates. 191 w'cuts. Spine sl chipped. *(Edwards)* £35

**Guiteras, Ramon Benjamin**
- Urology: the diseases of the urinary tract in men and women. New York & London: D. Appleton, 1912. 2 vols. xxii,701; xix,757 pp. 947 text ills, 7 plates. *(Poitras)* $75

**Gulick, John T.**
- Evolution: racial and habitudinal. Wash, DC: 1905. 1st edn. 269 pp. Rebnd in cloth, orig wraps bnd in. *(Scientia)* $40

**Gulliver, G.**
- The works of William Hewson, F.R.S. Sydenham Society, 1846. lvi,360 pp. Port, 8 plates. Orig cloth, dull, t.e.g. *(Whitehart)* £40

**Gully, James Manby**
- The water cure in chronic diseases, an exposition of the causes, progress and termination of the various chronic diseases ... New York: 1846. xi,405 pp. Frontis. Some foxing on prelims. Orig cloth, crnrs & edges bumped. *(Jenner)* **£20**

**Gunter, Edmund**
- The description and use of the sector, the crosse-staffe & other instruments. London: ... Weaver, 1624. 1st edn, 2nd issue. 4to. [6]ff,143,[1] pp. Frontis, engvd title. Occas spotting. Tear across E1, lower portion A4 cut away. Mod qtr calf. *(Zeitlin)* **$950**

**Guthrie, Douglas**
- A history of medicine. 1945. 1st edn. 72 plates. *(Robertshaw)* **£12**
- A history of medicine. London: 1945. 1st edn. 448 pp. 72 plates. *(Oasis)* **$30**

**Guttman, Paul**
- A handbook of physical diagnosis comprising the throat, thorax and abdomen. London: 1879. 1st English translation. 441 pp. *(Fye)* **$40**
- A handbook of physical diagnosis comprising the throat, thorax and abdomen. London: New Sydenham Society, 1879. Translated from the 3rd German edn. xii,441 pp. Orig olive cloth. *(Jenner)* **£10**

**Gwynne, C.W.**
- Monograph on the manufacture of wire and tinsel in the United Provinces. Allahabad: 1910. 4to. iii,27 pp. 11 plates. Orig gilt-lettered cloth, a bit worn & loose, inscrbd by the author. *(Weiner)* **£75**

**Gypendole, Evariste de**
- A salve for the bite of the black viper. Translated from the French ... Louisville: 1852. Sm 8vo. 141 pp. Lib stamp in text, one one removed from title. Title faded. Rebacked with black tape. Religious allegory of poison, quasi-medical. *(Jenner)* **£50**

**Haab, O.**
- Atlas and epitome of operative ophthalmology. Phila: 1905. 1st English translation. 377 pp. 30 cold lithos. *(Fye)* **$40**
- Atlas and epitome of operative ophthalmology. Phila: Saunders, 1905. 377 pp. 30 cold lithos, 155 text cuts. *(Xerxes)* **$50**
- Atlas and epitome of ophthalmoscopy and ophthalmoscopic diagnosis. Phila: 1901. 1st English translation. 85 pp. 152 cold lithos with text. *(Fye)* **$75**
- Atlas and epitome of ophthalmoscopy and ophthalmoscopic diagnosis. Phila: Saunders, 1901. 1st edn. 85 pp. 152 cold lithos. *(Xerxes)* **$50**

- Atlas of the external diseases of the eye including a brief treatise on the pathology and treatment. Phila: 1899. 228 pp. 76 cold plates. *(Fye)* **$60**
- Atlas of the external diseases of the eye. Phila: Saunders, 1903. 2nd edn. 232 pp. 98 cold lithos on 48 plates. *(Xerxes)* **$60**

**Haagensen, C.D. & Lloyd, Wyndham E.B.**
- A hundred years of medicine. New York: 1943. 1st Amer edn. xii,443 pp. Plates. Cvrs sl worn. *(Jenner)* **£28**

**Haanel, Eugene**
- On the location and examination of magnetic ore deposits by magnetometric measurements. Ottawa: 1904. 1st edn. 9,[1],132 pp. Index. 5 photo ills, 8 fldg charts. Orig mor, rubbed at extremities. *(M&S)* **$50**

**Haas, Sidney Valentine**
- Management of celiac disease. Phila: J.B. Lippincott, 1951. 188 pp. Ills. *(Poitras)* **$30**

**Habershon, S.O.**
- Pathological and practical observations on diseases of the alimentary canal, esophagus ... Phila: 1859. 1st Amer edn. 312 pp. *(Fye)* **$45**

**Hachiya, Michihoko**
- Hiroshima diary. The journal of a Japanese physician, August 6 - September 30, 1945. Chapel Hill: University of North Carolina Press, 1955. 238 pp. Dw. *(Poitras)* **$20**

**Haggard, Howard W.**
- Devils, drugs and doctors. The story of the science of healing from medicine-man to doctor. London: Heinemann, n.d. [1903?]. 1st English edn. Caricature frontis, extensively illust. *(McDowell)* **£24**
- The lame, the halt, the blind. The vital role of medicine in the history of civilisation. New York: Harper's, 1932. 3rd printing. 8vo. Frontis, extensively illust. Pub cloth. *(McDowell)* **£38**

**Hahnemann, S.**
- The homeopathic medical doctrine, or, "Organon of the healing art" ... Translated ... Dublin: W.F. Wakeman, 1833. 1st edn in English. 8vo. xxv,[1],332 pp. Errata, 12 pp pub ctlg. Uncut. Orig bds, lightly soiled, crnrs & spine sl chipped, paper label. *(Rootenberg)* **$650**

**Haig, A.**
- Uric acid as a factor in the causation of disease ... 1894. 2nd edn. xi,400 pp. 36 figs. Orig cloth, sl stained. *(Whitehart)* **£15**

**Halbwachs, Maurice**
- The causes of suicide. Translated ... 1978.

xxx,372 pp. Few tables. Dw.    *(Jenner)* **£10**

**Haldane, J.B.S.**
- The causes of evolution. London: 1932. 1st edn. 235 pp.    *(Scientia)* **$50**
- Heredity and politics. New York: 1938. 1st Amer edn. 202 pp.    *(Scientia)* **$27.50**
- The Marxist philosophy and the sciences. New York: 1939. 214 pp.    *(Scientia)* **$27.50**
- New paths in genetics. New York: 1942. 1st Amer edn. 206 pp.    *(Scientia)* **$25**

**Haldane, J.S.**
- Methods of air analysis. 1912. x,130 pp. 23 ills, 1 plate. Orig cloth.    *(Whitehart)* **£18**
- The new physiology and other addresses. 1919. 1st edn. vii,156 pp. Orig cloth, lightly stained.    *(Whitehart)* **£18**

**Haldane, John Scott**
- Organism and environment as illustrated by the physiology of breathing. New Haven: 1917. 1st edn. xi,138 pp. Silliman Foundation Lectures.    *(Elgen)* **$55**

**Hale Enoch**
- Boylston medical prize dissertations for the years 1819 and 1821. Experiments and observations on the communications between the stomach and the urinary organs ... administering medicine by injection ... Boston: 1821. 1st edn. Orig wraps, soiled.    *(M&S)* **$65**

**Hale, Edwin M.**
- A systematic treatise on abortion. Chicago: 1866. 1st edn. xvi,[17]-347, [1 advts] pp. 2 cold litho plates, 1 b/w plate, text w'cuts. Marginal foxing, final 100 pp damp-stained. Rear cvr faded.    *(Elgen)* **$65**

**Hale, Enoch**
- History and description of an epidemic fever, commonly called spotted fever, which prevailed at Gardiner, Maine, in the spring of 1814. Boston: Wells & Lilly, 1818. 4to. xvi,246 pp. Half-title. Lib stamp on title. Uncut, unopened. Orig bds, sp bruised.    *(Hemlock)* **$175**

**Hales, Stephen**
- Vegetable staticks ... Also, a specimen of an attempt to analyse the air ... London: for Inny & Woodward; 1727. 1st edn. 8vo. [7],vii,[2],376 pp. 19 engvd plates. Minor wormtrails in blank margins of few leaves, 2 words of text crossed out. Mod calf.    *(Zeitlin)* **$1,750**

**Halford, Sir. H.**
- Essays and orations, read and delivered at the Royal College of Physicians; to which is added, an account of the opening of the tomb of Charles 1 ... 1842. 3rd edn. viii,424 pp. Orig cloth, worn, with two tears on spine.    *(Whitehart)* **£25**

**Hall, Granville Stanley**
- Adolescence: its psychology and its relations to physiology, anthropology, sociology, sex, crime ... New York & London: 1904. 1st edn. 2 vols. [iv],xxii,589,[3]; [iv],vi,784 pp. 10 pp advts. Red cloth, vol I reprd.    *(Gach)* **$75**
- Founders of modern psychology. New York & London: 1912. 1st edn. [x],470,[2] pp. 6 port photographs. Red cloth.    *(Gach)* **$40**

**Hall, J. Sparkes**
- The book of the feet: a history of boots and shoes ... New York: 1847. Lge 12mo. 216 pp. Extra elab chromo-litho title, many ills on 4 cold plates, ills in text. Light occas foxing. Contemp half-mor, worn, rebacked.    *(Weiner)* **£150**

**Hall, Marshall**
- A descriptive, diagnostic and practical essay on disorders of the digestive organs and general health ... Keene, N.H.: 1823. 1st Amer edn. 192 pp. Orig bds. Some light w'staining.    *(Whitehart)* **£80**

**Hall, Samuel**
- Samuel Hall's patent improvements in steam engines. Nottingham: S. Bennett, n.d. [ca 1835]. 8vo. 29 pp. 2 fldg plates. Portion of hd of title renewed without loss. Orig plain wraps, no backstrip.    *(Deighton Bell)* **£40**

**Hall, W.W.**
- Fun better than physic; or, everybody's life preserver. Chicago: Rand, McNally & Co., 1882. 8vo. 333 pp.    *(Poitras)* **$30**

**[Halley, Edmund]**
- Miscellanea curiosa: a collection of some of the principal phaenomena in nature ... London: ... John Knapton ..., 1726-23-27. 3 vols. 3rd, 1st, 2nd edns. 8vo. Frontis, 20 fldg plates. Some browning, a few marginal tears. Contemp calf, worn, hinges split.    *(Zeitlin)* **$650**

**Halsted, William S.**
- Surgical papers. Balt: 1924. 1st edn. 4to.    *(Scientia)* **$200**
- Surgical papers. Balt: 1924. 1st edn. 2 vols. 4to. 586; 683 pp. Backstrips worn with tears at hd & ft of spine.    *(Fye)* **$150**

**Hamilton, Alexander**
- Hamilton's itinerarium, being a narrative of a journey from Annapolis, through Delaware, N.Y., N.J., Conn., R.I., Mass and N.H. from May to September, 1744. St. Louis: William K. Bixby, 1901. Private circ only, ltd. Lea

crnrs & spine scuffed, worn.  *(Poitras)* **$75**

**Hamilton, Alice**
- Industrial poisons in the United States. New York: 1925. 1st edn.  *(Scientia)* **$175**

**Hamilton, Allan**
- Railway and other accidents with relation to injury and disease of the nervous system. New York: 1904. 1st edn. 351 pp. Num photographic ills.  *(Fye)* **$50**

**Hamilton, Frank**
- A practical treatise on fractures and dislocations. Phila: 1871. 4th edn. 789 pp.  *(Fye)* **$60**
- A practical treatise on fractures and dislocations. Phila: Lea, 1871. 4th edn. 8vo. 789 pp. Ills. Crnrs & spine ends v worn.  *(Xerxes)* **$25**
- A practical treatise on fractures and dislocations. Phila: 1891. 8th edn. 849 pp.  *(Fye)* **$40**

**Hamilton, Hugh**
- The works, collected and published, with some alterations and additions from his manuscripts, by Alexander Hamilton, his eldest son. London: William Bulmer, 1809. 1st coll edn. 2 vols. Lge 8vo. Port frontis, 20 fldg plates. Contemp mor, sl rubbed.  *(McDowell)* **£160**

**Hamilton, James**
- Observations on the utility and administration of purgative medicines in several diseases. Edinburgh: 1806. 2nd edn. xx,349 pp. Contemp tree calf, worn.  *(Whitehart)* **£40**
- Observations on the utility and administration of purgative medicines in several diseases. Edinburgh: 1806. 2nd edn. xx,349 pp. Lib stamp on title & 2 other leaves, some ink writing. Calf-backed mrbld bds, very rubbed.  *(Jenner)* **£35**
- Observations on the utility and administration of purgative medicines in several diseases ... Phila: James Webster ..., 1818. 4to. xix,122,168 pp. Contemp mottled calf, front hinge cracked, lea label.  *(Hemlock)* **$100**
- Observations on the utility and administration of purgative medicines in several diseases. Phila: James Webster, 1818. 2nd Amer edn. xix,122,168 pp. Contemp tree calf, cvrs sl worn.  *(Diamond)* **$75**

**Hamilton, John B.**
- Lectures on tumors. Phila: 1898. 3rd edn. 143 pp.  *(Fye)* **$25**

**Hamilton, Mary**
- Incubation: the cure of disease in pagan

temples and Christian churches. London & St. Andrews, 1906. 4to. 227 pp. Title sl foxed.  *(Poitras)* **$40**

**Hamilton, Sir William**
- Lectures on logic. Edited by Mansell & Veitch. Boston: Gould & Lincoln, 1860. xvi,731,[v] pp. Orig cloth, spine ends a little worn.  *(Pollak)* **£20**
- Lectures on metaphysics. Edited by Mansell & Veitch. Edinburgh: Blackwood, 1869. 4th edn. 2 vols. xix,444; x,568 pp. Orig cloth.  *(Pollak)* **£20**

**Hamilton, Sir William**
- Observations on Mount Vesuvius, Mount Etna, and other volcanos: In a series of letters addressed to the Royal Society. London: Cadell, 1774. New (2nd) edn. 8vo. Fldg map, 5 engvd plates. Contemp tree calf, elab gilt. Rebacked.  *(McDowell)* **£200**

**Hamilton, William A.**
- A treatise on the diseases of the nervous system. New York: D. Appleton & Co., 1881. 7th edn, rewritten, enlgd. 929 pp. 112 ills. 14 pp pub ctlg.  *(Poitras)* **$75**

**Hammer, William J.**
- Radium, and other radio-active substances. New York: D. Van Nostrand, 1903. 1st edn. 8vo. viii,72,7 [pub advts] pp. Frontis, num text ills. Orig dec cloth.  *(Antiq Sc)* **$125**

**Hammond, William**
- Sexual impotence in the male. New York: 1883. 1st edn. 274 pp.  *(Fye)* **$75**

**Hammond, William A.**
- Insanity in its medico-legal relations ... New York: 1867. 2nd edn. 81 pp. Spine faded & spine tips defective.  *(Diamond)* **$45**
- Sleep and its derangements. Phila: Lippincott, 1869. 1st edn. 318 pp. Cloth, shelfworn.  *(Gach)* **$50**
- Spiritualism and allied causes and conditions of nervous derangement. New York: 1876. 366 pp. Stamps on title. Cloth, sl stained, crnrs & spine ends worn. *(Epistemologist)* **$45**
- Spiritualism and allied causes and conditions of nervous derangement. London: H.K. Lewis, 1876. 1st English edn. xii,366,[ii] pp. 9 text ills. Orig cloth, spine & edges of bds marked.  *(Pollak)* **£35**

**Hampson, W.**
- Radium explained. A popular account of the relations of radium to the natural world, to scientific thought, and to human life. New York: 1905. 1st edn. 12mo. x,122 pp. Ills. Pict cloth.  *(Elgen)* **$125**

**Hanbury, Daniel**
- Notes on Chinese materia medica. 1862. 1st sep edn, reprinted from the Pharmaceutical Journal. Ills. Author's pres slip on front pastedown.                    *(Robertshaw)* £36
- Science papers, chiefly pharmacological and botanical. Edited ... London: Macmillan, 1876. x,[ii],543, [i]. Frontis, 11 plates, 48 text w'engvs. Some foxing. Tan mor, a.e.g.
                                    *(Pollak)* £35
- Science papers, chiefly pharmacological and botanical. Edited, with memoir, by Joseph Ince. 1876. 1st edn. Ills. A little browning at beginning. Orig cloth. Stamp of Pharmaceutical Society on front cvr.
                                *(Robertshaw)* £48
- See Fluckiger, Friedrich A. & Hanbury, Daniel

**Hancock, Thomas**
- Research into the laws and phenomena of pestilence; including a medical sketch and review of the Plague of London in 1665; and remarks on quarantine. With an appendix ... London: 1821. xv,379 pp. Title sl stained. Uncut in orig bds.        *(Whitehart)* £135

**Hand, William**
- The house surgeon and physician; designed to assist heads of families, travelers and seafaring people ... New Haven: 1820. 2nd edn. 288 pp. Mod cloth-backed bds, paper label.
                                    *(Fye)* $100

**Hanfmann, Eugenia & Kasanin, Jacob**
- Conceptual thinking in schizophrenia. New York: 1942. 1st edn. viii,115,[5] pp. Printed bds, rear bd stained.            *(Gach)* $35

**Harbord, F.W.**
- The metallurgy of steel. With a section on the mechanical treatment of steel by J.W. Hall. 1905. Thick 8vo. 2nd edn revised. 87 fldg plates, 280 text ills, many photos.
                                    *(Edwards)* £20

**Hardaway, W.A.**
- See Bangs, L.B. & Hardaway, W.A.

**Harden, Arthur**
- See Roscoe, Henry E. & Harden, Arthur

**Hardin, Willett L.**
- The rise and development of the liquefaction of gases. New York: Macmillan, 1899. viii,250 pp. 42 text figs.      *(Pollak)* £20

**Hardy, G.H.**
- Ramanujan. Twelve lectures on subjects suggested by his life and work. Cambridge: University Press, 1940. [viii],236 pp. Frontis. Orig cloth.                  *(Pollak)* £25

**Hardy, G.H. & Wright, E.M.**
- An introduction to the theory of numbers. Oxford: Clarendon Press, 1938. 1st edn. Royal 8vo. Pub cloth, faded & sl spotted.
                                *(McDowell)* £28

**Hardy, William**
- The miner's guide: or, compleat miner. Containing, I A succinct account of a vein in the earth. II The customs, laws ... III ... IV ... Sheffield: Francis Lister, 1748. 1st edn. 8vo. vii,234 pp. Errata. 3 w'cut plates. Foxed throughout. Contemp calf.
                            *(Deighton Bell)* £345

**Hare, H.A.**
- The pathology, clinical history and diagnosis of affections of the mediastinum. Phila: 1889. 1st edn. 150 pp. Plates.      *(Fye)* $60

**Harkavy, Joseph**
- Vascular allergy and its systemic manifestations. Washington: Butterworths, 1963. 304 pp. Ills.        *(Poitras)* $15

**Harker, A.**
- Natural history of igneous rocks. 1902. 8vo. 2 plates, 112 text figs. Cloth, trifle used, spine faded.            *(Wheldon & Wesley)* £15

**Harkins, Henry N.**
- The treatment of burns. Springfield: 1942. 1st edn. Spine lettering dull.    *(Scientia)* $55

**Harle, Jonathan**
- An historical essay on the state of physick in the Old and New Testament, and the Apocryphal Interval: with a particular account of the cases mentioned in scripture ... London: Richard Ford, 1729. 4to. 179 pp. Emblemata. New bds.        *(Poitras)* $225

**Harmony ...**
- The harmony of the ancient and modern geometry ... See Paman, Roger

**Harris, Chapin A.**
- A dictionary of medical terminology, dental surgery, and the collateral sciences. Phila: Lindsay & Blakiston, 1878. 4th edn, revsd & enlgd. xv,17-754,[ii] pp. Orig cloth, recased, spine faded, cvrs marked at top edge.
                                    *(Pollak)* £20
- The principles and practice of dental surgery. Phila: Lindsay & Blakiston, 1853. 5th edn, revsd, imprvd. 236 ills.      *(Poitras)* $100
- See Fox, Joseph & Harris, Chapin A.

**Harris, Henry**
- California's medical story. San Francisco: Grabhorn Press, 1932. 421 pp.    *(Oasis)* $65

**Harris, John**
- Lexicon technicum: or, an universal English dictionary of arts and sciences ... London: 1736. 5th edn. Folio. 2 vols. Unpaginated. 2 engvd frontis, 20 engvd plates (13 fldg), 2 fldg tables. Some leaves torn with loss of text. Contemp calf, worn, chipped. *(Zeitlin)* **$600**
- Lexicon technicum: or, an universal English dictionary of arts and sciences ... London: 1736. 5th, but 1st combined, edn. Folio. 2 vols. 2 ports, 21 engvd plates, 2 w'cut plates. Red & black titles. Contemp calf, jnts reprd.
*(Pickering)* **$1,500**

**Harris, Joseph**
- The description and use of the globes and the orrery, to which is prefixed by way of introduction a brief account of the solar system. 1745. 6th edn. viii,190 pp. 6 plates (1 sl cropped). A few insignificant stains. Contemp lea, rebacked, gilt spine.
*(Whitehart)* **£60**

**Harris, P.W.**
- See Scott-Taggart, John & Harris, P.W.

**Harris, Percy W.**
- The maintenance of wireless telegraph apparatus. 1917. xi,127 pp. Ills, diags. Cloth discoloured. *(Weiner)* **£20**

**Harris, W. Snow**
- On the nature of thunderstorms: and on the means of protecting buildings and shipping against the destructive force effects of lightning. 1843. Frontis, many ills. Cloth worn, lacks backstrip. *(Edwards)* **£17.50**
- Rudimentary electricity: being a concise exposition of the general principles of electrical science, and the purposes to which it has been applied. London: John Weale, 1848. 1st edn. 4 [advts],iv,160 pp. Frontis, 59 text figs. *(Pollak)* **£50**

**Harrison, Allen**
- A system of human anatomy, including its medical and surgical relations ... Phila: 1884. 1st edn. Large 4to. 812 pp. 109 full-page lithos, many in colour, 241 text w'cuts. 3/4 lea, crnrs scuffed. *(Elgen)* **$100**

**Harrison, H.H.**
- An introduction to the Strowger system of automatic telephony. 1924. vii,146 pp. Diags. Sl wear. *(Weiner)* **£18**

**Harrison, John**
- The library of Isaac Newton. Cambridge: 1978. 1st edn. 286 pp. Dw. *(Scientia)* **$50**

**Harrison, Newton**
- Wireless telephone construction. New York: 1909. 74 pp. Ills, diags. Orig limp cloth,

rather worn & shaken. *(Weiner)* **£38**

**Harrison, R.**
- The surgical anatomy of the arteries of the human body. Dublin: 1824-25. 1st edn. 2 vols in 1. xxii,201; vii,195 pp. Contemp calf, rebacked. *(Whitehart)* **£55**

**Harrison, Reginald**
- Lectures on the surgical disorders of the urinary organs. 1887. 3rd edn. xi,583 pp. 117 figs & plates in the text. Orig cloth, sl w'stained. *(Whitehart)* **£25**

**Harrison, Robert**
- The Dublin dissector, or manual of anatomy. New York: 1845. 2nd Amer edn. 541 pp. Full lea, rear bd nearly detchd. *(Fye)* **$25**

**Hart, D. Berry**
- Contributions to the topographical and sectional anatomy of the female pelvis ... Edinburgh & London: 1885. 1st edn. Folio. 8 pp,[1 advts]f. 12 plates, 2 text figs. Orig cloth. Backstrip gone, cvrs detchd. *(Zeitlin)* **$95**

**Hart, Ernest**
- Hypnotism, mesmerism and the new witchcraft. London: Smith, Elder, 1896. New edn. 8vo. Engvd & photogr ills. Pub cloth. *(McDowell)* **£30**

**Harte, Rev. Walter**
- Essays on husbandry. Essay I. A general introduction ... Essay ii. An account of some experiments ... London: W. Frederick, &c., 1770. 2nd edn. 2 parts in 1. 8vo. 5 copperplates, figs in text. Contemp calf, spine chipped, crnrs bruised. *(McDowell)* **£120**

**Hartenberg, Paul**
- Treatment of neurasthenia. Translated ... Edinburgh: 1914. 1st edn. *(Gach)* **$20**

**Hartley, David**
- A view of the present evidence for and against Mrs. Stephen's medicine, as a solvent for the stone. 1739. 1st edn. Contemp calf, rebacked. *(Robertshaw)* **£60**

**Hartmann, Franz**
- Buried alive. An examination into the occult cause of apparent death, trance and catalepsy. Boston: Occult Publishing Co., 1895. Sm 8vo. 147 pp. *(Xerxes)* **$90**

**Hartmann, Henri**
- Gynecological operations including non-operative treatment and minor gynecology. Phila: 1913. 1st English translation. 536 pp. *(Fye)* **$25**

**Hartree, D.R.**
- Calculating instruments and machines. Cambridge: 1950. 68 figs. *(Winterdown)* £20

**Hartshorne, Hugh & May, Mark A.**
- Studies in the nature of character by the Character Education Enquiry, Columbia University ... New York: 1928. 1st edn. 2 vols in 1. Green cloth.        *(Gach)* $27.50

**Harvey, Gideon**
- The vanities of philosophy and physick. The third edition ... enlarged ... London: for A. Roper ... R. Bassett ..., 1702. [14]ff,381 pp. Contemp blind-stamped panelled lea, front jnt tender.        *(Elgen)* $225

**Harvey, Samuel**
- The history of hemostasis. New York: 1929. 1st edn. 128 pp.        *(Fye)* $40

**Harvey, William**
- The anatomical exercises ... concerning the motion of the heart and blood ... to which is added ... discourse of the heart. London: for Richard Lowndes, 1653. 1st edn in English. 8vo. Without initial blank. Marginal worming, sev headlines cropped, 18th c calf.        *(Quaritch)* $9,500
- Movement of the heart and blood in animals. Translated from the original Latin ... Oxford: Blackwell, 1957. 1st edn thus. 8vo. Red & black title, cold frontis. Dw. *(McDowell)* £28
- The works ... Translated from the Latin with a life of the author by Robert Willis. London: Sydenham Society, 1847. 1st edn thus. Thick 8vo. Pub green blind-stamped cloth.        *(McDowell)* £55
- The works ... Translated from the Latin with a life of the author by Robert Willis. London: Sydenham Society, 1847. 624 pp. Orig cloth, extremities very worn.        *(Oasis)* $75
- The works ... Translated from the Latin with a life of the author by Robert Willis. London: Sydenham Society, 1847. 1st edn thus. 8vo. xcvi,624 pp. Minor spots & dust marks. Orig cloth, a little bumped, tips of crnrs worn, inner hinges strained.        *(Bow Windows)* £50

**Harwood, Sir John James**
- History and description of the Thirlmere water scheme. Manchester: Henry Blacklock, 1895. xv,277 pp. Frontis, 18 plates. Orig cloth gilt, t.e.g., spine ends bruised.        *(Pollak)* £50

**Harwood, William**
- On the curative influence of the southern Coast of England; especially that of Hastings: with observations on the diseases in which a residence on the coast is most beneficial. London: Colburn, 1828. 1t edn. viii,326 pp. Mod full green mor, gilt. *(Deighton Bell)* £50

**Hasheesh ...**
- The hasheesh eater ... See Ludlow, Fitz Hugh

**Hasse, Charles Ewald**
- An anatomical description of the diseases of the organs of circulation and respiration. Translated ... Sydenham Society, 1846. xiv,400 pp. Orig cloth, sl worn & dust stained.        *(Whitehart)* £40
- An anatomical description of the diseases of the organs of circulation and respiration. Translated ... Sydenham Society, 1846. xiv,[ii],400 pp. Some margins ragged, sm tear reprd, foxing. Orig cloth, spine ends worn.        *(Pollak)* £18

**Hastings, Charles**
- An experimental inquiry of the general nature of inflammation. Phila: J. Webster, 1821. 1st Amer edn. 8vo. 68 pp. Orig bds. Margin of one leaf torn away without loss of text.        *(Antiq Sc)* $100

**Hastings, Frank (ed.)**
- Artificial heart program conference: National Heart Institute Artificial Heart program. Washington: 1969. 1st edn. 1129 pp. Ex lib.        *(Fye)* $50

**Hatton, J.L.S.**
- The theory of the imaginary in geometry; together with the trigonometry of the imaginary. Cambridge: University Press, 1920. vi,[ii],215 pp. Orig cloth. *(Pollak)* £15

**Haubold, Herman**
- Preparatory and after treatment in operative cases. New York: 1910. 1st edn. 650 pp. Num ills, many photographic.        *(Fye)* $100

**Haughton, Graves Chamney**
- Prodromus, or, an enquiry into the first principles of reasoning: including an analysis of the human mind. 1839. viii,263 pp. Orig green cloth. Two sm stamps, inc one on title.        *(Jenner)* £25

**Hauksbee, F.**
- Physico-mechanical experiments on various subjects, containing an account of several surprising phaenomena ... 1719. 2nd edn. 8ff,336 pp. 8 fldg plates, few w'cut diags. 2 plates lightly w'stained & reprd at margins, few leaves frayed. Old calf, rebacked.        *(Weiner)* £150

**Haven, S.E.**
- See Toops, H.A. & Haven, S.E.

**Havens, W.P.**
- See Coates, J.B. & Havens, W.P.

**Haviland, A.**
- Scarborough as a health resort: its physical geography, geology, climate & vital statistics, with health guide, map, &c. 1883. vi,7,100 pp. Frontis view of Scarborough. Mod cloth, orig front & back pasted on.. *(Whitehart)* **£20**

**Haviland, Alfred**
- The geographical distribution of diseases in Great Britain. London: Swan Sonnenheim, 1892. 2nd edn. 406 pp. 4 cold engvd fold-out maps. Ills. *(Poitras)* **$60**

**Hawkins, C.C. & Wallis, F.**
- The dynamo, its theory, design and manufacture. 1903. 3rd edn, revsd & enlgd. xiii,925 pp. 413 pp. Orig cloth, sl worn & faded, hinges cracked. *(Whitehart)* **£15**

**Hawkins, H.P.**
- On diseases of vermiform appendix with a consideration of the symptoms and treatment of the resultant peritonitis. A dissertation ... 1895. vii,139 pp. 12 charts, 20 figs. Orig cloth, sl dust stained & faded. *(Whitehart)* **£18**

**Hay, William**
- Deformity: an essay. 1754. [iv],81 pp. Postscript. Some browning throughout. Mod calf gilt, new endpapers. *(Jenner)* **£50**

**Hayden, Horace H.**
- Geological essays; or, an enquiry into some of the geological phenomena to be found in various parts of America, and elsewhere. Balt: for the author, 1820. 1st edn. 8vo. 8,412 pp. Light marginal foxing. Later qtr-mor, mrbld bds, worn, upper cvr detchd. *(M&S)* **$150**

**Hayes, Albert Hamilton**
- Diseases of the nervous system: a treatise of psychological medicine. Boston: Peabody Medical Institute, [1873]. 1st edn. 204 pp. Spine tips rubbed. *(Gach)* **$35**
- Diseases of the nervous system: or, pathology of the nerves and nervous maladies. Boston: Peabody Medical Institute, 1875. 1st edn (?). 8vo. vi,204,[2 advts] pp. Engvd port, 18 text ills. A few prelims soiled. Orig cloth, rubbed, spine lettering flaked. *(Dailey)* **$45**

**Hayes, Charles**
- A treatise of fluxions: or an introduction to mathematical philosophy ... advances in mechanical philosophy ... London: for Tho. Leigh, 1704. 1st edn. Folio. [xvi],xii,315,[1 ad] pp. W'cut diag at ft of p 2, num w'cut text diags. Contemp calf, rebacked. *(Pickering)* **$2,450**

**Hayhoe, F.G.J.**
- Leukaemia. Research and clinical practice. Boston: Little, Brown, 1960. 335 pp. 12 cold plates, 196 b/w ills. *(Poitras)* **$30**

**Haymaker, Webb & Schiller, Francis (eds.)**
- The founders of neurology. Springfield: 1970. 2nd edn. 616 pp. Dw. *(Fye)* **$45**

**Hayward, C.B.**
- See Ashley, C.G. & Hayward, C.B.

**Hayward, George**
- Surgical reports, and miscellaneous papers on medical subjects. Boston: 1855. 1st edn. 452 pp. Rebound in cloth. *(Fye)* **$100**

**Head, Sir George**
- A home tour through the manufacturing districts of England, in the summer of 1835. London: Murray, 1836. 1st edn. 8vo. xi,434 pp. Some browning, neat ownership inscription on title. Half tan calf, red mor label. *(Deighton Bell)* **£125**
- A home tour through the manufacturing districts of England. New York: 1836. 8vo. Sl foxing. Orig cloth, spine defective. *(Marlborough)* **£45**

**Head, Henry**
- Studies in neurology. London: 1920. 1st edn. 2 vols. Rear cvr of Vol II sl faded. *(Scientia)* **$265**
- Studies in neurology. London: 1920. 1st edn. 2 vols. 4to. printed red cloth, recased. *(Gach)* **$250**

**Headland, Frederick William**
- The action of medicines in the system or, on the mode in which therapeutic agents ... produce their peculiar effects ... Phila: 1853. 1st Amer edn. Half-title, xii,[13]-560 pp. Light foxing. Orig blind-stamped cloth, rubbed. *(Elgen)* **$45**
- The action of medicines in the system. Phila: 1856. 2nd Amer edn. 408 pp. *(Fye)* **$30**

**Healde, Thomas**
- The pharmacopoeia of the Royal College of Physicians of London, translated into English, with notes, indexes of new names, preparations, etc., ... London: 1796. 7th edn. xx,390,[2 advts] pp. Full calf, lower bd detchd, worm hole in upper bd. *(Jenner)* **£28**

**Healing ...**
- The healing art; or, chapters upon medicine, diseases, remedies and physicians. London: 1887. 2 vols. viii,316; iv,377 pp. Pencil notes at end of each vol. Spines frayed, cvrs sl worn, plastic wallet. *(Jenner)* **£50**

**Health ...**
- Health restor'd, or, the triumph of nature, over physick, doctors, and apothecaries ... to which is added an essay on regimen. London:

for J. Torbuck & J. Noble ..., 1740. 1st edn.
iv,124 pp. Some dust-staining. Orig lea,
reprd, inner hinges cracked.        *(Elgen)* **$375**

**Healy, William & Tenney, Mary**
- Pathological lying, accusation, and swindling.
A study in forensic psychology. Boston:
Little, Brown & Company, 1926.
[ii],xii,286,[2] pp.        *(Gach)* **$25**

**Heath, C.**
- A manual of minor surgery and bandaging for
the use of house-surgeons, dressers, and
junior practitioners. London: 1886. 8th edn.
Sm 8vo. xvi,360,16 [advts] pp. 142 text figs.
Occas sm stains. Orig cloth, cvrs dull, upper
jnt sl torn.        *(Bow Windows)* **£15**

**Heath, Christopher**
- Injuries and diseases of the jaws. London:
1868. 1st edn. 416 pp. Lib b'plate & sm stamp
on title.        *(Fye)* **$300**
- Injuries and diseases of the jaws ... London:
John Churchill, 1868. 1st edn. 8vo. xii,416
pp. 40 pp pub advts. 100 text engvs. Orig
cloth, gilt spine. Author's pres inscrptn.
        *(Rootenberg)* **$250**
- Injuries and diseases of the jaws. The
Jacksonian Prize Essay ... London: Churchill,
1872. 2nd edn. xii,439,[i], 23 [ctlg], [i advts]
pp. 164 text w'engvs. Orig cloth, spine faded
& sl worn at hd.        *(Pollak)* **£25**

**Heath, Thomas**
- Aristarchus of Samos, the ancient
Copernicus. A history of Greek astronomy ...
Oxford: 1913. 1st edn. 425 pp. *(Scientia)* **$45**
- Aristarchus of Samos, the ancient
Copernicus. A history of Greek astronomy ...
Oxford: Clarendon Press, 1959. Reprint of
1913 edn. Dw.        *(Pollak)* **£30**

**Heather, J.F.**
- A treatise on mathematical drawing
instruments ... John Weale, 1849. 1st edn.
vi,183 pp. Frontis, plate, num text figs. Orig
limp cloth, hd of spine nicked, jnts a little
pulled.        *(Pollak)* **£25**

**Heaviside, Oliver**
- Electrical papers. London: Macmillan, 1892.
1st edn. 2 vols. xx,560; xvi,587 pp. Text figs.
Rear jnt vol II a little weak.  *(Pollak)* **£160**
- Electromagnetic theory. London: 1893 -
[1912]. 3 vols. xxi,466,32 [ctlg]; xvi,542,32
[ctlg]; [iv],519 pp. Num text figs. Orig cloth,
rebacked.        *(Pollak)* **£225**
- Electromagnetic theory. Vols 1 and 2.
1893-99. 2 vols. xxi,466; xvi,547 pp. Worn.
Vol 2 rebacked with old spine laid on. A third
volume was published in 1912. *(Weiner)* **£75**
- Electromagnetic theory. London: Benn Bros,
1922 reprint. 3 vols. xxi,466; xvi,547; [iv],519

pp. Num text figs. Spine ends a little worn.
        *(Pollak)* **£100**

**Hecker, John**
- The scientific basis of education. New York:
A.S. Barnes, 1868. 227 pp. 4 chromo-lithos.
        *(Gach)* **$40**

**Hedges, Killingworth**
- Continental electric light central stations with
notes on the methods in actual practice for
distributing electricity in towns. 1892. 4to.
x,210,11 [advts] pp. 25 plates, mostly fldg,
num ills & diags. Orig elaborate pict cloth
gilt, shaken.        *(Weiner)* **£40**

**Hediger, H.**
- Psychology and behaviour of animals in zoos
and circuses. London: 1955. 1st edn. 166 pp.
Ills.        *(Oasis)* **$40**

**Heisenberg, W.**
- Two lectures. 1. The present situation in the
theory of elementary particles; 2. Electron
theory of superconductivity. Cambridge:
University Press, 1949. 1st English edn. Slim
8vo. Dw.        *(McDowell)* **£25**

**Heitler, W.**
- The quantum theory of radiation. Oxford:
1936. 1st edn. Some bubbling on spine &
cvrs.        *(Scientia)* **$37.50**
- The quantum theory of radiation. Oxford:
1947. 2nd edn, 2nd printing. Dw.
        *(Scientia)* **$22.50**
- The quantum theory of radiation. Oxford:
1954. 3rd (final) edn. Cvrs lightly stained.
        *(Scientia)* **$45**

**Helferich, Heinrich**
- On fractures and dislocations ... illustrated
with 68 plates and 126 figures in the text.
London: New Sydenham Society, 1899. 4to.
162 pp. Cold plates.        *(Poitras)* **$60**

**Hellins, John**
- Select parts of Saunderson's elements of
algebra. For the use of students at the
universities. London: for C. Dilly, 1792. 5th
edn, revsd & crrctd. iv,417 pp. 2 plates. Tree
sheep, spine worn, some rubbing.
        *(Pollak)* **£35**

**Hellman, C. Doris**
- The comet of 1577; its place in the history of
astronomy. New York: 1944. 1st edn. 488 pp.
        *(Scientia)* **$50**

**Hellyer, S. Stevens**
- The plumber and sanitary houses. A practical
treatise on the principles of internal plumbing
work ... London: B.T. Batsford, [1884]. 3rd
edn. Pict title, 27 plates, 262 text ills. Orig

cloth gilt, spine ends nicked, sl wear to lower crnrs. *(Pollak)* **£25**

**Helmholtz, Hermann von**
- The description of an ophthalmoscope. Being an English translation ... Chicago: 1916. 1st edn in English. Lts (500). Lge 8vo. Frontis, 33 pp. Orig cloth, worn, spine edges & crnrs frayed. *(Elgen)* **$150**
- On the sensations of tone as a physiological basis for the theory of music. Translated from the fourth German edition ... London: Longmans, Green, 1885. 2nd English edn. xix,576 pp. Num text figs. *(Pollak)* **£85**
- On the sensations of tone as a physiological basis for the theory of music. London: 1895. 3rd edn. Rebound in buckram. Ex lib. *(Fye)* **$75**
- Popular lectures on scientific subjects. Translated ... London: Longmans, Green, 1893. New edn. 2 vols. [ii],xiv,348; vi,[ii],291 pp. 24 pp ctlg. 68 figs. Orig dec cloth. *(Pollak)* **£30**
- Popular lectures on scientific subjects. Translated ... first & second series. London: 1893. Sm 8vo. 2 vols. xiv,348; viii,291 pp. 68 figs. Some foxing. Contemp calf, gilt. Durham College arms in gilt on cvrs. *(Pollak)* **£65**

**Henderson, A.**
- The practical grazier; or, a treatise on the proper selection and management of livestock ... 1856. 3rd edn. xxxi,478 pp. Engvd title, frontis, many engvs, 4 plans. Orig embossed cloth. *(Phenotype)* **£80**

**Henderson, Alexander**
- An examination of the imposture of Ann Moore called the fasting woman, of Tutbury; illustrated by remarks on other cases of real and pretended abstinence. London: 1813. 1st edn. iv,52 pp. Paper-cvrd bds, some wear. *(Elgen)* **$125**

**Henderson, Ebenezer**
- Life of James Ferguson, F.R.S., in a brief autobiographical account and a further extended memoir ... Edinburgh, London & Glasgow: A. Fullerton, 1870. 2nd edn, with addtns. 8vo. xxxvi,503 pp. Port, map, num text ills & diags. Later blue binder's cloth. *(Burmester)* **£65**

**Henderson, William Augustus**
- The housekeeper's instructor; or, universal family cook. Being an ample and clear display of the art of cookery ... London: W. & J. Stratford, n.d. [1790?]. 1st edn. Frontis, 11 plates, subscribers' list. 2 leaves with minor reprs. 19th c half-calf, rebacked. *(McDowell)* **£220**

**Hendrick, James**
- See Ward, Grant & Hendrick, James

**Henfrey, Arthur**
- See Griffith, J.W. & Henfrey, Arthur

**Henle, Jacob**
- On miasmata and contagia, translated ... (reprinted Bull. Inst. Hist. Med.). Balt: 1938. Lge 8vo. 77 pp. Port. Orig printed bds. *(Weiner)* **£30**

**Henle, Mary (ed.)**
- Documents of gestalt psychology. Berkeley: 1961. 1st edn. 352 pp. Red & grey cloth. *(Gach)* **$50**

**Henoch, E.**
- Lectures on children's diseases. London: New Sydenham Society, 1889. 2 vols. 8vo. Bds of vol II sl discold. *(McDowell)* **£40**
- Lectures on children's diseases. London: New Sydenham Society, 1889. 2 vols. Orig cloth. *(Oasis)* **$80**
- Lectures on diseases of children. New York: 1882. 1st edn in English. *(Scientia)* **$125**

**Henry, Alfred Judson**
- Climatology of the United States [1870 - 1903]. 1906. 4to. 1012 pp. Tables, maps (some in color). Cloth. *(Diamond)* **$75**

**Henry, George W.**
- See Zilboorg, Gregory & Henry, George W.

**Henry, William**
- The elements of chemistry. 1829. 11th edn, comprehending all the recent discoveries. 2 vols. Thick 8vo. xvi,684; vii,753 pp. 10 plates, w'cuts. Plate I foxed, light foxing elsewhere. Uncut. Old grey bds, Vol I rebacked, sl cracking to jnts of Vol II. *(Weiner)* **£75**
- An epitome of experimental chemistry, in three parts ... to which are added, notes on various subjects ... Boston: 1810. 8vo. 507 pp. 8 engvd fldg copperplates. Qtr calf, spine worn. Ex lib. *(Argosy)* **$75**

**Henry, William Charles**
- Memoirs of the life and scientific researches of John Dalton. London: Cavendish Society, 1854. 1st edn. 8vo. Vignette frontis, 3 fldg charts. Orig green cloth, top of spine reprd. *(McDowell)* **£48**

**Henschen, Folke**
- The history and geography of disease. New York: Delacort Press, 1966. 344 pp. Ills. *(Poitras)* **$30**

**Henwood, William Jory**
- Address delivered at the spring meeting of the

Royal Institution of Cornwall ... 1871. Truro: James Netherton, 1871. [ii],65 pp. Interleaved with blanks. Old binder's cloth, discoloured & worn.          *(Pollak)* £15
Observations on metalliferous deposits and on subterranean temperature ... the eighth volume of the Transactions of the Royal Geological Society of Cornwall. Penzance: 1871. 2 vols. 8vo. xxxii,916 pp. 6 plates, 37 tables, ills. Uncut. Orig cloth-backed bds.
*(Weiner)* £85

**Herbart, Johann Friedrich**
- Herbart's ABC of sense-perception: and minor pedagogical works. New York: D. Appleton, 1896. 1st edn. 12mo. 288 pp.
*(Gach)* $25

**Herman, Leon**
- The practice of urology. Phila: 1938. 1st edn. 923 pp.          *(Fye)* $20

**Hermann, D.L.**
- Elements of human physiology. Translated from the 5th German edition ... 1875. Thick 8vo. xv,587 pp. Roughtrimmed, cvrs sl worn.
*(Jenner)* £20

**Hermes Trismegistus, Mercurius**
- The divine pymander ... in xvii books. Translated ... by that learned divine doctor Everard. London: ... Greg. Moule, 1650. 1st edn in English. Sm 8vo. [16],215 pp. Fldg engvd frontis. Mod qtr calf. Harvard b'plate & unobjectionable stamps. *(Dailey)* $1,500

**Herrick, James B.**
- A short history of cardiology. Springfield: 1942. 1st edn.          *(Scientia)* $55

**Herries, R.S.**
- See Monckton, H.W. & Herries, R.S.

**Herschel, J.F.W.**
- Outlines of astronomy. London: 1858. 8vo. 714 pp. 6 plates, text figs. Orig cloth. Ex lib.
*(Argosy)* $75
- A treatise on astronomy (Lardner's Cabinet Cyclopaedia, volume 43) ... London: Longman ..., 1833. 1st edn. Sm 8vo. 16 [advts],viii,422. Printed & engvd titles, 3 engvd plates. Uncut & unopened. Orig glazed cloth, printed paper label, spine faded.
*(Pickering)* $200

**Herschel, John Frederick William**
- Essays from the Edinburgh and Quarterly Reviews, with addresses and other pieces ... London: Longman ..., 1857. 1st coll edn. 8vo. iv,250 pp. 24 pp pub advts. Orig cloth. Signet Library b'plate.          *(Rootenberg)* $165
- Outlines of astronomy ... London: for Longman ..., 1849. 1st edn. xvi,[1 errata],661

pp. 32 pp pub advts. 6 engvd plates (1 fldg), plate foxed. Orig cloth, faded & sl frayed.
*(Pickering)* $300
- Outlines of astronomy. 1849. 2nd edn. xvi,661 pp. 6 plates (one fldg). Binding worn, rebacked. Ex lib.          *(Weiner)* £30
- Preliminary discourse on the study of natural philosophy. London: Longman, [1846]. New edn. [iv],372,16 [ctlg] pp. Engvd title, with name cut from top. Orig cloth. *(Pollak)* £25

**Hertwig, Oscar**
- The biological problem of today. Preformation or epigenesis? The basis of a theory of organic development. Translated ... London: 1896. 1st edn in English. 148 pp.
*(Scientia)* $35

**Hertz, Heinrich**
- Electric waves, being researches on the propagation of electric action with finite velocity through space. London: Macmillan, 1893. 1st English edn. xv,[iii],278,[ii] pp. 40 text figs.          *(Pollak)* £200
- Electric waves, being researches on the propagation of electric action with finite velocity through space. London: Macmillan, 1893. 1st English edn. 8vo. Pub cloth.
*(McDowell)* £120
- The principles of mechanics presented in a new form, with an introduction ... authorised translation ... 1899. xxviii,276 pp. Lib stamps.          *(Weiner)* £85

**Hertzler, A.E.**
- The peritoneum. 1919. 2 vols. Orig cloth, sl marked & dust stained.     *(Whitehart)* £15

**Hertzler, Arthur**
- Surgical pathology of the diseases of bones. Phila: 1931. 1st edn. 272 pp.     *(Fye)* $25
- Surgical pathology of the diseases of the mouth and jaws. Phila: 1938. 1st edn. 248 pp.
*(Fye)* $30
- Surgical pathology of the gastro-intestinal tract. Phila: 1936. 1st edn. 311 pp. Ills. Inscribed by the author.          *(Oasis)* $45
- A treatise on tumors. Phila: 1912. 1st edn. 725 pp. Photographic ills.          *(Fye)* $75

**Herzberg**
- The sewing machine: its history, construction and application. 1864. iv,112 pp. 7 lge fldg plates. Orig pict bds, cloth-backed, worn.
*(Weiner)* £240

**Hess, Alfred F.**
- Scurvy past and present. Phila: 1920. 1st edn.
*(Scientia)* $50

**Hess, Leo**
- See Eppinger, Hans & Hess, Leo

**Hevesy, George von**
- Chemical analysis by X-rays and its applications. New York: 1932. 1st edn. 333 pp. *(Scientia)* **$37.50**

**Hevesy, George von & Paneth, Frith**
- A manual of radioactivity. Oxford: 1926. 1st edn in English. 252 pp. Ills. Orig cloth. *(Oasis)* **$100**
- A manual of radioactivity. Translated by R.W. Lawson. London: 1926. 1st edn in English. 252 pp. *(Scientia)* **$45**

**Hewitt, Graily**
- The pathology, diagnosis and treatment of diseases of women ... edited with notes ... New York: 1883. New Amer edn. 2 vols. 469; 561 pp. *(Fye)* **$30**

**Hewitt, W.**
- An essay upon the encroachments of the German Ocean along the Norfolk Coast ... Norwich: 1844. Slim 8vo. 2 ills. Cloth. Sl loose in binding *(Thomas Crowe)* **£25**

**Hewson, William**
- The works of William Hewson, F.R.S., edited with an introduction and notes by George Gulliver. London: 1846. 1st edn. 260 pp. *(Fye)* **$175**

**Higgins, S.H.**
- Dyeing in Germany and America with notes on colour production. Manchester: 1916. 2nd edn. viii,143, 16 [ctlg] pp. T.e.g. Ex lib. *(Elgen)* **$35**

**Higinbotham, Norman**
- See Coley, Bradley & Higinbotham, Norman

**Hilbert D. & Ackerman, W.**
- Principles of mathematical logic. New York: 1950. 1st edn in English. 172 pp. *(Oasis)* **$30**

**Hilditch, T.P.**
- A concise history of chemistry. Methuen: 1911. ix,263 pp. 48 pp ctlg. *(Pollak)* **£15**

**Hill, A.V.**
- Trails and trials in physiology. A bibliography, 1909 - 1964. 1965. vii,374 pp. Few ills. Worn dw. *(Jenner)* **£15**

**Hill, J.**
- The family herbal, or an account of all those English plants, which are remarkable for their virtues ... Bungay: 1812. 8vo. viii,xl,376 pp. 54 hand-cold plates. Title browned, signs of use. Contemp tree calf, rebacked, trifle rubbed. *(Wheldon & Wesley)* **£80**

**Hill, Sir John**
- On the virtues of sage, in lengthening human

life. With rules to attain old age in health and cheerfulness. London: for the author, [1763]. 1st edn. 8vo. 32 pp. Mod bds. *(Quaritch)* **$250**
- The sleep of plants, and causes of motion in the sensitive plants, explain'd in a letter to C. Linnaeus ... London: R. Baldwin, 1757. 1st edn. 8vo. xii,57,[3] pp. Title soiled. Disbound, without final blank. *(Dailey)* **$225**
- Virtues of British herbs. With the history, description, and figures ... London: R. Baldwin ... 1771-2. 4th edn, with additions. 3 parts in one vol. 8vo. 106,[8],50,[2] pp. Lacking half-title. 31 engvd plates. Browning. Later qtr-calf. *(Dailey)* **$250**

**Hiller, L.**
- Surgery through the ages.: a pictorial chronicle. New York: 1944. 1st edn. 177 pp. Several dozen photographic ills. *(Fye)* **$75**

**Hillyard, C.**
- Practical farming and grazing, with observations on the breeding and feeding of sheep and cattle. 1844. 4th edn. ix,352 pp. Green cloth gilt. *(Phenotype)* **£38**

**Hilton, Harold**
- Homogenous linear substitutions. Oxford: Clarendon Press, 1914. 1st edn. 8vo. *(McDowell)* **£35**
- An introduction to the theory of groups of finite order. Oxford: Clarendon Press, 1908. 1st edn. 8vo. *(McDowell)* **£35**

**Hilton, John**
- On rest and pain. New York: 1879. 2nd Amer edn. 299 pp. *(Fye)* **$50**
- Rest and pain; a course of lectures on the influence of mechanical and physiological rest in the treatment of accidents ... London: 1896. 6th edn. xv,514 pp. Ills. Orig green cloth. *(Jenner)* **£15**

**Hind, H.L. & Randles, W.B.**
- Handbook of photomicrography. London: 1913. 44 plates. *(Winterdown)* **£12**

**Hind, John**
- The elements of plain and spherical trigonometry. Cambridge: Deighton, 1828. 2nd edn. xii,352 pp. Some foxing. Orig cloth-backed bds, front jnt weak. *(Pollak)* **£25**

**Hind, W.**
- A monograph of the British carboniferous lamellibrachiata. Pal. Soc., 1896-1905. 2 vols. 4to. 79 plates. Half-mor. *(Wheldon & Wesley)* **£60**

**Hinde, M., et al.**
- A new royal and universal dictionary of arts and sciences: or, complete system of human

knowledge. 1769-71. Folio. 2 vols. 88 plates, 11 (only, of 12) plates of constellations. New qtr calf.                    *(Weiner)* **£250**

**Hinds, J., et al.**
- A compendious pocket manual of the veterinary art; being a practical description of the true symptoms ... 1832. Sm 8vo. x,216 pp. Fldg frontis. Orig glazed cloth.
                    *(Phenotype)* **£30**

**Hines, Neal O.**
- Proving ground: an account of the radiobiological studies in the Pacific, 1946-61. Seattle: University of Washington Press, 1962. 4to. xvii,366 pp. Num ills, photographs.               *(Poitras)* **$30**

**Hippocrates**
- The genuine works of Hippocrates. Translated ... by Francis Adams. New York: William Wood & Co., 1886. 2 vols. 4to. v,390; 346 pp. 8 plates.      *(Poitras)* **$75**
- The genuine works. Translated and annotated by Francis Adams. London: Sydenham Society, 1849. 2 vols. 8 plates. Orig cloth.                 *(Oasis)* **$200**
- Upon air, water, and situation; upon epidemical diseases; and upon prognosticks in acute cases ... Translated by Francis Clifton. 1734. xxiv,389 pp. Errata, side-notes. Port frontis. Half-calf, mrbld bds, sl rubbed.
                    *(Jenner)* **£120**

**Hirach, August**
- Handbook of geographical and historical pathology. London: 1883-86. 1st English translation. 3 vols. Backstrip of vol 1 missing.
                    *(Fye)* **$100**

**[Hirsch, M.]**
- Hirsch's collection of examples, formulae and calculations, on the literal calculus and algebra. Translated ... London: Black [et al.], 1827. x,386 pp. 3 fldg tables. Some pencil scribblings erased, some foxing. Half-calf. Working copy.          *(Pollak)* **£20**

**Historical ...**
- An historical narrative of the Great Plague at London, 1665 ... and some account of other remarkable plagues ... London: W. Nicoll, 1769. 1st edn. 8vo. viii,456 pp. Contemp calf, rebacked. Crnrs & one e.p. renewed. Sl foxing. Lib stamp on title.  *(Dailey)* **$350**

**History ...**
- A history of a gentleman, cured of heats in his face. London: Printed for L. Hawes & Co, 1773. 8vo. 32 pp. New paper wraps.
                    *(Pollak)* **£75**

**Hitchcock, E.**
- Dystepsy forestalled and resisted: or lectures on diet, regimen and employment: delivered to the students at Amherst College, spring term, 1830. Amherst & New York: 1831. 2nd edn, crrctd & enlgd. 8vo. xii,452 pp. Orig linen-backed bds.        *(Hemlock)* **$75**

**Hitchcock, Edward**
- Illustrations of surface geology. Washington City: Smithsonian Institution, April, 1857. 1st edn. 4to. 5,[3],155 pp. Index, 2 fldg tables, 5 cold geolog maps (1 fldg), 7 litho views on 4 plates. Perf stamp on title. Orig printed wraps, chipped.      *(M&S)* **$75**
- The religion of geology and its connected sciences. Glasgow: Collins, [1851]. 408 pp. Frontis. Half-title wanting. Contemp calf, spine gilt, a little rubbed.    *(Pollak)* **£25**
- The religion of geology. Glasgow & London: [1851]. Cr 8vo. 408 pp. Frontis. Orig cloth, cvrs sl stained.    *(Wheldon & Wesley)* **£15**
- Report on the geology, mineralogy, botany, and zoology of Massachusetts ... Amherts: J.S. & C. Adams, 1833. 1st edn. 8vo. 12,700 pp. ills. Indices. Light scattered foxing. Orig cloth, faded, paper label. Ex lib. *(M&S)* **$60**

**Hitschmann, Eduard**
- Freud's theories of the neuroses. Translated ... New York: 1914. 8vo. 154 pp. Nervous and Mental Disease Monograph Series.
                    *(Argosy)* **$35**

**Hjort, Dr. Johan**
- See Murray, Sir John & Hjort, Dr. Johan

**Hoadley, Benjamin**
- Three lectures on the organs of respiration. London: W. Wilkins, 1740. 1st edn. Sm 4to. iv,112,20 pp. 3 engvd plates, 1 fldg. Marginal dampstaining. Contemp half-calf, bds rubbed.              *(Antiq Sc)* **$375**

**Hobhouse, L.T.**
- Mind in evolution. London: 1901. 415 pp. Mild shelfwear.      *(Epistemologist)* **$45**

**Hoblyn, Richard D.**
- A dictionary of terms used in medicine and the collateral sciences. Phila: Henry C. Lea, 1865. 522 pp. Lea, worn & scuffed.
                    *(Poitras)* **$20**

**Hobson, E.W.**
- The theory of functions of a real variable and the theory of Fourier's series. Cambridge: University Press, 1921-26. 2nd edn, revsd & enlgd. 2 vols. xv,671; x,780. Orig cloth.
                    *(Pollak)* **£30**

**Hodge, Hugh**
- On diseases peculiar to women including

displacements of the uterus. Phila: 1860. 1st edn. 469 pp. Hd & ft of spine worn. *(Fye)* **$75**

**Hodgkin, A.L.**
- The conduction of the nervous impulse (The Sherrington Lectures VII). 108 pp. Ills. Dw. *(Oasis)* **$40**

**Hodgkin, Thomas**
- Narrative of a journey to Morocco, in 1864 and 1864 ... with geological annotations. London: 1866. 1st edn. Sm folio. [20],xii,183, 24 [advts] pp. Errata slip & subscribers' list present. 2 ports, 4 cold litho plates & another plate. Orig green cloth. *(Hemlock)* **$450**

**Hodgson, Joseph**
- A treatise on the diseases of arteries and veins, containing the pathology and treatment ... London: for Thomas Underwood ..., 1815. 1st edn. 2 vols. 8vo & sm folio. xix,[1], 603,[1] pp; 27,[1] pp. 8 plates. Text vol lacks first blank. 19th c half-calf. *(Zeitlin)* **$1,500**

**Hofmeister, Wilhelm**
- On the germination, development, and fructification of the higher cryptogamia, and on the fructification of the coniferae. London: The Ray Society, 1862. 1st edn in English. 8vo. xvii,506 pp. 65 copperplates. Orig blind-stamped cloth, faded. *(Rootenberg)* **$500**

**Hogg, Jabez**
- The microscope: its construction and application ... London: 1856. 2nd edn. 16 plates, 218 figs. New cloth. *(Winterdown)* **£35**
- The microscope: its history, construction and application ... 1861. 5th edn. xiv, 621 pp. Over 500 ills. Cvrs sl rubbed. *(Jenner)* **£25**
- The microscope: its construction and application ... London & New York: George Routledge & Sons, 1869. 762 pp. Spine & endpapers reprd. Ex lib. *(Poitras)* **$75**
- The microscope: its construction and application ... London: 1898. 15th edn. 21 plates, 8 cold. 445 figs. *(Winterdown)* **£25**

**Holbrook, Martin Luther**
- Hygiene of the brain and nerves and the cure of nervousness. New York: Holbrook, 1879. 279 pp. Pub pebbled green cloth. *(Gach)* **$25**

**Holden, Harold**
- Noses. Cleveland: 1950. 1st edn. 252 pp. *(Fye)* **$50**

**Holland, G.C.**
- An experimental inquiry into the laws which regulate the phenomena of organic and animal life. Edinburgh: 1829. xxiii,462,5 pp. New bds. *(Whitehart)* **£35**

**Holland, H.**
- Essays on scientific and other subjects contributed to the Edinburgh and Quarterly Reviews. 1862. v,499 pp. Orig cloth. *(Whitehart)* **£25**

**Holland, Henry**
- Chapters on mental physiology. London: Longman, Brown, Green & Longmans, 1852. 1st edn. xii,301 pp. Advts. Lib stamp on title. Blind-blocked brown cloth. *(Gach)* **$75**

**Holland, John**
- A treatise on the progressive movement and present state of the manufactures in metal. London: Longman, Rees, 1831-34. 3 vols. viii,341,[iii]; viii,362,[iv]; x,414,[iv] pp. 3 engvd titles foxed. 303 figs. New cloth, paper labels. *(Pollak)* **£40**

**Hollander, Bernard**
- Brain, mind, and the external signs of intelligence. London: Allen & Unwin, [1931]. 1st edn. 288 pp. 47 half-tones. *(Gach)* **$40**
- Brain, mind, and the external signs of intelligence. London: Allen & Unwin, 1931. 1st edn. 288 pp. 47 plates. Dw. *(Pollak)* **£12**
- Mental symptoms of brain disease: an aid to the surgical treatment of insanity, due to injury, hemorrhage, tumours ... New York: Rebman, [1910]. 1st U.S. edn. xviii,237 pp. Front flyleaf torn. Hinges cracked. *(Gach)* **$22.50**
- The psychology of misconduct, vice and crime. London: Allen & Unwin [1922]. 220,4 [advts] pp. *(Gach)* **$35**

**Hollingworth, Leta Stetter**
- Gifted children: their nature and nurture. New York: Macmillan, 1927. 374 pp. Photo ills, charts. A few pencil notes. *(Xerxes)* **$35**
- The psychology of the adolescent. New York: D. Appleton, 1928. 1st edn. xiv,227 pp. *(Gach)* **$20**

**Holman, J.W.**
- Nurses' and mothers' preceptor: designed to aid nurses and mothers in the treatment of children, and the sick. Boston: Wright's Steam Power Press, [1845]. Sm 8vo. 108 pp. With commendatory leaf & frontis. Staining first 3 leaves. Disbound, loose. *(Hemlock)* **$85**

**Holmes, George & Ruggles, Howard**
- Roentgen interpretation. Phila: 1926. 3rd edn. 326 pp. Ills, num radiographs. *(Oasis)* **$30**

**Holmes, Oliver Wendell**
- Homoeopathy, and its kindred delusions; two lectures ... Boston: William D. Ticknor, 1842. 1st edn. 12mo. 5,[3],72 pp. Front

endpaper lacking. Orig bds, spine fairly shot, remnants of paper label.          *(M&S)* **$75**

**Holmes, Samuel J.**
- Studies in evolution and eugenics. New York: 1923. 261 pp.          *(Scientia)* **$25**
- The trend of the race: a study of present tendencies in the biological development of civilised mankind. New York: 1921. 1st edn. 396 pp. Joseph Grinnell's copy. *(Scientia)* **$25**

**Holmes, Timothy**
- A system of surgery theoretical and practical in treatises by various authors. London: 1870. 2nd edn. 5 vols. W'cuts, chromo-lithos.
          *(Fye)* **$250**

**Holt, J.**
- General view of the agriculture of the County of Lancaster. London: 1795, 1st 8vo edn. xii,241 pp. Fldg frontis, map, 2 fldg tables, 5 engvd plates. Contemp half-calf.
          *(Phenotype)* **£75**

**Holt, L. Emmet**
- The diseases of infancy and childhood. New York: 1897. 1st edn. Half lea, sl scuffed.
          *(Scientia)* **$150**

**Holtzappfel, Charles & John Jacob**
- Turning and mechanical manipulation, intended as a work of general reference ... 1866-1904. 5 vols (all published). 8,[7],462; xvi,[457]-1025; xx,796; xx,592; xx,656 pp. Num plates (many fldg), ills. Blind-stamped cloth, rebacked. 2 vols rather shaken.
          *(Weiner)* **£300**

**Homans, John**
- Circulatory diseases of the extremities. New York. 1939. 1st edn. Dw.          *(Scientia)* **$60**

**Hooke, Robert**
- An attempt to prove the motion of the earth from observations ... London: ... for John Martyn ..., 1674. 1st edn. 4to. [8],28 pp. Lge fldg plate. Title sl frayed, some browning. 3/4 mor.          *(Rootenberg)* **$850**
- The diary of Robert Hooke, M.A., M.D., F.R.S., 1672 - 1680. Transcribed from the original ... London: Taylor & Francis, 1935. 1st edn. Thick 8vo. Frontis, 10 other full-page plates. Interleaved throughout, extensively corrected & annotated. Red cloth.
          *(McDowell)* **£55**
- Micrographia: or some physiological descriptions of minute bodies made by magnifying glasses. London: Allestry ..., 1665. 1st edn. Folio. [18]ff,246 pp,[5]ff. 38 engvd plates (sm tears at folds rprd). Minor soiling, spotting, browning. Old calf, rebacked.          *(Zeitlin)* **$7,500**
- Philosophical experiments and observations

of the late eminent Dr. Robert Hooke ... London: by W. & J. Innys ..., 1726. 1st edn. 8vo. [viii],391, [7],[2 advts]. W'cut diags in text. Contemp calf, upper jnt cracked but sound.          *(Pickering)* **$1,250**

**Hooker, Worthington**
- Lessons from the history of medical delusions. New York: 1850. 1st edn. 12mo. 5,105 pp. Orig cloth, some foxing.
          *(M&S)* **$50**

**Hool, G.A. & Kinne, W.S.**
- Movable and long-span steel bridges. New York: 1923. xiv,496 pp. Fldg diags, many figs & ills in text. Library stamps on title & verso of fldg plates. New cloth.   *(Whitehart)* **£18**

**Hooper, Robert**
- The morbid anatomy of the human brain; being illustrations of the most frequent and important organic diseases ... London: Longman [et al.], 1826. 1st edn. Lge 4to. 15 col-ptd mezzo plates, finished by hand. Orig bds, backstrip rubbed & reprd. Mor box.
          *(Quaritch)* **$3,500**

**[Hooper, Robert]**
- The surgeon's vade-mecum: containing the symptoms, causes, diagnosis, prognosis, and treatment of surgical diseases ... London: John Murray, 1809. 1st edn. 8vo. xvi,269,[1] pp, 8ff. Red pebbled cloth.   *(Hemlock)* **$85**

**Hoopes, Penrose R.**
- Connecticut clockmakers of the eighteenth century. Hartford: Edwin Valentine ..., 1930. 4to. [4]ff, 178,[2] pp. Frontis, 56 figs. Orig linen, paper label. Dw.          *(Zeitlin)* **$100**

**Hooton, Ernest A.**
- Why men behave like apes and vice-versa, or body and behaviour. Princeton, NJ: Princeton University Press, 1940. 1st edn. xxvi,234 pp. 26 plates. Green cloth, lea label.          *(Gach)* **$17.50**

**Hopkins, B.S., et al.**
- Chapters in the chemistry of the less familiar elements. Stipes Publishing Co., Illinois, 1938-40. 2 vols in 1. 263; 286 pp. Num ills. Binder's cloth. Roneo typescript. *(Pollak)* **£15**

**Hopkins, N.M.**
- Experimental electrochemistry. 1905. xiv,284 pp. 130 ills. Orig cloth, worn on spine. Stitching loose, one section partly detchd.
          *(Whitehart)* **£15**

**Hopkinson, Bertram**
- The scientific papers. Cambridge: 1921. Lge 8vo. xxvii,480 pp. Port, plates, diags.
          *(Weiner)* **£40.**

**Hopkinson, John**
- Original papers. Cambridge, 1901. 2 vols. lxvi,294; vii,393 pp. 2 ports, diags. Cloth darkened. Ex lib. *(Weiner)* £50

**Horner, Gustavus Richard Brown**
- Medical and topographical observations upon the Mediterranean; and upon Portugal, Spain and other countries ... Phila: Haswell, Barrington ..., 1839. 1st edn. 8vo. 212 pp. 8 plates. Light browning on prelims & last leaves. Calf-backed bds. *(Rootenberg)* $225

**Horner, William**
- A treatise on special and general anatomy. Phila: 1830. 2nd edn. 2 vols. 535; 528 pp. Endpapers vol 2 missing. Orig lea, front bds of both vols detchd, lacks labels. *(Fye)* $75

**Horning, Eric**
- See Burrows, Harold & Horning, Eric

**Horsley, J. Shelton**
- Surgery of the stomach and small intestine. New York: 1926. 1st edn. 325 pp. *(Fye)* $40

**Hosack, Alexander**
- A memoir upon staphyloraphy; with cases, and a description of the instruments requisite for the operation. New York: 1833. 21 pp. Fldg engvd plate. Cvr soiled, sev leaves w'stained. Wraps. *(Fye)* $250

**Hoskold, H.D.**
- The engineer's valuing assistant: being a practical treatise on the valuation of collieries and other mines ... 1877. Spotting. Half-calf, rubbed, lea label. *(Quinto Charing Cross)* £20

**Hospital ...**
- Hospital transports. A memoir of the embarkation of the sick and wounded from the Peninsula of Virginia in the summer of 1862. Boston: Ticknor, 1863. 167 pp. Contemp half-calf, mrbld bds, rubbed. *(M&S)* $30

**Hot-water cure ...**
- A hot-water cure, sought out in Germany ... See Blenkinsop, Adam

**Housing ...**
- Housing of the working classes: History of the schemes, and description, &c. of the Corporation dwellings. Manchester: ... Sanitary Committee, 1904. 59 pp. 36 plates, fldg plans, sketch details of houses &c., tables. Orig cloth-backed printed bds. Shaken. *(Weiner)* £35

**Houson, Edwin J.**
- A dictionary of electrical words, terms and phrases. New York: 1894. Sm 4to. vi,667 pp.

582 w'cuts. *(Elgen)* $75

**Howard, Richard Baron**
- An inquiry into the morbid effects of deficiency of food, chiefly with reference to ... the destitute poor. London: Simpkin, Marshall ... & Manchester: George Sims, 1839. 1st edn. 8vo. iv,77,[1] pp. Disbound. *(Dailey)* $100

**Howard, Thomas**
- On the loss of teeth; and on the best means of restoring them ... London: Simpkin, Marshall, 1853. 2nd edn. Sm 8vo. 93 pp, [1]f. Aquatint frontis with overlay slip. Orig green stamped cloth. Inscribed "with the Author's compliments". *(Zeitlin)* $250

**Howe, H.A. & Bodian, D.**
- Neural mechanisms in poliomyelitis. New York: 1942. vii,234 pp. 35 plates, 1 fldg table. *(Whitehart)* £18

**Howe, Joseph**
- Emergencies and how to treat them. The etiology, pathology and treatment of the accidents, diseases, and cases of poisoning, which demand prompt action. New York: 1871. 1st edn. 265 pp. *(Fye)* $75

**Howe, Lucien**
- The muscles of the eye. New York: 1907-1908. 1st edn. 2 vols. xi,467; xiv,481 pp. 13 ports, num ills. Ex lib. *(Elgen)* $75

**Huarte, Juan**
- Examen de Ingenios: or, the tryal of wits, discovering the great difference of wits among men, and what sort of learning suits best with each genius ... London: for Richard Sare, 1698. [xl],502,[2] pp. Some ink-scrawling to title. Crudely rebacked. *(Gach)* $185

**Hubbell, Alvin Alvace**
- The development of ophthalmology in America, 1800 to 1870. Chicago: 1908. 1st edn. *(Scientia)* $65

**Huckel, Oliver**
- Mental medicine: some practical suggestions from a spiritual standpoint. New York: Thomas Y. Cruell, 1909. 1st edn. xxxii,214 pp. Library b'plate. *(Gach)* $17

**Hudson, Alfred**
- See Davidson, Wm. & Hudson, Alfred

**Hudson, P.S. & Richens R.H.**
- The new genetics in the Soviet Union. Cambridge: 1946. 88 pp. Rebound in bds. *(Scientia)* $55

**Hughes, Brodie**
- The visual fields. A study of the applications of quantitative perimetry ... Oxford: Blackwells, 1954. ix,174 pp. Ills. Orig blue cloth. Dw.                    *(Jenner)* **£15**

**Hughes, Wendell**
- Reconstructive surgery of the eyelids. St. Louis: 1943. 1st edn. 160 pp.     *(Fye)* **$125**

**Hulke, J.W.**
- A practical treatise on the use of the ophthalmoscope. Being the essay for which the Jacksonian Prize was awarded ... London: John Churchill, 1861. 1st edn. 8vo. viii,70,[2] pp. 4 full-page cold plates, leaf of explanation. Mostly unopened. Orig cloth.
                    *(Rootenberg)* **$350**

**Hull, C.L.**
- Principles of behavior. New York: 1954. 422 pp. V sl shelfwear. Stanley Milgram's copy.
                    *(Epistemologist)* **$35**

**Hull, Edward**
- A treatise on the building and ornamental stones of Great Britain and foreign countries, arranged according to their geological distribution and mineral character. London: Macmillan, 1872. 1st edn. 8vo. 2 photographic ills, cuts in text. Contemp calf.
                    *(McDowell)* **£45**

**Hulls, Jonathan**
- A description and draught of a new-invented machine ... for carrying vessels or ships ... London: for the author, 1737. 1st edn. 12mo. 48 pp. Fldg engvd frontis, dust soiled, torn & reprd with loss. Title & last leaf soiled & browned. 19th c calf.    *(Pickering)* **$3,500**
- A description and draught of a new-invented machine ... for carrying vessels or ships ... London: for the author, 1737 [1855 facsimile reprint]. [vii],8-48 pp. Lge fldg frontis. Half green mor, mrbld bds, rubbed. *(Pollak)* **£125**

**Humboldt, Alexander von**
- Aspects of nature, in different lands and different climates, with scientific elucidations. Translated by Mrs. Sabine. Phila: 1849. 1st Amer edn. 475 pp. Spine chipped.                    *(Scientia)* **$35**

**Humphrey, J.**
- See White, E. & Humphrey, J.

**Humphreys, W.J.**
- Physics of the air. New York: 1940. 3rd edn, 6th imp. xiv,676 pp. 226 figs, 2 fldg graphs. Orig cloth sl rubbed.    *(Whitehart)* **£15**

**Humphris, Francis Howard**
- Electro-therapeutics for practitioners, being

essays on some useful forms of electrical apparatus and on some diseases which are amenable to electrical treatment. London: Henry Frowde [et al.], 1921. 8vo. x,300 pp. Ills.                    *(Poitras)* **$35**

**Hunt, H. Lyons**
- Plastic surgery of the head, face and neck. Phila: 1926. 404 pp. 342 text ills, 10 cold plates.                    *(Oasis)* **$40**
- Plastic surgery of the head, face and neck. Phila: 1926. 1st edn. 404 pp. Extensive red ink underlining and occas marginal notations.
                    *(Fye)* **$150**

**Hunt, J. McV.**
- Personality and the behavior disorders. New York: 1944. 2 vols. 618 pp. Both vols inscrbd by the author.    *(Epistemologist)* **$35**

**Hunt, Robert**
- A manual of photography, third edition. 1853. x,321 pp. Cold frontis, ills. Occas grubbiness or marks. Orig pict dec cloth, rather worn & grubby. Griffin's illus ctlg of photographic and other apparatus bound in at end.                    *(Weiner)* **£125**
- The poetry of science, or studies of the physical phenomena of nature. 1848. 1st edn. xxiv,463 pp. Half-cloth, mrbld bds.
                    *(Weiner)* **£40**
- A popular treatise on the art of photography, including daguerrotype, and all the new methods of producing pictures by the chemical agency of light. Glasgow: 1841. 1st edn. viii,96 pp. Frontis. Orig dec blind-stamped cloth, rebacked, new endpapers.
                    *(Weiner)* **£380**

**Hunt, Sterry**
- Chemical and geological essays. Boston: Osgood, 1875. 1st edn. Sm 8vo. xxii,489 pp. Orig cloth. Author's pres copy.
                    *(Antiq Sc)* **$110**

**Hunter, Donald**
- The diseases of occupation. 1962. 3rd edn. Thick 8vo. xvii,1180 pp. Ills throughout. Orig red cloth. Dw.    *(Jenner)* **£14**
- Harvey and his contemporaries. London: B.M.A., 1957. Slim 8vo. Orig red cloth.
                    *(McDowell)* **£20**

**Hunter, John**
- A treatise on the blood, inflammation and gun-shot wounds, by the late John Hunter. To which is prefixed ... author's life. London: for John Nicol, 1794. 1st edn. 4to. lxvii,[1],575 pp. Frontis port, 9 plates. Marginal foxing & browning. Mod half-mor.
                    *(Zeitlin)* **$1,500**
- A treatise on the blood, inflammation and gun-shot wounds ... to which is prefixed ... a

short account of the author's life. London: John Richardson, 1794. 1st edn. 4to. Engvd port, 9 engvd plates. V sl occas marginal foxing. Prize mottled calf. *(Quaritch)* **$2,200**
- A treatise on the blood, inflammation, and gun-shot wounds. Phila: 1823. 2nd Amer edn. 480 pp. 8 engvd plates. Full lea, front hinge cracked. *(Fye)* **$400**
- A treatise on venereal disease. London: 1786. 1st edn. 4to. [6]ff, 398pp, [13]ff. 7 plates. Mod grained brown calf, gilt lettering. Lib withdrawn stamp on prelim. *(Zeitlin)* **$850**

**Hunter, Richard & MacAlpine, Ida**
- Three hundred years of psychiatry 1535 - 1860. London: Oxford University Press, 1963. 1st edn. Lge thick 8vo. Text ills. Discreet lib stamp on endpaper. Dw.
*(McDowell)* **£48**
- Three hundred years of psychiatry 1535 - 1860. A history presented in selected English texts. Oxford University Press, 1963. 1st edn. Num ills. *(Robertshaw)* **£75**

**Hunter, Robert**
- A practical treatise on the diseases of the throat and lungs; with their treatment by inhalation. New York: 1854. 1st edn. 16mo. 12,96 pp. Orig printed wraps. *(M&S)* **$37.50**

**Hurdon, Elizabeth**
- See Kelly, Howard & Hurdon, Elizabeth

**Hurst, G.H.**
- Painters' colours, oils and varnishes: a practical manual. 1896. 2nd edn, revsd & enlgd. xiii,499 pp. 73 ills in text. Orig cloth. *(Whitehart)* **£18**

**Hurwitz, Alfred & Degensheim, G.A.**
- Milestones in modern surgery. New York: 1958. 1st edn. *(Scientia)* **$70**
- Milestones in modern surgery. New York: 1958. 1st edn. 520 pp. *(Fye)* **$50**

**Hutchinson, G. Evelyn**
- The biogeochemistry of vertebrate excretion. New York: 1950. 1st edn. 554 pp. Orig wraps, sgnd by author. *(Scientia)* **$65**

**Hutchinson, H.A.**
- A treatise on the practical drainage of land. 1844. vii,207 pp. Frontis, 4 fldg plans. E.p.s browned. Orig half-calf, cloth sides. *(Phenotype)* **£38**

**Hutchinson, Horace (ed.)**
- Life of Sir John Lubbock, Lord Avebury. London: 1914. 1st edn. 2 vols. 338; 334 pp. *(Scientia)* **$60**

**Hutchinson, J.**
- Hernia and its radical cure. London: 1923.

1st edn. 264 pp. *(Fye)* **$40**

**Hutchinson, Jonathan**
- A clinical memoir on certain diseases of the eye and ear, consequent on inherited syphilis ... London: 1863. 1st edn. Half-title. xii,259 pp. Uncut. Sunned cloth. Author's pres copy. *(Goodrich)* **$450**
- The pedigree of disease. Being six lectures on temperament, idiosyncrasy and diathesis. London: Churchill, 1884. 1st edn. 8vo. Pub cloth. *(McDowell)* **£40**
- The pedigree of disease. Being six lectures on temperament, idiosyncrasy and diathesis. New York: 1885. 1st Amer edn. [3]ff,113pp. Cvrs sl soiled. *(Elgen)* **$100**

**Hutchinson, Robert**
- Food and principles of diatetics. 1906. 2nd edn. xx,582,[4 advts]. Sev plates, some cold. Orig red cloth, spine faded, hinges rubbed. *(Jenner)* **£10**

**Hutt, Fred**
- Genetics of the fowl. New York: 1949. 1st edn. 590 pp. *(Scientia)* **$50**

**Hutter, R.**
- See Frankel, J. & Hutter, R.

**Hutton, Charles**
- A course of mathematics. Composed ... for the use of the gentlemen cadets in the Royal Military Academy at Woolwich. London: 1800-01-11. 3rd, 3rd, 1st edns. 3 vols. 8vo. iv,iv,382,[1]; iv,364; viii,[iv],379 pp. Num diags. Contemp half-calf, sl rubbed. *(Burmester)* **£90**
- A course of mathematics. In two volumes. For the use of academies as well as private tuition. London: for J. Johnson, 1810. 6th edn, enlgd & crrctd. viii,384; iv,414. Text figs, 4 plates on 2 leaves. Some foxing. Half-calf, worn. *(Pollak)* **£25**
- A course of mathematics. In two volumes. Composed for the use of The Royal Military Academy. London: Longman, Orme, 1841-43. 12th edn. viii,535; xii,548 pp. One gathering cracked. New paper bds, old cloth spines. *(Pollak)* **£25**
- A mathematical and philosophical dictionary containing mathematics, astronomy ... London: J. Johnson, 1796-95. 1st edn. 2 vols. 4to. viii,650; ii,756 pp. 37 engvd plates. Contemp tree sheep, rebacked. Contemp signature of Thos. Maugham. *(Pickering)* **$650**
- A mathematical and philosophical dictionary. London: J. Johnson, 1796-95. 1st edn. 2 vols. 4to. viii,650; 756 pp. Half-title vol 2, 37 engvd plates. Contemp tree calf, jnts vol 2 partially cracked. *(Antiq Sc)* **$450**
- A mathematical and philosophical dictionary.

London: J. Johnson, 1796-95. 2 vols. 4to. viii,650; [ii],756 pp. 37 engvd plates. Contemp half-russia, mrbld bds, rebacked with old spine laid back, crnrs reprd. Lacks both half-titles.          *(Pollak)* £175
- Mathematical tables: containing common, hyperbolic, and logistic logarithms. London: for J. & J. Robinson, 1785. 1st edn. xii,176,343 pp. Tree calf, worn. B'plate of Daniel Cresswell, mathematician.
*(Pollak)* £40
- A philosophical and mathematical dictionary. Containing an explanation of the terms ... a new edition with numerous additions and improvements. 1815. 4to. 2 vols. 41 copper plates. Full calf, 2 bds detchd.
*(Edwards)* £150
- Recreations in science and natural philosophy: Dr. Huttons translation of Montucla's edition of Ozanam ... Revised ... 1844. xiv,826 pp. W'cuts. Full prize calf gilt.
*(Weiner)* £85
- Tracts on mathematical and philosophical subjects; comprising ... the theory of bridges ... the force of gunpowder ... 1812. 1st edn. 3 vols. x,[1],485; 384 pp. Frontis, 10 fldg plates. Mod paper-cvrd bds, linen spines, paper labels.          *(Whitehart)* £80
- A treatise on mensuration, both in theory and practice. London: for ... Robinson et al., 1788. 2nd edn. 8vo. xvi,703 pp. Plate, text engv, text w'cuts. First 15 leaves stained in gutter. Diced calf gilt, spine reprd.
*(Pollak)* £40
- A treatise on mensuration, both in theory and practice. London: 1802. 3rd edn. 8vo. 530 pp. Plate, text engv, text w'cuts. Some foxing. Speckled calf, rebacked.          *(Pollak)* £30

**Hutton, Charles & Ramsay, William**
- A course of mathematics. Composed for the use of the Royal Military Academy. London: Tegg, 1833. New edn. Thick 8vo. Text figs. Pub blue stamped cloth, faded.
*(McDowell)* £30

**Hutton, F.R.**
- The gas engine, a treatise on the internal combustion engine using gas, gasoline, kerosene or other hydrocarbon as source of energy. New York: 1904. 2nd edn. xx,483 pp. 243 ills. Spine faded.          *(Whitehart)* £18

**Huxham, John**
- An essay on fevers ... with dissertations on slow nervous fevers ... on the smallpox and on pleurisies and peripneumonies. London: 1750. 1st edn. 288 pp. Sl worming lower margin on first few leaves without loss. Old calf, worn, no label.          *(Oasis)* $400
- Medical and chemical observations upon antimony. 1756. 78 pp. Sl browning at front & end. Half-calf, worn, spine very cracked &

frayed.          *(Jenner)* £65

**Huxley, Julian**
- Evolution, the modern synthesis. 1942. 1st edn, 1st iss. 645 pp. Endpaper trifle marked. Orig cloth.          *(Wheldon & Wesley)* £25
- Problems of relative growth. New York: 1932. 1st Amer edn. 276 pp. Dw.
*(Scientia)* $45

**Huxley, Julian (ed.)**
- The new systematics. Oxford: 1941. 2nd printing. 583 pp.          *(Scientia)* $35

**Huxley, Julian, et al. (eds.)**
- Evolution as a process. London: 1954. 1st edn. 367 pp. Dw.          *(Scientia)* $40

**Huxley, Leonard (ed.)**
- The life and letters of Sir Joseph Dalton Hooker. New York: 1918. 1st Amer edn. 2 vols. 546; 569 pp.          *(Scientia)* $65
- Life and letters of Thomas Henry Huxley. London: Macmillan, 1900. 2nd edn. 2 vols. 8vo. 12 ills. Half red mor.          *(McDowell)* £70

**Huxley, Thomas Edward**
- Science and education. New York: 1902. 381 pp. Frontis. Front free endpaper removed.
*(Whitehart)* £15

**Huxley, Thomas Henry**
- American addresses, with a lecture on the study of biology. New York: 1877. 1st Amer edn. 164 pp. Spine faded & lightly shelfworn.          *(Scientia)* $30
- Collected essays. New York: 1897. 9 vols. Half lea, mrbld bds.          *(Scientia)* $100
- Critiques and addresses. 1883. 8vo. xiv,350 pp. Orig cloth.          *(Wheldon & Wesley)* £15
- Darwiniana. London: 1893. 1st edn. 475 pp.
*(Scientia)* $27.50
- Diary of the voyage of H.M.S. Rattlesnake. Edited from the unpublished Ms. by Julian Huxley. London: Chatto & Windus, 1935. 1st edn. Roy 8vo. Cold frontis, 12 other ills. Pub blue cloth.          *(McDowell)* £45
- Diary of the voyage of H.M.S. Rattlesnake. Edited from the unpublished Ms. by Julian Huxley. 1935. Roy 8vo. 372 pp. Map, 13 plates. Cloth, reprd. *(Wheldon & Wesley)* £45
- Diary of the voyage of H.M.S. Rattlesnake. Edited from the unpublished Ms. by Julian Huxley. New York: 1936. 1st Amer edn. 301 pp.          *(Scientia)* $40
- Evidence as to man's place in nature. London: Williams & Norgate, 1863. 1st edn. 8vo. Pub green pebbled cloth.          *(McDowell)* £110
- Evidence as to man's place in nature. London: Williams & Norgate, 1863. 1st edn. 8vo. [8],159 pp. Frontis, 52 text figs. Orig green pub cloth, inner hinges cracked, short marginal tear in first few leaves. Author's pres

copy. *(Dailey)* **$450**
- Evidence as to man's place in nature. New York: 1863. 8vo. 184 pp. Frontis, 32 ills. Orig cloth, trifle worn, sl signs of use.
*(Wheldon & Wesley)* **£30**
- Evidence as to man's place in nature. London: Williams & Norgate, 1863. 1st edn. 8vo. [6],159,8 pp. Frontis, text ills. Orig pebbled cloth. Pub advts dated February, 1863.
*(Rootenberg)* **$350**
- An introduction to the classification of animals. 1869. 147 pp. Ills. Some ink annotation. Worn. *(Weiner)* **£25**
- Lectures on the elements of comparative anatomy ... 1864. xi,303 pp. Ills. pencil annotations. Inner front hinge broken, worn.
*(Weiner)* **£30**
- A manual of the anatomy of invertebrated animals. [1877]. 596 pp. Ills. Pub ctlg dated 1885 or 1886. *(Weiner)* **£30**
- A manual of the anatomy of the vertebrated animals. 1871. 431 pp. 110 figs in text. Orig cloth. *(Whitehart)* **£18**
- A manual of the anatomy of the vertebrate animals. New York: 1878. 596 pp.
*(Scientia)* **$30**
- A manual of the anatomy of vertebrated animals. 1871. 1st edn. 431 pp. Ills. G.O. Mitchell's copy. *(Weiner)* **£50**
- On our knowledge of the causes of the phenomena of organic nature. 1863. 1st edn. 156 pp. Orig blind-stamped green cloth, gilt.
*(Whitehart)* **£50**
- On the origin of species: or, the causes of phenomena of organic nature ... New York: D. Appleton, 1863. 1st Amer edn. 8vo. [2],150,[8] pp. With text ills & 6 pp pub advts. Orig cloth, backstrip & edges soiled,
*(Rootenberg)* **$150**
- On the origin of species: or, the causes of the phenomena of organic nature. A course of six lectures to working men. New York: 1863. 1st Amer edn. 150 pp. Spine worn. *(Scientia)* **$50**
- On the origin of species: or, the causes of the phenomena of organic nature. New York: 1872. 1st Amer edn. 12mo. 150 pp. Orig cloth, spine faded. *(M&S)* **$40**

**Huygens, [Christian]**
- The celestial worlds discover'd: Or, conjectures concerning the inhabitants, plants and productions of the worlds in the planets. London: for Timothy Childe, 1698. 1st edn in English. 8vo. vi,160 pp. 5 fldg engvd plates, Full-calf, new endpapers.
*(Rootenberg)* **$800**

**Hymers, J.**
- The elements of the theory of astronomy. Cambridge: Deighton, 1840. 2nd edn, revsd & impvd. vii,354 pp. 4 fldg plates. Orig cloth-backed bds, new label, jnts pulled.
*(Pollak)* **£30**

**Hyndman, H.H. Francis**
- Radiation: an elementary treatise on electromagnetic radiation and on Roentgen and cathode rays. London: 1898. 1st edn. Sm 8vo. xviii, 307 pp. Ills. Sl fraying at hd of spine. *(Elgen)* **$85**

**Hyslop, Theophilus Bulkeley**
- The borderland: some of the problems of insanity. London: 1924. 1st edn. 310 pp. Spine tips rubbed, front hinge very weak.
*(Gach)* **$25**
- Mental physiology especially in its relation to mental disorders. Phila: 1895. Cloth worn.
*(Gach)* **$25**
- Mental physiology especially in its relation to mental disorders. 1895. xv,552 pp. Orig cloth. *(Whitehart)* **£25**
- Mental physiology especially in its relation to mental disorders. London: J. & A. Churchill, 1895. 1st edn. [xvi],552,16 [advts] pp. Pub blind-blocked mauve cloth. Pres stamp on title. *(Gach)* **$85**

**Hytten, Frank & Leitch, Isabella**
- The physiology of human pregnancy. Oxford: 1964. 1st edn. 463 pp. Dw. *(Fye)* **$17.50**

**Iffy, L.**
- See Kaminetzky, H.A. & Iffy, L.

**Improved ...**
- The improved American family physician; or, sick man's guide to health. New York: 1833. 8vo. viii,144 pp. *(Poitras)* **$37.50**

**Infeld, Leopold**
- See Einstein, Albert & Infeld, Leopold

**Ingalls, Walter Renton**
- The metallurgy of zinc and cadmium. New York & London: 1903. xviii,[ii], 701,[iii] pp. 408 ills, plates & fldg plans. *(Pollak)* **£17.50**

**Ingen-Housz, Jan**
- Experiments upon vegetables, discovering their great power of purifying the common air ... To which is joined, a new method ... London: P. Elmsly & H. Payne, 1779. 1st edn. 8vo. lxviii, 302 pp, 9ff. Engvd plate. Contemp calf, back gilt. *(Offenbacher)* **$1,750**

**Ingersoll, C.J.**
- A discourse concerning the influence of America on the mind ... oration delivered before the American Philosophical Society ... Phila: Abraham Small, 1823. 67,[i] pp. A trifle foxed, few crnrs dog-eared. Orig wraps, stitched. *(Pollak)* **£20**

**Inhelder, Barbel**
- See Piaget, Jean & Inhelder, Barbel

**Inman, Rev. J.**
- Navigation and nautical astronomy, for the use of British seamen. 1849. 7th edn. iv,280 pp. 3 plates. Orig 3/4 roan, mrbld bds very worn, spine defective, one section loose.
*(Whitehart)* £18

**Inskip, Rev. R.M.**
- Navigation and nautical astronomy: containing practical rules, notes and examples. Portsea: 1865. 1st edn. viii,170 pp. Many figs. Orig cloth, sl worn with sm ink stains.              *(Whitehart)* £18

**Instructions ...**
- Instructions for cutting out apparel for the poor ... London: ... J. Walter, Charing Cross, 1789. 1st edn. 8vo. xii,85,[7] pp. 13 lge fldg plates. Imprint crossed out & rewritten in manuscript. Uncut in orig bds.
*(Rootenberg)* $1,250

**Ireland, William W.**
- The mental affections of children: idiocy, imbecility and insanity. Edinburgh: 2nd edn.
*(Gach)* $75

**Ives, John**
- Electricity as a medicine, and its mode of application. New York: 1879. 1st edn. 12mo. 123 pp. Ills. Cvr rubbed & worn at ends & crnrs.              *(Xerxes)* $45

**Ivy, Robert & Curtis, Lawrence**
- Fractures of the jaws. Phila: 1931. 1st edn. 180 pp. Ills. Spine rubbed.       *(Oasis)* $25

**Ivy, Robert (ed.)**
- Manual of standard practice of plastic and maxillo-facial surgery. Phila: 1943. 1st edn. 432 pp.              *(Fye)* $50

**J.L.S.**
- Sugar; how it grows, and how it is made. A pleasing account for young people. London: Darton & Clark, [1844]. 1st edn. 4to. Hand-cold litho frontis & half-title, 6 hand-cold litho plates. Some thumbing & foxing. Pub dec cloth, spine sl snagged. *(McDowell)* £70

**Jablon, Seymour**
- See Walker A. Earl & Jablon, Seymour

**Jackman, W.J. & Russell, Thos. H.**
- Flying machines: construction and operation. A practical book which shows ... how to build and navigate the modern airship. Chicago: Thompson, 1910. 1st edn. Sm 8vo. 221,1 [advts] pp. Num figs, ills. Orig cloth, spine ends rubbed, inner hinges broken.
*(M&S)* $150

**Jackson, Arnold**
- Goiter and other diseases of the thyroid gland. New York: 1926. 1st edn. 401 pp. Inscribed & autographed by the author.
*(Fye)* $40

**Jackson, C.**
- Diseases and injuries of the larynx. New York: 1942. 1st edn. 633 pp.      *(Fye)* $30

**Jackson, C. & Jackson, C.L. (eds.)**
- Diseases of the nose, throat and ear including bronchoscopy and esophagoscopy. Phila: 1946. 844 pp.              *(Fye)* $30

**Jackson, Charles T.**
- First annual report on the geology of the State of New Hampshire. Concord, N.H.: Barton & Caroll, 1841. 1st edn. 8vo. 164 pp. Orig wraps, a little chipped,      *(Antiq Sc)* $40
- A manual of etherization, containing directions for the employment of ether, chloroform and other anaesthetic agents ... Boston: J.B. Mansfield, 1861. 1st edn. 8vo. 134 pp. Orig cloth. Lib duplicate, with b'plate & stamps.       *(Hemlock)* $375

**Jackson, Chevalier**
- Bronchoesophagology. Phila: 1950. 1st edn. 366 pp.              *(Fye)* $25
- Bronchoscopy and esophagoscopy: a manual of peroral endoscopy and laryngeal surgery. Phila: 1927. 2nd edn. 457 pp.      *(Fye)* $40
- Diseases of the air and food passages of foreign-body origin Phila: 1936. 1st edn. 4to. 636 pp.              *(Fye)* $55
- Foreign bodies in the air and food passages. 1924. 1st edn. 174 pp. Photographs. *(Fye)* $75
- The life of Jackson Chevalier - an autobiography. New York: 1938. 1st edn. 229 pp. Autographed by the author.      *(Fye)* $50

**Jackson, Edward**
- Skiascopy and its practical application to the study of refraction. Phila: 1895. 1st edn. 112 pp. Author's printed card tipped onto front endpaper.              *(Fye)* $70

**Jackson, James**
- Another letter to a young physician: To which are appended some other medical papers. Boston: 1861. 1st edn. 12,179 pp. 12mo. Orig cloth.              *(M&S)* $50
- A syllabus of the lectures delivered at the Massachusetts Medical College to the medical students of Harvard University. N.p., [1816]. 1st edn. Sm 8vo. 108 pp. Interleaved with blanks throughout. Contemp bds, 19th c mor spine. B'plate of Wm. E. Channing.
*(M&S)* $200

**Jackson, John**
- Lepers. Thirty-one years' work amongst

them, being the history of the Mission to Lepers in India and the East, 1874 - 1905. 1906. Thick 8vo. xviii,390 pp. 2 maps, many ills. Frontis port detchd. Orig red cloth.
*(Jenner)* **£10**

**Jackson, Ruth**
- The cervical syndrome. Springfield: Charles C. Thomas, 1966. 3rd edn. 333 pp.
*(Poitras)* **$30**

**Jacobi, Mary Putnam**
- The question of rest for women during menstruation. New York: 1877. 1st edn. 232,2 [pub ctlg] pp. 14 plates. Spine edges frayed.
*(Elgen)* **$145**

**Jacobi, Professor**
- Portfolio of dermachromes. 1903. 2 vols plus supplement. Num cold plates. 2 plates & supplement index plate detchd, inscription cut from title. Cvrs sl worn.
*(Jenner)* **£25**
- Portfolio of dermachromes. London: Rebman, 1904. 2nd enlgd edn. 2 vols. 4to. Cold photog ills. Green cloth, mor spine.
*(McDowell)* **£40**

**Jaensch, E.R.**
- Eidetic imagery and typological methods of investigation: their importance for the psychology of childhood ... translated ... New York: Harcourt, 1930. [viii],136,8 [pub advts] pp. Green cloth, flecked.
*(Gach)* **$25**

**Jagielski, Apollinaris Victor**
- On Marienbad Spa and the diseases curable by waters and baths. 1873. 186 pp. Fldg map frontis. Shaken. Orig purple cloth, spine very faded & worn, upper bd w'stained.
*(Jenner)* **£25**

**James, Sir Henry**
- Instructions for taking meteorological observations; with notes for their correction and notes on meteorological phenomena. London: Eyre & Spottiswoode, 1860. 1st edn. Frontis, 19 litho plates, some fldg, some cold. Lge fldg chart. Pub cloth.  *(McDowell)* **£110**

**James, R.**
- Pharmacopoeia universalis: or a new universal English dispensary. 1764. 3rd edn. Lacks free endpapers. Contemp calf, some wear, red labels.  *(Robertshaw)* **£25**

**James, W.**
- Wireless valve transmitters, the design and operation of small power apparatus. 1925. viii,271 pp. 8 plates, diags. Few marks.
*(Weiner)* **£25**

**James, William**
- The principles of psychology. 1890. 1st

English edn (same year as 1st Amer). 2 vols. xii,689; vi,704. Half-calf, mrbld bds, very worn spines cracking and lacking top half to vol I.  *(Jenner)* **£40**
- The principles of psychology. New York: Henry Holt & Co., 1890. 1st edn. 2 vols. 8vo. xii,689; vi,704,8 [advts] pp. Text figs. Orig cloth, a little worn, hinges reprd.
*(Antiq Sc)* **$450**
- The principles of psychology. New York: 1905. 2 vols. 689; 704 pp. Moderate shelfwear, hinges sl cracked.
*(Epistemologist)* **$45**

**Jameson, Thomas**
- A treatise on Cheltenham waters, and bilious diseases. 1809. 2nd edn. xxx,219 pp. Fldg frontis plan, plate. Uncut in orig cloth-backed blue bds.  *(Jenner)* **£30**

**Janet, Pierre**
- Psychological healing. A historical and clinical study. Translated ... London: [1925]. 1st edn in English. 2 vols. 1266 pp.
*(Elgen)* **$110**

**Janovski, N.A.**
- Color atlas of gross gynecologic and obstetric pathology. New York: 1969. 1st edn. 297 pp. Dw.  *(Fye)* **$27.50**

**Jarcho, Julius**
- Postures and practices during labor among primitive peoples... New York: 1934. 1st edn. 4to. xiv,175 pp. 130 ills. Errata slip tipped in.
*(Elgen)* **$75**

**Jastrow, Joseph**
- The subconscious. Boston & New York: 1906. 549 pp. Straight grained blue cloth gilt. Front hinge cracked.  *(Gach)* **$28.50**

**Jeaffreson, John Cordy**
- A book about doctors. n.d. [1862?]. xii,324,[6 advts]. Port frontis. Orig cloth gilt, bds w'stained, spine sl bumped.  *(Jenner)* **£14**
- A book about doctors. N.d. [ca 1861]. 1st edn. Frontis.  *(Robertshaw)* **£20**

**Jeancon, J.A.**
- Pathological anatomy, pathology and physical diagnosis. A series of clinical reports comprising the principal diseases of the human body ... Cinn: 1883. Folio. 100 full page cold plates. Orig printed wraps.
*(M&S)* **$85**

**Jeans, James H.**
- Astronomy and cosmogony. Cambridge: 1928. 1st edn. x,420 pp. 16 full-page plates. Spine faded.  *(Whitehart)* **£25**
- Astronomy and cosmogony. Cambridge: Deighton, 1929. 2nd edn. x,420 pp. 16 plates.

Occas marginal mark.          *(Pollak)* **£30**
- Atomicity and quanta. Being the Rouse Ball
lecture delivered on May 11, 1925.
Cambridge: University Press, 1926. 1st edn.
64 pp. Orig paper bds, dusty, spine wearing
a little on one edge.          *(Pollak)* **£15**
- The dynamical theory of gases. Cambridge:
1904. 1st edn. Lge 8vo. vi,352 pp. Diags.
Label removed from front cvr. *(Weiner)* **£40**
- The mathematical theory of electricity and
magnetism. Cambridge: University Press,
1908. 1st edn. vi,[ii],536 pp. 137 text figs.
Recased.          *(Pollak)* **£65**
- The mathematical theory of electricity and
magnetism. Cambridge: University Press,
1918. 2nd edn. vi,[ii],584 pp. 137 text figs.
          *(Pollak)* **£25**
- Problems of cosmogony and stellar dynamics.
Cambridge: University Press, 1919. 1st edn.
Roy 8vo. Ills. Pub blue cloth. *(McDowell)* **£45**

**Jeans, T.T.**
- Reminiscences of a naval surgeon. 1927.
xiv,310 pp. Port frontis, 6 plates. Orig cloth,
sl marked & faded.          *(Whitehart)* **£18**

**Jeffereys, W. Hamilton & Maxwell, James
L.**
- The diseases of China, including Formosa
and Korea. Phila: 1910. 1st edn. xvi,716 pp.
5 cold plates, 11 noso-geographical plates,
360 text ills. Spine sunned.          *(Elgen)* **$75**

**Jeffreys, Harold**
- The Earth: its origin, history and physical
constitution. Cambridge: 1924. 1st edn. 4to.
278 pp.          *(Scientia)* **$75**
- The Earth: its origin, history and physical
constitution. Cambridge: University Press,
1962. 4th edn. xvi,438 pp. 10 plates, 28 text
figs. Dw.          *(Pollak)* **£10**
- Theory of probability. Oxford: Clarendon
Press, 1939. 1st edn. 8vo.   *(McDowell)* **£30**

**Jeffries, B. Joy**
- Color-blindness: its dangers and its detection.
Boston: 1879. 1st edn. 312 pp.     *(Fye)* **$75**
- The eye in health and disease. Boston: 1871.
1st edn. 119 pp.          *(Fye)* **$60**

**Jelliffe, Smith Ely**
- Sketches in psychosomatic medicine. New
York: 1939. 1st edn. v,155,3 [pub ctlg] pp.
Ills. Paper-cvrd bds.          *(Elgen)* **$45**

**Jelsma, Franklin**
- Primary tumors of the calvaria. Springfield:
1959. 1st edn. 116 pp. Dw.     *(Fye)* **$17.50**

**Jenkins, C. Francis**
- The boyhood of an inventor. Washington,
DC: 1931. xix,273 pp. Port, num ills.
          *(Weiner)* **£50**

**Jenkins, R.**
- See Dickinson, H.W. & Jenkins, R.

**Jenner, Edward**
- An inquiry into the causes and effects of the
variolae vaccinae ... known by the name of the
cow pox. London: for the author by Sampson
Low, 1800. 2nd edn. 4to. 3 parts in 1 volume.
4 hand-cold engvd plates. (with) Report ... On
vaccination, 1807. 13 pp. *(Quaritch)* **$2,250**

**Jennings, H.C.**
- See Eschauzier, J.S. & Jennings, H.C.

**Jenyns, L.**
- Observations in meteorology: relating to
temperature, the winds, atmospheric
pressure, the aqueous phenomena of the
atmosphere, weather-changes ... 1858.
ix,[1],415 pp.          *(Whitehart)* **£15**

**Jepson, Glenn, et al. (eds.)**
- Genetics, paleontology and evolution.
Princeton: 1949. 1st edn. Top of spine
creased.          *(Scientia)* **$35**

**Jervis, W.P.**
- The mineral resources of central Italy:
including geological, historical and
commercial notices of the mines and marble
quarries ... 1868. 132 pp. Plates, ills, map,
fldg tables. Fore-edge of cloth discoloured.
Few lib stamps. Author's pres copy.
          *(Weiner)* **£30**

**Jess, Zachariah**
- A compendious system of practical surveying,
and dividing of land ... Phila: 1814. 2nd edn,
impvd. 8vo. 9,227 pp. [with] Tables of
difference of latitude and departure ... Phila:
1814. 154 pp. Contemp tree calf, lea label.
          *(M&S)* **$60**

**Jessop, William**
- Facts and arguments ... containing the report
of William Jessop ... See Macartney, Sir J.

**Jewett, Paul**
- New England farrier; or, a compendium of
earriery (sic), in four parts ... intended for the
use of private gentlemen and farmers.
Newburyport: 1795. 1st edn. 1st iss. 18mo.
46,[2] pp. Sewn. Top margin cropped
affecting some page numbers. *(M&S)* **$325**

**Jex-Blake, Sophia**
- Medical women. Two essays: medicine as a
profession ... medical education ...
Edinburgh: 1872. 1st edn.   *(Scientia)* **$85**

**Johnson, C.N.**
- Principles and practice of filling teeth. 1906.
3rd edn. [3],305 pp. 121 figs in text. Orig

cloth, sl worn & dust stained. *(Whitehart)* **£18**

**Johnson, Charles**
- British poisonous plants. London: John E. Sowerby, 1856. 1st edn. 8vo. iv,59 pp. 28 hand-cold plates. Orig cloth, gilt. Spine lightly faded. *(Rootenberg)* **$250**

**Johnson, Christopher Turner**
- A practical essay on cancer ... Phila: Edward Parker, 1811. 1st Amer edn. 12mo. 136 pp. Contemp calf, some scuffing of extremities. *(M&S)* **$85**

**Johnson, Edward**
- The water cure: a lecture on the principles of hydropathy ... London: 1843. vii,43,[1 advts]. Title spotted, last leaf detchd. Disbound. *(Jenner)* **£14**

**Johnson, Edward J.**
- Practical illustrations of the necessity for ascertaining the deviations of the compass; with explanatory diagrams ... notes on magnetism, etc. London: G. Barclay, 1847. 1st edn. 4to. vi,85,[1] pp. 2 engvd charts, (1 fldg). Contemp cloth. *(Antiq Sc)* **$150**

**Johnson, Francis R.**
- Astronomical thought in renaissance England. A study of the English scientific writings ... Balt: 1937. 1st edn. 357 pp. *(Scientia)* **$37.50**

**Johnson, George**
- Medical lectures and essays. 1887. xxxii,900 pp. 46 figs in text. Orig cloth, dust stained. Inscrbd "to Dr. Wm Jenner with regards from the Author". *(Whitehart)* **£40**

**Johnson, I.D.**
- Guide to homeopathic practice; designed for use of families and private individuals. Phila: Boericke, 1879. 1st edn. Sm 4to. 494 pp. Front hinge cracked. *(Xerxes)* **$50**

**Johnson, James**
- Change of air, or the philosophy of travelling; being autumnal excursions through Switzerland ... and Belgium. With observations on ...the medicinal influence of travelling exercise. New York: Samuel Wood, 1831. 326 pp. W'staining, foxing. Mod lea. *(Poitras)* **$100**
- Change of air, or the philosophy of travelling ... With observations on ...the medicinal influence of travelling exercise. New York: Samuel Wood, 1831. Roy 8vo. 326 pp. Occas foxing. Top crnr of front blank endpaper torn out. Cvr v worn. *(Xerxes)* **$90**
- Change of air, or the philosophy of travelling, being autumnal excursions through France, Switzerland ... with observations on the ...

medicinal influence of travelling-exercise. New York: 1831. 8vo. viii,326,[2] pp. Orig green pebbled cloth, spine taped. *(Hemlock)* **$65**
- An essay on morbid sensibility of the stomach and bowels, as the proximate cause or characteristic condition of indigestion, nervous irritability ... 1828. 5th edn. viii,174 pp. Uncut, edges sl soiled. New qtr calf gilt, mrbld bds. *(Jenner)* **£40**
- The influence of tropical climates on European constitutions: being a treatise on the principal diseases incidental to Europeans ... 1821. 3rd edn. xiv,531 pp. Rebnd in cloth-backed mrbld bds, sl rubbed. *(Jenner)* **£48**
- The influence of tropical climates on European constitutions: being a treatise on the principal diseases incidental to Europeans ... New York: 1826. viii,[9]-416 pp. Browning & foxing. Staining on last 30 pp. Orig mottled calf, scuffed. *(Elgen)* **$125**
- A treatise on derangements of the liver, internal organs and nervous system. Phila: 1826. 12mo. xii,233 pp. Light browning. Orig calf, scuffed. *(Elgen)* **$95**
- A treatise on derangements of the liver, internal organs and nervous system. Concord [Mass?]: Horatio Hill, 1832. 1st Amer edn. vi,[13]-234 pp. Foxed. Bds worn, spine tips taped. *(Diamond)* **$50**

**Johnson, Louisa**
- Every lady her own gardener. Addressed to the industrious and economical only. London: W. Kent ..., 1851. 15th edn. vi,[ii],136 pp. Hand-cold frontis & title vignette. Orig dec cloth. *(Pollak)* **£15**

**Johnson, Stephen L.**
- The history of cardiac surgery 1896-1955. Balt: 1970. 1st edn. Dw. *(Scientia)* **$30**

**Johnston, J.F.W.**
- Lectures on agricultural chemistry and geology with an appendix containing suggestions for experiments in practical agriculture. 1844. 1st edn. 911,116,xx pp. Contemp 3/4 roan, spine gilt, lea label. Binding worn & sl rubbed. *(Whitehart)* **£45**
- Lectures on agricultural chemistry and geology. Edinburgh: 1847. 2nd edn. xx,1117,[16] pp. Orig cloth rebacked, orig spine laid on, cloth sl stained. *(Whitehart)* **£38**

**Johnston, W.J.**
- Telegraphic tales and telegraphic history. New York: 1880. 254 pp. Elab pict cloth, back cvr lightly stained. *(Weiner)* **£25**

**Johnstone, J.**
- An account of the mode of draining land, according to the system practised by Mr.

Elkington. 1801. 2nd edn. 8vo. xvi,164 pp. 19 fldg engvd plates. New bds.
*(Wheldon & Wesley)* £30

**Jones, Bence**
- The life and letters of Faraday. London: Longmans, 1870. 1st edn. 2 vols. 8vo. Port frontis to each vol. Titles spotted. Pub cloth, snagged at top of spines, rubbed.
*(McDowell)* £55
- The life and letters of Faraday. London: Longmans, Green, 1870. 2nd edn, revsd. 2 vols. viii,[iv], 385,[iii], 44 [ctlg]; [viii],491,[i] pp. 2 frontis, plate, 6 ills. Orig cloth, faded, unopened.
*(Pollak)* £55

**Jones, Bennett M. & Griffiths, J.C.**
- Aerial surveying by rapid methods. Cambridge University Press, 1925. 1st edn. Sm 4to. xiv,[2],159 pp. 5 plates, 17 full-page diags (2 fldg), 2 fldg plates in rear pocket. Lacks oblique stereo photographs.
*(Diamond)* $25

**Jones, Charles Handfield**
- Clinical observations on functional nervous disorders. London: 1864. 1st edn. Orig cloth. Lib b'plate.
*(Gach)* $35

**Jones, F. Wood**
- Structure and function as seen in the foot. 1944. 1st edn. iv,329 pp. Figs in text.
*(Whitehart)* £20

**Jones, Harry Clarry & Strong, W.W.**
- A study of the absorption spectra of solutions of certain salts of potassium, cobalt, nickel ... affected by chemical agents and by temperature. Washington, DC: 1910. 1st edn. 4to xi,[1],159 pp. 98 plates. Orig green cloth, gilt lettering, sl worn.
*(Zeitlin)* $75

**Jones, John**
- The mysteries of opium revealed ... London: Richard Smith, 1701. 1st edn. 8vo. [4],371 pp. Lge fldg chart "A table of the doses of the best and safest opiates". Text browned. Full calf, antique.
*(Dailey)* $325

**Jones, Kathleen**
- Lunacy, law, and conscience 1744 - 1845. The social history of the care of the insane. 1955. 1st edn.
*(Robertshaw)* £10

**Jones, Robert**
- Notes on military orthopaedics. 1917. xiv,132 pp. 128 figs. Orig cloth, sl dust stained.
*(Whitehart)* £18
- Notes on military orthopaedics. London: Cassell, 1918. 2nd imp. xiv,132 pp. 128 figs.
*(Pollak)* £20

**Jones, Robert & Lovett, Robert**
- Orthopedic surgery. New York: 1924. 1st edn, 699 pp.
*(Fye)* $200
- Orthopedic surgery. New York: 1924. 1st edn, 2nd printing. 699 pp.
*(Fye)* $125

**Jones, Robert (ed.)**
- Orthopaedic surgery of injuries by various authors. London: 1921. 1st edn. 2 vols. 540; 692 pp. Ills.
*(Fye)* $150

**Jones, Thomas Wharton**
- Evolution of the human race from apes, and of apes from lower animals. London: Smith, Elder, 1876. 8vo. xix,69 pp. Dark brown cloth. Ex lib.
*(Blackwell's)* £45

**Jones, W.**
- Heating by hot water, ventilation and hot water supply ... with information and suggestions ... 1890. 116 pp, 8 pp advts. Plans & ills throughout. Spine faded.
*(Quinto Charing Cross)* £12
- Heating by hot water, ventilation and hot water supply ... with information and suggestions ... 1904. 3rd edn. xv,344,xxxii [advts] pp. 142 figs in text. Orig cloth.
*(Whitehart)* £18

**Jones, William H.S.**
- Malaria and Greek history. To which is added the history of Greek therapeutics and the malaria theory by E.T. Withington. Manchester: 1909. 1st edn.
*(Scientia)* $75

**Jongh, L.J. de**
- The three kinds of cod liver oil; comparatively considered with reference to their chemical and therapeutic properties ... Phila: Lea & Blanchard, 1849. 8vo. 211 pp. Sl stained. Lacks spine, hinges worn.
*(Poitras)* $50

**Jordan, David Starr**
- The heredity of Richard Roe: a discussion of the principles of eugenics. Boston: 1911. 1st edn. 165 pp.
*(Scientia)* $25

**Jordan, Henry H.**
- Workmen's compensation and the physician. A manual for the use of general practitioners and insurance carriers. New York: Oxford University Press, 1941. 180 pp.
*(Poitras)* $17.50

**Joslin, Elliott**
- Diabetes - its control by the individual and state. Cambridge: Harvard University Press, 1931. Harvard Health Talks. 70 pp. Inscribed by author.
*(Poitras)* $35
- The treatment of diabetes mellitus. Phila: 1917. 2nd edn, enlarged & largely re-written. 559 pp. Ills.
*(Oasis)* $30

**Journal ...**
- The journal of a naturalist ... See Knapp, John Leonard
- Journal of the history of medicine and allied sciences. New York: Henry Schuman [&c.], 1946-78. Vol 1, No 1 to Vol 33, No 4, plus index vol for vols 1-30. Roy 8vo. Orig stiff paper wraps. *(McDowell)* **£450**

**Joyce, Rev. J.**
- Scientific dialogues; intended for the instruction and entertainment of young people ... Halifax: 1851. Sm 8vo. Engvd title. Orig cloth, rebacked, orig spine laid on. *(Whitehart)* **£15**

**Judovich, Bernard & Bates, William**
- Pain syndromes. Treatment by paravertebral nerve block. Phila: F.A. Davis, 1949. 3rd edn. 357 pp. 181 ills. *(Poitras)* **$30**
- Segmental neuralgia in painful syndromes. Phila: 1944. x,313 pp. 178 ills. Orig green cloth. *(Jenner)* **£18**

**Jukes, J.B.**
- Popular physical geology. 1853. xvi,359 pp. 20 hand-cold plates. Cloth, spine defective. *(Wheldon & Wesley)* **£25**

**Jung, Carl Gustav**
- Psychology of the unconscious: a study of the transformations and symbolisms of the libido. A contribution to the history of the evolution of thought. New York: Moffat ..., 1916. 1st edn in English. lvi,566,[2] pp. Lge 8vo. 6 plates. Blue cloth. *(Gach)* **$150**
- Studies in word-association: experiments in the diagnosis of psychopathological conditions ... London: Heinemann Medical Books, [1918]. x,575 pp. *(Gach)* **$150**

**Kahlden, C. von**
- Methods of pathological histology. Translated and edited ... London: Macmillan, 1894. xi,[i], 171,[i] pp. Uncut in orig cloth. *(Pollak)* **£20**

**Kahn, D.**
- The codebreakers. The story of secret writing. New York: 1967. Many plates & ills. *(Whitehart)* **£30**

**Kallman, Franz**
- The genetics of schizophrenia: a study of heredity and reproduction in the families of 1,087 schizophrenics. New York: J.J. Augustin, 1938. 1st edn. xvi,291 pp. Pub green cloth. Ex lib. *(Gach)* **$75**
- Heredity in health and mental disorders: principles of psychiatric genetics in the light of comparative twin studies. New York: 1953. 1st edn. 315 pp. *(Scientia)* **$30**

**Kaminetzky, H.A. & Iffy, L.**
- New techniques and concepts in maternal and fetal medicine. New York: Van Nostrand & Reinhold, 1979. 1st edn. 390 pp. Num charts. Dw. *(Poitras)* **$25**

**Kammerer, Paul**
- The inheritance of acquired characters. Translated ... New York: 1924. 1st edn in English. 414 pp. *(Scientia)* **$50**

**Kammerer, Percy Gamble**
- The unmarried mother: a study of five hundred cases. Boston: Little, Brown, 1920. xvi,342,[2] pp. Criminal Science Monograph No. 3. *(Gach)* **$30**

**Kanavel, Allen**
- Infections of the hand. Phila: 1912. 1st edn. 447 pp. *(Fye)* **$250**
- Infections of the hand. Phila: 1914. 2nd edn. 463 pp. 147 ills. *(Fye)* **$150**
- Infections of the hand. Phila: 1921. 4th edn. 500 pp. *(Fye)* **$100**
- Infections of the hand. Phila: 1933. 6th edn. 552 pp. *(Fye)* **$75**

**Kantor, Jacob R.**
- Principles of psychology. New York: Alfred A. Knopf, 1924. 1st edn. 2 vols. 473; 524 pp. *(Gach)* **$35**

**Kaplan, Emanuel**
- Functional and surgical anatomy of the hand. Phila: 1953. 1st edn. 288 pp. Dw. *(Fye)* **$60**

**[Karman, Theodore von]**
- Contributions to applied mechanics and related subjects by the friends of Theodore von Karman on his sixtieth birthday. Pasadena: 1941. 4to. 337 pp. Sgnd pres copy from von Karman. *(Scientia)* **$60**

**Karpinski, Louis C.**
- Bibliography of mathematical works printed in America through 1850. Ann Arbor, MI: 1940. 1st edn. 4to. 697 pp. *(Scientia)* **$200**

**Kasanin, Jacob**
- See Hanfmann, Eugenia & Kasanin, Jacob

**Kasanin, Jacob S. (ed.)**
- Language and thought in schizophrenia: collected papers presented at the meeting of the American Psychiatric Association, May 12, 1939 ... Berkeley & Los Angeles: 1946. 2nd printing. *(Gach)* **$25**

**Kasanjian, V.H. & Converse, J.M.**
- The surgical treatment of facial injuries. Balt: 1949. 1st edn. 574 pp. *(Fye)* **$40**

**Kassabian, M.K.**
- Roentgen rays and electro-therapeutics, with chapters on radium and phototherapy. Phila: 1910. 2nd edn. xxxv,540 pp. 245 ills & plates in the text. Orig cloth, sl worn.
*(Whitehart)* £18

**Kater, Henry**
- See Lardner, Dionysius & Kater, Henry

**Kawamura, Rinya**
- Studies on Tsutsugamushi disease (Japanese flood fever). Cincinnati: 1926. 1st edn in English. ix,229 pp. 2 maps, 25 plates. Ex lib.
*(Elgen)* $40

**Kay, William**
- Report on the sanitary condition of Bristol & Clifton. Clifton [Somerset]: 1844. Folio. 32 pp. Tables. Qtr calf. Author's pres copy.
*(Goodrich)* $90

**Kean, F.J.**
- The petrol engine. A text book dealing with the principles of design and construction ... 1915. xiv,124 pp. 71 figs in text. Orig cloth, sl marked.
*(Whitehart)* £15

**Keating, J.M.**
- The Yellow Fever epidemic of 1878, in Memphis, Tenn. Memphis, Tenn: for the Howard Association, 1879. 1st edn. 4to. 454 pp. Orig cloth.
*(M&S)* $60

**Keats, W.A.**
- See English, Frank P. & Keats, W.A.

**Keele, K.D.**
- Leonardo da Vinci on movement of the heart and blood. 1952. Ltd (1000). xviii,142 pp. Qtr lea.
*(Whitehart)* £35

**Keen, William & White, J. William (eds.)**
- An American text-book of surgery. Phila: 1893. 1st edn. 1209 pp. Full lea. *(Fye)* $100

**Keen, William (ed.)**
- Surgery: its principles and practice by various authors. Phila: 1907-13. 1st edn. 6 vols.
*(Fye)* $200

**Keen, William W.**
- The surgical complications and sequels of typhoid fever. Based upon tables of 1700 cases ... Phila: W.B. Saunders, 1898. 386 pp. Ills. Sl staining lower edge back cvr.
*(Poitras)* $60

**Keen, William Williams**
- The treatment of war wounds. Phila & London: W.B. Saunders Company, 1917. 8vo. 169,14 [pub ctlg] pp. Ills. *(Poitras)* $40

**Keill, James**
- The anatomy of the human body abridg'd; or, a short and full view of all the parts of the body. Together with their several uses ... London: for John Keblewhite, 1698. 1st edn. 12mo. [12]ff, 328pp, [4]ff. Mod lea. Outer edge of margins gnawed slightly.
*(Zeitlin)* $400
- The anatomy of the human body abridg'd. 1731. 8th edn, crrctd. 12mo. Contemp calf, hd & ft of spine crudely reprd.
*(Robertshaw)* £25

**Keill, John**
- Euclid's elements of geometry, from the Latin translation of Commandine, to which is added. a treatise on the nature and arithmetic of logarithms ... London: for W. Strahan, 1782. 12th edn. [xvi],399 pp. 18 plates. Orig calf, rebacked, crnrs little worn. *(Pollak)* £40

**Keith, Arthur**
- The antiquity of man. 1915. 1st edn. xx,519 pp. Frontis, 189 figs. Orig cloth, embossed stamps on title. *(Whitehart)* £15
- Menders of the maimed. London: 1919. 1st edn. *(Scientia)* $85
- New discoveries pertaining to the antiquity of man. 1931. 512 pp. 186 figs. Orig blue cloth, edges bumped, hinges cracked, jnts rubbed.
*(Jenner)* £15
- New discoveries relating to the antiquity of man. Williams & Norgate, 1931. 512 pp. Frontis, 186 ills. *(Pollak)* £20

**Keith, George Skene**
- Tracts on weights, measures and coins. London: Murray, 1791. 4to. Sewn as issued, edges frayed. *(Marlborough)* £85

**Keith, William**
- See Pirrie, William & Keith, William

**Keller, A.**
- See Fulton John F. & Keller, A.

**Kellogg, Edward**
- The duodenum. New York: 1933. 1st edn. 4to. 855 pp. *(Fye)* $30

**Kellogg, John Harvey**
- A household manual of hygiene, food and diet, common disease, accidents and emergencies ... Battle Creek: Office of the Health Reformer, 1877. 1st edn. 12mo. 172 pp. 3 ills, 4 pp advts. A few pencil marks. Dec cvrs, worn. *(Diamond)* $45

**Kellogg, Vernon**
- Darwinism today: A discussion of present-day scientific criticism of the Darwinian selection theories, together with a brief account of ... other, alternative theories ... New York: 1907.

1st edn. 403 pp.                   *(Scientia)* **$50**

**Kelly, Emerson Crosby**
- Encyclopedia of medical sources. Balt:
Williams & Wilkins Company, 1948. 4to.
v,476 pp.                          *(Poitras)* **$30**

**Kelly, George A.**
- Psychology of personal contructs. New York:
1955. 2 vols. 1218 pp. Spine faded, sl
shelfworn.               *(Epistemologist)* **$65**

**Kelly, Howard**
- Appendicitis and other diseases of the
vermiform appendix. Phila: 1909. 502 pp.
Inner hinges cracked.              *(Fye)* **$125**
- Medical gynecology. New York: 1908. 1st
edn. 662 pp.                        *(Fye)* **$50**
- Operative gynecology. New York: 1898. 1st
edn. 2 vols. 569; 557 pp. Ills by Broedel.
                                   *(Fye)* **$150**
- Operative gynecology. New York: 1901. 1st
edn, reprinted. 2 vols. 569; 557 pp. Ills by
Broedel.                           *(Fye)* **$100**

**Kelly, Howard & Burnham, Curtis**
- Diseases of the kidneys, ureters and bladder.
New York: 1914. 1st edn. 2 vols. 582; 652 pp.
Num ills by Max Brodel.            *(Oasis)* **$100**

**Kelly, Howard & Cullen, Thomas**
- Myomata of the uterus. Phila: 1909. 1st edn.
723 pp. Scattered lib stamps. Inscrbd &
autographed by Cullen.             *(Fye)* **$250**

**Kelly, Howard & Hurdon, Elizabeth**
- The vermiform appendix & its diseases.
Phila: 1905. 1st edn. 827 pp. Num ills, some
in color, many by Max Brodel. Orig cloth.
                                   *(Oasis)* **$200**
- The vermiform appendix & its diseases.
Phila: W.B. Saunders, 1905. xx,827 pp. Cold
frontis, several fldg plates, hundreds of text
ills. Orig cloth.                 *(Hemlock)* **$150**
- The vermiform appendix and its diseases.
Phila: 1905. 1st edn. 827 pp. Binding rubbed,
shaken.                            *(Fye)* **$150**
- The vermiform appendix and its diseases.
Phila: 1911. 1st edn, reprinted. 827 pp.
Inscrbd & autographed by Kelly with an
original photo of Kelly mounted above the
inscrptn.                          *(Fye)* **$500**

**Kelly, Howard & Noble, Charles**
- Gynecology and abdominal surgery. Phila:
1907-08. 1st edn. 2 vols. 851; 862 pp. Num
ills by Max Broedel.               *(Fye)* **$100**
- Gynecology and abdominal surgery. Phila:
1910. 1st edn, 2nd printing. 2 vols. 851; 862
pp. Half lea.                      *(Fye)* **$100**

**Kelly, Howard & Ward, Grant**
- Electrosurgery. Phila: 1932. 1st edn. 305 pp.

Ills.                              *(Oasis)* **$50**
- Electrosurgery. Phila: 1932. 1st edn. 305 pp.
                                   *(Fye)* **$60**
- Electrosurgery. Phila: W.B. Saunders, 1932.
305 pp. 382 ills.                  *(Poitras)* **$75**

**Kelly, Howard (ed.)**
- The Surgical Clinic No. 21: Dr. Samuel T.
Earle's operation for hemorrhoids. Consisting
of 23 mounted stereo photographs on loose
leaves with explanatory text. Complete as
issued. N.d. [1900's ?]. Orig slipcase.
                                   *(Oasis)* **$45**

**Kelly, James**
- See Roberts, John & Kelly, James

**Kelly, P.**
- A practical introduction to spherics and
nautical astronomy; being an attempt to
simplify those useful sciences ... London:
1822. Roy 8vo. xvi,236 pp. Leaf of
instructions to binder, sep title to 2nd part. 20
engvd plates, fldg table. Half-calf, rebacked.
                                 *(Burmester)* **£25**

**Kelsey, Charles**
- Diseases of the rectum and anus. New York:
1890. 3rd edn. 483 pp.             *(Fye)* **$40**
- Diseases of the rectum and pelvis. New York:
1897. 1st edn. 573 pp. 300 ills.   *(Fye)* **$75**

**Kempf, Edward J.**
- The autonomic functions and the personality:
Nervous and Mental Diseases Monograph
Series No. 28. New York: 1918. 156 pp. A bit
loose.                             *(Gach)* **$25**
- Psychopathology. St. Louis: Mosby, 1920.
Lge 8vo. xxiii,[1],762 pp. 87 text ills. Orig
olive green ribbed cloth, a little rubbed &
bumped at crnrs.                   *(Zeitlin)* **$85**

**[Kendall, Francis]**
- A descriptive catalogue of the minerals, and
fossil organic remains of Scarborough, and
the vicinity. Scarborough: Coutas, 1816. Sole
edn. Engvd title, 5 hand-cold plates, 1 fldg
engvd plate. Half-title, subscribers' list. Pub
bds, hinges cracked.            *(McDowell)* **£550**

**Kennedy, A.B.W.**
- The mechanics of machinery. 1886. xv,652
pp. 400 figs in text. Cloth worn & stained.
                                 *(Whitehart)* **£18**

**Kennedy, Alex Mills**
- See Worster-Drought & Kennedy, Alex Mills

**Kennedy, Donald**
- On diseases of the skin. Roxbury, Mass.:
[1871]. 2nd edn. 8vo. 128 pp. 3 cold plates.
Tear in one leaf without loss of text. Orig
printed wraps.                    *(Hemlock)* **$65**

**Kennedy, Evory**
- Observations on obstetric auscultation, with an analysis of the evidences of pregnancy, and an enquiry ... with an appendix containing legal notes ... New York: 1843. 1st Amer edn. Sm 8vo. vi, [3]ff,311 pp. 17 full-page litho plates, foxed. Bndg worn.        *(Elgen)* **$95**
- Observations on obstetric auscultation, with an analysis of the evidences of pregnancy. New York: 1843. 1st Amer edn. 311 pp. Engvd plates.        *(Fye)* **$100**

**Kennedy, Rankin**
- Electrical installations of electric light, power, traction and industrial electrical machinery. 1902-03. 1st edn. Many plates & ills in the text. Orig pict cloth, vol II sl marked.        *(Whitehart)* **£55**

**Kerr, James**
- The fundamentals of school health. London: Allen & Unwin, 1926. xvi,859,[v] pp. Cloth a little rubbed, new endpapers.        *(Pollak)* **£40**

**Kerr, Richard**
- Nature through microscope and camera. With sixty-five photomicrographs by Arthur E. Smith. London: Religious Tract Society, 1909. 1st edn, 2nd imp. 8vo. 197 pp. 65 plates. Orig dec cloth.        *(Antiq Sc)* **$50**

**Kerrison, Robert M.**
- An enquiry into the present state of the medical profession in England ... a comparative view of the profession in Scotland, Ireland ... and Europe. London: 1814, 1st edn. 96 pp. Old bds. Inscrbd by author.        *(Goodrich)* **$250**

**Kersey, John**
- The elements of that mathematical law called algebra ... numerical resolution of the same ... by Edmund Halley. London: ... Mount, 1717. 2nd edn. Sm folio. [1]f,24 pp,323,[1] pp. Frontis. Light browning, damp-stain in inner margin. Contemp calf, label worn.        *(Zeitlin)* **$275**

**Kettilby, Mary**
- A collection of above three hundred receipts in cookery, physick and surgery; for the use of all good wives, tender mothers and careful nurses. To which is added ... London: ... Parker, 1746. 6th edn. 8vo. 2 titles. Some spotting. Contemp roan, rebacked.        *(McDowell)* **£240**

**Key, Ancel, et al.**
- The biology of human starvation. Minneapolis: 1950. 1st edn. 2 vols. 1835 pp. Ills.        *(Oasis)* **$60**

**Keynes, Geoffrey**
- A bibliography of Robert Hooke. Oxford: Clarendon Press, 1960. 1st edn. 4to. Dw.        *(McDowell)* **£75**
- A bibliography of Sir Thomas Browne. Cambridge: 1924. 1st edn. Ltd (500). 4to. xii,255,[1] pp. Orig cloth, sl rubbed.        *(Hemlock)* **$200**
- Dr. Timothie Bright, 1550 - 1615. A survey of his life with a bibliography of his writings. London: Wellcome, 1962. 1st edn. 4to. Plates.        *(McDowell)* **£28**
- John Ray: A bibliography. London: 1951. 1st edn. Ltd (650). 163 pp.        *(Scientia)* **$100**
- John Ray: A bibliography. London: Faber & Faber, 1951. Ltd (650). xv,163 pp. 4 collotypes, 16 title-page reproductions. Orig cloth.        *(Pollak)* **£60**
- The personality of William Harvey. Cambridge: University Press, 1945. 1st edn. Slim 8vo. Pub beige cloth.        *(McDowell)* **£25**

**Keynes, Geoffrey (ed.)**
- Blood transfusion. Balt: 1949. 1st Amer edn. 574 pp.        *(Fye)* **$50**

**Keynes, John Neville**
- Studies and exercises in formal logic ... London: Macmillan, 1887. 2nd edn, revsd & enlgd. xii,455 pp. Orig cloth, a little faded.        *(Pollak)* **£45**

**Keys, Thomas E.**
- The history of surgical anesthesia. New York: 1945. 36 plates. Bibliog.        *(Winterdown)* **£35**
- See Faulconer, Albert & Keys, Thomas E.

**Kidd, John**
- On the adaptation of external nature to the physical condition of man. London: William Pickering, 1833. 2nd edn. 8vo, xvi,375 pp. Minor foxing. Contemp calf, cvrs trifle scraped & marked.        *(Bow Windows)* **£70**
- On the adaptation of external nature to the physical condition of man. 1837. 8vo. xvi,375 pp. Tree calf, gilt, jnts weak.        *(Wheldon & Wesley)* **£15**
- On the adaptation of external nature to the physical condition of man. 1837. 5th edn. xvi,375 pp. Sm lib stamps on title verso. New cloth, rebacked.        *(Jenner)* **£10**

**Kidd, Joseph**
- The laws of therapeutics or the science and art of medicine. A sketch. Kegan Paul, 1878. [viii],232 pp. Orig cloth. Spine ends sl worn, jnts weak.        *(Pollak)* **£15**

**Kilduffe, Robert & DeBakey, Michael**
- The blood bank and the technique and therapeutics of transfusions. St. Louis: 1942. 1st edn. 558 pp.        *(Fye)* **$50**

**King, Henry C.**
- The history of the telescope. Cambridge: 1955. 1st edn. 456 pp. Dw torn. *(Scientia)* **$85**

**King, James**
- Local anesthesia in otolaryngology and rhinology. New York: 1926. 1st edn, 205 pp. Fldg chart. *(Fye)* **$75**

**King, John H.**
- Man an organic community, being an exposition of the law that the human personality ... is the multiple of many sub-personalities. 1893. 1st edn. 2 vols. *(Robertshaw)* **£18**

**King, William (ed.)**
- Behaviourism: a battle line. Nashville, Tennessee: Cokesbury Press, 1930. 1st edn. 376 pp. Black cloth, dull & soiled. Some lib stamps. *(Gach)* **$25**

**Kinne, W.S.**
- See Hool, G.A. & Kinne, W.S.

**Kinsey, A., et al.**
- Sexual behavior in the human male. Phila: 1948. 1st edn. 804 pp. *(Fye)* **$35**

**Kirby, William**
- On the power, wisdom and goodness of God as manifested in the creation of animals and in their history, habits and instincts. London: 1835 1st edn. 2 vols. 406; 542 pp. Kirby's Bridgewater Treatise. *(Scientia)* **$85**

**Kirk, Edward C. (ed.)**
- The American text-book of operative dentistry. Phila: 1897. 1st edn. Lge 8vo. 702,16 [pub ctlg] pp. 751 text engvs. Orig sheep, rubbed. *(Elgen)* **$85**

**Kirkbride, Thomas S.**
- Report of the Pennsylvania Hospital for the Insane for the year 1854. Phila: 1855. 54,6,[2] pp. Engvd frontis. Mod wraps. *(Gach)* **$30**

**Kirkland, Thomas**
- An essay on the inseparability of the different branches of medicine, towards improving the study and practice of medical surgery. London: [1783]. vi,148 pp. Contemp half-calf. Author's pres slip tipped in. *(Goodrich)* **$150**

**Kirkpatrick, Henry**
- Cataract and its treatment. London: 1921. 1st edn. 201 pp. *(Fye)* **$35**

**Kirwan, Richard**
- An essay on the analysis of mineral waters. London: J.W. Myers for D. Bremner, 1799. 1st edn. 8vo. Tables, some fldg, errata pasted-in. Orig bds, spine lacks most of paper. *(McDowell)* **£110**

**Kistler, W.P.**
- Practical, medical and surgical family guide in emergencies. Hints and helps on health, home nursing and remedies. 1894. 339 pp. *(Poitras)* **$17.50**

**Klebs, Arnold C. (ed.)**
- Tubercolosis: A treatise by American authors ... New York: 1909. 1st edn. *(Scientia)* **$65**

**Klein, E.**
- Studies in the bacteriology and etiology of Oriental plague. 1906. 301 pp. 89 photo ills. Dye stains on prelims. Orig red cloth, spine sunned, bds badly w'stained. *(Jenner)* **£12**

**Klein, E. & Smith, E. Noble**
- Atlas of histology. London: Smith, Elder, 1880. Folio. x,iv,448,[ii advts] pp. 48 plates. Occas faint foxing, one plate loose & a little dusty at edges. Half-calf, little rubbed, front cvr marked. *(Pollak)* **£65**

**Klein, Felix**
- The Evanston Colloquium: lectures of mathematics delivered ... 1893 before members of the Congress of Mathematics ... World's Fair in Chicago ... New York: 1894. ix,109 pp. Diags. Horace Lamb's copy. *(Weiner)* **£50**

**Klemperer, Otto (compiler)**
- Electron optics by the research staff of Electric and Musical Industries Ltd. Cambridge: 1939. Plate, many figs. Wraps. *(Winterdown)* **£15**

**Kline, Morris**
- Mathematical thought from ancient to modern times. New York: 1972. 1st edn. 1238 pp. Dw. *(Scientia)* **$65**

**Kluver, Heinrich**
- Mescal: The 'Divine' plant and its psychological effects. London: Kegan Paul, Trench, Trubner, 1928. 1st edn in English. 16mo. [xiv],[5]-111 pp. Orig cloth-backed printed bds, paper label. *(Dailey)* **$125**

**Kluver, Henrich**
- Visual mechanisms. Lancaster: 1942. 322 pp. *(Fye)* **$20**

**Knapp, H.**
- A treatise on intraocular tumours. New York: 1869. 1st English translation. 323 pp. 16 engvd plates. Ex lib. *(Fye)* **$125**

**[Knapp, John Leonard]**
- The journal of a naturalist. London: John

Murray, 1829. 1st edn. 8vo. xii,403,[1] pp.
Fldg engvd frontis, 10 engvd plates. Contemp
half-calf gilt, red label.        *(Burmester)* **£45**

**Knott, Cargill**
- Napier tercentary memorial volume. London:
1915. 1st edn. 441 pp.        *(Scientia)* **$65**

**Knuthsen, L.F.B.**
- Obstinate    hiccough:    the    physiology,
pathology and treatment ... 1902. viii,169,[16
advts] pp. Orig black pebbled cloth.
                                *(Jenner)* **£16**

**Kober, G.M. & Hanson, W.C.**
- Diseases of occupation and vocational
hygiene. Phila: Blakiston, 1919. 1st edn. 918
pp.                                *(Oasis)* **$30**

**Kocher, Theodor**
- Text-book of operative surgery. London:
1895. 1st English translation. 303 pp.
                                *(Fye)* **$150**
- Text-book of operative surgery. London:
1911. 3rd English edn. 723 pp.    *(Fye)* **$75**

**Koehler, Alban**
- Roentgenology: the borderlands of the
normal and early pathological in the
skiagram. 1935. 2nd English, from 5th
German edn. Lge 8vo. xvi,681 pp. many ills.
Orig maroon cloth, spine sl faded.
                                *(Jenner)* **£21**

**Kohl, W.H.**
- See Burton, E.F. & Kohl, W.H.

**Kohler, Wolfgang**
- Gestalt psychology. New York: Horace
Liveright, 1929. 1st edn. [xii],403,[1] pp.
Shelfworn.                        *(Gach)* **$25**
- The mentality of apes. Translated ... London
& New York: [1927]. 2nd edn, revsd & reset.
viii,336 pp. 9 plates. Green cloth, crown
chipped.                        *(Gach)* **$30**
- The place of value in a world of facts. New
York: Liveright Publishing Corporation,
[1938]. [xiv],418 pp. Blue cloth. Worn dw.
                                *(Gach)* **$35**
- The task of psychology. NJ: Princeton
University Press, [1969]. 2nd printing.
viii,164,[2] pp. Worn dw.        *(Gach)* **$15**

**Kohlrausch, F.**
- An introduction to physical measurements ...
Translated from the fourth German edition ...
London: J. & A. Churchill, 1883. 2nd edn.
xii,344, xvi [ctlg] pp. 36 text figs. *(Pollak)* **£50**

**Kolle, Frederick Strange**
- Plastic and cosmetic surgery. New York:
1911. 1st edn. Lge 8vo. xxi,511 pp. Frontis,
cold plate, 522 ills. Sl shelf wear. *(Elgen)* **$135**

- Plastic and cosmetic surgery. New York:
1911. 1st edn. 511 pp. Water stain affecting
bottom inch of front cvr.        *(Fye)* **$350**

**Kolliker, Rudolph Albert von**
- Manual of human histology. London: The
Sydenham Society, 1853-54. 1st edn in
English. 2 vols. 8vo. xiii,[1],498; ix,[1],434
pp. Many text w'cuts. Orig cloth, gilt
lettering.                    *(Rootenberg)* **$250**

**Kolmer, John Albert**
- Serum diagnosis by complement-fixation
with special reference to syphilis ... Phila: Lea
& Febiger, 1928. 1st edn. 8vo.
xix,[1],[17]-583 pp. Cold plate, 65 text ills.
Green cloth, spine gilt.        *(Zeitlin)* **$75**

**Kooy, J.M.J. & Uytenbogaart, J.W.H.**
- Ballistics of the future, with special reference
to the dynamical and physical theory of the
rocket weapons. New York & London: 1946.
472 pp. 11 fldg plates, ills, diags.
                                *(Weiner)* **£50**

**Kopetzky, Samuel**
- The surgery of the ear. New York: 1908. 1st
edn. 368 pp.                    *(Fye)* **$50**

**Koplik, Henry**
- The diseases of infancy and childhood. New
York: [1910]. 3rd edn, revsd & enlgd. Lge
8vo. xii, 17-944 pp. 39 plates (sev in color),
num ills. Hd of spine sl frayed. *(Elgen)* **$55**

**Kraepelin, Emil**
- General    paresis.    Authorized    English
translation ... New York: Nervous and
Mental Disease Publishing Company, 1913.
[ii],vi,200 pp. Puncture to inner margins of
first few signatures. Later fabricoid, orig
wraps bound in.                *(Gach)* **$50**
- One hundred years of psychiatry. New York:
1962. 1st edn in English.        *(Scientia)* **$35**

**Krafft-Ebing, Richard F. von**
- Text-book of insanity based on clinical
observations for practitioners and students of
medicine. Authorized translation ... Phila:
F.A. Davis, 1904. 1st edn in English.
xvi,638,[2] pp. Blue cloth, recased.
                                *(Gach)* **$85**

**Kramers, H.A. & Holst, Helge**
- The atom and the Bohr theory of its
structure. With a foreword by Sir Ernest
Rutherford. New York: 1924. xiii,210 pp.
Frontis, ills, fldg plate. Spine worn. Ex lib.
                                *(Elgen)* **$40**

**Kraus, B., et al.**
- Developmental anatomy of the face with
special reference of normal developmental

anatomy of the face. New York & London: Hoeber ..., 1966. 378 pp. 1224 ills.
(*Poitras*) **$60**

**Krause, Allen K., et al.**
- Studies on tuberculous infection. Balt: privately printed, 1928. Ltd (250). 1st edn. Sm 4to. xiii, pp 1-291, 551-591. Frontis, 4 mounted partial color slides, plates (sev with printed overlays), text figs, &c. Orig calf, spine sl rubbed.          (*Diamond*) **$75**

**Krause, Ernst**
- Erasmus Darwin. Translated by W.S. Dallas. With a preliminary notice by Charles Darwin. New York: 1880. 1st Amer edn. 216 pp.
(*Scientia*) **$100**

**Krause, Fedor**
- Surgery of the brain and spinal cord. New York: 1909-12. 1st English translation. 3 vols. 1201 pp. 62 cold plates.          (*Fye*) **$250**

**Krauss, J.S.**
- Aerial navigation: how far is it practicable? London & Manchester: 1901. 23 pp. Halfmor, t.e.g.          (*Pollak*) **£25**

**Kremers, Edward & Urdang, George**
- History of pharmacy. A guide and a survey. Phila: Lippincott, 1940. 1st edn. 4to. ix,466 pp. 30 ills. Dw.          (*Poitras*) **$40**

**Kretschmer, Ernst**
- Heredity and constitution in the aetiology of psychic disorders ... instinct and hysteria. London: British Medical Association, [1937]. 39 pp. Self-wraps.          (*Gach*) **$40**
- Physique and character: an investigation of the nature of constitution and of the theory of temperament.. London: Kegan Paul, Trench, Trubner, 1936. 2nd edn. xvi,282,[2] pp. Advts. 32 half-tones. Shelfworn. (*Gach*) **$30**

**Kronfeld, Peter C., et al.**
- The human eye in anatomical transparencies. Rochester: Bausch & Lomb, 1944. 99 pp. Cold ills. Dw.          (*Poitras*) **$50**

**Kropotkin, Peter**
- Mutual aid; a factor of evolution. New York: 1902. 1st Amer edn. 348 pp. (*Scientia*) **$30**

**Krumbhaar, Edward B.**
- Pathology. New York: 1937. 1st edn. Clio Medica Series.          (*Scientia*) **$27.50**

**Krusen, Frank Hammond**
- Light therapy. New York: Hoeber, 1933. 1st edn. 186 pp. 33 photo ills.          (*Xerxes*) **$45**

**Kuhn L.**
- Hand-book of the science of facial expression

or the new system of diagnosis. Translated from the 9th German edition. Leipzig: 1902. Sm 4to. Orig cloth, badly stained.
(*Whitehart*) **£25**

**Kuhne, Louis**
- Science of facial expression. Butler, N.J.: Benedict Lust, 1917. 1st edn. 88 pp. Many line drawings.          (*Xerxes*) **$45**

**Kulpe, O.**
- Outlines of psychology. London: 1909. 462 pp. B'plate removed from endpaper. Shelfworn.          (*Epistemologist*) **$50**

**Kuntz, A.**
- The autonomic nervous system. Phila: 1945, reprinted 1947. 687 pp. 91 figs in text. Orig cloth.          (*Whitehart*) **£25**

**Kutter, W.R.**
- The new formula for mean velocity of discharge of rivers and canals. 1876. x,95,clx pp. 2 plates (1 fldg). Orig cloth, new endpapers.          (*Whitehart*) **£15**

**Kyan, John H.**
- On the elements of light, and their identity with those of matter, radiant and fixed. London: Longman, 1838. 1st edn. Tall 8vo. xiv,130 pp. 4 engvd plates (2 hand-cold). Orig cloth. Author's pres copy.          (*Antiq Sc*) **$250**

**La Beche, Sir H.T. de**
- A geological manual. 1832. 2nd edn, crrctd & enlgd. xiv,564 pp. Lib stamps on title. Binder's cloth.          (*Whitehart*) **£30**
- The geological observer. 1853. 2nd edn, revsd. xxviii,740 pp. 308 figs in text. Mod cloth.          (*Whitehart*) **£35**

**La Garde, Louis**
- Gunshot injuries: how they are inflicted, their complication and treatment. New York: 1916. 2nd edn. 457 pp.          (*Fye*) **$50**
- Gunshot injuries: how they are inflicted, their complication and treatment. New York: William Wood & Company, 1916. 2nd rvsd edn. 4to. xii,457 pp. Ills.          (*Poitras*) **$30**

**Labat, Gaston**
- Regional anesthesia. Phila: 1922. 1st edn, 1st printing. 496 pp.          (*Fye*) **$150**
- Regional anesthesia; its technic and clinical application. Phila: 1922. 1st edn.
(*Scientia*) **$75**
- Regional anesthesia. Phila: 1930. 2nd edn. 576 pp.          (*Fye*) **$60**

**Lacey, Thomas**
- See Andrews, Edmund & Lacey, Thomas

**Lack, David**
- The natural regulation of animal numbers. Oxford: 1954. 1st edn. 343 pp. *(Scientia)* **$45**

**Ladd, William & Gross, Robert**
- Abdominal surgery of infancy and childhood. Phila: 1941. 1st edn. 455 pp.        *(Fye)* **$40**

**Laennec, R.T.H.**
- A treatise on the diseases of the chest and on mediate auscultation. London: Underwood, 1827. 2nd English edn, greatly enlgd. 8vo. Engvd frontis (sl discold), 8 plates. Contemp half-calf, rebacked.        *(McDowell)* **£350**

**Laing, Samuel**
- National distress; its causes and remedies. Londman, Brown, 1844. viii,169,[i]. Orig cloth.        *(Pollak)* **£32**

**Lamb, Horace**
- A treatise on the mathematical theory of the motion of fluids. Cambridge: University Press, 1879. 1st edn. x,258,40 [ctlg] pp. 9 text figs. Recased.        *(Pollak)* **£40**

**Lanchester, F.W.**
- Aerodynamics ... aerodonetics ... 1907-10. 2 vols. 8vo. xvi,442; xv,433 pp. Few plates, fldg chart, diags. Hd of vol 2 spine torn. Vol 2 2nd edn.        *(Weiner)* **£80**
- The part played by skin-friction in aeronautics. Royal Aeronautical Society, 1936. Advance proof. 47 pp. Fldg chart, diags. Pencil annotation. Outer leaves grubby. Stapled as issued.        *(Weiner)* **£15**

**Landolt, H.**
- Handbook of the polariscope and its practical applications. Translated ... 1882. 1st edn. xvi,262 pp. 57 ills. Endpaper & half-title sl holed. Orig cloth.        *(Whitehart)* **£38**

**Langdon, W.E.**
- The application of electricity to railway working. 1897. 2nd edn. xvi,331 pp. Frontis, 4 full-page ills, 142 ills in text. Orig cloth.        *(Whitehart)* **£25**

**Langley, S.P.**
- Experiments in aerodynamics. Washington: 1891. 115 pp. 7 double-page & 3 single-page plates. 11 ills. Unopened, with wide margins. Half lea.        *(Whitehart)* **£120**

**Langley, Samuel Pierpoint**
- Researches on solar heat, and its absorption by the earth's atmosphere ... Washington, DC: Govt Printing Office, 1884. 1st edn. 4to. 242 pp. Plates, some fldg, text figs. Orig cloth, rebacked.        *(Diamond)* **$150**

**Langley, Samuel Pierpoint & Manley, Charles M.**
- Langley memoir on mechanical flight. Part I. 1887 to 1896 ... Part II. 1897 to 1903. Washington: Smithsonian Institution, 1911. 1st edn. Folio. 10,[2],320 pp. Index. 100 plates. Orig printed wraps detchd, backstrip defective. Minor defect on title. *(M&S)* **$150**

**Lankester, E. Ray**
- The advancement of science. Occasional essays and addresses. London: 1890. 1st edn. 387 pp. Shelfworn.        *(Scientia)* **$30**

**Lankester, Edwin**
- Vegetable substances used for the food of man. 1832. 12mo. viii,396 pp. W'cuts. Cloth.        *(Weiner)* **£35**

**Lankester, Edwin (ed.)**
- The correspondence of John Ray ... Ray Society, 1848. xvi,502 pp. Frontis, plate. Orig cloth, faded, rebacked, old spine relaid.        *(Pollak)* **£65**
- Memorials of John Ray, consisting of his life ... biographical and critical notices ... London: Ray Society, 1846. xii,220 pp. Tinted litho frontis. Orig cloth, faded, recased.        *(Pollak)* **£50**
- Memorials of John Ray, consisting of his life ... biographical and critical notices ... London: 1846. Cloth worn.        *(Winterdown)* **£37.50**

**Lardner, D.**
- The electric telegraph, a new edition, revised and edited ... [1867]. xii,272 pp. Num ills. Cloth discoloured.        *(Weiner)* **£25**

**Lardner, Dyonysius**
- An elementary treatise on the differential and integral calculus. London: John Taylor, 1825. xxxiii,[v],520 pp. Some foxing. Orig cloth-backed bds.        *(Pollak)* **£35**
- An elementary treatise on the differential and integral calculus. 1825. xxxiii,520 pp. Errata leaf. Uncut, unopened. Orig cloth-backed bds with paper label. Hd of spine torn.        *(Weiner)* **£18**
- The first six books of the elements of Euclid, with a commentary and geometrical exercises. London: John Taylor, 1830. 2nd edn, crrctd & enlgd. xix,332 pp. Occas foxing. New half-calf.        *(Pollak)* **£30**
- The museum of science and art. London: Walton & Maberly, 1854-56. 1st edn. 12 vols in 6. viii,208 each vol (vol III, 203 pp; vol XII, xii,206 pp). Contemp half-mor, sl rubbed.        *(Pickering)* **$225**
- Popular lectures on science and art ... New York, Greeley & McElrath, 1848. 1st edn. 2 vols. 8vo. 608; 568,[8 pub advts] pp. Frontis, 2 plates. Orig cloth.        *(M&S)* **$60**

**Lardner, Dyonysius & Kater, Henry**
- A treatise on mechanics. Phila: 1831. 290 pp. 21 full-page engvd plates. Orig cloth-backed bds. *(M&S)* **$40**

**Lardy, H.A. (ed.)**
- Respiratory enzymes. Minneapolis: 1949. Revsd edn. 4to. iii,290 pp. *(Whitehart)* **£18**

**Larmor, Joseph**
- Aether and matter. A development of the dynamical relations of the aether to material systems on the basis of the atomic constitution of matter ... Cambridge: University Press, 1900. xxviii,365 pp. Text figs. *(Pollak)* **£100**
- Aether and matter; a development of the dynamical relations of the aether to material systems on the basis of the atomic constitution of matter ... Cambridge: 1900. 1st edn. 356 pp. *(Scientia)* **$75**

**Larner, E.T.**
- Practical television, with a foreword by John L. Baird. 1928. xv,175 pp. Plates, diags. *(Weiner)* **£50**

**Lashley, K.S.**
- Brain mechanisms and intelligence - a quantitative study of injuries to the brain. Chicago: University of Chicago Press, [1929]. 1st edn. 8vo. xiv, 186 pp. 11 plates. Orig cloth. *(Antiq Sc)* **$90**

**Latham, John**
- On rheumatism, and gout; a letter addressed to Sir George Baker. 1796. 1st edn. 80 pp. Mod mor-backed bds, unlettered. *(Robertshaw)* **£42**

**Latham, P.M.**
- Lectures of subjects connected with clinical medicine, comprising diseases of the heart. London: Longman, 1845-46. 1st edn. 2 vols. 8vo. Half-titles & advts in both vols. Pub dark green cloth, rubbed, spines sl snagged. *(McDowell)* **£180**
- Lectures on ... diseases of the heart. Phila: 1847. 1st Amer edn. 365 pp. F.e.p. torn. Half vell, sl worn & soiled. *(Oasis)* **$80**
- Lectures on subjects connected with clinical medicine comprising diseases of the heart. Phila: 1847. 1st Amer edn. Half-title, 365 pp. Some foxing. New cloth back. *(Elgen)* **$95**

**Laughlin, Harry H.**
- Eugenical sterilisation in the United States. Chicago: 1922. 1st edn. 502 pp. Ex lib. Spine frayed, bds worn. *(Scientia)* **$47.50**

**Laurance, Lionel**
- Visual optics and sight testing. London: 1912. 1st edn. 396 pp. Binding worn & soiled.

*(Fye)* **$15**

**Laurence, John Z. & Moon, Robert C.**
- A handy-book of ophthalmic surgery. Phila: H.C. Lea, 1866. 1st Amer edn. 8vo. 191 pp. Text w'cuts. Orig cloth. *(Antiq Sc)* **$60**
- A handy-book of ophthalmic surgery. Phila: 1866. 1st Amer edn. 191 pp. *(Fye)* **$75**

**Laurens, Georges**
- Oto-rhino-laryngology. New York: 1919. 1st edn. 339 pp. *(Fye)* **$15**

**Laurent, Auguste**
- Chemical method, notation, classification and nomenclature, translated ... for the Cavendish Society, 1855. xxii,382 pp. Orig cloth, little faded & stained, rebacked. *(Weiner)* **£75**

**Lavater, John Caspar**
- Essays on physiognomy ... also one hundred physiognomical rules, taken from a posthumous work ... and a memoir of the author. N.d. 17th edn. Lge thick 8vo. cxxviii,507 pp. Port frontis, over 400 ills. Some pages detchd, but complete. *(Jenner)* **£24**
- Essays on physiognomy, designed to promote the knowledge and the love of mankind ... London: John Murray, 1789-92-98. 1st English edn. 3 vols in 5. Folio. Complete with all blanks, half-titles, subscr list. Occas foxing & w'stains. Contemp calf, rebacked. *(Rootenberg)* **$850**

**Laveran, A.**
- Paludism. London: New Sydenham Society, 1893. 1st English edn. Roy 8vo. 6 plates, 2 cold. Orig cloth. *(McDowell)* **£35**
- Paludism. London: New Sydenham Society, 1893. xii,197,[i] pp. 6 plates, some part cold, 7 text figs. Sm nick at lwr edge of last few leaves. Spine ends knocked. *(McDowell)* **£30**

**Lavoisier, Antoine Laurent**
- Elements of chemistry in a new systematic order ... Edinburgh: for William Creech, 1790. 1st edn in English. 8vo. L,511,[1] pp. 2 fldg tables, 13 fldg engvd plates. Some foxing & staining, lower crnr of 1 plate torn off. Contemp calf, rebacked. *(Zeitlin)* **$950**
- Elements of chemistry. Edinburgh: W. Creech, 1790. 1st edn in English. 8vo. l,511 pp. 2 fldg tables, 13 fldg engvd plates. With the half-title. Sev plates torn, without loss, reprd. Full calf, lea label. *(Antiq Sc)* **$1,100**

**Law, Henry**
- A rudimentary treatise on logarithms. London: John Weale, 1851. 4,[iv],165 pp. Orig cloth. *(Pollak)* **£15**

**Lawrence, J.**
- The horse in all his varieties and uses. His breeding, rearing and management ... preservation from disease. 1829. xx,319,1[pub advts] pp. Orig paper bds, spine rubbed.                    *(Phenotype)* **£32**
- The modern land steward. In which the duties and functions of stewardship are considered and explained ... 1806. 2nd edn, with additions. xiii,499 pp. Calf, a little marked.                     *(Phenotype)* **£42**
- The new farmer's Calendar, or monthly remembrancer, for all kinds of country business ... with the management of live stock. 1802. 4th edn. xxxvi,554,4 [index] pp. Fldg frontis. Rebnd half-calf, paper sides.
                                *(Phenotype)* **£42**

**Lawrence, William**
- Lectures of comparative anatomy, physiology, zoology, and the natural history of man. London: 1840. 8th edn. 396 pp. Bds with linen spine.          *(Scientia)* **$45**
- Lectures on physiology, zoology, and the natural history man ... London: 1822. 1st edn. 500 pp. 7 engvd plates. Rec cloth.
                                 *(Goodrich)* **$150**

**Lawrie, L.G.**
- A bibliography of dyeing and textile printing comprising a list of books from the sixteenth century to the present time. London: Chapman & Hall, 1949. 8vo. Pub cloth. Dw.
                                *(McDowell)* **£40**

**Lawson, Andrew C. (Chairman ...)**
- The California earthquake of April 18, 1906. Report of the State Investigation Committee. Washington, DC: Carnegie Institute, 1908-10. 2 text vols in 3. Very lge 8vo. xviii,451; ix,192 pp. Atlas vol. Lge folio. Num maps & plates. Binder's & orig cloth.
                                 *(Weiner)* **£195**

**Lawson, George**
- Injuries of the eye, orbit and eyelids: their immediate and remote effects. Phila: 1867. 1st Amer edn. 408 pp.          *(Fye)* **$60**

**Layton, T.B.**
- Catalogue of the Onodi collection in the museum of the Royal College of Surgeons of England. [London]: 1934 xxiv,131 pp. 47 plates. Ex lib.          *(Elgen)* **$115**

**Le Bon, Gustav**
- The crowd: a study of the popular mind. London: T. Fisher Unwin, 1897. 2nd edn. xxii,219 pp.          *(Gach)* **$25**

**Le Loyer, Pierre**
- A treatise of specters or straunge sights, visions and apparitions ... nature of spirites,

angels, and divels ... newly done out of French into English ... London: 1605. 1st English edn. 4to. Title & first 10 leaves defective. 18th c calf, hinge broken.
                                *(Hemlock)* **$350**

**Leake, Chauncey D.**
- The amphetamines. Their actions and uses. Springfield: Charles C. Thomas, 1958. Ex lib.                         *(Poitras)* **$25**

**Leakey, Louis**
- The Stone Age cultures of Kenya Colony. Cambridge: 1931. 1st edn. 288 pp.
                                 *(Scientia)* **$125**

**Lean, Thomas, & brother ...**
- Historical statement of the improvements made in the duty performed by the steam engines in Cornwall. London: 1839. vii,152 pp. Tables (1 fldg). Orig cloth, paper label.
                                  *(Weiner)* **£60**

**Lee, Robert**
- Three hundred consultations in midwifery. 1864. Sm 8vo. 226 pp. Foxing on endpapers. Orig blue cloth, upper hinge rather tender.
                                  *(Jenner)* **£28**

**Lees, F. Arnold**
- See Davis, James W. & Lees, F. Arnold

**Leeson, John Rudd**
- Lister as I knew him [Joseph Lister]. 1927. xii,212 pp. 7 plates inc 1 fldg. Orig cloth, sl worn, spotting on endpapers.    *(Jenner)* **£20**

**Leftwich, R.W.**
- The preservation of the hair. Bristol: 1901. 127 pp. Frontis. Orig cloth, sl marked.
                                *(Whitehart)* **£18**

**Legendre, A.M.**
- Elements of geometry and trigonometry; with notes ... translated (by Thomas Carlysle) from the French ... Edinburgh: 1824 xvi,367 pp. Diags, errata leaf. Contemp polished calf, rubbed.                       *(Weiner)* **£50**
- Elements of geometry and trigonometry; with notes. Translated ... by David Brewster. Revised and altered for the use of the Military Academy at West Point. New York: 1828. 1st edn. 16,316 pp. Ills. Orig cloth-backed bds, uncut.                         *(M&S)* **$20**

**Lehmann, C.G.**
- Physiological chemistry. With illustrations selected from Funke's Atlas of physiological chemistry and an appendix of plates. Phila: Blanchard & Lea, 1855. 1st Amer edn. 2 vols. 8vo. 648; 547 pp. 24 w'cut plates, w'cuts in text. Orig cloth.           *(Antiq Sc)* **$75**

**Leibowitz, Joshua O.**
- The history of coronary heart disease. London: 1970. 1st edn. Dw. *(Scientia)* **$35**
- The history of coronary heart disease. London: Wellcome Institute, 1970. xvii,227 pp. Cold frontis, 14 plates. Orig red cloth. Dw. *(Jenner)* **£14**

**Leidy, Joseph**
- An elementary treatise on human anatomy. Phila: Lippincott, 1861. 663 pp. 392 ills. Light foxing. Full sheep, rubbed.
*(Goodrich)* **$125**

**[Leifchild, John R.]**
- Our coal and coal pits; the people in them, and the scenes around them. By a traveller underground. London: Longman, Brown, 1862. 2nd edn. 12mo. 242 pp. Ills. Full prize calf gilt, sl cvr wear. *(Diamond)* **$45**

**Leigh, Denis**
- The historical development of British psychiatry. Volume I, 18th and 19th centuries. Oxford [etc.]: Pergamon Press, 1961. All published. 8vo. Dw.
*(McDowell)* **£40**

**Leighton, Gerald**
- Botulism and food preservation. (The Loch Maree tragedy). 1923. xiii,237 pp. Frontis detchd. Ills. Uncut. Cvrs worn with sm tear.
*(Jenner)* **£10**

**Leishman, William**
- A system of midwifery; including the diseases of pregnancy and the puerperal state. Glasgow: 1880. 3rd edn. xxiv,856 pp. 192 ills in text. Mod cloth, imitation watered silk.
*(Whitehart)* **£50**

**Leitch, Isabella**
- See Hytten, Frank & Leitch, Isabella

**Leith, C.K.**
- See Van Hise, C.R. & Leith, C.K.

**Leithauser, Daniel J.**
- Early ambulation and related procedures in surgical management. Springfield: 1946. xi,232 pp. Ills. Worn dw. *(Jenner)* **£10**

**Lemaitre, W.**
- Natural stability and the parachute principle in aeroplanes. London: Spon, 1911. 46,[ii], [xxviii ctlg]. Frontis, 33 figs. *(Pollak)* **£20**

**Lemery, Nicholas**
- A course of chymistry containing the easiest manner of performing those operations that are in use in physick ... Translated by Walter Harris ... London: Walter Kettilby, 1677. 1st English translation. 8vo. [16]ff, 323,[1]pp,

[10]ff. Orig calf, rebacked. *(Zeitlin)* **$750**
- A course of chymistry containing the easiest manner of performing those operations that are in use in physick ... London: ... for Walter Kettilby, 1698. 3rd English edn. 8vo. [12]ff, 815,[1]pp, [8]ff. 7 plates, 5pp chemical symbols. Contemp polished calf.
*(Zeitlin)* **$600**
- New curiosities in art and nature: or a collection of the most valuable secrets in all arts and sciences ... translated into English ... 1711. Sm 8vo. 8ff,354 pp, 7ff. Frontis, 8 engvd plates. Third of text browned. Lib stamps. Some tears. Lib cloth. *(Weiner)* **£85**

**Leo-Wolf, W.**
- Remarks on the abracadabra of the nineteenth century; or, on Dr. Samuel Hahneman's homeopathic medicine ... New York: 1835. 1st edn. 273 pp. Uncut in antique bds.
*(Goodrich)* **$75**

**Leonardo, Richard A.**
- History of medical thought. From early Greek medical philosophy to the 19th and 20th centuries. New York: Froben Press, 1946. 92 pp. 14 full-page ports. *(Poitras)* **$35**
- History of surgery. New York: 1943. 1st edn. xvii,504 pp. 100 plates. *(Elgen)* **$65**

**Leonardus, Camillus**
- The mirror of stones, in which the nature, generation, properties, virtues and various species of more than 200 different jewels ... are distinctly described. London: for J. Freeman, 1750. 1st edn in English. 12mo. 240 pp. Contemp sheep, rebacked.
*(Burmester)* **£375**

**Leriche, R. & Policard, A.**
- The normal and pathological physiology of bone: its problems. St. Louis: 1928. 1st English translation. 236 pp. *(Fye)* **$40**

**Leslie, John**
- Elements of geometry, and plane trigonometry. With an appendix, and copious notes and illustrations. Edinburgh: Constable. 1817. 3rd edn, imprvd & enlgd. viii,423,2 [advts] pp. Occas foxing. Orig paper bds, new cloth spine. *(Pollak)* **£35**

**Lesser, L. von**
- Surgical emergencies. New York: 1883. 1st English translation. 215 pp. *(Fye)* **$40**

**Lessius, Leonardus & Cornaro, Luigi**
- A treatise of health and long life, with the sure means of attaining it; in two books ... Translated by Timothy Smith. 1747. 12mo. Contemp unlettered calf. *(Robertshaw)* **£60**

**Letchworth, William Pryor**
- Care and treatment of epileptics. New York: Putnams, 1900. xii,244 pp. Num plates. Inner hinge split, uncut. Ex lib.
*(Goodrich)* **$95**

**Letsome, Sampson & Nichol, John (eds.)**
- A defence of natural and revealed religion: being a collection of sermons preached at the lecture founded by ... Robert Boyle. London: for D. Midwinter [et al.], 1739. Folio. 3 vols. A little spotting, one prelim loose. Contemp calf, worn, all jnts weak.
*(Pollak)* **£75**

**Lettsom, John Coakley**
- Memoirs of John Fothergill, M.D., &c. London: for C. Dilly, 1786. 4th edn. 8vo. v,[iii], 280,[8] pp. Engvd title, 6 engvd ports. Contemp polished tree calf, red label, spine richly gilt.
*(Burmester)* **£100**
- Observations on the cowpock. J. Mawman, 1801. 1st edn, 100 copies, only, published. 4to. vi,88 pp. Engvd title, lightly foxed, engvd ports. Institutional stamps on title verso. Lacking half-title. Contemp calf, rebacked.
*(Hemlock)* **$500**

**Levens, Peter**
- A right profitable booke for all diseases called, The Path-way to Health wherein are to bee found most excellent and approved medicines ... London: John Beale for Richard Bird, 1632. 4to. [2],114,[6]ff. Tears in blanks. Contemp calf, sl warped. *(Rootenberg)* **$1,200**

**Levinson, Abraham (ed.)**
- Medical leaves. Chicago. 1939. 4to. 196 pp. Ills. Dec cloth.
*(Jenner)* **£20**

**Lewes, George Henry**
- The physiology of common life. Edinburgh & London: William Blackwood, 1859-60. 1st edn. 2 vols. 12mo. 455,485 pp. Polished calf, edges rubbed, front bd to vol I detchd.
*(Gach)* **$75**
- The physiology of common life. London: 1859. 2 vols in 1. 455; 485 pp. Full lea, sl rubbed. *(Epistemologist)* **$135**

**Lewin, Kurt**
- A dynamic theory of personality: selected papers. Translated ... New York: McGraw-Hill, 1935. Later printing, same year as 1st edn. Sm 8vo. [x],286 pp. *(Gach)* **$25**
- Principles of topological psychology. New York: 1936. 6th printing. 231 pp. Cvr sl spotted. *(Epistemologist)* **$35**

**Lewin, Kurt, et al.**
- Frustration and regression. 1941. 314 pp.
*(Epistemologist)* **$35**
- Studies in topological and vector psychology. Iowa City: University of Iowa Press, 1940.

307 pp. Printed grey wraps. Studies in Child Welfare Vol 16, No. 3.          *(Gach)* **$50**

**Lewin, Louis**
- The incidental effects of drugs; A pharmacological and clinical hand-book. Translated by W.T. Alexander. New York: 1882. 1st edn in English.          *(Scientia)* **$150**

**Lewinski-Corwin, E.H.**
- The hospital situation in Greater New York; report of a survey of hospitals ... Knickerbocker Press, 1924. xvi,356 pp. Ills, fldg map. Orig red cloth, spine sl bumped.
*(Jenner)* **£20**

**Lewis, C.A.**
- Broadcasting from within. [1924]. ix,176 pp. Ports.          *(Weiner)* **£25**

**Lewis, Gilbert N.**
- Valence and the structure of atoms and molecules. New York: 1923. 1st edn. 172 pp.
*(Scientia)* **$95**

**Lewis, Henry Carvill**
- Papers and notes on the genesis and matrix of the diamond, edited ... 1897. 72 pp. 2 plates, ills.          *(Weiner)* **£30**
- Papers and notes on the glacial geology of Great Britain and Northern Ireland. 1894. lxxxi,469 pp. 82 figs in text, 10 maps. New cloth.          *(Whitehart)* **£28**
- Papers and notes on the glacial geology of Great Britain and Northern Ireland. London: Longmans, Green, 1894. lxxxi,469,[iii],16 pp. 10 maps, num text ills. Some foxing.
*(Pollak)* **£20**

**Lewis, John Ransome**
- The surgery of scars. New York: 1963. 1st edn. 201 pp. Num ills. Dw.          *(Oasis)* **$25**
- The surgery of scars. New York: McGraw-Hill, 1963. 201 pp. Frontis, num ills.
*(Poitras)* **$20**

**Lewis, L.V.**
- Picture telegraphy (Post Office Green Papers No. 17). [1935]. 4to. 14 pp. 8 plates. Orig pict wraps, worn.          *(Weiner)* **£18**

**Lewis, Sir Thomas**
- Clinical electrocardiography, London: Shaw & Sons, 1918. 2nd edn. xvii,120 pp. 103 figs. Some notes on front endpaper & in text. Orig cloth.          *(Pollak)* **£15**
- Diseases of the heart described for practitioners and students. London: Macmillan, 1937. xx,297,[iii] pp. 45 text figs. Dw.          *(Pollak)* **£10**
- Diseases of the heart. New York: 1933. 1st Amer edn. 297 pp.          *(Oasis)* **$35**
- The mechanism of the heart beat with

especial reference to its clinical pathology. London: Shaw, 1911. 1st edn. 4to. Cold plate, 5 fldg plates, many ills in text. Pub cloth, lettered in gilt. *(McDowell)* **£140**
- The soldier's heart and the effort syndrome. London & New York: Shaw & Sons, 1918. 1st edn. 8vo. Pub gilt-lettered cloth.
*(McDowell)* **£90**
- Vascular disorders of the limbs. Described for practitioners and students. New York: Macmillan, 1936. 111 pp. Ex lib.
*(Poitras)* **$20**
- Vascular disorders of the limbs. Described for practitioners and students. London: Macmillan, 1946. 2nd edn. 118 pp. Dw.
*(Poitras)* **$15**
- Vascular disorders of the limbs. London: 1949. 2nd edn. 118 pp. Dw. *(Fye)* **$15**

**[Lewis, William]**
- The new dispensatory: containing the theory and practice of pharmacy. A distribution of medical simples ... correction and improvement of Quincy. London: for J. Nourse, 1753. 1st edn. 8vo. xii,32,664 pp. Contemp gilt-ruled calf, lower jnt split, spine worn. *(Zeitlin)* **$250**

**Ley, Willy**
- Rockets: the future of travel beyond the stratosphere. New York: 1944. 1st edn. Dw.
*(Oasis)* **$85**

**Leybourn, Thomas**
- The mathematical questions proposed in the ladies' diary, and their original answers, together with some new solutions ... 1704 to 1816. London: J. Mawman, 1817. 4 vols. xi,415; [iv],416; [iv],400; [iv],440, [ii errata] pp. Half-calf, rubbed. *(Pollak)* **£75**
- The new series of the Mathematical Repository. London: J. Mawman, 1806. 2 vols. Tree calf, rubbed. *(Pollak)* **£55**

**Libby, W.F.**
- Radiocarbon dating. Chicago: 1955. 2nd edn. ix,175 pp. *(Whitehart)* **£15**

**Liddell, E.G.T. & Sherrington, Charles**
- Mammalian physiology: a course of practical exercises. Oxford: 1929. 2nd edn. xii,162 pp. Ills throughout text, some cold. Some pen underscoring. Orig red cloth, sl worn.
*(Jenner)* **£15**

**Liebig, Justus von**
- Animal chemistry, or organic chemistry in its application to physiology and pathology ... edited ... by William Gregory ... London: for Taylor & Walton, 1842. 1st edn in English. 8vo. xxiv,354 pp. Contemp calf.
*(Zeitlin)* **$250**
- Animal chemistry, or organic chemistry in its

application to physiology and pathology. London: Taylor & Walton, 1842. 1st edn in English. 8vo. xxiv,354 pp. 2 pp pub ctlg. Orig cloth, lightly faded, crnrs worn.
*(Rootenberg)* **$300**
- Chemistry in its applications to agriculture and physiology. Edited by Lyon Playfair. Taylor & Walton, 1842. 2nd edn, with v num addtns. xii,409,[x ctlg] pp. Orig ribbed cloth, a little faded. *(Pollak)* **£75**
- Chemistry in its applications to agriculture and physiology. Edited by Lyon Playfair. London: 1842. 2nd edn. xii,409 pp. Orig dec cloth faded, hinges weak. *(Jenner)* **£24**
- Chemistry in its applications to agriculture and physiology. Edited by Lyon Playfair and W. Gregory. New York: 1849. From 4th London edn. 401 pp. Foxed. *(Scientia)* **$35**
- Organic chemistry in its applications to agriculture and physiology ... London: for Taylor & Walton, 1840. 1st edn in English. 8vo. xxiv,[2],387,[1], [8] pp. Half-title lightly browned. Orig stamped green cloth, gilt lettering, hinges & back reprd. *(Zeitlin)* **$240**
- Principles of agricultural chemistry, with special reference to the late researches made in England. London: Walton & Maberly, 1855. 1st edn in English. 8vo. vii,[1],136 pp, 3ff & 12pp (pub advts). Partially unopened. Orig cloth, spine sunned, some wear.
*(Zeitlin)* **$200**
- Researches on the chemistry of food ... edited ... by William Gregory. London: Taylor & Walton, 1847. 1st edn in English. 8vo. xx,156,[16 advts] pp. Light foxing. Orig cloth, reprs to spine. *(Zeitlin)* **$325**
- Researches on the chemistry of food, and the motion of the juices in the animal body. Edited ... from the English edition by Eben N. Horsford. Lowell: 1848. 1st Amer edn. 219 pp. Lacks f.e.p. *(Scientia)* **$65**

**Lief, Alfred**
- The commonsense psychiatry of Dr. Adolf Meyer ... with biographical narrative. New York: McGraw-Hill, 1948. 1st edn. xviii,677 pp. Ltd iss printed on rag paper. Tan buckram, boxed. *(Gach)* **$50**

**Lilienthal, Howard**
- Thoracic surgery: the surgical treatment of thoracic disease. Phila: 1925. 1st edn. 2 vols. 694; 600 pp. *(Fye)* **$125**

**Lilienthal, Otto**
- Birdflight as a basis of aviation ... with a biographical introduction ... Longman, Green & Co., 1911. 1st edn in English. 8vo. xxiv,139,[5] pp. Frontis, advt leaf, 8 fldg tables, 94 text ills. Orig cloth.
*(Rootenberg)* **$275**

**Lillie, Frank R.**
- Problems of fertilization. Chicago: 1919. 1st edn. 278 pp.                    *(Scientia)* **$35**

**Lilly, W.**
- An introduction to astrology: with numerous emendations, adapted to the improved state of the science in the present day ... 1860. xiv,492,64 pp. 2 fldg plates, 33 ills. Scattered foxing. 3/4 lea, mrbld bds & edges, cvrs rubbed.                    *(Whitehart)* **£35**

**Limbeck, R.R. Van**
- The clinical pathology of the blood. London: New Sydenham Society, 1901. 1st English edn. 8vo. Ills. Pub blind-stamped cloth.
                    *(McDowell)* **£35**

**Lin, Tsung-Yi**
- See Caudill, William & Lin, Tsung-Yi

**Lincoln, David F.**
- Sanity of mind: a study of its conditions, and of the means to its development and preservation. New York: G.P. Putnam's Sons, 1900. 1st edn. 12mo. vi,177 pp. Orig cloth.
                    *(Gach)* **$30**

**Lind, James**
- An essay on diseases incidental to Europeans in hot climates. With the method of preventing their fatal consequences ... London: for T. Becket, 1777. 3rd edn, enlgd & imprvd. 8vo. 16,379, [1],[8] pp. Contemp calf, lea label, upper cvr detchd. *(M&S)* **$650**
- An essay on diseases incidental to Europeans in hot climates. With the method of preventing their fatal consequences ... London: J. & J. Richardson, et al., 1808. 6th edn. 4to. xiv,402 pp. New half lea, new endpapers.                    *(Poitras)* **$350**
- A treatise on the scurvy ... containing an inquiry into the nature, causes and cure, of that disease ... Edinburgh: ... for A. Millar. 1753. 1st edn. 8vo. xvi,456 pp. Contemp sprinkled calf, rebacked in mor. Scattered foxing & marginal dust-soiling.
                    *(Zeitlin)* **$15,500**

**Lindeboom, G.A.**
- Herman Boerhaave. The man and his work. London: 1968. 35 plates, 15 figs.
                    *(Winterdown)* **£25**

**Linfoot, E.H.**
- Recent advances in optics. Oxford: 1955. 8 plates, 113 figs.    *(Winterdown)* **£10**

**Lingg, Claire**
- See Cohn, Alfred E. & Lingg, Claire

**Linnell, E.H.**
- The eye as an aid to clinical diagnosis: a

handbook for the use of students and general practitioners. Phila: 1897. 248,[3] pp. 4 plates. Orig red cloth, bds & spine sunned.
                    *(Jenner)* **£8**

**Linsley, J.S.**
- Jersey cattle in America. New York: 1885. 4to. 741 pp. 2 silhouettes, 69 ports, 56 charts &c. Orig cloth. Some amateur colouring of plates.                    *(Phenotype)* **£120**

**Lister. Joseph**
- Collected papers. Oxford: 1909. 1st edn. 2 vols. 4to. Bottom of spine of Vol I frayed.
                    *(Scientia)* **$350**

**Liston, Robert**
- Elements of surgery. Phila: 1837. 1st Amer edn. 540 pp. Full lea.    *(Fye)* **$150**
- Practical surgery, with one hundred and twenty engravings on wood ... with notes ... Phila: 1842. 2nd Amer edn. 588 pp. Full lea.
                    *(Fye)* **$100**

**Litchfield, W.F.**
- Diptheria in practice. 1908. 94,[4 advts] pp. Damp-spots in later text. Cloth. Ex lib.
                    *(Jenner)* **£8**

**Little, A.D.**
- See Griffin, R.B. & Little, A.D.

**Little, David**
- Controlled hypotension in anesthesia and surgery. Springfield: 1956. 1st edn. 159 pp.
                    *(Fye)* **$25**

**Lives ...**
- Lives of British physicians. London: John Murray, 1830. 1st edn. Sm 8vo. 341 pp. 3/4 calf, mrbld edges. Edited by William Macmichael                    *(Hemlock)* **$80**

**Livingston, Edward M.**
- A clinical study of the abdominal cavity and peritoneum. New York: 1932. 1st edn. 4to. 866 pp.                    *(Fye)* **$40**

**Livingston, William Kenneth**
- The clinical aspects of visceral neurology with special reference to the surgery of the sympathetic nervous system. London: Bailliere, Tindall & Cox, 1935. 1st London edn. 8vo. xi,254 pp. Many text ills. Orig cloth, lib stamp.                    *(Rootenberg)* **$225**

**Lloyd, Humphrey**
- Elementary treatise on the wave-theory of light. Longmans, Green, 1873. 3rd edn, revsd & enlgd. xi,247,24 [ctlg] pp. Text figs. Spine ends bumped.                    *(Pollak)* **£30**
- Elements of optics. Dublin: 1849. 115 pp. 2 fldg plates. Orig cloth, spine cracked, spine &

bds sunned & watermarked.      *(Jenner)* **£17**

**Lloyd, J.F., et al.**
- Wireless telegraphy and how to make the apparatus. ('Work' Handbooks). 1913. viii,152 pp. Diags. Orig pict card cvrs, worn.
*(Weiner)* **£20**

**Lloyd, Wyndham E.B.**
- See Haagensen, C.D. & Lloyd, Wyndham E.B.

**Lobb, Theophilus**
- Medicinal letters. In Two parts. 1763. 12mo. [viii],75 pp. Pub ctlg. Title reprd. Sl spotting. Mod cloth gilt, new endpapers. *(Jenner)* **£60**
- A practical treatise of painfull distempers, with some effectual methods of curing them ... London: James Buckland, 1739. 8vo. xxx,[ii advts], 344 pp. Sl foxing & offsetting. Contemp calf, mor label.
*(Frew Mackenzie)* **£120**
- Rational methods of curing fevers; deduced from the structure, and oeconomy of human bodies ... London: John Oswald, 1734. 1st edn. 8vo. xxii,ii,403, xxxiii [index], iii pp. 3 plates. Occas marginal notes. Contemp calf, mor label. *(Frew Mackenzie)* **£140**

**Lobstein, J.F. Daniel**
- Researches and observations on the use of phosphorus, in the treatment of various diseases. Phila: for the Author, 1825. 1st edn in English. 8vo. 114 pp. Linen-backed blue bds, antique style. *(Antiq Sc)* **$175**

**Lock, C.G. Warnford & Newlands, B.E.R. & J.A.R.**
- Sugar: a handbook for planters and refiners; being a comprehensive treatise on the culture of sugar-yielding plants ... the distillation of rum. 1888. 8vo. xxiv,920,24 [advts] pp. Fldg plates, ills, bibliog. Jnts shaken, tear at hd of spine, frontis detchd.      *(Weiner)* **£40**

**Lock, Robert H.**
- Recent progress in the study of variation, heredity and evolution. New York: 1906. 1st Amer edn. Top of spine frayed, spine faded.
*(Scientia)* **$37.50**

**Locke, John**
- Elements of natural philosophy. Whitehaven: Sheperd, 1764. Lge 12mo. Dusty & thumbed. New qtr calf.      *(Marlborough)* **£110**

**Lockwood, C.B.**
- Aseptic surgery. 1896. 1st edn. xiv,[1],233 pp. Orig cloth, dull.      *(Whitehart)* **£25**

**Lockwood, Charles**
- Cancer of the breast: an experience of a series of operations and their results. London: 1913.

1st edn. 234 pp.      *(Fye)* **$100**

**Lockyer, J. Norman**
- The chemistry of the sun. London: 1887. 1st edn. Uncut & unopened.      *(Elgen)* **$75**
- The chemistry of the sun. London: Macmillan, 1887. 1st edn. Some marginal notes. Orig cloth, recased, a little dirty.
*(Pollak)* **£45**
- The meteoritic hypothesis. A statement of the results of a spectroscopic inquiry into the origin of cosmical systems. London: Macmillan, 1890. 1st edn. xvi,560 pp. 7 plates, 101 ills. Orig cloth, recased.
*(Pollak)* **£50**
- The spectroscope and its applications. London: Macmillan, 1873. 2nd edn. [iv],xii,127 pp. Fldg cold frontis, 60 text ills. Cloth dull, front jnt weak, dusty at edges.
*(Pollak)* **£12**
- Studies in spectrum analysis. London: Kegan Paul, 1878. 2nd edn. xii,258,32 [ctlg] pp. Frontis, 7 plates, 51 text w'cuts. *(Pollak)* **£15**

**Locomotives ...**
- The locomotives of the London, Brighton & South Coast Railway ... See Burtt, G.F.

**Lodeman, E.G.**
- The spraying of plants. A succinct account of the history ... of the application of liquids and powders to plants ... New York: Macmillan, 1909. xvii,[i], 399,[vii] pp. 92 text ills.
*(Pollak)* **£15**

**Lodge, Sir Oliver**
- Electrons or the nature and properties of negative electricity. London: Bell & Sons, 1907. 2nd edn, revsd. xv,230 pp. 24 text figs.
*(Pollak)* **£25**
- Electrons, or the nature and properties of negative electricity. 1907. 2nd edn. xv,230 pp. Light pencil underlining. Spine sl dulled.
*(Whitehart)* **£35**
- The ether of space. New York & London: Harper & Bros., 1909. 1st edn. xix,168 pp. Frontis, 19 ills.      *(Pollak)* **£20**
- Modern views of electricity. London: 1889. 1st edn. 422 pp.      *(Scientia)* **$45**
- Modern views of electricity. London: Macmillan, 1906. 3rd edn, revsd. xiv,518 pp. 65 text figs.      *(Pollak)* **£12**
- Past years, an autobiography. London: Hodder & Stoughton, 1931. 364 pp. Frontis, 15 plates.      *(Pollak)* **£15**
- Signalling through space without wires, being a description of the work of Hertz and his successors ... [1900]. 3rd edn. ii,133 pp.
*(Weiner)* **£40**
- Signalling through space without wires, being a description of the work of Hertz and his successors ... New York & London: n.d. [ca 1901]. 3rd edn. Sm 8vo. [2],2,[2], 133 pp. 32

pp pub advts dated July 1901. Some soiling in text. Orig cloth, worn, soiled.    *(M&S)* **$50**
- Signalling through space without wires. Being a description of the work of Hertz and his successors ... [1914]. 4th enlgd edn. [ii],ii, 154,[ii] pp. 24 pp pub ctlg. Text ills. Orange cloth gilt.    *(Weiner)* **£25**
- The work of Hertz and some of his successors. being the substance of a lecture ... London: 'The Electrician', [1897]. 2nd edn. 58,[ii],32 [advts] pp. Frontis, 32 text figs. Orig orange cloth.    *(Pollak)* **£20**

**Loeb, H.W.**
- Operative surgery of the nose, throat and ear. St. Louis: 1916. 1st edn. 2 vols. 390; 427 pp. 885 ills.    *(Oasis)* **$40**
- Operative surgery of the nose, throat and ear. St. Louis: 1924. 2 vols.    *(Fye)* **$50**

**Loeb, Jacques**
- Artificial parthogenesis and fertilization. Chicago: 1913. 1st edn. 312 pp. *(Scientia)* **$75**
- Comparative physiology of the brain and comparative psychology. London: John Murray, 1905. 1st edn in English. Spine faded.    *(Gach)* **$35**
- The dynamics of living matter. New York: Columbia University Press, 1906. 1st edn. xi,[1],233,4 [pub advts] pp. Text figs. Orig cloth.    *(Antiq Sc)* **$90**
- The dynamics of living matter. New York: 1906. 1st edn. 233 pp.    *(Scientia)* **$65**
- Forced movements, tropism and animal conduct. Phila: 1918. 1st edn. 209 pp.    *(Scientia)* **$47.50**
- Forced movements, tropisms and animal conduct. Phila & London: Lippincott, [1918]. 1st edn. 8vo. 209 pp. 4 plates, text figs. Orig cloth.    *(Antiq Sc)* **$85**
- The mechanistic conception of life. Chicago: University of Chicago Press, [1912]. 1st edn. 8vo. [4],232 pp. Text figs. Orig cloth.    *(Antiq Sc)* **$110**
- The organism as a whole from a physiochemical viewpoint. New York: 1916. 1st edn. 379 pp. William M. Wheeler's copy.    *(Scientia)* **$50**
- The organism as a whole from a physiochemical viewpoint. New York: G.P. Putnam's Sons, 1916. 1st edn. x,379 pp. Rear hinge cracked.    *(Gach)* **$35**
- Studies in general physiology. 2 parts. Chicago: 1905. 1st edn. 782 pp.    *(Scientia)* **$150**

**Loeb, Leo**
- The venom of Heloderma. Wash, DC: 1913. 1st edn.    *(Scientia)* **$75**

**Loening, Grover, C.**
- Military aeroplanes, simplified - enlarged. An explanatory consideration of their

characteristics, performances, construction, maintenance & operation ... 1918. 2nd edn. 202 pp.    *(Scientia)* **$85**
- Our wings grow faster. Garden City, NY: 1935. 1st edn. 203 pp.    *(Scientia)* **$65**

**[Loftus, William R,]**
- The brewer. A familiar treatise on the art of brewing ... London: Wm. R. Loftus, 1867. 12mo. 173,34 [pub ctlg] pp. Spine tips defective, sl cvr staining & rubbing.    *(Diamond)* **$45**

**Lomax, Montagu**
- The experiences of an asylum doctor with suggestions for asylum and lunacy law reform. London: Allen & Unwin, [1921]. 255 pp. Black cloth. Sl musty.    *(Gach)* **$30**
- The experiences of an asylum doctor with suggestions for asylum and lunacy law reform. London: Allen & Unwin, 1921. 255 pp. Orig cloth.    *(Pollak)* **£15**

**Lombroso-Ferrero, Gina**
- Criminal man according to the classification of Cesare Lombroso. New York & London: 1911. 1st edn in English. 322 pp. 15 plates. Marginal pencilling. Green buckram, front hinge broken.    *(Gach)* **$35**

**Lommel, Eugene**
- The nature of light, with a general account of physical optics. New York: D. Appleton, 1881. 1st Amer edn. 8vo. xiii,[1],356 pp. Cold frontis, num text figs. Orig cloth.    *(Antiq Sc)* **$50**

**Long, Esmond R.**
- Selected readings in pathology from Hippocrates to Virchow. Springfield: 1961. 2nd edn. Stained dw.    *(Scientia)* **$45**

**Long, John St. John**
- A critical exposure of the ignorance and malpractice of certain medical practitioners in their theory and treatment of disease ... 1831. 1st edn. Uncut in orig bds, spine torn, paper label rubbed.    *(Robertshaw)* **£55**

**Long, W.H.**
- See Currie, J.R. & Long, W.H.

**Longacre, J.J. (ed.)**
- Craniofacial anomalies: pathogenesis and repair. Phila: 1968. 389 pp. 1st edn. Ex lib.    *(Fye)* **$30**

**Longley, W.R. & Van Name, R.G. (eds.)**
- The collected works of J. Willard Gibbs. New Haven: 1928. 1st edn. 2 vols. *(Scientia)* **$100**

**Longridge, C.N.**
- The anatomy of Nelson's ships. Hemel

Hempstead: 1961. 4to. xii,283 pp. Num plates, inc fldg plans, ills.  *(Weiner)* £25

**Loomis, Elias**
- Elements of analytical geometry and of the differential and integral calculus. New York: Harper, 1851. 1st edn. xii,[9]-278,[6 advts] pp. Some foxing & a little pencilling. Orig calf cvrs worn & re-attached. *(Diamond)* $75

**Lorentz, Hendrik A.**
- The theory of electrons and its applications to the phenomena of light and radiant heat. Leipzig: 1909. 1st edn. 332 pp.
*(Scientia)* $125
- The theory of electrons and its application to the phenomena of light and radiant heat, a course of lectures ... in 1906. Leipzig: 1909. 332 pp. Cloth, worn. Ex lib.  *(Weiner)* £38

**Lorenzo, N.**
- See Fowler, Orson Squire & Lorenzo, N.

**Lotze, Hermann**
- Microcosmus: an essay concerning man and his relation to the world. New York: 1887. 2nd edn. 740 pp. B'plate. Spine edges worn.
*(Epistemologist)* $65

**Loudon, J.C.**
- An encyclopaedia of agriculture. Comprising the theory and practice of the valuation, transfer, laying out ... cultivation and economy ... general history of agriculture ... 1825. xvi,1226. Half-mor.  *(Phenotype)* £80
- An encyclopaedia of agriculture. Comprising the theory and practice of the valuation, transfer, laying out ... London: for Longman ..., 1835. 3rd edn. 3 vols. Engvs throughout. Orig calf, v sl scuffing & w'stain on vol 1.
*(Ivelet)* £125

**Lougheed, Victor**
- Vehicles of the air. Chicago: [1909]. 1st edn. Lge 8vo. 479 pp. Ills. Gilt dec cloth.
*(Argosy)* $50

**Louis, Pierre Charles Alexandre**
- Anatomical, pathological and therapeutic researches on the yellow fever of Gibraltar of 1828 ...Translated ... Boston: Little & Brown, 1839. 1st edn. xxiii,374 pp. Dec blind-stamped cloth, some wear. Spine worn, chipped & scuffed.  *(Diamond)* $150
- Pathological researches on phthisis. Translated, with introduction, notes, additions, and an essay on treatment by Charles Cowan. London: 1835. 1st edn. 51,388 pp. Orig cloth, paper label.
*(Argosy)* $175
- Pathological researches on phthisis. Translated from the French ... revised by Henry I. Bowditch. Washington: 1836. 293

pp. Light foxing. Qtr calf, mrbld bds.
*(Goodrich)* $100
- Pathological researches on phthisis. Translated from the French ... revised by Henry I. Bowditch. Boston: 1836. 1st Amer edn. lxxii,550 pp. Light foxing. Orig embossed cloth bds, worn, jnts rubbed.
*(Goodrich)* $125
- Researches on the effect of bloodletting in some inflammatory diseases ... translated ... Boston: Hilliard, Gray, & Company, 1836. 1st edn in English. xxxii,171 pp. Brown pebbled cloth, paper label.  *(Hemlock)* $275

**Love, Augustus Edward Hough**
- A treatise on the mathematical theory of elasticity. Cambridge: University Press, 1892. 1st edn. 2 vols. 8vo. Pub green cloth.
*(McDowell)* £70

**Lovett, Robert**
- Lateral curvature of the spine and round shoulders. Phila: 1907. 1st edn. 188 pp.
*(Fye)* $75
- See Jones, Robert & Lovett, Robert

**Lovett, William**
- Elementary anatomy and physiology, for schools and private instruction: with lessons on diet, intoxicating drinks, tobacco and disease. 1851. 1st edn. 10 cold lithos. Some foxing throughout. Orig cloth, recased, new endpapers.  *(Robertshaw)* £15

**Lovibond, J.W.**
- An introduction to the study of colour phenomena explaining a new theory of colour based entirely on experimental facts ... 1905. 48 pp. 10 hand-cold plates, figs in text. Orig cloth. Inscrbd by author.  *(Whitehart)* £18

**Low, D.**
- Elements of practical agriculture. Comprehending the cultivation of plants, husbandry of domestic animals and the economy of the farm. 1847. 5th edn. xx,811,24 [pub advts] pp. Orig cloth.
*(Phenotype)* £55

**Low, R. Cranston**
- Carbonic acid snow as a therapeutic agent in the treatment of diseases of the skin. Edinburgh: 1911. xi,117 pp. 16 plates. Orig green cloth.  *(Jenner)* £9

**Low, R.B.**
- Local Government Board. Reports and papers on bubonic plague. An account of the progress and diffusion of plague throughout the world, 1898 - 1901 ... xi,446 pp. 8 fldg maps. Later bds, cloth spine. *(Whitehart)* £35

**[Lowe, T.S.C.]**
- The airship City of New York; a full description of the airship and the apparatus ... in the aerial voyage to Europe ... New York: Baker & Goodwin, 1859. 1st edn. 12mo. 24 pp, inc frontis & 1 other full-page ill. Staining. Orig printed wraps, chipped.
*(M&S)* **$1,250**

**Lowell, Percival**
- Mars and its canals. New York: 1906. 1st edn. Spine shelfworn. *(Scientia)* **$60**
- Mars and its canals. New York: Macmillan, 1906. 1st edn. 8vo. xv,[1],393 pp. 3 photogravs, 19 Martian maps (4 cold), text figs. Orig cloth. *(Antiq Sc)* **$110**
- Mars as the abode of life. New York: 1908, reprinted 1909. xix,288 pp. 8 plates, num figs in text. Orig cloth, sl stained. *(Whitehart)* **£18**
- Mars. Boston & New York: Houghton, Mifflin & Co., 1895. 1st edn. 8vo. x (misnumbered viii),228 pp. 24 plates (1 cold, & 1 a map), 3 text ills. Light browning, ownership inscr. Orig red gilt dec cloth, sl worn. *(Zeitlin)* **$95**
- The solar system. Six lectures delivered at the Massachusetts Institute of Technology in December 1902. Boston: 1903. 1st edn. 134 pp. Red & black title, fldg chart, ills. Sl shelf wear. *(Elgen)* **$50**

**Lowenfield, Viktor**
- The nature of creative activity. Experimental and comparative studies of visual and non-visual sources of drawing ... Translated ... New York: Harcourt, 1939. 272 pp. 1st U.S. edn. 272 pp. Sl musty. Red cloth.
*(Gach)* **$28.50**

**Lower, W.E.**
- See Crile, George & Lower, W.E.

**Lowry, T.M.**
- Historical introduction to chemistry. Macmillan, 1926. Reprinted, with addtns. xv,581 pp. 57 ills. Dw. *(Pollak)* **£25**

**Lowson, G.**
- The modern farrier; containing the causes, symptoms, and most approved methods of preventing and curing diseases of horses, cows, oxen ... N.d. [ca 1830s]. New edn. 616 pp. Frontis, few plates. Sl soiled & damp-stained. Calf, very worn, cvrs almost detchd.
*(Jenner)* **£40**
- The modern farrier; containing the causes, symptoms, and most approved methods of preventing and curing diseases of horses, cows and sheep ... Stokesley: 1845. 12,234 pp. Frontis & plates. Orig cloth, gilt.
*(Phenotype)* **£26**

**Lucas, A.**
- Forensic chemistry and scientific criminal investigation. 1931. 2nd edn. 324 pp. Orig cloth, sl marked. Spine sl worn.
*(Whitehart)* **£18**

**Ludlam, William**
- An introduction and notes on Mr. Bird's method of dividing astronomical instruments. To which is added, a vocabulary of English and French technical terms. London: John Sewell, 1786. 1st edn. Lge 4to. 3ff,32 pp,1f. Mod 3/4 red mor. *(Offenbacher)* **$450**
- Two mathematical essays: the first on ultimate ratios, the second on the power of the wedge. Cambridge: for T. Cadell, 1770. 1st edn. 8vo. [ii],90 pp. 2 fldg engvd plates. Contemp mrbld bds, new calf spine.
*(Burmester)* **£240**

**[Ludlow, Fitz Hugh]**
- The hasheesh eater: being passages from the life of a Pythagorean. New York: Harper & Bros, 1857. 1st edn. 8vo. 371 pp. Orig cloth, spine sl chipped, front jnt loose.
*(Rootenberg)* **$200**
- The opium habit. With suggestions as to the remedy. New York: Harper & Bros, 1868. 8vo. [6],335,[2 advts] pp. Orig green ribbed cloth. *(Dailey)* **$200**

**Lufkin, Arthur W.**
- A history of dentistry. Phila: Lea & Febiger, 1938. 8vo. 255 pp. 80 engvs. *(Poitras)* **$35**
- A history of dentistry. Phila: 1948. 2nd edn. *(Scientia)* **$37.50**

**Luisinus, Aloysius**
- Aphrodisiacus, containing a summary of the ancient writers on the venereal diseases ... London: for John Clarke, 1736. liii,[2],343,[2] pp. Stamp on title. Contemp panelled calf, rec rebacking. *(Goodrich)* **$695**

**Lukin, James**
- The lathe and its uses.; or, instruction in the art of turning wood and metal ... 1868. 1st edn. v,284 pp. Plates, some fldg, many ills. Top third of spine torn. *(Weiner)* **£40**
- Turning for amateurs: being descriptions of the lathe and its attachments and tools ... use on wood, metal, ivory and other materials. [1888]. 204 pp. 144 ills. Orig pict cloth. *(Whitehart)* **£35**
- Turning lathes: a manual for technical schools and apprentices. 1904. 6th edn. [2],228,[5] pp. 225 ills inc 33 plates. 200 pp ctlg of engineer's tools dated 1905 at end, also illus. Orig pict cloth. *(Whitehart)* **£35**

**Lummer, Otto**
- Contributions to photographic optics. Translated ... 1900. xi,135 pp. 55 ills.

*(Whitehart)* **£35**
- Contributions to photographic optics. Translated ... London: Macmillan, 1900. xi,135 pp. Text figs. Cloth a little faded, t.e.g.
*(Pollak)* **£45**

**Lund, Edward**
- Hunterian lectures. On some of the injuries and diseases of the head and neck, the genito-urinary organs ... 1886. 116 pp. 4 plates. Light foxing. Cvrs sl rubbed & bumped.
*(Jenner)* **£20**
- On the removal of the entire tongue by the Walter Whitehead method, with full details of the operation and after treatment. 1880. 36 pp. Blue cloth, spine faded, upper hinge cracked. *(Jenner)* **£25**

**Luria, A.R.**
- Nature of human conflicts. New York: 1932 (not 1st printing). 431 pp. Dw.
*(Epistemologist)* **$35**

**Lusk, William T.**
- The science and art of midwifery. New York: 1885. 2nd edn. 697 pp. *(Fye)* **$45**
- The science and art of midwifery. New York: 1887. 3rd edn. 763 pp. Full lea. *(Fye)* **$35**

**Lustgarten, J.**
- See Zeidler, J. & Lustgarten, J.

**Lyell, Charles**
- Elements of geology. London: John Murray, 1838. 1st edn. 8vo. xix,[1],543,[1] pp. Hand-cold frontis, w'cuts in text. Orig diced cloth, a little worn. *(Antiq Sc)* **$285**
- Elements of geology. London: Murray, 1838. 1st edn. xix,[i],543,[i] pp. Hand-cold frontis (misbound after contents), 294 text w'cuts. Some early margins thumbed. Lib buckram, lea label, sm lib stamps on plates. *(Pollak)* **£50**
- Elements of geology. Phila: 1845. 2nd edn. 316 pp. Pages browned and lightly stained along bottom edge. *(Scientia)* **$75**
- Elements of geology, or the ancient changes of the earth and its inhabitants ... 1865. 6th edn. 8vo. xvi,794 pp. 769 text figs. Full prize calf. *(Wheldon & Wesley)* **£40**
- The geological evidences of the antiquity of man with remarks on the origin of species by variation. London: J. Murray, 1863. 1st edn. 8vo. xii,520, 32 [pub ctlg] pp. 2 plates, text w'cuts. Contemp cloth, front jnt reprd.
*(Antiq Sc)* **$185**
- The geological evidences of the antiquity of man, with remarks on theories of the origin of species by variation. 1863. 1st edn. 8vo. xii,520 pp. 32 pp pub ctlg dated Jan 1863 at end. 2 plates, text figs. Orig cloth, trifle worn. *(Wheldon & Wesley)* **£80**
- The geological evidences of the antiquity of man with remarks on the origin of species by

variation. 1863. 1st edn. xii,520 pp. Plates, w'cuts. Lib stamp on title verso. New green buckram. *(Weiner)* **£50**
- The geological evidences of the antiquity of man with remarks on the origin of species by variation. London: J. Murray, 1863. 1st edn. 8vo. xii,520 pp, 32 pp pub ctlg. 2 plates, text w'cuts. Orig cloth, recased, spine faded.
*(Rootenberg)* **$225**
- The geological evidences of the antiquity of man, with remarks on theories of the origin of species by variation. Phila: 1863. 1st Amer edn. 518 pp. *(Scientia)* **$125**
- A manual of elementary geology. 1851. 3rd, revsd, edn. 8vo. xvi,512 pp. Frontis, 520 text figs. New cloth. *(Wheldon & Wesley)* **£30**
- Principles of geology, being an attempt to explain the former changes of the earth's surface ... London: John Murray, 1830-32-33. 3 vols. Approx 1500 pp. 3 engvd frontis, 3 maps, 8 engvd plates. Orig & later matching bds, paper labels. In cloth case.
*(Rootenberg)* **$2,000**
- Principles of geology. London: J. Murray, 1830-33. 1st edn. 3 vols. 8vo. xv,[1],511,[1]; xii,330,[1]; xxxi,[1],398, 109,[1] pp. Half-titles vols 1 & 3 (not iss vol 2), 3 frontis, 5 maps (2 cold), 9 plates (2 cold, 2 fldg). Contemp 3/4 calf, rebacked.
*(Antiq Sc)* **$1,800**
- Principles of geology. 1837. 5th edn. 4 vols. Sm 8vo. Engvd frontis, 15 engvd plates (10 fldg & some hand cold). Bds rebacked with strong card, orig labels. *(Edwards)* **£75**
- Principles of geology. London: 1837. 5th edn. 4 vols. Sm 8vo. 15 plates, inc sev extending & 4 hand-cold. Few inked marginalia, trivial spotting. Recent qtr calf.
*(Bow Windows)* **£166**
- Principles of geology. London: J. Murray, 1837. 5th edn. 4 vols. 12mo. 15 plates, half-titles to vols 3 & 4 only. Lib buckram, with lib stamp on all plates. *(Pollak)* **£60**
- Principles of geology. New York: 1857. 9th edn, entirely revised. 834 pp. Half lea, mrbld bds. *(Scientia)* **$60**
- Principles of geology. Phila: J. Kay, 1837. 1st Amer edn. 2 vols. 8vo. 546; 553; [2 pub advts] pp. W'cut frontis, 15 engvd & w'cut plates, sev hand cold & num text w'cuts. Orig cloth-cvrd bds. *(Antiq Sc)* **$285**
- Principles of geology ... London: John Murray, 1853. 9th edn. 8vo. xii,835 pp. 32 pp pub ctlg. Frontis, fldg map, Orig cloth, sl marked, spine faded & sl frayed.
*(Burmester)* **£30**
- The student's elements of geology. London: John Murray, 1871. 1st edn. xix,624,16 [pub ctlg] pp. Frontis, 636 text figs. Orig cloth, recased. Neat contemp annotation.
*(Pollak)* **£30**
- Travels in North America; with geological observations of the United States, Canada,

and Nova Scotia. London: J. Murray, 1845.
1st edn. 2 vols. 8vo. xiii,[3],316; viii,272,[16
pub ctlg] pp. 3 hand-cold litho, 4 litho &
w'cut plates. Orig cloth, recased.
*(Antiq Sc)* **$350**

**Lyle, Donald**
- Neuro-ophthalmology. Springfield: 1945. 1st
edn. 395 pp.                      *(Fye)* **$30**

**Lynch, Bernard**
- A guide to health through the various stages
of life ... London: for the Author, 1744. 1st
edn. xxxii,480 pp. Some browning. Contemp
calf, jnts tender.             *(Elgen)* **$350**

**Lynch, Charles**
- See Blech, G.M. & Lynch, Charles

**Lynch, Jerome**
- Diseases of the rectum and colon and their
surgical treatment. Phila: 1914. 1st edn. 596
pp. Over 200 engvs.            *(Fye)* **$35**

**Lynn, T.**
- Azimuth tables, showing a true bearing of the
sun, or other celestial object   ... 1829.
vi,366,[12] pp. Contemp 3/4 lea, rebacked,
worn & rubbed. New label. *(Whitehart)* **£25**
- Horary tables, for finding the time by
inspection, to facilitate the operations for
obtaining the longitude at sea ... 1827. xl,307
pp. 2 plates. Contemp paper-cvrd bds
rebacked, with paper label. *(Whitehart)* **£25**

**Lyons, Israel**
- A treatise on fluxions. London: 1758. 1st edn.
8vo. xxiii,[1],269, [1 errata],[2 advts] pp. 7
fldg engvd plates. Light marginal brown
stains. Uncut in red binder's cloth.
*(Burmester)* **£225**

**Lysenko, T.D.**
- Heredity and its variability. Translated ...
New York: 1946. 1st edn in English. 65 pp.
Orig printed wraps, spine torn. *(Elgen)* **$50**

**,M'Culloch, J.R.**
- A dictionary of commerce. London:
Longman, 1856. New edn. Thick 8vo. 3 fldg
maps (1 torn), num text ills. Contemp half-
calf, a little rubbed. *(Marlborough)* **£180**

**M.G.**
- See Markam, Gervase

**Macadam, J.L.**
- Report from Select Committee on Mr.
McAdam's petition, relating to his improved
system of constructing and repairing the
public roads of the kingdom. 1823. Folio. 100
pp. Mod buckram.           *(Weiner)* **£120**

**MacAlpine, Ida**
- See Hunter, Richard & MacAlpine, Ida

**Macartney, Sir J.**
- Facts and arguments respecting the great
utility of an extensive plan of inland
navigation in Ireland. With an appendix
containing the report of William Jessop ...
Dublin: William Porter, May 1800. 8vo.
[2],77. Uncut later wraps.
*(Deighton Bell)* **£110**

**MacBride, David**
- Experimental essays on the following
subjects. I ... fermentation ... II ... properties
of fixed air ... III ... IV ... On the scurvy ...
London:   1764.   1st   edn.   265   pp.
Copperplates. New cloth.   *(Goodrich)* **$125**

**MacCulloch, John**
- Malaria; an essay on the production and
propagation of this poison, and on the nature
and localities of the places by which it is
produced ... Phila: Thomas Kite, 1829. 1st
Amer edn. 8vo. 219 pp. Lightly browned.
Uncut, unopened. Contemp bds, rebacked.
*(Rootenberg)* **$150**

**MacDonald, Duncan**
- The new London family cook; or, town and
country housekeeper's guide... cookery for the
sick and for the poor ... general directions for
servants ... London: Albion Press, 1808. 1st
edn. 8vo. Engvd frontis, 9 plates. Some
spotting. Contemp calf, rebacked.
*(McDowell)* **£120**

**MacDonald, J.D.**
- A guide to the microscopical examination of
drinking water ... London: 1883. 2nd edn. 25
litho plates.          *(Winterdown)* **£12.50**

**MacDonald, William Rae**
- The construction of the wonderful canon of
logarithms by John Napier. Translated from
Latin into English ... Edinburgh & London:
1889. Sm 4to. xix,[iii], 169 pp. Orig cloth, lea
label.                         *(Pollak)* **£60**

**Macfarlane, R.G.**
- See Biggs, Rosemary & Macfarlane, R.G.

**Macgregor, Frances, et al.**
- Facial deformities and plastic surgery. A
psychosocial study. Springfield: 1953. 1st
edn. Ex lib.                  *(Fye)* **$50**

**Mach, Ernst**
- Contributions to the analysis of the
sensations. Translated by C.M. Williams.
Chicago: 1897. 1st edn in English. 208 pp.
*(Scientia)* **$60**
- History and root of the principle of the

conservation of energy. Translated by P.E.B. Jourdain. Chicago: 1911. 1st edn in English. 116 pp. *(Scientia)* **$45**

**MacIntosh, Robert**
- From Comte to Benjamin Kidd; the appeal to biology or evolution for human guidance. New York: 1899. 1st edn. 312 pp. *(Scientia)* **$35**

**Mackay, Andrew**
- A collection of mathematical tables. London: 1804. 1st edn. 260 pp. Half-mor, sl worn. *(Oasis)* **$60**
- The commencement of the nineteenth century, determined upon unerring principles. Aberdeen: for the Author, 1800. 1st edn. 8vo. 62 pp. Small hole in final leaf with loss of page number only. Prelim sl soiled. Mod half-calf. *(Deighton Bell)* **£50**

**Mackenzie, Colin**
- Five thousand receipts in all the useful and domestic arts, constituting a complete and universal library and operative cyclopaedia. 1824. 3rd edn. iv,828 pp. Calf gilt, cvrs worn, spine cracked. *(Jenner)* **£28**

**Mackenzie, James**
- Angina pectoris. London: Oxford University Press, 1927. 1st edn. 4to. Pub red cloth. *(McDowell)* **£110**
- Diseases of the heart. London: Oxford University Press, 1908. 1st edn. 4to. Plates & textual ills. Pub red cloth, spine reprd. *(McDowell)* **£130**
- Heart disease in pregnancy. London: 1921. 1st edn. 138 pp. *(Fye)* **$100**
- Principles of diagnosis and treatment in heart affections. London: Oxford University Press, 1916. 1st edn, 2nd imp. 8vo. Pub red cloth, top of spine sl snagged. *(McDowell)* **£40**
- Principles of diagnosis and treatment in heart affections. London: Oxford University Press, 1916. 1st edn. 8vo. Pub red cloth. *(McDowell)* **£60**
- The study of the pulse arterial, venous, and hepatic and of movements of the heart. Edinburgh: 1902. 1st edn. 8vo. Ills in text. Pub cloth. *(McDowell)* **£150**
- The study of the pulse, arterial, venous and hepatic, and of the movements of the heart. Edinburgh: 1902. 1st edn. Ex lib. *(Scientia)* **$200**

**Mackenzie, Sir James**
- Angina pectoris. 1923. 4to. xvi,253 pp. Diags. *(Weiner)* **£50**

**Mackenzie, Morell**
- Diptheria; its nature and treatment, varieties and local expressions. Phila: 1879. 1st Amer edn. 104 pp. *(Fye)* **$60**

**Mackenzie, P.**
- Practical observations on the medical powers of the most celebrated mineral waters and of the various modes of bathing ... London: 1819. iii,151 pp. Orig bds, rebacked. *(Whitehart)* **£40**

**Mackenzie, William**
- A practical treatise on diseases of the eye. Boston: 1833. 1st Amer edn. Tall 8vo. Half-title, xii,719 pp. Orig cloth-backed, paper-cvrd bds, sl soiled. *(Elgen)* **$375**

**MacKinney, Loren**
- Medical illustrations in medieval manuscripts. California University Press, 1965. 1st edn. Sm 4to. Plates, some in colour. Dw sl soiled. *(Robertshaw)* **£25**

**Mackintosh, John**
- Principles of pathology and principles of physic ... second American from the fourth London edition. Phila: Edward C. Biddle, 1837. 2 vols. 4to. xxiii,563; xii,538 pp. Foxing. Full lea. *(Poitras)* **$75**

**Mackintosh, T.S.**
- The 'electrical theory' of the universe. Or the elements of physical and moral philosophy. London & Manchester: Simpkin ... & Heywood, n.d. [1838]. 1st edn. 12mo. viii.[4],468 pp. Lge fldg chart. Contemp cloth, lea label. Cloth rubbed, a little shaken. *(Antiq Sc)* **$685**

**Maclachlan, Daniel**
- A practical treatise on the diseases and infirmities of advanced life. 1863. xvi,718 pp. Orig blind-stamped cloth, faded & sl worn. *(Whitehart)* **£25**

**Maclaurin, Colin**
- An account of Sir Isaac Newton's philosophical discoveries. London: for the Author's children, 1748. 1st edn. Lge 4to, lge paper copy. [4],xx,[20, list of subsc & errata],392 pp. Half-title. 6 fldg engvd plates. Contemp speckled calf, rebacked. *(Antiq Sc)* **$550**
- An account of Sir Isaac Newton's philosophical discoveries. London: for the Author's children, 1748. 1st edn. 4to, lge paper copy. [14]ff,xx,392 pp. 6 fldg plates. Lightly browned, foxed. Old panelled calf, red lea labels, chipped, upper jnt split. *(Zeitlin)* **$275**
- An account of Sir Isaac Newton's philosophical discoveries. London: for the Author's children, 1748. 1st edn. 4to, lge paper copy. 28,392 pp. 6 fldg engvd plates. Contemp speckled calf. Subscriber's copy with engvd armorial b'plate. *(Pickering)* **$1,000**

- A treatise of algebra, in three parts ...
London: A. Millar & J. Nourse, 1748.
xiv,366, [ii],65,[i errata] pp. 12 fldg plates.
Calf, much worn, jnts weak.    *(Pollak)* **£100**
- A treatise of algebra, in three parts ...
London: A. Millar & J. Nourse, 1756. 2nd
edn. [xiv],432 pp. 12 fldg plates. later half-
calf, a little rubbed.          *(Pollak)* **£80**
- A treatise of fluxions, in two volumes. To
which is prefixed an account of his life
...London: for William Baynes & William
Davis, 1801. 2nd edn. 2 vols. 8vo. xxiv,412;
vii,342 pp. Port frontis, 41 plates. Contemp
calf, rebacked, a little rubbed. *(Pollak)* **£250**

**Maclean, John**
- Two lectures on combustion: supplementary
to a course of lectures on chemistry. Read at
Nassau Hall. Containing an examination ...
phlogiston and the decomposition of water.
Phila: T. Dobson, 1797. 1st edn. 8vo. 71 pp.
Disbound.              *(Offenbacher)* **$275**

**Maclean, William C.**
- Diseases of tropical climates. London:
Macmillan, 1886. 1st edn. 12mo. [xi],340 pp.
Fldg chart. Some cvr wear. Spine tips & part
of spine sl defective, spine faded.
                          *(Diamond)* **$35**

**MacLeod, John J.R. & Banting, Frederick
G.**
- The antidiabetic functions of the pancreas
and the successful isolation of the antidiabetic
hormone - insulin. St. Louis: 1925. 1st edn.
                          *(Scientia)* **$85**

**Macleod, John Macleod Henry**
- Practical handbook of the pathology of the
skin. An introduction to the histology ...
London: H.K. Lewis, 1903. 1st edn. 8vo.
xxiv,408 pp. 40 plates. Prize calf, backstrip
richly gilt, upper cvrs with arms of Adelaide
Hospital.                *(Dailey)* **$150**
- Practical handbook of the pathology of the
skin. An introduction to the histology ...
London: 1903. 40 plates, many in colour.
                        *(Winterdown)* **£15**

**Maclise, Joseph**
- Surgical anatomy. Phila: 1866. Folio. 156 pp.
Recent qtr lea.            *(Fye)* **$400**
- Surgical anatomy. Phila: Blanchard & Lea,
1866. 1st Amer edn. Folio. 156 pp. 68 cold
plates. Occas light spotting. Bds present but
detchd, lacks backstrip, binding broken.
                          *(Xerxes)* **$250**

**Macmichael, William**
- Lives of British physicians, 1830. Plates.
Half-calf, worn, lacking label.
                      *(Bow Windows)* **$50**

**Macmillan, Lieut. Cdr. D.H.**
- Precision echo sounding and surveying. N.d.
[ca 1939]. 4to. [vii],87 pp. Plates.
                          *(Weiner)* **£20**

**MacMunn, Charles A.**
- The spectroscope in medicine. London:
Churchill, 1880. 1st edn. 8vo. xiii,[1],198 pp.
3 chromo-litho plates, text w'cuts. Orig cloth
                        *(Antiq Sc)* **$175**

**[Maconochie, Allan, Lord Meadowbank]**
- Directions for preparing manure from peat.
Edinburgh: 1815. 50 pp. Disbound.
                          *(Weiner)* **£30**

**Maddock, Alfred Beaumont**
- Practical observations on the efficacy of
medicated inhalations in the treatment of
pulmonary consumption ... 1845. 2nd edn.
xiv,137 pp. Fldg cold frontis, sl torn along
fold, few ills. Sl soiled. Uncut. Cvrs sl worn.
                          *(Jenner)* **£18**
- Pulmonary consumption, bronchitis, asthma,
chronic cough ... successfully treated by
medical inhalations. 1851. 4th edn. xvi,172
pp. Orig green cloth, spine & edges worn &
tattered. Tired copy.      *(Jenner)* **£25**

**Magendie, Francois**
- Physiological and chemical research of the
use of prussic or hydro-cyanic acid in the
treatment of the breast ... New Haven: 1820.
1st Amer edn. xv,89 pp. Uncut, old bds,
rebacked.                *(Goodrich)* **$175**
- A summary of physiology (1816-1817).
Translated by J. Reeve. Balt: 1822. 1st edn in
English. Full lea.        *(Scientia)* **$125**

**Maier. Julius**
- Arc and glow lamps: a practical handbook.
1886. viii,375 pp. Ills. Worn.  *(Weiner)* **£35**

**Main, R.**
- Practical and spherical astronomy for the use
chiefly of students in the universities.
Cambridge: 1863. xvi,392 pp. Figs in text.
Spine sl worn.          *(Whitehart)* **£18**

**Major, Ralph H.**
- Classic descriptions of disease with
biographical sketches of the authors.
Springfield: 1932. 1st edn. 630 pp. Cloth
rubbed.                  *(Goodrich)* **$45**
- Classic descriptions of disease with
biographical sketches of the authors.
Springfield: 1939. 2nd edn, with additions.
727 pp. Ills.              *(Oasis)* **$50**
- Classic descriptions of disease with
biographical sketches of authors. Oxford:
Blackwell, 1948. 3rd edn. Roy 8vo. Ills.
                        *(McDowell)* **£45**
- A history of medicine. Springfield: 1954. 2

vols. Worn dw. *(Goodrich)* **$85**

**Malcolm, Alexander**
- A new system of arithmetick, theoretical and practical. London: J. Osborn, Longman, et al., 1730. 4to. Contemp calf, sl wear.
*(Pollak)* **£150**

**Malcolm, James**
- A compendium of modern husbandry principally written during a survey of Surrey ... London: for the Author, 1805. 1st edn. 8vo. 3 vols. Frontis, full-page fldg engvd plates. Orig tree calf, front hinge of one vol worn. *(Ivelet)* **£145**

**Malcolm, John**
- The physiology of death from traumatic fever. A study in abdominal surgery. London: 1893. 1st edn. 129 pp. Inscribed by the author. *(Fye)* **$75**

**Maliniak, Jacques**
- Sculpture in the living: rebuilding the face and form by plastic surgery. New York: Lancet, 1934. 1st edn. 203 pp. Photo ills. Front hinge cracked. Inscrbd & sgnd by author. *(Xerxes)* **$60**
- Sculpture in the living: rebuilding the face and form by plastic surgery. New York: 1934. 1st edn. 203 pp. *(Fye)* **$40**

**Maloff, I,G, & Epstein, D.W.**
- Electron optics in television. With theory and application of television cathode-ray tubes. New York: 1938. 1st edn, 3rd imp. Num tables & figs. *(Winterdown)* **£12.50**

**Malor, Ralph, H.**
- A history of medicine. Springfield: 1954. 1st edn. 2 vols. 1155 pp. Num ills. Sl frayed dws. *(Oasis)* **$80**

**Malthus, T.R.**
- An essay on the principle of population: or, a view of its past and present effects on human happiness ... a new edition, very much enlarged. London: 1803. [2nd edn]. 4to. 8,[4],610 pp. New full brown speckled calf, lea label. *(M&S)* **$1,500**
- An essay on the principle of population: or, a view of its past and present effects on human happiness; with an enquiry into our prospects ... 1807. 4th edn. 2 vols. xvi,580; vii,484,[16] pp. Light foxing, name in ink on title. Tree calf gilt, a.e.g. *(Whitehart)* **£190**

**Maltz, Maxwell**
- New faces - new futures: rebuilding character with plastic surgery. New York: 1936. 1st edn. 315 pp. *(Fye)* **$100**

**Maltzman, Irving**
- See Cole, Michael & Maltzman, Irving

**Manley, Charles M.**
- See Langley, Samuel Pierpoint & Manley, Charles M.

**Mann, Ida**
- The development of the human eye. Cambridge: 1928. 1st edn. *(Scientia)* **$60**

**Mann, J.D.**
- Forensic medicine and toxicology. 1893. 1st edn. [2],639 pp. Frontis, 23 figs in text. Orig cloth, sl stained, front inner hinge cracked. *(Whitehart)* **£25**

**Mann, Robert James**
- Health and diet or, the philosophy of food and drink. 1882. 1st edn. W'engvd ills. Orig dec cloth. *(Robertshaw)* **£9**

**Manning, Henry**
- Geometry of four dimensions. New York: 1914. 1st edn. 348 pp. *(Oasis)* **$35**

**Mansfield, Charles Blanchford**
- A theory of salts: a treatise on the constitution of bipolar chemical compounds. London: Macmillan, 1865. 1st edn. 8vo. lii,608 pp. 2 fldg diag plates. Orig cloth. *(Antiq Sc)* **$125**

**[Mansfield, Jared]**
- Essays, mathematical and physical: containing new theories and illustrations of some very difficult subjects of the sciences. New Haven: [1801]. 1st edn. 8vo. 10,274, [42],[5] pp. 13 fldg plates. Contemp calf, rebacked, orig spine & label laid down. *(M&S)* **$475**

**Manson, Patrick**
- Tropical diseases. New York: Wood, 1903. Revsd & enlgd edn. 767 pp. Cold & b/w ills. Some wear. *(Xerxes)* **$45**
- Tropical diseases; A manual of the diseases of warm climates. New York: 1898. 1st Amer edn. Lib stamp on spine. Shelfworn. *(Scientia)* **$75**

**Mantell, Gideon**
- The geology of the south-east of England. London: Longman ..., 1833. 1st edn. 8vo. xix,[1], v-viii [subscribers], 415,[1] pp. Litho frontis, 5 plates (1 fldg), fldg hand-cold map. Orig cloth with paper label, uncut, unopened. *(Antiq Sc)* **$225**
- The geology of the south-east of England. London: 1833. 8vo. xix,415 pp. Cold map, 6 plates, 69 w'cuts. Plates sl foxed, sm tear in map. Orig bds, trifle worn. *(Wheldon & Wesley)* **£85**
- The journal of Gideon Mantell ... See

Curwen, E. Cecil
- The medals of creation; or, first lessons in geology and in the study of organic remains. London: 1844. 1st edn. 2 vols. 1016 pp. Both volumes rebacked.            *(Scientia)* **$65**
- Petrifactions and their teachings. Bohn, 1851. xi,496 pp. Frontis, 115 text w'cuts. Some marginal marks. Orig cloth, new back.
*(Pollak)* **£20**
- The wonders of geology. 1838. 2 vols. 8vo. 1 plain, 8 cold, plates, 81 text figs. Cloth, reprd & refixed. 2 gatherings in vol I bound out of order.            *(Wheldon & Wesley)* **£45**

**Manuel, Frank E.**
- Isaac Newton historian. Cambridge: 1963. 1st edn. 328 pp. Dw.            *(Scientia)* **$27.50**
- A portrait of Sir Isaac Newton. Cambridge: 1968. 1st edn. 478 pp. Dw.            *(Scientia)* **$35**

**[Marcet, Mrs. Jane]**
- Conversations on natural philosophy ... for the comprehension of young pupils. London: Longman, Hurst, et al., 1824. 4th edn, revsd & crrctd. 12mo. x,[ii],429 pp. 23 plates. New buckram, lea label.            *(Pollak)* **£30**

**Marchant, James (ed.)**
- Alfred Russel Wallace. Letters and reminiscences. New York: 1916. 507 pp. Shelfworn.            *(Scientia)* **$40**

**Marchiafava, E., et al.**
- Two monographs on malaria and the parasites of malarial fever. London: New Sydenham Society, 1894. 1st English edn. Roy 8vo. 6 cold plates. Pub blind-stamped cloth.            *(McDowell)* **£58**

**Marcou, Jules**
- Life, letters and works of Louis Agassiz. Boston: 1876. 319 pp.            *(Scientia)* **$50**

**Marcy, Henry**
- The anatomy and surgical treatment of hernia. New York: 1892. 1st edn. 4to. Rebacked.            *(Scientia)* **$225**

**Marey, E.J.**
- Animal mechanism. A treatise on terrestrial and aerial locomotion. London: Henry S. King. 1874. 1st English edn. xvi,283 pp. 117 ills. Lacks half-title. Occas foxing. Later half-mor, t.e.g.            *(Pollak)* **£50**

**Mariani, Angelo**
- Coca and its therapeutic derivatives. New York: 1892. 2nd edn. 78 pp.            *(Fye)* **$150**

**Marie, P.**
- Lectures on diseases of the spinal cord. New Sydenham Society, 1895. 1st edn in English. xix,511 pp. 244 figs in text. Orig cloth.

*(Whitehart)* **£55**

**Mariotte, Edme**
- The motion of water, and other fluids. Being a treatise of hydrostaticks ... London: for J. Senex & W. Taylor, 1718. 1st English trans. xxiii,[1],290 pp,[1 advts]f. Lacks last blank. 7 fldg engvd plates. A few minor stains. Contemp calf, label worn.            *(Zeitlin)* **$475**
- The motion of water, and other fluids. Being a treatise of hydrostaticks ... [translated by] J.T. Desaguliers ... London: J. Senex & W. Taylor, 1718. 1st English trans. 8vo. 7 fldg engvd plates. Contemp panelled calf.
*(Quaritch)* **$650**

**Mark, Leonard P.**
- Acromegaly; a personal experience. London: 1912. 1st edn.            *(Scientia)* **$85**

**Markham, Gervase**
- The inrichment of the Weald of Kent, or a direction to the husbandman, for the true ... inriching of all the grounds within the Wealds of Kent, and Sussex ... London: for G. Sawbridge, 1660. Sm 4to. [iv],20 pp. Faint damp-staining. 19th c half-calf.
*(Deighton Bell)* **£175**
- Markham's masterpiece, containing all knowledge belonging to the smith, farrier or horse leach ... divided into two books ... to which is added ... also The Compleat Jockey. 1717. 19th edn. Title,4 [index], 319, iii[i.e. ii],64 pp. Some worm. Early calf.
*(Phenotype)* **£90**

**Marks, E.C.R.**
- Notes on the construction of cranes and lifting machinery. Manchester, 1899. xi,183 pp. 155 figs in text. Orig cloth, inner hinges cracked.            *(Whitehart)* **£25**

**Marmor, Leonard**
- Arthritis surgery. Phila: Lea & Febiger, 1976. 548 pp. Profusely illust.            *(Poitras)* **$40**

**Marr, James Pratt**
- Pioneer surgeons of the Woman's Hospital: the lives of Sims, Emmett ... Phila: 1957. Ltd. ix,148 pp. Plates throughout. Orig brown cloth, slipcase, rubbed at edges.            *(Jenner)* **£8**

**Marsh, George P.**
- Man and nature; or, physical geography as modified by human action. New York: Charles Scribner, 1864. 1st edn. 8vo. 19,[1],560 pp. Index. Orig cloth, worn at edges, backstrip defective.            *(M&S)* **$175**

**Marsh, H. & Watson, C. Gordon**
- Diseases of the joints and spine. 1910. 3rd edn. xv,632 pp. 12 plates, 108 figs in text.            *(Whitehart)* **£15**

**Marsh, Howard**
- Diseases of the joints ... London: Cassell, 1886. 1st edn. Sm 8vo. x,461 pp, [4 advts]ff. Cold litho frontis, text ills. Orig blue cloth, sl wear to spine. *(Zeitlin)* **$75**
- Diseases of the joints and spine. London: 1895, new & revsd edn. xvi,532,8[pub ctlg] pp. 79 text w'cuts. *(Elgen)* **$50**

**Marsh, O.C.**
- Dinocerata, a monograph of an extinct order of gigantic mammals. Washington: 1884. 4to. xviii,237 pp. 56 lithos, 200 w'cuts. Orig cloth, trifle used & sl dust-soiled. U.S. Geological Survey. *(Wheldon & Wesley)* **£60**
- The dinosaurs of North America. Washington: 1895. 4to. 102 pp. 85 plates. Cloth. U.S. Geological Survey. *(Wheldon & Wesley)* **£50**

**Marshall, A.**
- Explosives, their manufacture, properties, tests and history. 1915. xv,624 pp. 137 ills. Spine sl faded. *(Whitehart)* **£40**

**Marshall, Arthur Milnes**
- Lectures on the Darwinian theory, edited by C.F. Marshall. David Nutt, 1894. 8vo. xx,236 pp. 37 ills. Tree calf gilt, red lea label, backstrip faded, mrbld edges & endpapers. *(Blackwell's)* **£45**

**Marshall, Charles**
- Plain and easy introduction to the knowledge and practice of gardening, with hints on fishponds. [London]: 1813. Half-calf, rubbed. *(Argosy)* **$75**

**Marshall, Henry Rutgers**
- Consciousness. London: Macmillan, 1909. 1st British edn. [xvi],685,[3] pp. Pub blue cloth. Inscribed "from the author". *(Gach)* **$40**

**Marshall, Mr.**
- See Marshall, William

**Marshall, William**
- Minutes, experiments, observations, and general remarks, on agriculture, in the Southern Counties. London: for G. Nicol, 1799. New edn. 2 vols. 8vo. xxiv,414,[2]; xi,387,[5]. Fldg table, 5 double-page plates. Contemp half-calf, jnts cracked, crnrs worn. *(Deighton Bell)* **£85**
- Minutes, experiments, observations, and general remarks, on agriculture, in the Southern Counties. London: for G. Nicol, 1799. New edn. 2 vols. 6 plates, map. Orig calf. *(Ivelet)* **£100**

**Martin, A.**
- Atlas of obstetrics and gynecology. Phila:

1881. 2nd edn. 98 engvd plates (sev cold) with accompanying text. Lib stamp on title & verso of plates. *(Fye)* **$150**

**Martin, C.F.**
- See Adami, J. & Martin, C.F.

**Martin, Robert (ed.)**
- The collected works of Dr. P.M. Latham, with memoir ... New Sydenham Society, 1876-78. 2 vols. xlvii,[i],480; xlii,575,[i]. Occas foxing. Wear to spine ends, one weakening. *(Pollak)* **£35**

**Martin, Thomas C. & Wetzler, Joseph**
- The electric motor and its applications. 2nd edn, enlarged. New York: 1888. Sm folio. 10,282 pp. 300 ills, fldg plate. Orig cloth, slight wear. *(M&S)* **$47.50**

**Martin, Staff Comm. W.R.**
- A treatise on navigation and nautical astronomy. 1888. 1st edn. xi,356 pp. 177 figs, 9 plates (2 fldg). Orig cloth, sl worn, spine defective, crnrs worn. *(Whitehart)* **£18**

**Martine, George**
- Essays medical and philosophical. London: A. Millar, 1740. 1st edn. 8vo. [12],376 pp. With the fldg engvd plate. Contemp calf, jnts partially cracked. *(Antiq Sc)* **$1,200**
- Essays medical and philosophical. London: A. Millar, 1740. 1st edn. 8vo. 8ff, 376pp. Engvd fold-out table. Contemp calf, rebacked. *(Offenbacher)* **$450**

**Martyn, Thomas**
- Letters on the elements of botany, addressed to a lady. Translated into English with notes and 24 letters fully explaining the system of Linnaeus. 1787. 2nd edn with crrctns. xxv,[1],500,[28] pp. Index, fldg table. Contemp calf rebacked, gilt spine. *(Whitehart)* **£85**

**Maseres, Francis**
- Scriptores logarithmici; or, a collection of several curious tracts on the nature and construction of logarithms .... London: for B. White & Son, 1791 - 1807. 6 vols. 4to. 98 tracts. Plates, some fldg. Occas foxing. Contemp tree calf, all rebacked. *(Pollak)* **£550**

**Mason, Francis**
- On the surgery of the face with one hundred illustrations. Phila: 1879. 170 pp. Bds soiled. *(Goodrich)* **$100**

**Massachusetts Medical Society**
- Acts of Incorporation and acts regulating the practice of physic and surgery with the Bye-Laws and Orders of the ... Boston: T.B. Wait & Son, 1826. 100 pp. Paper cvrs.

*(Poitras)* **$75**
- Acts of Incorporation, Bye-Laws and Orders, of the Massachusetts Medical Society in the Year of our Lord, 1761. Boston: John Eliot, 1816. 54 pp. Paper cvrs. Ex lib. *(Poitras)* **$60**

**Massey, H.S.W.**
- See Mott, Nevil & Massey, H.S.W.

**Mathematical ...**
- Mathematical tables ... See Sherwin, Henry

**Mathematicall ...**
- Mathematicall magick ... See Wilkins, John

**Matheson Commission**
- Epidemic encephalitis. Etiology, epidemiology, treatment. Report of a survey by the Matheson Commission. New York: Columbia University Press, 1929. 8vo. xiii,849 pp.                    *(Poitras)* **$40**

**Matheson, Ewing**
- Works in iron: bridge and roof structures. 1873. Lge 8vo. Num ills. Orig cloth, gilt.
*(Edwards)* **£60**

**Mathews, G.B.**
- See Gray, Andrew & Mathews, G.B.
- Theory of numbers. Part 1 [all published]. Cambridge: Deighton, Bell, 1892. 1st edn. 8vo.                              *(McDowell)* **£30**

**Mathews, Joseph M.**
- A treatise on diseases of the rectum, anus, and sigmoid flexure. New York: 1892. 1st edn. 537 pp. Half lea.              *(Fye)* **$60**
- A treatise on diseases of the rectum, anus, and sigmoid flexure. New York: D. Appleton, 1896. 2nd edn, revsd. 545 pp. 6 chromolithos, num ills.              *(Poitras)* **$45**

**Mathews, Joseph McDowell**
- How to succeed in the practice of medicine. Phila: 1905. 1st edn. ix, 215 pp. Frontis, 5 plates.                           *(Elgen)* **$30**

**Mathias, Andrew**
- The mercurial disease. An inquiry into the history and nature of the disease, produced in the human constitution by the use of mercury ... Phila: 1811. 1st Amer edn. Sm 8vo. [4]ff, xiv,[15]-250 pp. Some browning. Tree calf, front jnt tender.              *(Elgen)* **$150**

**Matho ...**
- Matho; or, the Cosmotheoria puerilis ... See Baxter, Andrew

**Matijaca, Anthony**
- Principles of electro-medicine, electro-surgery and radiology. A practical treatise for students and practitioners ... Butler, N.J.:

Benedict Lust, 1917. 210,[xiv advts] pp. Frontis, 19 plates, 104 text ills. *(Pollak)* **£20**

**Matson, Donald**
- The treatment of acute compound injuries of the spinal cord due to missiles. Springfield: 1948. 1st edn. 64 pp.              *(Fye)* **$30**

**Matthews, Chas. Geo. & Lott, Francis E.**
- The microscope in the brewery and malthouse. 1889. Num ills. Spine faded & frayed, inner hinges cracked.
*(Quinto Charing Cross)* **£20**

**Matthews, D.N.**
- The surgery of repair, injuries and burns. Oxford: Blackwell, 1943. xii,386 pp. 198 ills. Dw.                           *(Pollak)* **£20**

**Matthews, Leslie G.**
- The antiques of perfume. 1973. 1st edn. 88 ills. Dw.                  *(Robertshaw)* **£12.50**
- Antiques of the pharmacy. 1971. 1st edn. Num ills. Dw.            *(Robertshaw)* **£14**
- History of pharmacy in Britain. 1962. 1st edn. 37 plates. Dw.       *(Robertshaw)* **£18**
- History of pharmacy in Britain. Edinburgh: 1962. xiv,427 pp. 37 plates. *(Whitehart)* **£25**
- The Royal apothecaries. Wellcome Historical Medical Library, 1967. 16 ills. Dw.
*(Robertshaw)* **£8**

**Matthews, Martin**
- Engine turning 1680 - 1980. The tool and technique ... [n.p.: ca. 1984]. 4to. [2]ff, 175,[5] pp. Ills, in sepia. Sgnd by author.
*(Zeitlin)* **$50**

**Mattson, M.**
- Directions for the employment of injections in various diseases, with remarks upon the nature and treatment of habitual constipation ... Boston: 1855. 3rd edn. Sm 8vo. 165 pp. 4 plates. Dampstained throughout. Wraps sl soiled.                           *(Jenner)* **£12**

**Mauborgne, J.O.**
- Practical uses of the wave meter in wireless telegraphy. 1913. 74 pp. Diags. *(Weiner)* **£30**

**Maudsley, Henry**
- Body and mind: an inquiry into their connection and mutual influence, specially in reference to mental disorders. New York: D. Appleton, 1871. 1st U.S. edn. Sm 8vo. [ii],155,[15] pp. Pebbled mauve cloth.
*(Gach)* **$65**
- Organic to human: psychological and sociological. London: Macmillan, 1916. 1st edn. viii,386,[2] pp.            *(Gach)* **$50**
- The physiology and pathology of the mind. New York: Appleton, 1890. x,580 pp. Advts.
*(Gach)* **$30**

**Maunder, E. Walter**
- The Indian eclipse, 1898. Report of the expeditions organised by the British Astronomical Association to observe the total solar eclipse of 1898 ... 1899. Lge 8vo. Orig cloth, gilt. *(Edwards)* **£17.50**

**Maunsell, Henry**
- The Dublin practice of midwifery. London: Longman, 1856. New edn, revsd. xii,272,32 [ctlg] pp. Some marginal pencil notes. Recased. *(Pollak)* **£25**

**Maurice, Frederick Denison**
- The conscience: lectures on causistry, delivered in the University of Cambridge. 1883. 3rd edn. ix,175 pp. Stamps on half-title & title. Orig maroon cloth. *(Jenner)* **£13.50**

**Mauriceau, Frank**
- The diseases of women with child, and in child-bed ... to which is prefix'd an exact description of the parts of generation in women ... the fifth edition, translated ... London: Bell, 1716. xliv,373,[7] pp. Plates some reprd. Contemp calf, jnts cracked. *(Goodrich)* **$250**

**Maury, F.**
- Treatise on the dental art ... Translated from the French, with notes and additions, by J.B. Savier. Phila: Lea & Blanchard, 1843. 1st Amer edn. 8vo. 324 pp. Ills & advts. 20 litho plates. Staining of first 30pp & foxing throughout. Contemp sheep, very worn. *(M&S)* **$85**

**Maury, M.F.**
- The physical geography of the sea. New York: Harper, 1855. 1st edn. 274pp. 8 fldg plates, 4 plates in the text. Lacking front fly-leaf. Orig gilt cloth, a little frayed. *(Antiq Sc)* **$250**
- The physical geography of the sea. New York: 1855. 1st edn. 8vo. 24,274pp. Orig cloth, light stain on front cvr, spine sl faded. B'plate. *(M&S)* **$375**
- Physical survey of Virginia. Geographical position of: its commercial advantages and national importance. (Preliminary report) ... December, 1868. Richmond: Nye, 1868. 1st edn, 8vo. 90 pp, errata leaf. 2 fldg maps. Orig printed wraps, top crnr torn away. *(M&S)* **$85**

**Mavor, F.J.**
- See Burness, Alexander G. & Mavor, F.J.

**Mawe, John**
- Familiar lessons on mineralogy and geology ... 1830. 12th edn. Sm 8vo. 4 hand-cold plates, 1 other plate. Calf backed bds, sl worn. *(Edwards)* **£60**

**Max-Muller, Friedrich**
- Three introductory lectures on the science of thought. Chicago: Open Court Publishing Company, 1888. 1st edn. *(Gach)* **$40**

**Maxwell, James Clerk**
- The electrical researches of the Honourable Henry Cavendish, F.R.S. ... Cambridge: University Press, 1879. 1st edn. 8vo. 3 plates. Pub plum cloth, lettered in gilt. *(McDowell)* **£180**
- An elementary treatise on electricity. Oxford: Clarendon Press, 1881. 1st edn. 8vo. Pub cloth. *(McDowell)* **£110**
- An elementary treatise on electricity. Edited ... Oxford University Press, 1888. 2nd edn. xvi,208,80 [pub ctlg] pp. 6 plates. Sl cvr staining & rubbing. *(Diamond)* **$35**
- Matter and motion (Manuals of Elementary Science). 1876, 1st edn. Sm 8vo. 128 pp. Diags. *(Weiner)* **£38**
- Matter and motion. London: S.P.C.K., 1888. 1st edn. viii,9-128, [iv ctlg] pp. 16 text figs. *(Pollak)* **£50**
- The scientific papers, edited by W.D. Niven. Cambridge: 1890. 4to. 2 vols. xxix,607; viii,806 pp. Ports, plates, diags. Orig cloth, old spines laid on. Ex lib. *(Weiner)* **£280**
- Theory of heat. London: Longmans, Green, 1872. 2nd edn. xii,312 pp. 40 text figs. Faded, foxed at ends. *(Pollak)* **£40**
- A treatise on electricity and magnetism. New York: [n.d.]. 3rd edn. 2 vols in 1. xxxii,560; xxiv,500 pp. 20 plates. *(Elgen)* **$45**
- A treatise on electricity and magnetism. Oxford: Clarendon Press, 1873. 1st edn. 2 vols. 8vo. xxx,[3],425; xxiii,[1],444 pp. Complete with both errata slips, 15 pp advts, & 20 plates. Orig cloth, rebacked, orig spine laid down. *(Rootenberg)* **$1,000**
- A treatise on electricity and magnetism. Oxford: Clarendon Press, 1892. 3rd edn. 2 vols. xxxii,506,[ii], [ii advts]; xxiv,500,[ii],8 [ctlg] pp. 2 errata slips, 20 plates, text figs. Full new calf, gilt spine. Ex Inner Temple lib, with sm stamps. *(Pollak)* **£175**
- A treatise on electricity and magnetism. Oxford: Clarendon Press, 1892. 3rd edn, re-issue. 2 vols. Orig cloth, spine ends nicked. *(Pollak)* **£145**
- A treatise on electricity and magnetism. Oxford University Press, 1892. 3rd edn. 2 vols. xxiii,506; xxiv,500 pp. Cvrs sl rubbed. *(Diamond)* **$60**
- A treatise on electricity and magnetism. Oxford: 1892. 3rd edn. 2 vols. 506; 500 pp. Unopened. *(Scientia)* **$95**

**Maxwell, James L.**
- See Jeffereys, W. Hamilton & Maxwell, James. L.

**[Maxwell, Robert ?]**
- See Treatise ... concerning the manner of fallowing of land ...

**May, Charles & Worth, Claud**
- A manual of diseases of the eye. London: 1906. 4th edn. 400 pp. Shaken.  *(Fye)* **$10**

**May, Edward**
- A most certaine and true relation of a strange monster or serpent found in the left ventricle of the heart of John Pennant ... London: George Miller, 1639. Sole edn. Sm 4to. [8],40 pp. 2 plates (1 fldg). Catchword of E4 & plate margin sl shaved. Mor.  *(Rootenberg)* **$1,850**

**May, Hans**
- Reconstructive and reparative surgery. Phila: F.A. Davis Company, 1947. xxi,964 pp. 963 ills (17 cold). Back hinge loose. *(Poitras)* **$50**
- Reconstructive and reparative surgery. Phila: 1949. 1st edn. 964 pp. 967 ills.  *(Fye)* **$50**
- Reconstructive and reparative surgery. Phila: 1958. 2nd edn. 1115 pp.  *(Fye)* **$50**

**May, Mark A.**
- See Hartshorne, Hugh & May, Mark A.

**Mayer, Alfred Marshall**
- Sound. A series of simple, entertaining and inexpensive experiments in the phenomena of sound for the use of students ... London: Macmillan, 1891. xv,156, [iv ctlg] pp. 61 text figs.  *(Pollak)* **£25**

**Maygrier, J.P.**
- Midwifery illustrated. Translated from the French, with notes ... New York: J.K. Moore, 1833. 1st Amer edn. Roy 8vo. 186,[2] pp. 80 litho plates (1 fldg). Text cracked after p 72, text & plates rather heavily foxed. Contemp cloth, worn.  *(M&S)* **$150**
- Midwifery illustrated. Translated ... New York: 1834. 4to. 179 pp. 82 lithos. *(Fye)* **$300**

**Mayo ...**
- Mayo's compound vegetable anaesthetic. A safe and pleasant substitute for ether, chloroform ... and all substances used to destroy pain in dentistry and surgery. Boston: 1883. 1st edn. 12mo. 24 pp. Orig printed wraps.  *(M&S)* **$37.50**

**Mayo, George Elton**
- The human problems of an industrial civilization. New York: Macmillan, 1933. 1st edn. [viii],194,[6] pp. Maroon cloth.  *(Gach)* **$50**

**Mayr, Ernst**
- Animal species and evolution. Cambridge: 1963. 1st edn. 797 pp.  *(Scientia)* **$37.50**

**McBride, C.A.**
- The modern treatment of alcoholism and drug narcotism. 1910. vii,376 pp. Orig blue cloth.  *(Jenner)* **£9**

**McCallum, Alex**
- The navigation of the air. Reprinted from the 'Glasgow Herald'. London: Aeronautical Society, 1897. 20 pp. Half-mor, orig printed wraps bound in, t.e.g.  *(Pollak)* **£25**

**McCallum, David**
- The globotype telegraph: a recording instrument, by which small coloured balls are released one-by-one ... by the force of their own gravity. 1856. 8vo. 32 pp. W'engvd frontis, 8 figs in text, one hand-cold. A few leaves soiled. Mod bds, paper label.  *(Deighton Bell)* **£95**

**McCarrison, R.**
- The etiology of endemic goitre. 1913. vi,216 pp. 57 figs & plates. Orig cloth, rebacked. Milroy Lectures delivered at the Royal College of Physicians of London, January 1913.  *(Whitehart)* **£25**

**McClellan, George**
- Anatomy in its relation to art ... illustrated by 338 drawings and photographs made by the author ... Phila: 1900. Lge 4to. 141 pp, plus plates. Uncut in orig cloth, rubbed & recased.  *(Goodrich)* **$250**
- Regional anatomy in its relation to medicine and surgery. Phila: 1891-92. 2 vols. Lge 4to. xvi,436; xvi,414 pp. 97 photographic plates "hand-coloured by the author". Cloth, lightly shaken, hinges weak.  *(Goodrich)* **$125**
- Regional anatomy in its relation to medicine and surgery. Phila: 1894. 2nd edn. 2 vols. 4to. 436; 414 pp. Many of the plates with manuscript notations. Half lea, backstrips worn, rubbed with some tears.  *(Fye)* **$100**

**McCollom, Elmer V.**
- A history of nutrition. Boston: 1957. 1st edn. Ex lib. Stamp marks on f'edges. *(Scientia)* **$60**
- A newer knowledge of nutrition. The use of food for the preservation of life and health. New York: Macmillan, 1918.  *(Poitras)* **$40**

**McComb, Samuel**
- See Worcester, Elwood & McComb, Samuel

**McConnell, Anita**
- Geomagnetic instruments before 1900. An illustrated account of their construction and use. [London]: Harriet Wynter, 1980. Ltd (500). 8vo. 75 pp. 19 figs, 17 plates. Orig blue buckram.  *(Zeitlin)* **$30**

**McCosh, James**
- Intuitions of the mind. New York: 1872. 3rd

edn. 451 pp. Spine ends worn, front internal hinge cracked.  *(Epistemologist)* **$40**

**McCrae, John**
- See Adami, J. George & McCrae, John

**McDougall, William**
- Character and the conduct of life: practical psychology for every man. London: Methuen & Co., [1927]. 1st British edn.  *(Gach)* **$15**

**McDowell, F.**
- See Brown, J.B. & McDowell, F.

**McDowell, Frank, et al.**
- Surgery of face, mouth and jaws. St. Louis. 1954. 1st edn. 213 pp.  *(Fye)* **$40**
- Surgery of face, mouth and jaws. St. Louis. C.V. Mosby Company, 1954. vii,213 pp. 168 ills.  *(Poitras)* **$50**

**McGillicuddy, Timothy J.**
- Functional disorders of the nervous system in women. New York: William Wood, 1898. vi,367 pp. 45 w'engvs, 2 chromo-lithos. Cvrs stained & very musty, hinges broken. Very poor.  *(Gach)* **$50**

**McGlannan, Alexius**
- Collected papers of ... 1905-1939. Balt: 1940. 1st edn. Orig cloth.  *(Oasis)* **$50**

**McGowan, Frank**
- See Pool, Eugene & McGowan, Frank

**Mcilwain, G.**
- Memoirs of John Abernethy, F.R.S., with a view of his lectures, writing and character. 1853. 2 vols. xii,342; 376 pp. Frontis. Orig blind-stamped cloth, faded & sl worn.  *(Whitehart)* **£40**

**McKay, H.**
- See Moseley, Sydney A. & McKay, H.

**McKinley, E.B.**
- A geography of disease. A preliminary survey of the incidence and distribution of tropical and certain other diseases. Washington: 1935. xxv,495 pp. Light damp stains to margins of final few pages.  *(Whitehart)* **£38**

**Mclachlan, H. (ed.)**
- Sir Isaac Newton. Theological manuscripts. Liverpool: 1950. 1st edn. 147 pp. Dw.  *(Scientia)* **$35**

**McMichael, John (ed.)**
- Circulation: Proceedings of the Harvey Tercentenary Congress held ... 1957, Royal College of Surgeons of England. Oxford: 1958. xxiii,503 pp. Worn dw.  *(Jenner)* **£26**

**McVail, John C.**
- Vaccination vindicated: being an answer to the leading anti-vaccinators. London: 1887. 176 pp. Fldg table.  *(Goodrich)* **$45**

**McWilliam, Robert**
- An essay upon the origin and operation of the dry rot, with a view to its prevention or cure. London: Taylor, 1818. 4to. xx,420 pp. 3 plates, sl foxed. Errata slip & printer's instructions at end. Contemp bds, rebacked in calf.  *(Frew Mackenzie)* **£180**

**Mead, G.H.**
- The philosophy of the act. Chicago: 1938. 696 pp. Sm spot on spine.  *(Epistemologist)* **$40**
- The philosophy of the present. Chicago: 1932. 199 pp. Sl foxing. Spine ends sl worn.  *(Epistemologist)* **$40**

**Mead, Richard**
- A discourse on the plague. London: Millar & Brindley, 1744. 9th edn, crrctd & enlgd. 8vo. viii,xl,164 pp. Contemp calf.  *(Frew Mackenzie)* **£75**
- A mechanical account of poisons, in several essays. 1745. 3rd edn, with lge addtns. xlviii,318 pp. Errata slip. 4 fldg plates at end. Full calf gilt, sl worn, rebacked, new endpapers.  *(Jenner)* **£90**
- Medical precepts and cautions. London: J. Brindley, 1755. 2nd edn in English. 8vo. xvi,311,[1] pp. Lacks 1st blank. Orig calf, cvrs somewhat worn.  *(Rootenberg)* **$200**
- A short discourse concerning pestilential contagion, and the methods to be used to prevent it. 1722. 8th edn, with lge addtns. Roy 8vo. xxxvi,150 pp. Light browning of title. Calf, rebacked, rubbed.  *(Jenner)* **£100**
- A treatise concerning the influence of the sun and moon upon human bodies, and the diseases thereby produced ... translated from the Latin ... London: for J. Brindley, 1748. 2nd English edn. 8vo. xxiii,[1],130 pp. Title & final page dust-soiled. Mod cloth.  *(Zeitlin)* **$350**

**Meade, Richard**
- A history of thoracic surgery. Springfield: 1961. Thick 8vo. 670 pp. Dw. *(Goodrich)* **$65**
- An introduction to the history of general surgery. Phila: 1968. 1st edn. 403 pp.  *(Fye)* **$50**

**Meader, C.L.**
- See Pillsbury, W.B. & Meader, C.L.

**Means, James**
- Twentieth century energy. A pamphlet which treats briefly of an unseen yet potent form of matter. Boston: W.B. Clarke, 1896. 1st edn. Sq 8vo. 19,[1] pp. Orig printed wraps. Sheets

loose in binding.        *(M&S)* **$100**

**Medical ...**
- Medical extracts: on the nature of health ...
See Thornton, Robert John

**Medical Directory ...**
- The medical directory for Scotland, 1858.
[24],x,[14], 212,[106 advts] pp. Orig cloth,
inner hinges cracked.        *(Whitehart)* **£25**
- Nisbet's practical medical directory 1908 in
two parts. Part I, directory of medical
practitioners; Part II, the local directory.
1908. xvi,790,[1] pp. Orig cloth, rebacked.
*(Whitehart)* **£35**

**Meduna, Ladislas Joseph**
- Carbon dioxide therapy: a neuro-
physiological treatment of nervous disorders.
Springfield: Charles C. Thomas, [1950]. 1st
edn. xvi,236,[4] pp. Lightly worn dw.
*(Gach)* **$50**

**Meigs, Arthur V.**
- The origin of disease, especially disease
resulting from intrinsic as opposed to
extrinsic causes ... Phila: 1897. 1st edn.
xiv,229 pp. 61 plates containing 137 etchings
with facing text. Lower spine edge frayed.
*(Elgen)* **$55**

**Meigs, Charles**
- Females and their diseases. Phila: 1848. 1st
edn. 670 pp. Full lea.        *(Fye)* **$100**
- Obstetrics: the science and the art. Phila:
1852. 2nd edn. 759 pp. Full lea. Backstrip
cracked & dry, some w'stains.        *(Fye)* **$25**
- A treatise on the acute and chronic diseases of
the neck of the uterus. Phila: 1854. 1st edn.
116 pp. 22 full-page cold litho plates.
*(Fye)* **$150**

**Meirowsky, Arnold (ed.)**
- Neurological surgery of trauma. Washington:
1965. 1st edn. 604 pp.        *(Fye)* **$35**

**Meldola, Raphael**
- The chemical synthesis of vital products ...
London: Arnold, 1904. Volume I (all
published). xvi,338, [ii],4 pp. Front bd
spotted.        *(Pollak)* **£15**

**Mellet, John William**
- Cotton: the chemical, geological and
meteorological conditions involved in its
successful cultivation ... (in the) Cotton States
of North America. London: Chapman & Hall,
1862. 1st edn. Cold frontis, lge cold fldg map
in pocket. Pub pebbled cloth.
*(McDowell)* **£140**

**Mello, Rev. J. Magens**
- Handbook to the geology of Derbyshire.

London: Bemrose & Sons, n.d. [ca 1860].
12mo. 72,[viii] pp. Fldg cold map, 7 plates (2
double-page. Orig lettered cloth. *(Pollak)* **£15**

**Mellor, William (ed.)**
- Bookbinding Trades Journal. Manchester: for
the Bookbinders' and Machine Rulers'
Consolidated Union, 1904-14. Sole edn. 2
vols in 1. Vol I, Nos. 1-24; vol II, Nos. 1-16
[all published]. 8vo. Ills throughout, 8
samples of mrbld paper. Contemp half-mor.
*(McDowell)* **£650**

**Memoirs ...**
- Memoirs on diptheria, from the writings of
Bretonneau, Guersant, Trousseau [et al.].
Translated ... New Sydenham Society, 1859.
407 pp. Orig olive cloth, crnrs bumped. Ex
lib, with stamps.        *(Jenner)* **£14**

**Memoranda ...**
- Memoranda, references and documents
relating to the Royal Hospitals of the City of
London. Reprinted, 1863. Orig cloth, spine
faded & soiled.        *(Robertshaw)* **£15**

**Mendel, Gregor**
- Experiments in plant hybridisation -
Mendel's original paper in English translation
... Edinburgh: 1965. ix,95 pp. Orig green
cloth. Torn dw.        *(Jenner)* **£16**

**Mendeleef, D.**
- The principles of chemistry, translated from
the Russian ... 1891. 1st edn in English. 2
vols. xvi,611; vi,487 pp. Fldg table, ills.
Cloth a little worn & soiled, front jnts shaken.
*(Weiner)* **£75**

**Menninger, Karl A.**
- The human mind. New York & London:
1930. Lge 8vo. xiv,447,xi pp. Few ills. Cvrs
sl soiled.        *(Jenner)* **£18**

**Menninger, William Claire**
- A psychiatrist for a troubled world: selected
papers ... New York: The Viking Press,
[1967]. 1st edn, deluxe format. 2 vols. Blue
buckram, boxed.        *(Gach)* **$40**

**Mercier, Charles**
- Sanity and insanity. London: Walter Scott,
1890. 12mo. xx,395 pp.        *(Gach)* **$40**

**Mercury ...**
- Mercury, or the secret and swift messenger ...
See Wilkins, John

**Merendino, K. Alvin (ed.)**
- Prosthetic valves for cardiac surgery.
Springfield: Charles C. Thomas, 1961. 586
pp. Many ills. Ex lib.        *(Poitras)* **$40**

**Merrett, H.S.**
- A practical treatise on the science of land and engineering surveying, levelling, estimating quantities, &c. ... 1878. 3rd edn. vi,317 pp. 41 plates, some fldg. Title amateurishly reprd. Orig cloth, new endpapers, hinges cracked. *(Whitehart)* **£18**

**Merrill, George P.**
- Contributions to a history of American state geological and natural history surveys. Wash. DC: 1920. 1st edn. Orig wraps, unopened. Smithsonian Inst Bull 109. *(Scientia)* **$45**

**Merz, John T.**
- A history of European thought in the nineteenth century. Edinburgh: 1907-14. 4 vols (3rd; 2nd; 1st; 1st edns). *(Scientia)* **$95**

**Metchnikoff, Elie**
- The prolongation of life ... edited ... London: Heinemann, 1907. 1st edn in English. 8vo. xx,343 pp. Orig cloth, a little shaken. *(Dailey)* **$75**

**Metz, A.**
- The anatomy and histoloy of the human eye. Phila: 1868. 1st edn. 184 pp. *(Fye)* **$50**

**Meyer, F.S.**
- A handbook of art smithing for the use of practical smiths, designers of ironwork, technical and art schools, architects, etc. 1896. Trans from the 2nd German edn. viii,207 pp. 214 ills. Orig cloth, spine faded. *(Whitehart)* **£18**

**Meyer, Lothar**
- Outlines of theoretical chemistry, translated ... 1892. xii,220 pp. 2 fldg tables. *(Weiner)* **£38**

**Meyer, Osker Emil**
- The kinetic theory of gases. Elementary treatise with mathematical appendices. Translated ... London: Longmans, Green, 1899. xvi,472,32 [ctlg] pp. 4 text figs. Cvrs faded. *(Pollak)* **£100**

**Meyer, William**
- An analysis of the de Generatione Animalium of William Harvey. Stanford: 1936. 167 pp. Ills. Dw. *(Oasis)* **$35**

**Meyrick, W.**
- The new family herbal: or, domestic physician. Birmingham: 1790. 8vo. xxiv,498 pp. Engvd frontis, 14 hand-cold plates. Without leaf of advts & errata. Title somewhat foxed, minor foxing elsewhere, 2 margins sl defective. Mod calf, antique style. *(Wheldon & Wesley)* **£190**

**Michell, John**
- A treatise of artificial magnets. Cambridge: printed by J. Bentham ..., 1750. 1st edn. 8vo. 81 pp. Engvd fldg plate. Title a little dust-soiled. Lea-backed mrbld bds. *(Antiq Sc)* **$375**

**Michelson, A.A.**
- Light waves and their uses. Chicago: University of Chicago Press, 1907. 2nd imp of 1st edn of 1903. [xii],166 pp. 2 cold plates, 108 text figs. *(Pollak)* **£25**
- Studies in optics. Chicago: University of Chicago Press, [1927]. 1st edn. Small 8vo. [4],176 pp. 6 plates, 1 cold. Text figs. Orig cloth. *(Antiq Sc)* **$100**

**Mickle, Wm. Julius**
- General paralysis of the insane. London: 1886. 2nd edn, enlgd & revsd. 466 pp. Cloth, needs rebinding. Ex lib. *(Gach)* **$25**

**Middleton, John**
- View of the agriculture of Middlesex; with observations on the means of its improvement ... 1798. xvii,597 pp. 2 fldg cold maps. Lib stamps on map & other leaves. *(Weiner)* **£85**

**Midon, F.**
- A course of lectures, upon several curious and important points of natural philosophy. Particularly the nature and properties of air and water ... Newcastle-upon-Tyne: I. Thompson, 1753. 8vo. [iv],12 pp. Red & black title. Orig gray wraps. *(Burmester)* **£250**

**Miles, W. Ernest**
- Rectal surgery. 1944. 2nd edn. vii,359 pp. Cold frontis. Ills. B'plate. Spine faded. *(Jenner)* **£9**

**Miles, W.J.**
- Modern practical farriery. A complete system of the veterinary art. Mackenzie, [1899]. 4to. xiii,538,96 pp. 51 plates (19 col-printed), figs in text. Contemp half-calf gilt, some surface wear. *(Deighton Bell)* **£70**
- Modern practical farriery. A complete system of all that relates to the horse ... forming a complete system of the veterinary art. London: n.d. 536,96,vii pp. Cold frontis, 38 plates, inc 12 cold by Benj Herring. Half-calf, sl worn, top of spine cracked. *(Jenner)* **£60**

**Milford, Lee**
- The hand. St. Louis: 1971. 282 pp. *(Fye)* **$30**

**Military ...**
- Military roentgenology. Washington: War Department, 1944. 447 pp. Profusely illust. *(Poitras)* **$75**

**Mill, Hugh Robert**
- The record of the Royal Geographical Society

1830 - 1930. London: R.G.S., 1930. 1st edn.
Tall 8vo. Frontis, extensively illust.
*(McDowell)* **£30**

**Mill, John Stuart**
- Examination of Sir William Hamilton's
philosophy. New York: 1877. 2 vols. 330; 345
pp. Few pages carelessly opened. Spine ends
chipped, crnrs worn, hinges sl cracked.
*(Epistemologist)* **$37.50**

**Millar, G.H.**
- A new complete and universal body or system
of natural history. London: [1785]. Folio. iv,
5-618 pp. Frontis, 85 plates of figs. Calf,
rebacked.        *(Wheldon & Wesley)* **£165**

**Millar, James**
- Practical observations on cold and warm
bathing; and descriptive notices of watering
places in Britain. Edinburgh: 1821. 1st edn.
Contemp half-calf, sl rubbed.
*(Robertshaw)* **£18**

**Millar, John**
- Observations on antimony. London: J.
Johnson & D. Wilson, 1774. 1st edn.
viii,103,[1 pub advt],[4 pub ctlg] pp. Title &
verso final leaf dust-soiled, reprd tear on title.
Early 19th c lea-backed mrbld bds.
*(Antiq Sc)* **$150**

**Miller, Charles**
- Cosmetic surgery: the correction of featural
imperfections. Phila: 1924. 1st edn. 213 pp.
Ex lib.        *(Oasis)* **$20**

**Miller, Genevieve**
- The adoption of inoculation for smallpox in
England and France. Phila: University of
Pennsylvania Press, 1957. 8vo. 355 pp. 14
ills. Dw. Sgnd by author.     *(Poitras)* **$35**

**Miller, Henry**
- Lectures on inflammation and ulceration of
the cervix uteri. [Louisville]: 1855. 71 pp.
Somewhat browned. Mod wraps. *(Oasis)* **$35**

**Miller, Hugh**
- The old red sandstone; or, new walks in an
old field ... Edinburgh: Constable, 1858. 7th
edn. xxxi,[ii drctns to binder], 33-385 pp.
Cold fldg map, 14 plates. Contemp polished
calf, a.e.g., a little rubbing.    *(Pollak)* **£25**
- The old red sandstone ... to which is
appended a series of geological papers read
before the Royal Physical Society of
Edinburgh. Boston: 1864. 403 pp.
*(Scientia)* **$15**
- The testimony of the rocks. Edinburgh: 1857.
xi,500 pp. Frontis, 152 figs in text. New
cloth.        *(Whitehart)* **£18**
- The testimony of the rocks; or, geology in its

bearings on the two theologies, natural and
revealed. Edinburgh: Constable, 1857. 1st
edn. 8vo. xii,500 pp. Frontis, 152 w'cuts in
text. Occas foxing. Publisher's blind-stamped
cloth.        *(Frew Mackenzie)* **£68**

**Miller, James**
- The principles of surgery. Edinburgh: 1844.
1st edn. 716 pp. Name torn from title, not
affecting text. Inner hinges cracked. Ex lib.
*(Fye)* **$75**
- The practice of surgery. Phila: 1853. 3rd
Amer edn. 720 pp. Num w'cuts. Full lea.
*(Fye)* **$75**

**Miller, John A.**
- The practical handbook for the working
miner and prospector and for the mining
investor. 1897. xx,234 pp. Diags.
*(Weiner)* **£18**

**Miller, Philip**
- The gardener's dictionary ... abridged from
the last folio edition. 1754. 8vo. 3 vols.
Frontis, 3 plates. Contemp calf.
*(Wheldon & Wesley)* **£130**
- The gardener's kalendar, directing what
works are necessary to be done every month in
the kitchen, fruit, and pleasure gardens ...
London: 1757. 11th edn. 8vo. xviii,352,[12]
pp. Engvd frontis. Contemp calf gilt, upper
jnt split.        *(Burmester)* **£65**

**Miller, S.A.**
- The American palaeozoic fossils: a catalogue
of the genera and species ... Cinncinnati: by
the Author, 1877. 1st edn. Lge 8vo.
xv,[1],253 pp. Orig cloth. Top of spine a little
chipped.        *(Antiq Sc)* **$70**

**Miller, S.C. & Fink, D.G.**
- Neon signs manufacture, installation,
maintenance. New York: 1935. xiii,288 pp.
Frontis, 12 tables, 103 figs in text.
*(Whitehart)* **£18**

**Millikan, Robert A.**
- The electron. Its isolation and measurement
and the determination of some of its
properties. Chicago: 1917. 1st edn. 268 pp.
Spine faded & shelfworn.    *(Scientia)* **$75**
- The electron. Its isolation and measurement
and the determination of some of its
properties. Chicago: University of Chicago
Press, 1927. 5th imp of 2nd edn. xiv,293 pp.
42 ills.        *(Pollak)* **£20**

**Millingen, J.G.**
- Curiosities of medical experience. London:
Bentley, 1839. 2nd edn.    *(Xerxes)* **$95**

**Milne, E.A.**
- The aims of mathematical physics. An

inaugural lecture delivered before the University of Oxford on 19 November 1929. Oxford: Clarendon Press, 1929. 28 pp. Orig wraps. *(Pollak)* £12

**Milner, Esther**
- Human neural and behavioral development: a relational inquiry, with implications for personality. Springfield: Charles C. Thomas, 1967. xxvi,393 pp. Dw. *(Gach)* $30

**Milstein, B.B.**
- Cardiac arrest and resuscitation. Chicago: Year Book Medical Publishers, 1963. 231 pp. Ills. Some damp-staining. *(Poitras)* $25

**Minot, Charles Sedwick**
- The problem of age, growth and death. Lectures delivered at the Lowell Institute, Boston, 1907. 523 pp. Paper cvrs. Compiled from the Popular Science Monthly.
*(Poitras)* $35

**Minow, Helmut (ed.)**
- Historical surveying instruments. List of collections in Europe ... Wiesbaden: Verlag Chmielorz ..., 1982. 4to. 468 pp. Tri-lingual text. Orig wraps. *(Zeitlin)* $50

**Miscellanea ...**
- Miscellanea curiosa ... See Halley, Edmund

**Mitchell, Sir Arthur**
- Dreaming, laughing and blushing. Edinburgh: 1905. [1],157 pp. Orig cloth, sl marked. *(Whitehart)* £20

**Mitchell, Clifford**
- A clinical study of disease of the kidneys. Chicago: 1890. xii,431,4 [pub ctlg] pp. Inner hinge starting, sl shelf wear. *(Elgen)* $45

**Mitchell, John Kearsley**
- On the cryptogamous origin of malaria and epidemic fevers. Phila: Lea & Blanchard, 1849. 8vo. vi,137 pp. *(Poitras)* $75

**Mitchell, P. Chalmers**
- Thomas Henry Huxley. A sketch of his life and work. New York: 1901. 2nd imp. 6 plates. *(Winterdown)* £20

**Mitchell, S. Weir**
- Lectures on the diseases of the nervous system, especially in women. Phila: 1885. 2nd edn. 287 pp. *(Fye)* $65

**Mitchell, S. Weir & Reichart, Edward T.**
- Researches upon the venoms of poisonous serpents. Wash, DC: 1886. Folio. ix,186 pp. 5 full-page cold litho plates. *(Elgen)* $300

**[Mitchell, William Andrew]**
- An essay on capacity and genius; to prove there is no mental superiority between the most illiterate and the most learned of mankind ... London: Simpkin & Marshall, n.d. [ca 1820]. [ii],xix, 21-537,[iii] pp. Some foxing. New paper bds, uncut, spine faded.
*(Pollak)* £45

**Mittendorf, W.F.**
- A manual on diseases of the eye and ear. New York: 1881. 1st edn. 432 pp. 10 chromo-lithos. *(Fye)* $30

**Mivart, St. George J.**
- On the genesis of species. London: 1871. 1st edn. 296 pp. *(Scientia)* $100
- On the genesis of species. New York: 1871. 1st Amer edn. 314 pp. Cvrs somewhat mottled. *(Scientia)* $60

**Modern ...**
- The modern practice of the London Hospitals ... Second edition to which is added an index of diseases and their remedies. 1766. 12mo. Sgntr on title. Contemp calf, ruled in gilt, some wear, new mor label. *(Robertshaw)* £75

**Moellenbroek, Andreas Valentine**
- Cochlearia curiosa; or the curiosities of scurvygrass ... London: William Cademan, 1676. 1st edn in English. 8vo. [14],195,[28] pp. 4 fldg engvd plates. Some light browning. Full-calf in blind, rebacked. *(Rootenberg)* $950

**Mohr, Francis & Redwood, Theophilus**
- Practical pharmacy: the arrangements, apparatus, and manipulations of the pharmaceutical shop and laboratory. 1849. 1st edn. 400 w'engvs in text. Some foxing. Orig cloth, spine soiled. *(Robertshaw)* £30

**Moissan, Henri**
- The electric furnace. London: E. Arnold, 1904. 1st edn in English. 8vo. x,[2],307,[1] pp. Text figs. Orig cloth. *(Antiq Sc)* $125

**Moissenet, H.**
- Observations on the rich parts of the lodes of Cornwall, their form, and their relations with the directions of the stratigraphic systems, translated ... London & Truro: 1877. xii,150 pp. 8 plates (4 fldg), diags, subscribers' list.
*(Weiner)* £50

**Moll, Aristides**
- Aesculapius in Latin America. Phila: 1944. 1st edn. *(Scientia)* $45
- Aesculapius in Latin America. Phila: 1944. xii,639 pp. Ills. *(Jenner)* £45

**Moller, F. Peckel**
- Cod-liver oil and chemistry. London &

Christiana: Peter Moller, 1895. 4to. cxxiii,508 pp. Frontis, map, 2 fldg tables. Some neat marginalia. Orig gilt dec cloth, rebacked. Pres copy. *(Pollak)* £60

**Molloy, Edward & Curwen, M.D. (eds.)**
- Chemistry in commerce. A comprehensive, practical and authoritative guide ... Newnes, n.d. [ca 1910]. 4 vols. Roy 8vo. 1544 pp. Profusely illust. Orig cloth. *(Pollak)* £20

**Monckton, H.W. & Herries, R.S.**
- Geology in the field: the Jubilee Volume of the Geologists' Association. 1910. 2 vols. xxiv,916 pp. 32 plates, fldg maps, ills. *(Weiner)* £40

**Monro, Alexander**
- The anatomy of the human bones, nerves and lacteal sac and duc. Edinburgh: 1763. 7th edn. vii,410 pp. Lib stamp on title, affecting text. Contemp lea, rebacked. Gilt spine. *(Whitehart)* £50
- The works of Alexander Monro, M.D. ... published by his son, Alexander Monro (Secundus). Edinburgh: ... Charles Elliott, 1781. 1st edn. 4to. [2],xxiv, 791,[1] pp. Frontis, 7 fldg plates. Some offsetting & sl browning. Mod 3/4 calf, mrbld bds. *(Elgen)* $800

**Monro, Alexander Secundus**
- Observations on the communication of the ventricles of the brain with each other; and on internal hydrocephalus ... Edinburgh: Neill, 1797. 3 works in 1. 4to. 263 pp. 24 plates (one cold). Foxing. Uncut. Bds, rebacked. *(Goodrich)* $1,950

**Monro, Donald**
- An account of the diseases which were most frequent in the British military hospitals in Germany ... To which is added ... preserving the health of soldiers ... London: A. Millar ..., 1764. 8vo. xiii,408 pp. Part of title removed, some staining. Lea. *(Poitras)* $150

**Monro, John**
- Remarks on Dr. Battie's treatise on madness. London: Clarke, 1758. [2],60 pp. New qtr calf. *(Goodrich)* $395

**Monro, P.A.G.**
- Sympathectomy. An anatomical and physiological study with clinical applications. London: 1959. 1st edn. 290 pp. Dw. *(Fye)* $20

**Monro, T.K.**
- The physician as man of letters, science and action. Glasgow: 1933. viii,212 pp. Orig cloth. *(Whitehart)* £18

**Montagu, Ashley**
- Adolescent sterility - a study in the comparative physiology of the infecundity of the adolescent organism in mammals and man. Springfield: 1946. 1st edn. 148 pp. Dw (soiled). *(Fye)* $25

**[Montagu, Basil]**
- Some enquiries into the effects of fermented liquors. By a water drinker. London: R. Hunter, 1818. 2nd edn. 8vo. [4],iii,365 pp. 7 plates & engvd tailpiece. Orig bds, uncut, cloth backstrip worn at jnts, bds stained. *(Dailey)* $90

**Montagu, M.F. Ashley (ed.)**
- Studies and essays in the history of science and learning offered in homage to George Sarton on the occasion of his sixtieth birthday 31 August 1944. New York: [1946]. 597 pp. *(Scientia)* $45

**Montagu, Lady Mary Wortley**
- The works ... including her correspondence, poems, and essays. London: for Richard Philips, 1805. 5th edn. (Together with): An additional volume to the letters of ... For Becket & de Hondt, 1797. 1st edn. Some foxing. Contemp sheep. *(Pollak)* £28

**Montaigne, Michael de**
- The essayes or morall, politike and militarie discourses of Lord Michael de Montaigne ... whereunto is now newly added an index ... London: ... for Rich. Royston, 1632 [1631]. Folio. [12],631 (mispag 161),[12] pp. 3 separate titles. 19th c full-calf. *(Rootenberg)* $500

**Montgomery, E.E.**
- Practical gynaecology. A comprehensive textbook for students and physicians. Phila: P. Blakiston's Sons, 1900. xxviii,819 pp. 527 ills. Fly-leaf missing, spine & backing loose. *(Poitras)* $35

**Montgomery, W.F.**
- An exposition of the signs and symptoms of pregnancy, the period of gestation and the signs of delivery. Phila: 1839. 1st Amer edn. 344 pp. Light foxing. Antique style cloth. *(Goodrich)* $125

**Monti, Achille**
- The fundamental data of modern pathology, history, criticisms ... London: New Sydenham Society, 1900. 1st English edn. 8vo. Pub cloth. *(McDowell)* £25
- The fundamental data of modern pathology, history, criticisms ... London: New Sydenham Society, 1900. 266 pp. Orig olive cloth, crnrs sl worn. *(Jenner)* £10

**Moon, Robert C.**
- See Laurence, John Z. & Moon, Robert C.

**Moon, Robert O.**
- Hippocrates and his successors in relation to the philosophy of their time. London: 1923. 1st edn. *(Scientia)* **$37.50**

**Moore, Col. E.C.S.**
- Sanitary engineering - a practical treatise on the collection, removal and final disposal of sewage and on the design and construction of works ... London: 1898. 8vo. viii,621 pp. 534 ills, 70 lge fldg plates. Foxing. Orig cloth, spine & crnrs bumped. *(Jenner)* **£65**

**Moore, Francis D.**
- Give and take: the development of tissue transplantation. Phila & London: W.B. Saunders Company, 1964. xii,182 pp. 19 ills. *(Poitras)* **$25**

**Moore, G.**
- The use of the body in relation to the mind. 1847. 2nd edn. viii,433 pp. Orig blind-stamped cloth, faded & worn. *(Whitehart)* **£25**

**Moore, Henry Thomas**
- The sense of pain and pleasure. New York: Moffat, Yard, 1917. 1st edn. 174 pp. Cloth a little dingy. *(Gach)* **$15**

**Moore, J.H.**
- The new practical navigator; being an epitome of navigation ... the whole exemplified in a journal kept from England to Tenerife. 1796. 1st edn. viii,309,[205] pp. Frontis, 8 plates, num figs. Contemp scribbling on endpapers. Old lea, worn, rebacked. *(Whitehart)* **£50**

**Moore, J.W.**
- Text-book of the eruptive and continued fevers. Dublin: 1892. xxv,535 pp. Double-page frontis, 6 fldg charts. Orig cloth, sl worn. Dust stained spine. *(Whitehart)* **£18**

**Moore, Norman**
- The history of the study of medicine in the British Isles. Fitzpatrick Lectures delivered 1905-06. 1908. viii,202 pp. Roughtrimmed, cvrs sl rubbed, sl wear at top of spine. *(Jenner)* **£28**

**Moorhead, John**
- Traumatic surgery. Phila: 1917. 1st edn. 760 pp. Photographic & X-ray ills. *(Fye)* **$45**

**Moran, Lord**
- On credulity. London: British Medical Association, 1952. Slim 8vo. Orig cloth. *(McDowell)* **£20**

**Morant, G.M. & Welch, B.L.**
- A bibliography of the statistical and other writings of Karl Pearson. Cambridge: 1939. 1st edn. 119 pp. *(Scientia)* **$40**

**More, L.T.**
- Isaac Newton, a biography. New York: 1934. Plate. *(Winterdown)* **£20**

**Morfit, C.**
- A practical treatise on the manufacture of soaps ... 1871. x,270 pp. 16 fldg plates (5 cold), ills, tables. *(Weiner)* **£30**

**Morfit, Campbell**
- Chemistry applied to the manufacture of soap and candles. Phila: Carey & Hart, 1847. 1st edn. 8vo. 544 pp. 170 w'cut figs. Some w'staining at beginning & end. Contemp blind-stamped cloth. *(Antiq Sc)* **$75**

**Morgan, Augustus de**
- The differential and integral calculus, containing differentiation, integration ... also elementary illustrations of ... calculus. London: Baldwin & Cradock (for S.D.U.K.), 1842. 1st edn. Thick 8vo. Pub blind-stamped cloth. *(McDowell)* **£110**

**Morgan, Conway Lloyd**
- Animal life and intelligence. Boston: 1891. 1st Amer edn. 512 pp. *(Scientia)* **$75**
- Animal sketches. London: Edward Arnold, [1891]. 1st edn. [iv],312 pp. Advts. 53 photo-engvs. Sm stamp on title. Cloth-backed pict bds, hinges cracked. *(Gach)* **$25**
- The emergence of novelty. London: Williams & Norgate, 1933. 207 pp. Pub green cloth, some scuffing & flecking. *(Gach)* **$27.50**
- Habit and instinct. London & New York: Edward Arnold, 1896. 1st edn. [viii],351,[1] pp. 32 pp advts. Pub blue cloth. *(Gach)* **$50**
- An introduction to comparative psychology. London: Walter Scott, 1894. 1st edn. xvi,320 pp. Advts. Lacking front endpaper. Lib stamps on title. *(Gach)* **$50**
- Mind at the crossways. London: Williams & Norgate, [1929]. 1st edn. [xii],275 pp. Beige cloth. Crown shelfworn. *(Gach)* **$27.50**

**Morgan, Sir Gilbert & Burstall, Francis H.**
- Inorganic chemistry. A survey of modern developments. Cambridge: Heffer, 1936. ix,462 pp. Front hinge pulled. *(Pollak)* **£10**

**Morgan, John Edward**
- University Oars. Being a critical enquiry into the after health of the men who rowed in the Oxford and Cambridge boat-race from 1829 to 1869 ... London: 1873. 1st edn. xvi,397,2[pub ctlg] pp. Pict cloth, inner hinges cracked, spine frayed. *(Elgen)* **$65**

**Morgan, Sidney**
- The preparation of plantation rubber. With a chapter on ... vulcanisation by Henry P. Stevens. London: Constable, 1928. 2nd edn. vi,357,[iii] pp. Num ills. Faded. *(Pollak)* **£15**

**Morgan, Sir T.C.**
- Sketches of the philosophy of life. London: 1819. 8vo. x,[ii],466 pp. Contemp calf, sl wear on crnrs, bumped. *(Bow Windows)* **£36**

**Morgan, Thomas H.**
- A critique of the theory of evolution. Princeton: 1916. 1st edn. 197 pp. Crnrs bumped.                        *(Scientia)* **$40**
- The development of the frog's egg: an introduction to experimental embryology. New York: 1897. 1st edn. 192 pp.
                              *(Scientia)* **$165**
- Evolution and adaptation. New York: 1903. 8vo. xiii,470 pp. 7 text figs. Cloth.
                        *(Wheldon & Wesley)* **£60**
- Evolution and adaptation. New York: 1903. 1st edn. 470 pp.       *(Scientia)* **$75**
- Evolution and adaptation. New York: 1908. 2nd printing. 470 pp.     *(Scientia)* **$50**
- Heredity and sex. The Jesup lectures 1913. New York: 1913. 1st edn. ix,282 pp. 121 figs. Orig cloth, t.e.g. Spine faded. *(Whitehart)* **£25**
- The physical basis of heredity. Phila & London: 1919. 8vo. 305 pp. 117 ills. Stamp on title & last leaf. New cloth. *(Whitehart)* **£50**
- The physical basis of heredity. [1919]. 1st edn. 305 pp. 117 ills.    *(Whitehart)* **£18**
- Regeneration. New York: 1901. 1st edn. 316 pp. Ex lib. Spine discoloured. *(Scientia)* **$75**
- The scientific basis of evolution. New York: 1932. 1st edn. 286 pp. Spine faded.
                              *(Scientia)* **$45**
- The theory of the gene. New Haven: 1926. 1st edn. 343 pp. Silliman Lectures.
                              *(Scientia)* **$85**

**Morgan, Thomas H., et al.**
- The mechanism of Mendelian heredity. New York: 1915. 1st edn. 262 pp. Spine faded.
                              *(Scientia)* **$225**
- The mechanism of Mendelian heredity. New York: 1926. Revsd edn. xiv,357 pp. 73 text figs. Cloth.    *(Wheldon & Wesley)* **£30**
- The mechanism of Mendelian heredity. New York: 1923. Revsd edn. 357 pp. *(Scientia)* **$95**

**Morgan, William**
- The homoepathic treatment of indigestion, constipation and haemorrhoids. Phila: Rademacher & Sheek, 1854. 8vo. 166 pp. Foldout plate. Dec bds.    *(Poitras)* **$40**

**Morganstern, Oskar**
- See Von Neumann, John & Morganstern, Oskar

**Morley, Muriel**
- Cleft palate and speech. Edinburgh: 1945. 1st edn. 160 pp.                *(Fye)* **$60**
- Cleft palate and speech. Edinburgh: 1954. 3rd edn. 173 pp.              *(Fye)* **$35**

**Morris, Henry**
- Surgical diseases of the kidney. London: 1885. 1st edn. 548 pp. Num w'cuts, 6 chromo-lithos.            *(Fye)* **$100**

**Morris, Sir Henry**
- Surgical diseases of the kidney and ureter, including injuries, malformations and misplacements. Chicago: 1904. 2 vols. ix,682; vii,670 pp. 2 cold plates, over 200 engvs.
                              *(Elgen)* **$110**

**Morris, Sir Malcolm**
- The story of English public health. London: 1919. 1st edn.              *(Scientia)* **$30**

**Morris, Robert T.**
- Lectures on appendicitis and notes on other subjects. New York: 1897. Revsd & enlgd. viii,173,2 [advts] pp. 67 text ills. *(Elgen)* **$40**

**Morrow, Albert**
- Diagnostic and therapeutic technic. Phila: 1915. 2nd edn. 834 pp.            *(Fye)* **$50**

**Morse, Frederick H.**
- Electro-therapy with the Morse wave generator. New York: Privately printed by the Author, 1921. 2nd edn. 4to. 59 pp. Ills.
                              *(Poitras)* **$30**

**Mortality ...**
- The mortality experience of life assurance companies, collected by the Institute of Actuaries. 1869. vii,282 pp. Mainly tables, little text. Cvrs sl bumped. Ex lib.
                              *(Jenner)* **£28**

**Mortensen, Otto**
- Jens Olsen's clock: A technical description. Copenhagen: Technological Institute, 1957. 4to. 156pp, [2]ff. 2 cold plates, 81 figs. Cloth-backed dec blue paper bds. Dw. *(Zeitlin)* **$45**
- Jens Olsen's clock: A technical description. Copenhagen: 1957. 156pp. 83 ills.
                              *(Whitehart)* **£25**

**Mortimer, W. Golden**
- Peru, history of coca "the divine plant" of the Incas. With an introductory account of the Incas ... New York: J.H. Vail, 1901. 1st edn. Thick 8vo. xxxi,576 pp. Frontis, 178 ills in the text, many full-page. Orig burgundy cloth.            *(Dailey)* **$250**

**Morton, Dudley J.**
- The human foot. Its evolution, physiology

and functional disorders. New York: Columbia University Press, 1935. xiii,[i], 244,[iv] pp. 100 ills. Dw torn. *(Pollak)* £15

**Morton, G.A.**
- See Zworykin, V.K. & Morton, G.A.

**Morton, Richard**
- Phthisiologia: or, a treatise of consumption ... London: for Sam. Smith & Benj. Walford, 1694. 1st edn in English. 8vo. [4]ff, 360 pp, [8]ff. Engvd frontis. Contemp panelled calf, rebacked. Minor spotting. *(Zeitlin)* $750

**Morton, Samuel George**
- Crania Aegyptiaca; or, observations on Egyptian ethnography, derived from anatomy, history and the monuments. Phila & London: 1844. 1st edn. Lge thin 4to. 14 litho plates, other text ills. New bds. *(Argosy)* $150
- Crania Americana; or, a comparative view of the skulls of various Aboriginal nations of North and South America. Phila: ... & London: ..., 1839. 1st edn. Folio. [4],v,296,[2], [1 errata] pp. Frontis, 78 plates, cold map. Old half-mor, jnts split. *(Dailey)* $675
- Illustrations of pulmonary consumption, its anatomical character, causes, symptoms and treatment. Phila: Key & Biddle, 1834. 1st edn. 8vo. xiii,[2],183,[2] pp. Half-title. 12 litho plates (11 hand-cold). Minimal browning. Orig full-calf, a little worn. *(Rootenberg)* $350

**Morton, Thomas**
- Engravings illustrating the surgical anatomy of the head and neck, axilla, bend of the elbow, and wrist, with descriptions. 1845. Roy 8vo. 24 pp. 8 fldg cold plates. Sl staining. Cvrs rubbed & faded. *(Jenner)* £50

**Morton, William J.**
- The X Ray; or, photography of the invisible and its value in surgery ... New York: 1896. 1st edn. Sm 8vo. 196 pp. Cold frontis, 32 half-tone photographic plates, num text ills. Orig silver pict cloth. Ex lib. *(Elgen)*

**Moschzisker, F.A. von**
- The ear, its diseases and their treatment. Phila: 1864. 319 pp. *(Fye)* $75

**Moseley, Benjamin**
- A treatise on sugar. With miscellaneous medical observations. London: John Nichols, 1800. 2nd edn, "with considerable additions". 8vo. Contemp half-russia, mrbld bds. *(McDowell)* £175
- A treatise on the lues bovilla or cow pox ... second edition with considerable additions. London: 1805. Half-title. 142 pp. Old style bds. *(Goodrich)* $95

**Moseley, Rev. H.**
- A treatise on mechanics, applied to the arts; including statics and hydrostatics. 1839. viii,306 pp. Num ills. Orig blind-stamped cloth, spine faded with small nick. Sl watermark inside both cvrs. *(Whitehart)* £18

**Moseley, H.F.**
- Shoulder lesions. Springfield: 1945. 1st edn. 181 pp. *(Fye)* $40

**Moseley, Sydney A. & Barton-Chapple, H.J.**
- Television today and tomorrow, with a foreword by John L. Baird. 1940. 5th edn. xix,179 pp. Fldg map, num plates & diags. Cloth, soiled & worn. *(Weiner)* £40

**Moseley, Sydney A. & McKay, H.**
- Television: a guide for the amateur. [1936]. 144 pp. 31 plates, diags. *(Weiner)* £25

**Motamed, Hosein**
- Color anatomy and kinesiology of the hand. Chicago: 1973. 1st edn. 4to. 145 pp. Cold ills. *(Fye)* $75
- Color anatomy and kinesiology of the hand. Published and distributed by the author. Not for sale by any publishing company. *(Poitras)* $50

**Motherby, George**
- A new medical dictionary; or, general repository of physic. Containing an explanation of the terms, and a description of ... anatomy, physiology, physic, surgery ... London: 1775. 1st edn. Folio. 23 engvd plates. Qtr calf, rebacked. *(Goodrich)* $350
- A new medical dictionary; or, general repository of physic. Containing an explanation of the terms ... London: for J. Johnson, 1775. Folio. vi,[584] pp. 25 engvd plates. Orig calf, some wear. *(Pollak)* £105

**Mott, Nevil & Massey, H.S.W.**
- The theory of atomic collisions. Oxford: 1933. 1st edn. 283 pp. *(Scientia)* $75

**Motte, Andrew**
- A treatise of the mechanical powers, wherein the laws of motion, and the properties of those powers are explained ... London: for Benj. Motte, 1727. 1st edn. 8vo. [viii],222,[1 errata],[1 advt]. 3 engvd plates. Contemp panelled calf, worn, rebacked. *(Pickering)* $450

**Motz, L.**
- See Boorse, H. & Motz, L.

**Moullin, C.W. Mansell**
- Surgery. Phila: 1893. 2nd Amer edn. 1238 pp. Cold litho frontis, over 600 ills. Full lea.

*(Fye)* **$50**

**Mountaine, William**
- A description of the lines drawn on Gunter's scale, as improved by Mr. John Robertson ... with their use and application ...London: ... Nairne & Blunt, 1788. 1st edn, re-iss prob with cancel title. 8vo. xi,88 pp. 4 fldg engvd plates. Contemp blue wraps. *(Antiq Sc)* **$350**

**Moxon, Joseph**
- A tutor to astronomie and geographie, or an easie and speedy way to know the use of both the globes, celestial and terrestrial ... London: Moxon, 1659. 1st edn. 4to. xiv,240,40 pp. Engvd title, 12 engvs in the text. Stained, soiled. Contemp vell bds. *(Pickering)* **$1,850**
- A tutor to astronomy and geography, or an easie and speedy way to know the use of both the globes, celestial and terrestrial in six books ... London: for Joseph Moxon, 1686. 4th edn. 4to. [4],271,[9] pp. Frontis, many text w'cuts. Half-calf. *(Rootenberg)* **$300**

**Moynihan, B.G.A.**
- Abdominal operations. Phila: 1905. 1st Amer edn. 694 pp. *(Fye)* **$100**
- Gall-stones and their surgical treatment. Phila: 1905. 2nd edn. 458 pp. Inner hinges cracked, shaken. *(Fye)* **$30**
- Gall-stones and their surgical treatment. Phila: 1905. 2nd, enlgd, edn. 458 pp. Num ills, some in color. *(Oasis)* **$35**

**Mudie, Robert**
- Man, in his physical structure and adaptations. Boston: 1838. 295 pp. Rubbed & sl spotted. *(Epistemologist)* **$37.50**

**Muirhead, James Patrick**
- Historical eloge of James Watt by M. Araga ... translated with additional notes by Muirhead. London: John Murray & Edinburgh: William Blackwood, 1839. 1st edn. 4to. x,261 pp. Engvd port frontis, foxed. Orig blind-stamped black cloth, upper jnt split at hd. *(Pickering)* **$300**
- The origin and progress of the mechanical inventions of James Watt, illustrated by his correspondence with his friends ... London: John Murray, 1854. 1st edn. 3 vols. 8vo. Port frontis vols I & II, 24 fldg engvd plates. Contemp half-calf. *(McDowell)* **£220**

**Mulhall, Michael G.**
- The dictionary of statistics. 1892. Cr 8vo. 10 diags. Unopened. Upper hinge tender. *(Edwards)* **£25**

**Mulins, John & Sons**
- The divining rod. Its history, truthfulness & practical utility. Bath: 1914. Sm 8vo. Advts at rear. *(Edwards)* **£12.50**

**Muller, Fritz**
- Facts and arguments for Darwin. London: John Murray, 1869. 1st English edn. 8vo. Ills in text. Some little spotting, damp affecting front endpapers. Contemp half red polished calf, crack in rear bd. *(McDowell)* **£55**

**Muller, Hermann**
- The fertilisation of flowers, translated and edited by D'Arcy W. Thompson. With a preface by Charles Darwin. 1883. xiii,669 pp. Ills. Prize calf gilt, worn, rebacked, old spine laid on. *(Weiner)* **£40**
- The fertilisation of flowers. Translated by D'Arcy W. Thompson. With a preface by Charles Darwin. London: 1883. 1st edn in English. 669 pp. *(Scientia)* **$125**

**Muller, Hermann J.**
- Out of the night: a biologist's view of the future. London: 1936. Left Book Club edn. 160 pp. Orig wraps. *(Scientia)* **$40**

**Muller, John**
- Elements of mathematics. Containing geometry ... mechanics ... gunnery ... a theory of pumps ... For the use of the Royal Academy of Artillery at Woolwich. J. Millan, 1765. 28 engvd plates. Occas foxing. Contemp calf gilt, rebacked. *(Edwards)* **£75**

**Mummery, J.H.**
- The microscopic anatomy of the teeth. Oxford: 1919. 1st edn. viii,382 pp. 243 figs in text. New cloth. *(Whitehart)* **£25**

**Muncie, Wendell**
- Psychobiology and psychiatry: a textbook of normal and abnormal human behavior. St. Louis: C.V. Mosby, 1939. 1st edn. 620 pp. *(Gach)* **$30**

**Munde, Paul**
- A sketch of the management of pregnancy, parturition and the puerperal state, normal and abnormal. Detroit: 1887. 1st edn. 110 pp. *(Fye)* **$40**

**Murchison, C.**
- Functional derangements of the liver. 1874. xvi,182 pp. 6 figs in text. Orig cloth. The Croonian Lectures delivered at the Royal College of Physicians, March 1874. *(Whitehart)* **£35**

**Murchison, Carl**
- Social psychology: the psychology of political domination. Worcester, Mass: Clark University Press, 1929. 1st edn. x,210 pp. Red buckram. *(Gach)* **$40**

**Murchison, Carl (ed.)**
- Foundations of experimental psychology.

1930. 907 pp. Shelfworn. *(Epistemologist)* **$35**
- Handbook of child psychology. 1931. 710 pp. Rubbed, spine ends frayed. R. Leeper's copy with pen & pencil annotations.
*(Epistemologist)* **$37.50**
- Handbook of general experimental psychology. 1934. 1125 pp. Spine darkened & dull. *(Epistemologist)* **$37.50**
- A handbook of social psychology. 1935. 1195 pp. *(Epistemologist)* **$40**
- Psychologies of 1930. 1930. 497 pp. Recased. *(Epistemologist)* **$35**
- Psychologies of 1930. Worcester, Clark University Press, 1930. 1st edn. 497 pp. Some pencil underlining. *(Oasis)* **$30**

**Murchison, Roderick I.**
- Siluria. The history of the oldest known rocks containing organic remains. London: J. Murray, 1854. 1st edn. 8vo. xv,[1], 523,[1] pp. Hand-cold fldg engvd map, fldg litho map, 37 litho plates of fossils by Sowerby. Orig dec cloth, recased. *(Antiq Sc)* **$200**
- Siluria. The history of the oldest known rocks containing organic remains. 1854. 1st edn. 8vo. xv,[1],523 pp. Fldg cold geolog map, another map, 37 plates, text figs. A little minor foxing. Orig cloth, trifle used, spine faded. *(Wheldon & Wesley)* **£90**
- Siluria. The history of the oldest fossiliferous rocks and their foundations. 1859. xx,592 pp. 8vo. Fldg cold geolog map, cold frontis, table, sketch map, 41 plates, text figs. Sl foxing. Half-calf, trifle used, spine faded. *(Wheldon & Wesley)* **£65**

**Murphy, John B.**
- The surgical clinics of John B. Murphy, M.D. at Mercy Hospital, Chicago. Phila: W.B. Saunders, 1912-16. 1st edn. 30 vols (6 vols per year for 5 years). Royal 8vo. Lib stamp in gilt on spines. A complete set. *(McDowell)* **£160**

**Murray, Henry A.**
- Explorations in personality. New York: 1938. 761 pp. Cvr sl faded. Robert Challman's copy, sgnd. *(Epistemologist)* **$30**

**Murray, John**
- A treatise on pulmonary consumption, its prevention and remedy. London: 1830. 1st edn. 156 pp. Orig cloth, extremities worn. *(Oasis)* **$100**

**Murray, Sir John & Hjort, Dr. Johan**
- The depths of the ocean. A general account of the modern science of oceanography. London: Macmillan, 1912. xx,821,[iii] pp. 2 ports, 4 maps, 9 plates (7 cold), num text ills. Orig cloth gilt, recased. Pres copy to Walter E. Archer. *(Pollak)* **£50**
**Murray, Thomas Edward**

- Applied engineering. New York: 1928. 1st edn. ix,183 pp. Frontis, profusely illust. *(Elgen)* **$35**

**Murray, William**
- Rough notes on remedies. London & Phila: 1901. 4th edn. 8vo. xi,176 pp. Fold-out map. 24 pp pub ctlg. *(Poitras)* **$35**

**Muspratt, James Sheridan**
- Lectures on chemistry, theoretical, practical and analytical, as applied and relating to the arts and manufactures. 1860. 2 vols, bound in 3. Lge 8vo. 836,9; 1186,10. Extra engvd titles, 29 engvd ports, num w'cuts. Half-calf gilt, mrbld edges. *(Weiner)* **£75**

**Muter, Robert**
- Practical observations on the lateral operation of lithotomy; and on various improved and new modes of performing this operation ... with remarks on the recto vesical operation. New York: 1824. 1st Amer edn. 8vo. 107 pp, 2 plates. Orig bds detchd. *(M&S)* **$47.50**

**Muys, John**
- A rational practice of chyrurgery: or chyrurgical observations resolved according to the solid fundamentals of true philosophy. London: F. Collins, 1686. [8],248 pp. Engvd frontis. Light foxing. New calf. *(Goodrich)* **$795**

**My ...**
- My station and its duties: a narrative for girls going to service, by the author of 'The Last Day of the Week'. 1855. Frontis, 5 plates. Pebble-grained cloth, sl grubby & marked, hinge cracked. *(Quinto Charing Cross)* **£10**

**Myers, Charles Samuel**
- Shell shock in France 1914-18, based on a war diary. Cambridge: At the University Press, 1940. 1st edn. 12mo. xii,146 pp. Grey cloth. *(Gach)* **$20**

**Myers, Frederic W.**
- Human personality and its survival of bodily death. New York: 1904. 2 vols. 700; 660 pp. *(Epistemologist)* **$45**

**Myers, Grace W.**
- History of the Massachusetts General Hospital June 1872 to December 1900. 1929. 1st edn. *(Scientia)* **$37.50**

**Myerson, Abraham**
- The nervous housewife. Boston: Little, Brown, 1920. 1st edn. 273 pp. Worn dw. *(Gach)* **$25**
- The psychology of mental disorders. New York: Macmillan, 1927. 1st edn. x,135 pp.

Worn dw.                    *(Gach)* **$20**

**Myrtle, A.S. & Myrtle, J.A.**
- Practical observations on the Harrogate mineral waters, and chronic diseases with cases. Harrogate: 1893. 4th edn. [1],242 pp. Orig blind-stamped cloth.   *(Whitehart)* **£18**

**Nagel. Joseph Darwin**
- Nervous and mental diseases. A manual for students and practitioners, with an appendix on insomnia. Phila & New York: Lea & Febiger, 1914. 2nd edn. 293 pp. 50 engvs, 1 cold plate. The Medical Epitome Series.
                              *(Poitras)* **$22.50**

**Nakaya, Ukichiro**
- Snow crystals: natural and artificial. Cambridge: 1954. 1st edn. 510 pp. 188 plates.
                                    *(Oasis)* **$50**

**Nancrede, Charles**
- Lectures upon the principles of surgery. Phila: 1905. 2nd edn. 407 pp.    *(Fye)* **$25**

**Nasmyth, J. & Carpenter, J.**
- The moon considered as a planet, a world, and a satellite. 1874. 1st edn. Lge 4to. xvi,189 pp. Frontis, 23 plates. Advt at end dated Dec, 1873. Inner front hinge & some inner margins reprd with sellotape. Orig pict cloth, worn & marked. Lacks rear e.p.    *(Whitehart)* **£90**

**Naunton, W.J.S.**
- Synthetic rubber. London: Macmillan, 1937. xvi,162 pp. Frontis, 12 plates, 20 figs.
                                   *(Pollak)* **£12**

**Naunyn, B.**
- A treatise on cholelithiasis. London: 1896. 1st English translation. 197 pp. One-half inch torn from top of spine.    *(Fye)* **$60**
- A treatise on cholelithiasis. London: New Sydenham Society, 1896. 1st English edn. 8vo. Pub blind-stamped cloth..
                                *(McDowell)* **£45**

**Neal, E. Virgil (ed.)**
- Hypnotism and hypnotic suggestion; a scientific treatise of the use and possibilities ... Rochester: New York State Publishing Co., 1900. 259 pp. Tiny chip on spine.
                                  *(Xerxes)* **$45**

**Needham, Joseph**
- Clerks and craftsmen in China and the West. Lectures and addresses on the history of science and technology. Cambridge: 1970. 40 plates, 99 figs.    *(Winterdown)* **£40**
- A history of embryology. Cambridge: 1934. 1st edn. xviii,274 pp. Frontis, 15 plates, text ills.    *(Elgen)* **$85**

**Needham, Joseph, et al.**
- Heavenly clockwork: The great astronomical clocks of medieval China - a missing link in horological history. Cambridge: University Press ..., 1960. 1st edn. 8vo. xv,253 pp. Frontis, 21 plates, other ills. Orig cloth. Dw.
                                   *(Zeitlin)* **$90**

**Neil, E. Virgil & Clark, C.S. (eds.)**
- Hypnotism and hypnotic suggestion. A scientific treatise on the uses and possibilities ... Rochester, N.Y. [1906]. 1st edn. xiii,259 pp.    *(Diamond)* **$45**

**Neil, John**
- Outlines of the arteries with short descriptions ... Phila: 1852. 2nd edn. 28 pp. 7 hand-cold plates. Foxing. Cloth, spine defective.    *(Goodrich)* **$75**

**Neilson, Robert M.**
- The steam turbine. With numerous illustrations. 1902.    *(Edwards)* **£15**

**Neisser, Albert**
- On modern syphilotherapy with particular reference to Salvarsan. Translated ... Balt: 1946. Roy 8vo. iv,42 pp. Port frontis. Biog & bibliog. Bds sl soiled.    *(Jenner)* **£10**

**Neligan, J. Moore**
- Medicines, their uses and modes of administration. Edinburgh: 1851. 3rd edn. xxvii,555 pp. Orig purple cloth, spine & bds faded, crnrs bumped.    *(Jenner)* **£22**
- Medicines, their uses and modes of administration. Edited by R. MacNamara. Edinburgh: 1864. 6th edn. xxx,758 pp. Cvrs rubbed.    *(Jenner)* **£20**

**Nernst, Walther**
- The new heat theorem, its foundations in theory and experiment. Translated by G. Barr. New York: 1926. 2nd English edn (from 2nd German edn). 281 pp. Shelfworn.
                                 *(Scientia)* **$50**
- Theoretical chemistry from the standpoint of Avogadro's rule and thermodynamics. Translated ... London: Macmillan, 1895. 1st English edn. xxv,697.[iii] pp. 26 figs. Name cut from tip of half-title. Orig cloth, front jnt pulled.    *(Pollak)* **£100**

**Nesbit, A.**
- A complete treatise on practical land surveying, in seven parts. Designed chiefly for the use of schools and private students ... 1820. 2nd edn, enlgd. 160 w'cuts, 12 engvd plates. Mottled calf, spine splitting.
                               *(Edwards)* **£37.50**

**Neubauer, C. & Vogel, J.**
- A guide to the qualitative and quantitative

analysis of the urine ... London: New
Sydenham Society, 1863. 4th edn in English.
8vo. 4 plates, 2 with colour. Pub cloth, top of
spine torn.                        *(McDowell)* **£20**
- A guide to the qualitative and quantitative
analysis of the urine. Translated ... and
revised ... New York: 1879. 1st Amer edn.
xxiv,551 pp. 4 plates, 3 in colour, ills. Cvrs
worn & faded, hinges cracked.  *(Jenner)* **£25**

**Neumann, Caspar**
- The chemical works of Caspar Neumann ...
Abridged ... by William Lewis. London: for
W. Johnston ..., 1759. 1st edn in English. 4to.
[8]ff,586 pp,[19]ff. Contemp calf, hinges
split, spine chipped, rubbed.  *(Zeitlin)* **$450**

**Neumann, John, von & Morganstern,
Oskar**
- Theory of games and economic behavior.
Princeton: Princeton University Press, 1944.
1st edn. 8vo. xviii,625 pp. Errata sheet. Orig
cloth.                           *(Antiq Sc)* **$285**

**New ...**
- The new dispensatory ... See Lewis, William
- The new family physician, and guide to
health and long life; with a variety of valuable
tables on medical statistics ... London:
Thomas Allman, n.d. [ca 1830]. 216 pp.
Frontis port. Occas marginal mark & pencil
line. New paper cvrs.             *(Pollak)* **£25**

**New, Gordon & Erich, John**
- The use of pedicle flaps of skin in plastic
surgery of the head and neck. Springfield:
1950. 1st edn. Ills. Orig pebbled cloth.
                                   *(Oasis)* **$40**
- The use of pedicle flaps of skin in plastic
surgery of the head and feet. Springfield:
1950. 1st edn.                       *(Fye)* **$45**

**Newlands, B.E.R.**
- See Lock, C.G. Warnford & Newlands,
B.E.R.

**Newlands, John A.R.**
- On the discovery of the periodic law, and on
relations among the atomic weights. London:
E. & F.N. Spon, 1884. 1st edn. 12mo.
viii,39,16 [pub ctlg] pp. 2 fldg tables. Orig
cloth.                           *(Antiq Sc)* **$175**
- On the discovery of the periodic law, and on
relations among the atomic weights. London:
E. & F.N. Spon, 1884. 1st edn. 8vo. viii,39
pp. 16 pp pub ctlg. 2 fldg tables. Orig cloth.
                               *(Rootenberg)* **$250**
- On the discovery of the periodic law, and on
relations among the atomic weights. London:
E. & F.N. Spon, 1884. 1st edn. 8vo.
viii,39,[1] pp. 16 pp advts. 2 fldg tables. Orig
cloth. Inscribed by the author.
                                 *(Pickering)* **$250**

**Newman, Charles**
- The evolution of medical education in the
nineteenth century. London: 1957. 1st edn.
Dw.                              *(Scientia)* **$55**

**Newman, Ehlers & Impey**
- Prize essays on leprosy. London: New
Sydenham Society, 1895. 1st edn. 8vo. Lge
fldg map. Pub cloth.            *(McDowell)* **£30**

**Newman, Sir George**
- The building of a nation's health. London:
1939. 1st edn. Dw.               *(Scientia)* **$65**
- The rise of preventive medicine. London:
1932. 1st edn.                   *(Scientia)* **$65**
- The rise of preventive medicine. London:
Oxford University Press, 1932. 1st edn. 8vo.
Pub olive cloth.                *(McDowell)* **£35**

**Newman, W.A.C.**
- See Rose, Sir Thomas Kirke & Newman,
W.A.C.

**Newsholme, Arthur**
- Epidemic diptheria. A research on the origin
and spread of the disease from an
international standpoint. Swan
Sonnenschein, 1898. iv, 196 pp. 60 text figs.
Stamp neatly erased from title.  *(Pollak)* **£25**
- Epidemic diptheria. A research on the disease
from an international standpoint. 1900. 2nd
edn. iv,196 pp. Lib stamp on title, last few
leaves soiled. Cvrs sl worn, lib label on spine.
                                 *(Jenner)* **£18**

**Newton, Isaac**
- The correspondence of Isaac Newton ...
Cambridge: ... at the University Press,
1959-60-61-67. 4 vols. 4to. Frontis, ports, text
ills. Orig cloth. Dws.         *(Rootenberg)* **$225**
- Mathematical elements of natural philosophy
confirmed by experiments ... Translated ...
1720. 1st English edn. xxi,259,[2] pp. 33 fldg
plates (2 loose). Title margin reprd. Contemp
lea, new endpapers. Spine & edges sl worn.
                               *(Whitehart)* **£180**
- The mathematical principles of natural
philosophy ... the laws of the moon's motion
... London: Benjamin Notte, 1729. 1st edn in
English. 2 vols. 8vo. [38],320; [2],393,[13];
viii,71,[1] pp. 3 frontis, 47 fldg plates, 2
tables. Contemp calf. Large paper.
                              *(Rootenberg)* **$2,750**
- Opticks: or, a treatise of the reflexions,
refractions, inflexions and colours of light.
Also two treatises ... London: S. Smith & B.
Walford. 1704. 1st edn. 144; 211,[1 errata]
pp. 19 fldg plates. Contemp panelled calf,
rebacked.                       *(Scientia)* **$5,500**
- Opticks: or, a treatise of the reflexions,
refractions, inflexions and colours of light.
Also two treatises ... London: S. Smith & B.
Walford. 1704. 1st edn, 1st iss. Red & black

title. 4to. 19 fldg plates. Contemp panelled calf, rebacked.        *(Pickering)* **$9,500**
- Opticks: or, a treatise of the reflexions, refractions, inflexions and colours of light ... London: for W. & J. Innys, 1718. 2nd edn, 2nd iss. 8vo. viii,382,[2 advts]. 12 fldg engvd plates. Paper sl discoloured. Contemp panelled calf, rebacked.        *(Pickering)* **$1,500**
- Opticks: or, a treatise of the reflections, refractions, inflections and colours of light. London: for W. & J. Innys, 1718. 2nd edn, 2nd issue, with addtns. 8vo. 12 fldg engvd plates, advt leaf. Contemp panelled calf, red label.        *(McDowell)* **£850**
- Opticks: or, a treatise of the reflections, refractions, inflections and colours of light. London: 1721. 3rd edn, crrctd. 382 pp. 12 fldg plates. Extensive 18th c ink notations. Early lea, rebacked.        *(Scientia)* **$375**
- Sir Isaac Newton's philosophy explained ... See Carter, Elizabeth
- Universal arithmetick: or, a treatise of arithmetical composition ... translated ... revised and corrected ... London: for Senex & Innys, 1728. 2nd edn. [iv],iii,[i advt], 271,[i advt] pp. 8 fldg plates. Occas foxing. Orig calf, rebacked, crnrs reprd.        *(Pollak)* **£250**

**Newton, John**
- Trigonometria Britannica: or, the doctrine of triangles ... London: R. & W. Leybourn, 1658. 1st edn. Folio. [4]ff,96 pp,[94]ff, [46]ff, [14 fldg sheet with errata & diag]. Title browned & trimmed, some light browning. Old sprinkled calf, rebacked.        *(Zeitlin)* **$775**

**Nichol, J.P.**
- The planet Neptune: an exposition and history. Edinburgh, 1848. vi,133 pp. 6 plates. Orig cloth, rebacked, new endpapers.        *(Whitehart)* **£35**
- Views of the architecture of the heavens in a series of letters to a lady. Edinburgh: 1837. 1st edn. viii,226 pp. 22 plates. 3/4 mor, badly rubbed & spine defective.        *(Whitehart)* **£35**
- Views of the architecture of the heavens ... Edinburgh: 1839. 3rd edn. xii,[1],219 pp. 23 plates. Orig watered silk, spine defective, 4 pp loose.        *(Whitehart)* **£25**
- Views of the architecture of the heavens in a series of letters to a lady. New York: 1840. 12mo. 2 fldg cold plates, 23 lithos. Full calf.        *(Argosy)* **$100**

**Nichol, John**
- See Letsome, Sampson & Nichol, John

**Nichols, John**
- Biographical and literary anecdotes of William Bowyer, printer, F.S.A., and of many of his learned friends. London: Nichols, 1782. 1st edn. viii,666. Copper engvd port. Sl sporadic foxing. Full contemp calf gilt, edges

rouged, sl wear, jnts tender.        *(Deighton Bell)* **£155**

**Nicholson, George**
- On the primeval diet of man; arguments in favour of vegetable food; on man's conduct to animals. Poughnill, near Ludlow: the Author, 1801. 1st edn. 12mo. ii,221,[3] pp. Engvd title, some foxing of first leaves, tear on p 3. Mod bds.        *(Dailey)* **$135**

**Nicholson, William**
- A dictionary of chemistry, exhibiting the present state of the theory and practice of that science ... 1795. 1st edn. 2 vols. 4 plates. Contemp calf, gilt edged. Sl rubbed.        *(Edwards)* **£250**
- The first principles of chemistry. London: for G.G.J. & J. Robinson, 1790. 1st edn. 8vo. xxviii,532,[5 index] pp. Fldg engvd plate. Sm wormhole in margin of first few leaves, title a little dust soiled. Contemp calf, a little rubbed.        *(Pickering)* **$420**
- The first principles of chemistry. London: Robinson, 1796. 3rd edn. 8vo. xxi,[3],564,[4] pp. Fldg engvd plate. Light, uniform browning. Contemp tree calf. *(Antiq Sc)* **$100**
- The first principles of chemistry. London: Robinson, 1796. 3rd edn, revsd by author. xxi,[iii],564,[iv index] pp. Fldg plate. Contemp tree calf, a little chafed. *(Pollak)* **£55**
- An introduction to natural philosophy. London: for J. Johnson, 1782. 1st edn. 2 vols. 8vo. xx,383,[1 blank],[12 index]; xi,[i blank],441,[14 index]. 25 fldg engvd plates. Contemp speckled half-calf, hds of spines chipped.        *(Pickering)* **$850**

**Nicolson, Marjorie H.**
- Pepys' diary and the new science. Charlottesville VA: 1965. 1st edn. 198 pp. Dw.        *(Scientia)* **$25**
- Voyages to the moon. New York: 1948. 1st edn. 297 pp. Dw, torn.        *(Scientia)* **$30**

**Niekurk, Willem A. van**
- True hermaphroditism. Clinical, morphologic and cytogenetic aspects. Harper & Row: 1974. xiii,200 pp. Ills. *(Jenner)* **£12**

**Nightingale, Florence**
- Army sanitary administration and its reform under the late Lord Herberts "read at the London meeting of the Congres de Bienfaisance, June 1862". London: McCorquodale, n.d. 11 pp. Orig blue wraps.        *(Xerxes)* **$85**
- Life or death in India with an appendix on life or death by irrigation. London: Spottiswoode & Co., 1874. 1st edn. 8vo. 63 pp. Orig blue wrapper (front only) bound into half-calf. Pres copy to Lord Robert C. Napier.        *(Rootenberg)* **$475**

- Notes on nursing; What it is and what it isn't. London: 1860. 1st edn, 3rd issue. 79 pp. Orig black pebbled cloth. *(Scientia)* **$200**
- Notes on nursing; What it is and what it isn't. London: 1860. 1st edn, 3rd issue, with advts & "Right of Translation Reserved" on title. 79 pp. Side-notes, owners' inscriptions on title. Orig pebbled cloth, sl worn. *(Jenner)* **£75**
- Notes on nursing; What it is and what it isn't. New York: 1860. 1st Amer edn. Lacks rear e.p. *(Scientia)* **$95**

**Nitchie, Edward**
- Lip reading principles and practice: a handbook for teachers and for self instruction. New York: Stokes, 1912. 2nd edn. Sm 8vo. 324 pp. *(Xerxes)* **$30**

**Noad, Henry M.**
- Lectures on chemistry; including its applications in the arts; and the analysis of organic and inorganic compounds. 1843. 505 pp. Fldg table, w'cuts. Orig dec cloth, worn & soiled. *(Weiner)* **£30**

**Noble, Charles**
- See Kelly, Howard & Noble, Charles

**Noble, Mark**
- Two dissertations upon the Mint and coins of the Episcopal-Palatines of Durham ... Birmingham: for the Author, 1780. 1st edn. 4to. vi,91 pp. 21 engvd ills in text. Prelims foxed. Recent qtr calf, red mor label. *(Deighton Bell)* **£90**

**Noguchi, Hideyo**
- Serum diagnosis of syphilis and luetin reaction, together with the butyric acid test for syphilis. Phila: [1912]. 3rd edn. 306 pp. 6 cold plates. Sl wear to spine edges. *(Elgen)* **$85**
- Serum diagnosis of syphilis. Phila: 1910. 1st edn. 173 pp. Ills. Orig cloth, extremities sl worn. *(Oasis)* **$75**

**Nohl, Johannes**
- The Black Death. A chronicle of the plague. Translated ... 1926. 284 pp. Frontis, sev plates & ills. Spotting on edges. Cvrs sl faded. Ex lib. *(Jenner)* **£15**

**Norie, J.W.**
- A new and complete epitome of practical navigation, containing all necessary instruction for keeping a ship's reckoning at sea ... including a journal of a voyage from London to Madeira ... 1831. 10th edn. Orig lea, rebacked. Cloth sl worn. *(Whitehart)* **£40**

**Norman, John C.**
- Cardiac surgery. New York: Appleton ...,

1967. 703 pp. 1st page of table of contents reprd. Ex lib. *(Poitras)* **$50**

**Norman, Robert & Borough, William**
- The new attractive. Containing a short discourse of the magnes or loadstone ... corrected and amended by M.W.B. London: E. Allde for Hew Astley, 1592. 3rd edn. Sm 4to. Two parts with separate titles. 48,30ff. Minor w'staining. 18th c diced half-russia. *(Pickering)* **$12,500**

**Norris, George**
- Contributions to practical surgery. Phila: 1873. 1st edn. 318 pp. *(Fye)* **$100**

**North, Elisha**
- A treatise on a malignant epidemic commonly called spotted fever. New York: T. & J. Swords, 1811. 1st edn. 8vo. xi,[1],249, [1 errata] pp. Fldg table. Title worn, without loss, & soiled. Some foxing. Mod lea. *(Antiq Sc)* **$200**

**Northcott, W.H.**
- A treatise on lathes and turning, simple, mechanical and ornamental. 1868. xiv,298 pp. Plates, few fldg, many ills. Sl worn. *(Weiner)* **£50**

**Nott, John**
- On the Hotwell Waters near Bristol. Bristol: 1793. 1st edn. 94 pp. Uncut. Mod cloth. *(Robertshaw)* **£38**

**Nott, Josiah Clark & Gliddon, Geo. R.**
- Types of mankind: or, ethnological researches, based upon the ancient monuments .... London: Trubner, 1854. 2nd edn. 4to. lxxvi,738 pp. 6 fldg litho plates, num ills & diags in text. Pub embossed cloth, hd of spine chipped, backstrip sunned. *(Dailey)* **$125**

**Numbers, Ronald (ed.)**
- The education of American physicians. Los Angeles: 1980. 1st edn. 345 pp. Dw. *(Fye)* **$30**

**Nuttall, George H.F.**
- Blood immunity and blood relationship: a demonstration of certain blood-relationships amongst animals by means of the precipitation test for blood. Cambridge: 1904. xii,444 pp. Plate, many tables. Orig cloth, sunned in places. Ex lib. *(Jenner)* **£48**

**O'Doherty, D.S.**
- See Ramey, E.R. & O'Doherty, D.S.

**O'Gorman, Mervyn**
- Problems relating to aircraft. London: Inc Inst of Automobile Engineers, 1911. 44 pp. 4

plates, 18 figs. Half-mor, t.e.g. *(Pollak)* **£25**

**O'Malley, Austin**
- The ethics of medical homicide and mutilation. New York: [1919]. 1st edn. vii,273 pp. Spine ends sl frayed. *(Elgen)* **$35**

**O'Malley, C.D. (ed.)**
- The history of medical education. Berkeley: 1970. 1st edn. 548 pp. Dw.        *(Fye)* **$25**

**O'Shea, M.V.**
- Tobacco and mental efficiency. New York: Macmillan, 1923. 12mo. xxx,258 pp. Leta Hollingworth's copy with occas annotation.
*(Gach)* **$17.50**

**Oatman, Edward**
- Diagnostics of the fundus oculi. Troy: 1913. 1st edn. 3 vols (1 vol text, 2 portfolios containing 79 stereoscopic cards). *(Fye)* **$150**

**Observations ...**
- Observations on the report of the Select Committee ... relative to the timber trade ... See Cock, Simon

**Ochsner, Albert & Percy, Nelson**
- A new clinical surgery. Chicago: 1911. 3rd edn. 924 pp.        *(Fye)* **$75**

**Ochsner, Albert & Sturm, Meyer**
- The organisation, construction and management of hospitals. Chicago: 1907. 1st edn. 4to. 600 pp. Num ills & plans.
*(Oasis)* **$75**

**Oesterlen, F.**
- Medical logic. Translated and edited by G. Whitley. Sydenham Society, 1855. xii,437 pp. B'plates. Cvrs bumped & worn, hinges sl cracked.        *(Jenner)* **£25**

**Oesterreich, Traugott Konstantin**
- Possession: demoniacal and other among primitive races ... authorised translation ... London: Kegan Paul, Trench, Trubner, 1930. 1st edn in English. [xii],400,[2] pp. Black buckram, edges bumped. *(Gach)* **$50**

**Ogle, John W.**
- The Harveian Oration, 1880, with additional notes and an appendix. 1881. 209 pp. Frontis. Cvrs stained.        *(Jenner)* **£20**

**Oliver, Henry K.**
- An elementary treatise on the construction and use of the mathematical instruments usually put into portable cases. Boston: 1830. 68 pp, 6 fldg plates, errata leaf. Orig bds, cloth back, paper label.        *(M&S)* **$50**

**Oliver, Thomas**
- Diseases of occupation from the legislative, social and medical points of view. London: [1908]. 1st edn. xix,427,[32 pub ctlg] pp. 2 plates. Ex lib.        *(Elgen)* **$85**

**Oliver, William**
- A practical dissertation on bath-waters. To which is added, a relation of an extraordinary sleepy person at Tinsbury near Bath ... London: for H. Hammond, 1719. 2 parts in 1. 12mo. viii,168,28 pp, advt leaf. Some browning of text. Mod sheep-backed bds.
*(Deighton Bell)* **£95**

**Olmstead, Denison**
- The mechanism of the heavens or familiar illustrations of anatomy. London: 1850. 1st edn in English. 399 pp. Engvd frontis, 23 blue & white plates. Orig cloth. *(Oasis)* **$100**
- The mechanism of the heavens. 1850. xii,404 pp. Frontis, pict title, 15 plates, 77 figs in text. New cloth.        *(Whitehart)* **£30**

**Olmsted, J.M.D.**
- Claude Bernard, Physiologist. London: 1939. 318 pp. 7 plates, 1 cold. Orig black cloth.
*(Jenner)* **£15**

**Onania ...**
- Onania: or, the heinous sin of self-pollution, and all its frightful consequences (in both sexes) considered. 1756. 18th edn. Contemp calf, worn.        *(Robertshaw)* **£135**

**Ontyd, Conrad George**
- A treatise on mortal diseases, containing a particular view of the different ways in which they lead to death. London: 1798. Sole English edn. xix,643 pp. Foxing on early pages. Rebnd in black cloth, red lea label.
*(Jenner)* **£70**

**Opium ...**
- Opium eating. An autobiographical sketch. By an habituate. Phila: Claxton, Remsen & Haffelfinger, 1876. 1st edn. 12mo. 150 pp. Orig green cloth, cvrs stamped in blind. Wear to spinal extremities.        *(Dailey)* **$200**
- The opium habit ... See Ludlow, Fitz Hugh

**Oppenheim, H.**
- Diseases of the nervous system. Phila: 1904. 2nd edn, enlgd. Num ills.        *(Oasis)* **$40**

**Oppenheimer, J. Robert**
- The flying trapeze. Three crises for physicists. London: 1964: 1st edn. Dw.
*(Antiq Sc)* **$17.50**

**[Oppenheimer, J. Robert]**
- In the matter of J. Robert Oppenheimer - transcript of hearing before personnel

security board. Washington: G.P.O., 1954. 1st edn. 8vo. 992 pp. Advance copy. Orig printed wraps. *(Antiq Sc)* **$125**

**Oppenheimer, Jane M.**
- Essays in the history of embryology and biology. Cambridge, Mass: 1967.
*(Winterdown)* **£20**

**Ord, W.M. & Garrod, A.E. (eds.)**
- The climates and baths of Green Britain, being the Report of the Sub-Committee of the Royal Medical and Chirurgical Society of London. Macmillan, 1895 – 1902. 2 vols. xvi,640; xvi,628 pp. 8 maps, fldg chart. Occas pencil note. Some fading of cvrs. *(Pollak)* **£40**

**Orfila, M.**
- A general system of toxicology, or, a treatise on poisons ... Translated ... 1819. 2nd edn. 2 vols. xxxi,517; xvi,568 pp. Port frontis laid down, but detchd. Occas spotting & browning, sporadic pencilling. Rebnd in grey cloth, orange mor labels. *(Jenner)* **£60**
- A popular treatise on the remedies to be employed in cases of poisoning and apparent death ... translated from the French. Phila: Solomon W. Conrad, 1818. 169,8[index] pp. Sl tear in 1 lf of index. Orig binding.
*(Poitras)* **$150**

**Orley, Alexander**
- Neuroradiology. Springfield: 1949. 1st edn. 421 pp. Num radiographic ills. Bibliog.
*(Oasis)* **$30**
- See Wakeley, Cecil & Orley, Alexander

**Ormerod, W.P.**
- On the sanatory conditions of Oxford. Oxford: Ashmolean Society, 1848. 48 pp. Tables, lge fldg plan of Oxford. Unopened. Orig printed wraps. *(Weiner)* **£15**

**Ornstein, Martha**
- The role of scientific societies in the seventeenth century. Chicago: 1928. 1st edn. 308 pp. *(Scientia)* **$30**

**Orr, E. Winnett**
- The treatment of osteomyelitis and other infected wounds by drainage and rest. 1927. 1st edn. 54 pp. *(Fye)* **$15**
- Wounds and fractures: a clinical guide to civil and military practice. Springfield: 1941. 1st edn. 227 pp. *(Fye)* **$30**

**Orr, William S. (ed.)**
- Orr's circle of the sciences. A series of treatises on the principles of science ... London: Orr & Co., 1854-55. 2nd edn. 3 vols. xvi,393; xvi,491; xvi,538 pp. Orig blue cloth gilt, a little wear to spine ends. *(Pollak)* **£30**

**Orth, Johannes**
- A compend of diagnosis in pathological anatomy. Translated ... sole authaurized English translation. New York: 1878. 440 pp. Plates. *(Goodrich)* **$75**

**Osborn, Henry F.**
- The evolution of mammalian molar teeth to and from the triangular type, including collected and revised researches ... Edited by W.K. Gregory. New York: 1907. 1st edn. 250 pp. *(Scientia)* **$75**
- Fifty-two years of research, observation and publication ... New York: 1930. 1st edn. 160 pp. *(Scientia)* **$25**
- The origin and evolution of life. On the theory of action, reaction and interaction of energy. London: G. Bell, 1918. xxxi,322 pp. Frontis. 135 ills, fldg table. Spine faded, a bit slack. *(Pollak)* **£15**

**Osler, William**
- The diagnosis of abdominal tumors. New York: 1898. 1st edn, reprinted. 192 pp.
*(Fye)* **$60**
- The evolution of modern medicine. New Haven: 1921. 1st edn. 4to. 243 pp. Num plates. Rubbed cloth. Sgntr of E.N. da C. Andrade on pastedown. *(Goodrich)* **$135**
- The evolution of modern medicine. New Haven: 1923. Lge 8vo. xv,243 pp. Ills. Spine ends & crnrs a little worn. *(Weiner)* **$50**
- Incunabula medica. A study of the earliest printed medical books 1467-1480. London: Oxford University Press, 1923. 1st edn. Tall 8vo. xi,[1], 137,[1] pp, [1]f. Frontis port, 16 facsimile plates. Red & black title. Orig cloth-backed bds. *(Zeitlin)* **$475**
- Men and books. Collected and reprinted from the Canadian Medical Association journal ... Pasadena: Private Printed, Castle Press, 1959. 1st edn. Ltd (200). *(Scientia)* **$125**
- The old humanities and the new science. With an introduction by Harvey Cushing. Boston: 1920. 1st edn. Dw. *(Scientia)* **$37.50**
- The principles and practice of medicine. New York: 1892. 1st edn, later printing (advts dated September, 1892). Half lea, worn.
*(Scientia)* **$400**
- The principles and practice of medicine. New York: Appleton, 1894. Roy 8vo. Ills. advts. Orig cloth, bumped, sl soiled, spine ends worn. *(Xerxes)* **$75**
- The principles and practice of medicine. New York: 1909. 7th edn. 1143 pp. Some ills. Orig maroon cloth, sl shaken, cloth extensively blistered. *(Jenner)* **£22**
- Science and immortality. London: 1904. 12mo. 94 pp. Bds, quite worn. *(Goodrich)* **$45**
- Selected writings of ... with an introduction by G.L. Keynes. London: 1951. 1st edn. Sl bubbling of front cvr. *(Scientia)* **$47.50**

**Ostwald, Wilhelm**
- Manual of physico-chemical measurements. Translated ... London: Macmillan, 1894. 1st English edn. xii,255 pp. 3 sets of tables in rear pocket, 188 text figs.          *(Pollak)* **£35**
- Outlines of general chemistry. Translated ... by James Walker. London: Macmillan, 1890. 1st English edn. xii,396 pp. 57 text figs. Orig cloth, spine darkened, wearing at edges, front jnt pulled.          *(Pollak)* **£35**
- Outlines of general chemistry. Translated ... by W.W. Taylor. London: Macmillan, 1912. 3rd edn. xvii,596 pp. 67 figs. Pub pres copy to Sir William Crookes, with his b'plate.          *(Pollak)* **£25**
- The scientific foundations of analytical chemistry. Treated in an elementary manner. Translated ... London: 1900. 2nd English edn (from 2nd German edn). 215 pp.          *(Scientia)* **$50**

**Otis, George**
- A report on amputation at the hip-joint in military surgery. Washington: Surgeon General's Office, 1867. Circular No. 7, War Department. Folio. 87 pp, 9 cold plates. Later half-calf, some unobtrusive lib markings.          *(Goodrich)* **$225**
- A report on excisions of the head of the femur for gun-shot injury. Washington: 1869. 1st edn. 4to. 143 pp. Recent cloth.          *(Fye)* **$125**

**Ottley, Drewry**
- Observations on surgical diseases of the head and neck. London: 1848. 1st edn. 293 pp.          *(Fye)* **$100**
- Observations on surgical diseases of the head and neck, selected from the memoirs of the Royal Academy of Surgery of France. Sydenham Society, 1848. x,293 pp. Orig blind-stamped cloth, sl dust stained & worn.          *(Whitehart)* **£40**
- Observations on surgical diseases of the head and neck ... Sydenham Society, 1848. x,293 pp. Prelims rather grubby. Orig green cloth, spine badly rubbed.          *(Jenner)* **£14**
- Observations on surgical diseases of the head and neck. London: Sydenham Society, 1848. 293 pp.          *(Goodrich)* **$75**

**Our ...**
- Our coal and coal pits ... See Leifchild, John R.

**Overman, Frederick**
- Practical mineralogy, assaying and mining. Phila: Lindsay & Blakiston, 1851. 1st edn. 12mo. x,12-230 pp. Orig blind-stamped cloth.          *(Antiq Sc)* **$50**

**Owen, Charles**
- An essay towards the natural history of serpents: In two parts ... London: for the author, 1742. 1st edn. 4to. xxiii,240 pp. 12 pp index (sm tear on last leaf), 7 full-page ills, 15 pp list of subscribers, errata, directions to binder. Half-calf.          *(Rootenberg)* **$350**
- An essay towards the natural history of serpents: In two parts ... 1742. xxiii,240,[12] pp (49-56 misbound). Additional pages of ms information & comments. Contemp bds, later half-calf with lea label.          *(Whitehart)* **£285**

**Owen, Charles Alfred**
- A treatise on weighing machines. A guide to the principles ... London: C. Griffin, 1922. 1st edn. xii,207 pp. 175 text ills. Ex lib.          *(Diamond)* **$45**

**Owen, Richard**
- Description of the fossil reptilia of South Africa in the collection of the British Museum. 1876. 4to. xii,88 pp. 70 plates, many fldg. Orig cloth. Ex lib, with stamps on title & plates.          *(Wheldon & Wesley)* **£180**
- Description of the fossil reptilia of South Africa in the collection of the British Museum. 1876. 4to. xii,88 pp. With an atlas of 70 plates, many fldg. Binder's cloth.          *(Wheldon & Wesley)* **£250**
- A history of British fossil mammals and birds. 1846. 1st edn. xlvi,560 pp. Fldg table, 236 w'cuts. Contemp half-calf gilt, mrbld bds, worn.          *(Weiner)* **£50**
- A history of British fossil mammals and birds. 1846. 8vo. xlvi,560 pp. Fldg table, 237 w'cuts. Orig cloth, trifle used.          *(Wheldon & Wesley)* **£50**
- A history of British fossil reptiles. 1849-84. Ltd (170). 4to. 4 vols. 286 plates. Orig buckram.          *(Wheldon & Wesley)* **£400**
- On parthogenesis ... London: John Van Voorst, 1849. 1st edn. 8vo. 76 pp. Frontis. Occas browning. Orig blue cloth, spine with minor defect. Inscribed by the author.          *(Rootenberg)* **$250**
- On the classification and geographical distribution of the mammalia ... London: John W. Parker, 1859. 1st edn. 8vo. [2],103,[5] pp. Text ills, pub ctlg. Orig cloth, somewhat faded. Lib label. *(Rootenberg)* **$275**
- Palaeontology or a systematic summary of extinct animals and their geological relations. 1860. 1st edn. 8vo. xv,420 pp. Fldg table, 142 text figs. Orig cloth. trifle used.          *(Wheldon & Wesley)* **£45**
- Palaeontology. Edinburgh: 1861. 2nd edn. 8vo. xvi,463 pp. 173 text figs. Orig cloth, reprd.          *(Wheldon & Wesley)* **£35**
- Paleontology or a systematic summary of extinct animals & their geological relations. Edinburgh: 1861. 2nd edn. 463 pp. Shelfworn.          *(Scientia)* **$75**

**Owen, Robert Dale**
- Moral physiology; or, a brief and plain

treatise on the population question. Boston:
Mendum, 1875. 10th edn. Sm 8vo. 88 pp.
One page of drwngs. Front hinge cracking.
*(Xerxes)* **$65**

**Owen, William O. (compiler)**
- The medical department of the United States
Army ... during the period of the Revolution
[1776-1786]. New York: 1920. 1st edn. Sm
8vo. Frontis, 3 other ports.      *(Elgen)* **$65**

**Packard, Alphaus**
- Lamarck, the founder of evolution. His life
and work. New York: 1901. 1st edn. 449 pp.
Ex lib.                          *(Scientia)* **$45**
- Lamarck, the founder of evolution. New York
& London: Longmans, Green, 1901. 1st edn.
8vo. Etched port frontis in orange, ills. Pub
blue ribbed cloth, spine faded.
*(McDowell)* **£26**

**Packard, Francis R.**
- Text-book of diseases of the nose, throat and
ear. Phila: 1909. 1st edn. 369 pp. *(Fye)* **$25**

**Padgett, Earl C.**
- Plastic   and   reconstructive   surgery.
Springfield: 1948. 1st edn. 4to. 945 pp. Ills.
Orig cloth, somewhat worn.       *(Oasis)* **$75**
- Skin   grafting   from   a   personal   and
experimental viewpoint. Springfield: 1942.
1st edn. 149 pp.                   *(Fye)* **$75**

**Page, John**
- Receipts for preparing and compounding the
principal medicines made use of by the late
Mr. Ward. Together with an introduction
etc. 1763. 1st edn. Title lightly browned,
occas light marginal dampmarks. Mod cloth.
*(Robertshaw)* **£48**

**Page, Victor**
- Modern aircraft. Basic principles, operation,
application,   construction,   repair,
maintenance. A complete practical treatise ...
New York: Henley Pub. Co., 1928. 1st edn.
xvi,855,39 [pub ctlg] pp. 400 ills & text figs.
Sl cvr wear, soiling & staining. *(Diamond)* **$45**

**Paget, Stephen (ed.)**
- Memoirs and letters of Sir James Paget. 1901.
2nd edn. 438,[32 advts] pp. Port frontis.
Spotting on prelims. Orig blue cloth, spine sl
faded.                          *(Jenner)* **£14**

**Paine, Martyn**
- Essays on the philosophy of vitality as
contradistinguished   from   chemical   and
mechanical philosophy, and on the modus
operandi of remedial agents. New York: for
the Author, 1842. 1st edn. 70pp. Minor water
stain on some bottom margins. Mod binding.
*(Xerxes)* **$100**

**Paley, William**
- Natural   theology;   or,   evidences   of   the
existence and attributes of the Deity. London:
1817. New edn. Roy 8vo. 468 pp. Orig bds,
worn & broken.      *(Wheldon & Wesley)* **£15**
- Natural   theology;   or,   evidences   of   the
existence   and   attributes   of   the   Deity,
Collected from the appearances of nature ...
Boston: 1831. 336 pp. 36 plates.
*(Scientia)* **$37.50**
- Paley's natural theology, with selections from
the illustrative notes and the supplementary
dissertations of Sir Charles Bell and Lord
Brougham. Edited by Elisha Bartlett. Boston:
1839. 2 vols. 365; 454 pp.      *(Scientia)* **$65**

**Palmer, Henry R.**
- Description of a railway on a new principle;
with   observations   on   those   hitherto
constructed ... friction of axles ... resistance of
floating vessels and carriages ... London: J.
Taylor, 1823. 1st edn. 8vo. 2 fldg engvd
plates. Mod half-calf, gilt back.
*(Deighton Bell)* **£285**

**Palmer, Sir Thomas**
- An essay on the meanes how to make travailes
into forraine countries the more profitable
and honourable. London: Lownes, 1606. Sole
edn. 4to. 4 fldg tables. Some w'staining.
Contemp calf, rebacked. *(Marlborough)* **£350**

**Palmieri, Luigi**
- The eruption of Vesuvius in 1872 ... with
notes   ...   present   state   of   knowledge   of
terrestrial volcanicity ... by Robert Mallet.
1873. 148 pp. 8 plates. Orig pict cloth gilt,
worn, stained on back, spine stained & torn.
*(Weiner)* **£30**

**[Paman, Roger]**
- The harmony of the ancient and modern
geometry asserted: In answer to the call of the
author of the "Analyst" ... their
obscure analytics. London: J. Nourse, 1745.
1st edn. 4to. [4]67,[1] pp. 8 engvd fldg plates.
Contemp calf, rebacked.    *(Rootenberg)* **$450**

**Pancoast, Joseph**
- A treatise on operative surgery; comprising a
description of the various processes of the art
... Phila: 1846. 2nd edn. 389 pp. 80 engvd
plates. Lib stamp on title & verso of plates.
Recent qtr lea.                  *(Fye)* **$500**

**Paneth, Frith**
- Radio-elements as indicators. New York:
1928. 1st edn. 164 pp. Orig cloth. *(Oasis)* **$40**
- See Hevesy, George von & Paneth, Frith

**Pannekoek, A.**
- A history of astronomy. London: 1861. 1st
edn in English. 521 pp. 24 plates, 42 text figs.

*(Oasis)* **$30**

**Panton, Arthur W.**
- See Burnside, William S. & Panton, Arthur W.

**Papez, James W.**
- Comparative neurology. A manual and text for the study of the nervous system of vertebrates. New York: 1929. xxv,518 pp. Ills. Sl worn dw. *(Jenner)* **£15**

**Pare, Ambroise**
- The apologie and treatise of Ambroise Pare containing the voyages made into diverse places ... edited by Geoffrey Keynes. Chicago: 1952. 1st Amer edn. 227 pp. *(Fye)* **$50**

**Paris, John Ayrton**
- The elements of medical chemistry; embracing only those branches of chemical science which are calculated ... London: Phillips, 1825. [2],xxxi, [1], 586,[12] pp. 1st ed. Contemp half-calf. *(Goodrich)* **$150**
- The life of Sir Humphrey Davy, Bart., ... London: 1831. Frontis. New half-calf. *(Winterdown)* **£75**
- Pharmacologia, being an extended inquiry into the operations of medicinal bodies, upon which are founded the theory and art of prescribing. 1843. 9th edn. xvi,622 pp. Sm stain on front cvr. *(Jenner)* **£40**
- Pharmacologia; corrected and extended in accordance with the London Pharmacopoeia of 1824 ... 3rd Amer edn, from the 6th London edn ... New York: 1825. 2 vols. 322; 376 pp. Foxing & browning. Volvule (medicinal dynometer) mtd inside front cvr. Orig bds. *(Elgen)* **$125**

**Parker, G.**
- The early history of surgery in Great Britain. Its organization and development. 1920. ix,204 pp. Frontis, 7 plates. Bibliog. Orig cloth. Medical History Manuals Series. *(Whitehart)* **£18**

**Parker, Raymond C.**
- Methods of tissue culture ... New York: Paul B. Hoeber, 1950. 2nd edn, revised. 294 pp. 113 ills. *(Poitras)* **$30**

**Parker, T. Jeffery**
- William Kitchen Parker, F.R.S. Sometime Hunterian Professor of Anatomy and Physiology ... London: 1893. 1st edn. Sm 8vo. Frontis, xv,145 pp. Ex lib. *(Elgen)* **$50**

**Parker, W.K.**
- On mammalian descent. The Hunterian Lectures for 1884. Being nine lectures delivered in the theatre of the Royal College of Surgeons during February, 1884. 1885. xii,229 pp. 16 figs in text. New cloth. *(Whitehart)* **£18**

**Parkes, Samuel**
- The rudiments of chemistry; illustrated by experiments ... For the Author, 1810. 12mo in sixes. xii,294 pp. 8 plates a little foxed. Contemp calf, spine rubbed & wearing at edges. *(Pollak)* **£25**

**Parkinson, J.**
- Organic remains of a former world, An examination of the mineralized remains ... of the antediluvian world ... London: 1820,1810-11. 2nd, 1st, 1st edns. 4to. 3 vols. 3 frontis (2 cold), 3 title vignettes, plate of strata, 50 plates (48 cold). Half-mor. *(Wheldon & Wesley)* **£375**

**Parkinson, R.**
- The experienced farmer ... or, complete practice of agriculture according to the latest improvements 1807. 2 vols. xix,477; 565, 32 [index]. 4 plates. Half-calf, rebacked. *(Phenotype)* **£110**

**Parnell, Edward Andrew (ed.)**
- Applied chemistry in manufactures, arts, and domestic economy ... New York & Phila: Appleton, 1844. 1st Amer edn. 8vo. 16,175 pp. 41 text figs, 4 fabric swatches (2 v faded). Occas spotty foxing. Orig cloth, light wear to extremities. *(M&S)* **$60**

**Parr, Bartholomew**
- The London medical dictionary; including, under distinct heads, every branch of medicine ... with whatever relates to medicine in natural philosophy ... and natural history. Phila: 1819. 1st Amer edn. 2 vols. Thick 4to. Contemp calf, cvrs detchd. *(M&S)* **$150**

**Parr, G.**
- The cathode ray tube and its applications. 1941. 2nd edn. viii,180 pp. 2 plates, diags. Bibliog. Ex lib. *(Weiner)* **£15**

**Parson, Charles**
- Sea-air and sea-bathing. Their influence on health. Practical guide for the use of visitors at the sea-side. Phila: Lindsay & Blakiston, 1877. 1st edn. 12mo. 119 pp. Some spots in text. *(Xerxes)* **$60**

**Parson, James**
- Philosophical observations on the analogy between the propagation of animals and that of vegetables ... London: 1752. xvi,288 pp. Fldg plate. Full calf, jnts split. *(Phenotype)* **£110**

**Parsons, J. Inglis**
- The operative treatment of prolapse and retroversion of the uterus. New York: 1906. 1st Amer edn. 90 pp.                *(Fye)* **$20**

**Parsons, Usher**
- Directions for making anatomical preparations formed on the basis of Pole, Marjolin, and Breschet ... Phila: 1831. xxvi,316 pp. 4 plates. Foxed. Old calf, rebacked.               *(Goodrich)* **$95**
- A lecture, on the connexion and reciprocal influence, between the brain and stomach, delivered before the American Institute of Instruction, at Providence, 1840. Providence: Cranston, 1841. Tall 8vo. 16 pp. Brown printed wraps.           *(Hemlock)* **$40**

**Partington, Charles F.**
- A manual of natural and experimental philosophy, being the substance of a series of lectures ... n.d. [?ca 1830]. xxviii,404,x pp. Frontis, 3 plates (1 fldg), w'cuts. Orig dec cloth, worn & discoloured.      *(Weiner)* **£38**

**Partington, J.R.**
- A history of Greek fire and gunpowder. Cambridge: Heffer, 1960. 1st edn. 4to Frontis, ills. Cloth, dw.     *(McDowell)* **£48**
- A short history of chemistry. Macmillan, 1951. 2nd edn.         *(Pollak)* **£12**

**Pasteur, Louis**
- Studies on fermentation. The diseases of beer, their causes and means of preventing them. London: Macmillan, 1879. 1st English edn. 8vo. 12 plates with tissues. Pub cloth, sm repair to jnt.          *(McDowell)* **£160**

**Patent ...**
- Patent artificial slate manufactury ... See Cook, Henry

**Paterson, Donald G.**
- Physique and intellect. New York: 1930. 304 pp. Rubbed, spine bit dull. From lib of Harry & Leta Hollingworth.     *(Epistemologist)* **$35**

**Paton, Stewart**
- Psychiatry: a text-book for students and physicians. Phila: Lippincott, 1905. 1st edn. xii,618 pp.            *(Gach)* **$30**

**Patterson, T.S.J.**
- See Peet, Eric W. & Patterson, T.S.J.

**Paul, Alexander**
- The vaccination problem in 1903 and the impracticability of compulsion. 1903. vii,130,[1 advts]. Prelims foxed. Orig green cloth, hinges cracked inside.    *(Jenner)* **£17**

**Paul, Benjamin H.**
- Manual of technical analysis: a guide for the testing and valuation of the various ... substances employed in the arts and in domestic economy. London: H.G. Bohn, 1857. 1st edn. 12mo. xii,426 pp. 92 text figs. Contemp calf, sl worn & soiled.
                *(Diamond)* **$50**

**Paul, Constantin Charles T.**
- Diagnosis and treatment of diseases of the heart. Translated from the French. New York: William Wood & Co., 1884. 1st edn in English. 335 pp. Ills.     *(Poitras)* **$75**

**Paul, John R.**
- A history of poliomyelitis. Yale University Press, 1971. [iv],xv,[i], 486,[viii]. 61 ills, 8 tables.           *(Pollak)* **£20**

**Pauli, Wolfgang**
- Theory of relativity [1921]. Translated by G. Field with supplementary notes by the author. New York: 1958. 1st edn in English. 241 pp.           *(Scientia)* **$65**

**Pauling, Linus**
- General chemistry. An introduction to descriptive chemistry and modern chemical theory. San Francisco, 1948. xi,618 pp. Num figs,              *(Pollak)* **£10**
- The nature of the chemical bond and the structure of molecules and crystals. An introduction to modern structural chemistry. Ithaca, NY: 1939. 1st edn. 429 pp. Spine stained, bubbling in cvrs.    *(Scientia)* **$125**
- The nature of the chemical bond and structure of molecules and crystals. New York: Cornell University Press, 1960. 3rd edn. xx,644 pp. Num figs. Torn dw.
                *(Pollak)* **£15**

**Pauling, Linus & Goudsmit, Samuel**
- The structure of line spectra. New York: 1930. 1st edn. 263 pp.    *(Scientia)* **$60**

**Pavlov, Ivan Petrovich**
- Conditioned reflexes. An investigation of the physiological activity of the cerebral cortex. Translated ... Oxford: 1927, reprinted 1940. Orig cloth stained & marked. *(Whitehart)* **£40**
- Conditioned reflexes. An investigation of the physiological activity of the cerebral cortex. Translated ... Oxford University Press: 1946 (from the sheets of the 1927 1st edn). xv,[i], 430,[ii] pp. 18 text ills.      *(Pollak)* **£20**
- Conditioned reflexes: an investigation of the physiological activity of the cerebral cortex ... translated and edited ... [London]: Oxford University Press, 1927. 1st edn in English. [xvi],430,[2] pp. Black cloth, scratched & rubbed.           *(Gach)* **$150**
- Lectures on conditioned reflexes: twenty-five

years of objective study ... London: 1928. 414 pp. Cvrs sl warped & shelfmarked.
*(Epistemologist)* **$20**
- Lectures on conditioned reflexes: twenty-five years of objective study of the higher nervous activity (behaviour) of animals. 1928. 1st edn in English. [10],414 pp. Frontis, 9 ills. Orig cloth, rebacked. *(Whitehart)* **£35**
- Lectures on conditioned reflexes: twenty-five years of objective study of the higher nervous activity (behaviour) of animals. New York: Liveright, [1936]. 414 pp. Cloth. Worn dw.
*(Gach)* **$25**
- The work of the digestive glands. Lectures by I.V. Pavlov ... London: 1902. 1st English edn. Orig cloth. Ex lib. *(Goodrich)* **$295**
- The work of the digestive glands. Lectures by I.V. Pavlov ... translated ... London: Charles Griffin, 1910. 2nd English edn. [ii],xiv, 266,[2] pp. Maroon cloth. *(Gach)* **$175**

**Pawsey, J.L. & Bracewell, R.N.**
- Radio astronomy. Oxford: 1955. 1st edn. 361 pp, 23 plates. *(Scientia)* **$35**

**Paxton, Peter**
- An essay concerning the body of man, wherein its changes or diseases are consider'd ... London: for Rich. Wilkin, 1701. [i title],[i blank],[vi preface],[xv contents],[i errata], 392 pp. Sl damp-staining, contemp ink notes, no f.e.p. Contemp calf, rubbed. *(Pollak)* **£180**

**Payne, B.O.**
- Microscope design and construction. York: Cooke, Troughton & Simms, 1954. Num ills. *(Winterdown)* **£15**

**Peach, B.N., et al.**
- Geology of the neighbourhood of Edinburgh. Me. Geol. Survey, 1910. 2nd edn. 8vo. Maps & 12 plates. Cloth, trifle used.
*(Wheldon & Wesley)* **£20**

**Peacock, Rev. D.M.**
- A comparative view of the principles of the fluxional and differential calculus. Cambridge: Deighton, et al. 1819. [iv],95 pp. Orig paper wraps. *(Pollak)* **£50**

**Peacock, George**
- Life of Thomas Young. London: 1855. 1st edn. 514 pp. Spine & cvrs chipped, worn, bumped. *(Scientia)* **$55**

**Pear, T.H.**
- See Smith, G. Elliott & Pear, T.H.

**Pearce, C.T.**
- Vaccination: its tested effects on health, mortality and population. An essay by ... London: Bailliere, 1868. viii,-120 pp.
*(Goodrich)* **$60**

**Pearl, Raymond**
- The biology of population growth. New York: 1925. 1st edn. 260 pp. *(Scientia)* **$27.50**
- Modes of research in genetics. New York: 1915. 1st edn. 182 pp. *(Scientia)* **$40**
- The natural history of population. New York: 1939. 416 pp. Dw. *(Scientia)* **$35**
- Studies in human biology. Balt: 1924. 1st edn. 651 pp. *(Scientia)* **$37.50**

**Pears, Francis**
- The skin, baths, bathing and soap. 1859. 1st edn. Later cloth-backed mrbld bds, lea label.
*(Robertshaw)* **£25**

**Pearson, George**
- Observations and experiments for investigating the chymical history of the tepid springs of Buxton; together with an account ... London: J. Johnson, 1784. 1st edn. 2 vols. 8vo. xvi,[4],327; [2 errata],227, [29] pp. Engvd plate. Contemp 3/4 calf.
*(Antiq Sc)* **$285**

**Pearson, Karl**
- The chances of death and other studies in evolution. London: 1897. 1st edn. 2 vols. 388; 460 pp. Cvrs bubbled. *(Scientia)* **$160**
- The grammar of science. London: 1892. 1st edn. 493 pp. Rear cvr somewhat stained.
*(Scientia)* **$65**
- The grammar of science. London: 1900. 2nd edn, rvsd & enlgd. 548 pp. *(Scientia)* **$60**
- The life, letters and labours of Francis Galton. Cambridge: 1914 - 1930. 1st edn. 3 vols in 4. *(Scientia)* **$400**
- On the handicapping of the first-born. London: 1914. 1st edn. 68 pp. Orig wraps.
*(Scientia)* **$50**

**Peaslee, E.R.**
- A monograph on the foetal circulation. New York: 1854. 1st sep edn. 26 pp. 3 w'cuts. Inner margin stained. Orig printed wraps, worn. *(Elgen)* **$95**

**Pechey, John**
- A general treatise on cancerous complaints: with an account of some diseases which have been confounded with the cancer. Also ... operations performed in cancerous cases. London: for the author, 1793. 1st edn. Mod half-calf. *(Quaritch)* **$425**

**Peer, Lyndon A.**
- Transplantation of tissues. Balt: 1955-59. 1st edn. 2 vols. 421; 690 pp. Ills. Dws sl frayed.
*(Oasis)* **$60**

**Peers, G.R.**
- Electricity made plain. [1912]. viii,133 pp. 54 figs in text. Orig printed card cvrs, linen spine. Cvrs sl worn. *(Whitehart)* **£18**

**Peet, Eric W. & Patterson, T.S.J.**
- The essentials of plastic surgery. Oxford: 1963. Roy 8vo. ix,448 pp. Ills. *(Jenner)* **£10**

**Pelly, Anthony**
- See Clarkson, Patrick & Pelly, Anthony

**Pemberton, Henry**
- The dispensatory of the Royal College of Physicians, London, translated into English with remarks. 1746. 1st edn. Contemp calf, ruled in gilt, new label.    *(Robertshaw)* **£65**
- A view of Sir Isaac Newton's philosophy. London: 1728. 1st edn. 4to. 407 pp. 12 fldg engvd plates, several engvd decorations. Some staining of mid-section, mostly unobtrusive. Lib stamp on title. Re-bound in half-calf.
  *(Oasis)* **$150**
- A view of Sir Isaac Newton's philosophy. London: S. Palmer, 1728. 1st edn. Demy 4to. [25]ff,407 pp. Engvd title vignette, 12 fldg plates. A few stains & light spotting. Contemp calf, rebacked.    *(Zeitlin)* **$450**
- A view of Sir Isaac Newton's philosophy. London: S. Palmer, 1728. 1st edn. 4to. [50],407 pp. 12 fldg engvd plates. Contemp sprinkled calf, lower jnt strengthened.
  *(Pickering)* **$850**
- A view of Sir Isaac Newton's philosophy. London: S. Palmer, 1728. 1st edn. 4to. [48],407 pp. 12 fldg engvd plates. Title a little dust-stained. Contemp calf, rebacked.
  *(Antiq Sc)* **$375**

**Penfield, Wilder**
- See Roberts, Iamar & Penfield, Wilder

**Penington, John**
- An inaugural dissertation on the phenomena, causes and effects of fermentation ... Phila: Joseph James, 1790. 1st edn. 12mo. 30 pp. Title lightly stained, top margin cropped, wants the err lf but with early ms correction. Old mrbld wraps in fldg case. *(M&S)* **$275**

**Penn, W.A.**
- The soverane herbe, a history of tobacco. 1901. 8vo. ix,326 pp. 5 ills. Cloth, trifle used.
  *(Wheldon & Wesley)* **£25**

**Pennington, John**
- Aerostation, or steam aerial navigation ... [Caption title]. [Balt: 1838]. 1st edn. Sm 8vo. 8 pp. Frontis. Text browned. Self-wraps, sewn into new plain wraps. *(M&S)* **$1,000**

**Penrose, L.S.**
- The biology of mental defect. London: 1949. 1st edn. 285 pp. 7 plates.    *(Oasis)* **$30**

**People ...**
- The people's vade-mecum comprising a collection of valuable recipes ... simple and curious experiments in chemistry: including medicine, perfumery ... Buffalo, 1849. 1st edn. 18mo. 46 pp. Some stains. Orig printed wraps.    *(M&S)* **$45**

**Pepper, John Henry**
- The boy's playbook of science ... London: Routledge, 1860. 1st edn. vii,440 pp. 3 plates, 470 w'engvs. One gathering weak, plates foxed. Orig dec cloth, a little rubbed, jnts weak.    *(Pollak)* **£20**

**Pepper, William (ed.)**
- An American text-book of the theory and practice of medicine. Phila: 1893-94. 2 vols. Lea, rubbed, jnts tender, labels chipped.
  *(Goodrich)* **$125**
- A system of practical medicine. By American authors. Phila: Lea Brothers & Co., 1885-86. 5 vols. Ills. Full lea.    *(Poitras)* **$150**

**Pepys, Lady Charlotte-Maria**
- Thoughts of home; or, counsel and consolation for expatriated invalids. With some remarks on climate. London: William Skeffington, 1864. xi,[iii], 326,[ii advts] pp. A little foxing, few leaves creased at top crnr. Orig ribbed cloth.    *(Pollak)* **£20**

**Percy, Cornelius McLeod**
- The mechanical engineering of collieries ... London: "Colliery Guardian" Office, 1885-86. Tall 8vo. 2 vols. 465 figs on 178 plates (72 fldg), 2 ports. Some spotting & light browning. Orig brown cloth, stamped in gilt & black, rubbed & sl shaken. *(Zeitlin)* **$175**

**Percy, Nelson**
- See Ochsner, Albert & Percy, Nelson

**Percy, T. & Kirkpatrick, C.**
- History of the medical teaching in Trinity College Dublin and of the School of Physic in Ireland. Dublin: 1912. xi,363 pp. Frontis, 2 plates. Orig cloth, t.e.g. Spine sl faded.
  *(Whitehart)* **£30**

**Pereira, Jonathan**
- The elements of materia medica and therapeutics. With notes and additions by Joseph Carson. Phila: 1843. 1st Amer edn from 2nd English edn. 2 vols. Full lea, scuffed.    *(Scientia)* **$85**
- The elements of materia medica and therapeutics. Phila: Lea & Blanchard, 1846. 2 vols. Roy 8vo. 724; 862 pp. Num ills. A few minor stains. Full lea, rubbed & worn, lacking one spine label.    *(Xerxes)* **$85**

**Perez, Bernard**
- First three years of childhood. New York: 1888. 292 pp. Cvr sl rubbed.
  *(Epistemologist)* **$37.50**

**Perkins, Benjamin Douglas**
- The influence of metallic tractors on the human body in removing various painful inflammatory diseases ... 1799. 2nd edn. Uncut in mod wraps.  *(Robertshaw)* **£125**

**Perkins, John J.**
- Principles and methods of sterilization. Springfield: Charles C. Thomas, 1960. 2nd printing. 340 pp. Ex lib.  *(Poitras)* **$35**

**Perrault, Claude**
- Memoirs for a natural history of animals ... to which is added an account of the measure of a great circle of the earth. London: 1688. Sm folio. 266; 40 pp. Engvd frontis, red & black title, num engvs. Damp-staining & browning. New qtr calf.  *(Goodrich)* **$195**

**Perrin, Jean**
- Atoms. Authorised translation ... 1916. 1st English edn. xiv,211 pp. Ills, diags. Book sl bowed, last page apparently pasted to free endpaper.  *(Weiner)* **£40**
- Atoms. Translated ... London: Constable, 1920. 1st English edn, 2nd imp. xiv,211 pp. 16 text figs. Cvrs shabby.  *(Pollak)* **£20**

**Perry, Sampson**
- A disquisition of the stone and gravel, with strictures on the gout. London: 1785. 7th edn. 16 mo. xix,248 pp. Last 5 pp sl browned. Mod half-calf, mrbld bds.  *(Jenner)* **£80**

**'Peter Progress' (pseud.)**
- The electric telegraph, comprising a brief history of former modes of telegraphic communication, an account of the electric clock ... 1847. 12mo. 84 pp, 2 plates. 12 pp ctlg of books at end. Frontis foxed. Orig printed card wraps.  *(Weiner)* **£45**

**Peter, Robert**
- The history of the medical department of Transylvania University. Louisville: John P. Morton, 1905. 193 pp. Many full-page ills. Uncut. Soft bound.  *(Poitras)* **$70**

**Peterson, Frederick**
- See Church, Archibald & Peterson, Frederick

**Pettigrew, T.J.**
- On superstitions connected with the history and practice of medicine and surgery. Phila: 1844. Half-title. 239 pp. Plate. New cloth, w'stained.  *(Goodrich)* **$65**

**Pfister, Oscar**
- Some applications of psycho analysis. London: George Allen & Unwin, [1923]. 1st edn in English. 352 pp.  *(Gach)* **$30**

**Pharmacopoeia ...**
- Pharmacopoeia Bateana: or, Bate's Dispensatory. Translated from the second edition of the Latin copy. Published by Mr. James Shipton. Containing ... 1694. 1st edn in English. [xvi],965,[19] pp. Ill. Light browning. Contemp panelled calf, rubbed.  *(Jenner)* **£175**
- Pharmacopoeia Bateana: or, Bate's Dispensatory. Translated from the last Latin edition ... 2nd ed, enlarged by William Salmon. London: for S. Smith & B. Walford, 1700. [8]ff, 747,[12] pp. Index, advt leaf. Some sl browning. Orig calf bds, rebacked.  *(Elgen)* **$275**
- Pharmacopoeia Edinburgensis: or, the dispensatory of the Royal College of Physicians in Edinburgh. Fifth and most correct edition. 1753. Contemp calf, ruled in gilt.  *(Robertshaw)* **£60**
- Pharmacopoeia Nosocommi Neo-Eboracensis; or, the pharmacopoeia of the New York Hospital ... To which is added, an appendix ... New York: 1816. x,[1],180 pp. Foxed. Qtr calf, worn, weak jnts.  *(Goodrich)* **$275**
- The pharmacopoeia of the United States of America. Boston: for Charles Ewer, December, 1820. 272 pp. Latin American text. Some leaves heavily browned & difficult to read. Rebound.  *(Poitras)* **$200**
- The pharmacopoeia of the United States of America. Boston: Charles Ewer, 1828. 4to. 272 pp. Latin American index. Full lea, spine sl chipped.  *(Poitras)* **$225**
- Pharmacopoeia Officinalis & Extemporanea: or, a compleat English dispensatory. In four parts .... London: 1718. 1st edn. xvi,618,[70] pp. Contemp panelled calf, worn & rubbed. Hinges cracked.  *(Whitehart)* **£125**
- The pharmacopoiea of the United States of America, by the authority of "The General Convention ..." held in 1830. New York: S. Converse, 1830. 2nd edn, from the 1st with additions & corrections. 176 pp. Little age-staining. Rebnd in cloth. Ex lib.  *(Diamond)* **$150**
- The pharmocopoiea of the United States of America, by the authority of the National Medical Convention ... 1850. Phila: Lippincott, Grambo, 1851. xxiii,317,27 [pub ctlg]. Orig calf cvrs, worn. Ex lib.  *(Diamond)* **$75**

**Phelps, Charles**
- Traumatic injuries of the brain and its membranes. New York: 1897. 1st edn. 582 pp. Tear in fore-edge of first 25 leaves, not affecting text. Half lea.  *(Fye)* **$90**

**Philip, A.P.W.**
- A treatise on febrile diseases, intermitting, remitting and continued fevers ... symptoms,

cause and cure ... Hartford: 1809. 1st Amer edn. 5 vols in two. 8vo. 501; 615 pp. Browning. Contemp calf, front hinge of Vol 2 cracked. *(Hemlock)* **$150**
- A treatise on indigestion, and its consequences, called nervous and bilious complaints; with observations on organic diseases, in which they sometimes terminate. 1821. xiv,363 pp. Orig half-calf, mrbld bds, orig spine laid on. Interleaved with contemp notes. *(Whitehart)* **£85**
- A treatise on indigestion, and its consequences, called nervous and bilious complaints ... Phila: 1822. 2nd edn. 205 pp. Browned. Uncut. Rebacked. *(Goodrich)* **$40**
- A treatise on indigestion, and its consequences. Phila: Carey & Lea, 1823. 3rd edn. 195 pp. Bds stained, backstrip nearly worn away. *(Xerxes)* **$85**
- A treatise on the nature and cure of those diseases, either acute or chronic, which precede change of structure. Balt: Edward Coale, 1831. 1st Amer edn. 328 pp. Foxed. Lea, backstrip worn, front bd detchd, rear bd tender. *(Xerxes)* **$85**

**Philip, R.W.**
- Pulmonary tuberculosis - etiological and therapeutic based on an experimental investigation. 1891. iv,55 pp. Orig cloth. *(Whitehart)* **£18**

**Philipson, John**
- Harness, as it has been, as it is, and as it should be ... with remarks on traction, and the use of the Cape Cart by Nimshivich ... Newcastle-upon-Tyne & London: 1882. vii,80 pp. 25 plates. ills, errata slip, 12 pp illus advts. Orig pict cloth, stained. *(Weiner)* **£85**

**Phillips, A.J.**
- See Stone, Janet & Phillips, A.J.

**Phillips, B.**
- Scrofula; its nature, its causes, its prevalence and the principles of treatment. 1846. v,379 pp. Frontis. Later cloth. Lib stamp on title. *(Whitehart)* **£35**

**Phillips, J.**
- Illustrations of the geology of Yorkshire. Part 1 ...; Part 2 ... 1835-36. 2nd, 1st edns. 2 vols in 1. 8vo. xii,184,[1]; xx,253,[1] pp. Cold geolog map, 9 plates of sections (7 cold), 29 other plates. Sl foxing. Contemp half-calf, worn, rebacked, recased. *(Wheldon & Wesley)* **£220**

**Phillips, Richard**
- Translation of the pharmacopoiea of the Royal College of Physicians of London, with notes and illustrations. London: 1851.

xiii,567 pp. Text diags. Full calf, hinges rather rubbed, last panel at hd of spine missing. *(Jenner)* **£38**
- Translation of the pharmacopoiea of the Royal College of Physicians of London, with notes and illustrations. London: 1851. xiii,[iii], 567,[i] pp. Text diags. Full calf, hd of spine reprd, front jnt weak. *(Pollak)* **£30**

**Phillips, Sarah**
- The ladies handmaid: or a compleat system of cookery,; on the principals of elegance and frugality ... London: J. Coote, 1758. Sole edn. 8vo. Frontis, 4 plates. Title finger-marked, occas spotting. Last leaf of index in facsimile. Contemp calf, chipped. *(McDowell)* **£200**

**Phipson, T.L.**
- Meteors, aerolites and falling stars. London: Lovell Reeve, 1867. 1st edn. 8vo. Tinted litho frontis, ills in text. Pub cloth. *(McDowell)* **£30**
- Phosphorescence or, the emission of light by minerals, plants and animals. London: Lovell Reeve, 1862. 1st edn. 8vo. Tinted litho frontis, cuts in text. Pub cloth.
*(McDowell)* **£55**

**Physician, A. (pseud.)**
- Eupaedia; or letters to a mother on the watchful care of her infant ... London: Sherwood, Gilbert & Piper, n.d. [ca 1836]. viii,144 pp. Occas foxing. Orig lettered cloth, a.e.g., backstrip reprd. *(Pollak)* **£150**

**Physicians ...**
- Physicians of the Mayo Clinic and Mayo Foundation with portraits. Phila: 1927. 1st edn. 578 pp. *(Fye)* **$40**

**Piaget, Jean**
- The child's conception of number. 1969. 4th English impression. ix,248 pp. Dw. *(Jenner)* **£10**
- The child's conception of physical causality. London & New York: 1930. viii,309,[3] pp. Inserted advts dated 1947. Pub green cloth. *(Gach)* **$60**
- The child's conception of physical causality. 1970. 4th English printing. viii,309 pp. Dw. *(Jenner)* **£10**
- The child's conception of the world. 1967. 5th English printing. ix,397 pp. Dw. *(Jenner)* **£10**
- Judgment and reasoning in the child ... translated ... New York & London: 1928. 1st edn. viii,260 pp. *(Gach)* **$50**
- Judgment and reasoning in the child. 1969. 5th English impression. viii,260 pp. Dw sl worn. *(Jenner)* **£10**
- The mechanisms of perception. Translated ... New York: Basic Books, [1969]. *(Gach)* **$25**
- The moral judgment of the child. New York & London: 1932. 1st edn in English, Amer

sue. [xii],418,[2] pp. Green cloth. *(Gach)* **$50**
- The origin of intelligence in the child. 1970.
3rd English impression. xi,425 pp. Dw sl
worn & soiled.               *(Jenner)* **£10**
- Play, dreams and imitation in childhood.
New York: W.W. Norton, [1951]. 1st edn in
English. [x],296 pp. Cloth. Worn dw.
                              *(Gach)* **$20**
- The psychology of intelligence. London:
Routledge & Kegan Paul, [1950]. 1st edn in
English. [viii],182,[8] pp. Cloth. Worn dw.
                              *(Gach)* **$25**
- The psychology of intelligence. 1967. 5th
English impression. viii,182 pp. Dw sl soiled.
                              *(Jenner)* **£10**

**Piaget, Jean & Inhelder, Barbel**
- The child's conception of space. 1971. 4th
English imp. xii,490 pp. Few ills. Dw.
                              *(Jenner)* **£10**
- The early growth of logic in the child. 1972.
2nd English edn. xxv,302 pp. Ills.
                              *(Jenner)* **£10**
- The growth of logical thinking from
childhood to adolescence. 1972. 4th English
imp. xxvi,356 pp. Few ills. Dw. *(Jenner)* **£10**

**Piaget, Jean, et al.**
- The child's conception of geometry. London:
1960. 411 pp. Adhesive mark on front
endpaper. Dw.           *(Epistemologist)* **$35**
- The child's conception of geometry. 1970.
3rd English printing. vii,411 pp. Dw.
                              *(Jenner)* **£10**

**Pickering, Sir George**
- Physician and scientist, the Harveian Oration
1964. London: British Medical Association,
1964. Slim 8vo. Orig red cloth.
                              *(McDowell)* **£20**

**Piesse, G.W. Septimus**
- The art of perfumery and the methods of
obtaining the odour of plants ... 1879. 4th
edn. Ills.              *(Robertshaw)* **£35**

**Piffard, Henry G.**
- A treatise on the materia medica and
therapeutics of the skin ... New York: 1881.
1st edn. 351pp. Text ills..   *(Elgen)* **$45**

**Pike, Nicholas**
- A new and complete system of arithmetic ...
Newbury-Port: ... John MyCall, 1788. 1st
edn. 8vo. 512 pp. Errata slip pasted on
endpaper. Browned, with light foxing, some
marginal w'staining at end. Contemp calf, red
mor label, hd of spine reprd. *(Zeitlin)* **$250**
- A new and system of arithmetic, composed
for use of citizens of the United States.
Newbury-Port: John Mycall, 1788. 1st edn.
8vo. [16],512 pp. Marginal stains. Contemp
calf, rebacked, cvrs rubbed. With the scarce

recommendation leaf.     *(Rootenberg)* **$250**

**Pilch, Richard B.**
- History of the Institute (of Chemistry of
Great Britain and Ireland): 1877 - 1914. For
the Institute, 1914. 4to. Lge paper copy.
[iv],5-307. Frontis, 20 plates. Fore-edge of
cvrs a little affected by damp. *(Pollak)* **£15**

**Pilcher, Cobb**
- See Bancroft, Frederic & Pilcher, Cobb

**Pillsbury, W.B. & Meader, C.L.**
- Psychology of language. New York: 1928.
306 pp. Spine lettering dull.
                       *(Epistemologist)* **$25**

**Pillsbury, Walter Bowers**
- Attention. London & New York: 1908. 1st
edn in English. [xii],346,[2] pp. Mauve
buckram.                      *(Gach)* **$25**
- The history of psychology. New York: W.W.
Norton, [1929]. 1st edn. [x],326,[2] pp. Front
hinge broken.                 *(Gach)* **$25**
- Psychology of reasoning. New York: 1910.
306 pp. Cvr spotted, sl shelfworn.
                       *(Epistemologist)* **$27.50**

**Pinchot, Gifford**
- A primer of forestry. Washington, DC:
G.P.O., 1899, 1905. 2 vols. 1st edn. 16mo.
88; 88 pp. 65 plates, 130 text figs. Pict blind-
stamped cloth.            *(Diamond)* **$45**

**Pinkerton, James N.**
- Sleep and its phenomena. An essay. 1839. 1st
sep edn. Orig cloth, rebacked, inner hinges
reprd.                    *(Robertshaw)* **£9**

**Pirrie, William & Keith, William**
- Acupressure: an excellent method of arresting
surgical haemorrhage and of accelerating the
healing of wounds. Illustrated by engravings
on wood by Bagg. London, Edinburgh &
Dublin: 1867. 1st edn. Tall 8vo. 190 pp. Orig
cloth, top of spine chipped.   *(M&S)* **$75**
- Acupressure: an excellent method of arresting
surgical haemorrhage and of accelerating the
healing of wounds. London: John Churchill,
1867. 1st sep edn. 8vo. 190 pp. 46 text figs.
Orig cloth, cvrs lightly faded & soiled. Pres
copy.                     *(Rootenberg)* **$250**

**[Pitt, Robert]**
- The craft and frauds of physick expos'd ...
with instructions to prevent being cheated
and destroy'd by the prevailing practice.
London: 1702. [10],192 pp. Light worming.
Contemp panelled calf, recased.
                          *(Goodrich)* **$250**
- The craft and frauds of physick expos'd ...
1703. 2nd edn. Contemp calf, rebacked, mor

label. B'plate. *(Robertshaw)* £140
- The craft and frauds of physick expos'd ...
London: Tim. Childe, 1703. 2nd edn, imprvd
& augmented. [xvi],203,[i blank],[viii index].
Sm stain lower crnr last few leaves. Contemp
panelled calf, spine ends & edges rubbed.
*(Pollak)* £120

**Pittman, E.F.**
- The mineral resources of New South Wales
(Geological Survey of New South Wales).
Sydney: 1901. viii,487 pp. Cold frontis, fldg
cold map, fldg cold sections, very many
plates. Orig printed bds, worn. Ex lib.
*(Weiner)* £40

**Planck, Max**
- The origin and development of the quantum
theory: being the Nobel Prize address ... at
Stockholm 2 June 1920. Translated by H.T.
Clarke ... Oxford: 1922. 1st edn in English.
23 pp. Orig wraps. *(Scientia)* $65
- The theory of heat radiation. Translated by
M. Masius. Phila: 1914. 1st edn in English
(from 2nd German edn). 225 pp.
*(Scientia)* $100
- Treatise on thermodynamics. Translated ...
1921. New imp. xii,272 pp. Few diags.
Underlining on one page. *(Weiner)* £25
- Treatise on thermodynamics. Translated ...
London: Longmans, Green, 1927. 3rd edn,
from the 7th German edn. xiv,297,[vii] pp. 4
text figs. Spine worn. *(Pollak)* £20
- The universe in the light of modern physics.
Translated by W.H. Johnston. London: 1931.
1st edn in English. 110 pp. *(Scientia)* $15
- Where is science going? Prologue by Albert
Einstein. Translated and biographical notes
by J. Murphy. New York: 1932. 1st edn in
English. 221 pp. *(Scientia)* $40

**Plat, Sir Hugh [Platt]**
- The jewel house of art and nature containing
divers rare and profitable inventions ... art of
distillation ... discourse of minerals ...
London: ... Alsop, 1653. 2nd edn. Sm 4to.
[4]ff,232 pp. Text w'cuts. Lightly browned,
tear on 1 leaf. Mod calf. *(Zeitlin)* $1,250

**Plate-Glass-Book**
- The plate-glass-book, consisting of the
following authentic tables. I, The value ... II.
The glass-house table ... The compleat
appraiser. London: for W. Owen, 1771. 9th
edn, crrctd. Tall 12mo. Contemp roan,
rubbed, rebacked. Rider Haggard's b'plate.
*(McDowell)* £380

**Platen, M.**
- The new curative treatment of disease:
handbook of hygienic rules of life, health
culture and the cure of ailments, without the
use of drugs. Translated ... Bong & Co., 1898.

2 vols. 8vo. iii,1579 pp. 3 fldg cold anatomical
models. Orig cloth, spines sl worn.
*(Jenner)* £50

**Playfair, John**
- Elements of geometry; containing the first six
books of Euclid, with a supplement ...
Edinburgh: Bell & Bradfute, 1814. 4th edn,
enlgd. xvi,17-461 pp. 2 pp advts. Orig sheep,
worn, hinges weak. *(Pollak)* £25
- Outlines of natural philosophy, being heads
of lectures delivered in the University of
Edinburgh. 1819-16. 3rd & 2nd edns. 2 vols
(all published). xi,323; vii,341 pp. 7 plates.
Contemp bds, paper spines defective, one bd
loose. *(Whitehart)* £45

**Playfair, W.S.**
- A treatise on the science and practice of
midwifery. London: Smith, Elder, 1882. 4th
edn. Roy 8vo. 2 vols. 405,418 pp. Ills. One
hinge cracked, one signature loose.
*(Xerxes)* $30
- A treatise on the science and practice of
midwifery. Phila: 1889. 5th Amer edn. 671
pp. Full lea. *(Fye)* $20

**Pleasonton, A.J., et al.**
- Influence of the blue ray of the sunlight, and
of the blue colour of the sky. Phila: Claxton,
Remsen, 1877. Roy 8vo. 185 pp. Printed on
blue paper. Frontis. Back cvr & spine sl
wrinkled. *(Xerxes)* $65

**Pliny**
- The historie of the world. Commonly called
the naturall historie ... Translated ... by
Philemon Holland ... London: Adam Islip,
1601. 1st edn in English. Folio. 2 vols in 1.
[29]ff, 614pp, index [21]ff; [6]ff, 632 pp. 3
leaves in facsimile. Full sheep. *(Elgen)* $1,200
- The historie of the world: Commonly called,
the Natural Historie of C. Plinius Secundus
... London: Adam Islip, 1634. 2nd edn in
English. 2 vols in 1. Folio. [56],614,[42];
[10],632,[86] pp. Sep titles. Errata Vol II.
Contemp calf, rebacked. *(Rootenberg)* $750

**Plumbe, Samuel**
- A practical treatise on the diseases of the skin
... Phila: 1837. 1st Amer edn. 396,8[pub
advts] pp. Hand-cold frontis, 3 plates (2 cold,
1 fldg). Contemp calf, front jnt tender.
*(Elgen)* $95

**Plunket, Emmeline M.**
- Ancient calendars and constellations.
London: 1903. 8vo. 14 plates, 10 fldg charts.
Cloth. *(Argosy)* $50

**Plurality ...**
- The plurality of worlds ... See Whewall,
William

**Podmore, Frank**
- Mediums of the 19th century. New Hyde Park, NY: University Books, [1963]. 2 vols. xxviii,307,[1]; x,374 pp. Cloth. Slipcase.
*(Gach)* **$35**

**Policard, A.**
- See Leriche, R. & Policard, A.

**Pollen, Andrew G.**
- Fractures and dislocations in the child. Edinburgh & London, 1973. Sm 4to. vii,234 pp. Ills. Dw.        *(Jenner)* **£10**

**Pollock, Horatio, et al.**
- Hereditary and environmental factors in the causation of manic-depressive psychoses and dementia praecox. New York: State Hospitals Press, 1939. 473,[3] pp. Blue cloth.
*(Gach)* **$35**

**Polya, G.**
- Mathematics & plausible reasoning. Princeton: 1954. 1st edn. 2 vols. 280; 190 pp. Dws.        *(Oasis)* **$35**

**Polyak, S.L.**
- The retina. The anatomy and histology of the retina in man, ape and monkey ... Chicago: 1941. 1st edn. 4to. x,607 pp. Plus an atlas of 100 plates.        *(Elgen)* **$165**

**Pomeroy, Oren**
- The diagnosis and treatment of diseases of the ear. New York: 1886. 2nd edn. 413 pp.
*(Fye)* **$25**

**Pomet, Pierre**
- A compleat history of druggs, written in French by Monsieur Pomet ... to which is added what is further observable on the same subject. London: for R. Bonwicke, 1712. 1st edn in English. 2 vols in 1. Demy 4to. Orig dec panelled calf, old rebacking. *(Ivelet)* **£460**

**Pontey, William**
- The forest pruner, or timber owner's assistant ... with remarks on the old and outlines of a new system for the management of oak wood. London: 1808. 2nd edn. 8vo. 8 plates, some fldg & in color. Mod wraps.   *(Argosy)* **$125**
- The forest pruner, or timber owner's assistant: a treatise on the training or management of British timber. London: 1808. 2nd edn. 8vo. 277,[3] pp. Engvd frontis, 7 engvd plates (some fldg & tinted). Orig salmon-pink bds, one jnt a little split.
*(Deighton Bell)* **£45**

**Ponton, Mungo ·**
- Earthquakes, their history, phenomena, and probable causes. 1888. New & revsd edn. Sm 8vo. Orig cloth.        *(Edwards)* **£20**

**Pontopiddan, E.**
- The natural history of Norway: containing a particular and accurate account of the temperature of the air, the different soils, waters ... 1755. Folio. xxiv,206, vii,291,[xii] pp. Fldg map, 28 engvd plates. Minor foxing. Contemp calf, rebacked.
*(Wheldon & Wesley)* **£550**

**Pool, Eugene & McGowan, Frank**
- Surgery at the New York Hospital one hundred years ago. New York: 1930. 1st edn. 188 pp.        *(Fye)* **$35**

**Pool, J.L., at al.**
- Acoustic nerve tumors, early diagnosis and treatment. Springfield: 1970. 2nd edn. 232 pp. Dw.        *(Fye)* **$20**

**Poole, J.L. & Potts, J.D.**
- Aneurysms and arteriorenous anomalies of the brain. New York: 1965. xv,463 pp. Cold frontis, 267 ills. Cvrs rubbed & sl stained.
*(Jenner)* **£25**

**Poore, George Vivian**
- Essays on rural hygiene. New York & Bombay: 1903. 3rd edn. 426 pp. Frontis, 11 ills. B'plate. Cvrs sl rubbed & bumped.
*(Jenner)* **£30**

**Popenoe, Paul**
- See Gosney, E.S. & Popenoe, Paul

**Porcher, Francis Peyre**
- Resources of the Southern fields and forests, medical, economical and agricultural; being also a medical botany of the Southern States. Charleston: 1869. New edn, revsd & lgely augmntd. 15,[1],733, [3],[32],[12] pp. Light damp-staining. Orig cloth, rubbed.
*(M&S)* **$200**

**Porter, Eliot**
- Galapagos, the flow of wildness. Sierra Club. Folio. 2 vols. Dw, torn, in box.
*(Scientia)* **$135**

**[Porter, George R.]**
- A treatise on the origin, progressive improvement, and present state of the manufacture of porcelain and glass. Phila: 1834. 1st Amer edn. 12mo. 252 pp, index. Ills. Orig cloth-backed bds, paper label.
*(M&S)* **$35**

**[Porter, Rufus]**
- A select collection of valuable and curious arts, and interesting experiments ... Concord: Rufus Porter, 1826. 2nd edn. 16mo. [2],132 pp. Half-title, frontis, full-page ill. Some minor stains & foxing. Contemp mrbld bds, paper spine clumsily re-glued. *(M&S)* **$450**

**Porter, W.E.**
- See Turner, A. Logan & Porter, W.E.

**Portmann, Georges**
- Ear, nose and throat treatment in general practice. London: 1924. 1st English translation. 180 pp. *(Fye)* **$15**

**Posey, W.C. & Spiller, W.G.**
- The eye and nervous system: their diagnostic relations by various authors. Phila: 1906. 1st edn. 988 pp. Inner hinge cracked, loose in binding with moderate wear. *(Fye)* **$20**

**Post Office ...**
- The Post Office telephone service; illustrated description of the central and other exchanges in the metropolitan areas. 1903. v,89 pp. Many diags (1 fldg) & ills. Reprints of articles from 'The Electrician'. Tipped-in notice of rates of pay. *(Weiner)* **£75**
- The Post Office telephone service; illustrated description of the trunk, central and other exchanges in the metropolitan areas. n.d. [1905]. v,118 pp. Many diags (1 fldg) & ills. Orig printed card wrappers, a little worn. Tipped-in notice of rates of pay. *(Weiner)* **£60**

**Pott, Percival**
- The chirurgical works of Percivall Pott. Dublin: 1778. 2 vols. 1st edn thus. 508; 493 pp.5 plates. Messy ink scratchings on both titles. Tree calf, rebacked, crnrs worn. *(Jenner)* **£180**
- The chirurgical works, a new edition with his last corrections, to which are added, a short account of the life of the author ... 1803. 3 vols. Over 1200 pp. 22 plates. Lacks port. Uncut. One or two leaves torn or spotted. Orig grey bds, very loose. *(Weiner)* **£75**
- The chirurgical works. A new edition. 1779. 3 vols. 12 plates. Some worming in vol II, affecting title & a few leaves of text. Calf, worn & recently rebacked. Vol III also includes "On palsy of the lower limbs ... Pybus, 1614" *(Oasis)* **$300**
- The chirurgical works. A new edition, with his last corrections. London: For J. Johnson & others, 1790. 3 vols. viii,xiv,477, [i advts]; iv,487,[i]; vi,505,[i],[xxxi index],[i] pp. Port frontis, 19 plates. Browning, sl tear to plate. Recent half-calf. *(Pollak)* **£180**

**Potter, Irving W.**
- The place of version in obstetrics. St. Louis: 1922. 1st edn. 138 pp. 42 ills. *(Elgen)* **$40**
- The place of version in obstetrics. St. Louis: 1922. 1st edn. 138 pp. *(Fye)* **$40**

**Potts, J.D.**
- See Poole, J.L. & Potts, J.D.

**Potts, Percival**
- Observations on the nature and consequences of those injuries to which the head is liable from external violence. To which are added some few general remarks on fractures and dislocations. London: Hawes, 1768. 276,126 pp. New qtr calf, mrbld bds. *(Goodrich)* **$495**

**Potts, Robert**
- Elementary arithmetic, with brief notes of its history. Cambridge: Metcalfe & Son, 1876. 12 sections. 26; 48; 26; 20,[ii]; 14; 35,[iii]; 33; 14; 41; 30; 28,[ii]; 33 pp. Half-calf, rubbed. *(Pollak)* **£25**
- Euclid's elements of geometry. The first six books, and the portions of the eleventh and twelfth read at Cambridge ... London: Longman, 1865. xvi,504 pp. Orig cloth, faded. *(Pollak)* **£20**

**Pouchet, F.A.**
- The universe. Or, the infinitely great and the infinitely little. 1871. New edn. Thick roy 8vo. Gilt dec cloth, a.e.g. *(Edwards)* **£25**

**Poulet, Alfred**
- A treatise on foreign bodies in surgical practice. New York: 1880. 1st English translation. 2 vols. 271; 320 pp. *(Fye)* **$25**

**Poulton, Edward B.**
- Charles Darwin and the theory of natural selection. New York: 1896. 1st Amer edn. 224 pp. *(Scientia)* **$30**
- The colours of animals, their meaning and use, especially considered in the case of insects. New York: 1890. 1st Amer edn. Spine faded. *(Scientia)* **$37.50**

**Powell, Baden**
- On the nature and evidence of the primary laws of motion. Oxford: Ashmolean Society, 1837. 86 pp. Unopened. Orig printed wraps. *(Weiner)* **£15**
- On the theory of parallel lines. Oxford: Ashmolean Society, 1842. 46 pp. Plates. Unopened. Orig printed wraps. *(Weiner)* **£10**

**Power, d'Arcy**
- A short history of St. Bartholomew's Hospital 1123 - 1923. Printed for the Hospital, 1923. xv,201 pp. Cold frontis, 33 plates, 18 plans, 2 fold-outs, 13 text ills. Orig bds a bit faded, spine sl grubby. *(Jenner)* **£22**
- Wounds in war: their treatment and results. London: 1915. 1st edn. 108 pp. Ex lib. *(Fye)* **$25**

**Power, d'Arcy & Thompson, C.J.S.**
- Chronologia medica. A handlist of persons, periods and events in the history of medicine. New York: 1923. 1st Amer Edition. *(Scientia)* **$30**

**Power, Henry**
- Experimental philosophy, in three books; containing new experiments ... London: ... for John Martin ... 1664. 1st edn. 4to. [xxiv],193,[1 blank]. Errata leaf. Fldg engvd plate. Title & prelims dust soiled. Contemp calf, chipped, worn, jnts weak.
*(Pickering)* **$3,000**

**Power, Henry & Sedgwick, Leonard W.**
- The New Sydenham Society's lexicon of medicine and the allied sciences. 1881-1899. 5 vols. Orig half-mor, spines sl scuffed.
*(Oasis)* **$75**
- The New Sydenham Society's lexicon of medicine and the allied sciences. 1881-1899. Sm 4to. 5 vols. Unpaginated. Sl soiled. Ex lib with stamps, & labels on spines. *(Jenner)* **£75**

**Poynting, J.H. & Thomson, J.J.**
- A text-book of physics. Properties of matter. London: Griffin, 1902. vi,228 pp. 168 text figs. *(Pollak)* **£20**

**Poynting, John Henry**
- Collected papers. Cambridge: 1920. Lge 8vo. xxxii,768 pp. Frontis, diags. Sm lib stamp on title verso & ft of last page. *(Weiner)* **£60**

**Practical ...**
- The practical surveyor ... See Warner, Samuel

**Prain, D[avid]**
- On the morphology, teratology, and diclinism of the flowers of cannabis. Calcutta: Government Printing Office, 1904. 1st edn. Thin 4to. [2],51-82 pp. 5 plates. Orig printed bds, cloth backstrip. *(Dailey)* **$150**

**Pratt, J.G.**
- See Rhine, Joseph Banks & Pratt, J.G.

**Pratt, John Henry**
- The mathematical principles of mechanical philosophy, and their application ... Cambridge: Deighton, 1842. 2nd edn, revsd & imprvd. xxxii,620 pp. 5 fldg plates. Orig cloth-backed bds, spine ends worn, jnts weak. *(Pollak)* **£30**

**Pratt, Joseph Gaither, et al.**
- Extra-sensory perception after sixty years: a critical appraisal of the research ... New York: Henry Holt, [1940]. 1st edn. [ii],xiv,463 pp. Worn dw. *(Gach)* **$30**

**Prentice, Charles**
- Ophthalmic lenses. Phila: 1907. 2nd edn. 192 pp. *(Fye)* **$20**

**Prescott, Frederick**
- See Bicknell, Franklin & Prescott, Frederick

**Prescott, George B.**
- Electricity and the electric telegraph. New York: D. Appleton, 1877. 1st edn. 8vo. iv,5-978 pp. Fldg frontis, 564 text engvs. Orig cloth. Author's pres copy. *(Antiq Sc)* **$125**

**Preston, George Junkin**
- Hysteria and certain allied conditions. Phila: 1897. Ills. Spine tips rubbed. *(Gach)* **$35**

**Preston, Thomas**
- The theory of heat. London: Macmillan, 1894. 1st edn. xvi,719 pp. 190 text figs. *(Pollak)* **£15**

**Prestwich, J.**
- Geology: chemical, physical and stratigraphical. Oxford: 1886-88. 1st edn. xxvi,606 pp. 256 figs in text, num fldg maps & charts. Orig cloth. *(Whitehart)* **£28**

**Prestwich, Sir John**
- Dissertation on mineral, animal and vegetable poisons, containing a description of poisons in general, and respective antidotes. London: 1775. 331 pp. 10 engvd plates. Occas foxing throughout. Half-calf, mrbld bds, hinges tender. *(Jenner)* **£70**

**Pribram, Karl H.**
- Languages of the brain: experimental paradoxes and principles in neuropsychology. Englewood Cliffs, NJ: Prentice-Hall, [1971]. 1st edn. [xvi],432 pp. Worn dw. *(Gach)* **$50**

**Price, Frederick W.**
- Diseases of the heart. Their diagnosis, prognosis, and treatment by modern methods... 1918. xiv,472 pp. Cold frontis, ills. Lower hinge cracked. Pres inscrptn. *(Jenner)* **£12**

**Price, George McCready**
- The new geology. Mountain View, CA: 1923. 726 pp. *(Scientia)* **$45**
- The phantom of organic revolution. New York: 1924. 219 pp. *(Scientia)* **$30**

**Prichard, James Cowles**
- The natural history of man; comprising inquiries into the modifying influence ... 1845. 2nd edn. xviii,596 pp. 44 cold plates, 5 b/w plates, 97 figs in text. Orig blind-stamped pict cloth rebacked, orig spine laid on. *(Whitehart)* **£35**
- The natural history of man; comprising inquiries into the modifying influence of physical and moral agencies on the different tribes of the human family. London: Bailliere, 1855. 5th edn. 2 vols. xxiv,343; vii,[343]-720 pp. 19th c polished calf, sl wear. *(Gach)* **$275**
- The natural history of man; comprising inquiries into the modifying influence of

physical and moral agencies on the different tribes of the human family. London: Bailliere, 1855. 4th edn. 2 vols. 8vo. 62 cold plates. Pub cloth, blind & gilt.          *(McDowell)* **£240**
- Researches into the physical history of mankind. [1836-1847]. 3rd edn. 5 vols. xvi,376; xiv,373; xxii,507; xv,631; xv,570 pp. 19 plates, some cold, cold fldg map. Orig cloth, sl worn & dust stained. *(Whitehart)* **£90**
- The natural history of man. Comprising inquiries into the modifying influence of ... different tribes of the human family. 1848. 3rd edn, enlarged. Thick 8vo. 50 hand-cold, 5 plain, steel engvs. Mod half-calf.
                                          *(Edwards)* **£60**
- Researches into the physical history of mankind. London: Houlston & Stoneman, 1851, 1841-4-7. 4th, 3rd & 1st edns. 5 vols. 8vo. 22 plates, inc 9 cold. Orig cloth, gilt titles. A few library stamps, o/w a pristine set.
                                          *(Dailey)* **$250**
- A treatise on insanity and other disorders affecting the mind. London: Sherwood, Gilbert & Piper, 1835. xvi,483 pp. Lightly foxed.                            *(Gach)* **$385**

**Priestley, Joseph**
- Heads of lectures on a course of experimental philosophy particularly including chemistry, delivered at New College ... Dublin: for Wm. Jones ..., 1794. Pirated edn. 12mo. [ii blank],xxxi,[i blank],208,[ii blank]. Lib stamp. Mottled calf, jnts sl cracked.
                                          *(Pickering)* **$450**
- The history and present state of electricity, with original experiments ... London: for J. Dodsley ..., 1767. 1st edn. 4to. [iv],xxxi,[2 bibliog],[5 index],[1 ad]. Advt plate, 7 fldg engvd plates. Some foxing, soiling. Contemp sprinkled calf, rebacked.   *(Pickering)* **$1,500**
- The history and present state of discoveries relating to vision, light, and colours. London: J. Johnson, 1772. 1st edn. 4to. v,[1],xvi, [6, list of subsc],[2, errata],812,[12, index & catalogue] pp. Fldg engvd frontis, 24 fldg engvd plates. Orig bds.   *(Antiq Sc)* **$1,500**

**Prince, Morton**
- Clinical and experimental studies in personality. Cambridge, Mass: Sci-Art Publishers, 1929. 1st edn. xvi,559 pp. Thick 8vo. Pencilled. Red cloth, shelfworn.
                                          *(Gach)* **$35**

**Prince, Morton (ed.)**
- Contributions to psychology: psychopathology of everyday life and others. Boston: Richard G. Badger, [1918]. [ii],436 pp. Pub red buckram, paper label. *(Gach)* **$30**

**Pringle, A.**
- See Bailey, J. & Culley, G. (General view of the agriculture ...)

**Pringle, J.J.**
- An atlas of skin diseases. [New York: Rebman Co., ca 1900]. Folio. 50 chromo-litho plates printed by Lemercier. Orig red cloth. Lacking text (?).                         *(Dailey)* **$175**

**Pringle, Sir John**
- Six discourses, delivered ... when President of the Royal Society; on occasion of six annual assignments of Sir Godfrey Copley's Medal. London: for W. Strahan & T. Cadell, 1783. 1st edn. 8vo. Erratum leaf at end. Contemp mrbld bds, rebacked in calf. *(Quaritch)* **$650**

**Pritchard, Andrew**
- A history of infuoria, Including the Desmidiaceae and Diatomaceae British and Foreign. 1861. 4th edn, enlgd & revsd. Thick 8vo. 40 plates. Orig cloth, hinges tender, shaken.                       *(Edwards)* **£12**

**Pritchard, Rev. C.**
- Analogies in the progress of nature and grace ... to which are added two sermons preached before the British Association in 1866 and 1967. Cambridge: 1868. xxxiv,144 pp. Roughtrimmed, spine sl rubbed. Hulsean Lectures & essay attacking the new Darwinism.                       *(Jenner)* **£45**

**Proceedings ...**
- Antiquarian horology and the Proceedings of the Antiquarian Horological Society. Vols 1 through 4. 1953-1965. 4 vols. Half-calf, & buckram. All published.    *(Zeitlin)* **$100**
- The proceedings of the Charaka Club. Volumes 1-10. 1902-41. Ltd edns. Lib call numbers on spine, rebound in blue buckram.
                                          *(Fye)* **$650**
- Proceedings of the Tenth Annual Meeting of the Association of Medical Superintendents of American Institutions for the Insane. Utica: at the Asylum, 1855. 65 pp. Wraps.
                                          *(Poitras)* **$50**
- The situation in biological science. Proceedings of the Lenin Academy of Agricultural Sciences of the U.S.S.R., July 31 - August 7, 1948. Verbatim Report. Moscow: 1949. 631 pp. Lysenko affair. *(Scientia)* **$50**

**Procter, R.A.**
- The stars in their seasons, an easy guide to the knowledge of the stars ... 1883. 7 pp. 12 double-page maps. Ex lib with library stamps.
                                          *(Whitehart)* **£15**

**Proctor, Richard A.**
- Old and new astronomy. London: 1888. 4to. 816 pp. 31 plates. Half lea. *(Scientia)* **$85**

**Progress, Peter**
- See 'Peter Progress' (pseud.)

**Prout, William**
- Chemistry, meteorology and the functions of digestion considered with reference to natural theology. London: Pickering, 1834. 1st edn. 8vo. [xxviii],564 pp. Table, fldg cold map. Damp mark on end few leaves. Contemp calf, a little rubbed & insect gnawed.
*(Bow Windows)* **£70**
- An inquiry into the nature and treatment of gravel, calculus, and other diseases ... 1821. viii,227 pp. Advts. 9 cold panels on final leaf. Occas light markings, tear on one leaf without loss. Some worming at end. Mrbld bds, rebacked with mod calf gilt.    *(Jenner)* **£100**

**Pruitt, Basil**
- See Salisbury, Roger & Pruitt, Basil

**Pryor, William**
- The treatment of pelvic inflammations through the vagina. Phila: 1899. 1st edn. 248 pp.    *(Fye)* **£30**

**Puchkovskaya, N.**
- Corneal transplantation in complicated leukomas. Moscow: [ca 1959]. 1st English translation. 211 pp. Dw.    *(Fye)* **£40**

**Pullan, J.M.**
- The history of the abacus. London: 1968. Many ills.    *(Winterdown)* **£12**

**Punnett, R.C.**
- Heredity in poultry. London: 1923. 1st edn. 204 pp. Rear cvr stained.    *(Scientia)* **$65**
- Mendelism. Cambridge: 1905. 1st edn. Sm 8vo. vii,63 pp. Little foxing. Orig cloth.
*(Wheldon & Wesley)* **£40**
- Mendelism. Cambridge: 1907. 2nd edn. 85 pp.    *(Scientia)* **$30**

**Purdy, Avis B.**
- See Bennett, A.E. & Purdy, Avis B.

**Pusey, William**
- The history of dermatology. Springfield: 1933. 1st edn.    *(Scientia)* **$50**
- The history of dermatology. Springfield: 1933. 1st edn. Frontis, xiii,223 pp. Ills, ports.
*(Elgen)* **$55**

**Putnam, J.**
- The metric system of weights and measures. Second edition, revised and enlarged. Boston: American Metric Bureau, 1877. 8vo. 70,13 pp. 3 charts (1 long, cold & fldg). Orig cloth. Author's pres copy to Edward Pickering.
*(M&S)* **$85**

**Putnam, James Jackson**
- A memoir of Dr. James Jackson, with sketches of his father ... by James Jackson Putnam, M.D. Boston & New York: 1906.

4to. 456 pp. 32 ills.    *(Poitras)* **$75**

**Pye-Smith, P.H.**
- The Lumleian Lectures on certain points in the aetiology of disease delivered before the R.C.P. 1892, to which is added ... 1895. [2],236 pp. Cloth, dust stained.
*(Whitehart)* **£25**

**Quain, Jones**
- Elements of anatomy. New York: 1882. 9th edn. 2 vols. 747; 947 pp. 380 engvs (78 cold). Rebound, orig spines laid down.    *(Fye)* **$75**
- Human anatomy, edited by Richard Quain and William Sharpey. Phila: 1849. 1st Amer edn. 2 vols. 638; 639 pp.    *(Fye)* **$75**

**Quick, Armand**
- The physiology and pathology of hemostasis. Phila: 1951. 1st edn. 188 pp.    *(Fye)* **$15**

**Quincy, John**
- A complete English dispensatory in four parts. 1742. 12th edn, enlgd & crrctd. Contemp calf, very worn.    *(Robertshaw)* **£20**
- Medicina statica: being the aphorisms of Sanctorius, translated into English with large explanations. London: William Newton, 1718. lvi,112 [i.e. 312] pp. Frontis, lge fldg plate. Leaves P1 & P2 misbound following P4. Mod mrbld paper bds.    *(Pollak)* **£70**
- Pharmacopoiea officinalis & extemporanea. Or, a complete English dispensatory, in four parts ... London, Thomas Longman, 1739. 11th edn, enlgd & crrctd. xvi,700,lx pp. Occas foxing. Contemp calf, rubbed, crnrs worn.    *(Pollak)* **£30**

**[Quincy, John]**
- Quincy's      Lexicon      Physico-Medicum improved: or a dictionary of the terms employed in medicine ... with many amendments and additions, expressive of discoveries lately made ... New York: 1802. ·1st Amer edn. 8vo. 4,646,[2] pp. Full contemp calf.    *(M&S)* **$75**

**Quinn, John Philip**
- Gambling and gambling devices, being a complete systematic educational exposition designed to instruct the youth of the world to avoid all forms of gambling. Canton, Ohio: 1912. ii,306,[2] pp. Port, many ills. Orig pict cloth gilt.    *(Weiner)* **£95**

**Rachford, Benjamin Knox**
- Neurotic disorders of childhood including a study of auto and intestinal intoxications ... New York: E.B. Treat, 1905. 1st edn. 440,[8] pp. Olive cloth.    *(Gach)* **$85**

**Radar ...**
- Principles of radar. Cambridge, MA: M.I.T.,

1944. 1st edn. [922] pp. Num ills. Inner hinges cracked, sl shaken. Ex lib. *(Elgen)* **$50**

**Radcliffe, Charles B., et al.**
- On diseases of the spine and of the nerve. Phila: Lea, 1871. 196 pp. Uncut. New cloth. *(Goodrich)* **$90**

**Radford, Thomas**
- Observations on the Caesarian section, and on other obstetrical operations, with an appendix of cases. London: 1865. 68,xlviii pp. 9 fldg plates. Orig soft blue cloth, bound into mod cloth bds. Author's sgnd pres copy. *(Jenner)* **£18**

**Raffald, Elizabeth**
- The experienced English housekeeper ... nearly eight hundred original receipts ... and the plan of a fire stove whereby any common fuel may be burnt ... 1771. 2nd edn. iv,384 pp. 3 fldg plates. Some heavy foxing. Old calf, worn, crudely rebacked. *(Weiner)* **£85**
- The experienced English housekeeper, for the use and ease of ladies, housekeepers, cooks, &c. ... London: for Osborne & Griffin, 1794. 8vo. Port frontis, fldg plate, 2 lge fldg plates. 1 leaf reprd. Later roan. *(McDowell)* **£140**
- The experienced English housekeeper, for the use and ease of ladies, housekeepers, cooks, &c. Phila: 1818. New edn. 3 engvd plates. Early pages stained, plates misfolded. Old sheep, jnts broken. *(Allen)* **$150**

**Railway-Engine ...**
- The railway-engine driver's guide ... See Flachat, E. & Petiet, J.

**Rainbird, W. & H.**
- The agriculture of Suffolk, including the report to which the prize was given by the R.A.S.E. 1849. viii,324 pp. 70 ills, map. Orig cloth. *(Phenotype)* **£42**

**Ramadge, Francis Hopkins**
- Consumption curable; and the manner in which nature ... operates in effecting a healing process in cases of consumption ... London: Longman ..., 1836. 3rd edn. 8vo. li,[1], 213,[1] pp. 8 cold plates. Some browning, marginal worming. Mod qtr cloth. *(Dailey)* **$100**

**Ramey, E.R. & O'Doherty, D.S. (eds.)**
- Electrical studies on the unanesthetized brain. New York: 1960. 1st edn. 423 pp. Ills. *(Oasis)* **$25**

**Ramon Y Cajal, Santiago**
- Neuron theory or reticular theory? Objective evidence of the anatomical unity of nerve cells. (1933). Translated by M.U. Purkiss & C.A. Fox. Madrid: 1954. 1st edn in English.

Dw. *(Scientia)* **$100**
- The structure of the retina [1892, 1894, 1933]. Translated by S.A. Thorpe & M. Glickstein. Springfield: 1972. 1st edn in English. Dw. *(Scientia)* **$75**
- Studies on the cerebral cortex. (1901-02). Translated by L.M. Kraft. Chi: 1955. 1st edn in English. *(Scientia)* **$75**
- Studies on the diencephalon. Translated by E. Ramon-Moliner. Springfield: 1966. 1st edn in English. Dw. *(Scientia)* **$50**
- Studies on vertebrate neurogenesis (1929). Translated by L. Guth. Springfield: 1960. 1st edn in English. Dw. *(Scientia)* **$75**

**Ramsay, Alexandar**
- Anatomy of the heart, cranium, and brain, adapted to the purposes of the medical ... practitioner ... Constable, 1813; (with) A series of plates ... Edin: Constable, 1813. 4to, 2nd edns, much enlgd. [2],66 pp. 15 handcold plates. Orig wraps, orig folder. *(Antiq Sc)* **$750**

**Ramsay, Professor A.C.**
- The physical geology and geography of Great Britain; a course of six lectures ... London: Stanford, 1863. [iv],145 pp. 9 figs. Sm stamp on title. Orig blind-dec cloth, front jnt a little weak. *(Pollak)* **£15**

**Ramsay, William**
- Essays biographical and chemical. London: Constable, 1908. 1st edn. 8vo. Pub cloth. *(McDowell)* **£28**
- The gases of the atmosphere. The history of their discovery. London: Macmillan, 1896. 1st edn. 8vo. Ports. Pub cloth. *(McDowell)* **£110**
- The gases of the atmosphere. The history of their discovery. London: Macmillan, 1905. 3rd edn. xiii,296 pp. Frontis, 8 plates. Ex lib. A working copy. *(Pollak)* **£10**
- See Hutton, Charles & Ramsay, William
- A system of inorganic chemistry. 1891. xv,700 pp. Ills. Worn. *(Weiner)* **£30**

**Ramsbotham, Francis H.**
- The principles and practice of obstetric medicine and surgery ... London: 1844: 2nd edn. 732 pp. 110 ills. Orig blue cloth, spine torn, bds very worn & bumped, hinges cracked. *(Jenner)* **£22**
- The principles and practice of obstetric medicine and surgery, in reference to the process of parturition. 1844. 2nd edn, enlgd. 90 steel-engvd plates, w'engvs in text. *(Robertshaw)* **£56**
- The principles and practice of obstetric medicine and surgery ... Phila: 1847. 4th Amer edn. 527 pp. 55 litho plates. Full lea. *(Fye)* **$30**

**Ramsbotham, John**
- Practical observations in midwifery ... with notes by William P. Dewees. Phila: 1822. 1st Amer edn. 379 pp. Some staining. Full lea. *(Fye)* **$200**

**Ranby, John**
- The method of treating gunshot wounds. London: John & Paul Knapton, 1744. 1st edn. 4to. [14],84 pp. Text w'cut. Wrappers. In slipcase. *(Rootenberg)* **$450**

**Rand, C.W.**
- See Cuneo, H.M. & Rand, C.W.

**Randles, W.B.**
- See Hinds, H.L. & Randles, W.B.

**Rank, B.K., et al.**
- Surgery of repair as applied to hand injuries. Edinburgh: 1968. 350 pp. Dw. *(Fye)* **$40**

**Rankin, Egbert Guernsey**
- A digest of external therapeutics with numerous formulae arranged for reference. New York: Boericke & Runyon, 1900. 2nd edn, enlgd & rvsd. 754 pp. *(Poitras)* **$30**

**Ranney, Ambrose**
- Lectures on nervous diseases from the standpoint of cerebral and spinal localization ... Phila: 1888. xiv,778 pp. Num plates. *(Goodrich)* **$65**

**Ransommet, Baron Eugene de**
- Sketches of the inhabitants, animal life & vegetation ... of Ceylon, as well as the submarine scenery near the coast, taken in a diving bell. Vienna: for the author, 1867. Folio. 59,[i] pp. 26 litho plates, 4 cold. Foxing on edges. Orig cloth, new spine. *(Pollak)* **£375**

**Ranvier, Louis**
- See Cornil, A. Victor & Ranvier, Louis

**Rathborne, Aaron**
- The surveyor in foure bookes. London: W. Stansby for W. Burre, 1616. 1st edn. Folio. 6,228 pp. 2 engvd port, engvd title, text w'cuts. Title mounted on old blank. 20th c full calf. *(Antiq Sc)* **$1,700**

**Raven, Canon Charles E.**
- John Ray, naturalist. His life and works. Cambridge: 1942. Port. *(Winterdown)* **£40**

**Ravitch, Mark (ed.)**
- The papers of Alfred Blalock. Balt: 1966. 1st edn. 2 vols. Slipcase. *(Fye)* **$80**

**Ray, John**
- Miscellaneous discourses concerning the dissolution and changes of the world. Edited by C. Moxon. Wernerian Club, 1850. Roy 8vo. viii,169 pp. Binder's cloth. *(Wheldon & Wesley)* **£30**
- Observations topographical, moral ... made in a journey through part of the Low-Countries, Germany, Italy, and France ... London: for John Martyn, 1673. [xvi],499,[viii], sub-title, 115 pp. 4 engvd plates, 3 w'cuts. Prelims dampmarked. New half-calf. *(Pollak)* **£250**
- Three physico-theological discourses, concerning I ... II ... III The dissolution of the world and future conflagration ... London: for William Innys, 1732. "Fourth edition" (but 5th). xxxi,456 pp. Port frontis, 4 plates. Newly rebnd with old bds. *(Pollak)* **£50**
- The wisdom of God manifested in the works of the creation: in two parts ... London: for William Innys, 1714. 6th ed, crrctd. [xvi],17-405,[iii] pp. Lacking port (although not called for by Keynes 65). Minor wormholes. Contemp panelled calf, rebacked. *(Pollak)* **£50**

**Rayleigh, Lord [Strutt, John William]**
- Scientific papers. New York: Dover Publications, 1964. 6 vols in 3. Reprint of Cambridge University Press "Collected Papers", 1899-1920, 6 vols. Addtnl bibliog. *(Pollak)* **£100**
- The theory of sound. London: Macmillan, 1877-78. 1st edn. 2 vols. 8vo. xi,[1], 326,[2]; x,302,[2] pp. Text figs. Orig cloth. *(Antiq Sc)* **$450**
- The theory of sound. London: Macmillan, 1894-86. 2nd edn, revsd & enlgd. 2 vols. 8vo. xiv,480; xvi,504 pp. Num text ills. *(Pollak)* **£150**
- The theory of sound. London: Macmillan, 1894. 2nd edn, revsd & enlgd. 2 vols. 8vo. Pub dark brown cloth, spine gilt *(McDowell)* **£60**

**Raymond, Rossiter W.**
- Statistics of mines and mining in the States and territories west of the Rocky Mountains for the year 1870. Washington: 1872. 1st edn. 8vo. [5],566 pp. Ills, index, 5 fldg tables. Orig cloth. *(M&S)* **$50**

**Raynaud**
- Raynaud's two essays on local asphyxia. London: New Sydenham Society, 1888. Sl foxing & dust marks. Orig cloth. *(Bow Windows)* **£36**

**Read, J.**
- The alchemist in life, literature and art. 1947. xii,100 pp. Cold frontis, 29 plates. Orig cloth, t.e.g. *(Whitehart)* **£18**
- Humour and humanism in chemistry. 1947. 1st edn. xxiii,388 pp. Frontis, 89 ills. Orig cloth. *(Whitehart)* **£18**

## Reade, T.M.
- The origin of mountain ranges considered experimentally, structurally, dynamically. 1886. 8vo. xviii,359 pp. 42 plates. Cloth trifle damp-stained. *(Wheldon & Wesley)* £30

## Reamur, Rene A.F.
- Memoirs on steel and iron [1722]. Translated by A.G. Sisco ... Chicago: 1956. xxxxiv,396 pp. 17 plates. Dw. *(Scientia)* $30

## Red Cross Research Committee
- Trench fever. 1918. Lge 8vo. vii,446 pp. 7 plates, 7 charts, 65 tables. Cvrs sl soiled & faded. *(Jenner)* £40

## Redwood, Iltyd I.
- A practical treatise on mineral oils and their by-products including a short history of the Scotch shale industry. ... 1897. xiv,336 pp. Frontis, fldg plate, ills, tables. *(Weiner)* £50

## Redwood, T.
- See Bell, J. & Redwood, T.

## Reece, D.M.
- A plain and practical treatise on the epidemic cholera, as it prevailed in the City of New York, in the summer of 1832 ... 1833. 110 pp. Frontis fldg plan of New York. Orig cloth, sl worn. *(Whitehart)* £60

## Reece, Richard
- The medical guide for the use of families and young practitioners in medicine and surgery ... 1808. 5th edn, considerably enlgd & imprvd. 2 plates. Contemp calf, rubbed. *(Robertshaw)* £25
- The medical guide, for the use of clergy, heads of families, and practitioners in medicine and surgery ... comprising the latest and most important discoveries in medicine. 1810. xx,515 pp. Contemp tree calf, rubbed, worn. Hinges weak. *(Whitehart)* £65

## Reese, David Meredith
- Phrenology known by its fruits, being a brief review of Doctor Brigham's late work ... New York: Howe & Bates, 1836. [ii],195,[3] pp. *(Gach)* $50

## Reese. Algernon
- Tumors of the eye. New York: 1951. 1st edn. 574 pp. *(Fye)* $10

## Reich, Wilhelm
- Character-analysis. Translated by Theodore P. Wolfe. Third, enlarged edition. New York: 1949. 2nd edn in English. xxvi,516 pp. *(Gach)* $30

## Reichart, Edward T.
- See Mitchell, S. Weir & Reichart, Edward T.

## Reichenbach, Baron Karl von
- Researches on magnetism, electricity, heat, light, crystallization and chemical attraction in the relations to the vital force. Parts I, II. Translated & edited ... by W. Gregory. London: 1850. 1st edn in English. 463 pp. 3 plates. Rebnd in blue cloth. *(Scientia)* $65
- Researches on magnetism, electricity, heat, light, crystallization and chemical attraction in the relations to the vital force. Parts I & II, including the second edition of the first part. 1850. xlv,[1],463 pp. 3 fldg plates. Orig cloth, spine worn. *(Whitehart)* £50

## Reid, David Boswell
- Academical examinations on the principles of chemistry ... Edinburgh & London: 1825. 1st edn. 2 vols. 12mo. Occasional spotting & ink stains, lib stamps, & a few contemp marginal notes. Orig half-calf, rebacked, new endpapers. Pres copy. *(Zeitlin)* $225

## Reid, Hugo
- A catechism of chemistry; exhibiting a condensed view of the facts and principles of that science. Edinburgh: Oliver & Boyd, 1837. Sole edn. 12mo. Lge fldg table, w'cuts in text. Pub cloth. *(McDowell)* £24

## Reid, John
- Essays on hypochondrical and other nervous affections. Phila: Carey, 1817. 1st Amer edn. 209 pp. Old calf, disbound. *(M&S)* $85
- An experimental investigation into the functions of the eighth pair of nerves, or the glosso-pharyngeal, pneumogastric, and spinal accessory ... Phila: New Orleans, 1840. 1st Amer edn. 8vo. 59,[1] pp. Disbound, some foxing, library stamp. *(Zeitlin)* $75

## Reid, T.
- An inquiry into the human mind, on the principles on common sense. Edinburgh: 1818. 8vo. 400 pp. Lacking half-title. Some foxing. Contemp calf, rubbed, upper jnt cracked at head. *(Bow Windows)* £48

## Reid, Thomas
- Treatise on clock and watch making, theoretical and practical. Edinburgh: John Fairburn, 1826. 1st edn. 8vo. xii,476 pp. 20 plates. Some foxing & plate offsetting. Mod blue cloth. Robert W. Coltman association copy. *(Zeitlin)* $700
- Treatise on clock and watch making, theoretical and practical ... Phila: Carey & Lea, 1832. 1st Amer edn. 8vo. xiii,476 pp. 20 plates (browned & dust-stained). Mod half-calf. *(Zeitlin)* $500

## Reid, Lieut.-Col. W.
- An attempt to discover the law of storms. By means of facts ... and hence to point out a

cause for the variable winds ... 1838. Lge 8vo.
Fldg charts, text ills. Orig cloth, worn, hinges
tender.                          *(Edwards)* **£30**

**Reid. St. George**
- Bacteriological diagnosis. 1897. iv,64 pp.
Some soiling. Cvrs soiled, label on cvr. Pub
file copy.                       *(Jenner)* **£10**

**Reinhold, August F.**
- Nature vs. drugs. A challenge to the drugging
fraternity. New York: Privately published,
[1898]. 1st edn. Frontis, 546,vii,2 [advts] pp.
Num ills. Gilt pict cloth.       *(Elgen)* **$50**

**Reinhold, August F. (trans.)**
- Louis Kuehne's facial diagnosis. A free and
abridged translation with notes. New York:
A.F. Reinhold, 1897. 1st edn. 8vo. 106 pp.
Num ills. Cloth with gilt vignette on front.
                                 *(Dailey)* **$45**

**Reinnel, F.**
- The carpenters, joiners, cabinet makers, and
gilders' companion. London: Brodie &
Middleton, n.d. [ca 1876]. 8vo. 89,[1], [12],40
pp. Disbound.                    *(Burmester)* **£25**

**Religio ...**
- Religio medici ... See Browne, Sir Thomas

**Religion ...**
- The religion of nature ... See Wollaston,
William

**Relph, John**
- An inquiry into the medical efficacy of a new
species of Peruvian bark ... observations
respecting the choice of bark in general.
London: J. Phillips, 1794. 1st edn. 8vo.
viii,177 pp. Mod grey bds. From the library
of the Edinburgh Medical Society.
                                 *(Deighton Bell)* **£175**

**Remarks ...**
- Remarks upon Dr. William Redmond's
principles and constituence of antimony, and
several other of the Doctor's opinions in
chemistry, by a chemist. 1764. 55 pp.
Disbound.                        *(Weiner)* **£65**

**Remington, Joseph F.**
- The practice of pharmacy: a treatise on the
modes of making and dispensing officinal,
unofficinal,      and      extemporaneous
preparations, with ... properties, uses and
dosage. Phila: 1886. 1st edn. Lge 8vo, 1080
pp. 500 ills. Orig pebble cloth.  *(Elgen)* **$85**

**Rendu, C. le**
- Theory of the glaciers of the Savoy ...
[translated and edited]. 1874. 1st English edn.
216 pp. 1 plate & facsimile title of orig 1840

edn.                             *(Whitehart)* **£25**

**Renshaw, Samuel, et al.**
- Children's sleep. New York: 1933. 242 pp.
Adhesive stain on flyleaf. V sl spotted.
                                 *(Epistemologist)* **$25**

**Report ...**
- Eighth annual report of the New-England
Female Medical College. College Rooms,
274, Washington Street, Boston: 1857. 8vo.
24 pp. Orig green printed wraps.
                                 *(Hemlock)* **$65**
- Report of the Commissioners of ...
Massachusetts, on the routes of canals from
Boston Harbour, to Connecticut and Hudson
Rivers. Boston: True & Green, 1826. 1st edn.
8vo. 185,[1], [2],62 pp. Lge fldg map sl
browned. Orig printed wraps.     *(M&S)* **$125**
- Report of the Select Committee of the Senate
of the United States on the sickness and
mortality on board emigrant ships.
Washington: 1954. 147 pp.        *(Poitras)* **$150**
- Report on insanity and idiocy in
Massachusetts. By the Commission on
Lunacy, under Resolve of the Legislature of
1854. House Report No. 144. Boston:
William White, 1855. 4to. x,228 pp.
                                 *(Poitras)* **$37.50**
- Report on the experiments made in 1888 in
the treatment of the downy mildew and black
rot of the grape vine. Washington, DC:
G.P.O., 1889. 1st edn. 61 pp. 2 plates. Orig
wraps.                           *(Diamond)* **$45**
- A report on vaccination and its results, based
on the evidence taken by the Royal
Commission during the years 1889 - 1897.
Vol 1: The text ... [all published]. New
Sydenham Society, 1898. 493 pp. Prelims
foxed. Orig olive cloth.         *(Jenner)* **£18**
- Report to Her Majesty's Principal Secretary
of State on ... sanitary conditions ... See
Chadwick, Edwin
- Seventh report to the directors of the
American Asylum at Hartford for the
education and instruction of the deaf and
dumb, exhibited to the Asylum. Hartford:
1823. 8vo. 40 pp. Sisbound, sewn.
                                 *(Hemlock)* **$45**

**Reuleux, Franz**
- The constructor. A hand-book of machine
design. Translated ... Phila: 1893. Lge 4to.
xviii,312 pp. Frontis, over 1200 ills. Inner
hinges cracked, lacking front free endpaper.
                                 *(Whitehart)* **£55**
- The kinematics of machinery ... translated.
London: Macmillan, 1876. Sm 4to. xvi,622
pp. 451 text figs. Pict cloth, rebacked, sl wear.
Ex lib.                          *(Diamond)* **$60**

**Revesz, Geza**
- Psychology and the art of the blind.

Translated ... London: Longmans, Green, [1950]. 1st edn in English. xiv,338 pp. Ills. *(Gach)* **$30**

**Revy, Julian John**
- See Bateman, John Frederic & Revy, Julian John

**Reymond, Arnold**
- History of the sciences in Greco-Roman antiquity. London: 1927. 1st edn. 245 pp. *(Oasis)* **$25**

**Reynolds, Sir J. Russell**
- Epilepsy: its symptoms. treatment and relation to other chronic convulsive diseases. London: 1861. 1st edn. xxix,360,32 [pub ctlg] pp. Uncut & unopened. Orig blind-stamped cloth, spine edges frayed. *(Elgen)* **$300**

**Reynolds, R.S.**
- An essay on the breeding and management of draught horses. 1882. vi,104 pp. Orig cloth, gilt. *(Phenotype)* **£32**

**Rhees, William Jones**
- The Smithsonian Institution. Documents relative to its origin and history, 1835 - 1899. Washington: G.P.O., 1901. 1st edn. 2 vols. liii,1983 pp. 2 fldg maps. Sl cvr staining & sl wear to one spine & cvr. *(Diamond)* **$75**

**Rhind, William**
- A treatise on the nature and cure of intestinal worms of the human body arranged according to the classification of Rudolphi and Bremser ... London: 1829. 152 pp, 6 engvd plates. Uncut in recent cloth. *(Goodrich)* **$125**

**Rhine, Joseph Banks**
- New world of the mind. London: Faber & Faber, [1954]. 1st British edn. [xii],291,[1] pp. Cloth. *(Gach)* **$15**

**Rhine, Joseph Banks & Pratt, J.G.**
- Parapsychology: frontier science of the mind. A survey of the field, the methods, and the facts of ESP and PK research. Springfield: Charles C. Thomas, [1957]. 1st edn. 220 pp. Dw. *(Gach)* **$20**

**Rhine, Joseph Banks (ed.)**
- Progress in parapsychology. Parapsychology Press, [1971]. xvi,313 pp. Worn dw. *(Gach)* **$17.50**

**Ribot, Th.**
- Diseases of memory. New York: Humboldt, 1883. 48 pp. Wraps. *(Xerxes)* **$80**
- The psychology of the emotions. New York: 1911. 2nd edn. *(Epistemologist)* **$35**

**Rice, Nathan P.**
- Trials of a public benefactor as illustrated in the discovery of etherization. New York: 1859. 1st edn. Ex lib. Top of spine worn. *(Scientia)* **$135**
- Trials of a public benefactor as illustrated in the discovery of etherization. New York: Pudney & Russell, 1859. 1st edn. [4],460 pp. Sev spots of foxing on title. Orig cloth. *(M&S)* **$125**
- Trials of a public benefactor, as illustrated in the discovery of etherization. New York: 1859. 1st edn. 460 pp. Hd & ft of spine torn. With Logan Clendening's b'plate. *(Fye)* **$200**

**Rich ...**
- A rich cabinet with variety of inventions ... See White, John

**Richard, D.W.**
- See Fishman, Alfred & Richard D.W

**Richards, John Morgan**
- A chronology of medicine: ancient, mediaeval and modern. London: Bailliere, Tindall & Cox, 1880. 314 pp. Ills. *(Poitras)* **$75**

**Richards, Theodore**
- The scientific work of Morris Loeb. Harvard University Press, 1913. 1st edn. 349pp. *(Oasis)* **$60**

**Richards, Theodore & Willard, H.H.**
- Determinations of atomic weights. Washington: 1919. 1st edn. 113 pp. Carnegie Institute publication No. 125. *(Oasis)* **$125**

**Richards, Vivyan**
- From crystal to television ... with a foreword by J.L. Baird. 1928. x,116 pp. Frontis, diags. *(Weiner)* **£25**

**Richardson, Sir Benjamin Ward**
- Vita medica: chapters of medical life and work. London: 1897. xvi,496,[32 advts] pp. Orig maroon cloth. *(Jenner)* **£35**

**Richardson, C.G.**
- Corn and cattle producing districts of France. 1887. xiv,528, 8 [pub advts] pp. Fldg cold map, ills. Brown cloth, a little grubby. *(Phenotype)* **£32**

**Richardson, G.F.**
- Geology for beginners, comprising a familiar explanation of geology ... London: Bailliere, 1842. xx,530,[i advt] pp. Frontis, title vignette, 251 text w'cuts. Occas foxing & mark. Orig dec cloth, sl slack. *(Pollak)* **£16**

**Richardson, Robert**
- The scalpel and the heart. New York: 1970. 1st Amer edn. 323 pp. Dw. *(Fye)* **$20**

**Richens R.H.**
- See Hudson, P.S. & Richens, R.H.

**Richerand, A.**
- Elements of physiology ... translated from the French ... London: Thomas & George Underwood, 1819. 3rd edn. 4to. xxiv,523,[11 index] pp. Staining on endpaper. Qtr lea, mrbld bds, spine damaged.        *(Poitras)* **$75**
- Elements of physiology ... translated from the French ... with notes and improvements. Phila: 1823. viii,621,xvi pp. Foxing. Orig sheep, rubbed.        *(Goodrich)* **$75**
- Elements of physiology. Translated from the French ... Phila: 1825. 5th Amer edn. viii,[9],448,111 pp. Browning & foxing. Tree calf, scuffed.        *(Elgen)* **$60**

**Richter, Derek**
- Addiction and brain damage. London: Croon Helm, 1980. 305 pp.        *(Poitras)* **$17.50**

**Ricketts, H.T.**
- Infection immunity and serum therapy, in relation to the infectious diseases of man. Chicago: 1911. 2nd edn, revsd & enlgd. xv,785 pp. Some shelf wear.        *(Elgen)* **$90**

**[Ricketts, H.T.]**
- Contributions to medical science by Howard Taylor Ricketts, 1870-1910. Published as a tribute to his memory ... Chicago: [1911]. 1st edn. Lge 8vo. ix,497 pp. Frontis, 22 plates (one cold). Orig buckram, inner hinges cracked.        *(Elgen)* **$150**

**Riddell, J. Scott**
- A manual of ambulance. London: 1897. 3rd edn. xvi,115 pp. Photo frontis, 169 ills, plates. Orig brown cloth, spine sunned.        *(Jenner)* **£9**

**Riddell, Robert**
- The carpenter and joiner, stair builder and hand-railer. n.d. [ca 1870]. Imp 4to. 124 pp explanatory text. 58 litho plates of plans, 4 plates duplicated on card with hinged pieces. Contemp half-calf, some rubbing, sides a little soiled.        *(Deighton Bell)* **£110**

**Riddle, Edward**
- Recreations in science and natural philosophy. Dr. Hutton's translation of Montucla's edition of Ozanam. Revised and corrected ... by Edward Riddle. William Tegg, 1844. New edn. xiv,826 pp. Num ills. Orig cloth, spine faded.        *(Pollak)* **£40**
- A treatise on navigation, and nautical astronomy, adapted to practice, and to the purposes of elementary instruction ... 1824. 1st edn. viii,299,[252] pp. Contemp tree calf, rebacked, new lea label.        *(Whitehart)* **£40**

**Ridge, C. Harold**
- Stage lighting. Cambridge: 1928. xvi,201 pp. Cold frontis, plates of sets, diags (2 fldg), ills of equipment, &c.        *(Weiner)* **£20**

**Rigby, Edward**
- A system of midwifery. London: Whittaker, 1841. xi,314 pp. Text figs. Some margins sl marked. Orig cloth, a bit worn at spine ends.        *(Pollak)* **£30**

**Rigg, Arthur**
- A practical treatise on the steam engine. 1878. Thick 4to. xiv,312 pp. Num diags on 96 plates. Elab engvd title. Orig cloth, worn, rebacked.        *(Weiner)* **£100**

**Riley, Henry Alsop**
- See Tilney, Frederick & Riley, Henry Alsop

**Rimington, C.**
- See Goldberg, A. & Rimington, C.

**Rimmel, Eugene**
- The book of perfumes. 1865. 1st edn. Over 250 ills. Prelims a little foxed. Orig dec cloth gilt, a.e.g., worn at hd & ft of spine.        *(Robertshaw)* **£30**
- The book of perfumes. 1865. 3rd edn. xx,266 pp. Plates (one cold), ills. First & last few leaves stained. Orig dec cloth gilt, worn, rebacked.        *(Weiner)* **£40**
- The book of perfumes. London: Chapman & Hall. 6th edn. Pub heavily gilt cloth, bds rubbed & grubby.        *(McDowell)* **£55**

**Rindfleisch, Eduard**
- A manual of pathological histology to serve as an introduction to the study of morbid anatomy. London: New Sydenham Society, 1872-73. 1st English edn. 2 vols. 8vo. Cuts in text. Pub blind-stamped cloth, top of spines sl pulled.        *(McDowell)* **£50**

**Ritchie, Archibald Tucker**
- The dynamical theory of the formation of the earth ... assumption of its non-rotation during the whole period called 'The Beginning'. London: J. Nisbet, 1854. 2nd edn. xv,704 pp. Orig cloth, recased.        *(Pollak)* **£30**

**Ritchie, William Thomas**
- Auricular flutter. Edinburgh: Green & Son, 1914. 1st edn. Roy 8vo. Ills. Pub dark red cloth.        *(McDowell)* **£40**

**Ritson, Joseph**
- An essay on abstinence from animal food as a moral duty. 1802. [iv],236 pp. 19th c half-roan & mrbld bds, rubbed.        *(Weiner)* **£180**

**Riverius, Lazarus**
- The practice of physick, in seventeen several

books. Wherein is plainly set forth, the nature, cause ... and several sorts of signs ... London: Streater, 1672. Folio. [5],645, [6],463, [16] pp. Engvd frontis. C2 shaved, affecting text. New panelled calf.
*(Goodrich)* **$595**

**Rivers, W.H.R.**
- Medicine, magic and religion. London: Kegan Paul, 1924. 1st edn. 8vo. Pub cloth.
*(McDowell)* **£40**

**Roback, A.A.**
- Behaviorism at twenty-five. 1937. 256 pp.
*(Epistemologist)* **$20**
- The psychology of character. With a survey of temperament. New York: 1931. 605 pp. Sl shelfworn.
*(Epistemologist)* **$20**

**Robb, Hunter**
- Aseptic surgical technique: with especial reference to gynaecological operations, together with notes on the technique employed in certain supplementary procedures. Phila: 1894. 1st edn. 264 pp. Num photographic ills.
*(Fye)* **$100**

**Roberts, Isaac**
- A selection of photographs of stars, star-clusters and nebulae, together with information concerning the instruments and the methods employed in the pursuit of celestial photography. London: [1893-99]. 1st edn. Tall 4to. 2 vols. 81 photo plates. Cloth.
*(Argosy)* **$250**

**Roberts, James**
- The grant and validity of British patents for inventions. New York: Dutton, 1903, 1st Amer edn. liii,647 pp. Ills. Cvrs sl damp-stained & rubbed.
*(Diamond)* **$37.50**

**Roberts, John**
- Paracentesis of the pericardium. A consideration of the surgical treatment of pericardial effusions. Phila: 1880. 1st edn. 100 pp.
*(Fye)* **$100**

**Roberts, John & Kelly, James**
- Treatise on fractures. Phila: 1916. 1st edn. 677 pp. Nearly 1,000 ills.
*(Fye)* **$25**

**Roberts, John B.**
- Surgery of deformities of the face including cleft palate. New York: 1912. 1st edn. Lacks front free e.p.
*(Scientia)* **$135**

**Roberts, Lamar & Penfield, Wilder**
- Speech and brain-mechanisms. Princeton: 1959. xiii,286 pp. Cold frontis, ills. Cvrs sl soiled.
*(Jenner)* **£10**

**Robertson, Abraham**
- A manual on extracting teeth ... second edition. Phila: Lindsay & Blakistan, 1868. 12mo. 200 pp. Ills, index. Later buckram. Ex lib.
*(M&S)* **$30**

**Robertson, Rev. Abram**
- A geometrical treatise of conic sections. In four books. To which is added ... Oxford; Clarendon Press, 1802. 1st edn. xii,268 pp. 28 fldg plates. Orig calf, a little worn.
*(Pollak)* **£25**

**Robertson, William**
- A practical treatise on the human teeth: showing the causes of their destruction ... Phila: Lea & Blanchard, 1841. 1st Amer edn. 8vo. xxii,[3], 26-229,[3] pp. 8pp pub advts. 6 full-page plates. Dampstains on prelims & end. Minimal browning. Orig cloth.
*(Rootenberg)* **$150**

**Robins, Lee N.**
- Deviant children grown up: a sociological and psychiatric study of sociopathic personality. Balt: The Williams & Wilkins Company, 1966. xiv,351,[3] pp.
*(Gach)* **$25**

**Robins, Robert**
- Injuries and infections of the hand. Balt: 1961. 1st edn. 220 pp.
*(Fye)* **$20**

**Robinson, Beverley**
- The treatment of ordinary diseases. Notes from the record book of an old practitioner. New York: American Medical Publishing Company, 1921. 8vo. 132 pp.
*(Poitras)* **$27,50**

**Robinson, Bryan**
- A dissertation of the aether of Sir Isaac Newton. Dublin: Geo. Ewing & Wil. Smith, 1743. 1st edn. 8vo. [2],124 pp. Fldg plate. Light soiling on prelims. Mrbld bds, rebacked.
*(Rootenberg)* **$500**

**Robinson, George**
- On the prevention and treatment of mental disorders. London: Longman ..., 1859. Sole edn. 8vo. [8],228,[4,24 advts] pp. Orig cloth, blind- & gilt-stamped.
*(Dailey)* **$175**

**Robinson, H.P.**
- Picture-making by photography. London: Hazell, Watson & Viney, 1889. 2nd edn. vi,146,xvii [advts]. Frontis. Occas foxing. Spine ends sl worn.
*(Pollak)* **£75**

**Robinson, James**
- The surgical, mechanical, and medical treatment of the teeth: including dental mechanics ... London: W. Webster, 1846. 1st edn. 12mo. xx,320 pp. 3 plates (1 cold), 139

engvs. Sm lib stamp on title. Mod half-calf.
*(Rootenberg)* **$550**

**Robinson, N.**
- A new method of treating consumption ... to
which is added ... curing ulcers of the lungs.
London: A. Bettesworth & T. Warner, et al.,
1727. 1st edn. 2 parts in 1. 8vo. 218; [6],160
pp, 12 pp pub advts. Flyleaf reprd, minimal
browning. Contemp calf, rebacked.
*(Rootenberg)* **$425**

**Robinson, Samuel**
- A course of fifteen lectures on medical botany
... Columbus: 1832. 12mo. 206,[2] pp. Calf,
jnts weak.                    *(Goodrich)* **$60**
- A course of fifteen lectures on medical
botany, denominated Thomson's new theory
of medical practice ... Columbus: Pike, Platt,
1832. Sm 8vo. 206,[2] pp. Staining of last
section. Old calf, lacking spine, defective.
*(Hemlock)* **$65**
- A course of fifteen lectures on medical botany
... Boston: 1835. 216 pp. Some foxing. Cloth
sl blistered.                   *(Elgen)* **$35**

**Robson, A.W. Mayo & Cammidge, P.J.**
- The pancreas: its surgery and pathology.
Phila: 1907. 1st Amer edn. 546 pp. *(Fye)* **$50**

**Rockwell, A.**
- Lectures on electricity in its relations to
medicine and surgery. New York: 1879. 1st
edn. 99 pp.                      *(Fye)* **$75**
- See Beard, G.M. & Rockwell, A.

**Rocque, B.**
- A practical treatise on cultivating lucern
grass, improved and enlarged; and some hints
relative to burnet and timothy grasses, [and a
new method of improving land]. For R.
Davis, 1765. 1st coll edn. 8vo. 75 pp. Half-
title. New mrbld bds.    *(Deighton Bell)* **£40**

**Roddis, Louis**
- James Lind, founder of nautical medicine.
London: Heinemann, 1951. 1st English edn.
8vo. Dw.                   *(McDowell)* **£35**
- A short history of nautical medicine. New
York: 1941. 2nd printing.    *(Scientia)* **$35**

**Rodman, William**
- Diseases of the breast with special reference
to cancer. Phila: 1908. 1st edn. 385 pp.
*(Fye)* **$75**

**Roesler, H.**
- See Dressler, Wilhelm & Roesler, H.

**Rogers, J.E.T.**
- A history of agriculture and prices in
England, 1259 - 1400. Oxford: 1866. 2 vols.
xvi,711; xviii,714 pp. Orig cloth, soiled.

*(Phenotype)* **£25**

**Rogers, Stephen**
- Can chloroform be used to facilitate robbery?
New York: 1871. 1st sep edn. 8vo. 21 pp.
Orig printed wraps.            *(M&S)* **$47.50**

**Rohde, Eleanour Sinclair**
- The old English herbals. 1922. 4to. xii,243
pp. Cold frontis, 17 ills. Occas sl foxing. Cvrs
sl worn.                       *(Jenner)* **£75**

**Rohr, M. von**
- Geometrical investigation of the formation of
images in optical instruments. Embodying
the results of scientific researches constructed
in German optical workshops. 1920. xxiii,612
pp. 133 figs.               *(Whitehart)* **£25**

**Rokitansky, Carl**
- A manual of pathological anatomy. London:
Sydenham Society, 1854. 4 vols. Orig cloth,
worn.                       *(Goodrich)* **$225**
- Pathological anatomy. Containing: the
abnormal conditions of the organs of
respiration. Translated from the German ...
New York: 1855. 5th thousand. xii,164 pp.
Foxed. Lacks front blank. Spine sunned.
*(Goodrich)* **$125**

**Rolleston, H.D.**
- Diseases of the liver, gall-bladder and bile-
ducts. 1905. viii,794 pp. 97 figs, other plates.
Orig cloth, sl dust stained. Lib stamps on
title.                      *(Whitehart)* **£35**
- Diseases of the liver, gall-bladder and bile-
ducts. 1912. Thick 8vo. xv,811 pp. Cold
frontis & plates, num ills. T.e.g. Cvrs sl worn.
*(Jenner)* **£14**

**Rolleston, Sir Humphrey**
- Internal medicine. New York: 1930. 1st edn.
Clio Medica Series.          *(Scientia)* **$25**

**Rollins, William**
- Notes on X-light. Boston: 1904. 1st edn. 4to.
xlii, errata leaf, 400 pp. 152 full-page plates,
each with facing page of explanatory text.
Orig cloth, t.e.g.            *(Elgen)* **$325**

**Rolt, L.T.C.**
- Tools for the job. A short history of machine
tools. London: Batsford, 1965. 1st edn. 8vo.
Extensively illust. Pub cloth. *(McDowell)* **£20**

**Romanes, George John**
- An examination of Weismannism. Chicago:
1893. 1st Amer edn. 221 pp. *(Scientia)* **$45**
- Jelly-fish, star-fish, and sea-urchins. London:
1885. "2nd edn". 323 pp.     *(Scientia)* **$40**
- Mental evolution in animals. With a
posthumous essay on instinct by Charles
Darwin. London: Kegan Paul, Trench & Co.,

1883. 1st edn. 8vo. 411,32 [pub advts] pp. Frontis, fldg chart, errata, text ills. Occas browning. Orig cloth, recased, some wear. *(Rootenberg)* **$250**
- Mental evolution in animals. With a posthumous essay on instinct by Charles Darwin. New York: 1884. 1st Amer edn. 411 pp. *(Scientia)* **$65**
- The scientific evidences of organic revolution. London: Macmillan, 1882. 1st edn. viii,88 pp. Cloth. *(Frew Mackenzie)* **£25**

**Ronalds, Francis**
- Descriptions of an electrical telegraph, and some electrical apparatus. London: R. Hunter, 1823. 1st edn. 8vo. [4],83 pp. 8 plates (7 engvd, 1 w'cut, 1 fldg). 19th c 3/4 calf, front jnt partially cracked. *(Antiq Sc)* **$575**

**Ronayne, Philip**
- A treatise of algebra in two books. London: William & John Innys, 1727. 2nd edn, with addtns. 8vo. [viii],v,[iii], 461,[iii advts] pp. Contemp panelled calf, rebacked, crnrs worn. *(Pollak)* **£85**

**Roscoe, Henry E.**
- Spectrum analysis. Six lectures, delivered in 1868, before the Society of Apothecaries of London. New York: 1869. 1st Amer edn. 8vo. 15,348 pp. Ills. Fldg colour frontis, 6 plates (1 in colour). Later cloth, worn, inner hinges cracked. *(M&S)* **$37.50**

**Roscoe, Henry E. & Harden, Arthur**
- A new view of the origin of Dalton's atomic theory; a contribution to chemical history ... New York: 1896. 1st edn. 191 pp. *(Scientia)* **$60**

**Rose, Sir Thomas Kirke & Newman, W.A.C.**
- The metallurgy of gold. London: Griffin, 1937. 7th edn, revsd & reset. xii,561,[iii] pp. Frontis, 5 plates, 233 ills. *(Pollak)* **£12**

**Rosen, George**
- The history of miners' diseases. A medical and social interpretation. New York: 1943. 1st edn. Spine & cvrs soiled. *(Scientia)* **$35**

**Rosenau, Milton**
- Preventive medicine and hygiene. New York: 1914. 1st edn. 1074 pp. Ills. *(Oasis)* **$50**

**Rosenstein, I.G.**
- Theory and practice of homoeopathy. First part ... [all published]. Louisville: 1840. 1st edn. 12mo. 11,288 pp. Heavily foxed. Orig cloth, damp-stained. *(M&S)* **$85**

**Rosenthal, M.**
- A clinical treatise on diseases of the nervous

system. With a preface by Professor Charcot. New York: 1879. 1st edn in English. 555 pp. Ills. F.e.p. damaged. *(Oasis)* **$65**
- A clinical treatise on diseases of the nervous system. With a preface by Professor Charcot. New York: 1879. 2 vols. 278; 284 pp. Rubbed, extremities frayed. *(Epistemologist)* **$37.50**

**Ross, Sir Ronald**
- Studies on malaria. London: John Murray, 1929. 1st edn. 196 pp. Ills. Dw. *(Poitras)* **$35**

**Rosser, W.H.**
- How to find the stars, and their use in determining latitude, longitude, and the error of the compass ... [1883]. 2nd edn. 70 pp. 4 fldg plates. Orig cloth, bndg damp-stained. *(Whitehart)* **£15**

**Rotch, Thomas Morgan**
- Pediatrics. The hygienic and medical treatment of children. Phila: Lippincott, 1896. 1st edn. 1124 pp. Num plates & photos, some cold. Full sheep, rubbed. *(Goodrich)* **$195**

**Roth, Bernard**
- The treatment of lateral curvature of the spine with appendix giving an analysis of 1000 consecutive cases ... London: 1899. Roy 8vo. 2nd edn. viii,141,[32 advts] pp. 7 plates. Orig cloth, bevelled bds, crnrs & spine bumped. *(Jenner)* **£25**
- The treatment of lateral curvature of the spine ... London: Lewis, 1899. Roy 8vo. 2nd edn. viii,141,[32 advts] pp. 6 plates, 2 fldg charts on linen, 46 text figs. Some pencil underlining. *(Pollak)* **£20**

**Rousseau, J.J.**
- Letters on the elements of botany, Addressed to a lady. Translated ... and twenty-four additional letters fully explaining the system of Linnaeus. London: White, 1791. 3rd edn, with crrctns. xxiii,503,[xxix] pp. Fldg table. Orig bds, uncut. *(Pollak)* **£35**

**Rout, Ettie A.**
- Native diet, with numerous practical recipes. 1926. ix,140 pp. 10 plates. *(Weiner)* **£30**

**Routh, Edward John**
- A treatise on analytical statics. With numerous examples. Cambridge: University Press, 1909-02. 2nd edn. 2 vols. xii,391; xiv,376 pp. Orig cloth. *(Pollak)* **£25**

**Rowbotham, G.F.**
- Acute injuries of the head and their diagnosis, treatment, complications and sequels. Balt: 1942. 1st Amer edn. 288 pp. *(Fye)* **$35**
- Acute injuries of the head. Balt: 1942. 288

pp. Ills.                    *(Oasis)* **$45**

**Rowe, John**
- An introduction to the doctrine of fluxions. London: J. & J. March, 1767. 3rd edn, with addtns & altrtns. 8vo. xii,218,[ii] pp. Errata. 13 plates. Contemp sheep, rebacked, crnrs worn.                    *(Pollak)* **£100**

**Rowland, Alex**
- A treatise on human hair, describing the causes of its decay and the means of restoring it ... Lyons: n.d. [ca 1833]. 24 pp. 8 engvs. Printed wraps.              *(Goodrich)* **$55**

**Rowland, Henry A.**
- The physical papers of Henry Augustus Rowland. Balt: 1902. 1st edn. 704 pp. Ex lib. Spine frayed.              *(Scientia)* **$70**

**Rowley, William**
- A letter to Dr. William Hunter ... on the dangerous tendency of medical vanity, occasioned by the death of the late Lady Holland. London: for F. Newbery, 1774. 1st edn. 8vo. [ii],34 pp. Half-title. Disbound.
                          *(Burmester)* **£250**

**Rowntree, B. Seebohm**
- Poverty. A study of town life. 1901. xviii,437 pp. Lge fldg cold map of York, num tables. Uncut. Upper hinge sl cracked. *(Jenner)* **£40**

**Rowntree, Leonard G.**
- Amid masters of twentieth century medicine. Springfield: 1958. xviii,684 pp. Frontis & ills. Front hinge cracked. Dw sl soiled.
                          *(Jenner)* **£20**

**Royle, John Forbes**
- An essay on the antiquity of Hindoo medicine, including an introductory lecture to the course of materia medica and therapeutics delivered at King's College. London: W.H. Allen, 1837. 1st edn. 8vo. iv,196 pp. Orig cloth, printed paper label.
                          *(Hemlock)* **$165**

**Rucker, C. Wilbur**
- A history of the ophthalmoscope. Rochester, Minnesota: 1971. 1st edn. 127 pp. *(Fye)* **$25**
- A history of the ophthalmoscope. Rochester, Minnesota: Whiting, 1971. 1st edn. Sm 8vo. Section cut from top of free endpaper. Pub cloth.              *(McDowell)* **£28**

**Ruggles, Howard**
- See Holmes, George & Ruggles, Howard

**Ruhmer, Ernst**
- Wireless telephony in theory and practice, translated ... 1908. xiii,224 pp. Ills, diags.
                          *(Weiner)* **£40**

**Rules ...**
- Rules, orders, constitutions, and ordinances, made by The Master ... of the Guild ... of Pargettors ... or Plaisterers of the City of London ... 1787. 50,[i declaration],[i authorisation] pp. Notes on title verso. Contemp mrbld wraps, new cloth spine.
                          *(Pollak)* **£50**

**Rumpel, O.**
- Cystoscopy as adjuvant in surgery with an atlas of cystoscopic views and concomitant text for physicians and students. New York: 1910. 1st English translation. 4to. 131 pp. 85 mtd cold ills.              *(Fye)* **$150**

**Ruoff**
- Ruoff's repertory of homoeopathic medicine, nosologically arranged. Translated from the German ... Phila: J. Dobson, &c., 1840. 354 pp. Embossed cvrs.          *(Poitras)* **$40**

**[Ruscelli, Girolamo]**
- See Alexis of Piemount

**Rush, Benjamin**
- An inquiry into the effects of ardent spirits upon the human body and mind with an account of the means of preventing, and of the remedies for curing them. Boston: Loring, 1823. 8th edn, with addtns. 36 pp. Sewn.
                          *(Goodrich)* **$100**
- Medical inquiries and observations upon the diseases of the mind ... Phila: Kimber & Richardson, 1812. 1st edn, variant or 2nd issue. 8vo. 367,5 [pub advts] pp. Mod brown cloth, lightly browned.     *(Zeitlin)* **$750**
- Medical inquiries and observations upon the diseases of the mind ... Phila: Kimber & Richardson, 1812. 1st edn, variant or 2nd issue. 8vo. 367 pp. Contemp tree calf, rebacked. Browned, some spotting.
                          *(Zeitlin)* **$850**
- The works of Thomas Sydenham M.D., on acute and chronic diseases; with their histories and modes of cure ... Phila: Benjamin & Thomas Kite, 1809. 4to. xl,473,[9 index] pp. Some staining, title reprd. Rebnd in full lea.   *(Poitras)* **$300**

**Rush, James**
- The philosophy of the human voice: embracing its physiological history ... Phila: J, Maxwell, 1827. 1st edn. 8vo. 7,586 pp. Ills. Occas light scattered foxing. Rec 3/4 calf.
                          *(M&S)* **$250**

**Ruspini, Bartholomew**
- A concise relation of the effects of an extraordinary styptic, lately discovered in a series of letters from several Gentlemen of the Faculty ... London: 1787. xiii,124 pp. Some foxing throughout, small section cut from

title. Rebnd in brown cloth.    *(Jenner)* **£35**

**Russell, Bertrand**
- The ABC of relativity. London: Kegan Paul, 1925. 1st edn. [viii],231 pp.    *(Pollak)* **£30**
- A critical exposition of the philosophy of Leibniz with an appendix of leading passages. Cambridge: at the University Press, 1900. 1st edn. 8vo. xvi,[2], 311,[1] pp. Faint marginal w'stains. Partly unopened. Orig cloth.    *(Rootenberg)* **$250**
- An essay on the foundations of geometry. Cambridge: University Press, 1897. 1st edn. 8vo. xvi,202 pp. Cloth, cvrs sl worn.    *(Frew Mackenzie)* **£225**
- Introduction to mathematical philosophy. London: Allen & Unwin, 1938. Reprint of 2nd edn of 1920. xv,208 pp.    *(Pollak)* **£25**
- The principles of mathematics. Vol.I. (all published). Cambridge: University Press, 1903. 1st edn. 4to. xxix,[1],534 pp. Index reprd with tape, margins of some leaves chipped. Orig cloth.    *(Antiq Sc)* **$250**

**Russell, J.S.**
- On the nature, properties and applications of steam, and on steam navigation ... 1841. xii,378 pp. 15 fldg plates, 47 figs in text. New half lea, gilt spine.    *(Whitehart)* **£50**

**Russell, James**
- A treatise on scrofula. Edinburgh: ... for Archibald Constable ..., 1808. Sole edn. 8vo. vi,[2],144 pp. Very sl foxing. Rec bds.    *(Dailey)* **$125**

**Russell, K.F.**
- British anatomy 1525 - 1800. A bibliography. Melbourne: 1963. Ltd, 750 copies. xvii,254 pp. Frontis, 51 ills. In slip-case.    *(Whitehart)* **£40**
- British anatomy 1525 - 1800. A bibliography. Melbourne: 1963. Ltd. 254 pp. Slipcase. Sgnd by author.    *(Fye)* **$125**

**Russell, Patrick**
- A treatise of the plague: Containing an historical journal and medical account of the plague at Aleppo in ... 1760, 1761 & 1762. London: G.G.J. & J. Robinson, 1791. 1st edn. 4to. [24],583, [1],clix,[1],[8 index] pp. Recent qtr calf, mrbld bds.    *(Dailey)* **$300**

**Russell, Richard**
- The oeconomy of nature in acute and chronical diseases of the glands. Translated under the author's inspection. 1755. 1st edn in English. 253 pp. 1 plate. Light browning. Full calf, scored & rubbed.    *(Jenner)* **£68**

**Russell, Thos. H.**
- See Jackman, W.J. & Russell, Thos. H.

**Ruston, Thomas**
- An essay in inoculation for the small pox ... London: J. Payne, 1767. 8vo. viii, 74 pp, leaf of errata. Last 3 leaves foxed. Complete with half-title. Wellcome Medical Library stamps on title-verso.    *(Dailey)* **$325**

**Rutherford, Ernest**
- The collected papers ... Published under the scientific direction of Sir James Chadwick, F.R.S. London: Allen & Unwin, London. 1962-65. 3 vols.    *(Pollak)* **£60**
- Radio-activity. Cambridge: University Press, 1905. 2nd edn. xi,[iii],580 pp. 108 text figs.    *(Pollak)* **£100**
- Radioactive substances and their radiations. Cambridge: 1913. 1st edn. 699 pp. Spine sl bubbled & shelfworn.    *(Scientia)* **$50**
- Radioactive substances and their radiations. Cambridge: 1913. 1st edn. vii,699 pp. 5 plates, text diags. Sl shaken, spine ends sl frayed.    *(Elgen)* **$125**
- Radioactive substances and their radiations. Cambridge: University Press, 1913. 1st edn. 8vo. vii,[1], 699,[1] pp. 5 plates & various diags. Light foxing. Orig dark green cloth, some wear. Inscrbd pres copy. *(Zeitlin)* **$475**
- Radioactive transformation. New Haven: 1911. 2nd printing. 287 pp. Top of spine frayed.    *(Scientia)* **$50**
- Radioactive transformations. 1912. 287 pp. Diags. Dw.    *(Weiner)* **£25**
- Radioactivity. Cambridge: 1905. 2nd edn. 508 pp. Edges of spine rubbed.    *(Scientia)* **$175**

**Rutherford, Ernest, et al.**
- Radiations from radioactive substances. 1930. 1st Amer edn. 588 pp. Spine faded.    *(Scientia)* **$50**
- Radiations from radioactive substances. Cambridge: 1930. 1st edn. xi,588 pp. Ills, 5 plates. Spine sunned.    *(Scientia)* **$100**

**Rutley, Frank**
- Granites and greenstones. A series of tables and notes for students of petrology. London: Murby, 1894. 48 pp. Text fig. Orig cloth-backed paper bds, label on front cvr erased.    *(Pollak)* **£12.50**

**Rutty, John**
- An account of some new experiments and observations on Joanna Stephen's medicine for the stone; with some hints on reducing it. London: 1742. 56 pp. Some soiling. Uncut. Old style bds.    *(Goodrich)* **$150**
- An account of some new experiments and observations on Joanna Stephen's medicine for the stone ... London: J. Manby, 1745. 2nd edn. 8vo. Some browning. Wraps.    *(Dailey)* **$125**

**Ryall, E.C.**
- Operative cystoscopy. St. Louis: 1925. 1st edn. Folio. 47 pp. 115 full-page plates, each with 6 ills, mostly in color. Minimal damp-staining to lower crnrs. Binding sl worn.
*(Oasis)* **$75**

**Ryan, M.**
- A manual of midwifery, and diseases of women and children ... including one hundred and twenty figures ... a companion to all obstetric works. London: by the Author, 1841. 4th edn, re-written & enlgd. 8vo. 40 engvd plates. Pub green cloth.
*(McDowell)* **£35**

**Ryle, John**
- Gastric function in health and disease. Oxford: 1926. 1st edn. 156 pp. Orig cloth.
*(Oasis)* **$40**

**Sachs, Ernest**
- The diagnosis and treatment of brain tumors. St. Louis: 1931. 1st edn. 396 pp.   *(Fye)* **$35**

**Sacks, Oliver W.**
- Migraine: The evolution of a common disorder. London: 1970. Frontis. Some ills. Orig blue cloth. Dw.        *(Jenner)* **£14**

**Sadler, Wm. S.**
- The physiology of faith and fear. Or the mind in health and disease. Chicago: A.C. McClurg, 1925. xxiv,602,[2] pp. Hinges cracked.        *(Gach)* **$25**

**Sajous, Charles**
- Hayfever and its successful treatment by superficial organic alteration of the nasal-mucous membrane. Phila: 1885. 1st edn. 103 pp.        *(Fye)* **$50**
- Lectures on diseases of the nose and throat. Phila: 1886. 1st edn. 439 pp. Half lea.
*(Fye)* **$40**

**Salisbury, Roger & Pruitt, Basil**
- Burns of the upper extremity. Phila: 1976. 1st edn. 180 pp.        *(Fye)* **$40**

**Salmon, William**
- The family dictionary: or, household companion. Containing: I. Cookery ... II. Pastry ... VII. Preparations galenick and chymick relating to physick ... London: H. Rhodes, 1710. 4th edn. 8vo. Sm repair to half-title & title. Contemp calf, hinge split.
*(McDowell)* **£280**

**Salmon, William (trans. & ed.)**
- Pharmacopoeia Londinensis: or the New London Dispensatory. In IV books ... as also the praxis of chymistry, as it's now exercised. London: for Chiswell, 1707. 7th edn, crrctd &

amended. 8vo. [16],896, 865-87,[3] pp. Modest browning. Panelled calf.
*(Hemlock)* **$125**

**Salomons, Sir David**
- Electric light installations. 1893-94. 7th edn (1st in 3 vols). 3 vols. Over 700 pp. Fldg plates, ills.        *(Weiner)* **£30**

**Salomonsen, C.J.**
- Bacteriological technology for physicians. New York: W. Wood, 1890. 1st edn in English. 8vo. 162 pp. Ills. Orig cloth.
*(Antiq Sc)* **$90**

**Salt, T.P.**
- A practical treatise on rupture; its causes, management, and cure. London: 1865. 2nd edn. Sm 8vo. xx,112 pp. 22 diags inc one cold plate. A few leaves carelessly opened. Orig cloth.        *(Bow Windows)* **£30**

**Samuelson, Arnold**
- Flight-velocity. Hamburg: Boysen & Maasch, 1906. 42,[ii] pp. 5 plates. Half-mor, t.e.g.
*(Pollak)* **£25**

**[Sanders, J. Milton]**
- A system of instruction in the practical use of the blowpipe. New York: H. Bailliere, 1858. 1st edn. 8vo. 269,16 [pub ctlg] pp. Text w'cuts. Orig cloth.        *(Antiq Sc)* **$85**

**Sanitary ...**
- Sanitary economy. Its principles and practice; and its moral influence on the progress of civilisation. Edinburgh: 1850. 320 pp. Half-calf.        *(Goodrich)* **$85**

**Sansom, Arthur**
- Chloroform, its action and administration. Phila: 1865. 1st Amer edn. 279 pp. Stain affecting upper crnr of one-qtr of the book, advt leaves chewed. Recent leatherette.
*(Fye)* **$75**

**Sappington, John**
- The theory and treatment of fevers ... revised and corrected by Ferdinando Stith ... Arrow Rock: the Author, 1844. Sole edn. Sm 8vo. 216 pp. Title lightly soiled, occas light foxing. Mod calf.        *(Dailey)* **$300**
- The theory and treatment of fevers ... revised and corrected by Ferdinando Stith ... Arrow Rock: 1844. 1st edn. 216 pp. Foxing. Qtr calf.
*(Goodrich)* **$175**

**Sargant, William**
- The unquiet mind - the autobiography of a physician in psychological medicine. London: 1967. xvi,240 pp. Port frontis. Orig black cloth. Dw.        *(Jenner)* **£12**

**Sargeaunt, Captain R.A.**
- Notes on the climate of the earth past and present. Smith, Elder, 1875. x,[ii],76 pp. 3 fldg plates, 2 figs. Spine & crnrs rubbed.
*(Pollak)* £20

**Sargent, F.W.**
- On bandaging, and other operations of minor surgery, with an additional chapter on military surgery. Phila: 1862. 283 pp.
*(Fye)* $100

**Sarton, George**
- A history of science. Hellenistic science and culture in the last three centuries B.C. Harvard: 1959. Sm 4to. xxiv,554 pp. 112 figs in text. *(Whitehart)* £25
- Introduction to the history of science. Balt: 1927-1948. 1st edns, 1st printings. 3 vols in 5. Thick lge 8vo. *(Elgen)* $450

**Saunders, John Cunningham**
- The anatomy of the human ear ... with a treatise on the diseases of that organ, the causes of deafness ... Phila: Benjamin Warner, 1821. 1st Amer edn. 4to. viii,1f [advt], 128 pp. Browning. Contemp tree calf, worn, hinges partially split. *(Hemlock)* $125

**Saunders, P.**
- Edward Jenner. The Cheltenham years, 1795 - 1823. Being a chronicle of the vaccination campaign. Hanover, N.H.: 1982. Ills.
*(Winterdown)* £35

**Saunders, William**
- A treatise on the chemical history and medical powers of some of the most celebrated mineral waters; with practical remarks ... London: Phillips & Fardon, 1805. 2nd edn. 8vo. [4],viii,xx, 570,[1 advt] pp. Fldg table. Old bds rebacked in cloth. Lib stamp.
*(Dailey)* $100

**Saunderson, Nicholas**
- The method of fluxions applied to a select number of useful problems: together with the demonstration ... London: for A. Millar ..., 1756. 1st edn. xxiv,309,[1 errata]. 12 fldg engvd plates. Some browning. Rebound in calf-backed bds. *(Pickering)* $650

**Saunier, Claudius**
- A treatise on modern horology in theory and practice. Translated from the French ... by Julien Triplin & David Rigg. London: Crosby Lockwood, 1887. 2nd English edn (1st in book form?). Roy 8vo. xvi,844 pp. 22 fldg cold plates, 78 text figs. Orig cloth.
*(Zeitlin)* $120

**Savage, Henry**
- The surgery, surgical pathology and surgical

anatomy of the female pelvic organs in a series of plates taken from nature ... New York: 1880. 3rd edn. 115 pp. 60 full-page engvd plates. *(Fye)* $60

**Saveur, A.**
- The metallography of iron and steel. Cambridge, Mass: 1912. xvi. ca 400 pp (pagination irregular). Ills & diags in text. New cloth. *(Whitehart)* £25

**Savory, John**
- A compendium of domestic medicine: and companion to the medicine chest. London: John Churchill, 1852. 4th edn. xv,357,[iii] pp. 19 figs. Orig cloth, uncut, a little worn at spine ends, & crnrs, bds shabby, stitching strained. *(Pollak)* £30

**Sawer, J. Ch.**
- Odorographia, a natural history of raw materials and drugs used in the perfume industry ... ( ... including the aromatics used in flavouring, Second Series). London & Brighton: 1892-94. 2 vols. xxiii,383; 523,[11] pp. Fldg map, ills, bibliog. *(Weiner)* £150

**Sawyer, W.E.**
- Electric lighting by incandescence, and its application to interior illumination, a practical treatise. New York: 1881. 189 pp. Ills. Lacks front free endpaper. *(Weiner)* £40

**Saxe, Arthur Wellesley**
- Report on Hawaiian leprosy! Read before the California State Medical Society at San Francisco, April 20, 1881. Pamphlet. 26,[11] pp. 11 (ex 12) photographic plates laid down. Paper cvrs, upper cvr torn but reprd. 4 sm ink scorings across front edge. *(Jenner)* £1,300

**Sayre, Lewis**
- Lectures on orthopedic surgery and diseases of the joints. New York: 1885. 2nd edn. 569 pp. 324 ills. *(Fye)* $100

**Scales, F.S.**
- Practical microscopy: an introduction to microscopical methods. 1926. 3rd edn. viii,332 pp. 122 figs. *(Whitehart)* £15

**Scammon, Richard & Calkins, Leroy**
- The development and growth of the external dimensions of the human body in the fetal period. Minneapolis: 1929. 1st edn. 4to. 367 pp. *(Fye)* $35

**Scarpa, Antonio**
- A treatise on hernia, translated from the Italian ... Edinburgh: 1814. 1st English edition. 8vo. xxv,548 pp. 14 mezzotint plates. Contemp mottled calf, partial splitting of hinges. *(Hemlock)* $375

- A treatise on hernia. Edinburgh: 1814. 1st
English translation. 548 pp. 14 engvd plates.
Full lea.                            *(Fye)* **$600**

**Schaeberle, J.M.**
- Report on the total eclipse of the sun,
observed at Mina Bronces, Chile on April 16,
1893. 1st edn. 8vo. [6],126,[1] pp. Mounted
silver print photog frontis, 9 plates. Orig
cloth. Author's pres copy.    *(Antiq Sc)* **$85**

**Schaeffer, J. Parsons**
- The nose, paranasal sinues, nasolacrimal
passage-ways, and olfactory organ in man ...
Phila: 1920. 1st edn. 370 pp.     *(Fye)* **$40**

**Schafer, Paul**
- Pathology in general surgery. Chicago: 1950.
4to. 581 pp. Cold plates, radiographs, &c.
                                  *(Fye)* **$15**

**Schall, W.E.**
- X-rays; their origin, dosage and practical
application. Bristol: 1923. viii,136 pp. Num
figs.                     *(Winterdown)* **£15**

**Scheele, Carl Wilhelm**
- The chemical essays of Charles William
Scheele. Translated ... with a sketch of the life
... London: Scott, Greenwood, 1901. 1st edn
thus. 8vo. Pub cloth.         *(McDowell)* **£90**

**Schenk, Leopold**
- Schenk's theory. The determination of sex.
Chicago: 1898. 1st English translation. 222
pp.                              *(Fye)* **$15**
- Schenk's theory. The determination of sex.
Authorised translation. 1898. 173 pp. B'plate.
Cvrs sl worn.                  *(Jenner)* **£8**

**Schleip, Karl**
- Haematological atlas with a description of the
technic of blood examination. London:
Rebman, 1908. 1st English edn. 4to. 45 cold
ills laid in on card. Pub green cloth, green
mor spine.                  *(McDowell)* **£55**

**Schmalhausen, I.I.**
- Factors of evolution: the theory of stabilizing
selection. Translated ... Edited ... Phila:
1949. 1st edn in English. 327 pp. Shelfworn.
                              *(Scientia)* **$55**

**Schmidt, Rudolph**
- Pain, its causation and diagnostic significance
in internal diseases. Phila: 1908. 1st English
translation. 326 pp.             *(Fye)* **$25**

**Schnabel, Dr. Carl**
- Handbook of metallurgy. Translated by
Henry Louis. 1905. 2nd edn. 2 vols. Thick
8vo. Num ills.               *(Edwards)* **£20**

**Schofield, Alfred T.**
- Functional nerve diseases. New York: 1908.
1st Amer edn. Cloth a little dingy. *(Gach)* **$20**
- The unconscious mind. New York: Funk &
Wagnall, 1901. 1st Amer edn. xviii,426 pp.
                                *(Gach)* **$20**
- Unconscious therapeutics: or, the personality
of the physician. London: J. & A. Churchill,
1904. 1st edn. x,317 pp. Lib b'plate & stamp
on rear paste-down.             *(Gach)* **$25**

**Schrenk-Notzing, A. von**
- Therapeutic suggestion in psychopathia
sexualis ... with especial reference to contrary
sexual instinct. Translated ... Phila: 1895. 1st
edn in English. xix,320 pp. Orig cloth.
                               *(Elgen)* **$50**

**Schron, Ludwig**
- Seven-figure logarithms of numbers 1 to
108000 and of sines, cosines ... with a
description of the tables by A. de Morgan.
London: Williams & Norgate, 1865. 5th edn.
ix,474,76 pp. Orig cloth, spine split at ft.
                               *(Pollak)* **£25**

**Schubert, Hermann**
- Mathematical essays and recreations.
Translated ... Chicago: Open Court
Publishing, 1910. 3rd edn. [viii],140 pp.
Faded & wearing at spine ends & crnrs.
                               *(Pollak)* **£15**

**Schuck, H., et al.**
- Nobel: the man and his prizes. Amsterdam:
1962. 2nd enlgd edn. 690 pp.    *(Oasis)* **$40**

**Schultz, Jackson S.**
- The leather manufacture in the United States;
a dissertation on the methods and economies
of tanning, to which is added a report .... New
York: 1876. 305,62 pp. Frontis, port. Plates
& engvs of machinery, tools, &c. Half-calf,
worn.                          *(Weiner)* **£50**

**Schuster, Arthur & Shipley, Arthur E.**
- Britain's heritage of science. Constable, 1917.
xv,334 pp. Frontis, 14 plates.  *(Pollak)* **£15**

**Schwartz, Morris S.**
- See Stanton, Alfred H. & Schwartz, Morris S.

**Science ...**
- Science lectures at South Kensington.
London: Macmillan, 1878-79. 1st edn. 2 vols.
Sm 8vo. vi,[2],290, [2],26 [pub ctlg] pp. Text
figs. Orig cloth.            *(Antiq Sc)* **$135**

**Scofield, Samuel**
- A practical treatise on vaccina or cowpock.
New York: 1810. xvi,139 pp. Cold plate.
Foxing. Orig calf.           *(Goodrich)* **$195**

## Scoresby, W.
- An account of the Arctic regions, with a history ... of the Northern whale-fishery. Edinburgh: Constable, 1820. 2 vols. xx,551,82 [appendix]; viii,574 pp. 2 fldg frontis, 22 plates (foxed), 4 tables. Lacking half-titles. Occas foxing. Later half-calf.
*(Pollak)* £180

## Scott, D.H.
- Studies in fossil botany. 1909. 2nd edn. 8vo. xxiv,683 pp. 213 ills. Cloth.
*(Wheldon & Wesley)* £18
- Studies in fossil botany. 1920-23. 3rd edn. 2 vols. 8vo. 326 text figs. Cloth, spine faded.
*(Wheldon & Wesley)* £35

## Scott, George
- Select remains of the learned John Ray ... with his life ... London: Ja. Dodsley, 1760. vii,336 pp. Port frontis, 3 text engvs. Errata slip pasted to ft of last page. Antique style calf, old label. *(Pollak)* £80

## Scott, J.F.
- The scientific work of Rene Descartes. Taylor & Francis, [1952]. [x],211 pp. Frontis, 82 figs. Ex lib, occas stamps. *(Pollak)* £25

## Scott, Sir Walter
- Letters on demonology and witchcraft, addressed to J.G. Lockhart, Esq. London: John Murray, 1830. 1st edn. [iv],ix,[i],402 pp. 16 pp pub ctlg bound in. Frontis. Orig cloth, rebacked with orig spine laid on. *(Pollak)* £50

## Scott-Taggart, John & Harris, P.W. (eds.)
- The Radio Press Year Book 1926. 1926. 169 pp. Ills, diags. 28 pp advts. Orig pict card cvrs. First year of issue (all published?).
*(Weiner)* £20

## Scripture ...
- Scripture illustrated, by means of natural science ... See Taylor Charles

## Scrivenor, J.B.
- The geology of Malaya. 1931. xx,217 pp. 33 figs in text, lge fldg cold map in pocket at rear. Cloth sl marked. *(Whitehart)* £18

## Scrope, George Poulett
- The geology and extinct volcanos of Central France. 1858. 2nd edn, enlgd & imprvd. 1858. xvii,258 pp. 17 tinted plates on 15 sheets (7 fldg), w'cuts. Orig green dec blind-stamped cloth, crnrs worn, rebacked, new endpapers. *(Weiner)* £85
- Volcanos, the character of their phenomena. 1862. 2nd edn, revsd & enlgd. 8vo. xi,[1],490 pp. Cold frontis, fldg cold map, num text figs. Frontis sl foxed, a few pencil markings. Orig cloth, faded. *(Wheldon & Wesley)* £50

## Scudamore, Charles
- Observations on the use of the colchicum autumnale in the treatment of gout. 1825. 1st edn. Some light foxing to title. Orig bds. Pres copy to the Duke of Northumberland.
*(Robertshaw)* £65
- A treatise on the nature and cure of gout and rheumatism, including ... morbid states of the digestive organs ... Phila: 1819. 1st Amer edn. xix,335 pp. Scattered foxing & browning. Full lea, chipped. *(Elgen)* $85

## Scudder, Charles
- The treatment of fractures. Phila: 1901. 2nd edn. Num X-ray photographic ills (1st edn so illustrated). 457 pp. *(Oasis)* $80

## Scudder, John M.
- The eclectic family physician. Cincinnati: 1924. 2 vols in 1. 884 pp. Frontis. Ills. Mod mor. *(Jenner)* £30
- The eclectic practice in diseases of children. Cincinnati: 1894. 7th edn. xv,486 pp. Mod mor. *(Jenner)* £25

## Seaman, Valentine
- A dissertation on the mineral waters of Saratoga. Including an account of the waters of Ballston. New York: 1809. 2nd edn, enlgd. 12mo. 131 pp. Fldg map. Sheep.
*(Goodrich)* $175

## Searle, A.B.
- Refractory materials, their manufacture and use. 1940. 3rd edn, revsd. xvi,895 pp. 173 ills in text. Cloth marked on back.
*(Whitehart)* £15

## Searle, William S.
- What is finest in homoeopathy and likely to survive. An address ... N.p., n.d. [ca 1875]. 4to 19 pp. Printed wraps. *(Hemlock)* $35

## Sedgwick, Leonard W.
- See Power, Henry & Sedgwick, Leonard W.

## Sedgwick, William T.
- Principles of sanitary science and the public health, with special reference to the causation and prevention of infectious diseases. New York: 1905. 1st edn, 3rd printing. xix,368 pp. Sl shelf wear. T.e.g. *(Elgen)* $45

## See, Germain
- Diseases of the lungs ... the bronchites, infectious pneumonia, gangrene, syphilis ... Translated ... New York: [1885]. 1st edn in English. xviii,398 pp. *(Elgen)* $30

## Seguin, E.
- Medical thermometry and human temperature. New York: 1876. 1st edn. 466 pp. *(Fye)* $75

**Seguin, Edouard C.**
- Idiocy and its treatment by the physiological method. New York: William Wood, 1866. 1st edn. Photog frontis. Title foxed, some internal stains, minor pencilling. Orig pebbled cloth, recased.      *(Gach)* **$150**

**Seiler, Carl**
- Compendium of microscopical technology. Phila: D.G. Brinton, 1881. 1st edn. 8vo. 130,[4 advts] pp. Text figs. Orig cloth.
                          *(Antiq Sc)* **$45**

**Select ...**
- A select collection of valuable and curious arts ... See Porter, Rufus

**Selected ...**
- Selected monograms on dermatology. London: New Sydenham Society, 1893. 613 pp. 2 plates. Orig cloth, spine sl faded.
                          *(Oasis)* **$30**

**Selesnick, S.**
- See Alexander, Franz & Selesnick, S.

**Seltzer, Albert**
- Plastic surgery of the nose. Phila: 1949. 1st edn. 305 pp. Margins of several leaves w'stained. Binding rubbed.      *(Fye)* **$40**

**Semple, R.H.**
- See Field, Henry & Semple, R.H.

**Semple, Robert Hunter**
- A manual of the diseases of the heart. London: 1875. viii,296,[23 advts] pp. Orig maroon cloth, hinges cracked inside, spine worn, chipped & faded.      *(Jenner)* **£12**

**Semple, Robert Hunter (ed.)**
- Memoirs on diptheria. From the writings of Bretonneau, Guersant ... & Daviot. London: New Sydenham Society, 1859. 1st edn thus. 8vo. Cloth. Top of spine pulled.
                          *(McDowell)* **£28**

**Senac, Jean**
- A treatise on the hidden nature, and the treatment of intermitting and remitting fevers ... in two books. Translated ... Phila: 1805. 1st Amer edn & 1st edn in English. [8]ff, 299 pp. 1f [advt]. Contemp tree calf, rubbed.
                          *(Elgen)* **$395**

**Sendivogius, Michael**
- A new light of alchemye ... To which is added a treatise of sulphur ... Also nine books ... chymical dictionary. London: by R. Cotes for T. Williams, 1650. 1st edn in English. Sm 4to. [14], 147,[1 blank],[3 contents]; [6],145; 48 pp. Contemp calf rebacked.
                          *(Antiq Sc)* **$775**

**Senn, Nicholas**
- Intestinal surgery. Chicago: 1889. 1st edn. 269 pp.                *(Fye)* **$125**
- Medico-surgical aspects of the Spanish American War. Chicago: 1900. 1st edn. 379pp. Num ills, plates, ports, fold-out chart on typhoid fever cases, fold-out plans of hospital. Lacks front flyleaf.      *(Elgen)* **$150**
- Medico-surgical aspects of the Spanish American War. Chicago: 1900. 379pp. Photos & ills.         *(Goodrich)* **$75**
- The pathology and surgical treatment of tumors. Phila: 1900. 2nd edn. 718 pp.
                          *(Fye)* **$30**
- Practical surgery. Phila: 1902. 1133 pp. Full lea.                *(Fye)* **$60**
- Principles of surgery. Phila: 1891. 1st edn. 611 pp. Advts wrinkled. Cvrs spotted.
                          *(Fye)* **$100**
- Principles of surgery. Phila: 1896. 2nd edn. 656 pp.                *(Fye)* **$35**
- Surgical bacteriology. Phila: 1871. 2nd edn. 271 pp.                *(Fye)* **$75**
- Tuberculosis of the genito-urinary organs, male and female. Phila: 1897. 1st edn. vi,317,30 [pub ctlg] pp. 7 cold plates, text ills.
                          *(Elgen)* **$90**

**Sewall, Charles Henry**
- Wireless telegraphy; its origins, development, inventions and apparatus ... 1903. 229 pp. Frontis map (detchd), ills, diags. *(Weiner)* **£75**

**Seward, A.C. (ed.)**
- Darwin and modern science. Essays in commemoration of the centenary of the birth of Charles Darwin and of the fiftieth anniversary of the publication of The Origin of Species. Cambridge: 1909. 1st edn. 595 pp.
                          *(Scientia)* **$60**

**Seybert, Adam**
- An inaugural dissertation: Being an attempt to disprove the doctrine of putrefaction in the blood of living animals. Phila: R. Dobson, 1793. 1st edn. 8vo. 78 pp. Linen-backed blue bds, antique style. Author's pres copy.
                          *(Antiq Sc)* **$400**

**Shadwell, Charles F.A.**
- Tables for facilitating the reductions of lunar observations. London: J.D. Potter, 1860. viii,63 pp. Full calf, worn.      *(Pollak)* **£30**

**Shaffer, Newton**
- Selected essays on orthopaedic surgery from the writings of Newton Melman Shaffer, M.D. New York: 1923. 1st edn. 636 pp.
                          *(Fye)* **$100**

**Shankland, E.C.**
- Dredging of harbours and rivers, a work of descriptive and technical reference ...

Glasgow: 1931. xii,248 pp. 83 ills, 3 fldg plans. *(Whitehart)* **£25**

**Sharp, A.**
- Bicycles and tricycles. An elementary treatise on their design and construction with examples and tables. 1896. 1st edn. xviii,536 pp. 565 ills. Orig cloth. Author's pres copy. *(Whitehart)* **£40**

**Sharp, Samuel**
- A treatise on the operations of surgery, with a description and representation of the instruments used in performing them ... London: 1761. 8th edn. 234 pp. Engvd plates. Recent qtr lea. *(Fye)* **$400**
- A treatise on the operations of surgery, with a description and representation of the instruments used in performing them ... London: 1772. 19th edn. 247 pp. Faint lib stamps. Recent qtr lea. *(Fye)* **$325**

**Sharpe, Ella Freeman**
- Dream analysis - a practical handbook for psychoanalysts. Hogarth Press: 1937. 211 pp. Orig green cloth. *(Jenner)* **£21**

**Sharpe, William**
- Diagnosis and treatment of brain injuries. Phila: 1920. 1st edn. 757 pp. *(Fye)* **$25**

**Sharpe, William & Sharpe, Norman**
- Neurosurgery: principles, diagnosis and treatment. Phila: 1928. 1st edn. 762 pp. Ex lib, rebound in buckram. Inscribed & autographed by the authors. *(Fye)* **$35**

**Sharrock, Robert**
- The history of the propagation and improvement of vegetables by the occurrence of art and nature, etc., etc. Oxford: for Tho. Robinson, 1660. Sm 8vo. Plate. Orig calf, rebacked. *(Ivelet)* **£210**

**Shattuck, Lemuel**
- The vital statistics of Boston: containing an abstract of the bills of mortality for the last twenty-nine years ... Phila: 1841. 1st sep edn. 8vo. 35 pp. Orig plain wraps. *(M&S)* **$175**

**Shaw, John**
- Further observations on the lateral or serpentine curvature of the spine, and on the treatment of contracted limbs. With an enquiry into the effects of various exercises ... London: 1825. 1st edn. Half-title, xi,195,2 [advts] pp. Orig bds. Ex lib. *(Elgen)* **$250**

**Sheehan, J. Eastman**
- A manual of reparative surgery. Oxford University Press, 1938. 1st edn. 311 pp. 18 plates, 314 text ills. Spine sl dull. *(Oasis)* **$30**
- Plastic surgery of the nose. New York: Paul

B. Hoeber, 1925. xix,249 pp. 177 ills, 9 plates. *(Poitras)* **$45**
- Plastic surgery of the orbit. New York: 1927. 1st edn. 348 pp. *(Fye)* **$100**

**Sheldon, J. Prince**
- Livestock in health and disease. The breeding and management of horses, cattle, sheep ... N.d. [ca 1901]. 4to. xi,627 pp. Cold & b/w plates. Half-mor, cloth sides. *(Phenotype)* **£52**

**Sheldon, W.H.**
- The varieties of human physique: an introduction to constitutional psychology ... New York & London: 1940. 1st edn. [xiv],347,[7] pp. 30 plates. B'plate. *(Gach)* **$35**

**Sheppard, John**
- On dreams, in their mental and moral aspects ... in two essays. London: 1847. 12mo. xxiv,179 pp. Victorian cloth. *(Goodrich)* **$85**

**Sherer, J.**
- Rural life described and illustrated in the management of horses, cattle, sheep ... and a complete system of modern veterinary practice. n.d. [ca 1860]. 4to. 5 vols. 1016 pp. Frontis, engvd title, 86 engvs on 63 plates. Orig cloth. *(Phenotype)* **£140**

**Sherlock, William**
- A practical discourse concerning death. 1690. 2nd edn. vi,352 pp. Lacking A1 (presumably blank). Title soiled, some stains. Half red mor, new endpapers. *(Jenner)* **£35**

**Sherrin, G.C.**
- The Montagu motor book, edited by Lord Montagu. [1913]. 288 pp. Frontis (pencil 'enhancement'). Num ills. *(Weiner)* **£35**

**Sherrington, Charles**
- The integrative action of the nervous system. London: Constable, 1911. 2nd printing. 411 pp. Orig blue cloth. *(Goodrich)* **$395**
- See Liddell, E.G.T. & Sherrington, Charles

**Sherrington, Sir Charles**
- Selected writings of Sir Charles Sherrington; A testimonial ... London: Hamish Hamilton, 1939. 1st edn. 4to. Frontis, ills in text. Pub black cloth. *(McDowell)* **£30**

**[Sherwin, Henry]**
- Mathematical tables ... a most comprehensive method; viz, a table of logarithms ... London: for R. & W. Mount & T. Page, 1717. 8vo. [6]ff,64 pp; Tables [152]ff,29,[1] pp. Engvd plate. Light browning. Lacks the blanks. Contemp calf gilt, rubbed. *(Zeitlin)* **$290**
- Mathematical tables, contrived after a most comprehensive method ... London: ... Mount, 1726. Probably re-issue of 1717 edn. 8vo.

[4]ff,64 pp, fldg engvd plate; tables
[152]ff,39,[1] pp. Light browning, damp-stain
at end. Contemp calf, cvrs detchd.
*(Zeitlin)* **$175**
- Mathematical tables, contained in an easy and
comprehensive manner ... Fifth edition,
revised ... London: for J. Mount & T. Page,
1771. 116 pp text, logarithm tables, errata
leaf. Orig calf cvrs, worn, rprd, rebacked.
Lacks fldg plate & table.       *(Diamond)* **$45**

**Sherwood, H.H.**
- The Astro-Magnetic Almanac for 1843.
Calendar by David Young. No. 1 - To be
continued annually. New York: [1843]. 12mo.
72pp. Ills. (All published).       *(M&S)* **$45**

**Sherwood-Dunn, B.**
- Regional   anesthesia   (Victor   Pauchet's
technique). Phila: 1922. 1st edn. 294 pp.
*(Fye)* **$50**

**Shiercliffe, E.**
- The Bristol and Hotwell guide: containing an
historical account ... of that opulent city; also
of the Hotwell; the nature, properties, and
effects of its medicinal water ... Bristol: 1793.
2nd edn. 8vo. Frontis soiled & rprd. Rebound
in black cloth.       *(Deighton Bell)* **£68**

**Ship-master's ...**
- Ship-master's medical assistant; or, physical
advice to all masters of ships who carry no
surgeons ... diseases especially those peculiar
to seamen in long voyages .. London: for
Wilkie & Baldwin, 1777. 299 pp. Lea bds,
worn & detchd, backstrip worn. *(Xerxes)* **$125**

**Shipley, Arthur E.**
- See Schuster, Arthur & Shipley, Arthur E.

**Shipley, Maynard**
- The war on modern science: a short history of
the fundamentalist attacks on evolution and
modernism. New York: 1927. 1st edn. 415
pp.       *(Scientia)* **$45**

**Shoemaker, William**
- Retinitis pigmentosa with an analysis of
seventeen cases occuring in deaf mutes. Phila:
1909. 1st edn. 106 pp.       *(Fye)* **$75**

**Short, Thomas**
- Discourses on tea, sugar, milk, made-wines,
spirits ... with plain and useful rules for gouty
people. London: for T. Longman & A.
Millar, 1750. 1st edn. 8vo. [2],vi, [6],424 pp.
Pub advts. Occas browning & ms notations.
Contemp calf, spine chipped.
*(Rootenberg)* **$675**
- The natural, experimental, and medicinal
history of the mineral waters of Derbyshire,
Lincolnshire, and Yorkshire, 1734. [and] ...

Cumberland,        Northumberland,
Westmorland, 1740. 2 vols in 1. Thick 4to. 4
fldg plates. Dampstained throughout. Bds
rebacked.       *(Jenner)* **£200**

**Shuchardt, Karl (ed.)**
- Treatment of patients with clefts of lip,
alveolus and palate. New York: 1966. 1st edn.
237 pp. 654 ills.       *(Fye)* **$40**

**Shurly, Ernest**
- A treatise on diseases of the nose and throat.
New York: 1900. 1st edn. 744 pp. Half lea.
*(Fye)* **$40**

**Shute, D.K.**
- See Coues, Elliot & Shute, D.K.

**Sibly, Ebenezer**
- The medical mirror, or, treatise on the
impregnation of the human female ... New
edition, with large additions and anatomical
plates. N.d. [ca 1799?; 3rd edn?]. iv,218 pp.
12 plates, extra illustrated, lacking one plate.
Half-calf, hinges worn, rubbed. *(Jenner)* **£55**

**Sidis, Boris**
- The foundations of normal and abnormal
psychology. Boston & Toronto: [1914]. 413
pp.       *(Gach)* **$25**
- Nervous ills: their cause and cure. Boston:
The Gorham Press, [1922]. 379,[3] pp. Green
cloth, damp-spotted, rear hinge cracked.
*(Gach)* **$17.50**
- Psychology of suggestion. New York: 1898.
386 pp. Spine dull & sl frayed, rubbed &
spotted.       *(Epistemologist)* **$20**
- Psychopathological researches. Studies in
mental dissociation. New York: 1902. 329 pp.
Sl bumped.       *(Epistemologist)* **$37.50**
- The source and aim of human progress.
Boston: Richard G. Badger, [1919]. 63 pp.
*(Gach)* **$25**

**Siegbahn, Manne**
- The spectroscopy of X-rays. Translated, with
the author's additions, by G.A. Lindsay.
London: 1925. 1st edn in English. 287 pp.
*(Scientia)* **$50**

**Siemens, Sir William**
- On the conservation of solar energy. A
collections   of   papers   and   discussions.
London: Macmillan, 1883. 1st edn. 8vo.
xii,111 pp. Plates & diags in text. Sl occas
spotting. Cvrs rather soiled. Author's pres
inscrptn.       *(Frew Mackenzie)* **£50**

**Sigerist, Henry E.**
- American medicine. New York: 1934. 1st edn
in English. Spine lettering dull. *(Scientia)* **$45**
- The great doctors. A biographical history of
medicine. New York: 1933. 1st edn in

English.  *(Scientia)* $45
- Hieronymus Brunschwig and his work. New York: [1946]. 4to. 45 pp. Ills. Cloth-backed dec bds.  *(Argosy)* $30
- A history of medicine. New York: 1951, 1961. 1st edns. 2 vols. Dws.  *(Scientia)* $60
- Man and medicine. An introduction to medical knowledge. New York: 1932.
*(Scientia)* $35
- Medicine and health in the Soviet Union. New York: 1947. 364 pp. Chipped dw. Special edn sgnd by Sigerist for members of the American - Soviet Medical Society.
*(Oasis)* $50
- Socialised medicine in the Soviet Union. London: Gollancz, 1937. 397,[iii] pp. 24 ills. Some pencil lines in text. Orig limp orange cvrs.  *(Pollak)* £15

**Silberstein, Ludwik**
- Elements of the electromagnetic theory of light. London: Longmans, Green, 1918. vii,48 pp. 2 text figs..  *(Pollak)* £20
- Report on the quantum theory of spectra. London: Adam Hilger, 1920. 42 pp. New cloth.  *(Pollak)* £30
- The theory of relativity. London: 1914. 1st edn. 295 pp.  *(Scientia)* $40

**Silliman, Benjamin, Jr.**
- First principles of chemistry ... Phila: 1851. Sm 8vo. 480 pp. Text w'cuts. Full sheep, worn.  *(Elgen)* $80

**Simmons, George H. & Fishbein, Morris**
- The art and practice of medical writing. Chicago: 1925. 163 pp. Cvrs worn.
*(Jenner)* £12

**Simmons, Samuel F.**
- Elements of anatomy and the animal economy. From the French of M. Person, corrected ... augmented with notes. London: Wilie, 1775. 1st edn. xii,396 pp. Errata leaf. 3 engvd plates. Light pencilling. Old qtr calf, worn.  *(Goodrich)* $75
- Practical observations on the treatment of consumptions. 1780. 87 pp. Some old ink markings. Mod bds.  *(Weiner)* £40

**Simms, F.W.**
- Practical tunnelling. Explaining in detail, the setting out ... shaft sinking and heading driving ... as exemplified by the particulars of Blechingley and Saltwood Tunnels. 1844. 1st edn. 4to. xii,174 pp. Frontis, 12 fldg plates. Orig blind-stamped cloth.  *(Whitehart)* £200
- A treatise on the principal mathematical instruments, employed in surveying, levelling, and astronomy: explaining their construction, adjustments and use. Balt: F. Lucas, n.d. [1836]. 1st Amer edn. 110,[15] pp. Text w'cuts. Orig cloth-backed bds.

*(Antiq Sc)* $100
- A treatise on the principal mathematical instruments ... Balt: F. Lucas, n.d. [1844]. 2nd Amer edn. xvii,[1],134,[18 tables],[2],[12 James Green's scientific instrument catalogue] pp. Orig cloth, soiled. Some staining.  *(Antiq Sc)* $100

**Simms, William**
- The achromatic telescope, and its various mountings, especially the equatorial. To which are added some hints on private observatories. London: 1852. 56 figs. 16 pp price list of instruments by Troughton & Simms. Orig cloth, sl faded.
*(Winterdown)* £25

**Simon, John**
- English sanitary institutions, reviewed in their course of development ... London: Cassell, 1890. xv,[i], 496,[xvi advts] pp. Orig cloth, sm square removed from spine & rprd, spine ends & crnrs a little worn, new end-papers at front.  *(Pollak)* £75
- English sanitary institutions, reviewed in their course of development ... London: Cassell, 1897. 2nd edn. xix,516 pp. New cloth.  *(Pollak)* £45
- Filth-diseases and their prevention. Boston: 1876. 1st Amer edn.  *(Scientia)* $75

**Simon, Th.**
- See Binet, Alfred & Simon, Th.

**Simonds, James B.**
- A practical treatise on varida ovina, or small-pox in sheep, containing ... recent introduction into England ... best means to avoid its fatal consequences. 1848. viii,157 pp. Cold frontis, 4 cold plates (1 detchd). Foxing. Rec cloth, bumped, worn.
*(Jenner)* £25

**Simpson, George G.**
- A catalogue of the mesozoic mammalia in the Geological Department of the British Museum. London: 1928. 1st edn. 4to. 215 pp. 12 plates.  *(Scientia)* $100
- Horses: the story of the horse family in the modern world and through sixty million years of history. New York: 1951. 1st edn. 247 pp.
*(Scientia)* $30
- Tempo and mode in evolution. New York: 1944. 1st edn. 237 pp. Dw.  *(Scientia)* $60
- This view of life: the world of an evolutionist. New York: 1964. 1st edn. 308 pp.
*(Scientia)* $22.50

**Simpson, J.Y.**
- Remarks on the superinduction of anaesthesia in natural and morbid parturition: with cases illustrative of the uses and effects of chloroform ... William B. Little & Co.,

Chemists & Druggists, 1848. 1st Amer edn.
8vo. 48 pp. Orig printed wraps. *(M&S)* **$300**

**Simpson, James**
- Anaesthesia, or the employment of
chloroform and ether in surgery, midwifery,
etc. Phila: 1849. 1st edn. 248 pp. Recent qtr
lea, mrbld bds.                      *(Fye)* **$750**

**Simpson, Sir James Young**
- Acupressure. A new method of arresting
surgical haemorrhage and of accelerating the
healing of wounds ... Edinburgh: Adam &
Charles Black, 1864. 1st edn. 8vo. xiv,580 pp.
42 text figs. Light foxing. Orig cloth. Wear to
crnrs & spinal extremities.    *(Dailey)* **$250**
- Clinical lectures on diseases of women. Phila:
Blanchard & Lea, 1863. 4to. xii,510 pp. 102
engvs.                              *(Poitras)* **$75**

**Simpson, Thomas**
- The doctrine and application of fluxions.
London: for J. Nourse, 1750. 1st edn. 2 parts
in 1 vol. Contemp calf, rubbed. *(Pollak)* **£125**
- Elements of geometry; with their application
to the mensuration ... London: J. Nourse,
1760. 2nd edn, with lge altrtns & addtns.
xi,276 pp. Sl worming in lower margin not
affecting text. Contemp calf, relaid, old label
rebacked.                           *(Pollak)* **£35**
- Mathematical dissertations on a variety of
physical and analytical subjects. London: T.
Woodward, 1743. 1st edn. Sm 4to. viii,168
pp. Text w'cuts. Light unif browning & occas
foxing. 3/4 calf.                *(Antiq Sc)* **$250**
- Select exercises for young proficients in the
mathematicks ... to which is prefixed, an
account of the life and writings of the author,
by Charles Hutton. London: for F. Wingrave,
1792. New edn. [iv],iv, xxiii,[i advts], 252 pp.
Orig sheep, edges worn.            *(Pollak)* **£30**
- A treatise of algebra ... London: John Nourse,
1775. 4th edn, revsd. [x],402 pp. Orig sheep,
rebacked, fore edges of bds worn. *(Pollak)* **£35**
- A treatise of algebra, wherein the principles
are demonstrated ... London: John Nourse,
1755. 2nd edn, with lge addtns. [xii],402 pp.
Some foxing. Speckled calf, crnrs worn,
rebacked with old spine relaid. Sgntr of James
Whatman on end-paper.             *(Pollak)* **£45**

**Simpson, W.J.**
- A treatise on plague, dealing with the
historical, epidemiological, clinical,
therapeutic and preventive aspects of the
disease. 1905. xxiv,466 pp. Many maps,
charts & ills included in text. Orig cloth, sl
worn.                           *(Whitehart)* **£35**

**Sims, J. Marion**
- Clinical notes on uterine surgery. New York:
1866. 1st edn. 401 pp. One inch tear at top of
spine.                               *(Fye)* **$400**

**Simson, Robert**
- The elements of Euclid, viz the first six
books, together with the eleventh and twelfth.
Glasgow: 1756. 1st Simson edn in English.
4to. [viii],431 pp. W'cut text diags. A little
paper discolouration. Contemp calf,
rebacked, crnrs rprd. Mor label.
                                  *(Pickering)* **$350**
- The elements of Euclid, viz the first six
books, together with the eleventh and twelfth.
Glasgow: Andrew Foulis, 1781. [x],466 pp. 3
fldg plates. Some old damp-staining, occas old
ink mark, plates frayed. Lacks Gg2 (blank?).
New half-calf.                     *(Pollak)* **£35**
- The elements of Euclid, viz the first six books
... London & Edinburgh: 1799. vii,9-520 pp.
3 plates. Some pencil marginalia. Orig sheep,
spine worn, jnts weak.             *(Pollak)* **£25**
- Elements of the conic sections. Translated
from the Latin original ... Edinburgh: for
James Dickson & William Creech, 1792. 2nd
edn. [viii],284,[iv] pp. 14 plates. Sgntr of
Thomas Bazely on title. Orig sheep, rubbed.
                                     *(Pollak)* **£35**

**Simson, Thomas**
- An inquiry how far the vital and animal
actions of the more perfect animals can be
accounted for independent of the brain ...
Edinburgh: ... Neill, 1752. 1st edn. 4to.
[4],16, 270,[2] pp. Errata, 2 fldg plates.
Minimal browning. Contemp calf, rebacked.
                               *(Rootenberg)* **$600**

**Sinclair, George**
- The hydrostaticks; or, the weight, force, and
pressure of fluid bodies ... Together with
some miscellany observations ...Edinburgh:
George Swintoun ..., 1672. 1st edn. 4to.
x,319,[1 blank] pp. Engvd title, 8 fldg engvd
plates. Contemp mottled calf.
                                *(Pickering)* **$1,850**

**Sinclair, J.**
- History of shorthorn cattle. 1907. xiv,895 pp.
26 ports, many ills. Half-calf, worn. Spine
chipped.                        *(Phenotype)* **£40**

**Sinclair, Maurice**
- The Thomas splint and its modifications in
the treatment of fractures. London: 1927. 1st
edn. 168 pp.                         *(Fye)* **$50**

**Singer, Charles**
- The earliest chemical industry: an essay in the
historical relations of economics and
technology. London: Folio Society, 1943. Ltd
(1,100). Folio. xviii,337,[4] pp. 181 ills. Red
cloth, black mor label, gilt lettering on spine
(sl faded).                       *(Zeitlin)* **$200**
- The evolution of anatomy. New York: 1925.
1st Amer edn. 209 pp. 22 plates, 117 text ills.
                                    *(Oasis)* **$50**

- The evolution of anatomy: a short history of anatomical and physiological discovery to Harvey. New York: 1925. 1st edn. 209 pp. *(Fye)* **$50**
- From magic to science. Essays on the scientific twilight. London: 1928. 47 plates, 14 cold, 60 figs. *(Winterdown)* **£40**
- A short history of anatomy and physiology from the Greeks to Harvey. New York: 1957. 2nd edn. 209 pp. Wraps. *(Fye)* **$10**
- A short history of biology. Oxford: Clarendon Press, 1931. xxxv,572 pp. Frontis, 193 ills. *(Pollak)* **£18**

**Singer, Charles & Underwood, E.A.**
- A short history of medicine. New York: 1962. Rvsd & enlgd edn. Dw. *(Scientia)* **$40**

**Singer, Charles, et al.**
- A history of technology. New York: 1957-59. Library of Science edn. 5 vols. Dw. *(Scientia)* **$200**
- A history of technology. Oxford: Clarendon Press, 1954. 5 vols. Thick 4to. 204 plates. Dws. *(Edwards)* **£250**

**Skelton, C.A.**
- The Cyanide Plant Supply Co. supply complete cyanide plants and steel or wooden vats ... London, 1902. 4to. 300 pp. Occas marginal mark. Front jnt weak. A trade catalogue. *(Pollak)* **£20**

**Skelton, Dr.**
- Botanic record and family herbal. Leeds: 1855. Sev ills. Rebound in calf. *(Jenner)* **£40**

**Skelton, John**
- A plea for the botanic practice of medicine. 1853. 1st edn. Frontis. *(Robertshaw)* **£18**

**Skene, Alexander**
- Electro-hemastasis in operative surgery. New York: 1899. 1st edn. 173 pp. *(Fye)* **$75**
- Medical gynecology. New York: 1900. 1st edn. 529 pp. *(Fye)* **$65**

**Skey, Frederic C.**
- Operative surgery. London: 1850. xii,709 pp. Half-title. Ill. Some pages crudely opened. Orig cloth. *(Goodrich)* **$125**

**Skey. Frederic Carpenter**
- Hysteria: remote causes of disease in general. Treatment of disease ... London: Longmans [et al], 1870. 3rd edn. x,122 pp. *(Gach)* **$35**

**Skinner, B.F.**
- See Ferster, C.B. & Skinner, B.F.
- Verbal behavior. N.J.: 1957. 478 pp. *(Epistemologist)* **$35**

**Skoog, Tord**
- Plastic surgery. New methods and refinements. Phila: W.B. Saunders, 1974. 500 pp. Profusely illust in color. Ex lib. *(Poitras)* **$75**

**Skrimshire, Fenwick**
- A series of popular chymical essays: containing a variety of instances of the application of chymistry to arts and manufactures ... London: J. Johnson, 1804. 2nd edn. Sm 8vo. Occas foxing. Contemp half-calf, mrbld bds rubbed. *(McDowell)* **£70**

**Slade, Daniel D.**
- Diptheria: Its nature and treatment. With an account of its prevalence in various countries. Phila: 1864. 2nd rvsd edn. 164 pp. Orig cloth, faded, some shelf wear. *(Elgen)* **$40**

**Slater, John C.**
- Quantum theory of matter. New York: 1951. 1st edn. 528 pp. *(Scientia)* **$30**

**Slocum, Donald**
- An atlas of amputations. St. Louis: 1949. 1st edn. Ills. Orig cloth. *(Oasis)* **$75**

**Sluder, Greenfield**
- Nasal neurology: headaches and eye disorders. St. Louis: 1927. 1st edn. 272 pp. Ills. *(Oasis)* **$45**

**Sluss, John**
- Emergency surgery. Phila: 1910. 2nd edn. 748 pp. Full lea. *(Fye)* **$25**

**Smart, John**
- Tables of interest, discount, annuities, &c. London: J. Darby & T. Browne, 1726. 4to. [viii],123 pp. Blank margin of title & 1 other leaf rprd. Contemp calf, rebacked, 2 crnrs rprd. other 2 worn. *(Pollak)* **£50**

**Smeaton, John**
- Experimental enquiry concerning the natural powers of wind and water to tun mills and other machines ... 1813. 3rd edn. vii,110 pp. 5 engvd fldg plates. Uncut. Orig paper-cvrd bds, worn. *(Weiner)* **£110**

**Smedley, John**
- Practical hydropathy. Including plans of baths, and remarks on diet, clothing, and habits of life. 1870. 13th edn. Thick 8vo. xxx,450 pp. Frontis, 160 ills. Sl foxing. Cvrs loose, spine sl worn. *(Jenner)* **£10**

**Smee, Alfred**
- The source of physical science. Being an introduction to the study of physiology through physics. London: H. Renshaw, 1843. 1st edn. 8vo. xx,296 pp. Orig cloth. Hd of

spine chipped. *(Antiq Sc)* **$110**

**Smellie, William**
- A set of anatomical tables ... and an abridgement of the practice of midwifery. Worcester, Mass.: Isaiah Thomas, 1793. 1st Worcester edn. 8vo. 84 pp. 41 plates. Plates lightly foxed, with some offsetting. Contemp sheep, edges scuffed, jnts tender. *(M&S)* **$850**
- A set of anatomical tables ... of the practice of midwifery with a view to illustrate a treatise on the subject. London: 1754. 1st edn. Imp folio. [44] pp. 38 (of 39) plates. Some lib stamps. Half-mor, cvrs loose. *(Hemlock)* **$1,000**
- A set of anatomical tables ... of the practice of midwifery with a view to illustrate a treatise on the subject. London: 1761. 2nd edn. Atlas folio. 22ff. 39 engvd plates. Title heavily soiled, w'stains on some margins. New pebbled bds, new endpapers. *(Jenner)* **£950**

**Smethurst, Gamaliel**
- Tables of time: whereby the day of the month ... Manchester: 1749. Sm 8vo. viii,132,48 pp. Lib label on front cvr, embossed stamp on title & first few pages. Later lib binding, cloth sl dust stained, spine dull. *(Whitehart)* **£40**

**Smethurst, Thomas**
- Hydrotherapia; or, the water cure ... together with a short sketch of the history ... and remarks on sea bathing. London: John Snow, 1843. 2nd edn. 8vo. xvi,17-282 pp. Litho port frontis, plate. Cloth *(Hemlock)* **$85**

**Smiles, Samuel**
- Lives of Boulton & Watt ... a history of the invention and introduction of the steam-engine, 1865. 1st edn. 8vo. [xvi],521. 2 engvd ports, num wood engravings in the text. Sl browning. Contemp prize calf, gilt arms on side, rebacked. *(Pickering)* **$150**
- Lives of Boulton & Watt ... a history of the invention and introduction of the steam-engine, London: John Murray, 1865. 1st edn. Thick 8vo. Port frontis, one other port, many ills in text. Orig cloth. *(McDowell)* **£55**
- Lives of the engineers. London: John Murray, 1874. New & revised edn. 5 vols. 8vo. Full contemp tree calf, spines heavily gilt, hinges tender & some chipping to hd of spines. *(McDowell)* **£130**

**Smith, A.H.**
- Dental microscopy. London: 1899. 2nd edn. I cold, 8 other litho plates. 67 engvd figs. *(Winterdown)* **£10**

**Smith, Clement**
- The physiology of the newborn infant. Springfield: 1946. 1st edn, 2nd printing. 312

pp. *(Fye)* **$20**

**Smith, Cyril S.**
- A history of metallurgy. The development of ideas on the structure of metals before 1890. Chicago: 1965. 2nd printing with additions. 293 pp. Ex lib, somewhat worn. *(Scientia)* **$30.**

**Smith, David E.**
- History of mathematics. Boston: 1923-25. 2 vols. 596; 725 pp. Shelfworn, spine lettering rubbed. *(Scientia)* **$35**
- Rara arithmetica. A catalogue of the arithmetics written before the year 1501. With a description of those in the library of George Arthur Plimpton. Boston & London: Gunn & Co., 1908. 1st edn. 8vo. *(McDowell)* **£80**

**Smith, E. Noble**
- See Klein, E. & Smith, E. Noble

**Smith, Edgar C.**
- A short history of naval and marine engineering. Cambridge: 1937. 16 plates, 46 figs in text. Cloth sl stained. *(Whitehart)* **£25**

**Smith, Edgar F.**
- Chemistry in America: chapters from the history of the science in the United States. New York: 1914. 1st edn. 356 pp. *(Scientia)* **$50**
- Chemistry in old Philadelphia. Phila: 1919. 1st edn. 106 pp. *(Scientia)* **$45**
- Old chemistries. New York: 1927. 1st edn. 89 pp. Stain on rear cvr. *(Scientia)* **$45**

**Smith, Elisha**
- The botanic physician: being a compendium of the practice of physic, upon botanical principles ... New York: Murphy & Bingham, 1830. viii,624 pp. Foxing. Orig calf, worn. *(Goodrich)* **$75**

**Smith, Ernest A.**
- A manual on dental metallurgy. London: Churchill, 1898. 1st edn. 8vo. W'cut ills in text. Title sl spotted. Pub cloth, crnrs rubbed. *(McDowell)* **£28**

**Smith, Eustace**
- Clinical studies of disease in children: diseases of the lungs, acute tubercolosis. 1876. xv,303 pp. Some foxing on prelims. Orig green cloth, upper hinge cracked. *(Jenner)* **£16**

**Smith, Franklin**
- See Davison, Charles & Smith, Franklin

**Smith, G. Elliott & Pear, T.H.**
- Shell shock and its lessons. Manchester &

London: 1917. xii,135 pp. Shelfworn.
*(Gach)* **$25**

**Smith, G. Geoffrey**
- Gas turbines and jet propulsion for aircraft ...
New York: 1944. 1st U.S. edn. [5],123 pp.
Ills, diags. Ex lib with stamps. *(Weiner)* **£20**

**Smith, J.B.**
- A treatise upon wire, its manufacture and
uses ...1891. 4to. xxii,347 pp. 95 figs, 33
tables. Orig cloth, sl stained, sm nick on
spine. *(Whitehart)* **£25**

**Smith, J.G.**
- Abdominal surgery. London: 1887. 1st edn.
606 pp. *(Fye)* **$60**

**Smith, J.H.**
- Elementary principles of algebra explained
and exemplified. Cambridge: for private
circulation by Jonathan Palmer, n.d. [ca
1840]. [ii],72 pp. Orig cloth. *(Pollak)* **£20**

**Smith, James**
- The panorama of science and art; embracing
the sciences of aerostation ... chemistry,
electricity ... experiments. Liverpool: 1815. 2
vols. x,626; xii,862 pp. Frontis, 49 plates.
Browning & sl damp-staining. Tree calf,
worn, jnts weak. *(Pollak)* **£45**

**Smith, Joe T.**
- American pediatric directory, 1935. 1st edn.
A listing of the pediatricians of the United
States ... Knoxville, Tenn: 1935. 128 pp.
*(Poitras)* **$50**

**Smith, John**
- Hand-book of dental anatomy and surgery for
the use of students and practitioners. London:
J. & A. Churchill, 1871. 2nd edn. 8vo. Pub
blind-stamped cloth. *(McDowell)* **£85**

**Smith, John Augustine**
- Select discourses on the functions of the
nervous system, in opposition to phrenology,
materialism and atheism ... New York:
Appleton, 1840. 1st edn. Sm 8vo. 210 pp.
Lightly foxed. *(Xerxes)* **$100**

**Smith, John Gordon**
- The principles of forensic medicine
systematically arranged, and applied to
British practice. London: for T. & G.
Underwood, 1821. 1st edn.xv,[1],503, [2],10
[index] pp. Marginal damp staining. Owner's
stamp on title. Orig bds, worn & stained,
rebacked. *(Diamond)* **$125**

**Smith, Joseph Mather**
- Elements of the etiology and philosophy of
epidemics. In two parts. New York: for J. &

J. Harper, 1824. 1st edn. 8vo. 223 pp.
Staining in margins of prelims. Orig bds,
front hinge & spine shaken. *(Hemlock)* **$175**

**Smith, Marcus J.**
- Error and variation in diagnostic radiology.
1967. 1st edn. 191 pp. Ills. Dw. Author's
sgnd pres copy. *(Oasis)* **$20**

**Smith, Mary**
- The complete housekeeper, and professed
cook. Calculated for the greater ease of ladies,
housekeepers, cooks, &c., &c. Newcastle: for
S. Hodgson, 1803. New edn. 8vo. Contemp
roan, rebacked. *(McDowell)* **£160**

**Smith, Nathan**
- Medical and surgical memoirs. Balt: 1831. 1st
edn. 374 pp. Recent leatherette. Inscribed &
autographed by Sarah Smith, the author's
wife. *(Fye)* **$300**

**[Smith, R.C., et al.]**
- The astrologer of the nineteenth century: or,
the master keye of futurity, and guide to
ancient mysteries ... London: Knight &
Lacey, 1825. 7th edn. 8vo. Hand-cold frontis
& title, printed title, 3 hand-cold plates. Plates
a little marked. Contemp bds. *(McDowell)* **£65**

**Smith, Robert**
- A compleat system of opticks in four books ...
and a philosophical treatise ... Cambridge: for
the author, 1738. 1st edn. 2 vols. 4to.
[4],vi,[8],280; 282-455, 1-171,[13] pp. 83 fldg
plates, list of subscribers, errata. Contemp
calf, jnts strengthened. *(Rootenberg)* **$1,000**
- A compleat system of opticks in four books ...
and a philosophical treatise ... Cambridge: for
the author, 1738. 1st edn, lge paper copy. 2
vols in 1. 4to. 83 fldg engvd plates. Contemp
red mor, gilt edges, jnts reprd.
*(Quaritch)* **$2,000**
- Harmonics or the philosophy of musical
sounds. Cambridge: J. Bentham, 1749. 1st
edn. 8vo. Fldg tables, 25 fldg engvd plates.
Contemp calf. *(Quaritch)* **$500**
- Harmonics or the philosophy of musical
sounds ... London: for T. & J. Merrill, [etc],
1759. 2nd edn. 8vo. xx,280,[13,1 blank]. 28
fldg engvd plates, tables (3 fldg). Title a little
stained, some spotting. Contemp sprinkled
calf, rebacked. *(Pickering)* **$450**

**Smith, Samuel Stanhope**
- An essay on the causes of the variety of
complexion and figure in the human species
... Phila: Robert Aiken, 1787. 1st edn. 8vo.
[2],111,31 pp. Short tear in title without loss,
another leaf defective in margin. Orig blue
wraps, backstrip mostly lacking.
*(Antiq Sc)* **$500**
- An essay on the causes of the variety of

complexion and figure in the human species ... New Brunswick: J. Simpson, 1810. 2nd edn. 411 pp. Foxing. Contemp calf, scuffed. *(Elgen)* **$150**
- An essay on the causes of the variety of complexion and figure in the human species ... New Brunswick: J. Simpson, 1810. 2nd edn, enlgd & impvd. Browning. Calf, rubbed. *(Goodrich)* **$125**

**Smith, Stephen**
- Hand-book of the principles and practice of operative surgery. Phila: 1884. 5th edn. 689 pp. Inner hinges cracked. *(Fye)* **$40**
- The principles and practice of operative surgery. Phila: 1887. New & thoroughly revsd edn. 877 pp. 1005 w'cuts. Orig sheep, rubbed. *(Goodrich)* **$45**
- Scientific research: a view from within. [1901]. vii,72 pp. 9 (on 8) plates of experiments. Uncut. Edge of cloth discoloured. (Vivisection.) *(Weiner)* **£25**

**Smith, Truman**
- An examination of the question of anaethesia, arising on the memorial of Charles Thomas Wells ... New York: John A. Gray, printer, 1858. Tall 8vo. 135 pp. Uncut in orig embossed cloth, backstrip loose. *(Hemlock)* **$265**
- An examination of the question of anaethesia, arising on the memorial of Charles Thomas Wells ... New York: 1859. 154 pp. Lib stamp & pencil notations on title & front paste down. Lacks front endpaper. *(Fye)* **$100**

**Smith, W.**
- The chemistry of hat manufacturing. 1906. vii,124 pp. 16 ills. *(Whitehart)* **£15**

**Smith, William**
- A dissertation upon the nerves; containing an account ... of the nature of man ... of brutes ... of all nervous diseases. London: for the Author ..., 1768. 1st edn. 8vo. vi,[2],302 pp, [1]f. Contemp gilt-ruled calf, back reprd. Lge paper copy. *(Zeitlin)* **$325**

**Smith, Wm. R.**
- The laws concerning public health. Including the various sanitary Acts passed in the Session 1883, and the circulars issued ... 1883. xlviii,812 pp. Orig cloth, faded & worn. Lib stamp on title. *(Whitehart)* **£38**

**Smyth, A.L.**
- John Dalton, 1766-1844. A bibliography of works by and about him. Manchester: 1966. 1st edn. 114 pp. *(Scientia)* **$60**
- John Dalton, 1766-1844. A bibliography of works by and about him. Manchester: University Press, 1966. 1st edn. 4to. Plates. *(McDowell)* **£28**

**Smyth, H.D.**
- Atomic energy for military purposes. The official report of the development of the atomic bomb under the auspices of the United States government, 1940 - 1945. Princeton: 1945. 8vo. 8 photo plates. Orig printed wraps. *(Argosy)* **$100**
- A general account of the development of methods of using atomic energy for military purposes under the auspices of the United States Government 1940-1945. London: H.M.S.O., 1945. 1st English edn. 8vo. Some spotting to printed wraps. *(McDowell)* **£30**
- A general account of the development of methods of using atomic energy for military purposes under the auspices of the United States Government 1940-1945. Washington, DC: 1945. 1st Government Printing Office edn. 182 pp. Orig wraps. *(Scientia)* **$275**

**Smyth, W.H.**
- A cycle of celestial objects, observed, reduced and discussed. Oxford: 1881. 2nd edn. xxii,696 pp. Cold frontis, 51 other ills. Later cloth. *(Whitehart)* **£25**

**Snell, Albion T.**
- Electric motive power. "The Electrician": [1899]. vi,409,[xi advts], 32 [ctlg] pp. 224 ills. Spine faded, sl worn at ends & crnrs. *(Pollak)* **£20**

**Soame, John**
- Hampstead Wells: or, directions for the drinking of those waters. Shewing ... the diseases in which they are most prevalent ... London: for the Author, 1734. 110 pp. Sev vignettes. Cvrs rubbed, worn. *(Xerxes)* **$400**

**Sobotta, Johannes**
- Atlas of human anatomy. New York: 1927. 3 vols. Num leaves loose in binding, 5 leaves torn without loss of text. Bindings rubbed, vol 3 shaken. *(Fye)* **$45**

**Soddy, Frederick**
- The chemistry of the radio-elements. Parts I, II. London: 1915-14. 2nd edn (rvsd & rewrttn); 1st edn. 151; 46 pp. *(Scientia)* **$85**
- The interpretation of radium and the structure of the atom. London: John Murray, 1922. 4th edn, revsd and enlgd. xvi,260,[iv advts] pp. 44 text figs. *(Pollak)* **£25**
- The interpretation of radium, being the substance of six free popular experimental lectures ... London: John Murray, 1909. 1st edn. 8vo. Ills. Pub red blind-stamped cloth. *(McDowell)* **£38**
- The interpretation of radium. New York: 1912. 3rd edn. Rvsd & enlgd. 284 pp. *(Scientia)* **$25**
- The interpretation of the atom. 1932. xviii,355 pp. Fldg charts, plates, diags.

Inscribed 'G.O. Griffith, with the author's thanks for his help, FS, Oct. 1932'.
*(Weiner)* **£40**
- The interpretation of the atom. New York: 1932. 1st Amer edn. 355 pp. *(Scientia)* **$35**
- Matter and energy. London: Williams & Norgate, n.d. [ca 1910] 256,[iv ctlg] pp.
*(Pollak)* **£20**
- The story of atomic energy. London: Nova Atlantis, 1949. 1st edn in book form. 4to. viii,136 pp. Orig cloth. *(Antiq Sc)* **$50**

**Solis-Cohen, J.**
- Diseases of the throat: a guide to the diagnosis and treatment of affections of the pharynx, esophagus ... New York: 1872. 1st edn. 582 pp. *(Fye)* **$125**

**Some ...**
- Some enquiries into the effects of fermented liquors ... See Montagu, Basil
- Some thoughts on the woollen manufactures of England ... See Bindon, David

**Somerville, Mary**
- On molecular and microscopic science. London, J. Murray, 1869. 1st edn. 2 vols. 8vo. xi,[1],432; 320,32[pub ctlg, Sept 1868] pp. 10 plates printed in blue, num text w'cuts. Orig blue cloth gilt. *(Antiq Sc)* **$100**

**Sommerfeld, Arnold**
- Atomic structure and spectral lines. London: Methuen, [1923]. 1st edn in English. 8vo. xiii,[1],626, 8 [pub ctlg] pp. Text figs. Orig cloth. *(Antiq Sc)* **$90**

**Soper, Fred L. & Wilson, D.B.**
- Anopheles Gambiae in Brazil 1930 - 1940. New York: 1943. xviii,262 pp. Frontis, ills, tables. Cvrs sl soiled. *(Jenner)* **£10**

**Soyer, Alexis**
- The modern housewife or menagere, comprising nearly one thousand receipts ... and those for the nursery and the sick room. London: Simpkin, Marshall, 1849. 2nd edn. Half-title, engvd frontis, occas cuts, advts at end. Orig embossed cloth, rubbed, stained.
*(McDowell)* **£130**

**Spaeth, Edmund**
- Newer methods of ophthalmic plastic surgery. Phila: 1925. 1st edn. 258 pp. 168 ills. *(Fye)* **$175**

**Spargo, John**
- The bitter cry of the children. New York: Macmillan, 1906. xxiii,337,[iii] pp. Frontis, 32 plates. Orig dec cloth. *(Pollak)* **£25**

**Sparhawk, Ebenezer**
- Discourse delivered January 18, 1794, at the internment of of Benjamin Shuttock, Esq., an eminent physician in Templeton. Worcester, Mass.: 1795. 22 pp. Edges frayed. Wraps.
*(Xerxes)* **$100**

**Spear, Jesse S.**
- The family physician: a brief treatise on the origin and nature of the principal diseases which afflict humanity ... Boston: 1848. 8vo. 62 pp. Sm defect upper outer blank margin of title, tear without loss on rear page. Sewn, in wraps. *(Hemlock)* **$65**

**Spearman, C.**
- The nature of intelligence and the principles of cognition. London: 1923. 1st edn. 358 pp.
*(Oasis)* **$75**

**Spectral ...**
- Spectral visitants, or journal of a fever; by a convalescent. Portland: S.H. Colesworthy, 1845. Sole edn. Sm 8vo. 75,[1] pp. Slightly browned. Printed wraps. *(Dailey)* **$150**

**Spemann, Hans**
- Embryonic development and induction. New Haven: 1938. 1st edn. 401 pp. Cvrs faintly stained. Silliman Lectures. *(Scientia)* **$85**

**Spence, James**
- Lectures on surgery. Edinburgh: 1882. 2 vols. xxvii,510; xxiv,511-1226 pp. Many ills, some cold plates. Orig brown cloth, cvrs & spines defective, one spine detchd.
*(Jenner)* **£30**

**Spencer, Herbert**
- An autobiography. New York: 1904. 1st Amer edn. 2 vols. 655; 613 pp. *(Scientia)* **$35**
- Principles of biology. London: 1864-67. 2nd thous. 2 vols. 492; 574 pp. Spines faded.
*(Scientia)* **$75**
- The principles of psychology. 1890. 3rd edn. 2 vols. xiv,640; 696 pp. Tear on title to vol I. Orig dec cloth, sl faded, hinges to vol II weak.
*(Jenner)* **£30**
- The principles of psychology. London: Williams & Norgate, 1870. 2nd edn, stereotyped. *(Gach)* **$75**
- The principles of psychology. London: 1890. 3rd edn, 5th thousand. 2 vols. 640; 696 pp. Sm piece torn from title of vol I. Dec cloth, sl shelfwear, spine faded.
*(Epistemologist)* **$67.50**

**Spencer, L.J.**
- The world's minerals. 1911. 8vo. xi,212 pp. 40 cold plates. Sl foxing. Cloth, trifle used, spine faded. *(Wheldon & Wesley)* **£18**

**Speransky, A.D.**
- A basis for the theory of medicine. New York: International Publishers, 1943. 417 pp. 46

photographic plates.          *(Poitras)* **$40**

**Spiegel, Capt. J.**
- See Grinker, Lt. Col. Roy R. & Spiegel, Capt. J.

**Spiller, W.G.**
- See Posey, W.C. & Spiller, W.G.

**Spilsbury, Francis**
- Free observations on the scurvy, gout, diet, and remedy. Rochester: T. Fisher, 1783. 2nd edn. Upper crnr in last third of text nibbled. Later bds, unlettered.          *(Robertshaw)* **£45**

**Spitzka, Edward Charles**
- Insanity: its classification, diagnosis and treatment. A manual for students and practitioners of medicine. New York: Bermingham & Co., 1883. 1st edn. 12mo. 415 pp. Green cloth.          *(Gach)* **$65**

**Spottiswoode, William**
- Polarisation of light. Macmillan, 1874. viii,[ii],129 pp. Cold double frontis. 29 figs. Author's pres copy.          *(Pollak)* **£25**
- Polarisation of light. Macmillan, 1879. 3rd edn. viii,149,[iii] pp. Cold double frontis. 29 figs.          *(Pollak)* **£20**

**Sprat, Thomas**
- The history of the Royal Society of London ... London: for Rob. Scot ... 1702. 2nd edn. Sm 4to. [8]ff,438 pp. 2 fldg engvd plates. Small wormtrail affecting lower blank margin. Contemp panelled calf, label gone, jnts split.          *(Zeitlin)* **$300**
- The history of the Royal Society of London. London: J. Knapton ..., 1722. 3rd edn, corrected. 4to. [12],438 pp. Red & black title, engvd armorial frontis, 2 fldg engvd plates. Contemp blind-stamped polished calf. Jnts cracked.          *(Antiq Sc)* **$160**
- The history of the Royal-Society of London, for the improving of natural knowledge. London: J. Martyn, 1667. 1st edn. Lge 8vo. 2 plates. Contemp reverse calf, later rebacking, red calf label.          *(McDowell)* **£375**

**Spratt, G.**
- Obstetric tables: comprising graphic illustrations, with descriptions and practical remarks ... with additional notes and plates. Phila: 1847. 1st Amer edn. 4to. Unpaginated text. 19 engvd plates, mostly fldg & hand-cold. Scattered foxing & soiling.          *(Fye)* **$500**

**Sprengell, C.J.**
- The aphorisms of Hippocrates, and the sentences of Celsus ... to which are added aphorisms upon the small-pox, measles, and other distempers. 1708. 1st edn. 2 ports. Red & black title. Mod lib cloth, ex Lincoln's Inn

Library.          *(Robertshaw)* **£25**

**Sprunt, Thomas P.**
- See Barker, Lewellys F. & Sprunt, Thomas P.

**Spurgin, John**
- The physician for all; his philosophy, his experience, and his mission. London: 1855. viii,226 pp. Half-title. Author's pres copy.          *(Goodrich)* **$70**

**Spurzheim, Johann Caspar**
- The anatomy of the brain, with a general view of the nervous system ... Translated ... by R. Willis ... London: S. Highley, 1826. 1st edn & 1st appearance in English. 8vo. xxiv,234 pp. 11 plates. Half-calf. Lightly browned & spotted. Lib stamp on title.          *(Zeitlin)* **$285**
- The anatomy of the brain, with a general view of the nervous system ... Translated ... by R. Willis ... Boston: 1836. 2nd Amer edn. xxvii,[9]-244 pp. 18 litho plates. Foxed. Orig cloth, upper jnt starting, spine ends chipped off.          *(Elgen)* **$100**
- Observations on the deranged manifestations of the mind, or insanity. Boston: Marsh, Capen & Lyon. 1833. 1st Amer edn. viii,260 pp. 4 engvd plates. Rose cloth, faded, paper label chipped.          *(Gach)* **$175**
- Observations on the deranged manifestations of the mind, or insanity ... Boston: 1833. 1st Amer edn. viii,260 pp. 4 litho plates. Inner margin w'stained throughout. Orig cloth, new label.          *(Elgen)* **$165**
- Phrenology, in connexion with the study of physiognomy ... Boston: 1833. 1st Amer edn. Lge 8vo. Engvd frontis. 191 pp. 34 litho plates, tipped-in errata note. Scattered foxing. Orig cloth, faded. Shelf wear.          *(Elgen)* **$175**
- Phrenology, in connexion with the study of physiognomy. Illustrations of characters with 35 plates. Boston: Marsh, Capen & Lyon, 1836. 272 pp. 2 pp reprd, not affecting text. Spine split. Ex lib.          *(Poitras)* **$75**
- A view of the elementary principles of education, founded on the study of the nature of man. Edinburgh: for Archibald Constable & Co., 1821. 1st edn. Sm 8vo. [xvi],360 pp. Orig bds, spine quite worn.          *(Gach)* **$125**
- A view of the philosophical principles of phrenology. 1825. 3rd edn, greatly improved. viii,216 pp. Contemp half lea, rebacked. Dust stained & worn.          *(Whitehart)* **£45**

**Stackhouse, J.**
- Nereis Britannica; containing all the species of Fuci, natives of the British coasts. Bath: [1795] - 1801. Folio. xl,112,7 pp. 2 title-vignettes, 17 cold plates, 7 watercolour drawings (issued in subscribers' copies only). Contemp half-mor, worn.          *(Wheldon & Wesley)* **£700**

**Stanley, Rupert**
- Text book on wireless telegraphy. With illustrations. London: Longmans, 1914. 1st edn. 8vo. 11,[3],344 pp. 201 text figs, fldg diagram. Orig cloth.               *(M&S)* **$40**
- Text book on wireless telegraphy. 1919-23. New edn. 2 vols. xiii,471; xi,394 pp. 2 frontis ports, fldg plate, num other ills. Cloth dust-stained.                   *(Whitehart)* **£35**

**Stanton, Alfred H. & Schwartz, Morris S.**
- The mental hospital. A study of institutional participation in psychiatric illness and treatment. 1954. xx,492 pp. Figs & tables. Roughtrimmed. Worn dw.       *(Jenner)* **£20**

**Stark, Richard Boies**
- Plastic surgery. New York: Hoeber ..., 1962. xiii,718 pp. 891 ills.          *(Poitras)* **$40**

**Starr, M. Allen**
- Brain surgery. New York: 1893. 1st edn. 295 pp.                          *(Fye)* **$100**

**Starrat, William**
- The doctrine of projectiles demonstrated and apply'd to all the most useful problems in practical gunnery ... new mathematical instrument ... curious properties of projectiles ... Dublin: S. Powell, 1733. 1st edn. 8vo. xi,[xiii],176 pp. Contemp calf.
                                *(Burmester)* **£325**

**State ...**
- The state of the corn trade considered: in answer to all the objections against the bounty granted to encourage the exportation of corn, and its influence ... For S. Birt, [1753]. 8vo. 30 pp. Imprint trimmed & torn with some loss. Mod mrbld wraps. *(Deighton Bell)* **£80**

**Stebbing, F.C.**
- Navigation and nautical astronomy, 1896. 1st edn. xi,328 pp. 140 figs. Orig cloth, sl marked & worn.                  *(Whitehart)* **£18**

**Stebbins, G. Ledyard**
- Variation and evolution in plants. New York: 1950. 1st edn. 643 pp.        *(Scientia)* **$50**

**Steggall, John**
- An essay on mineral, vegetable, animal and aerial poisons. 1833. 2nd edn. 12 cold plates, some engvd, some litho. Uncut in orig cloth-backed mrbld bds, upper jnt partly split.
                                *(Robertshaw)* **£55**

**Steindler, Arthur**
- The traumatic deformities and disabilities of the upper extremities. Springfield: 1946. 1st edn. 494 pp.                      *(Fye)* **$45**

**Stekel, William**
- Peculiarities of behavior; wandering mania, dypsomania, cleptomania, pyromania and allied impulsive acts. Translated ... 1925. 2 vols. xiv,328; x,337 pp. Orig brown cloth, vol I a little shaken.            *(Jenner)* **£25**

**Stellwag (von Carion), Carl**
- Treatise on the diseases of the eye, including the anatomy of the organ. New York: 1868. 2nd Amer edn. 774 pp. 3 chromo-lithos.
                                    *(Fye)* **$50**

**Stenger, Erich**
- The march of photography, translated by Edward Epstean ... 1958. 302 pp. Lib labels at front. Cloth soiled.       *(Weiner)* **£75**

**Sterling, J.W. (trans.)**
- Report ... on the cholera-morbus. New York: 1832. 1st edn in English. 234 pp. Orig cloth, spine worn & label damaged.    *(Oasis)* **$50**

**Stern, W.**
- General psychology from the personalistic standpoint. New York: 1938. 589 pp. Cvrs sl bumped & soiled. *(Epistemologist)* **$37.50**

**Sternberg, George M.**
- Report on the etiology and prevention of yellow fever. Wash, DC: 1890. 1st edn. 271 pp. 4 cold plates, 17 plates photomicrographs. Orig pebble cloth, spine sl frayed. *(Elgen)* **$75**

**Sternberg, Maximilian**
- Acromeagaly. London: New Sydenham Society, n.d. 1st English edition. Slim 8vo. Num photographic plates. Binder's cloth, spine sl stained.       *(McDowell)* **£20**

**Steuert, W.M.**
- Street and electrical railways. Washington: Government Printing Office, 1905. 4to. Num tables, many ills.          *(Edwards)* **£60**

**Steven, John**
- The pathology of mediastinal tumours with special reference to diagnosis. London: 1892. 1st edn. 100 pp.                  *(Fye)* **$75**

**Stevens, Edward F.**
- The American hospital of the twentieth century. New York: 1921. Revsd edn. Sm 4to. viii,380 pp. Profusely illust. Sgnd by the author.                   *(Elgen)* **$65**

**Stevens, William**
- Observations on the healthy and diseased properties of the blood. 1832. xx,504 pp. Endpapers soiled. Diced calf, worn.
                                  *(Jenner)* **£75**

**Stevenson, Alan**
- Account of the Skerryvore lighthouse with notes on the illumination of lighthouses. Edinburgh & London: 1848. Lge 4to. 439 pp. Engvd frontis (nearly detchd), 33 plates (4 double-page, 1 fldg), ills. Plates w'stained. Orig gilt-dec cloth, worn, rebacked.
*(Weiner)* £40

**Stevenson, David**
- The principles and practice of canal and river engineering. Edinburgh: 1872. 2nd edn. Fldg frontis, 3 fldg plans, num plates. Sl shaken, spine faded. *(Edwards)* £100

**Stevenson, John**
- Deafness; its causes, prevention, and cure. London: Henry Colburn, 1828. 1st edn. 8vo. iv,262,[2] pp. Uncut in orig bds. Geo. Arbuthnott's sgntr on front fly leaf.
*(Rootenberg)* $425

**Stewart, Alexander (ed.)**
- The medical and legal aspects of of sanitary reform. London: 1867. 100 pp. New bds. Pres copy from author to Lord Houghton, with a.l.s. tipped in. *(Goodrich)* $150

**Stewart, Balfour**
- The conservation of energy. Being an elementary treatise on energy and its laws. London: King, 1877. 4th edn. xv,180,32 [ctlg] pp. 14 text figs. Cvrs sl faded.
*(Pollak)* £20

**Stewart, J. Purves & Evans, Arthur**
- Nerve injuries and their treatment. London: 1919. 2nd edn. 249 pp. Ex lib. *(Fye)* $20

**Stewart, James Purves**
- Intracranial tumours and some errors in their diagnosis. London: 1927. 1st edn. 206 pp. Tear at hd of spine. *(Fye)* $55

**Stewart, Matthew**
- The distance of the sun from the earth determined ... Edinburgh: for A. Millar [etc], 1763. 1st edn. 8vo. viii,103 pp. 2 fldg engvd plates. Contemp calf, spine gilt. B'plate of Dugald Stewart, son of the author. Early text crrctns (by the author?). *(Pickering)* $1,250

**Stewart, Purves**
- The diagnosis of nervous disease. 1906. 1st edn. xi,380 pp. 192 figs, 2 plates. Orig cloth, spine faded. *(Whitehart)* £20
- The diagnosis of nervous diseases. 1906. xi,380 pp. 2 cold plates, many ills. Rebound in red cloth, orig backstrip pasted down. Ex lib with many lib stamps. *(Jenner)* £28

**Stiles, R. Cresson**
- The life and doctrines of Haller. An

anniversary address before the Kings County Medical Society. New York: 1867. 4to. 24 pp. Frontis port. Printed wraps. *(Hemlock)* $40

**Still, George Frederic**
- Common disorders and diseases of childhood. London: Oxford University Press, 1910. 1st edn, 2nd imp. 8vo. Text ills. Pub red cloth.
*(McDowell)* £25

**Stillingfleet, Benjamin**
- Miscellaneous tracts relating to natural history, husbandry, and physick. London: 1762. 2nd edn. xxxi,391 pp. 11 engvd plates. Lib stamp on title. Contemp calf, rebacked. Author's pres copy. *(Goodrich)* $145

**Stillman, J.D.B.**
- The horse in motion, as shown by instantaneous photography; with a study on animal mechanics founded on anatomy and the revelations of the camera ... theory of quadrupedal locomotion. Boston: 1882. 1st edn. Sm folio. 107 plates. Dec cloth, rubbed.
*(Argosy)* $400

**Stimson, Lewis**
- A manual of operative surgery. Phila: 1885. 2nd edn. 506 pp. *(Fye)* $65
- A practical treatise on fractures and dislocations. Phila: 1899. 1st edn. 822,16 [ctlg]. 20 X-ray plates, num text ills. Orig red cloth. *(Oasis)* $75
- A practical treatise on fractures and dislocations. Phila: 1905. 4th edn. 837 pp. Half lea. *(Fye)* $75

**Stockton, Rev. Owen**
- A warning to drunkards, delivered in several sermons to a congregation at Colchester. Upon the occasion of a sad providence towards a young man dying in the act of drunkeness. 1682. 12mo. [xi],196 pp. Browning throughout. Shaved. Calf, worn, rebacked. *(Jenner)* £80

**Stodola, Dr. A.**
- Steam turbines. With an appendix on gas turbines, and the future of heat engines. Translated from the 2nd enlarged and revised German edition. 1905. 3 litho tables in pocket at rear. *(Edwards)* £20

**Stoker, William**
- A treatise on fever, with observations on the practice adopted for its cure, in the fever hospital and house of recovery, in Dublin. 1815. xxiv,195 pp. 2 tables. Light foxing. Disbound, without cvrs. *(Jenner)* £60

**Stokes, George G.**
- Burnett lectures. On light. London: Macmillan, 1887. 1st edn. Sm 8vo.

xiv,342,[2] pp. Orig cloth with sl wear.
*(Antiq Sc)* **$100**

**Stokes, William**
- The diseases of the heart and the aorta ...
Dublin: Hodges & Smith, 1854. 1st edn. 8vo.
xvi,689 pp. Uncut. Orig black stamped cloth,
spine reprd.            *(Rootenberg)* **$850**

**Stone, Edward**
- A new mathematical dictionary: wherein is
contained, not only ... but likewise ...
London: W. Innys, 1743. 2nd edn, with lge
addtns. xii,[278] pp. 1 gathering weak. Old
calf, rebacked, crnrs worn.    *(Pollak)* **£100**

**Stone, Capt. J.E.**
- Hospital organisation and management
(including planning and construction). 1932.
2nd edn. xxi,797 pp. Orig red cloth. Dw.
*(Jenner)* **£12**

**Stone, Janet & Phillips, A.J.**
- Contact lenses. A textbook for practitioner
and student. 1972. [xii],507 pp. Num plates,
some in colour. Ills. Sl worn dw. *(Jenner)* **£18**

**Stone, William L[eete].**
- Letter to Dr. A. Brigham on animal
magnetism ... New York: George Dearborn,
1837. 1st edn. 8vo. 66 pp. Some foxing.
Disbound.            *(Dailey)* **$50**

**Stoney, B.B.**
- The theory of strains in girders and similar
structures, with observations on the
application of theory to practice ... 1873. New
edn, revsd & enlgd. xxxi,632 pp. 5 fldg plates,
123 figs in text. Orig cloth rebacked, orig
spine laid on.        *(Whitehart)* **£35**

**Stookey, Byron**
- Surgical and mechanical treatment of
peripheral nerves. Phila: 1922. 1st edn. 475
pp.                *(Fye)* **$125**

**Stopes, Marie**
- Contraception (birth control), its theory,
history and practice: a manual for the medical
and legal professions. London: 1927. 2nd
edn. xxvi,480 pp. 5 b/w plates. Orig green
cloth, spine sl rubbed.    *(Jenner)* **£15**
- A letter to working mothers on how to have
healthy children and avoid weakening
pregnancies. Surrey: 1919. Pamphlet.
*(Goodrich)* **$50**

**Story-Maskelyne, Nevil**
- Crystallography. A treatise on the
morphology of crystals. Oxford: Clarendon
Press, 1895. 1st edn. Sm 8vo. xii,521 pp.
Text figs. Orig cloth. Author's pres copy.
*(Antiq Sc)* **$100**

**Stoughton, John**
- Worthies of science. R.T.S., n.d. [ca 1880].
vi,[ii], 342,[ii]. One gathering weak. Spine
ends bruised.            *(Pollak)* **£12**

**Stout, George Frederick**
- Analytic psychology. London: Swan
Sonnenschen, 1909. 3rd edn. 2 vols. Tall 8vo.
289; 314 pp. Pub red cloth. H.L.
Hollingworth's copy, with his notes.
*(Gach)* **$45**
- The groundwork of psychology. New York:
Hinds & Noble, [1903]. [ii],[viii], 248,[14] pp.
1st Amer edn. Grey cloth.    *(Gach)* **$17.50**

**Stovin, G.H.T.**
- Gas and air analgesia in midwifery. London:
Staples Press, 1952. 2nd edn. 8vo. 78 pp. Ills.
*(Poitras)* **$25**

**Stratton, George Malcolm**
- Anger: its religious and moral significance.
New York: Macmillan, 1923. 1st edn.
[xii],277,[3] pp. Worn dw.    *(Gach)* **$30**
- Experimental psychology and its bearing
upon culture. New York & London: 1903. 1st
edn. [viii],331,[5] pp. Russet cloth, jnts
rubbed, shelfworn.        *(Gach)* **$40**
- psychology of the religious life. London:
1918. 376 pp. Sp sl faded & shelfworn.
*(Epistemologist)* **$27.50**

**Straus, Erwin W.**
- Phenomenological psychology: the selected
papers of Erwin W. Straus. Translated ...
New York: Basic Books, Inc., [1966]. 1st edn.
[xiv],353,[1] pp. Black cloth, rubbed.
Endpapers glued down.    *(Gach)* **$35**

**Stroganoff, W.**
- The improved prophylactic method in the
treatment of eclampsia. Translated ...
Edinburgh: 1930. 1st edn in English. vii,154
pp. Orig cloth.        *(Whitehart)* **£35**

**Strong, Edward W.**
- Procedures and metaphysics. A study in the
philosophy of mathematical physical science
in the sixteenth and seventeenth Centuries.
Berkeley: 1936. 1st edn. 301 pp.
*(Scientia)* **$35**

**Strong, Richard P., et al.**
- Typhus fever with particular reference to the
Serbian epidemic. Harvard University Press,
1920. Lge 8vo. viii,273 pp. 26 ills. Lib stamp
on title. Cvrs sl soiled.    *(Jenner)* **£18**

**Strong, T.B. (ed.)**
- Lectures on the methods of science. Oxford:
1906. 249 pp. Rubbed, sl shelfworn.
*(Epistemologist)* **$25**

**Strong, W.W.**
- See Jones, Harry Clarry & Strong, W.W.

**Stroud, T.B.**
- The elements of botany, physiological and systematical ... Greenwich ... & Reading: 1821. 1st edn. 8vo. 257,[93] pp. Contemp half-calf, richly gilt spine, rubbed & short split in the upper jnt.        *(Burmester)* **£60**

**Stroute, C.R.N., et al.**
- Chemical analysis, the working tools. Oxford: 1962. 3 vols. xvi,467; x,479; xii,273 pp. Plates & figs in the text.        *(Whitehart)* **£18**

**Strutt, John William**
- See Rayleigh, Lord

**Strutt, Robert John**
- The Becquerel rays and the properties of radium. London: Edward Arnold, 1904. 1st edn. 8vo. viii,214 pp. Advts at end. 3 plates, diags in text. Cloth.        *(Frew Mackenzie)* **£60**
- The Becquerel Rays and the properties of radium. London: 1904. 1st edn. 214 pp. Ills. Orig cloth.        *(Oasis)* **$150**
- The Becquerel Rays and the properties of radium. London: Edward Arnold, 1904. 1st edn. 8vo. viii,214,[4 advts] pp. W'engvd text ills. Largely unopened. Orig cloth, sl rubbed at hd & ft of spine.        *(Pickering)* **$150**
- The Becquerel rays and the properties of radium. London: Arnold, 1906. 2nd edn. vi,215,4 [ctlg] pp. 28 figs.        *(Pollak)* **£35**
- The Becquerel rays and the properties of radium. London: 1906. 2nd edn. 215 pp.        *(Scientia)* **$50**

**Struve, Christian Augustus**
- Asthenology: or, the art of preserving feeble life ... Translated from the German ... London: J. Murray & S. Highley ...,1801. 1st edn in English. 8vo. xxiii,[1],431,[1 advts] pp. Some foxing. Orig bds with paper label.        *(Dailey)* **$135**
- A practical essay on the art of recovering suspended animation ... Albany: for Whiting, Backus & Whiting, 1803. 1st Amer edn. 16mo. xxiv,210 pp, 6 pp pub list. Light browning & a few stains. Contemp calf, rebacked, one crnr reprd, some wear.        *(Zeitlin)* **$250**

**Stukeley, William**
- Memoirs of Sir Isaac Newton's life by William Stukeley ... 1752. London: Taylor & Francis, 1936. 1st edn. Sq 8vo. Port frontis, 4 ills. Pub green cloth.        *(McDowell)* **£40**
- Of the spleen, its description and history, uses and diseases ... to which is added some anatomical observations of the dissection of an elephant. London: for the Author, 1723. 1st edn. Folio. [6]ff,108 pp. Engvd frontis, 16

plates. Foxed. Mod full calf. *(Zeitlin)* **$2,000**

**Sturgeon, William**
- A course of twelve elementary lectures on galvanism ... London: Sherwood, Gilbert & Piper, 1843. xi,231,[iii advts] pp. Frontis, 103 text ills. Orig cloth, paper label. *(Pollak)* **£50**
- Scientific researches, experimental and theoretical, in electricity ... and electro-chemistry. Bury: Thomas Crompton, 1850. 1st edn. Lge 4to. 19 engvd plates. Orig blind-stamped cloth, spine reprd. *(McDowell)* **£220**

**Sturm, Meyer**
- See Achsner, Albert & Sturm, Meyer

**Sturrock, P.A.**
- Static and dynamic electron optics. An account of focusing in lens, deflector and accelerator. Cambridge: 1955.
        *(Winterdown)* **£10**

**Sullivan, John T.**
- Report of historical and technical information relating to the problem of interoceanic communication by way of the American isthmus. Wash, DC: 1883. Lge 4to. 219 pp. 29 maps, some fldg & in color. Spine ends frayed.        *(Elgen)* **$65**

**Sullivan, Robert**
- A dissertation on the sclerocele of the prostate gland ... why this affection occurs more particularly in old sedentary men ... New York: 1816. 51 pp. Heavily soiled, wraps detchd. Author's pres copy.        *(Goodrich)* **$75**

**Sully, James**
- Outlines of psychology with special reference to the theory of education. New York: D. Appleton, 1892. 1st U.S. printing of revsd edn. xviii,524 pp. Pub pebble-grained cloth, edges rubbed.        *(Gach)* **$25**
- Studies of childhood. New York: D. Appleton, 1896. 1st edn. viii,527 pp. Pebbled green cloth, shelfworn.        *(Gach)* **$50**

**Sumner, Thomas H.**
- A new and accurate method of finding a ship's position at sea ... Boston: T. Groom, 1845. 2nd edn. 8vo. 88 pp. 6 (5 fldg) litho plates. Orig cloth gilt. Front jnt partially cracked.
        *(Antiq Sc)* **$150**

**Suplee, Henry Harrison**
- The gas turbine. Progress in the design and construction of turbines operated by gases of combustion. 1910. Num ills. Upper hinge tender.        *(Edwards)* **£15**

**Surgeon ...**
- The surgeon's vade-mecum ... See Hooper, Robert

**Sutton, W.L.**
- A history of the disease usually called typhoid fever, as it had appeared in Georgetown and its vicinity, with some reflections as to its cause and nature. Louisville: 1850. iv,127 pp. Orig blind-stamped cloth, rebacked.
*(Whitehart)* £40

**Svedberg, T., et al.**
- The ultracentrifuge. Oxford: 1940. 154 figs.
*(Winterdown)* £60

**Swammerdam, Jan**
- The book of nature; or, the history of insects ... life of the author ... London: C.G. Seyffert, 1758. 1st edn in English. 2 parts in 1 vol. Folio. [2]ff,xx, [6],236; 153 pp, lxiii,liii (engvd plates), [6]ff (index). Subscriber's list. Contemp calf, rebacked. *(Rootenberg)* $1,250

**Swan, Joseph**
- Illustrations of the comparative anatomy of the nervous system. London: Longman, 1835. 4to. xxxii,311 pp. 35 litho plates. Inked stamp on verso of title & some plates. Recent cloth. *(Goodrich)* $750

**Swanzy, Henry R.**
- A handbook of the diseases of the eye and their treatment. Phila: 1897. 629 pp. Card of yarns for testing color vision. *(Fye)* $20
- A handbook of the diseases of the eye and their treatment. Phila: Blakiston, 1900. 7th edn. 8vo. xvii,607,24 [pub ctlg] pp. 165 ills.
*(Poitras)* $40

**Swediaur, Franz**
- A complete treatise on the symptoms, effects, nature and treatment of syphilis. Translated from the 4th French edition. Phila: Thomas Dobson, 1815. viii,539 pp. Some darkening of paper. Lea, scuffed, loose bds.
*(Poitras)* $150

**Sweet, William**
- See White, James & Sweet, William

**Sweetser, William**
- Mental hygiene: or, an examination of the intellect and passions, designed to illustrate their influence on health and the duration of life. Edinburgh: 1844. 1st British edn. [ii],69 pp. Foxed. Cloth-backed bds. *(Gach)* $75

**Swift, John**
- Adventure in vision. The first twenty-five years of television. London: Lehmann, 1950. vii,[xi, 18-223 pp. Frontis, 32 plates. Dw.
*(Pollak)* £15

**Swindin, Norman**
- The modern theory and practice of pumping. A treatise ... 1924. 364,[12] pp. 281 ills.
*(Whitehart)* £15

**Swinson, E.T.**
- The sanitation of buildings. 1928. viii,465 pp. 307 ills. Title & half-title sl foxed.
*(Whitehart)* £10

**Switzer, Stephen**
- An introduction to a general system of hydrostaticks and hydraulicks, philosophical and practical. London: for T. Astley [&c.], 1729. 1st edn. 2 vols. 4to. Engvd frontis, 61 plates, all but one fldg. 20th c plain dark brown half-calf, bds. *(McDowell)* £1,000
- An introduction to a general system of hydrostaticks and hydraulicks, philosophical and practical ... London: T. Astley, S. Austen & L. Gilliver, 1729. 1st edn. 2 vols in 1. 4to. Engvd frontis, 61 engvd plates, all but 7 fldg. Contemp calf, rebacked. *(Quaritch)* $1,250

**Sydenham, Thomas**
- The works ... See Rush, Benjamin

**Sykes, J.F.J.**
- Public health problems. London: 1892. 370 pp. Ills. *(Goodrich)* $50

**Syllabus ...**
- A syllabus of a course of lectures on chemistry ... See Davy, Sir Humphry

**Syme, James**
- Observations in clinical surgery. Edinburgh: 1862. 2nd edn. 217 pp. Orig cloth-backed printed bds. *(Fye)* $100

**Symonds, John Addington**
- A problem in modern ethics ... phenomenon of sexual inversion ... 1896. Ltd (100). 135 pp. Browning on endpapers. *(Jenner)* £60

**Symonds, Robert Wemyss**
- Thomas Tompion, his life & work. London: B.T. Batsford, [1951]. 1st edn. 4to. xvi,320 pp. Cold frontis, 3 cold plates, 272 figs on plates, 2 fldg plates. Orig cloth. Dw.
*(Zeitlin)* $100

**System ...**
- A system of ... the blowpipe ... See Sanders, J. Milton

**T.E.**
- Some considerations ... By T.E. a lay-man ... See Boyle, Robert

**Tachenius, Otto**
- ... Hippocrates Chymicus discovering the ancient foundation of the late viperine salt ... London: 1677. 1st English edn. Sm 4to. [11]ff,122 pp, [5]ff; Clavis [7]ff,120 pp (ie 124),[7]ff. Lightly foxed. Lacks license leaf. 3

margins torn away. Mod calf.  *(Zeitlin)* **$750**

**Tagen, C.H. von**
- Biliary calculi; perinorrhaphy; hospital gangrene, and its kindred diseases; with their respective treatments. New York: 1881. 1st edn. 154 pp.                            *(Fye)* **$40**

**Tait, Lawson**
- Diseases of women. New York: 1879. 2nd Amer edn. 192 pp.              *(Fye)* **$25**
- Diseases of women. New York: Wood, 1879. 2nd edn. 192 pp. Cvr worn.   *(Xerxes)* **$45**

**Tait, P.G.**
- Heat. London: Macmillan, 1884. 1st edn. xi,368,[iv ctlg] pp. Text figs. Spine ends wearing.                         *(Pollak)* **£30**
- Heat. London: Macmillan, 1892. 1st reprint, with crrctns. xii,372 pp. Text figs.
                                        *(Pollak)* **£15**
- Light. Edinburgh: Adams & Charles Black, 1889. 2nd edn, revsd & enlgd. xii,294,[ii] pp. 54 text figs. Shaky.          *(Pollak)* **£10**
- Newton's laws of motion. 1899. Sm 8vo. viii,53 pp. Diags.            *(Weiner)* **£30**
- Newton's laws of motion. London: Adam & Charles Black, 1899. vii,53,[iii] pp.
                                        *(Pollak)* **£30**
- Properties of matter. Edinburgh: Adam & Charles Black, 1885. 1st edn. viii,320,[iv] pp. 40 text figs. Recased.       *(Pollak)* **£35**
- Properties of matter. Edinburgh: Adam & Charles Black, 1899. 4th edn. xiv,340 pp. 41 text figs.                     *(Pollak)* **£15**

**Tait, Peter G.**
- Sketch of thermodynamics. Edinburgh: 1868. 1st edn. 128 pp. Rebacked, orig spine laid down.                           *(Scientia)* **$95**

**Talcott, Selden H[aines]**
- The insane diathesis. Middletown: Slauson & Boyd, 1881. Sole edn. 8vo. 21,[1] pp. Printed wraps, spine a little browned.  *(Dailey)* **$75**

**Tanner, T.H.**
- A practical treatise on the diseases of infancy and childhood. London: Henry Renshaw, 1858. 1st edn. 8vo. xiv,[2],408 pp. Orig cloth, worn.                     *(Rootenberg)* **$150**
- A practical treatise on the diseases of infancy and childhood. London: Renshaw, 1858. xiv,408 pp. Cloth.            *(Goodrich)* **$100**

**Tanzi, Eugenio**
- A text-book of mental diseases. Translated ... New York: Rebman Company, [1909]. 1st U.S. edn. xvi,803 pp. Pub grey cloth, lea label, front hinge hinge cracked. Shelfwear.
                                        *(Gach)* **$45**

**Tarnowsky, George de**
- Emergency surgery. The military surgery of the World War adapted to civil life. Phila & New York: Lea & Febiger, 1926. 4to. xvi,718 pp. 324 engvs.                 *(Poitras)* **$30**

**Tate, George**
- A treatise on hysteria. Phila: Carey & Hart, 1831. 1st Amer edn. [ii],240,[2] pp. Foxed. Cloth-backed bds.           *(Gach)* **$125**

**Taussig, Frederick**
- The prevention and treatment of abortion. St. Louis: 1910. 1st edn. 180 pp.   *(Fye)* **$45**

**Taussig, Helen**
- Congenital malformation of the heart. 1947. 1st edn, 2nd printing. 618 pp.  *(Fye)* **$150**

**Tavernier, A.**
- Elements of operative surgery with copious notes and additions by S.D. Gross. Phila: 1829. 448 pp. Full lea, hinges cracked, label missing.                        *(Fye)* **$200**

**Tawney, William**
- The complete measurer; or, the whole art of measuring. Etc., etc. London: for J. Knapton, 1763. 11th edn. 8vo in sixes. xi,[iii], 346,[ii advts] pp. Orig sheep, rebacked, crnrs a little worn.                           *(Pollak)* **£25**

**Tax, Sol (ed.)**
- Evolution after Darwin. Chicago: 1960. 3 vols. 629; 473; 310 pp. Dw.  *(Scientia)* **$45**

**Taylor, Alfred Swaine**
- Medical jurisprudence. Phila: 1853. 3rd Amer edn. 621 pp. Lea.        *(Fye)* **$30**
- On poisoning by strychnia, with comments on the medical evidence given at the trial of William Palmer for the murder of John Parsons Cook. 1856. viii,152 pp. Orig brown cloth.                        *(Jenner)* **£60**
- On poisons in relation to medical jurisprudence and medicine. Phila: 1859. 2nd Amer edn. 755 pp. Sl staining. Orig blind-stamped cloth, spine ends frayed. *(Elgen)* **$45**

**[Taylor, Charles]**
- Scripture illustrated, by means of natural science: in botany, geology, geography ... in two parts ... 1803. 4to. Ca 600 pp. Irregular pagination. Frontis, 30 engvd plates, 29 text engvs, 3 fldg & 2 full-page maps. Foxing. Tree calf, rebacked, crnrs wearing.
                                        *(Pollak)* **£55**

**Taylor, F.**
- A manual of the practice of medicine. 1891. 2nd edn. xiv,925 pp. 24 ills. Orig blind-stamped cloth, rebacked.   *(Whitehart)* **£25**

**Taylor, F. Sherwood**
- A history of industrial chemistry. Melbourne: 1957. xvi,467 pp. Frontis, 22 plates, 62 figs.
*(Whitehart)* £18

**Taylor, Frederick Winslow**
- The principles of scientific management. New York: Harper, 1934. 144 pp. Neat marginalia. Spine faded. *(Pollak)* £15

**Taylor, George**
- An exposition of the Swedish movement-cure, embracing the history of philosophy of this system of medical treatment ... New York: 1860. 1st edn. 396 pp. *(Fye)* $125

**Taylor, H.D.**
- A system of applied optics ... London: 1906. Num figs. Cloth worn. *(Winterdown)* £20

**Taylor, Hugh S. (ed.)**
- A treatise on physical chemistry. Macmillan, 1924. 2 vols. Text figs. Both vols a bit shaky & showing signs of wear. *(Pollak)* £15

**Taylor, J.**
- The complete weather guide; a collection of practical observations for prognosticating the weather; drawn from plants, animals ... philosophical instruments ... 1814. 2nd edn. viii,160 pp. Fldg frontis. Orig sheep, rubbed, spine sl cracked. *(Whitehart)* £45
- Luni-solar and honary tables with their applications in nautical astronomy. 1833. xi,233 pp. Polished calf, spine label missing. *(Whitehart)* £40

**Taylor, J.A.**
- History of dentistry. A practical treatise for the use of dental students and practitioners. Phila: Lea & Febiger, 1922. 238 pp. 42 engvs. *(Poitras)* $32.50

**Taylor, Mrs. Jane**
- Physiology for children. New York: Saxton & Miles, 1845. 24mo. 91 pp. Some staining. Wraps, with lea backstrip half-missing, quite worn. *(Xerxes)* $45

**Taylor, John Ellor**
- The sagacity and morality of plants. A sketch of the life and conduct of the vegetable kingdom. London: Chatto & Windus, 1884. 1st edn. 8vo. xi,311 pp, 32 pp pub ctlg. Cold frontis, 100 ills. Orig cloth, uncut. *(Rootenberg)* $125

**Taylor, Michael & Meskelyne, Nevil**
- Tables of logarithms of all numbers, from 1 to 101000; and of the sines and tangents ... London: Printed by Christopher Buxton ..., 1792. 1st edn. Lge 4to. [16],64,[68 tables]; [378 tables]. Occas light foxing, Contemp

reversed calf, ft of spine chipped.
*(Pickering)* $300

**Taylor, R. Tunstall**
- Orthopaedic surgery. Balt: 1907. 1st edn. 241 pp. Inscribed to R.W. Osgood & autographed by the author. *(Fye)* $40
- Surgery of the spine and extremities. Phila: 1923. 1st edn. 550 pp. *(Fye)* $50

**Taylor, T.K.**
- The pocket physician, or domestic medical adviser ... Boston: 1852. 110 x 70 mm (bound in 8vo). 128 pp. 128 pp. Correction slip on flyleaf. Orig blind-stamped & gilt-lettered cloth. *(Hemlock)* $65

**Taylor, W.T.**
- Distribution of electricity by overhead lines. 1928. vii,265 pp. Frontis, 57 ills, fldg chart.
*(Whitehart)* £12

**Taylor, William**
- On a new and successful treatment for febrile and other diseases, through the medium of the cutaneous surface. 1850. 1st edn. xi,170 pp. Orig blind-stamped cloth, rebacked.
*(Whitehart)* £25

**Teale, Thomas Pridgin**
- Dangers to health: a pictorial guide to domestic sanitary defects. 1881. 3rd edn. 70 two-colour plates. Dec cvrs, sl worn.
*(Jenner)* £18
- A treatise on neuralgic diseases, dependent upon irritation of the spinal marrow and ganglia of the sympathetic nerve. Phila: 1830. 1st Amer edn. iv,120 pp. Spotty foxing. Orig cloth-backed bds, worn. *(Elgen)* $125

**Teleky, Ludwig**
- History of factory and mine hygiene. New York 1948. 1st edn. *(Scientia)* $47.50
- History of factory and mine hygiene. New York: 1948. xvi,342 pp. *(Elgen)* $45

**'Telescope, Tom'**
- See 'Tom Telescope' (pseud.)

**Television ...**
- Television today; practice and principles clearly explained. N.d. [ca 1935]. 2 vols. Lge 8vo. 776 pp. Ills, diags. Orig pict cloth.
*(Weiner)* £60
- Television, the world's first television journal, edited by A. Dinsdale. Vols 1-4. March 1928 - February 1932. 4to. 4 vols. 5-600 pp per volume. Advt & contents leaves bound in, indexes at front of each vol. Gold-blocked pub cases. *(Weiner)* £600

**Tenney, Mary**
- See Healy, William & Tenney, Mary

**Terman, Lewis Madison (ed.)**
- Genetic studies of genius. Volume 1: Mental and physical traits of a thousand gifted children. Stanford: Stanford University Press, 1926. 2nd edn. Thick 8vo. Red cloth, spine rubbed.          *(Gach)* **$50**
- Genetic studies of genius. Volume 2: The early mental traits of three hundred geniuses. Stanford: Stanford University Press, 1926. 1st edn. Thick 8vo. Red cloth, spine rubbed.          *(Gach)* **$50**

**Teste, Alphonse**
- A practical manual of animal magnetism; containing an exposition of the methods employed ... Translated from the second edition ... London: Bailliere, 1843. xii,406,[x advts] pp. Orig cloth, recased.     *(Pollak)* **£35**

**Tewksbury, George E.**
- A complete manual of the Edison phonograph. Newark, N.J.: U.S. Phonograph Co., 1897. 1st edn. Sq 8vo. 92 pp. Extensively illust. Complete numbered index of 90 parts. Orig cloth, some wear.
          *(M&S)* **$125**

**Thacher, James**
- Observations on hydrophobia ... with an examination of the various theories and methods of cure ...Plymouth (Mass.): Joseph Avery, 1812. 1st edn. 8vo. 301,[1] pp. Hand-cold plate. Foxed. Contemp calf, worn & dry, upper cvr becoming detchd.     *(M&S)* **$175**
- Observations on hydrophobia, produced by the bite of a mad dog, or other rabid animal ... Plymouth (Mass.): Joseph Avery, 1812. 8vo. xi,[1], [13]-301,[1] pp. Cold plate of Skullcap Plant. Plate & title leaf on stubs. Browned & foxed. Mod bds.     *(Zeitlin)* **$450**
- Observations on hydrophobia, produced by the bite of a mad dog, or other rabid animal ... Plymouth: Avery, 1812. 8vo. xi,-302 pp. Hand-cold plate. Foxed. New qtr calf.
          *(Goodrich)* **$375**

**Thatcher, A.G.S.**
- Scaffolding. A treatise on the design and erection of scaffolds, gantries and stagings ... 1907. 2nd edn. xv,185 pp. 6 plates, 146 diags. Ink sgntr on title.     *(Whitehart)* **£15**

**Thatcher, Virginia S.**
- History of anesthesia, with emphasis on the nurse specialist. Phila: [1953]. 1st edn. xvii,298 pp. 7 plates, ills.     *(Elgen)* **$35**

**Thayer, Gerald H.**
- Concealing-coloration in the animal kingdom; an exposition of the laws of disguise through color and pattern: being a summary of Abbott H. Thayer's discoveries ... New York: 1909. 1st edn. 260 pp.     *(Scientia)* **$125**

- Concealing-coloration in the animal kingdom; an exposition of the laws of disguise through color and pattern ... New York: 1918. 2nd edn. 260 pp.     *(Scientia)* **$100**

**Thayer, W.S.**
- Lectures on the malarial fever. 1898. vii,326 pp. Orig cloth, sl marked. Spine faded. Lib stamp on title.     *(Whitehart)* **£35**

**Theobald, G.W.**
- Normal midwifery for midwives and nurses. Edinburgh: Humphrey Milford Press, 1927. 258 pp. Ills.     *(Poitras)* **$20**

**Theobald, Samuel**
- Prevalent diseases of the eye. Phila: 1907. 1st edn. 551 pp.     *(Fye)* **$30**

**Thirteen ...**
- Thirteen years a lunatic. Poems and essays written by a paranoiac lunatic while confined in the Nevada Hospital for Mental Diseases. Edited ... Reno: Wilson, 1907. Sole edn. [6],171,[1] pp. Ills. Cloth.     *(Dailey)* **$45**

**Thoma, Kurt H.**
- Clinical pathology of the jaws, with a histologic and Roentgen study of practical cases. 1934. xii,643 pp. 423 figs & plates in the text. Orig cloth.     *(Whitehart)* **£18**
- Traumatic surgery of the jaws. St. Louis: 1942. 1st edn. 315 pp.     *(Fye)* **$60**

**Thomas, E.E.**
- Lotze's theory of reality. London: 1921. 217 pp. Crnrs bumped, sl shelfworn.
          *(Epistemologist)* **$35**

**Thomas, K. Bryn**
- Curare. Its history and usage. Phila: 1963. 1st edn. Dw.     *(Scientia)* **$45**

**Thomas, K.B.**
- The development of anesthetic apparatus. Oxford: 1975. Ills.     *(Winterdown)* **£35**

**Thomas, T. Gaillard**
- A practical treatise on the diseases of women. Phila: 1872. 3rd edn. Tall 8vo. 784 pp. Cloth faded. Ex lib.     *(Argosy)* **$100**
- A practical treatise on the diseases of women. Phila: 1876. 4th edn. 801 pp.     *(Fye)* **$50**

**Thompson, C.J.S.**
- The history and evolution of surgical instruments. New York: 1942. 115 pp. 115 ills in text. Dw.     *(Whitehart)* **£120**
- The lure and romance of alchemy. 1932. 1st edn. Num ills. Light foxing at beginning.
          *(Robertshaw)* **£12**
- Magic and healing. 1946. 1st edn. 9 plates. Sl rubbed.     *(Robertshaw)* **£10**

- The mystery and art of the apothecary. 1929. 1st edn. 9 plates.          *(Robertshaw)* **£10**
- The mystery and art of the apothecary. London: John Lane, 1929. 1st edn. 287 pp. Ills.          *(Poitras)* **$30**
- The mystery and art of the apothecary. 1929. viii,287 pp. 10 plates, 18 ills in text.
*(Whitehart)* **£15**
- The mystery and lore of perfume. 1926. 1st edn. 26 ills. Prelims spotted. Orig cloth, a little rubbed.          *(Robertshaw)* **£10**
- The mystery and romance of alchemy and pharmacy. 1897. 1st edn. xv,335 pp. Orig cloth, sl marked.          *(Whitehart)* **£18**
- The mystery and romance of alchemy and pharmacy. 1897, 1st edn. Ills in text.
*(Robertshaw)* **£12.50**
- The mystic mandrake. London: Rider & Co., 1934. 4to. 253 pp. 30 ills.          *(Poitras)* **$50**
- The mystic mandrake. 1934. 1st edn. Ills. Dw.          *(Robertshaw)* **£12**
- The quacks of old London. 1928. 1st edn. Ills. Orig cloth-backed bds. *(Robertshaw)* **£16**
- The quacks of Old London. London: 1928. 1st edn. 356 pp. Many plates. Orig cloth.
*(Oasis)* **$60**
- The quacks of old London. [1928]. 1st edn. xvi,[1],356 pp. Frontis, 18 plates. Orig printed bds, linen spine. Back sl marked & a little foxing.          *(Whitehart)* **£35**
- The quacks of Old London. Phila: 1929. 1st Amer edn. 356 pp. Many plates. *(Oasis)* **$40**
- See Power, d'Arcy & Thompson, C.J.S.

**Thompson, d'Arcy W.**
- On growth and form. New York: 1942. 2nd edn. 1116 pp. Spine faded.          *(Scientia)* **$85**

**Thompson, J. Ashburton**
- Free phosphorus in medicine: with special reference to its use in neuralgia. 1874. 1st edn. Spine dull. Pres copy. *(Robertshaw)* **£20**

**Thompson, J. Harry**
- Report of Columbia Hospital for Women and Lying-in Asylum, Washington, D.C. Washington: 1873. 1st edn. 4to. 431 pp. 18 engvd plates. Half lea.          *(Fye)* **$150**

**Thompson, L.**
- See Deaderick, W.H. & Thompson, L.

**Thompson, S.**
- A short history of American railways. Chicago: 1925. 473 pp. 400 ills. Spine dull & sl worn.          *(Oasis)* **$25**

**Thompson, Silvanus P.**
- Dynamo-electric machinery. A manual for students of electrotechnics. London: 1886. 2nd edn, enlgd & revsd. 527 pp. Spine frayed.          *(Scientia)* **$50**
- The life of William Thomson, Baron Kelvin

of Largs. London: 1910. 1st edn. 2 vols. 1297 pp.          *(Scientia)* **$75**
- Light: visible and invisible. A series of lectures delivered at the Royal Institution of Great Britain, at Christmas, 1896. 1897. 1st edn. xii,294 pp. 158 figs. Orig cloth.
*(Whitehart)* **£25**
- Light: visible and invisible. A series of lectures delivered at the Royal Institution of Great Britain, at Christmas, 1896. 1897. xii,294 pp. Plates, one loose, & ills. Some pencil marks. Roughtrimmed. Cvrs sl rubbed & worn. Ex lib, with stamps.          *(Jenner)* **£38**

**Thompson, Theophilus**
- Annals of influenza or epidemic catarrhal fever in Great Britain from 1510 to 1837. Sydenham Society, 1852. Orig blind-stamped cloth, sl dust stained, t.e.g.   *(Whitehart)* **£40**

**Thompson, W. Gilman**
- Practical dietetics with special reference to diet in disease. New York: D. Appleton, 1896. 802 pp.          *(Poitras)* **$30**
- Practical dietetics with special reference to diet in disease. New York: D. Appleton, 1901. [iv],xxii, 802,[vi] pp. 9 plates, a few text figs.          *(Pollak)* **£15**

**Thoms, W.J.**
- Human longevity; its facts and its fictions. Including an inquiry into some of the more remarkable instances, and suggestions for testing reputed cases. 1873. xii,320 pp. Orig blind-stamped cloth. Ex lib. *(Whitehart)* **£25**

**Thomson, Anthony Todd**
- Atlas of delineations of cutaneous eruptions; illustrative of the descriptions in the practical synopsis of cutaneous diseases ... Thomas Bateman. London: Longman ... & Green, 1829. Lge 8vo. vii,[1],112 pp. 27 cold plates. Contemp cloth, faded & rubbed.
*(Rootenberg)* **$285**
- The London dispensatory. 1818. 2nd edn. 7 plates. Contemp calf, cvrs loose. Bodleian Library duplicate.          *(Robertshaw)* **£20**

**Thomson, Frederick**
- An essay on the scurvy: shewing effectual and practible means for its prevention at sea. With some observations on fevers ... London: for the Author, 1790. 1st edn. 8vo. xxiv,206 pp. Contemp sheep. Jnts cracked but holding.
*(Antiq Sc)* **$375**

**Thomson, Godfrey H.**
- See Brown, William & Thomson, Godfrey H.

**Thomson, J. Arthur**
- Heredity. 1912. 2nd edn. Thick 8vo. xvi,627 pp. Ills. Spine & cvrs sl faded. *(Jenner)* **£10**

- Progress of science in the century. Edinburgh: Chambers, 1906. 2nd edn. x,536 pp.                          *(Pollak)* **£15**

**Thomson, John**
- Lectures on inflammation, exhibiting a view of the general doctrines, pathological and practical, of medical surgery. Phila: 1817. 1st Amer edn. 509 pp. Sl browning & foxing. Orig calf, worn, jnts cracked.   *(Elgen)* **$195**

**Thomson, Joseph John**
- Applications of dynamics to physics and chemistry. London: Macmillan, 1888. 1st edn. viii,312,[ii] pp.       *(Pollak)* **£100**
- The conduction of electricity through gases. Cambridge: 1906. 2nd edn. 678 pp. Top of spine worn.          *(Scientia)* **$75**
- Conduction of electricity through gases. Cambridge: University Press, 1903. 1st edn. 8vo. vi,[2],566 pp. Text figs. Orig cloth.                            *(Antiq Sc)* **$200**
- Conduction of electricity through gases. Cambridge: University Press, 1903. 1st edn. viii,566 pp. Diags in text. Orig green cloth, sl worn.                   *(Pickering)* **$525**
- Conduction of electricity through gases. Cambridge: University Press, 1906. 2nd edn. vi,[ii], 678,[vi] pp. 205 text figs. Sm tear in one leaf without loss, some marginal pencil lines.                            *(Pollak)* **£75**
- The corpuscular theory of matter. New York: 1907. 1st Amer edn. 172 pp. *(Scientia)* **$60**
- The corpuscular theory of matter. London: Constable, 1907. 1st edn, 2nd imp. vi,172 pp. 29 figs. Stitching weak.   *(Pollak)* **£20**
- Electricity and matter. New York: 1908. Later printing. 162 pp. Silliman Lectures.                         *(Scientia)* **$50**
- Electricity and matter. Westminster: Constable, 1904. 1st edn. [viii],162 pp. 18 text figs. Cvrs faded & rubbed. *(Pollak)* **£50**
- The electron in chemistry. Phila: 1923. 1st edn. 144 pp.                *(Scientia)* **$35**
- Elements of the mathematical theory of electricity and magnetism. Cambridge: University Press, 1904. 3rd edn. vi,[ii],544 pp. 134 text figs.        *(Pollak)* **£20**
- Elements of the mathematical theory of electricity and magnetism. Cambridge: University Press, 1921. 5th edn. [viii],410 pp. 135 figs. Recased. Good working copy.                         *(Pollak)* **£10**
- Notes on recent researches in electricity and magnetism ... Oxford: at the Clarendon Press, 1893. 1st edn. 8vo. xvi,528,[2],8 [advts] pp. Orig green cloth, upper jnt splitting. Sgntr of W.H. Bragg, b'plate of W.L. Bragg, Nobel Prize winners.         *(Pickering)* **$400**
- Rays of positive electricity and their application to chemical analysis. London: Longmans, Green, 1931. 1st edn. vii,[i],132 pp. 50 ills. Cvrs rubbed.    *(Pollak)* **£80**

- Rays of positive electricity and their application to chemical analysis. London: 1921. 2nd edn. 237 pp.        *(Scientia)* **$45**
- A treatise on the motion of vortex rings. An essay ... London: Macmillan & Co., 1883. 1st edn. 8vo. xix,[1],124 pp. Orig cloth.                          *(Pickering)* **$350**

**Thomson, Samuel**
- A narrative of the life and medical discoveries of Samuel Thomson. Containing ... the manner of curing disease with vegetable medicine ... Boston: for the Author, 1822. 1st edn. 12mo. 180 pp. Port frontis. Some water stains & spots. Full lea, rubbed. *(Xerxes)* **$80**
- A narrative of the life and medical discoveries of Samuel Thomson. Containing an account of his system of practice ... Written by himself. Columbus: Jarvis Pike & Co., 1833. 9th edn. 16 mo. 256 pp. Upper part of title damaged. Mottled calf, scuffed, worn.      *(Poitras)* **$75**
- A new guide to health; or botanic family physician containing a complete system of practice ... To which is prefixed a narrative of the life and medical discoveries of the author. Boston: for the author, 1835. Port frontis.                              *(Poitras)* **$125**
- New guide to health; or, botanic family physician ... to which is prefixed a narrative of the life ... of the author. Boston: ... E.G. House, 1822. 1st edn. 12mo. 4,[13]-300pp, [1]f index. Frontis port. Contemp calf, very worn. Lightly browned.        *(Zeitlin)* **$350**

**Thomson, Thomas**
- History of the Royal Society, from its institution to the end of the eighteenth century. London: Baldwin, 1812. 1st edn. 4to. Pub grey bds, green linen spine, paper label, edges completely untrimmed.                         *(McDowell)* **£140**
- A system of chemistry of inorganic bodies. London & Edinburgh: 1831.'7th edn" (but first with this title). 2 vols. viii,742; ix,944 pp. Orig cloth, faded, shaken. *(Weiner)* **£50**

**Thomson, Sir William**
- Reprint of papers on electrostatics and magnetism. London: Macmillan, 1872. 1st edn. 8vo. xv,592 pp. 3 plates (2 fldg), text diags. Mod cloth.      *(Rootenberg)* **$150**

**Thomson, William**
- An outline of the necessary laws of thought; a treatise on pure and applied logic. London: William Pickering, 1849. 2nd edn, much enlgd. xiv,[ii],392, [iv advts] pp. Fldg plate. Some foxing. Orig cloth, faded & worn at spine.                          *(Pollak)* **£45**

**Thorburn, J.S.**
- Elements of bedside medicine and general

pathology, or, general disease discourse with a sketch ... and a confession ... London: 1836. xxiii,5,437 pp. Mod half cloth. "Vol I" only; but all published? *(Whitehart)* £50

**Thorburn, William**
- A contribution to the surgery of the spinal cord. London: 1889. 1st edn. 230 pp.
*(Fye)* $150

**Thorek, Max**
- The face in health and disease. Phila: 1946. 1st edn. 781 pp. 636 ills, mainly photographic. *(Fye)* $175
- Modern surgical technic. Phila: 1939. 1st edn, 2nd printing. 3 vols. Inscrbd & autographed by the author. *(Fye)* $200

**Thorndike, Augustus**
- Athletic injuries: prevention, diagnosis and treatment. Phila: 1938. 1st edn. 208 pp.
*(Fye)* $50

**Thorndike, Edward Lee**
- Educational psychology. New York: 1920-21. 3 vols. 327; 452; 408 pp. Rubbed.
*(Epistemologist)* $75
- The elements of psychology. New York: A.G. Seiler, 1911. 2nd edn, 2nd printing. xx,351 pp. Cloth. *(Gach)* $25

**Thorndike, Lynn**
- Science and thought in the XVth century. New York: 1929. 1st edn. 387 pp.
*(Scientia)* $30

**Thorne, R.**
- On the progress of preventive medicine during the era. Being the inaugural address delivered before the Epidemiological Society London, Session 1887-88. 1888. 1st edn. 63 pp. Red & black title. *(Whitehart)* £25

**Thornton, R.J.**
- A new family herbal: or popular account of the nature and properties of the various plants used in medicine, diet and the arts. 1810. Roy 8vo. xvi,901 pp. Num w'engvd ills by T. Bewick. Trifle foxed at beginning. Contemp diced calf, trifle worn.
*(Wheldon & Wesley)* £140

**[Thornton, Robert John]**
- Medical extracts: on the nature of health ... and the laws of the nervous and fibrous systems ... London: J.Johnson, et al., 1796-97. 1st edn (although "New Edition" on title). 4 vols. 8vo. 934 pp. 7 plates. Contemp half-calf, rebacked. Lib stamps. *(Dailey)* $750

**Thorpe, Sir Edward**
- History of chemistry. Watts, 1909. 2 vols. viii,148; vii,152 pp. 26 plates. Cvrs sl

marked, spines faded. *(Pollak)* £25

**Thorwald, Jurgen**
- The triumph of surgery. New York: 1960. 1st English translation. 454 pp. *(Fye)* $25

**Thudichum, J.L.W.**
- A treatise on the pathology of the urine ... a complete guide to its analysis. London: 1877. 2nd edn. 577 pp. Cloth sunned, inner hinges cracked. *(Goodrich)* $100

**Thurston, Albert P.**
- Elementary aeronautics or the science and practice of aerial machines. Whittaker, 1911. vii,126,[ii] pp. 125 ills. Binder's cloth, a little faded. *(Pollak)* £25

**Tibbits, Herbert**
- How to use the galvanic battery in medicine and surgery ... London: 1879. 2nd edn, revsd. 76 pp. New bds. *(Goodrich)* $65

**Tidswell, Herbert H.**
- The tobacco habit. Its history and pathology. London: Churchill, 1912. xii,246,[ii] pp. Author's pres copy. *(Pollak)* £12

**Tilden, William A.**
- Chemical discovery and invention in the twentieth century. London: Routledge, 1919. 3rd edn, revsd. xvi,487 pp. 11 ports, 150 ills. Shabby binding, a working copy. *(Pollak)* £10
- Introduction to the study of chemical philosophy. London: Longmans, Green, 1876. xvi,279,7 pp. *(Pollak)* £15

**Tilke, S.W.**
- Practical reflections on the nature and treatment of disease; founded upon fourteen years experience in the cure of gout, scrofula, fever ... 1842. 4th edn, rvsd & enlgd. xxcviii,179 pp. Frontis, w'stained. Orig blind-stamped cloth, faded & worn. *(Whitehart)* £38
- Random reflections on indigestion, bilious complaints, scrofula ... treatment of scarlet fever. 1837. 3rd edn. [clxxxvi], xxiv,179 pp. Port frontis. Orig embossed cloth, paper label, dust stained. *(Whitehart)* £49

**Tilney, Frederick**
- The brain from ape to man. New York: 1928. 1st edn. 2 vols. 1120 pp. Ills, some in color. Orig cloth. *(Oasis)* $250

**Tilney, Frederick & Riley, Henry Alsop**
- The forms and functions of the central nervous system ... New York: Paul B. Hoeber, 1938. 3rd edn. Tall thick 8vo. xxxvii,[3],851 pp. 600 text ills. W'stained. Orig black cloth, rubbed, shelf marks. Ex lib.
*(Zeitlin)* $150

**Tilt, Edward John**
- A handbook of uterine therapeutics and of diseases of women. New York: 1881. 4th edn. 326 pp.                              *(Fye)* **$20**
- On diseases of menstruation and ovarian inflammation, in connexion with sterility, pelvic tumours, and affections of the womb. New York: 1851. Sm 8vo. 286 pp. Sl browning, some marginal staining. Orig blind-stamped cloth.           *(Elgen)* **$40**

**Timoshenko. Stephen P.**
- History of the strength of materials. New York: McGraw-Hill, 1953. x,452 pp. 245 ills. Ex lib.                         *(Pollak)* **£30**

**Tinel, Jules**
- Nerve wounds; symptomatology of peripheral nerve lesions caused by war wounds. Translated by F. Rothwell. Revised & edited by C.A. Joll. New York: 1917. 1st Amer edn.                             *(Scientia)* **$175**
- Nerve wounds; symptomatology of peripheral nerve lesions caused by war wounds. Translation by F. Rothwell. Revised by Cecil A. Joll. New York: 1917. 1st Amer edn. 317 pp. Cloth rubbed.      *(Goodrich)* **$145**
- Nerve wounds; symptomatology of peripheral nerve lesions caused by war wounds. London: 1918. 1st English translation, 2nd printing. 317 pp.                *(Scientia)* **$150**

**Tissot [Simon Andre]**
- Three essays: first, on the disorders of people of fashion, second ... third ... Translated ... Dublin: for James Williams, 1772. 1st Dublin English translation. 8vo. Sep title pages & pagination. Contemp calf, front bd part detchd, rear hinge split.    *(Zeitlin)* **$300**

**Tissot, Simon Andre**
- Advice to people in general, with respect to their health. Translated ... to which are added ... inoculation ... lingering distempers. Dublin ... Potts, 1769. 5th edn, crrctd & impvd. 2 vols in one. Sm hole in title, damp-staining. Contemp calf, worn. *(Diamond)* **$75**
- An essay on the disorders of people of fashion. Translated from the French ... London: Richardson & Urquhart ..., [1771?]. 1st edn in English. 8vo. [4],xvi,163 pp. Qtr calf antique, red mor label. A tall copy mostly untrimmed.          *(Dailey)* **$200**

**Titchener, Edward Bradford**
- Experimental psychology: a manual of laboratory practice. New York: Macmillan, 1901. 1st edn. 214 pp. Brown cloth, shelfworn. Ex lib.            *(Gach)* **$25**
- Lectures on the experimental psychology of the thought-processes. New York: 1909. 318 pp. Sl shelfworn.     *(Epistemologist)* **$45**

**Todd, James**
- Experiments with oxygen on disease: tubercolosis, Bright's disease, et al. Pittsburgh: Privately printed, 1916. 1st edn. Sm 4to. viii,255 pp. 5 plates, num graphs. Spine ends worn, spine faded & rubbed.                              *(Elgen)* **$30**

**Todd, Robert B.**
- Clinical lectures on certain acute diseases. London: 1860. xl,487 pp. Cloth soiled.                          *(Goodrich)* **$150**

**Todd, Robert B. (ed.)**
- The cyclopaedia of anatomy and physiology. Sherwood, Gilbert & Piper, 1836-59. 5 vols in 6. New buckram with lea labels. *(Pollak)* **£175**

**Todhunter, I.**
- A history of the mathematical theory of probability from the time of Pascal to that of Laplace. London: Macmillan, 1865. 1st edn. xvi,624 pp. Lacks half-title. Half-mor gilt, inner jnts taped.           *(Pollak)* **£60**
- A history of the progress of the calculus of variations during the nineteenth century. London: Macmillan, 1861. 1st edn. xii,532 pp. Plate, foxed. Orig cloth, a little worn.                          *(Pollak)* **£60**
- A history of the theory of elasticity and of the strength of materials from Galelei to the present time. Cambridge: 1886-93. 3 vols. xiv,924,12; xiii,762; 546,12 pp. 3 frontis, 3 fldg plates. Prize lea, gilt spine, mrbld edges.                      *(Whitehart)* **£90**

**Todhunter, Isaac**
- An elementary treatise on Laplace's functions, Lame's functions, and Bessel's functions. London: Macmillan, 1875. 1st edn. Sm 8vo. viii,348 pp. Orig cloth.                        *(Antiq Sc)* **$90**

**Toilet ...**
- The toilet of flora ... See Buch'hoz, Pierre Joseph

**Tolman, Edward Chace**
- Collected papers in psychology. 1951. 269 pp. Dw.             *(Epistemologist)* **$35**
- Lectures on the elementary psychology of feeling and attention. New York: Macmillan, 1908.                           *(Gach)* **$60**

**Tolman, Richard C.**
- The theory of relativity of motion. Berkeley: 1917. 1st edn. 1917.      *(Scientia)* **$47.50**

**'Tom Telescope' (pseud.)**
- The Newtonian philosophy and natural philosophy in general explained and illustrated ... (on half-title 'fourth edition') 1838. Sm sq 8vo. xii,302 pp. Fldg frontis,

engvd title. Front jnt shaken.  *(Weiner)* **£40**
- The Newtonian system of philosophy. Adapted to the capacities of young ladies and gentlemen ... London: Ogilby & Speare, 1794. 12mo. [4], 136,[4] pp. Pub advts, 5 engvd plates, 16 wood-engvs. Signatures of previous owners. Contemp calf, worn.
*(Rootenberg)* **$150**
- The Newtonian system of philosophy: explained by familiar objects ... for the use of young persons. Chiswick: 1827. Sm 8vo. iv,158 pp. Fldg frontis, ills. Contemp qtr calf, rubbed. *(Weiner)* **£40**

**Tomes, John**
- A system of dental surgery. London: John Churchill, 1859. 1st edn. Sm thick 8vo. W'cut ills in text. Orig cloth, spine rather crinkled & bruised. *(McDowell)* **£120**

**Tomlinson, C.**
- The dew-drop and the mist: an account ... [1861]. xii,346 pp. 65 engvs. Orig cloth, inner hinge cracked. *(Whitehart)* **£15**
- The tempest: an account ... [1861]. xii,386 pp. 79 ills. Orig cloth. *(Whitehart)* **£15**
- The thunderstorm: an account ... [1859]. xii,348 pp. 65 engvs. Orig cloth, new endpapers. *(Whitehart)* **£15**

**Tomlinson, Charles (ed.)**
- Cyclopaedia of useful arts; mechanical and chemical, manufactures, mining and engineering. [1852-54]. 2 vols. clx,832; iv,1052 pp. 40 plates, 2477 figs in text. Light foxing of a few plates, title sl w'stained. Roan binding defective & worn. *(Whitehart)* **£45**
- Cyclopaedia of useful arts; mechanical and chemical, manufactures, mining and engineering. 1854. 2 vols. Thick cr 8vo. Engvd half-titles & frontis, 40 steel engvs, 2477 w'cuts. Prelims spotted. Half-calf. *(Edwards)* **£70**

**Toops, H.A. & Haven, S.E.**
- Psychology and the motorist. 1938. 265 pp. Ink line on spine. *(Epistemologist)* **$35**

**Topley, W.W.C. & Wilson, G.S.**
- The principles of bacteriology and immunity. 1929. 1st edn. 2 vols. xvi,1300 pp. 242 pp. Orig cloth. *(Whitehart)* **£38**

**Tosberg, William A.**
- Upper and lower extremity protheses. Springfield: Charles C. Thomas, 1962. 98 pp. Ills. Ex lib. *(Poitras)* **$30**

**Tournefort, J.P. de**
- Materia medica; or a description of simple medicines generally us'd in physick ... uses and virtues ... nature and use of mineral waters. Translated by Andrew Bell. 1716.

2nd edn. xx,406 pp. Some stains, sl tear on title. Contemp calf, rubbed. *(Jenner)* **£75**

**Tow, P. MacDonald**
- Personality changes following frontal leucotomy. Oxford University Press, 1955. xii,262 pp. Tables. Orig maroon cloth.
*(Jenner)* **£12**

**Townsend, John S.**
- The theory of ionization of gases by collision. London: Constable, 1910. 1st edn. xi,88 pp. 9 text figs. *(Pollak)* **£25**

**Townsend, Rev. Joseph**
- Elements of therapeutics: or, a guide to health. London: for J. Mawman, 1801. 3rd edn. xxiv,708,[viii index] pp. New qtr calf, mrbld bds. *(Pollak)* **£40**

**Toynbee, Joseph**
- The diseases of the ear; their nature, diagnosis and treatment ... with a supplement ... London: H.K. Lewis, 1868. 2nd edn. 8vo. Text ills. Old brown buckram.
*(McDowell)* **£95**

**[Trade catalogue]**
- Allen & Hanbury's: Supplement to catalogue of surgical instruments and appliances, ward requisites, &c., &c. 1905. Roy 8vo. xii,119 pp. *(Jenner)* **£75**
- Brooklyn Hospital Equipment Co: Aseptic metal hospital and surgical equipment and supplies. New York: 1930. 304 pp. Inner hinges cracked. *(Fye)* **$40**
- Buckman & Hickman Ltd.: General catalogue of tools and supplies for all mechanical trades. London: 1935. Thick 8vo. lxxxv,1158 pp. Num ills. Orig buckram, a trifle soiled.
*(Deighton Bell)* **£25**
- Cyanide Plant Supply Co.: ... See Skelton, C.A.
- Down Bros: Catalogue of surgical instruments and appliances with appendix. London: 1936 (Temporary edn). viii,[xiv], 2089, lxxxiii pp. Faded with faint damp-staining of rear cvr. *(Pollak)* **£50**
- Down Bros: Surgical instruments catalogue. N.d. [1930's]. 8vo. 1668 pp. Latter pages rather grubby, index very chipped & torn. Rebound in blue cloth. *(Jenner)* **£38**
- Eckels & Company: Derma surgery with complete catalogue of embalmer's supplies. Phila: n.d [ca early 1900s]. 317 pp.
*(Poitras)* **$50**
- Gardner, J.: Catalogue of surgical instruments and aseptic furniture. Edinburgh: 1929. 6th edn. 753 pp. Recased. *(Fye)* **$50**
- General Electric: Equipment and accessories for physical therapy. Chicago: N.d. [ca 1930]. Roy 8vo. 110 pp. *(Xerxes)* **$40**

- Hearson, Charles & Co: The problem solved. London: [1896]. 21st edn. 148 pp. New cloth with rear dec cvr laid down. Price ctlg of incubation equipment, chiefly medical but inc some agricultural.           *(Pollak)* **£25**
- Marks, A.A.: Manual of artificial limbs ... an exhaustive exposition of prosthesis. New York: 1905. 430 pp. Backstrip & front bd stained.                         *(Xerxes)* **$55**
- Marks, A.A.: Manual of artificial limbs: copiously illustrated ... an exhaustive exposition of prosthesis. New York: 1908. 431 pp. Several hundred w'cut ills. *(Fye)* **$75**
- Marks, A.A.: Manual of artificial limbs. New York: 1913.                      *(Xerxes)* **$45**
- Maw, S., Son & Thompson: The nurse's handbook and catalogue of nursing requisites. January, 1898. 3rd edn. viii,186 pp. Orig cloth, recased.              *(Pollak)* **£50**
- Mayer & Phelps: An illustrated catalogue of surgical implements and appliances. N.d. [ca 1920s]. Lge 8vo. xvi,568 pp. Cvrs sl worn.
                                      *(Jenner)* **£80**
- Milsom, A.: Hospitals and institutions handbook and buyer's guide of specialised instruments. 1930-31.         *(Jenner)* **£10**
- Milsom, A.: Hospitals and institutions handbook and buyer's guide of specialised instruments. 1934-35. 229 pp. Orig orange cloth.                         *(Jenner)* **£10**
- Morris, Herbert, Ltd.: Book 50: Modern lifting. Cranes, pulley-blocks, runways ... Loughborough, 1912. Sm sq 8vo. [iv],472 pp. 2 leaves with minor scribbles. Orig cloth, faded & worn.                   *(Pollak)* **£35**
- Thackery, Chas F. Ltd: A catalogue of surgical instruments, surgical appliances, hospital equipment ... Leeds & London: n.d. [ca 1940]. 4to. xxxviii,472 pp. Spine sl faded.
                                      *(Jenner)* **£55**
- Thayer, Henry: Descriptive catalogue of fluid and solid extracts, also pills, resinoids, and alkaloids. Cambridgeport: 1866. 270 pp.
                                      *(Fye)* **$100**
- Thompson, Skinner & Hamilton: Illustrated price list of chemical and scientific apparatus for chemist, assayers, smelters, mines, iron and steel works ... Glasgow: 1914. 882 pp. Orig red cloth, upper hinge cracked.
                                      *(Jenner)* **£65**
- Tiemann, George & Co: The American Armamentarium Chirurgicum. New York: 1879. 1st edn. Qtr lea, hd & ft of spine worn, crnrs bumped.              *(Fye)* **$325**
- Truax, Chas & Co: Mechanics of surgery comprising detailed descriptions, illustrations and lists of the instruments, appliances and furniture necessary in modern surgical art. Chicago: 1899. 1st edn. 1024 pp. *(Fye)* **$300**
- Truax, Chas & Co: Price list of physicians supplies. Chicago: 1890. 5th edn. 1080 pp. Inner hinges cracked, rear cvrs w'stained.
                                      *(Fye)* **$225**

- White & Wright: Aseptic hospital furniture. Liverpool, n.d. [ca 1930]. xii,175A [177] pp. Num ills. Cloth backed bds, lacking tear-off order form.                     *(Pollak)* **£25**

**Transactions ...**
- Transactions of the American Neurological Association, 63rd Annual Meeting, New Jersey 1937. xxxiv,199 pp. Title taped down. Sl bumped, front hinge cracked. *(Jenner)* **£20**
- Transactions of the section on surgery and anatomy of the American Medical Association. Chicago: 1904. 1st edn. 516 pp.
                                      *(Fye)* **$25**

**Travers, Morris W.**
- The discovery of the rare gases. Arnold, 1928. 1st edn. vii,128 pp. Frontis, 21 ills. Sm stamp at ft of title. Orig cloth, recased. *(Pollak)* **£45**
- The experimental study of gases. London: Macmillan, 1901. 1st edn. xiv,323 pp. 2 fldg diags, 1 plate, text ills. Orig cloth.
                                      *(Pickering)* **$100**

**Trease, George Edward**
- Pharmacy in history. 1964. 1st edn. Ills. Dw.
                                      *(Robertshaw)* **£12.50**

**Treatise ...**
- A treatise concerning the manner of fallowing of ground, raising of grass seeds ... for the increase and improvement of the linen manufacturers of Scotland ... Edinburgh: 1724. 173 pp. 6 fldg plates, 1 other plate. Contemp panelled calf. ? Robert Maxwell.
                                      *(Phenotype)* **£175**
- A treatise on ... porcelain and glass ... See Porter, George R.
- Two treatises ... nature of bodies ... See Digby, Kenelm

**Treves, Frederick**
- Intestinal obstruction: its varieties with their pathology, diagnosis and treatment. London: 1899. 2nd edn. Orig cloth, hinges cracked, fairly badly shaken. Ex lib. W.a.f.
                                      *(Jenner)* **£20**
- Intestinal obstruction: its varieties with their pathology, diagnosis and treatment. New York: 1899. 2nd Amer edn. 565 pp. *(Fye)* **$75**
- A manual of operative surgery. Phila: 1892. 1st Amer edn. 2 vols. More than 400 w'cuts.
                                      *(Fye)* **$125**

**Troltsch, Anton von**
- The diseases of the ear, their diagnosis and treatment. A text-book of aural surgery ... Translated from the second and last German edition. New York: 1864. 254 pp. Frontis. Cloth worn, jnts cracked.  *(Goodrich)* **$95**
- Treatise on the diseases of the ear, including the anatomy of the organ. New York: 1869. 2nd Amer edn. 566 pp. Engvs.   *(Fye)* **$100**

**Trotter, Thomas**
- An essay, medical, philosophical, and chemical, on drunkness ... London: 1810. 4th edn. 230 pp. Foxing.      *(Goodrich)* **$145**

**Troup, W. Annandale**
- Ultra-violet rays in general practice. 1926. xii,59. 12 ills. Orig red cloth.      *(Jenner)* **£8**

**Trousseau, Armand**
- Lectures on clinical medicine delivered at the Hotel-Dieu, Paris. Translated and edited ... New Sydenham Society, 1868. 5 vols. viii,712; xiii,630; xi,557; xii,470; xi,479 pp. Orig cloth, sl worn & some spines sl defective.      *(Whitehart)* **£40**
- Lectures on clinical medicine. London: New Sydenham Society, 1867-72. 1st edition in English. 5 vols. Orig cloth.      *(Oasis)* **$175**

**True, A.C.**
- The cotton plant; its history, botany, chemistry ... Washington: Government Printing Office, 1896. 433 pp. Frontis, 3 plates, 32 text figs. Title & last leaf torn at staples. New cloth. U.S. Dept. of Agric. bulletin.      *(Pollak)* **£25**

**Trueta, J.**
- Treatment of war wounds and fractures; with special reference to the closed method as used in the war in Spain. 1939. xiii,143 pp. 48 ills.      *(Whitehart)* **£25**
- Treatment of war wounds and fractures; with special reference to the closed method as used in the war in Spain. London: Hamish Hamilton, 1939. 1st edn. Sm 8vo. 143 pp. Many photo ills. Ex lib, label removed from front bd.      *(Xerxes)* **$60**

**Trueta, J., et al.**
- Studies of the renal circulation. Oxford: 1947. xix,187 pp. 83 figs.      *(Whitehart)* **£25**
- Studies of the renal circulation. Phila: 1947. 1st Amer edn. 187 pp. **$60**

**Tryon, Thomas**
- The way to health, long life and happiness ... the third edition, to which is added a discourse of the philosopher's stone ... London: 1697. [xvi],456,[24] pp. Browning on title, some margins dirtied & thumbed. Orig calf, very worn, bd nearly detchd.      *(Jenner)* **£225**

**Tuckey, C. Lloyd**
- Treatment by hypnotism and suggestion. London: 1907. 5th edn. xxviii,418, [4 advts] pp. Orig green pebbled cloth.      *(Jenner)* **£20**

**Tuke, Daniel Hack**
- Chapters in the history of the insane in the British Isles. London: Kegan Paul, 1882. 1st

edn. Top of spine badly torn. *(Scientia)* **$125**
- Chapters in the history of the insane in the British Isles. 1882. 1st edn. x,[1],548 pp. Frontis, 3 plates. Orig cloth. Front inner hinge cracked. Author's pres copy.      *(Whitehart)* **£65**

**Tuke, J. Batty**
- The insanity of over-exertion of the brain: being the Morison Lectures, session 1894. Edinburgh: Oliver & Boyd, [1894]. 1st edn. viii,66 pp. Fldg cold frontis.      *(Gach)* **$50**

**Tully, J.D.**
- The history of plague, as it has lately appeared on the Islands of Malta, Gozo, Corfu ... means adopted for eradication. 1821. xi,292 pp. Title sl soiled. Uncut. Half-calf, upper hinge cracked, lib stamps on spine & title.      *(Jenner)* **£70**

**Turnbull, A.**
- Treatment of diseases of the eye, by means of prussic acid vapour, and other medicinal agents. London: 1843. 1st edn. 89 pp. Backstrip lacking, front bd detchd. Ex lib. Willard Parker's copy with his autograph.      *(Fye)* **$50**

**Turnbull, Archibald D. & Lord, C.**
- History of United States naval aviation. New Haven: 1949. 1st edn. 345 pp. *(Scientia)* **$40**

**Turnbull, James**
- A practical treatise on disorders of the stomach with fermentation; the causes and treatment of indigestion ... London: 1856. x,160,[32 advts] pp. Frontis. Spine & crnrs v sl bumped. Inscribed by the author.      *(Jenner)* **£28**

**Turnbull, Laurence**
- The advantages and accidents of artificial anesthesia: a manual of anesthetic agents, and their employment in the treatment of disease. Phila: 1879. 2nd edn. 322 pp.      *(Fye)* **$125**

**Turner, A. Logan & Porter, W.E.**
- Skiagrophy of the accessory nasal sinuses. Edinburgh: 1912. 1st edn. 4to. 43 pp. 39 X-ray plates.      *(Fye)* **$60**

**Turner, Charles R.**
- The American text-book of prosthetic dentistry. 1907. 3rd edn. xiii,896 pp. 916 figs in text. Orig cloth, spine nicked.      *(Whitehart)* **£35**

**Turner, D.**
- The antient physician's legacy impartially survey'd. With a discourse on quicksilver ... To which is added, a preface ... 1734. 2nd edn. xvi,xi,306 pp. Browning & staining

throughout, sm hole in early leaves without loss. Calf, worn, rebacked.   *(Jenner)* **£100**

**Turner, Daniel**
- The art of surgery. London: 1741-42. 6th edn. 2 vols. 576; 520 pp. Frontis, engv. Worn.   *(Xerxes)* **$150**
- De Morbo Gallico. A treatise of the French diseases published above 200 years past, by Sir Ulrich Hutten ... London: for John Clarke, 1730. 110 pp. Title mounted, text browned. New qtr calf.   *(Goodrich)* **$135**

**Tuson, Edward**
- Spinal debility: its prevention, pathology and cure, in relation to curvatures, paralysis, epilepsy, and various deformities. London: 1861. 1st edn. 155 pp. Title chipped & detchd. Front endpaper lacking. Spine worn with sm pieces missing.   *(Fye)* **$50**

**Tuson, Edward William**
- Myology, illustrated by plates. In four parts ... London: Callow & Wilson, 1828. 2nd edn. Atlas folio. Title, dedication, 8 full-page litho plates of musculature, each with many movable overlays & accomp text. Contemp hand-cold. Orig bds, soiled, rebacked.   *(Dailey)* **$1,500**

**Tusser, Thomas**
- Five hundred points of good husbandry ... together with a book of huswifery, being a calendar of rural and domestic economy ... a new edition with notes. 1812. 338 pp. Uncut. Orig cloth, faded, rebacked, lea label.   *(Weiner)* **£50**
- Five hundred points of good husbandry ... together with a book of huswifery, being a calendar of rural and domestic economy ... a new edition with notes ... by William Mavor. 1812. 1st edn of Mavor's edn. 8vo. 338,2 [advts] pp. Mod polished half-roan.   *(Deighton Bell)* **£120**

**Tuttle, James**
- A treatise on diseases of the anus, rectum, and pelvic colon. New York: 1902. 1st edn. 961 pp. Qtr lea.   *(Fye)* **$75**

**Tutton, A.E.H.**
- Crystals. Kegan, Paul, 1911. x,301 pp. 120 ills, inc 24 plates.   *(Pollak)* **£15**

**Tweedie, Alexander**
- A system of practical medicine comprised in a series of original dissertations. Phila: Lea & Blanchard, 1842. 2nd Amer edn. 3 vols. 4to. viii,655,4 [pub ctlg]; xii,627; 734 pp. Some foxing. Full lea.   *(Poitras)* **$75**

**Tweney, C.F.**
- See Goodchild, G.F. & Tweney, C.F.

**Tyler, Albert**
- Roentgenotherapy. St. Louis: 1918. 1st edn. 162 pp. 111 ills.   *(Oasis)* **$35**

**Tyndall, John**
- Address delivered before the British Association assembled at Belfast, with additions. London: Longmans, 1874. viii,65,[i] pp. 8vo. Orig mauve cloth, lettered in gilt, faded.   *(Blackwell's)* **£75**
- Contributions to molecular physics in the domain of radiant heat. New York: Appleton, 1873. 1st Amer edn. 8vo. xiv,[2],446,[2 pub advts] pp. W'cut frontis & another w'cut plate. Contemp cloth.   *(Antiq Sc)* **$85**
- Contributions to molecular physics in the domain of radiant heat. New York: Appleton, 1885. 1st Amer edn. xiv,[ii], 446,[iv] pp. Frontis, plate, 31 text figs. Recased.   *(Pollak)* **£55**
- Essays on the floating matter of the air in relation to putrefaction and infection. London: 1881. 1st edn. 338 pp. Orig purple cloth, sl worn & soiled.   *(Oasis)* **$160**
- Essays on the floating matter of the air in relation to putrefaction and infection. London: Longmans, Green, 1881. 1st edn. xix,338,[2] pp. Text ills. Orig cloth, cvrs worn.   *(Rootenberg)* **$185**
- Essays on the floating matter of the air ... London: 1883. 2nd edn. 338 pp. Binding dull & sl damaged. Ex lib.   *(Oasis)* **$50**
- Essays on the floating-matter of the air in relation to putrefaction and infection. London: Longmans, 1883. 2nd edn. 8vo. Pub red cloth, spine faded & sl snagged at top. Ex lib with stamp on title, shelf number on spine.   *(McDowell)* **£30**
- Essays on the use and limit of the imagination in science. London: Longmans, 1870. 1st edn. Slim 8vo. Pub cloth.   *(McDowell)* **£48**
- Faraday as a discoverer. London: Longmans, 1868. 1st edn. 8vo. 2 ports. Pub brown cloth.   *(McDowell)* **£45**
- The forms of water in clouds ... Kegan, Paul, 1883. 8th edn. xix,192,40 [ctlg] pp. frontis. 67 ills.   *(Pollak)* **£10**
- The forms of water in clouds, rivers, ice, glaciers. 1872. 1st edn. Orig cloth, somewhat marked.   *(Wheldon & Wesley)* **£20**
- The glaciers of the Alps, a narrative of excursions and ascents. 1906. New edn. 8vo. xxvi, 445 pp. Frontis, 61 text figs. Cloth, sl faded & soiled.   *(Wheldon & Wesley)* **£20**
- Heat considered as a mode of motion. Being a course of twelve lectures delivered at the Royal Institution of Great Britain in the season of 1862. London: Longmans, Green, 1863. 1st edn. xix,[i], 468,31 [ctlg] pp. Fldg plate, 100 text figs. Recased.   *(Pollak)* **£18**
- Heat considered as a mode of motion ... London: Longmans, Green, 1865. 2nd edn with addtns & ills. xx,532,32 [ctlg] pp. Fldg

plate, 101 text figs. With sgntr of H.M. Brunel. Recased. *(Pollak)* **£55**
- Lectures in electricity at the Royal Institution 1875-76. London: Longmans, Green 1876. 1st edn. x,113,[i],ii [price list of apparatus],32 [ctlg] pp. 58 text figs. Jnts reprd. *(Pollak)* **£40**
- New fragments. London: Longmans, Green, 1892. 1st edn. [viii],500, [iv],24 [ctlg] pp. Faded, front jnt weak. *(Pollak)* **£30**
- Notes of a course of seven lectures on electrical phenomena and theories, delivered at the Royal Institution ... London: Longmans, Green, 1870. 1st edn. viii,40 pp. Recased. *(Pollak)* **£40**
- Notes of a course of seven lectures on electrical phenomena and theories. London: Longmans, Green, 1870. 1st edn. 8vo. viii,40 pp. Orig cloth, a bit faded. *(Antiq Sc)* **$65**
- On radiation. The "Rede" Lecture delivered in the Senate House before the University of Cambridge, May 16th, 1865. London: Longmans, Green, 1865. 1st edn. [vi],62,[ii] pp. Frontis. Recased. *(Pollak)* **£75**
- Researches on diamagnetism and magne-crystallic action ... London: Longmans, Green & Co., 1870. 1st edn. 8vo. x,361, [2],24 advts. Frontis, 9 plates. Orig cloth, a little worn. *(Pickering)* **$150**
- Six lectures on light delivered in America in 1872-73. London: Longmans, Green, 1875. 2nd edn. xvii,[iii],272 pp. Frontis, plate, 58 text figs. *(Pollak)* **£30**
- Sound. A course of eight lectures delivered at the Royal Institution of Great Britain. London: Longmans, Green, 1867. 1st edn. xiii,335,32 [ctlg] pp. Frontis, 169 text figs. Recased, cvrs shabby. *(Pollak)* **£50**
- Sound. A course of eight lectures ... London: Longmans, Green, 1869. 2nd edn. xv,341,32 [ctlg] pp. Frontis, 169 text figs. Recased. *(Pollak)* **£30**
- Sound. A course of eight lectures delivered at the Royal Institution of Great Britain. London: Longmans, Green, 1876. 1st edn. 8vo. xiii,[1],335 pp. Engvd frontis, numerous w'cuts. Orig cloth, uncut. *(Antiq Sc)* **$75**

**Tyson, James**
- A treatise on Bright's disease and diabetes. With special reference to pathology and therapeutics ... Phila: 1881. 1st edn. 312 pp. *(Fye)* **$100**

**Underwood, E. Ashworth**
- See Singer, Charles & Underwood, E.A.

**Underwood, E. Ashworth (ed.)**
- Science, medicine and history. Essays on the evolution of scientific thought and medical practice .... London: 1953. 1st edn. 2 vols. 4to. *(Scientia)* **$150**

**Underwood, Michael**
- A treatise on the diseases of children. With directions for the management of infants from the birth. With notes ... Three volumes in one ... Phila: 1818. 8vo. 18,186; [4],6,96; 11,[1],73 pp. Fldg table. Contemp calf, rubbed, hd of spine chipped. *(M&S)* **$65**
- A treatise on the diseases of children; with directions for the management of infants from the birth. 1827. 8th edn. xxxii,636 pp. Some foxing throughout. Mod half-calf. *(Jenner)* **£95**
- A treatise on the disorders of children, and the management of infants from birth. London: J. Callow, 1805. 2nd edn. 3 vols. 8vo. [2],xx, 311,[1]; xvi, xvi, 280,[1]; xiv,[1], 255,[1] pp. Half-titles, leaf of pub advts in Vol II. Half-calf. *(Rootenberg)* **$375**

**Unna, P.G.**
- The histopathology of the diseases of the skin. Translated from the German ... Edinburgh: Clay, 1896. xxviii,1205, [iii] pp. Double-page cold frontis, 42 text ills. Bndg a little slack. *(Pollak)* **£75**

**Upham, Thomas**
- Elements of mental philosophy. New York: 1841. 1st edn. 2 vols. 455; 470 pp. Some foxing. Old calf, spines worn & hinges weak. *(Oasis)* **$50**

**Upham, Thomas C.**
- Philosophical and practical treatise on the will. Portland: 1834. 400 pp. Spine reprd & taped, front inner hinge taped, edges v worn. *(Epistemologist)* **$45**

**Urdang, George**
- See Kremers, Edward & Urdang, George

**Ure, Andrew**
- A dictionary of arts, manufactures, and mines ... New York: Appleton, 1866. 2 vols. xiv,1118; [ii],998 pp. 1588 text w'engvs. Half-calf, mrbld bds, a little rubbing. *(Pollak)* **£60**
- A dictionary of chemistry. 1821. 1st edn. 14 plates. Contemp calf, some damp-staining at ft. *(Robertshaw)* **£24**
- A dictionary of chemistry. London: for Thomas Tegg, 1828. 3rd edn, with num addtns & crrctns. xii,829 pp. 9 plates. Occas foxing. Half-calf, a little rubbed. *(Pollak)* **£30**

**Urquhart, John W.**
- Electric light fitting, a handbook for working electrical engineers. London: Crosby, Lockwood, 1898. 3rd edn. 8vo. Frontis, ills throughout. Pub green cloth. *(McDowell)* **£28**

**Useful ...**
- The useful arts and manufactures of Great Britain. (First selection. S.P.C.K., n.d. [ca

1840's ?]. Sm 8vo. About 160 wood engvs. Orig blind-stamped cloth, rebacked.
*(Deighton Bell)* **£60**

**Uytenbogaart, J.W.H.**
- See Kooy, J.M.J. & Uytenbogaart, J.W.H.

**van Buren, W.H.**
- Lectures upon diseases of the rectum and the surgery of the lower bowel. New York: 1881. 2nd edn. 412 pp.            *(Fye)* **$50**

**Van der Kolk, Schroeder**
- On the minute structure and functions of the spinal cord and medulla oblongata and on ... epilepsy. London: New Sydenham Society, 1859. 1st English edn. 8vo. 5 litho plates. Pub blind-stamped cloth.        *(McDowell)* **£50**

**Van Hise, C.R.**
- A treatise on metamorphism. Washington: 1904. 4to. 1286 pp. 13 plates, 32 text figs. Cloth, worn. Monograph 47 U.S. Geological Survey.        *(Wheldon & Wesley)* **£30**

**Van Hise, C.R. & Leith, C.K.**
- Pre-Cambrian geology of North America. Washington: 1909. 8vo. 939 pp. 2 maps. Orig wraps, trifle worn. U.S. Geological Survey Bulletin 360.        *(Wheldon & Wesley)* **£18**

**Van't Hoff, J.H.**
- Studies in chemical dynamics. Translated ... Amsterdam & London: 1896. [x],vi,286 pp. 49 figs. Contemp white buckram, lea label.
*(Pollak)* **£35**

**Vaughan, Daniel**
- The destiny of the solar system: being an epitome of three lectures ... with an appendix on the theory of rain. Cincinnati: Marshall & Langtry, 1854. 1st edn. 8vo. 32 pp. Orig printed wraps.        *(M&S)* **$200**

**Vaughan, George Tully**
- Papers on surgery and other subjects. Washington: W.F. Roberts, 1932. 408 pp. Ex lib. Inscribed by author.    *(Poitras)* **$22.50**

**Vavilov, Nikolai I.**
- The origin, variation, immunity and breeding of cultivated plants: Selected writings of N.I. Vavilov. Translated ... Waltham, MA: 1951. 1st edn. 364 pp. Orig wraps. Chronica Botanica, vol 13.        *(Scientia)* **$50**

**Vegas, Marcelino Herrara**
- Hydatid cysts of the lung in children. Buenos Aires: 1928. 1st edn. 300 pp. Qtr lea. Autographed by the author.        *(Fye)* **$25**

**Velikovsky, Immanuel**
- Worlds in collision. New York: 1950. 1st edn.

Author's pres copy.        *(Minkoff)* **$375**

**'Velox' (pseud.)**
- Velocipedes, bicycles and tricycles. How to make and how to use them. With a sketch of their history, invention and progress. 1869. x,11-127 pp. 36 figs in text. Half-title marked. New cloth, orig pict card cvrs pasted on.
*(Whitehart)* **£65**

**Velpeau, A.**
- A complete treatise on midwifery: or, the theory and practice of tokology: including the diseases of pregnancy, labor and the puerperal state. Phila: 1852. 4th Amer edn. 652 pp. lea, worn.        *(Fye)* **$40**
- An elementary treatise on midwifery. Phila: 1831. 1st English translation. 584 pp. Full lea.        *(Fye)* **$300**
- An elementary treatise on midwifery; or, principles of tokology and embryology. Translated from the French ... Phila: John Grigg, 1831. 514 pp. 5 tables. Some foxing. Lea, spine reprd.        *(Poitras)* **$75**
- An elementary treatise on midwifery; or, principles of tokology and embryology. Translated from the French ... Phila: Grigg & Elliot, 1838. 2nd Amer edn. xxiii, [17]-592, 4[pub advts] pp. Little age-staining. New cloth & pattern bds.        *(Diamond)* **$50**
- A treatise on diseases of the breast. Translated from French ... Phila: 1840. 83 pp. Old style bds.        *(Goodrich)* **$55**
- A treatise on diseases of the breast and mammary region. Translated from French ... London: 1856. 608 pp. Cloth worn.
*(Goodrich)* **$95**
- A treatise on diseases of the breast and mammary region. London: 1856. 1st English translation. 608 pp.        *(Fye)* **$275**
- A treatise on surgical anatomy or the anatomy of regions ... translated from French ... New York: 1830. 2 vols. 14 plates. Foxed. Worn sheep.        *(Goodrich)* **$95**

**Venables, Robert**
- A practical treatise on diabetes: with observations on the tabes diuretica, or urinary consumption, especially as it occurs in children ... London: ... Underwood, 1825. 1st edn. 8vo. [2],xvi, 214,[2] pp. Uncut, unopened, in orig bds, rebacked.
*(Rootenberg)* **$225**

**Venn, John**
- The logic of chance. An essay on the foundations and province of the theory of probability. New York: Macmillan, 1888. 3rd edn. re-written & enlgd. xxix,508 pp. Orig cloth, a little rubbed.        *(Pollak)* **£65**
- The principles of empirical or inductive logic. London: Macmillan, 1889. 1st edn. xx,594,[ii advts] pp. Orig cloth, recased,

faded, crnrs worn.                    *(Pollak)* **£80**
- The principles of empirical or inductive logic. London: Macmillan, 1907. 2nd edn. xx,604 pp. Orig cloth, front cvr sl marked.
                                       *(Pollak)* **£55**
- Symbolic logic. London: Macmillan, 1881. 1st edn. xxxix,446, [ii advts] pp. Orig cloth, lower edge of rear cvr sl marked. *(Pollak)* **£90**

**Venturoli, Guiseppe**
- Elements of the theory of mechanics. Translated from the Italian ... Cambridge: Nicholson & Son, 1822. xi,192 pp. 3 fldg plates. Some foxing. Orig bds, new cloth spine.                      *(Pollak)* **£20**

**Ver Brugen, Adrian**
- Neurosurgery in general practice. Springfield: 1952. 1st edn. 665 pp.
                                       *(Oasis)* **$35**

**Vernon, H.M.**
- Health in relation to occupation. London: Oxford University Press, 1939. 1st edn. 8vo. Ex lib. House of Commons b'plate.
                                    *(McDowell)* **£30**

**Vernon, Philip, E.**
- See Allport, Gordon W. & Vernon, Philip E.

**Verrier, E.**
- Practical manual of obstetrics ... with revisions and anotations ... New York: 1884. 1st Amer edn. 395 pp.    *(Fye)* **$20**

**Vesling, Johann**
- The anatomy of the body of man ... Englished by N. Culpeper. London: Peter Cole, 1653. 1st English edn. Sm folio. xii,192 pp. 24 copperplates. Lacks engvd frontis. Some leaf edges worn, occas staining. Contemp panelled calf, rubbed.          *(Goodrich)* **$595**

**Vestiges ...**
- Vestiges of the natural history of creation ... See Chambers, Robert

**Vigo, Giovanni de**
- The most excellent works of chirurgerye ... Translated into English ... [London]: Edward Whytchurch, 1543. Folio, black letter. [6],cclcc,[11] pp. Wanting last 4 leaves of text & final blank. A few marginal stains & sl foxing. 19th century speckled calf.
                                   *(Dailey)* **$3,500**

**Villavecchia, Vittorio**
- Treatise on applied analytical chemistry. Translated ... London: Churchill, 1918. 2 vols. xvi,475; xv,536 pp. Pub ctlgs bound in. 11 plates, 157 text figs. Spine ends worn. Ex lib.                        *(Pollak)* **£25**

**Villiger, Emil**
- Brain and spinal cord. A manual for the study of the morphology and fibre-tracts of the central nervous system. Lippincott, 1912. Translated from the 3rd German edn. Lge 8vo. x,289 pp. 232 ills. Cvrs sl worn.
                                     *(Jenner)* **£12**

**Vogel, Alfred**
- A practical treatise on the diseases of children. Translated ... New York: 1890. 3rd Amer edn. Lge 8vo. xii,640 pp. 6 plates (4 cold). Orig 3/4 mor, rubbed.    *(Elgen)* **$45**

**Vogel, J.**
- See Neubauer, C. & Vogel, J.

**Von ...**
- For all surnames commencing with "von ...", as in "von Hevesy", "von Neumann", &c., see under the primary name "Hevesy", 'Neumann", & the like.

**Voronoff, Serge**
- The conquest of life. London: 1928. 1st edn. 201 pp. Ills. Orig cloth. Author's pres copy.
                                     *(Oasis)* **$40**
- Rejuvenation by grafting. London: 1925. 1st English edn. 223 pp. 38 ills. Orig red cloth, upper bd scuffed.              *(Jenner)* **£12**
- The sources of life. Boston: 1943. 1st edn. 240 pp. Plates. Dw sl frayed.    *(Oasis)* **$20**

**Vought, John G.**
- Treatise on bowel complaints ... for the use of physicians, ... masters of vessels &c., in the United States. Rochester, NY: ... for the Author, 1828. 1st edn. 16mo. 216 pp. Glossary, advts & list of pharmacists. Foxed. Contemp calf, worn. Hinge cracked.
                                   *(Diamond)* **$75**

**Vries, Hugo de**
- Intracellular Pangenesis [1899]; including a paper on fertilisation and hybridisation [1903]. Translated ... Chicago: 1910. 1st edn in English. 270 pp.    *(Scientia)* **$65**

**Wadd, William**
- Comments on corpulency; lineaments of leanness; ... on diets and dietetics. London: 1829. Sm 8vo. [3]ff,170 pp. Engvd frontis, 5 engvd plates. 3/4 lea, mrbld bds, sl rubbed.
                                     *(Elgen)* **£185**

**Waddell, J.A.L.**
- Bridge engineering. New York: 1916. 2 vols. lxxxv,2177 pp. Many figs & diags in the text, some fldg.            *(Whitehart)* **£35**

**Waddington, C.H.**
- The epigenetics of birds. Cambridge: 1952. 1st edn. 272 pp.        *(Scientia)* **$37.50**

**- An introduction to modern genetics.** New York: 1939. 1st edn. 441 pp. *(Scientia)* **$27.50**

**Waelsch, Heinrich (ed.)**
- Biochemistry of the developing nervous system. Proceedings of first Neurochemical Symposium, Oxford, 1954. New York: Academic Press, 1955. 537 pp. Ills. Ex lib. *(Poitras)* **$30**

**Wagner, Percy A.**
- The platinum deposits and mines of South Africa. Edinburgh: Oliver & Boyd, 1929. xv,326 pp. Frontis. 37 plates, some fldg. 37 text figs. Cvrs dusty. *(Pollak)* **£25**

**Waite, Arthur E.**
- Lives of the alchemystical philosophers ... with a philosophical demonstration ... to which is added a bibliography ... London: 1888. 1st edn. 315 pp. Ex lib. *(Scientia)* **$75**

**Wakeley, Andrew**
- The mariner's compass rectified; containing tables, shewing the true hour of the day, the sun being upon any point of the compass. London: J. Mount, 1765. 12mo. Foxed. Full lea, worn. *(Argosy)* **$125**

**Wakeley, C.P.G.**
- See Gladstone, R.J. & Wakeley, C.P.G.

**Wakeley, Cecil & Orley, Alexander**
- A textbook of neuroradiology. London: 1938. 1st edn. 336 pp. Ills. Ex lib. *(Oasis)* **$45**

**Walkden, S.L.**
- Aeroplanes in gusts: soaring flight and the stability of aeroplanes. 1913. 2nd edn, greatly enlgd. xxv,280 pp. Frontis, 4 fldg plates, diags. *(Weiner)* **£50**

**Walker, A. Earl**
- The primate thalamus. Chicago: 1938. 1st edn. 321 pp. *(Fye)* **$60**

**Walker, A. Earl & Jablon, Seymour**
- A follow up study of head wounds in World War II. Washington: 1961. 1st edn. 202 pp. Ex lib. *(Fye)* **$12.50**
- A follow up study of head wounds in World War II. Washington: 1961. 4to. x,202 pp. *(Poitras)* **$27.50**

**Walker, Adam**
- Analysis of a course of lectures on natural and experimental philosophy ... Second edition. Printed for, and sold by the Author. [Manchester, 1771?]. 8vo. 86,1 [glossary] pp. Title soiled, sl chipped. A little early inked addenda. Mod mrbld bds, mor label. *(Deighton Bell)* **£55**
- Analysis of a course of lectures on natural and

experimental philosophy ... Seventh edition. [London]: sold by the Author, [1795]. 8vo. 88 pp. Title soiled, last leaf torn on the inner margin with loss of a couple of letters. Recent half-calf, red label. *(Burmester)* **£75**

**Walker, Alexander**
- Intermarriage; or the mode in which, and the causes why, beauty, health and intellect result from certain unions; and deformity, disease and insanity from others ... New York: 1839. 1st Amer edn. 384 pp. Foxed. *(Scientia)* **$65**
- Intermarriage; or the mode in which, and the causes why, beauty, health and intellect result from certain unions; and deformity, disease and insanity from others ... New York: Langley, 1841. Sm 8vo. 384 pp. 8 engvd plates, darkened. Foxed. *(Xerxes)* **$65**

**Walker, Charles E.**
- Heredity characters and other modes of transmission. 1910. xii,239 pp. 21 ills. 3 lib stamps. *(Jenner)* **£28**

**Walker, G.A.**
- Gatherings from the graveyards; particularly those of London: with a concise history of the mode of interment ... unwise and revolting custom of inhuming the dead in the midst of the living. London: 1839. 258 pp. Foxing. Recased. *(Goodrich)* **$150**

**Walker, James**
- Introduction to physical chemistry. Macmillan, 1901. 2nd edn. xii,343 pp. 47 text figs. Rear jnt pulled. *(Pollak)* **£10**

**Walker, James (ed.)**
- Oxygen supply to the human foetus. Oxford: 1959. 1st edn. 313 pp. Dw. *(Fye)* **$20**

**Walker, N.**
- An introduction to dermatology. London: 1906. 3rd edn. 2nd imp. xiv,292 pp. 48 plates, some cold, 50 ills. Orig green cloth, upper hinge cracked, stain on upper bd. *(Jenner)* **£16**

**Walker, Thomas A.**
- The Severn tunnel; its construction and difficulties, 1872-1887 ... 1891. 3rd edn. xxi,195 pp. Many plates, most fldg & several tinted, 5 ports. Orig pict cloth. *(Weiner)* **£95**

**Wall, Martin**
- Dissertations on select subjects in chemistry and medicine. Oxford: for D. Prince & J. Cooke, 1783. 1st edn. 8vo. xv,[3],166 pp. Full page w'cut. Brown wraps. *(Zeitlin)* **$150**

**Wallace, A.B.**
- The treatment of burns. London: 1941. 1st edn. 113 pp. *(Fye)* **$15**

## Wallace, A.R.
- Is Mars habitable? A critical examination of Professor Percival Lowell's book "Mars and its Canals" with an alternative explanation. 1907. 1st edn. xii,100 pp. Frontis. Orig cloth.
*(Whitehart)* **£20**
- Is Mars habitable? London: 1907. 1st edn. 8vo. xii,110,2 [advt] pp. 2 plates. Sgntr on flyleaf. Orig cloth, cvrs v sl marked.
*(Bow Windows)* **£85**
- To Members of Parliament and others. Forty-five years of registration statistics, proving vaccination to be both useless and dangerous. London: 1885. 1st edn. 8vo. 38,6 [advts] pp. Extending table. Orig cloth.
*(Bow Windows)* **£75**

## Wallace, Alfred Russel
- Contributions to the theory of natural selection. A series of essays. London: 1870. 1st edn. 384 pp. Spine frayed. *(Scientia)* **$175**
- Darwinism, an exposition of the theory of natural selection with some of its applications. London: Macmillan, 1889. 3rd edn. 8vo. Port frontis, fldg cold map, ills. Pub green cloth. *(McDowell)* **£40**
- Darwinism, an exposition of the theory of natural selection ... London: Macmillan, 1889. 1st edn. 8vo. Port frontis, fldg map. Pub green cloth, sl shaken. *(McDowell)* **£55**
- Darwinism: an exposition of the theory of natural selection ... London: 1889. 1st edn. 494 pp. *(Scientia)* **$75**
- Darwinism: an exposition of the theory of natural selection ... London: Macmillan, 1889. 2nd edn. Orig cloth. *(Ivelet)* **£18**
- Darwinism: an exposition of the theory of natural selection ... London: 1897. 2nd edn, later printing. 494 pp. *(Scientia)* **$45**
- The geographical distribution of animals ... London: Macmillan, 1876. 1st edn. 2 vols. 8vo. 7 cold maps, some fldg, 20 plates. Occas spotting. Pub dark green cloth.
*(McDowell)* **£280**
- The geographical distribution of animals ... London: Macmillan, 1876. 1st edn. 2 vols. 8vo. xxi,[2],503; viii,[4],607 pp. 7 cold maps, text ills. Orig cloth. *(Rootenberg)* **$650**
- Island life or, the phenomena and causes of insular faunas and floras ... London: 1880. 1st edn. xix,526 pp. 26 maps & ills. Orig cloth, trifle used. A few pencil annotations.
*(Wheldon & Wesley)* **£95**
- Island life or, the phenomena and causes of insular faunas and floras ... New York: 1881. 1st Amer edn. 522 pp. *(Scientia)* **$85**
- Island life or, the phenomena and causes of insular faunas and floras ... London: Macmillan, 1892. 2nd, revsd, edn. xx,563 pp. Frontis map, 25 maps & plates. Orig cloth.
*(Pollak)* **£45**
- Island life or, the phenomena and causes of insular faunas and floras ... London: 1911.

3rd & revsd edn. 563 pp. *(Scientia)* **$45**
- The Malay archipelago. The land of the Orang-utan and the Bird of Paradise ... New York: 1869. 1st Amer edn. 638 pp.
*(Scientia)* **$85**
- The Malay archipelago. The land of the Orang-utan and the Bird of Paradise ... London: 1880. 7th edn. 653 pp.
*(Scientia)* **$37.50**
- Man's place in the universe. A study of the results of scientific research ... New York: 1903. 1st Amer edn. 326 pp. *(Scientia)* **$27.50**
- My life; a record of events and opinions. London: Chapman & Hall, 1905. 1st edn. 2 vols. 8vo. Frontis & other ills. Pub red cloth.
*(McDowell)* **£90**
- My life; a record of events and opinions. London: 1905. 1st edn. 2 vols. 435; 459 pp. Covrs mottled. *(Scientia)* **$65**
- My life; a record of events and opinions. New York: 1969 reprint of London 1905 edn. 2 vols. 40 plates, 5 figs. *(Winterdown)* **£30**
- A narrative of travels on the Amazon and Rio Negro ... London: 1889. 2nd edn. 363 pp. Spine shelfworn. *(Scientia)* **$65**
- Studies scientific and moral. London: 1900. 1st edn. 2 vols. 532; 535 pp. *(Scientia)* **$110**
- Tropical nature and other essays. London: 1878. 1st edn. 356 pp. Prize lea.
*(Scientia)* **$95**

## Waller, Augustus D.
- An introduction to human physiology. 1893. 2nd edn. xvi,632 pp. Errata slip. Ills. Some spotting throughout & a few marginal pencil marks. Orig cloth, spine faded. *(Jenner)* **£16**

## Wallis, F.
- See Hawkins, C.C. & Wallis, F.

## Wallis, George
- The art of preventing diseases, and restoring health, founded on rational principles, and adapted to persons of every capacity. London: 1793. xi,852,[12] pp. Little dog-eared. Mod 3/4 lea. *(Whitehart)* **£60**
- The art of preventing diseases, and restoring health, founded on rational principles, and adapted to persons of every capacity. 1793. xx,852 pp. Index. Orig calf, very rubbed & worn, hinges weak. *(Jenner)* **£60**

## Wallis-Taylor, A.J.
- Motor vehicles for business purposes. 1905. xv,298 pp. pp. Frontis, ills, 8 pp advts. Orig bevelled cloth, sl marked. *(Weiner)* **£75**
- Refrigerating and ice-making machinery. A descriptive treatise for the use of persons employing [such] installations, and others. 1897. 2nd edn. xviii,280 pp. 83 ills.
*(Weiner)* **£15**

**Walsh, James J.**
- The history of nursing. New York: P.J.
Kennedy & Sons, 1929. xxi,309 pp.
*(Poitras)* **$25**
- The popes and science. The history of papal
relations to science during the Middle Ages
and down to our own time. New York:
Fordham University Press, 1908. 431 pp.
*(Poitras)* **$30**

**Walsh, James Joseph**
- Cures: the story of cures that fail. New York:
D. Appleton, 1923. 1st edn. xii,291 pp.
Russet cloth.          *(Gach)* **$27.50**
- Psychotherapy: including the history of the
use of mental influence, directly and
indirectly in healing ... New York: D.
Appleton, 1912. 1st edn. xv,806 pp. Pub red
cloth.                  *(Gach)* **$75**

**Walshe, F.M.R.**
- Diseases of the nervous system, described for
practitioners and students. Edinburgh: 1942.
2nd edn. xvi,325 pp. Ills. Orig maroon cloth.
*(Jenner)* **£9**

**Walton, Thomas H.**
- Coal mining described and illustrated. Phila:
1885. xv,[9]-175 pp. 24 plates. Few text diags.
Orig dec cloth, a little worn & discoloured,
tear at hd of spine.      *(Weiner)* **£45**

**Wanklyn, J. Alfred**
- Water analysis: a practical treatise on the
examination of potable water. London: 1884.
6th edn. viii,192 pp. 2 text ills. Orig black
cloth, bds sl soiled, spine rubbed.
*(Jenner)* **£10**

**Ward, Grant**
- See Kelly, Howard & Ward, Grant

**Ward, Grant & Hendrick, James**
- Diagnosis and treatment of tumors of the
head and neck (not including the central
nervous system). Balt: 1950. 1st edn. 4to. 832
pp. Inscribed & autographed by both authors.
*(Fye)* **$75**

**Ward, Lester F.**
- Dynamic sociology, or applied social science.
New York: 1920. 2 vols. 706; 690 pp.
*(Epistemologist)* **$37.50**
- Psychic factors of civilisation. Boston: 1906.
2nd edn. 369 pp. V sl rubbed & shelfworn.
*(Epistemologist)* **$37.50**

**Ward, Mrs.**
- The microscope, or descriptions of various
objects of especial interest and beauty,
adapted for microscopic observation. London,
Groombridge, 1869. 3rd edn. 8vo. vi,154,[4
advts] pp. 8 cold plates. Orig gilt cloth, a.e.g.

*(Antiq Sc)* **$45**

**Ward, Ronald**
- The design and equipment of hospitals. 1949.
Sm 4to. xvi,360 pp. Plates & ills. Spine sl
nicked. Pub file copy with label on cvr.
*(Jenner)* **£20**

**Warden, Carl John**
- Animal motivation: experimental studies on
the albino rat. New York: Columbia
University Press, 1931. 1st edn. xii,502,[2]
pp. Blue cloth.          *(Gach)* **$50**

**Wardrop, James**
- Essays on the morbid anatomy of the human
eye. Volume 2. London: 1818. 1st edn. Vol 2
only (complete in itself). 274 pp. 8 hand-cold
engvd plates. Qtr lea.    *(Fye)* **$350**

**Waring, Edward John**
- Bibliotheca Therapeutica, or bibliography of
therapeutics, chiefly in reference to .... New
Sydenham Society, 1878-79. 2 vols. Orig
cloth.              *(Whitehart)* **£40**
- Bibliotheca therapeutica, or bibliography of
therapeutics, chiefly in reference to articles of
the materia medica ... London: New
Sydenham Society, 1878-79. 8vo. 2 vols. Orig
blind-stamped cloth, vol I rebacked. Lib
stamp on first title.    *(Zeitlin)* **$125**
- Bibliotheca therapeutica, or bibliography of
therapeutics, chiefly in reference to articles of
the materia medica ... London: New
Sydenham Society, 1878-79. 1st edn. 2 vols.
8vo. Pub blind-stamped cloth, sm tear to
hinge of vol II.      *(McDowell)* **£50**

**Warner, Deborah J.**
- Alvan Clark & Sons. Artists in optics.
Washington, D.C.: Smithsonian, 1968. 28
figs.              *(Winterdown)* **£15**

**Warner, Ferdinando**
- A full and plain account of the gout ...
London: for T. Cadell, 1768. 1st edn. 8vo.
xi,290 pp. Minor browning. Full calf, jnts
weakened.        *(Rootenberg)* **$250**
- A full and plain account of the gout. 1768. 1st
edn. Contemp calf.    *(Robertshaw)* **£85**
- A full and plain account of the gout, with
some new and important instructions for its
relief. London: for T. Cadell, 1768. 1st edn.
8vo. vi,290 pp. Contemp full calf, red mor
label, armorial b'plate. *(Deighton Bell)* **£100**

**Warner, Joseph**
- An account of the testicles, their common
coverings and coats; and the diseases to which
they are liable with the methods of treating
them. 2nd edn, with addtns. London: 1779.
100 pp. Title mounted. Old style bds.
*(Goodrich)* **$135**

- Cases in surgery, with introductions, operations, and remarks. London: J. & R. Tonson, 1760. 3rd edn. 8vo. [20],401,[1] pp. 9 engvd plates. Some browning. Full calf with raised bands, red mor label.  *(Dailey)* **$225**

**[Warner, Samuel]**
- The practical surveyor, or, the art of land-measuring made easy ... London: J. Hooke & J. Sisson, 1725. 1st edn. 8vo. xv,[1],182 pp. Fldg frontis, 5 other fldg plates. Orig calf, rebacked.  *(Rootenberg)* **$450**

**Warnes, John**
- On the cultivation of flax; the fattening of cattle with native produce; box feeding; and summer grazing. 1846. 1st edn. xv,321 pp. Orig cloth, spine faded.  *(Deighton Bell)* **£40**
- On the cultivation of flax; the fattening of cattle with native produce; box feeding and summer grazing. 1847. 2nd edn. xxii,362 pp. Black cloth. Spine marked, jnts split.  *(Phenotype)* **£38**
- On the cultivation of flax; the fattening of cattle with native produce ... London: 1847. 2nd edn. 8vo. xxii,362 pp. Sev un-numbered pages of w'cut ills, diags. One leaf a little crumpled. Orig embossed cloth, hd of spine worn, short tears on jnts. *(Bow Windows)* **£32**

**Warren, J. Collins**
- The healing of arteries after ligature in man and animals. New York: 1886. 1st edn. 184 pp. Plates.  *(Fye)* **$150**

**Warren, John C.**
- Address before the American Medical Association at ... Cincinnati, May 8, 1850. Boston: John Wilson, 1850. 1st edn. Tall 4to. 65 pp. Uncut in orig embossed red cloth cvrs. Author's pres copy.  *(Hemlock)* **$200**

**Warren, Kenneth**
- See Cattell, Richard & Warren, Kenneth

**Warren, Samuel**
- Passages from the diary of a late physician. N.d. [1837? 5th edn?]. xii,503,[4 advts] pp. Frontis. Serious foxing on prelims, spotted throughout. Uncut, unopened in orig cloth.  *(Jenner)* **£15**

**Wasmann, Erich**
- Instinct and intelligence in the animal kingdom. A critical contribution to modern animal psychology. St. Louis: 1903. 1st edn in English. 171 pp.  *(Scientia)* **$25**

**Waterhouse, Benjamin**
- Cautions to young persons concerning health ... delivered ... at Cambridge Nov. 20, 1804; shewing ... evil tendency of the use of tobacco ... [Cambridge, Ma.]: Univ. Press, 1805. 32

pp. Crnr of 1 leaf torn away. Cloth, paper label.  *(Antiq Sc)* **$175**
- The rise, progress, and present state of medicine. Boston: T. & J. Fleet, 1792. 1st edn. 8vo. xii,30 pp. Old repairs to sev leaves, without loss. 19th c cloth-backed mrbld bds.  *(Antiq Sc)* **$275**

**Waters, Charles**
- See Young, Hugh & Waters, Charles

**Watson, Chalmers (ed.)**
- Encyclopaedia medica. Edinburgh, 1899-1910. 15 vols (all published). 4to. Orig cloth.  *(Whitehart)* **£60**

**Watson, H.W. & Burbury, S.H.**
- A treatise on the application of generalised co-ordinates to the kinetics of a material system. Oxford: Clarendon Press, 1879. 1st edn. viii,[ii], 104,32 [ctlg]. 11 text figs.  *(Pollak)* **£35**

**Watson, Henry William**
- A treatise on the kinetic theory of gases. Oxford: Clarendon Press, 1893. 2nd edn. xiv,87 pp. A little shaky, spine ends wearing.  *(Pollak)* **£25**

**Watson, J.B. & McDougall, W.**
- Battle of behaviorism. London: 1928. 103 pp. Sl soiled & shelfworn.  *(Epistemologist)* **$35**

**Watson, James D.**
- The double helix, a personal account of the discovery of the structure of DNA. 1968. 1st edn. xvi,226 pp. Plates, diags. Dw. Sgnd photograph of Watson loosely inserted.  *(Weiner)* **£40**

**Watson, John**
- The medical profession in ancient times. An anniversary discourse ... November 7, 1855. New York: 1856. 1st edn. xii,9-222 pp. Errata leaf. Foxing. Orig blind-stamped cloth.  *(Elgen)* **$50**

**Watson, John Broadus**
- Behavior: an introduction to comparative psychology. New York: Henry Holt, [1929]. 12mo. 439 pp. Green cloth.  *(Gach)* **$25**
- Psychology from the standpoint of a behaviorist. 1919. 429 pp. Cvr spotted & sl shelfworn.  *(Epistemologist)* **$50**

**Watson, Thomas**
- Lectures on the principles and practice of physic, delivered at King's College, London. London: 1857. 2 vols. xvi,871; viii,984 pp. Ills. Half-calf.  *(Jenner)* **£45**
- Lectures on the principles and practice of physic ... 1857. 4th edn, rvsd & enlgd. 2 vols. xvi,871; viii,984 pp. 2 plates. New cloth.

*(Whitehart)* £35

**Watson-Jones, R.**
- Fractures and other bone joint injuries. Edinburgh: 1940. xiii,723. 1040 ills in text. Cloth sl worn & stained.     *(Whitehart)* £25

**Watson-Watt, R.A., et al.**
- Applications of the cathode ray oscillograph in radio research. London: 1935. 1st edn, 2nd printing. xvi,290 pp. 16 plates, 113 ills.
*(Elgen)* $75

**Watt, Robert**
- Cases of diabetes, consumption, &c., with observations on the history and treatment of disease in general. Edinburgh: 1808. 328 pp. Foxing. Later half-calf.     *(Goodrich)* $175

**Watts, Henry C.**
- The design of screw propellers with special reference to their adaptation for aircraft. 1920. xiii,340 pp. Plates, diags. *(Weiner)* £30

**Watts, Isaac**
- The knowledge of the heavens and the earth made easy: or, the first principles of astronomy ... London: J. Clark [&c.], 1726. 1st edn. 8vo. 5 fldg plates. Title reprd. Contemp calf, rebacked.     *(McDowell)* £160
- The knowledge of the heavens and the earth made easy: or, the first principles of astronomy ... 1728. 2nd edn. xi,222 pp. 6 fldg plates. Contemp calf, rebacked, gilt spine, new lea label.     *(Whitehart)* £85
- The knowledge of the heavens and the earth made easy: or, the first principles of astronomy ... London: for Richard Ford, 1736. 3rd edn crrctd. xiii,222,[xii] pp. 6 fldg plates. Sl worming, faded damp-staining at end. Orig calf, worn.     *(McDowell)* £50

**Watts, J.W.**
- See Freeman, Walter & Watts, J.W.

**Watts, John**
- The facts of the cotton famine by members of the Central Relief Committee. 1866. 1st edn. 8vo. xii,472 pp. Repairs to outer margins of some leaves, & 1 leaf loose. Half-calf, gilt, sl rubbed & worn.     *(Deighton Bell)* £110

**Watts, W. Marshall**
- Index of spectra. With a preface by H.E. Roscoe. London: Henry Gillman, 1872. xvi,74 pp. Cold frontis, 8 plates. One plate loose, marginal pencil notes at front.
*(Pollak)* £40

**Watts, W.W.**
- British geological photographs. Selected from the British Association collection ... Birmingham, 1902-04. 3 parts. xii,[viii],

9-18,[ii]; 19-30; [iv subscr list]. Duplicate text sheets, gummed for mounting. 71 [ex 72] platinotypes & 2 duplicates. In portfolio.
*(Pollak)* £200

**Weatherhead, George Hume**
- An account of the Beaulah saline spa at Norwood, Surrey ... medicinal properties ... London: 1832. 1st edn. 8vo. 39,[1] pp. Disbound. Pres inscrptn from the author.
*(Burmester)* £25

**Webb-Johnson, A.E.**
- Surgical aspects of typhoid and paratyphoid fevers ... amplified and revised. 1919. 190 pp. 28 plates, 2 cold. Orig red cloth. *(Jenner)* £16

**Webster, Arthur G.**
- The theory of electricity and magnetism being lectures on mathematical physics.. London & New York: Macmillan, 1897. 1st edn. 8vo. xii,576 pp. Text figs. *(Antiq Sc)* $90

**Webster, John**
- The displaying of supposed witchcraft wherein is affirmed that there are many sorts of deceivers and imposters ... London: by J.M. ..., 1677. 1st edn. Folio. [16],346,[4] pp. With the imprimatur leaf before the title. Light staining. Mod calf.    *(Rootenberg)* $475

**Webster, Joshua**
- Practical observations on the preservation of health ... pure sources of medical botany ... 1836. 5th edn. Port. Some foxing. Uncut in orig bds, lacks spine.     *(Robertshaw)* £20

**Webster, Malcolm R.**
- See Cescinsky, Herbert & Webster, Malcolm R.

**Weeks, John**
- A treatise on diseases of the eye. Phila: 1910. 944 pp.     *(Fye)* $40

**Wegener, Alfred**
- The origin of continents and oceans. Translated from the third German edition ... Methuen, 1924. 1st English edn. xx,212 pp. 44 figs. Cloth faded.     *(Pollak)* £25

**Weinberger, Bernhard W.**
- An introduction to the history of dentistry, with medical & dental chronology and bibliographical data. St. Louis: 1948. 1st edn. 2 vols. Dw.     *(Scientia)* $160
- Orthodontics, an historical review of its origin and evolution. St. Louis: C.V. Mosby, 1926. 1st edn. 2 vols. Sm 4to. 1011 pp. Many photo ills & diags. A few pages stuck together resulting in sl tears, without loss of text.
*(Xerxes)* $190
- Pierre Fauchard, Surgeon-Dentist. A brief

account of the beginning of modern dentistry ... Minneapolis: 1941. 1st edn. Ltd (950). xv,102 pp. Frontis, plates. Cloth-backed paper-cvrd bds. *(Elgen)* **$50**

**Weiner, Meyer & Alvis, Bennet**
- Surgery of the eye. Phila: 1939. 1st edn. 445 pp. Ills. *(Oasis)* **$45**

**Weinman, Joseph & Sicher, Harry**
- Bone and bones: fundamentals of bone biology. St. Louis: 1947. 1st edn. 464 pp. *(Fye)* **$20**

**Weissmann, August**
- Essays upon heredity and kindred biological problems. Edited by E.B. Poulton ... Oxford: 1891-1892. 2 vols. (2nd edn; 1st edn; in English). 471; 226 pp. *(Scientia)* **$95**
- Studies in the theory of descent. Translated ... by Raphael Meldola. With a prefatory notice by Charles Darwin. London: 1882. 1st edn in English. 729 pp. *(Scientia)* **$185**

**Welch, F.V.**
- See Barnard, J.E. & Welch, F.V.

**Welch, James A.**
- A popular treatise on tinea capitis, or, ringworm ... and a description of a medicated steam bath ... London: for the Author, [1837]. 8vo. xv,63 pp. Litho frontis, 7 chromo-litho ports. Plates browned at edges. Orig bds, upper cvr almost detchd.
  *(Frew Mackenzie)* **£125**

**Welch, William**
- Papers and addresses. Balt: 1920. 1st edn. 3 vols. *(Fye)* **$175**

**Welch, William H.**
- The causation of diptheria. N.p.: [1891]. 1st sep edn. 31 pp. Orig printed wraps.
  *(M&S)* **$100**

**Weldon, Walter**
- Observations on the different modes of puncturing the bladder, in cases of retention of urine; pointing out the advantages and disadvantages ... Southampton: 1793. 1st edn. 172 pp. Name torn from top of title, lib stamp on title, new endpapers. Full lea. *(Fye)* **$200**

**Wells, Edward**
- The young gentleman's astronomy, chronology, and dialling, containing such elements of the said arts or sciences, as are most useful and easy to be known, 1717-18. 2nd edn. 3 parts in 1. [2],148; [3],86; [3],54 pp. 34 plates. Contemp panelled calf.
  *(Whitehart)* **£180**

**Wells, Horace**
- An enquiry into the origin of modern anaethesia ... Hartford: Brown & Gross, 1867. 4to. 165 pp. Orig bds, spine chipped.
  *(Poitras)* **$150**

**Wells, J. Soelberg**
- On long, short, and weak sight, and their treatment by the scientific use of spectacles. N.d. [ca 1864]. 2nd edn. ix,214 pp. Some ills. Pencilling. Title foxed. Cvrs worn, spine frayed. *(Jenner)* **£20**
- A treatise on the diseases of the eye. Phila: 1869. 736 pp. 6 chromo-lithos, engvd test types. Full lea, worn, label missing. *(Fye)* **$45**

**Wells, William Charles**
- An essay of dew and several appearances connected with it. Phila: 1838. 71 pp. Antique style bds. *(Goodrich)* **$95**
- Two essays; one upon single vision with two eyes; the other on dew. [With] An account of a female of the white race ... whose skin resembles that of a negro. London: A. Constable, 1818. 1st coll edn. 8vo. lxxiv,[2], 439,[1] pp. Half-title. Half-calf.
  *(Antiq Sc)* **$475**
- Two essays; one upon single vision with two eyes; the other on dew ... an account of a female of the white race ... whose skin resembles that of a negro. London: A. Constable, 1818. 1st collected edn. 8vo. lxxiv,[2], 439,[1] pp. Half-titles. Half-calf.
  *(Rootenberg)* **$650**

**Werge, John**
- The evolution of photography with a chronological record of discoveries, inventions, etc. ... over forty years. 1890. viii,312 pp. 4 autotype plates. *(Weiner)* **£150**

**Wertham, Fredric**
- Seduction of the innocent. London: Museum Press, [1955]. [xii],397 pp. Dw. (Psychiatric study of the effect of comic books.) *(Gach)* **$50**

**Wesley, John**
- Primitive physics; or, an easy and natural way of curing most diseases. 1842. 12mo. 35th edn. 144 pp. Orig calf, sl rubbed. *(Jenner)* **£40**

**Wesolowski, Sigmund A.**
- Evaluation of tissue and prosthetic vascular grafts. Springfield: Charles C. Thomas, 1952. 167 pp. Ills. Some underlining. Ex lib.
  *(Poitras)* **$35**

**West Riding ...**
- West Riding Lunatic Asylum medical reports. London: 1871. Vols 1 - 6. Complete set in orig bds. *(Goodrich)* **$3,750**

**West, Charles**
- An inquiry into the pathological importance of ulceration of the os uteri. Phila: 1854. 1st Amer edn. 88 pp.                *(Fye)* **$75**
- Lectures on the diseases of women ... Part I ... Part II ... London: John Churchill, 1856-58. 1st edn. 2 vols. 8vo. Stamp on titles. Uncut in orig cloth.        *(Quaritch)* **$225**
- Lectures on the diseases of women. Phila: 1867. 3rd Amer edn. 543 pp. Half inch missing from top of backstrip.        *(Fye)* **$35**

**Westfall, Richard S.**
- Force in Newton's physics. London: 1971. 1st edn. 478 pp. Dw.        *(Scientia)* **$45**

**Westropp, Hodder M.**
- Pre-historic phases; or, introductory essays on pre-historic archaeology. Bell & Daldy, 1872. xxiii,202 pp. 6 litho plates, 59 text w'cuts. Top crnr of plates damp marked. *(Pollak)* **£20**

**Wetzler, Joseph**
- See Martin, Thomas C. & Wetzler, Joseph

**Weyl, Hermann**
- Space - Time - Matter. Translated by Henry Brose. New York: [1922]. 330 pp. Spine lettering rubbed.        *(Scientia)* **$45**
- Symmetry. Princetown: 1952. 1st edn. 168 pp. Dw.        *(Scientia)* **$30**

**Weymouth, Anthony**
- Through the leper-squint; A study of leprosy from pre-Christian times to the present day. London: [1938]. 1st edn. Badly torn dw.        *(Scientia)* **$60**

**Whately, Thomas**
- An improved method of treating strictures in the urethra ... the third edition with additions. London: 1816. Tall 8vo. 2ff,226 pp, 1f [pub advts]. Fldg engvd plate. Uncut in orig cloth-backed bds, spine defective.        *(Hemlock)* **$100**

**Wheatland, D.P.**
- The apparatus of science at Harvard, 1765 - 1800. Harvard: 1968. Num ills. Orig red cloth.        *(Winterdown)* **£27.50**

**Wheatstone, Sir Charles**
- The scientific papers. London: Taylor & Francis, 1879. 1st edn. 8vo. xiii,[3],380 pp. 21 plates (3 fldg), text ills. Light browning on prelims. Orig cloth.        *(Rootenberg)* **$425**

**Wheeler, Russell C.**
- Textbook of dental anatomy and physiology. Phila: W.B. Saunders, 1940. 4to. xiii,415 pp.        *(Poitras)* **$25**

**Wheeler, W.H.**
- The drainage of fens and low lands by gravitation and steampower. London: E. & F.N. Spon, 1888. 1st edn. iv,[3],175,48 [pub ctlg] pp. 18 ills on 7 plates. Small tear at spine tip, inner hinges starting.        *(Diamond)* **$45**

**Wheeler, William M.**
- Colony-founding among ants; with an account of some primitive Australian species. Cambridge: 1933. 1st edn. 179 pp.        *(Scientia)* **$30**
- Demons of the dust; a study in insect behaviour. New York: 1930. 1st edn. 378 pp.        *(Scientia)* **$35**
- Essays in philosophical biology. Cambridge: 1939. 1st edn. 261 pp. Dw.        *(Scientia)* **$30**
- The social insects, their origin and evolution. London: 1928. 1st edn. 378 pp. *(Scientia)* **$35**

**Whetham, William Cecil Dampier**
- The theory of experimental electricity. Cambridge: University Press, 1905. 1st edn. xi,334 pp. 123 text figs.        *(Pollak)* **£30**

**Whewell, William**
- Astronomy and general physics considered with reference of natural theology ... London: William Pickering, 1834. 4th edn. 8vo. xv,392 pp. Leaf of advts. Uncut in orig glazed cloth, printed paper label. The fourth Bridgewater treatise.        *(Pickering)* **$150**
- The doctrine of limits, with its applications. Cambridge: Deighton, 1838. xxii,[ii],172, [iv advts] pp. Orig cloth-backed bds, uncut, sl wear to spine ends & crnrs. *(Whitehart)* **£45**
- The doctrine of limits, with its applications ... Cambridge: at the University Press ..., 1838. 1st edn. 8vo. xxii,[1 errata, with additional errata slip],172,[4 advts]. Partially unopened in orig cloth-backed bds, spine reprd.        *(Pickering)* **$85**
- An elementary treatise on mechanics. Vol I. Containing statics and part of dynamics ... [all published]. Cambridge: Deighton & Sons, 1819. xxii,[ii],348 pp. 15 fldg plates, some heavily foxed. Later half-calf. *(Whitehart)* **£40**
- History of the inductive sciences from the earliest to the present time. 1847. 2nd edn. 3 vols. xliv,466; xi,602; xii,696 pp. Later cloth. Lib label on inner front cvr, gilt stamp on front cvr.        *(Whitehart)* **£80**

**[Whewell, William]**
- The plurality of worlds. With an introduction by Edward Hitchcock. New York: 1854. 1st Amer edn. 307 pp.        *(Scientia)* **$45**

**Whiston, William**
- Sir Isaac Newton's mathematick philosophy more easily demonstrated: with Dr. Halley's account of comets ... London: for J. Senex & W. Taylor, 1716. 1st English edn. 8vo.

[iv],443,[1 errata]. 9 fldg engvd plates. Contemp calf, spine worn, crnrs weak.
*(Pickering)* **$850**

**White, Andrew Dickson**
- The warfare of science. Henry S. King, 1876. Some foxing. *(Pollak)* **£25**

**White, Charles**
- An account of the regular graduation in man, and in different animals and vegetables; and from the former to the latter. London: C. Dilly, 1799. 1st edn. 4to. vii,138, cxl-clxvi, 140-146, xii pp. 5 plates (3 fldg). Occas browning. Half-calf. *(Rootenberg)* **$500**

**White, E. & Humphrey, J.**
- Pharmacopedia. A commentary on the British Pharmacopoeia 1898. 1904. New issue, with additions & corrections. 4to. xxii,[1],692 pp. Orig cloth, dull & faded. Spine worn.
*(Whitehart)* **£30**

**White, F.S.**
- A history of inventions and discoveries: alphabetically arranged. 1827. 1st edn. iv,547 pp. Orig cloth, rebacked with orig spine laid on, new paper label. *(Whitehart)* **£40**

**White, J.**
- New and exact observations on fevers. London: 1712. 1st edn. 188 pp. Mild browning. Unobtrusive lib stamp on title. Orig panelled calf, rebacked. *(Oasis)* **$200**

**White, J. William**
- See Keen, William & White, J. William

**White, James**
- A treatise on veterinary medicine, in four volumes. Containing a compendium of the veterinary art ... the eleventh edition. London: 1815. 4 vols. Copper plates, some cold. Tree calf. *(Goodrich)* **$195**

**White, James & Sweet, William**
- Pain and the neurosurgeon.: a forty-year experience. Springfield: 1969. 1st edn. 1000 pp. Dw. *(Fye)* **$50**

**[White, John]**
- A rich cabinet with variety of inventions: unlock'd and open'd ... being receipts ... of several natures for ... lovers of natural and artificial conclusions. London: William Whitewood, 1677. 16mo. Title reprd. W'engvs throughout. Half-calf, worn.
*(Argosy)* **$350**

**White, M.J.D.**
- Animal cytology and evolution. Cambridge: 1945. 1st edn. 375 pp. Spine faded.
*(Scientia)* **$45**

**White, R.P.**
- Catarrhal fevers, commonly called cold. The causes, consequences, control and cure. London: 1906. 1st edn. 8vo. viii,111 pp. 3 plates. Orig cloth. Cvrs dull.
*(Bow Windows)* **£15**

**White, William**
- Medical electricity. A manual for students ... New York: Samuel A. Wells, 1872. 1st edn. 12mo. 203,13 [advts] pp. Spine tips worn. Ex lib. *(Diamond)* **$25**

**White, William J.**
- Wireless telegraphy (Jack's Scientific Series). 1906. 173 pp. Ills. Orig pict cloth.
*(Weiner)* **£35**

**White, William Alanson**
- Essays in psychotherapy. New York: 1925. x,140 pp. *(Gach)* **$50**
- An introduction to the study of mind. New York: 1924. 1st edn. Orig bds. *(Gach)* **$50**
- Lectures in psychiatry. New York & Washington: 1928. 1st edn. Printed bds, spine moderately chipped. *(Gach)* **$27.50**

**Whitehead, A.N.**
- The principle of relativity with applications to physical science. Cambridge: University Press, 1922. 1st edn. xii,190,[ii] pp.
*(Pollak)* **£75**

**Whitehead, Alfred N.**
- A treatise on universal algebra with applications. Vol I [all published]. Cambridge: 1893. 1st edn. 586 pp. Hd & ft of spine chipped, crnrs of cvrs worn.
*(Scientia)* **$300**
- A treatise on universal algebra with applications. Vol I [all published]. Cambridge: University Press, 1893. 1st edn. xxvi,586 pp. Sgntr of J[ohn] Perry, F.R.S., on front pastedown & his notes in early part.
*(Pollak)* **£200**

**Whitehead, Alfred North**
- Adventures of ideas. Cambridge: 1933. xii,392 pp. Pencilled notes on endpapers. Cloth, a little worn & soiled. *(Weiner)* **£20**

**Whitehurst, J.**
- An enquiry into the original state and formation of the earth. London: 1786. 2nd edn. [x],283 pp. 4to. Port, 7 plates. Contemp calf, rebacked. *(Wheldon & Wesley)* **£140**

**Whiteside, D.T. (ed.)**
- The mathematical papers of Isaac Newton. Cambridge: University Press, 1967-[81]. Thick 4to. 8 vols. Frontis facsimile in each vol. Orig blue cloth, gilt on spines. Dws.
*(Zeitlin)* **$1,250**

- The mathematical papers of Isaac Newton. Cambridge: University Press, 1967-81. 8 vols. Vol 1 is out-of-print, Vols 2-8 new, being still in print at £100 per volume.
*(Pollak)* **£850**

**Whitlaw, Charles**
- A treatise on the causes and effects of inflammation, fever, cancer, scrofula, and nervous affections. London: by the Author, 1831. 1st edn. 8vo. xxxii,304 pp. Ms amendment to imprint. Contemp cloth, newly printed label.    *(Deighton Bell)* **£75**
- Whitlaw's new medical discoveries, with a defence of the Linnaean doctrine, and a translation of his vegetable materia medica ... London: F. Warr, 1829. 2 vols in 1. 272; 254 pp. Rebound in stiff bds, new endpapers.
*(Poitras)* **$150**

**Whitman, Edmund A.**
- Flax culture. An outline of the history and present of the U.S. flax industry ... Boston: 1888. 1st edn. 12mo, 102 pp. Author's inscribed copy.    *(Diamond)* **$35**

**Whitney, Daniel H.**
- The family physician, or every man his own doctor ... with the history, causes, symptoms and treatment of Asiatic cholera ... New York: 1835. 599 pp, errata leaf, foxed. Contemp calf, spine reprd.    *(M&S)* **$65**

**Whittaker, Sir Edmund T.**
- A history of the theories of aether and electricity ... London: 1910. 1st edn. xv,456 pp.    *(Elgen)* **$75**
- A history of the theories of aether and electricity ... London: Longmans, Green, 1910. xiii,[iii],475,[i] pp. Jnts reprd.
*(Pollak)* **£40**
- A treatise on the analytical dynamics of particles and rigid bodies ... Cambridge: 1927. 3rd edn. 4to. xiv,475 pp. *(Elgen)* **$65**

**Whitworth, William Allen**
- Choice and chance. Cambridge: Deighton, Bell, 1870. 2nd edn enlgd. xii,254 pp. Orig cloth.    *(Pollak)* **£20**

**Whytt, Robert**
- An essay on the virtues of lime-water and soap in the cure of the stone. Edinburgh: 1761. 3rd edn, enlgd. 12mo. Plate. Contemp calf, worn, upper cvr detchd.    *(Robertshaw)* **£45**
- Observations on the nature, causes and cure of those diseases which have been commonly called nervous, hypochondriac, or hysteric ... Edinburgh: T. Becket, 1765. 2nd edn, crrctd. Library blind-stamp on title. Contemp calf, rebacked.    *(McDowell)* **£220**
- Observations on the nature, causes and cure of those dis   es which have been commonly

called nervous, hypochondriac, or hysteric ... Edinburgh: for T. Becket ..., 1767. xiii,507,[23] pp. Contemp calf. Hd of spine worn, jnts tender.    *(Elgen)* **$350**

**Widdess, J.D.H.**
- An account of the Schools of Surgery, Royal College of Surgeons, Dublin, 1789-1948. Balt: 1949. 1st edn. 107 pp.    *(Fye)* **$30**

**Wiener, Norbert**
- Cybernetics: or control and communication in the animal and the machine. New York: 1948. 1st edn. Dw.    *(Scientia)* **$100**

**Wiggers, Carl J.**
- Physiology of shock. New York: 1950. 1st edn. xix,459 pp. Ills, tables. Spine faded, minor cvr staining. Ex lib.    *(Diamond)* **$25**

**Wightman, William P.D.**
- The growth of scientific ideas. Edinburgh: Oliver & Boyd, 1950. xii,495 pp. 8 plates, 33 figs. 2 sm lib stamps.    *(Pollak)* **£10**

**Wilder, Lucy**
- The Mayo Clinic. New York: 1938. 1st edn. 96 pp.    *(Fye)* **$20**

**Wiley, Harvey W.**
- Beverages and their adulteration. Origin, composition, manufacture ... alkaloidal and fruit juices. Phila: [1919]. 1st edn. xv,421 pp. 2 plates, 40 text ills. Orig buckram, spine faded.    *(Diamond)* **$45**

**Wilkenson, Erik A.**
- Dive bombing, a theoretical examination of ballistic aeronautical problems ... Norrkoping: 1947. 192 pp. 3 fldg diags, diags in text. Orig wraps.    *(Weiner)* **£18**

**Wilkins, Charles**
- The history of the iron, steel, tinplate, and other trades of Wales. Merthyr Tydfil: 1903. Orig cloth, sl worn, hinge tender.
*(Edwards)* **£75**

**[Wilkins, John]**
- Mathematical magick. Or, the wonders that may be performed by mechanical geometry ... London: Gellibrand, 1680. 3rd edn. 8vo. Frontis, title, xii,295 pp. Text diags, plates of contrivances inc a lay-over. 18th c calf gilt. Armorial b'plate.    *(Frew Mackenzie)* **£350**
- Mathematicall magick. Or, the wonders that may be performed by mechanicall geometry ... London: for Gellibrand, 1648. 1st edn. Sm 8vo. [8]ff,296,[1] pp. Engvd port, 8 lge text engvs. Port lightly browned, frayed at lower edge. Contemp calf, rebacked.    *(Zeitlin)* **$600**
- Mercury, or the secret and swift messenger: Shewing how a man may ... communicate his

thoughts ... at any distance. London: I. Norton, 1641. 1st edn. 8vo. [12],170 (mispaginated 180) pp. Minor tears. Full calf. B'plate of Sir Richard Wrottesley.

*(Rootenberg)* **$750**

**Wilkinson, Charles Henry**
- An enquiry into the natural history, chemical properties, and medical virtues, of the rock oil ... of Barbados ... observations on digestion ... London: for James Ridgeway ..., 1830. 1st edn. 8vo. [2]ff,vii,76 pp. A few ink stains. Mod bds. *(Zeitlin)* **$150**

**Wilks, S. & Daldy, T.M.**
- A collection of the published writings of the late Thomas Addison, M.D. Edited with introductory prefaces ... New Sydenham Society, 1868. xxxi,242 pp. 7 plates, 3 cold. Orig cloth, spine defective. *(Whitehart)* **£35**

**Willard, de Forest & Adler, Lewis**
- Artificial anaesthesia and anaesthetics. Detroit: 1891. 1st edn. 143 pp.  *(Fye)* **$75**

**Willard, H.H.**
- See Richards, Theodore & Willard, H.H.

**Willi, Charles**
- Facial rejuvenation, how to idealise the features and the skin of the face by the latest scientific methods. London: 1926. 1st edn. 160 pp. Photographic ills. *(Fye)* **$50**

**Williams, C.J.B.**
- Principles of medicine. An elementary view of the causes, nature, treatment, diagnosis, and prognosis, of disease, with brief remarks on hygienics or the preservation of health. 1856. 3rd edn. xxvii,603 pp. Orig blind-stamped cloth, sl stained & worn.
*(Whitehart)* **£30**

**Williams, Charles Wye**
- The combustion of coal and the prevention of smoke chemically and practically considered. London: J. Weale, 1854. [15],iii,244, 40 [pub ctlg] pp. 141 text ills. Rebacked with orig backstrip. *(Diamond)* **$45**

**Williams, Francis H.**
- The Roentgen rays in medicine and surgery ... New York: 1901. 1st edn. xxx,658 pp. 390 ills, plates. Orig cloth, spine ends sl frayed, inner hinges cracked. Ex lib. *(Elgen)* **$250**

**Williams, Henry**
- The diagnosis and treatment of diseases of the eye. Boston: 1882. 1st edn. 464 pp. Snellen charts & cold plates. *(Fye)* **$100**
- A practical guide to the study of the diseases of the eye: their medical and surgical treatment. Boston: 1862. 1st edn. 317 pp.

**Williams, J. Whitridge**
- Obstetrics. New York: 1927. 5th edn. 1076 pp. *(Fye)* **$35**

**Williams, John**
- On cancer of the uterus. London: 1888. 1st edn. 119 pp. 18 full-page engvd plates, some cold. *(Fye)* **$100**

**[Williams, John]**
- The case of indifferent thing used in the worship of God, proposed and stated, by considering these questions. Qu. I ... Qu. II ... For T. Moore, 1683. Med 4to. [2],49 pp. Advts on title verso. New mrbld bds, new blanks, uncut. *(Deighton Bell)* **£40**

**Williams, Ralph C.**
- The United States public health service, 1798 to 1950. Wash, DC:1951. 1st edn. Ex lib. Stamp marks on f'edges. *(Scientia)* **$40**

**Williams, W. Mattieu**
- A vindication of phrenology. 1894. xxii,428 pp. Port frontis. 44 ills. Spotting on prelims. Orig blue cloth. *(Jenner)* **£21**

**Williams, W. Roger**
- The influence of sex in disease. London: Churchill, 1885. [vi],39,[iii] pp. Lacks half-title. Author's pres inscrptn on title.
*(Pollak)* **£15**

**Williamson, George**
- Memorials of the lineage, early life, education and development of the genius of James Watt. 1856. 1st edn. 262 pp. Rebnd in brown cloth. *(Scientia)* **$50**

**Williamson, R.T.**
- Diseases of the spinal cord. London: 1911. 1st edn, 2nd imp. 432 pp. *(Fye)* **$100**

**Willich, A.F.M.**
- Lectures on diet and regimen. 1809. 4th edn. xxiii,448 pp. Orig paper cvrd bds.
*(Whitehart)* **£50**

**Willis, A.C.**
- The human face. Chicago: 1884. 59 pp. Wraps, a bit worn. *(Xerxes)* **$30**

**Willis, Robert**
- Principles of mechanism ... London: 1870. 2nd, rvsd, edn. 8vo. xxiv (i.e. xxxiv),[2],463 pp. [1]f. 374 text ills. Orig cloth, worn.
*(Zeitlin)* **$95**

**Willis, Thomas**
- The anatomy of the brain and nerves ... tercentenary edition 1664-1964. Montreal:

McGill University Press. Sm folio. 2 vols.
Ltd (2000). Port, 17 plates. Orig white paper
bds. *(Zeitlin)* **$225**
- The anatomy of the brain and nerves ...
tercentenary edition. Montreal: for McGill
University by Stinehour Press, 1965. 4to. 2
vols. 445 pp. Ills. Vell. Slipcase. *(Oasis)* **$300**
- A preservative from the infection of the
plague or any contagious distemper ...
Written in the year 1666 ... London: 1721. 58
pp. Browned. New qtr calf. *(Goodrich)* **$495**

**Wilm, E.C.**
- The theories of instinct. A study in the
history of psychology. New Haven: 1925. 1st
edn. 188 pp. *(Scientia)* **$27.50**

**Wilmer, E.N.**
- Retinal structure and colour vision: a
restatement and a hypothesis. Cambridge:
1946. 1st edn. 231 pp. *(Fye)* **$10**

**Wilmer, William**
- Atlas fundus oculi. New York: 1934. 1st edn.
100 chromo-lithos with text. *(Fye)* **$250**

**Wilson, D.B.**
- See Soper, Fred L. & Wilson, D.B.

**Wilson, Dorothy Clarke**
- Ten fingers of God. New York: [1965]. 1st
edn. 8vo. Ills. Cloth. (Paul Brand, & leprosy
in Vellore, India). *(Argosy)* **$25**

**Wilson, E.D.**
- See Zworykin, V.K. & Wilson, E.D.

**Wilson, Edwin Bidwell**
- Aeronautics: a class text. New York: 1920. 1st
edn. 265 pp. Author's sgnd pres copy.
*(Scientia)* **$40**
- Vector analysis. A text-book for the use of
students of mathematics and physics.
Founded upon the lectures of J. Willard
Gibbs. New Haven: Yale University Press,
1913 [1916, 3rd printing]. xviii,436 pp. 36
text figs. *(Pollak)* **£30**

**Wilson, Erasmus**
- Diseases of the skin. Phila: Blanchard & Lea,
1852. 3rd Amer edn, from 3rd London edn.
Roy 8vo. 483 pp. Cvrs worn. Ex lib.
*(Xerxes)* **$40**

**Wilson, G.S.**
- See Topley, W.W.C. & Wilson, G.S.

**Wilson, J.**
- The farmer's dictionary; or a cyclopaedia of
agriculture ... n.d. [ca 1860]. 2 vols.
xxxviii,744; 771 pp. Plates, some cold. Half-
calf. *(Phenotype)* **£65**

**Wilson, J.C.**
- Television engineering, with a foreword by
J.L. Baird. 1937. xv,492 pp. Frontis, num ills
& diags, fldg table. Ex lib. *(Weiner)* **£40**

**Wilson, Job**
- An enquiry into the nature and treatment of
the prevailing epidemic, called spotted fever,
&c., &c. In three parts. Boston: Bradford &
Read, 1815. 1st edn. 4to. 216,[3] pp. 6 plates
on 5 leaves. Orig bds, hinges & spine
cracking. *(Hemlock)* **$165**

**Wilson, Rev. Richard**
- A system of plane and spherical trigonometry.
Cambridge: Deighton, et al. 1831. xv,330 pp.
Some lower crnrs damp-marked. Prize calf
gilt, rebacked, a little worn. *(Pollak)* **£20**

**Wilson, S.D.**
- Applied and experimental microscopy.
Minneapolis: 1967. 3 plates, 2 cold.
*(Winterdown)* **£12.50**

**Wilton, Ake**
- Tissue reactions in bone dentine: a mono-
biological study of the formation and the
dissolving of bone and dentine. London:
1937. 1st edn. 194 pp. Wraps. Inscribed by
the author. *(Fye)* **$20**

**Winchester, Clarence**
- Flying men and their machines. London:
1916. 8vo. Num photographic ills. Cloth.
*(Argosy)* **$40**

**Wing, Vincent**
- An ephemerides of the coellestiall motions for
vii years, beginning anno 1652 ... London: for
the Company of Stationers, 1652. Sole edn.
Sm 4to. A-O4; 2A-3F4. Unpaginated.
Contemp signatures on fly leaves. Orig blind
ruled sheep. V sl wear to extremities.
*(Pickering)* **$1,200**
- Harmonicum coeleste: or, the coelestialle
harmony of the visible world ... London:
Robert Leybourn, 1651. 1st edn. 7 treatises in
1. Folio. [22],309 pp. Sep titles. W'cut diags.
Marginal stains, occas browning. Some
vignettes crudely colored. Full calf.
*(Rootenberg)* **$750**

**[Wingate, Edmund]**
- Mr. Wingate's arithmetick: containing a plain
and familiar method for attaining the
knowledge and practice of common
arithmetick ... London: for J. Phillips, 1726.
15th edn. 8vo. [viii],448 pp. A few leaves
wormed in edges. Contemp calf, spine reprd.
*(Pollak)* **£35**

**Winslow, Forbes Benignus**
- Obscure diseases of the brain and mind.

Phila: 1866. 2nd Amer edn from 3rd (revised) English edn. Spine faded. *(Scientia)* **$55**
- On obscure diseases of the brain, and disorders of the mind ... Phila: Blanchard & lea, 1860. 1st Amer. edn. 576,[2],32[pub advts]. Pebbled brown cloth, shelfworn. *(Gach)* **$125**

**Winslow, W.H.**
- The human ear and its diseases. New York: 1892. 1st edn. 526 pp. Num text ills. Orig cloth, spine worn & faded, inner hinges broken. *(Oasis)* **$30**

**Winter, George**
- Animal magnetism, history of; its origin, progress, and present state; its principles and secrets ... To which is added ... dropsy,; spasms ... Bristol: printed by G. Routh, n.d. [1801]. 1st edn. 8vo. [6],223 pp. Contemp cloth, sl frayed. *(Antiq Sc)* **$175**

**Winterburn, George William**
- The value of vaccination: a non-partisan review ... Phila: Hahnemann, 1886. 2nd edn. Sm 8vo. 182 pp. Orig cloth, sl stain, spine sl worn. *(Jenner)* **£14**

**Winthrop, John**
- Two lectures on comets, read in the chapel of Harvard College, in Cambridge, New England, in April 1759. Boston: Green & Russell, 1759. 1st edn. 8vo. 44,xviii pp. With the half-title. Light uniform browning. Disbound, preserved in a cloth folder, lea label. *(Antiq Sc)* **$550**

**Winton, John G.**
- Modern steam practice and engineering. 1885. Large thick 8vo. xv,1120 pp. Plates, some fldg, diags. Half-calf. *(Weiner)* **£30**

**Wintringham, Clifton**
- An enquiry into the exility of vessels of the human body: wherein animal identity is explained ... London: for Thomas Osborne, 1743. 1st edn. 8vo. Contemp calf. Wellcome Library duplicate with release stamp on verso of title. *(Quaritch)* **$325**
- A treatise of endemic diseases. York: 1718. 1st edn. 124 pp. Old calf, very worn. *(Oasis)* **$150**

**Wireless World ...**
- Wireless World, an illustrated monthly magazine ... Vols 1 - 78, lacking Vol 68. 1913-73. Various bindings. A few faults but generally a good run. *(Weiner)* **£750**
- Wireless World, an illustrated monthly magazine ... Vols 1 - 6. 1913-19. Lge 8vo. Pub cloth & half-mor. 2 vols without titles. *(Weiner)* **£150**

**Wise, T.A.**
- Commentary on the Hindu system of medicine. Calcutta & London: 1845. vii,431 pp. *(Poitras)* **$50**

**Wiseman, Richard**
- Several chirurgical treatises. The second edition. London: R. Norton & F. Macock ... 1686. [8],577,[7] pp. Folio. Contemp calf, rebacked. *(Goodrich)* **$695**

**Witham, Henry T.M.**
- The internal structure of fossil vegetables. Edinburgh: A. & C. Black, 1833. 1st edn. 4to. [2],84pp. Orig printed bds, rebacked & recrnrd. Author's pres copy. *(Antiq Sc)* **$300**

**Withering, William**
- An arrangement of British plants; according to the latest improvements of the Linnaean system ... illustrated with copperplates ...the third edition ... Birmingham: 1796. 4 vols. Gilt calf. *(Goodrich)* **$175**

**Withington, E.T.**
- See Jones, William H.S. (Malaria & Greek history ...)

**Withington, Edward Theodore**
- Medical history from the earliest times. A popular history of the healing art. London: 1894. 1st edn. viii,fldg plate, 424 pp. Frontis. Some foxing. Sl shaken. *(Elgen)* **$100**

**Wittie, Robert**
- Ouranoscopia: or, a survey of the heavens. A plain description ... of the heavenly bodies ... to which is added the gout-raptures. London: for the author, 1681. 1st edn. 8vo. [6],158,[2] pp. Sep title for Gout-Raptures. Ctlg of author's books. Half-calf. *(Rootenberg)* **$450**

**Witts, A.T.**
- Television cyclopaedia. 1937. 151 pp. Diags. Lib label on front f.e.p. *(Weiner)* **£20**

**Wolf, A.**
- A history of science, technology and philosophy in the 16th and 17th centuries. London: 1935. 1st edn. 692 pp. *(Scientia)* **$50**

**Wolf, C.W.**
- Apis mellifica: or, the poison of the honey bee considered as a therapeutic agent. Phila: 1858. 80 pp. Extensive foxing. Rebound in grey cloth. *(Jenner)* **£20**

**Wolf, Stewart, et al.**
- Life stress and essential hypertension. Balt: Williams & Wilkins, 1955. 1st edn. 8vo. Pub cloth. *(McDowell)* **£30**

**Wolff, Eugene**
- A pathology of the eye. London: 1934. 1st edn. 283 pp. 124 ills.        *(Fye)* **$60**

**Wollaston, Francis**
- A specimen of a general astronomical catalogue, arranged in zones of North Polar distance, and adapted to Jan 1, 1790 ... London: G. & T. Wilkie, 1789. 1st edn. Lge folio. 3 engvd diags in text. Some occas light foxing. Contemp tree calf, rebacked.
                                  *(Quaritch)* **$650**

**Wollaston, William**
- The religion of nature delineated. London: Sam. Palmer, 1724. 4to. [iv],5-218,[ii blank] pp. Orig speckled calf, rebacked, crnrs worn.
                                  *(Pollak)* **£45**

**Wood, C.A.**
- The fundus oculi of birds especially as viewed by the ophthalmoscope. A study in comparative anatomy and physiology. 1917. 180 pp. 145 drawings in the text, 61 cold plates. Orig cloth, v sl marked. Early pages sl w'stained in margins.        *(Whitehart)* **£85**

**Wood, Casey A. (ed.)**
- The American encyclopaedia and dictionary of ophthalmology. Chicago: 1913-21. 1st edn. 18 vols.        *(Fye)* **$600**
- An introduction to the literature of vertebrate zoology ... London: 1931. 1st edn. 4to. 643 pp.        *(Scientia)* **$175**
- A system of ophthalmic therapeutics. Chicago: 1909. 1st edn. 926 pp.        *(Fye)* **$50**

**Wood, Ernest**
- An atlas of myelography. Washington: 1948. 1st edn. 113 pp.        *(Fye)* **$25**

**Wood, George & Bache, Franklin**
- A treatise on therapeutics, and pharmacology or materia medica. Phila: 1856. 1st edn. 2 vols. Lea, wear to hd of spines. Ex lib.
                                  *(Fye)* **$75**

**Wood, George B.**
- Address on the occasion of the centennial celebration of the founding of the Pennsylvania Hospital delivered June 10, 1851 ... Phila: 1851. 1st edn. 141 pp. 2 steel engvs. Orig cloth.        *(Diamond)* **$45**
- A treatise of the practice of medicine. Phila: Grigg, Elliott & Co., 1849. 2nd edn. 2 vols. xvi,806; 816 pp. New endpapers.
                                  *(Poitras)* **$47**

**Wood, James**
- The elements of algebra, designed for the use of the students in the university. Cambridge: J. Deighton, et al., 1810. [iv],305 pp. New half-calf.        *(Pollak)* **£25**

**Wood, Rev. J.G.**
- Common objects of the microscope. Routledge, n.d. [ca 1880]. x,186 pp. 14 tinted plates. Orig dec yellow glazed bds, a little wear to crnrs & spine ends.        *(Pollak)* **£10**

**Wood, Robert W.**
- Physical optics. New York: 1905. 1st edn. xv,546 pp. Few plates, ills.        *(Weiner)* **£25**

**Woodcroft, Bennet**
- A sketch of the origin and progress of steam navigation ... London: Taylor & Watson, 1848. 1st edn. 4to. [8],[iv],140 pp. Tinted litho title, 16 litho plates. A few plates sl soiled in margin. Orig dec cloth gilt, little worn. Author's b'plate.        *(Pickering)* **$600**

**Woodforde, John**
- The strange story of false teeth. London: Routledge & Kegan Paul, 1968. 8vo. 1st edn. Pub green cloth.        *(McDowell)* **£30**

**Woodridge, W.E.**
- Report on the mechanical properties of steel. Chiefly with reference to gun construction on the Woodridge principle. Washington, DC: 1875. 1st edn. 246 pp. 23 plates. Spine faded, wear at spine tips.        *(Diamond)* **$50**

**Woods, Alan**
- Allergy and immunity in ophthalmology. Balt: 1933. 1st edn. 176 pp. Dw.        *(Fye)* **$25**

**Woodward, J.J., et al.**
- The medical and surgical history of the War of Rebellion, 1861-65. Washington: 1870-88. Sole edn, some vols 2nd issue. 6 vols. Orig green cloth. Some vols shaken with wear to extremities of binding.        *(Fye)* **$1,000**

**Woodward, John**
- The state of physick: and of diseases; with an inquiry into the causes of the late increase of them: But more particularly of the small-pox ... London: for T. Horne, 1718. [5]ff,274 pp, [5]ff. Contemp mottled calf, front cvr detaching.        *(Elgen)* **$300**

**Woodward, Joseph Janvier**
- Outlines of the chief camp diseases of the United States armies as observed during the present war. Phila: Lippincott, 1863. 1st edn. 8vo. xii,[9]-364 pp. Recent buckram.
                                  *(Hemlock)* **$125**

**Woodworth, Robert S.**
- Accuracy of voluntary movement. New York: 1899. 114 pp. Wraps chipped.
                                  *(Epistemologist)* **$50**

**Wooldridge, L.C.**
- On the chemistry of the blood and other

scientific papers ... London: 1893. Half-title, vi,354 pp. 3 plates (one cold). *(Elgen)* **$95**

**Woolgar, William**
- Youth's faithful monitor; or ... reading and writing made easy ... arithmetic ... mensuration ... astronomy ... London: 1770. Impvd, enlgd, crrctd. 12mo. xii,372 pp. Some ink marginalia. Contemp sheep, a little worn & shaky. *(Pollak)* **£25**

**Woolley, R.**
- See Dyson, Frank & Woolley, R.

**Wootton, A.C.**
- Chronicles of pharmacy. 1910. 1st edn. 2 vols. Num ills in text. *(Robertshaw)* **£60**
- Chronicles of pharmacy. London: Macmillan, 1910. 2 vols. xii,428; [viii],332 pp. 74 ills. Uncut, t.e.g. Num ills in text. *(Pollak)* **£40**

**Worcester, Elwood & McComb, Samuel**
- Body, mind and spirit. New York: Scribner's, 1932. [xx],367 pp. Blue cloth, shelfworn. *(Gach)* **$15**

**Worcester, Samuel**
- Repertory to the modalities in their relation to air, water, winds, weather and seasons ... Trubner, 1880. xii,160 pp. Orig blue cloth, all gatherings loose, bds a little spotted. *(Jenner)* **£14**

**Worster-Drought, C. & Kennedy, Alex Mills**
- Cerebro-spinal fever. The etiology, symptomatology, diagnosis and treatment of epidemic and cerebrospinal meningitis. London: 1919. xiii,514 pp. 8 plates, 56 ills. Orig red cloth, crnrs sl bumped. *(Jenner)* **£18**

**Worth, Claud**
- See May, Charles & Worth, Claud

**Wredden, J.H.**
- The microscope. Its theory and applications. 1947. xxiv,296 pp. 298 ills. *(Whitehart)* **£18**

**Wrenshall, Gerald A., et al.**
- The story of insulin: forty years of success against diabetes. Bloomington, In: 1963. 1st Amer edn. *(Scientia)* **$25**

**Wright, E.M.**
- See Hardy, G.H. & Wright, E.M.

**Wright, G.F.**
- The ice-age in North America and its bearing upon the antiquity of man. New York: 1889. 8vo. xviii,622 pp. Num maps & ills. Cloth, trifle used. *(Wheldon & Wesley)* **£20**

**Wright, Jonathan**
- The nose and throat in medical history. N.p., n.d. [1898]. 1st edn. 8vo. Orig red cloth, gilt lettered. *(Hemlock)* **$110**

**Wright, L.**
- A course of experimental optics chiefly with the lantern, London: 1882. 1st edn 8vo. xxiv,367 pp. 12 plates (4 cold). Some spotting. Orig cloth. *(Bow Windows)* **£15**

**Wright, Sewall**
- Statistical genetics in relation to evolution. Pais: 1939. 1st edn. 64 pp. Orig stiff wraps, unopened. *(Scientia)* **$45**

**Wright, Thomas**
- The romance of the shoe, being the history of shoemaking in all ages, and especially in England and Scotland. 1922. xvi,323 pp. 52 plates. Cloth a little faded. Inscribed by the author. *(Weiner)* **£50**

**Wright, Thomas (1561-1624)**
- The passions of the minde in generall. Corrected, enlarged, and with sundry new discourses augmented ... London: for Walter Burre, 1604. [xii],352,[4], 17,[3] pp. Lacking final blank & fldg table at p 258. Contemp vell, soiled, early marginal notes. *(Gach)* **$585**

**Wright, Thomas of Durham**
- Use of the globes or, the general doctrine of the sphere: Explaining propositions relating to astronomy ... doctrine of eclipses ... London: for John Senex, 1740. 1st edn. 8vo. iv,160 pp, [1]ff. Engvd front, 2 plates, 27 engvd fldg plates. Contemp calf. *(Zeitlin)* **$450**

**Wright, W[illiam]**
- An essay on the human ear, its anatomical structure and incidental complaints ... London: Longman, et al., [1817]. 1st edn. vii, 9-123,[7] pp. Engvd frontis. Straight grained mor. Contemp ms notes. *(Rootenberg)* **$625**

**Wrigley, William & Vergette, Louis**
- Wrigley's practical receipts in the arts, manufactures, trades & agriculture, including medicine, pharmacy ... Toronto: Wrigley & Vergette, 1870. 1st edn. 8vo. Pub black & sl shabby cloth. *(McDowell)* **£60**

**Wunderlich, C.A.**
- On the temperature in disease: a manual of medical thermometry. New Sydenham Society, 1871. Translated from the 2nd German edn. xii,468 pp. 7 fldg tables, 40 ills. Orig olive cloth, half of spine loose. Ex lib, with stamp on spine. *(Jenner)* **£30**

**Wunderlich, Carl & Seguin, Edward**
- Medical thermometry, and human temperature. New York: 1871. 1st edn. 280 pp. One inch clipped from top of title without loss of text. *(Fye)* **$150**

**Wundt, Wilhelm Max**
- Lectures on human and animal psychology. Translated from the second German edition. London & New York: 1896. 2nd edn in English. x,459 pp. *(Gach)* **$60**
- Outlines of psychology. Translated ... Leipzig: Wilhelm Engelmann, 1902. 2nd English edn, rvsd. xxii,390 pp. Lower margin of text & binding damp-stained. Blue cloth. *(Gach)* **$35**
- Outlines of psychology. Translated ... Leipzig: 1902. 2nd English edn from the 4th German. Cvrs rubbed, shelfworn & sl spotted. *(Epistemologist)* **$50**

**Wurtz, Adolphe**
- The atomic theory. Translated by E. Cleminshaw. New York: 1881. 344 pp. *(Scientia)* **$30**
- A history of chemical theory from the age of Lavoisier to the present time. Translated & edited by H. Watts. London: 1869. 1st edn in English. 220 pp. *(Scientia)* **$65**

**Wyeth, John**
- A text-book of surgery. New York: 1887. 1st edn. 777 pp. *(Fye)* **$50**

**Wylie, Francis E.**
- M.I.T. in perspective. A pictorial history of the Massachusetts Institute of Technology. Boston: 1975. 1st edn. 220 pp. Copy sgnd by various Presidents of M.I.T. *(Scientia)* **$45**

**Wynter, Andrew**
- The borderlands of insanity and other allied papers. New York: G.P. Putnam's Sons, 1875. 1st U.S. edn. viii,314 pp. Green cloth, shelfworn. Ex lib. *(Gach)* **$30**

**Wythes, Joseph H.**
- The microscopist: or, a complete manual on the use of the microscope. Phila: Lindsay & Blakistan, 1851. 1st edn. 12mo. 191,[1 advt] pp. Frontis, text figs. Orig cloth. *(Antiq Sc)* **$125**
- The microscopist: or, a complete manual on the use of the microscope. Phila: Lindsay & Blakistan, 1851. 1st edn. 12mo. 191 pp inc frontis. Num text ills. 1 p advts at end. Orig gilt dec cloth, some fading. *(M&S)* **$75**
- The microscopist: or, a complete manual on the use of the microscope. 1853. 2nd edn, impvd. Plates. *(Allen)* **$17.50**

**X-Ray ...**
- X-ray studies. Schenectady: General Electric

Co., 1919. 292 pp. Ills. Orig cloth. Containing 9 contributions by Coolidge. *(Oasis)* **$75**

**Yates, Dorothy H.**
- Psychological racketeers. Boston: The Gorham Press, [1932]. 1st edn. 232 pp. Lib stamp on title. Cloth faded, jnts worn. *(Gach)* **$15**

**Yates, R.F.**
- ABC of television or seeing by radio, a complete and comprehensive treatise dealing with the theory, construction and operation of telephotographic and television transmitters and receivers ... New York: 1929. viii,210 pp. Plates, diags. *(Weiner)* **£75**

**Year-Book ...**
- The year-book of wireless telegraphy & telephony. Marconi Press Agency, 1914. Thick 8vo. Jnts shaken, 2 leaves detchd. *(Weiner)* **£40**
- The year-book of wireless telegraphy & telephony. Marconi Press Agency, 1916. Thick 8vo. *(Weiner)* **£40**

**Yeaton, Charles**
- Manual of the Alden type-setting and distributing machine: an illustrated exposition of its mechanism ... New York: Francis Hart & Co., 1865. 1st edn. "Stockholder's copy". One of 100 only. Folio. [8],245,[3] pp. Orig 3/4 mor, rubbed, mor pres label. *(M&S)* **$2,500**

**Yeo, I. Burney**
- A manual of medical treatment or clinical therapeutics. London: 1893. 2 vols. x,631; vi,744 pp. Some ills. Orig green cloth. *(Jenner)* **£12**
- Therapeutics of mineral springs and climates. New York: Funk & Wagnall, 1910. 760 pp. *(Xerxes)* **$75**

**Yerkes, Robert M. & Yerkes, A.W.**
- The great apes. A study in anthropoid life. New Haven: 1929. 1st edn. 652 pp. *(Scientia)* **$65**
- The great apes. A study in anthropoid life. New Haven: 1929. Sm 4to. 172 ills. Cloth. *(Thomas Crowe)* **£40**

**Yerkes, Robert Mearns**
- Chimpanzees: a laboratory colony. New Haven & London: 1943. 1st edn. [xvi],321,[3] pp. 64 plates. Red cloth. Inscribed by author. *(Gach)* **$75**
- Introduction to psychology. New York: Henry Holt, 1911. 1st edn. 12mo. xii,427,[9] pp. Green cloth, shelfworn, pocket removed from rear pastedown. *(Gach)* **$27**
- See Yoakum, Clarence & Yerkes, Robert

Mearns

**Yerkes, Robert, et al.**
- A point scale for measuring mental ability. Balt: 1915. viii,218 pp. Ills, tables. Some spotting. Orig red cloth. Monograph No. 1 of the Psychopathic Hospital, Boston, Mass.
*(Jenner)* **£16**

**Yoakum, Clarence & Yerkes, Robert Mearns (eds.)**
- Army mental tests. New York: Henry Holt, 1920. 1st edn. 12mo. [xiv],303,[3] pp. Shelfworn.
*(Gach)* **$25**

**Yonge, James**
- Wounds of the brain proved curable, not only by the opinion and experience of many authors ... London: for Henry Faithorn & John Kersey, 1682. 1st edn. Sm 8vo. 3 ills in the text. Title lightly soiled, margins sl browned. Later calf. Wellcome Library duplicate.
*(Quaritch)* **$3,000**

**Youatt, W.**
- The complete grazier and farmers' and cattle breeders' assistant ...rewritten and enlarged ...1908. 14th edn. 1908. Cr 4to. xiv,1086 pp. Ills. Qtr mor.
*(Phenotype)* **£38**
- The horse, with a treatise on draught. 1838. vii,472 pp. Ills. Contemp calf. Marked internally.
*(Phenotype)* **£24**
- Sheep: their breeds and management and diseases. To which is added the Mountain Shepherd's Manual. 1837. viii,568,36 pp. Orig cloth. A little rubbed & shaken.
*(Phenotype)* **£28**

**Youmans, Edward L.**
- Chemical atlas or, the chemistry of familiar objects: Exhibiting the general principles of the science in a series of beautifully coloured diagrams. New York: 1855. 4to. 106 pp. Foxed, some dampstaining. Mod buckram.
*(Scientia)* **$65**

**Young ...**
- The young man's best companion or, a regular system of education ... grammar, writing, arithmetic, mensuration, land-surveying, navigation ... 1846. Vignette frontis, 4 plates. Foxing. Bds worn, soiled, crnrs bumped, spine faded & torn.
*(Quinto Charing Cross)* **£15**

**Young, A.**
- See Grace, J.H. & Young, A.

**Young, Arthur**
- The farmer's calendar, containing business necessary to be performed on various kinds of farms during every month of the year. 1805. 6th edn, enlgd & imprvd. 638 pp. Sl foxing &

fore-edge ragged & grubby. Mod mrbld bds, cloth back.
*(Quinto Charing Cross)* **£50**
- The farmer's tour through the East of England, etc. London: for W. Strahan, 1771. 4 vols. 28 plates, fldg table. Orig tree calf, spines gilt, hds of spines rubbed. B'plate of William Wickham.
*(Ivelet)* **£1771**
- A six months' tour through the North of England. Containing an account of the present state of agriculture, manufactures and population ... in 3 vols. Dublin: 1770. 1st Irish edn. 28 plates. 1 leaf torn in vol II with sl loss of text. Calf, sl worn. *(Edwards)* **£125**
- Travels in France during the years 1787, 1788, 1789. With an introduction, biographical sketch ... by M. Betham-Edwards. George Bell, 1890. 3rd edn. lix,366 pp. Frontis. Prize calf gilt, sl rubbing.
*(Pollak)* **£15**

**Young, C.A.**
- The Sun. London: Kegan Paul, 1882. 321,2,32 [advts] pp. Frontis, num ills. Some foxing. Orig cloth.
*(Pollak)* **£15**

**Young, D.**
- See Green, C.E. & Young, D.

**Young, George**
- A treatise on opium, founded on practical observations. London: 1754. xvi,182,[2 advts] pp. Rather w'stained. Full calf, v badly worn & scratched. Hinges, spine, &c., amateurishly reprd with brown paper tape. *(Jenner)* **£32**

**Young, Hugh**
- Genital abnormalities, hermaphroditism & related adrenal diseases. Balt: 1937. 1st edn. 649 pp. *(Fye)* **$125**
- Genital abnormalities, hermaphroditism & related adrenal diseases. Balt: Williams & Wilkins, 1937. xli,649 pp. 379 plates, 534 drawings. *(Poitras)* **$100**
- Genital abnormalities, hermaphroditism & related adrenal diseases. Balt: Williams & Wilkins, 1937. xli,649 pp. 379 plates. Orig cloth, front jnt weak, sm tear at spine hd.
*(Pollak)* **£30**

**Young, Hugh & Davis, David**
- Practice of urology. 1927. Reprinted. 2 vols. 746; 738 pp. Over 1000 ills, incl 20 cold plates. *(Oasis)* **$60**

**Young, Hugh & Waters, Charles**
- Urological roentgenology. New York: 1931. 2nd edn. 564 pp. Ills & drawings. *(Fye)* **$75**

**Young, James**
- A manual and atlas of orthopedic surgery including the history, etiology, pathology, diagnosis, prognosis ... of deformities. Phila: 1906. 1st edn. 4to. 942 pp. 720 ills, many

photographic.                    *(Fye)* **$200**

**Young, Matthew**
- An enquiry into the principal phaenomena of sounds and musical strings. Dublin: Joseph Hill, 1784. 1st edn. 8vo. [2],203,[2] pp. 2 plates (1 fldg). Old calf, rebacked. Inscribed by the author.          *(Rootenberg)* **$375**

**Young, W.H. & Young, G.C.**
- The theory of sets of points. Cambridge: University Press, 1906. 1st edn. 8vo.
                              *(McDowell)* **£40**

**Zeeman, P.**
- Researches in magneto-optics. with special reference to the magnetic resolution of spectrum lines. London: Macmillan, 1913. 1st edn. xiv,[ii], 219,[v] pp. 8 plates, 74 text figs. New endpapers.          *(Pollak)* **£95**

**Zeidler, J. & Lustgarten, J.**
- Electric arc lamps, their principles, construction and working. 1908. xvii,186 pp. 16 plates, ills. A few margins grubby. Cloth soiled.                       *(Weiner)* **£21**

**Zeuner, Gustav**
- Technical thermodynamics. Translated ... London: Constable, 1907. 1st English edn from "Grundzuge der Mechainischen Warmthecrie". 2 vols. xii,460; viii,488,lxviii pp. 117 text figs. Contemp half pigskin.
                              *(Pollak)* **£55**

**Ziehen, Theodore**
- Introduction to physiological psychology. Translated ... London: 1892. 1st English edn. xiv,284 pp. Some ills. Orig red cloth, upper hinge tender, jnts worn. Ex lib. *(Jenner)* **£10**
- Introduction to physiological psychology. Translated ... London & New York: 1899. 3rd edn. 112mo. xiv,305 pp. 21 ills. Printed red cloth.                     *(Gach)* **$40**

**Zilboorg, Gregory & Henry, George W.**
- A history of medical psychology. New York: 1941. 1st edn.          *(Robertshaw)* **£14**

**Zimmermann, J.G.**
- Essay on national pride. To which are added memoirs of the author's life ... Translated by S.H. Wilcocke. 1797. xliii,260,[23] pp. Paper-cvrd bds, paper label.       *(Whitehart)* **£60**

**Zinsser, F.**
- Diseases of the mouth for physicians, dentists, medical and dental students. New York: Rebman Company, 1912. 269 pp. 52 cold, 21 b/w ills.              *(Poitras)* **$45**

**Zinsser, Hans**
- Infection and resistance. An exposition of the biological phenomena underlying the occurrence of infection and the recovery ... from infectious disease. New York: Macmillan, 1914. 1st edn. xiii,546 pp. Ills. Little spine wear, inner hinges starting. Ex lib.                        *(Diamond)* **$50**
- Rats, lice and history. Being a study in biography, which ... deals with the life history of typhus fever. Boston: Little, Brown, 1938. 301 pp.                      *(Poitras)* **$20**

**Zirkel, Ferdinand**
- Microscopical petrography. Washington, DC: G.P.O., 1876. 1st edn. 4to. xv,[1],297 pp. 12 cold litho plates. Orig cloth.
                              *(Antiq Sc)* **$80**

**Zirkle, Conway**
- The beginnings of plant hybridization. Phila: 1935. 1st edn. 231 pp. Crnrs of cvrs bumped.
                              *(Scientia)* **$45**

**Zirkle, Conway (ed.)**
- Death of a science in Russia: the fate of genetics as described in Pravda and elsewhere. Phila: 1949. 1st edn. 319 pp.
                              *(Scientia)* **$35**

**Zittel, Karl A. Von**
- History of geology and paleontology to the end of the Nineteenth century. Translated ... London: 1901. 1st edn in English. 562 pp. Shelfworn.                   *(Scientia)* **$35**

**Zollinger, Robert**
- See Cutler, Elliott & Zollinger, Robert

**Zuckerkandl, Otto**
- Atlas and epitome of operative surgery. Phila: 1898. 1st English translation. 395 pp. 24 cold lithos, 217 engvs.                 *(Fye)* **$40**

**Zuckerman, J.**
- See Berens, C. & Zuckerman, J.

**Zuckerman, Solly**
- The social life of monkeys and apes. 1932. xii,357 pp. Frontis, 23 plates. Cloth sl stained, some plates w'stained in crnr.
                              *(Whitehart)* **£18**
- The social life of monkeys and apes. New York: Harcourt, Brace, [1932]. 1st U.S. edn. xii,356 pp. 24 plates.          *(Gach)* **$30**

**Zulch, K.J.**
- Brain tumors, their biology and pathology. New York: 1965. 2nd edn. 326 pp. *(Fye)* **$15**

**Zworykin, V.K. & Morton, G.A.**
- Television. The electronics of image transmission. New York: John Wiley, 1940. xi,654,[ii] pp.                   *(Pollak)* **£45**

# Catalogue Booksellers Contributing to IRBP

The booksellers who have provided catalogues during 1986 specifically for the purpose of compiling the various titles in the *IRBP* series, and from whose catalogues books have been selected, are listed below in alphabetical order of the abbreviation employed for each. This listing is therefore a complete key to the booksellers contributing to the series as a whole; only a proportion of the listed names is represented in this particular subject area volume.

The majority of these booksellers issue periodic catalogues free, on request, to potential customers. Sufficient indication of the type of book normally handled by each bookseller can be gleaned from the individual book entries set out in the main body of this work and in the companion titles in the series.

Catalogues have also been received from a number of further bookselling firms, unfortunately too late for inclusion in the current volumes.

| | | |
|---|---|---|
| Ad Orientem | = | Ad Orientem Ltd., 2 Cumberland Gardens, St. Leonards, Sussex TN38 0QR, England. (0424 427186) |
| Alec-Smith | = | Alex Alec-Smith, 31 Highgate, Beverley, North Humberside HU17 0DN, England. (0482 869453) |
| Allen | = | William H. Allen, Bookseller, 2031 Walnut Street, Philadelphia, Pa. 19103, U.S.A. (215 563 3398) |
| Allix | = | Charles Allix, Bradbourne Farmhouse, Sevenoaks, Kent TN13 3DH, England. (0732 451311) |
| Allsop | = | Duncan M. Allsop, 26 Smith Street, Warwick, England. (0926 493266) |
| Ampersand | = | Ampersand Books, P.O. Box 674, Cooper Station, New York City 10276, U.S.A. (212 674 6795) |
| Anderson | = | I.G. Anderson, Gribton, Irongray, Dumfries DG2 0YJ, Scotland. (0387 721071) |
| Antic Hay | = | Antic Hay Rare Books, P.O. Box 2185, Asbury Park, NJ 07712, U.S.A. (201 774 4590) |
| Antiq Sc | = | The Antiquarian Scientist, P.O. Box 367, Dracut, Mass. 01826, U.S.A. (617 957 5267) |
| Appelfeld | = | Appelfeld Gallery, 1372 York Avenue, New York, NY 10021, U.S.A. (212 988 7835) |
| Arader | = | Graham Arader III, 1000 Boxwood Court, King of Prussia, Pennsylvania 19406, U.S.A. (215 825 6570) |
| Argonaut | = | Argonaut Book Shop, 786-792 Sutter Street, San Francisco, California 94109, U.S.A. (415 474 9067) |
| Argosy | = | Argosy Book Store, Inc., 116 East 59th Street, New York, NY 10022, U.S.A. (212 753 4455) |
| Artcraft | = | B.R. Artcraft Company, Baldwin, Maryland 21013, U.S.A. (301 592 2847) |
| Ash | = | Ash Rare Books, 25 Royal Exchange, London EC3V 3LP, England. (01 626 2665) |
| Baker | = | A.P. & R. Baker Ltd., Laigh House, Church Lane, Wigtown, Newton Stewart, Wigtownshire DG8 9HT, Scotland. (098 84 3348) |
| Bannatyne | = | Bannatyne Books Ltd., 6 Bedford Road, London N8 8HL, England. (01 340 1953) |

| | | |
|---|---|---|
| Barbary | = | Barbary Books, Fortnight, Wick Down, Broad Hinton, Swindon, Wiltshire SN4 9NR, England. (079373 693) |
| Beasley | = | Beasley Books, 1533 W. Oakdale, Chicago, Ill 60657, U.S.A. (312 472 4528) |
| Bennett | = | Stuart Bennett, Rare Books & Manuscripts, 3 Camden Terrace, Camden Road, Bath BA1 5HZ, England. (0225 333930) |
| Bewdley | = | Bewdley Fine Books, Middle Habberley, Kidderminster, Worcestershire DY11 5RJ, England. (0562 743333) |
| Bickersteth | = | David Bickersteth, 38 Fulbrooke Road, Cambridge CB3 9EE, England. (0223 352291) |
| Blackwell's | = | Blackwell's Rare Books, B.H. Blackwell Ltd., Fyfield Manor, Fyfield, Abingdon, Oxon 0X13 5LR, England. (0865 390692) |
| Bookranger | = | Bookranger, 14 Hepburn Gardens, St. Andrews, Fife KY16 9DD, Scotland. (0334 75066) |
| Book Block | = | The Book Block, 8 Loughlin Avenue, Cos Cob, Connecticut 06807, U.S.A. (203 629 2990) |
| Bow Windows | = | Bow Windows Book Shop, 128 High Street, Lewes, East Sussex BN7 1XL, England. (0273 472839) |
| Box | = | Janet Box, Llanfachraeth, Holyhead, Gwynedd LL65 4UU, Wales. (0407 740374) |
| Box of Delights | = | The Box of Delights, 25 Otley Street, Skipton, North Yorkshire BD23 1DY, England. (0756 60111) |
| Boyle | = | Andrew Boyle, 21 Friar Street, Worcester WR1 2NA, England. (0905 611700) |
| Braiterman | = | Marilyn Braiterman, Antiquarian Bookseller, 20 Whitfield Road, Baltimore, Maryland 21210, U.S.A. (301 235 4848) |
| Bridge, Conachar | = | Bridge, Conachar, Swattenden Cottages, Cranbrook, Kent TN17 3PR, England. (0580 714283) |
| Bristow | = | David Bristow, Perth Antiquarian, Walnut Cottage, Marbrean Close, Fordingbridge, Hampshire, England. (0425 57337) |
| Burmester | = | James Burmester, Rare Books, 13 Riggindale Road, London SW16, England. (01 677 4161) |
| Burton-Garbett | = | A. Burton-Garbett, 35 The Green, Morden, Surrey SM4 4HJ, England. (01 540 2367) |
| Cathair | = | Cathair Books, 36 Parliament Street, Dublin 2, Eire. (01 792406) |
| Chanctonbury | = | Chanctonbury Books, Selborne, Cross Lane, Findon, Nr Worthing, West Sussex BN14 0UB, England. (090 671 2093) |
| Channel | = | The Channel Bookshop, 5 Russell Street, Dover, Kent CT16 1PX, England. (0304 213016) |
| Check Books | = | Check Books, The Bookshop, Tranquil Passage, Blackheath, London SE3, England. (01 318 9884) |
| Clark | = | Robert Clark, 24 Sidney Street, Oxford OX4 3AG, England. (0865 243406) |
| Clarke-Hall | = | J. Clarke-Hall Ltd., 7 Bride Court, Bride Lane, London EC4Y 8DU, England. (01 353 4116) |
| Coch-y-Bonddu | = | Coch-y-Bonddu Books, Penegoes, Machynlleth, Powys SY20 8NN, Wales. (0654 2837) |
| Collins | = | Louis Collins Books, 1083 Mission Street, 2nd floor, San Francisco, California 94103, U.S.A. (415 431 5134) |
| Cooper-Hay | = | Cooper-Hay Rare Books, 203 Bath Street, Glasgow G2 4HZ, Scotland. (041 226 3074) |
| Coracle | = | Coracle Books, 88 Ash Road, Leeds, West Yorkshire LS6 3HD, England. (0532 782531) |

| | | |
|---|---|---|
| Cox | = | Claude Cox, The White House, Kelsale, Saxmundham, Suffolk IP17 2PQ, England. (0728 2786) |
| Crowe | = | Thomas Crowe, Antiquarian Bookseller, 77 Upper Saint Giles Street, Norwich, Norfolk NR2 1AB, England. (0603 621962) |
| Dailey | = | William & Victoria Dailey Ltd., 8216 Melrose Avenue, P.O. Box 69160, Los Angeles, California 90069, U.S.A. (213 658 8515) |
| Dalian | = | Dalian Books, 81 Albion Drive, London Fields, London E8 4LT, England. (01 249 1587) |
| Davis & Schorr | = | Davis & Schorr Art Books, 14755 Ventura Boulevard, Suite 1-747, Sherman Oaks, CA 91403, U.S.A. (213 477 6636) |
| de Beaumont | = | Robin de Beaumont, 25 Park Walk, Chelsea, London SW10 0AJ, England. (01 352 3440) |
| Deighton Bell | = | Deighton, Bell & Co., 13 Trinity Street, Cambridge CB2 1TD, England. (0223 353939) |
| Diamond | = | Harold B. Diamond, Bookseller, Box 1193, Burbank, California 91507, U.S.A. (818 846 0342) |
| Drew's | = | Drew's Book Shop, Box 163, Santa Barbara, California 93101, U.S.A. (805 966 3311) |
| Eaton | = | Peter Eaton (Booksellers) Ltd., 80 Holland Park Avenue, London W11 3RE, England. (01 757 5211) |
| Edrich | = | I.D. Edrich, 17 Selsdon Road, London E11 2QF, England. (01 989 9541) |
| Edwards | = | Francis Edwards, The Old Cinema, Castle Street, Hay-on-Wye, via Hereford HR3 5DF, England. (0497 820071) |
| Elgen | = | Elgen Books, 336 DeMott Avenue, Rockville Centre, NY 11570, U.S.A. (516 536 6276) |
| Emerald Isle | = | Emerald Isle Books, 539 Antrim Road, Belfast BT15 3BU, Northern Ireland. (0232 771798) |
| English | = | Toby English, The Gallery, Lamb Arcade, Wallingford, Oxon OX10 0BS, England. (0491 36389) |
| Epistemologist | = | The Epistemologist, Scholarly Books, P.O. Box 63, Bryn Mawr, PA 19010, U.S.A. (215 527 1065) |
| Explorer | = | Explorer Books, Fallow Chase, Durfold Wood, Plaistow, W. Sussex RH14 0PL, England. (048649 524) |
| Farahar | = | Clive Farahar, XIV The Green, Calne, Wiltshire SN11 8DG, England. (0249 816793) |
| Fenning | = | James Fenning, 12 Glenview, Rochestown Avenue, Dun Laoghaire, County Dublin, Eire. (01 857855) |
| Fine Art | = | Fine Art Catalogues, The Hollies, Port Carlisle, Nr Carlisle, Cumbria, England. (096 55 1398) |
| Forest | = | Forest Books, Knipton, Grantham, Lincolnshire NG32 1RF, England. (0476 870224) |
| Frew Mackenzie | = | Frew Mackenzie plc, 106 Great Russell Street, London WC1B 3NA, England. (01 580 2311) |
| Fye | = | W. Bruce Fye, Antiquarian Medical Books, 1607 North Wood Avenue, Marshfield, Wisconsin 54449, U.S.A. (715 384 8128) |
| Gach | = | John Gach Books, 5620 Waterloo Road, Columbia, Md. 21045, U.S.A. (93010 465 9023) |
| Golden Age | = | Golden Age Books, "Valldemosa", 28 St. Peter's Road, Malvern, Worcestershire WR14 1QS, England. |
| Goodrich | = | James Tait Goodrich, 214 Everett Place, Englewood, New Jersey 07631, U.S.A. (201 567 0199) |

| Gough | = | Simon Gough Books, 5 Fish Hill, Holt, Norfolk, England. (026 371 2650) |
| Greyne | = | Greyne House, Marshfield, Chippenham, Wiltshire, England. (0225 891279) |
| Hadfield | = | G.K. Hadfield, Blackbrook Hill House, Ticklow Lane, Shepshed, Leicestershire LE12 9EY, England. (0509 503014) |
| Halsey | = | Alan Halsey, The Poetry Bookshop, 22 Broad Street, Hay-on-Wye, via Hereford HR3 5DB, England. (0497 820 305) |
| Hannas | = | Torgrim Hannas, 29a Canon Street, Winchester, Hampshire SO23 9JJ, England. (0962 62730) |
| Hawthorn | = | Hawthorn Books, 7 College Park Drive, Westbury-on-Trym, Bristol BS10 7AN, England. (0272 509175) |
| Hay-Cinema | = | Hay Cinema Bookshop Ltd., Castle Street, Hay-on-Wye, via Hereford HR3 5DF, England. (0497 820071) |
| Hazeldene | = | Hazeldene Bookshop, 61 Renshaw Street, Liverpool, Merseyside L1 2SJ, England. (051 708 8780) |
| Hemlock | = | Hemlock Books, 170 Beach 145th Street, Neponsit, New York 11694, U.S.A. (718 318 0737) |
| Heritage | = | Heritage Bookshop, 8540 Melrose Avenue, Los Angeles, California 90069, U.S.A. (213 659 3674) |
| High Latitude | = | High Latitude, P.O. Box 11254, Bainbridge Island, WA 98110, U.S.A. (206 842 0202) |
| Hodgkins | = | Ian Hodgkins & Co. Ltd., Upper Vatch Mill, The Vatch, Slad, Stroud, Gloucestershire GL6 7JY, England. (04536 4270) |
| House | = | J. & J. House Booksellers, 632 Broadway, San Diego, CA 92101, U.S.A. (619 265 1113) |
| Howes | = | Howes Bookshop, Trinity Hall, Braybrooke Terrace, Hastings, East Sussex TN34 1HQ, England. (0424 423437) |
| Hughes | = | Spike Hughes Rare Books, Leithen Bank, Leithen Road, Innerleithen, Peeblesshire, EH44 6HY, Scotland. (0896 830019) |
| Ivelet | = | Ivelet Books Ltd., 18 Fairlawn Drive, Redhill, Surrey RH1 6JP, England. (0737 64520) |
| Jenkins | = | The Jenkins Company, Postal Box 2085, Austin, Texas 78768, U.S.A. (512 280 2940) |
| Jenner | = | Jenner, Old & Rare Medical Books, The Old Fire Station, Castle Street, Hay-on-Wye, via Hereford HR3 5DF, England. (0497 820137) |
| Johnson | = | Johnson Architectural Books, Tynings House, Sherston, Malmesbury, Wiltshire SN16 0LS, England. (0666 840404) |
| C.R. Johnson | = | C.R. Johnson, Rare Book Collections, 21 Charlton Place, London N1, England. |
| Karmiole | = | Kenneth Karmiole, Bookseller, Post Office Box 464, Santa Monica, California 90406, U.S.A. (213 451 4342) |
| Knightsbridge | = | Knightsbridge Books Ltd., 32 Store Street, London WC1E 7BS, England. (01 636 0994/5/6) |
| Lamb | = | R.W. & C.R. Lamb, Talbot House, 158 Denmark Road, Lowestoft, Suffolk NR32 2EL, England. (0502 64306) |
| Landscape | = | Landscape Books, P.O. Box 483, Exeter, NH 03833, U.S.A. (603 964 9333) |
| Laywood | = | Anthony W. Laywood, Knipton, Grantham, Lincolnshire NG32 1RF, England. (0476 870224) |
| Leaves of Grass | = | Leaves of Grass, 2433 Whitmore Lake Road, Ann Arbor, Mi 48103, U.S.A. (313 995 2300) |

| | | |
|---|---|---|
| Lewcock | = | John Lewcock, 4 Cobble Yard, Napier Street, Cambridge CB1 1HP, England. (0223 312133) |
| Lloyd-Roberts | = | Tom Lloyd-Roberts, Old Court House, Caerwys, Mold, Clwyd CH7 5BB, England. (0352 720276) |
| Lopez | = | Ken Lopez, 51 Huntington Road, Hadley, MA 01035, U.S.A. (413 584 4827) |
| M&S | = | M & S Rare Books, Inc., P.O. Box 311, 45 Colpitts Road, Weston, Mass. 02193, U.S.A. (617 891 5650) |
| Mackey | = | Aiden Mackey, 15 Shaftesbury Avenue, Bedford MK40 3SA, England. (0234 57760) |
| Mair-Wilkes | = | Mair Wilkes Books, 3 St. Mary's Lane, Newport-on-Tay, Fife DD6 8AH, Scotland. (0382 542352) |
| Marlborough | = | Marlborough Rare Books Ltd., 35 Old Bond Street, London W1X 4PT, England. (01 493 6993) |
| Marlborough B'shop | = | The Marlborough Bookshop, 6 Kingsbury Street, Marlborough, Wiltshire, England. (0672 54074) |
| Mayou | = | David B. Mayou, 30 Denmark Road, London W13 8RG, England. (01 567 1383) |
| McDowell | = | Daniel McDowell, 56 Micklegate, York YO1 1LF, England. (0904 22000) |
| Miles | = | Mr. Miles of Leeds, 12 Great George Street, Leeds, West Yorkshire LS1 3DW, England. (0532 455327) |
| Minkoff | = | George Robert Minkoff Inc., Rare Books, Box 147, Great Barrington, Mass 01230, U.S.A. (413 528 4575) |
| Monroe | = | Monroe Books, 809 E. Olive, Fresno, CA 93728, U.S.A. (209 441 1282) |
| Moon | = | Michael Moon's Bookshop, 41-43 Roper Street, Whitehaven, Cumbria CA28 7BS, England. (0946 62936) |
| Moore | = | Peter Moore, P.O. Box 66, 200a Perne Road, Cambridge CB1 3PD, England. (0223 211846) |
| Morrell | = | Nicholas Morrell Ltd., 99 South End Road, Hampstead, London NW3 2RJ, England. (01 435 5538) |
| Mott | = | Howard S. Mott Inc., Sheffield, Massachusetts 01257, U.S.A. (413 229 2019) |
| Mountainbooks | = | Mountainbooks, Box 25589, Seattle, WA 98125, U.S.A. (206 365 9192) |
| Muns | = | J.B. Muns, Fine Art Books, 1162 Shattuck Avenue, Berkeley, California 94707, U.S.A. (415 525 2420) |
| Norton | = | The Norton Bookshop, 66 Bishopton Lane, Stockton, Cleveland, England. (0642 601676) |
| Nouveau | = | Nouveau Rare Books, P.O. Box 12471, 5005 Meadow Oaks Park Drive, Jackson, Mississippi 39211, U.S.A. (601 956 9950) |
| O'Neill | = | W.B. O'Neill, Old & Rare Books, 11609 Hunters Green Court, Reston, VA 22091, U.S.A. (703 860 0782) |
| O'Reilly | = | John O'Reilly, Mountain Books, 85 King Street, Derby DE1 3EE, England. (0332 365650) |
| Oasis | = | Oasis Books, P.O. Box 171067, San Diego, CA 92117, U.S.A. (619 272 0384) |
| Offenbacher | = | Emil Offenbacher, 84-50 Austin Street, P.O. Box 96, Kew Gardens, N.Y. 11415, U.S.A. (718 849 5834) |
| Old Cinema | = | The Old Cinema, Castle Street, Hay-on-Wye, via Hereford HR3 5DF, England. (0497 820071) |

| | | |
|---|---|---|
| Orient | = | Orient Books, Little Blakes, Halse, Taunton, Somerset TA4 3AG, England. (0823 432466) |
| Ottenberg | = | Simon Ottenberg, Bookseller, P.O. Box 15509, Wedgwood Station, Seattle, WA 98115, U.S.A. |
| Pacific | = | Pacific Book House, Kilohana Square, 1016G Kapahulu Avenue, Honolulu, Hawaii 96816, U.S.A. (808 737 3475) |
| Palladour | = | Palladour Books, Greenlands, Foot's Hill, Cann, Nr Shaftesbury, Dorset SP7 0BW, England. (0747 3942) |
| Phenotype | = | Phenotype Books, Wallridge, 39 Arthur Street, Penrith, Cumbria CA11 7TT, England. (0768 63049) |
| Pickering | = | Pickering & Chatto Ltd., 17 Pall Mall, London SW1Y 5NB, England. (01 930 2515) |
| Pirages | = | Phillip J. Pirages, Fine Books & Manuscripts, P.O. Box 504, 965 West 11th Street, McMinnville, Oregon 97128, U.S.A. (503 472 5555) |
| Poitras | = | Jean-Maurice Poitras & Sons, Antiquarian Medical Books, 107 Edgerton Road, Towson, Maryland 21204, U.S.A. (301 821 6284) |
| Pollak | = | P.M. Pollak, Ph.D, F.L.S., Scientific & Medical Books, "Moorview", Plymouth Road, South Brent, Devon, TQ10 9HT, England. (036 47 3457) |
| Popeley | = | Frank T. Popeley, 27 Westbrook Park Road, Woodston, Peterborough PE2 9JG, England. (0733 62386) |
| Post Mortem | = | Post Mortem Books, 58 Stanford Avenue, Hassocks, Sussex BN6 8JH, England. (07918 3066) |
| Quaritch | = | Bernard Quaritch Ltd., 5-8 Lower John Street, Golden Square, London W1R 4AU, England. (01 734 2983) |
| Quinto Bournemouth | = | Quinto Bookshops, Commins Bookshop, 18 Westover Road, Bournemouth, Dorset BH1 2BY, England. (0202 27504) |
| Quinto Charing Cross | = | Quinto of Charing Cross Road, 48A Charing Cross Road, London WC2H 0BB, England. (01 379 7669) |
| Quinto Marylebone | = | Quinto of Marylebone, 83 Marylebone High Street, London W1M 4AL, England. (01 935 9303) |
| Q Books | = | Q Books, The Cottage, Lower Snowden, Burnhill Green, Wolverhampton WV6 7HT, England. (074 65 421) |
| Rankin | = | Alan Rankin, 72 Dundas Street, Edinburgh EH3 6QZ, Scotland. (031 556 3705) |
| Reese | = | William Reese Company, 409 Temple Street, New Haven, Connecticut 06511, U.S.A. (203 789 8081) |
| Robertshaw | = | John Robertshaw, 5 Fellowes Drive, Ramsay, Huntingdon, Cambridgeshire PE17 1BE, England. (0487 813330) |
| Rootenberg | = | B. & L. Rootenberg, Fine & Rare Books, P.O. Box 5049, Sherman Oaks, California 91403-5049, U.S.A. (98180 788 7765) |
| Rostenberg | = | Leona Rostenberg & Madeleine B. Stern, 40 East 88 Street, New York, N.Y. 10128, U.S.A. (212 831 6628) |
| Rupert Books | = | Rupert Books, 59 Stonefield, Bar Hill, Cambridge CB3 8TE, England. (0954 81861) |
| Rybski | = | John Rybski, 2319 West 47th Place, Chicago, Ill 60609, U.S.A. (312 847 5082) |
| Sanders | = | Sanders of Oxford Ltd., 104 The High, Oxford OX1 4BW, England. (0865 242590) |
| Scientia | = | Scientia, Box 433, Arlington, Mass. 02174, U.S.A. (617 643 5725) |

| | | |
|---|---|---|
| Second Life | = | Second Life Books Inc., PO Box 242, Lanesborough, Ma 01237, U.S.A. (413 447 8010) |
| Serendipity | = | Serendipity Books, 1790 Shattuck Avenue, Berkeley, CA 94709, U.S.A. (415 841 7455) |
| Sherington | = | Nick Sherington, 11 Clifton Hall, Exeter EX1 2DL, England. (0392 216532) |
| Siddeley & Hammond | = | Siddeley & Hammond Ltd., 19 Clarendon Street, Cambridge CB1 1JU, England. (0223 350325) |
| Sinclair | = | Iain Sinclair Books, 28 Albion Drive, London E8 4ET, England. (01 254 8571) |
| Sklaroff | = | L.J. Sklaroff, Craiglea, The Broadway, Totland, Isle of Wight, England. (0983 754960) |
| Smith | = | Alan Smith, 15 Oakland Avenue, Dialstone Lane, Stockport, Cheshire, England. (061 483 2547) |
| John Smith | = | John Smith & Son, 57-61 St. Vincent Street, Glasgow G2 5TB, Scotland. (041 221 7472) |
| William Smith | = | William Smith (Booksellers) Ltd., 35-39 London Street, Reading, Berkshire RG1 4PU, England. (0734 59555) |
| Snowden-Smith | = | Snowden Smith Books, 41 Godfrey Street, London SW3 3SX, England. (01 352 6756) |
| Solomons | = | M. Solomons, 23 Culverhayes, Beaminster, Dorset DT8 3DG, England. (0308 862755) |
| Sotheran | = | Henry Sotheran Ltd., 2,3,4 & 5 Sackville Street, Piccadilly, London W1X 2DP, England. (01 734 1150) |
| Spelman | = | Spelman's Bookshop, 70 Micklegate, York YO1 1LF, England. (0904 24414) |
| Spink | = | Spink & Son Ltd., 5-7 King Street, Saint James's, London SW1Y 6QR, England. (01 930 7888) |
| Spire | = | Spire Books, 32 Rosebery Avenue, New Malden, Surrey KT3 4JS, England. (01 942 2111) |
| Sterling | = | Sterling Books, 43A Locking Road, Weston-Super-Mare, Avon BS23 3DG, England. (0934 25056) |
| Stewart | = | Andrew Stewart, 14 Middle Street, Rippingdale, Bourne, Lincolnshire PE10 0SU, England. (077 85 617) |
| Stillwell | = | Colin Stillwell, 25 Fossgate, York YO1 2TA, England. (0904 27467) |
| Stubbs | = | John H. Stubbs, 28 East 18th Street, 3rd Floor, New York, New York 10003, England. (212 982 8368) |
| Sykes & Flanders | = | Sykes & Flanders, P.O. Box 86, Weare, NH 03281, U.S.A. (603 529 7432) |
| Temple | = | Robert Temple, 65 Mildmay Road, London N1 4PU, England. (01 254 3674) |
| Thompson | = | Keith Thompson, 4 Sunset Close, Beachlands, Pevensey Bay, East Sussex BN24 6SA, England. (0323 766959) |
| Thornton | = | J. Thornton & Son, 11 Broad Street, Oxford OX1 3AR, England. (0865 242939) |
| Traylen | = | Charles W. Traylen, Castle House, 49-50 Quarry Street, Guildford, Surrey GU1 3UA, England. (0483 572424) |
| Trotter | = | John Trotter, 11 Laurel Way, London N20 8HR, England. (01 445 4293) |
| Typographeum | = | Typographeum Bookshop, The Stone Cottage, Bennington Road, Francestown, New Hampshire 03043, U.S.A. |

| | | |
|---|---|---|
| Upcroft | = | Upcroft Books Ltd., 66 St Cross Road, Winchester, Hants SO23 9PS, England. (0962 52679) |
| Virgo | = | Virgo Books, 'Little Court', South Wraxall, Bradford-on-Avon, Wiltshire BA15 2SE, England. (02216 2040) |
| Washton | = | Andrew D. Washton, 411 East 83rd Street, New York, New York 10028, U.S.A. (212 751 7027) |
| Waterfield's | = | Waterfield's, 36 Park End Street, Oxford OX1 1HJ, England. (0865 721809) |
| Weiner | = | Graham Weiner, 78 Rosebery Road, London N10 2LA, England. (01 883 8424) |
| Wheldon & Wesley | = | Wheldon & Wesley Ltd., Lytton Lodge, Codicote, Hitchin, Hertfordshire SG4 8TE, England. (0438 820370) |
| Whitehart | = | F.E. Whitehart, Rare Books, 40 Priestfield Road, Forest Hill, London SE23 2RS, England. (01 699 3225) |
| Wigram | = | Wigram Books, Lussacombe, Lustleigh, Newton Abbot, Devon TQ13 9SQ, England. (064 77 217) |
| Willow | = | Willow House Books, The Cottage Bookshop, 5 Hill Street, Chorley, Lancashire PR7 1AX, England. (025 72 69280) |
| Winterdown | = | Winterdown Books. P.O. Box 106, Folkestone, Kent CT20 1XR, England. (0304 853080) |
| Wolff | = | Camille Wolff, Grey House Books, 12A Lawrence Street, Chelsea, London SW3, England. (01 352 7725) |
| Words Etcetera | = | Words Etcetera, 327 Fulham Road, London SW10 9GL, England. (01 352 3186) |
| Wright | = | Vivian Wright, Fennelsyke, Raughton Head, Carlisle, Cumbria, England. (069 96 431) |
| Wrigley | = | John R. Wrigley, 185 The Wheel, Ecclesfield, Sheffield, South Yorkshire S30 3ZA, England. (0742 460275) |
| Xerxes | = | Xerxes, Fine & Rare Books & Documents, Box 428, Glenn Head, New York 11545, U.S.A. (516 671 6235) |
| Yesterday's Books | = | Yesterday's Books, 65-67 Bennet Road, Charminster, Bournemouth, Dorset BH8 8RH, England. (0202 302023) |
| Young's | = | Young's Antiquarian Books, Tillingham, Essex CM0 7ST, England. (062187 351) |
| Zeitlin | = | Zeitlin & Ver Brugge, 815 North La Cienaga Blvd, P.O. Box 69600, Los Angeles, CA 9069-0600, U.S.A. (213 655 7581) |
| Zwisohn | = | Jane Zwisohn Books, 524 Solano Drive N.E., Albuquerque, New Mexico 87108, U.S.A. (505 255 4080) |